The Evolution of the American Economy

Second Edition

The Evolution of the American Economy

Growth, Welfare, and Decision Making

Second Edition

Sidney Ratner *Professor Emeritus, Rutgers University*

James H. Soltow *Professor Emeritus, Michigan State University*

Richard Sylla *New York University*

Macmillan Publishing Company
New York

Maxwell Macmillan Canada
Toronto

Maxwell Macmillan International
New York   Oxford   Singapore   Sydney

Editor: Jill Lectka
Production Supervisor: Helen Wallace
Production Manager: Roger Vergnes
Text Designer: Debra Fargo
Cover Designer: Tom Mack
Cover illustration: Painting by Childe Hassam, *The Avenue in the Rain, 1917*. The White House, Washington, D.C.
Photo Researcher: Robert Schatz
Maps and figures: Maryland CartoGraphics

This book was set in 10/12 Palatino by Carlisle Communications, Ltd. and printed and bound by Book Press. The cover was printed by Phoenix Color, Corporation.

Macmillan Publishing Company
866 Third Avenue, New York, New York 10022

Macmillan Publishing Company is part of the Maxwell Communication Group of Companies.

Maxwell Macmillan Canada, Inc.
1200 Eglinton Avenue East
Suite 200
Don Mills, Ontario M3C 3N1

Library of Congress Cataloging in Publication Data
Ratner, Sidney,
    The evolution of the American economy : growth, welfare, and decision making / Sidney Ratner, James H. Soltow, Richard Sylla. — 2nd ed
      p.   cm.
    ISBN 0-02-398680-8
    1. United States—Economic conditions. 2. United States—Economic policy.   I. Soltow, James H.   II. Sylla, Richard Eugene. III. Title.
HC103.R34   1993
330.973—dc20
                                  92-11088
                                      CIP

About the Cover: *Avenue in the Rain, 1917* by (Frederick) Childe Hassam (1859–1935), showing flags waving in the rain, furnishes the patriotic theme of this painting of 1917, the year of U.S. entry into World War I. At the time, the U.S. economy was already the largest of any nation. The war set the stage for twentieth-century developments by greatly increasing the federal government's involvement in domestic economic affairs and by thrusting the United States into a role of economic, financial, and political leadership in the world.

Printing: 1 2 3 4 5 6 7 8   Year: 3 4 5 6 7 8 9 0 1 2

To Louise

To Martha Jane

To Edith

About the Authors

Sidney Ratner is Professor Emeritus at Rutgers University, where he taught economic history for thirty-two years. In 1956–1957, he was a member of the School of Historical Studies at the Institute for Advanced Study at Princeton. He was a lecturer on American economic history for the U.S. State Department in Japan in 1962 and in Nigeria in 1967. From 1942 to 1946, he served as an economist on the Board of Economic Warfare, as a senior economist for the Foreign Economic Administration, and as a principal economist in the U.S. State Department, in the planning division centered on the reconstruction of war-devastated areas. Professor Ratner is the author of *American Taxation, Taxation and Democracy in America*, and *The Tariff in American History*, and the editor of *Guide to Writings on American Economic History*. His articles and reviews have appeared in the *American Economic Review, Journal of Economic History, Journal of Economic Literature*, and other professional journals.

James H. Soltow is Professor Emeritus of History at Michigan State University, where he was a member of the faculty for twenty-five years, including a term as chairman of the Department of History. He also taught at Hunter College and Russell Sage College. Professor Soltow served as Business History Fellow at the Harvard Business School and Fulbright Research Fellow at the University of Louvain, Belgium. Among his books are *The Economic Role of Williamsburg and Origins of Small Business: Metal Fabricators* and *Machinery Makers in New England, 1890–1957*. His articles and reviews have appeared in the *Journal of Economic History, Economic History Review, Business History Review*, and other professional journals. Dr. Soltow is a past president and chief editor of the Economic and Business Historical Society and a former trustee of the Business History Conference.

Richard Sylla is the Henry Kaufman Professor of the History of Financial Institutions and Markets and Professor of Economics at the Stern School of Business of New York University and a Research Associate of the National Bureau of Economic Research. He is the author of *The American Capital Market, 1846–1914* (1975), and, with the late Sidney Homer, *A History of Interest Rates*, 3rd ed. (1991) and co-editor of *Patterns of European Industrialization—The Nineteenth Century* (1991). He has also written many articles, essays, and reviews on economics and economic history. A former editor of *The Journal of Economic History*, Professor Sylla teaches courses in economic, financial, and business history as well as economics at NYU.

Preface

This volume makes available to others the knowledge and insights that we collectively have gained from teaching and prolonged, far-ranging research in American economic history and policy making. We are, however, acutely aware of our great debt to the research and analysis of many other economists and historians. We feel a special obligation to those who have formulated and tested theories about the major factors and developments in American economic growth, welfare, and decision making. The range of our indebtedness to "old" and "new" economic historians is indicated by the variety of works cited in the text and by the suggested readings at the end of each chapter.

In this joint venture James Soltow, of Michigan State University, Emeritus, wrote the chapters on the colonial and early national period, American industry, 1860–1914, and the major economic trends in World War I, the 1920s, and the 1930s. Richard Sylla, of New York University, contributed the chapters on the period 1790–1860; banking and public finance, 1860–1914; transportation and communications, 1860–1914; and the dramatic, post-World War II economic changes, 1945–1990. Sidney Ratner, of Rutgers University, Emeritus, wrote the Introduction, the majority of the chapters in Part III, and the chapter on World

War II. His chapters on economic change, 1914–1979, in the first edition were an important basis for the chapters in Parts IV and V in the second edition written by his co-authors. He conceived the original plan for this book and as senior author had the responsibility of coordinating the various chapters.

This book has been the product of teamwork in grand design and in detail. Each author has contributed important ideas to the others. We wish to express our indebtedness to William Parker of Yale University, Gavin Wright of Stanford University, and to Lee Alson, University of Illinois; Ann M. Carlos, University of Colorado at Boulder; Barbara Sands, University of Arizona; Timothy E. Sullivan, Towson State University; and Spencer J. Pack, Connecticut College for valuable suggestions for the second edition; in the first edition we were equally indebted to Stanley Engerman of the University of Rochester. We are grateful to Jill Lectka, Helen Wallace, and their co-workers at Macmillan's for constructive criticism, wholehearted support, and great skill in expediting the production of our book.

We feel a great sense of indebtedness to our students. The stimulating interchange of ideas with them over the years in courses in American economic history has contributed much both to the substance and form of this book.

Sidney Ratner
James H. Soltow
Richard Sylla

Brief Contents

Part IV   *Prosperity, Depression, and World Wars*
          1914–1945   403

Part V   *The Postindustrial Economy and the New World Order*
          1945–1990s   513

Contents

List of Maps

Introduction

The Study of Economic Growth, Welfare, and Decision Making

THE SECOND EDITION OF *The Evolution of the American Economy* carves out a fresh perspective on the history of the American economy from the abundant new source materials, novel techniques, and challenging interpretations that have emerged in recent years. The old economic history is now considered obsolete. A new American economic history is being energetically created on both a quantitative and a qualitative level. Traditional assumptions about the structure, efficiency, and equity of the American economy are being reexamined. New questions are being raised about the customary methods of explaining the genesis and development of American institutions—economic, social, and political. Champions of the new economic history, such as Robert Fogel, call for enlarging the scope of quantitative measurement and the consideration of alternative ways in which different sectors of the economy might have evolved— for example, transportation without railroads. This is called *counterfactual history*. Radical economists urge paying more attention to the welfare of disadvantaged or oppressed groups. Concurrently, some scholars, e.g., Alfred Chandler, stress the importance of entrepreneurs in introducing creative innovations into the economic system, whereas others such as John K. Galbraith, underline the expanded role of government in dealing with the critical problems of depression, recovery, economic growth, and war.

The new winds of economic and historical thought have quickened interest in American economic history. In this volume, we explore the development of the economy of the United States, from the primitive economy of American Indians to the mercantile capitalism of Elizabethan England and Renaissance-Reformation Western Europe to the position that the United States holds in the late twentieth century as the greatest industrial country in the world with a higher standard of living than any other large country. This book is addressed to college and university students in economics and history courses who want not only to learn the important facts about the development of the American economy but also to see the complex factors involved in economic change through the prism of the best-tested theories advanced to explain it.

Three themes are emphasized in the text: economic growth, economic welfare, and decision making. Many American economic history texts in the past have been predominantly narrative. Some stress economic analysis by focusing on the special characteristics and growth patterns of different sectors of the economy. The few that dare to present a general theory of American economic growth tend to overstress certain factors or to advance an oversimplified stage theory of development. *The Evolution of the American Economy*, however, combines an analytical narrative of economic growth with an evaluation of economic welfare in five major economic periods. In addition, it focuses on the important role that the decisions of different social groups and their leaders played in shaping and changing the structure of the economy.

The conditions of economic progress are analyzed as well in order to shed light on the changes in the structure and the efficiency of the American economy (for example, the effects of an increasingly large percentage of the working population shifting from agriculture to manufacturing and then to the service industries). Attention is also given to subjects that often do not receive adequate treatment in textbooks, such as the relative distribution of wealth and income at different periods and among different social groups, the roles of the government and private enterprise, and the economic skills and contributions of various cultural and gender groups.

Because we cannot treat all phases of American economic development with equal thoroughness, this work centers on the main phases, turning points, and trends in American economic history. The epic sweep and increasingly complex processes of American economic growth can best be understood when studied in five periods: (1) From colonialism to national independence, 1607 to 1790; (2) the agricultural era and emerging industrialism, 1790 to 1860; (3) industrialization and the rise of big business, 1860 to 1914; (4) normalcy, the Great Depression, and two world wars, 1914 to 1945; and (5) the postindustrial economy and new world order, 1945 to the 1990s.

Economics and Economic History

The Scope of Economics

In order to comprehend the scope of economic history, students need some grasp of economics as an independent discipline as well as an understanding of the storehouse of tools used by economic historians. Economics has been characterized by noted economists in at least three different ways. Alfred Marshall, the great Victorian and neoclassical economist, stressed the quest for material welfare and defined economics as the study of the production, exchange, distribution, and consumption of goods and services needed to satisfy individual and group wants. A complementary approach to Marshall's is that of institutional economists like John K. Galbraith, who view economics as the study of relationships among different property-owning groups—landowners, merchants, and industrialists—and between these groups and their workers. This second approach has been used to reveal the social status and economic power position of different social groups within the same hierarchy.

A third approach, made famous by the English economist Lionel Robbins, defines economics as the "science which studies human behavior as a relationship between ends and scarce means which have alternative uses."[1]

Robbins's definition is accepted by nearly all contemporary economists. It has wide implications for the general public. All of us have to establish priorities or scales of preference among the things we want, and we have to allocate our limited time, energy, money, and materials in order to get as many of the desired things as possible. We often have to sacrifice certain things we want because getting them would require giving up other things we want more. Economics seeks to help us use our scarce resources to achieve our goals. It aids us in understanding how far the substitution of one thing or service for another can be used to satisfy some of our wants.

However, as important as Robbins's definition of economics has become, it supplements, rather than supplants or contradicts, the two prior definitions. In practice, most economists use all three approaches, depending on the kind of problem they are dealing with and the emphasis they wish to give to one approach as against the others. This situation inspired Jacob Viner, a distinguished American economist, to say, "Economics is what economists do."[2] His statement implies that any narrow definition is arbitrary and that economics is not a rigidly closed discipline but as broad as the various issues economists explore.

A list of the major subjects studied by economists and economic historians from both a theoretical and an empirical point of view embraces a study of (1) the factors of production—land and other natural resources, capital, labor, and management; (2) problems of supply and demand in markets ranging from pure competition to monopoly; (3) the allocation of scarce resources in agriculture, manufacturing, and the service industries under different forms of business and government organization; (4) the distribution of wealth and income; (5) the role of domestic and foreign trade; (6) the functions of money, banking, credit, and the price system; (7) the importance of taxes and government spending;

(8) the rate of economic growth; and (9) the overall levels of local, state, and national income.

Another way of viewing what economists do is to divide their field of activity into microeconomics and macroeconomics. *Microeconomics* is centered like a microscope on the study of individual decision units—individuals or households as consumers or as producers—and the process whereby their interrelated decisions determine the relative prices of goods and the factors of production. By contrast, *macroeconomics* is focused on broad aggregates of individuals and commodities for the whole economy or for major subdivisions of the entire economy, such as national income, total consumption, investment, government spending, the quantity of money, and the balance of payments. Hence, this division of economics is primarily concerned with the problems of depression and inflation, unemployment and high-level employment, and the rate of economic growth.

The Range of Economic History

Economic historians work on the same empirical subjects as economists do but from a long-term perspective. Although the variety of topics that economic historians explore can be staggering, in recent decades two subjects have acted as magnets. One is the economic growth of nations over long periods of time and the causes or determinants of that growth. Another is the economic welfare of groups within a society, especially as measured by the concentration or distribution of wealth, income, and other forms of economic power—for example, control divorced from ownership of property. These two subjects are major themes of this book.

Decision Making in Economic History

Most history texts present a narrative of past conditions and events as if the events occurred as inevitably as in classical Greek drama, with the sequence of actions undertaken by individuals seen only from the standpoint of the present. The author and the reader look back on a past that seems dead, finished, without the possibility of ever having developed in a different way. This retrospective view of a closed, rigidly determined universe is opposed to a history based on modern science, which presents an open universe in which individuals help to determine the course of events by making choices among several possible policies and risking in certain cases their lives, their careers, or their fortunes. The character and intelligence displayed by men and women in their decisions are crucial elements in the determination of their success or failure. This kind of history is written from the prospective point of view and presents history in the making. The focus is on decisions—such as those that led to the shaping of the colonial economy within the British Empire, the formation of the U.S. Constitution, the expansion of the frontier, the rise of the factory system, and the development of a unique mass-production and mass-consumption economy.

American economic history becomes most rewarding when scholars and students explore the important problems confronted by various decision makers—politicians, farmers, industrialists, merchants, bankers, workers—at various turning points in their personal careers and in American history. Insights into historic decision-making processes can be gained by examining (1) the various objectives desired, (2) the resources considered available, (3) the various courses of action that might have been adopted, (4) the gravity and extent of the risks that were taken, and (5) the consequences of the adopted policies for the decision makers and for those affected by their decisions. By doing so, we can better understand the significance of the choices made by the historical decision makers from their own points of view. Then we come to see more clearly how their wise or unwise decisions made their future, which we have inherited from them as our past. History becomes a laboratory in which we can reconstruct the experiments performed by the millions of diverse human beings who have inhabited this country and have made it what it is today. We, in turn, have to make our own decisions on critical economic issues—the national debt, government spending, the productivity slowdown, foreign trade, and unemployment. By so doing, we shall make our country's future and become part of the history that our children will explore. Most important, we can benefit from the experience of others by making decisions based on a historical perspective. We thereby link the past not only with the present but also with our vision of the future.

Endnotes

1. Lionel Robbins, *The Nature and Significance of Economic Science*, 2nd ed. (London: Macmillan Co., 1937), p. 16.

2. Alan A. Brown et al., eds., *Perspectives in Economics* (New York: McGraw-Hill, 1971), p. 3.

Suggested Readings

Some lively discussions on the nature of economics and economic history can be found in Ralph Andreano, ed., *The New Economic History* (New York: John Wiley, 1970); Alan A. Brown et al., eds., *Perspectives in Economics* (New York: McGraw-Hill, 1971); Nancy D. Ruggles, ed., *Economics* (Englewood Cliffs, N.J.: Prentice-Hall, 1970); and Douglass C. North, "Economics History," *International Encyclopedia of the Social Sciences*, vol. 6 (New York: Free Press, 1968). The most penetrating work on decision making in the real world of economic behavior is by Herbert A. Simon, the 1978 winner of the Nobel Prize in economics. Perhaps the best introductions to his ideas are *Administrative Behavior*, 3rd ed. (New York: Free Press, 1976); *The New Science of Management Decisions* (Englewood Cliffs, N.J.: Prentice-Hall, 1977); and *Models of My Life* (New York: Basic Books, 1991). See also William Baumol, "On the Contributions of Herbert A. Simon to Economics," *Scandinavian Journal of Economics*, 81 (1979). A technical but valuable supplement to Simon's work is Ralph L. Keeney and Howard Raiffa, *Decisions with Multiple Objectives: Preferences and Value Tradeoffs* (New York: Wiley, 1976).

Other more recent important studies include Karl W. Deutsch et al., eds., *Advances in the Social Sciences, 1900–1980* (Lanham, Md.: University Press of America, 1986); W. J. Fabrycky and G. J. Thuesen, *Economic Decision Analysis* (Englewood Cliffs, N.J.: Prentice-Hall, 1974); Michael E. Porter, *Competitive Strategy* (New York: Free Press, 1980); and John Friedman, *Planning in the Public Domain: From Knowledge to Action* (Princeton, N.J.: Princeton University Press, 1987).

Part I

From Colonialism to National Independence

1492–1790

THE COLONIAL PERIOD, COVERING ALMOST ONE-half of the total American experience, began in 1607 when an English trading company planted a small settlement of about a hundred men and boys in what is now Virginia. By 1790, America was not only an independent nation of almost four million people; more important, it also possessed a well-developed market economy, a relatively high level of wealth, and the economic institutions and entrepreneurial leadership to embark on the course of industrialization that was just getting under way in England. Part I of the text focuses on how transplanted Europeans and their descendants, by exploiting the abundant resources of the North American continent, created a rapidly growing market economy and moved toward autonomy in economic decision making even before winning political independence.

Settlement in America began at a time when middle-class, or entrepreneurial, values and market institutions were growing in importance in Europe. Through a process of selective migration, the colonies established by England attracted not a cross-section of society but an unusually large proportion of people who believed in the virtue of individual achievement and in the acquisition of material goods as a goal in life. In short, these men and women were willing to invest themselves and their capital in the process of colonization because they believed that hard work, frugality, and diligence would benefit them more in America than in Europe. In contrast to many other colonial societies, where the labor of the indigenous population was harnessed to the purpose of Europeans, English colonizers in America replaced the native people with members of their own race and with black slaves from Africa.

In the economy that evolved in the seventeenth and eighteenth centuries, staple commodities produced for export became the engine of growth, as settlers capitalized on an abundance of resources and especially on the fertility of the soil. However, as economist Melville H. Watkins points out in elaborating a staple theory of economic growth, most important was "the impact of export activity on domestic economy and society."[1] The southern mainland colonies, along with the West Indies, produced tropical and semitropical commodities for the European market but remained dependent on England for commercial services and most manufactured goods. They thereby fulfilled the economic role of a colony and perpetuated a pattern of dependence, leading eventually to a "staple trap," or the inability to change when their staples no longer served as an engine of growth. However, the northern provinces became integrated into the Atlantic economy focused on Europe in a distinctive way, with the unplanned result that more autonomy in decision making developed in the region than one would expect in a colony. From new centers of entrepreneurial initiative in this broad region came the direction for the basic transformation of American economic life in the nineteenth century.

British mercantilism did not impose a serious economic burden on the colonies in terms of growth or welfare. Indeed, ties with a strong British economy proved beneficial to Americans. Nevertheless, British regulation and British rule came to be viewed as obstacles to the attainment of a greater measure of autonomy for the northern colonies. British rule also came to be seen as the cause of the southern provinces' continuing economic dependence. Political independence accelerated the trend already under way toward economic independence, with businesspeople—the principal economic decision makers—taking advantage of the new opportunities created by the sweeping away of certain legal restrictions on enterprise. When the federal Constitution was adopted, providing a framework for the political problems that beset the new nation, America was a leading country in world commerce and ready to take economic advantage of the sweeping technological changes occurring in European industry.

Endnote

1. Melville H. Watkins, "A Staple Theory of Economic Growth," *Canadian Journal of Economic and Political Science,* 29 (1963): 144.

Chapter 1

America and the Developing World Economy

AMERICA HAD ITS BEGINNINGS AS PART OF A major economic expansion of Europe. Starting in the fifteenth century, Western Europeans moved to organize close and continuous economic relations with large parts of Africa, Asia, and the Western Hemisphere, trading with some regions and settling in others. It was intended to be a European-centered world economy, as the imperialists expected to derive most of the benefits from the economic ties they established with other continents. In the process, elements of the Western European economy were transferred to new environments.

Europe did not always possess the means and motivation for overseas expansion and eventual domination of so much of the world. The concepts and institutions that had developed as the European economy expanded over many centuries gave Europeans the ability to widen their economic horizons. Portugal, Spain, Holland, and France, together with England, supplied leadership in the creation of a world economy. As we will see in this chapter, however, not all national states practiced imperialism in precisely the same manner, nor did they all attain the same measure of success in the long term. Economic developments in England enabled it eventually to achieve leadership among European imperialist nations.

A Changing European Economy

Europeans were unable to take advantage of their first discovery of America, made by the Vikings around the year 1000. At that time, Europe was characterized by low levels of population, production, and consumption, with most people devoting their energies to subsistence agriculture. Economic life was conducted in small, largely self-sufficient communities where activities were carried out in traditional ways—a system called *manorialism*. For the or-dinary person, this organization of economic and social life held a basic security; a warrior class of lords of the manor provided protection for the inhabitants of the village, who in return gave their labor. But there existed little opportunity for ordinary individuals who lacked mobility, as they were often tied to the soil through the institution of serfdom.

At the time of the Viking discovery of America, though, Europe was on the eve of a long economic expansion that would extend over the next several centuries. As feudalism spread over much of Western Europe, it provided a greater measure of security (of both life and property), made possible a growth in population, and stimulated the expansion of settled areas and of innovations in agriculture. In turn, there came an increase in urban life and trade, with a growing emphasis on market-oriented economic activity carried on for profit. Businesspeople acquired greater power in economic decision making, a function previously performed almost exclusively by land-owners.

Business and International Trade

Stimulated by the growth in international trade between the eastern Mediterranean and Western Europe, a commercial revolution (from the late tenth century to the early fourteenth century) encouraged the development of business institutions and instruments. These, in turn, made possible the growth of a market-oriented economy. From Asia, Europeans imported a variety of luxury goods for the wealthy, spices being the most important. To the East they exported raw materials, such as copper, tin, and lumber, but manufactured goods like woolen and linen cloth grew in importance. Italy was the pivot of this trade. Merchants of Venice, Genoa, and other cities controlled much of the commerce around the Mediterranean basin. They established colonies, or trading posts, at strategic locations in the Levant where they could purchase goods brought by Arab middlemen along sea and land routes from the East Indies, India, and China, and distribute them throughout Western Europe. The Crusades helped to stimulate the expansion of this trade as merchants increased the capital at their disposal with the profits earned outfitting and transporting expeditions of Crusaders to the Holy Land. Another area of economic strength appeared in Flanders (a part of what is now Belgium); it centered on the manufacture of woolen cloth for export to Italy and other regions of Europe. Hand in hand with the growth of international commerce came an increase in regional and local trade as more and more people were incorporated into the evolving market economy of Europe.

The pioneer in developing new patterns of trade through western and central Europe was the traveling merchant, who personally accompanied the goods to market. Over time, sedentary merchants became the dominant figure in international trade; they concentrated on planning and directing their affairs from a countinghouse rather than spending much of their time in travel. As long-distance trade grew in volume, the merchants, led by those in the Italian commercial cities, began to make significant innovations in business methods. New forms of partnership were worked out, sometimes for a single venture and sometimes for a stipulated term of years. The invention of double-entry bookkeeping made it possible for individual businesspersons to know more precisely the state of their business (such as whether they were earning a profit or suffering a loss). Business correspondence carried by couriers to near and far places supplied a network of information on which to base decisions about projected ventures. Merchants assumed leadership in forming a body of international commercial law, including procedures to enforce contracts. Perhaps the single most important innovation made by medieval

business was banking, which evolved from money-changing. Merchants accepted deposits of funds for safekeeping, settled the affairs of clients by making transfers in their account books, and made loans. To settle balances arising from transactions at distant places without incurring the risk of shipping precious metals, merchant-bankers devised the bill of exchange, an instrument that resembles the modern check. The bill of exchange became a credit device; interest was charged but concealed in the rate of exchange to evade medieval regulations against usury.

A second commercial revolution, which occurred from the late fifteenth century to the sixteenth century, was characterized by further expansion of a market economy. Techniques that had been developed earlier for the rational conduct of business were now diffused throughout much of Europe. The invention of printing, for instance, facilitated the spread of information in published manuals about deposit banking, bills of exchange, and double-entry bookkeeping. It was during this period that economic leadership in Europe shifted from Italy and the Mediterranean to the Atlantic and northwestern Europe. The overall balance of economic strength within Europe was influenced by Portugal's development of a new route to Asia, Spain's discovery and exploitation of the treasures of the Western Hemisphere, and the vigorous commercial growth of England and Holland (topics we will return to later in the chapter).

As opportunities in international trade expanded, merchants developed a new form of association—the chartered company—to combine enterprise and capital in the conduct of commerce with distant areas. Such ventures usually required a relatively large amount of capital, carried a high degree of risk, and involved the conduct of business in an alien environment. A charter granted by the government of a national state conferred on a company special privileges, such as a monopoly of a branch of commerce and politico-judicial rights in its trading area abroad. One type of chartered company—the regulated company—evolved out of the medieval guild system. With only professional merchants eligible to join, individual members traded on their own accounts and earned profits from their own enterprises, but each had to accept the rules imposed by the company. Merchants were encouraged to invest capital in new forms of trade, since participation in a cartel-like organization protected them from competition by nonmembers. Slowly growing out of the regulated company was the joint stock company, which more nearly resembled today's corporation. The joint stock company also received a charter from the government, conferring economic and politico-judicial privileges, but it traded as a company in that it used pooled financial resources. Membership, not limited to merchants, was attained by the purchase of shares that later came to be traded on organized exchanges. The joint stock company mobilized large amounts of capital for risky ventures because its shares could be readily converted to cash and held by anyone with capital to invest, and its special privileges carried the potential of monopoly profits. The chartered company contributed to the organization of European economic relationships with other continents and played an important role in colony building.

Mercantilism

Although the expansion of the market economy widened the scope of individual economic decision making, there was a consensus among sixteenth- and seventeenth-century European leaders that the economy should be regulated by government for the purpose of increasing the power of the national state. This approach to economic policy later came to be called *mercantilism*. As the costs of government rose with the growth of bureaucratic administration and the escalation of military operations, rulers of national states seeking to enlarge their political authority became more aware of the relationship between the amount of revenues that could be raised and the wealth of the population (or at least of its richest members). Thus, the government of each national state held a vital interest in economic expansion. At the same time, various business groups searched for ways to advance their own welfare through specific measures or policies of government, particularly where they could argue that their own interests paralleled those of the state.

Mercantilists emphasized the importance of achieving national economic self-sufficiency, an understandable objective in an era of almost constant warfare among European nations. They directed special attention to gaining a favorable balance of trade: Exports should equal imports plus specie. One group of mercantilists known as the bullionists stressed the need for the nation to build up a store of gold and silver so that the national state would always be able to purchase military and other supplies when needed. But mercantilism embraced a broader sphere than trade balances and supplies of precious metals. Policymakers recognized the importance of manufactures; they put into effect tariff protection, grants of monopoly, and subsidies to encourage the establishment and growth of industries deemed essential to the national welfare. Authorities imposed maximum wage rates to keep labor costs low, but they also regulated the price of foodstuffs in order to reduce popular pressure for higher wages. Since a merchant marine and a strong business community brought to the nation earnings from carrying freight and performing commercial services, each national government imposed regulations and discriminatory taxes and duties to encourage its own shippers and traders at the expense of foreigners. Furthermore, colonies could contribute to the economic self-sufficiency of a nation by providing supplies of wanted goods not produced in the European national state (including not only tropical commodities like sugar but also defense materials such as naval stores and timber for shipbuilding and ship repair).

Toward a Market Economy

During the sixteenth and seventeenth centuries, the influence of the market extended more widely and penetrated more deeply than ever before. Agriculture still predominated in Europe in terms of the labor force and total product; the clergy and nobility continued to occupy top positions in the social structure. But a speculative spirit of gain had spread to large segments of European society. In contrast to the earlier predominant assumption that subsistence was the appropriate goal of economic activity, business values, particularly the belief in the legitimacy of profit taking, became more respectable. Writings began to reflect modern economic concepts and to recognize the link between prices and supply and demand as well as the relationship between risk and the taking of interest in moneylending. Of course, entrepreneurial values did not totally replace traditional doctrines, even among members of the business class. Merchants of the sixteenth and seventeenth centuries often headed their ledgers "In the name of God and profit." As a result of the commercial revolutions, though, a true market economy operated throughout much of Europe. It would eventually generate for Europeans the enterprise and capital to create economic bonds with Asia, Africa, and the Americas. Political leaders' interest in expanding the economic power of the national state, expressed in mercantilistic policies, encouraged business leaders to seek profits through overseas ventures.

Imperial Leaders

Many motives led Europeans to take part in the expanding overseas ventures of the fifteenth through the eighteenth centuries. Some individuals were guided by religious considerations—a desire to strike down or to convert the heathen. Some hoped to advance the glory of their national state. Others were stimulated by intellectual curiosity, seeking to determine the shape and nature of the earth. Still others looked for adventure as a way to escape a humdrum life. But most Europeans hoped to gain personal wealth from their overseas ventures.

Although a variety of motivations impelled Europeans to participate in overseas expansion, it was the technological progress of the fifteenth and sixteenth centuries that enabled them to undertake voyages of exploration to distant places and to extend their control over large areas of the world. Improvements in the rigging and the hull design of sailing vessels made it possible for ships to carry more cargo with smaller crews and on longer voyages. Advances in navigational techniques—the astrolabe to determine latitude, the compass to determine direction, and maps and charts to record geographical data—were essential as well. The development of nautical gunnery, particularly innovations in gun mounting that made possible the use of larger cannon, gave European ships a marked superiority in weaponry over non-European ships. When small bands of Europeans confronted large native forces in battle on land, the decisive factors for achieving victory included the former's military skill and discipline acquired in the constant warfare of Europe, the superiority of metal over stone weapons, and the diplomatic talent of encouraging divisions among rival political groups and leaders.

In sponsoring the exploration of what were then unknown areas outside of Europe, each national state sought to discover a route to the Far East—the source of spices and other luxury goods. The Venetians controlled access to the markets of the eastern Mediterranean through which the spice trade was then channeled, thereby enabling them to monopolize the distribution of those products throughout Western Europe. To break the monopoly, some Europeans sought to discover a southeast passage around southern Africa, while others tried to find a northeast passage across central Asia or to the north of that continent. Still others attempted to reach the Far East by sailing west, by way of either a southwest or a northwest passage (see Figure 1–1). Once a passage to the Far East was discovered by a national state, it would become a monopoly of that state.

Portugal

The geographical position of Portugal at the southwestern edge of Europe helps to explain why that small country was able to make the initial thrust into overseas expansion: It was in the best location from which to begin the search for a southeast passage around the south of Africa to the Far East. Moreover, the Portuguese had assumed an early leadership in maritime technology. As their expeditions explored farther and farther along the west coast of Africa throughout the fifteenth century, the Portuguese developed a profitable trade in slaves as well as in gold and other African commodities. They established fortified factories, or trading posts, at strategic points along the coast, to which they diverted trade that previously had moved across the Sahara. A by-product of the Portuguese activity in this area was their set-

tlement of the uninhabited Azores and Madeira Islands, where they established sugar plantations worked by slaves who were transported from factories on the African mainland.

Portugal's investment in the search for a southeast passage to the Far East paid off in the late fifteenth century. After reaching India, the Portuguese moved quickly to establish by naval force a widely dispersed seaborne empire in Asia. Throughout the sixteenth century, they dominated the maritime trade of the Indian Ocean from a series of forts and factories. Their sea power was superior to that of any native state in the region. From there the Portuguese organized regular shipments of spices and other Asian goods to Europe, thereby replacing the Venetians as the dominant figure in the distribution of spices in Western Europe. As in Africa, the Portuguese did little to impinge on domestic production and local trade in the Far East. In order to provide cargoes for their ships, they relied on an existing commercial network operated by native merchants. In the long run, however, Portugal lacked the military resources to maintain and defend its profitable commercial empire. When the more powerful European states of Holland and England challenged its supremacy in Asia in the seventeenth century, Portugal lost its Far Eastern empire almost as quickly as it had gained it.

The Portuguese were also present in the Western Hemisphere, claiming a vast area of eastern South America. However, Portugal initially displayed less interest in Brazil than in Africa and the Far East because in Brazil there were no trading systems already organized to bring valuable cargoes to the coast for sale and shipment to European markets. Brazil's major asset was an abundance of fertile land, but it soon became clear to the Portuguese that agricultural production would have to be organized under European direction if the region was to be integrated into the world economy. Lacking the ability to finance and organize

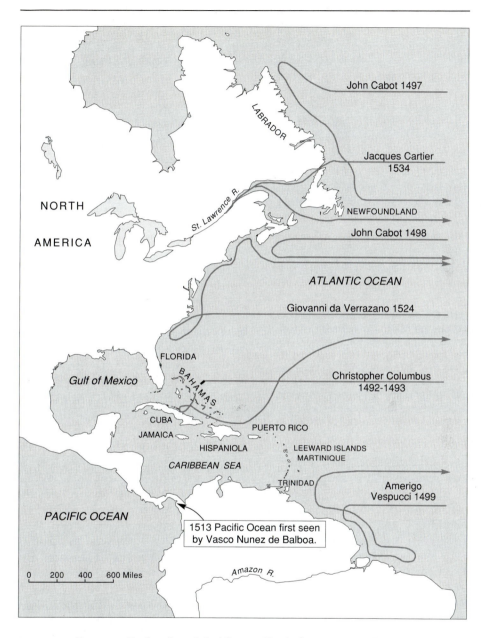

Figure 1-1 *European Exploration of the Western Hemisphere, 1492–1534*

Monument to the Discoveries, Lisbon. Erected in 1960 to celebrate the 500th anniversary of the death of Prince Henry the Navigator, the monumental ship includes figures representing the mixture of motives held by participants in overseas expansion by Portugal and other European powers—expanding the glory of the national state, converting non-Europeans to Christianity, and searching for personal material gain. (Courtesy of James Soltow)

colonization itself, the government of Portugal delegated those responsibilities to private individuals. The king made large grants of land and of political and judicial powers to individuals on the condition that they launch the settlement process. On the basis of their experience in the Azores and Madeira, the Portuguese already knew how to cultivate sugar; they also recognized the growing European demand for that commodity. The major obstacle was labor. Most of the Portuguese who migrated, whatever their social circumstances in the old country, had little intention of performing hard work in the New World. Settlers first sought to organize the natives into a labor force, but, again, drawing on their experience in the Azores and Madeira, they used their African connection to establish slavery as

the dominant labor system on the sugar plantations. Brazil quickly became a colony built on sugar. By the end of the sixteenth century, a leading planter could boast "that the sugar of Brazil was more profitable to the Iberian monarchy than all the pepper, spices, jewels, and luxury goods" imported by Portuguese merchants from the Far East. Although sugar remained the leading product of Brazil throughout the colonial period, new economic booms resulted from the discoveries of gold and diamonds in the late seventeenth and early eighteenth centuries, stimulating increases in immigration from Portugal and slave importations from Africa. Cattle ranching and stock raising also became important activities in several areas. But by the middle of the eighteenth century, the sugar-producing regions of the colony still accounted for more than 50 percent of Brazil's total population of about 1.5 million.

Even though Portugal was a pioneer in the expansion of Europe, the profits of imperialism did not contribute to its own economic strength. From almost the beginning of their overseas activity, the Portuguese had to use much of their earnings from commerce with the Far East and Brazil to pay for imported manufactured goods. Portugal, then a tiny country with a huge colony, literally lived on Brazil's productive energies. While the economic weakness of Portugal resulted in part from its small resource base and the drain of some of its most vigorous people to the colonies, a major factor was the lack of a strong business community. Genoese, then Dutch, and finally English merchants supplied much of the entrepreneurial services for Portugal as well as for Brazil. By the eighteenth century, England had become the major beneficiary of the colonial economy of Brazil. Portugal had become an economic colony of England.

Spain

While the Portuguese were exploring the west coast of Africa in search of a route to the Far

East, the Spanish were absorbed in creating a national state and completing the reconquest of their lands from the Moors; the latter task they accomplished in 1492. Once the Spanish did turn to overseas expansion in the late fifteenth century, they had to take into account Portuguese achievements. Under the then-existing international law recognized by treaties between the two Iberian nations and confirmed by papal authority, Portugal held a monopoly on the southeast passage to the Far East. Thus Spain, in authorizing and backing the voyages of Christopher Columbus, sought to discover a different route to Asia—a southwest passage. Belief in the feasibility of Columbus's proposition was encouraged by the notion that Asia lay not-too-far distant to the west, since existing geographical knowledge greatly underestimated the circumference of the earth. Instead of reaching the Far East, though, the Spanish discovered and laid claim to a vast new continent, whose extent and resources they only slowly came to realize.

From the beginning of Spain's interest in overseas expansion, it was gold that lured the military adventurers to organize the expeditions—first to Hispaniola and then to the mainland. Frontiers of plunder were opened to Spaniards with the conquest of Mexico and Peru, accomplished by the middle of the sixteenth century. But even the highly developed societies of the Aztecs and Incas produced little that was in demand in European markets. Thus, after seizing the treasures accumulated by the Indians, the Spaniards had to create an economic system to tap the great wealth of natural and human resources in the Western Hemisphere.

It was the spectacular silver discoveries in Peru and Mexico in the 1540s that opened up great new economic opportunities for the Spanish in America. For a century and a half, mining dominated the economies of those two provinces. Agriculture was organized to provide food supplies for the mining regions as well as for the large urban communities that developed at Mexico City and Lima to admin-

ister the political, economic, and religious affairs of the viceroyalties. In the eighteenth century, the Spanish undertook the development of peripheral areas that had previously been neglected. Colonies in and along the Caribbean—notably Cuba, Puerto Rico, Venezuela, and Colombia—became major producers of sugar, cocoa, and other tropical commodities for export to Europe. Ranching developed as the economic base of present-day Argentina and Paraguay, while production of wheat, wine, and fruit expanded in Chile.

In Mexico, Peru, and several other areas, the Spaniards encountered a native population with a highly organized society and economy in which the heavy work of agriculture was an accepted aspect of life for the ordinary person. The Spanish positioned themselves at the top level of that society, replacing the native upper class, and directed a reorientation of production to meet their own needs. The masses of the Indian population supplied the labor. Since the Spanish government prohibited enslavement of the native peoples of America, settlers devised other forms of forced labor. Under the *encomienda* system—a semifeudal institution transferred from Spain—Indians were forced to pay tribute in the form of labor. Later the Spanish introduced *peonage*, or debt bondage, by which large numbers of Indians, nominally free wage earners, were effectively tied to the *haciendas*, or large estates, on which they worked. To meet the need for labor in dangerous activities like mining, the Spanish borrowed an Inca system of forced labor—the *mita*, or a draft of Indian workers.

For the native populations, however, the most disastrous result of the Spanish Conquest and occupation was demographic. Within little more than a half-century after Columbus's first voyage, the Amerindian people of the Caribbean region were virtually annihilated, a result of European diseases and the unaccustomed pattern of disciplined labor imposed by the Spanish. To replace the native population as a labor force, Spain imported slaves from Africa.

Potosí, in the High Andes in Present-Day Bolivia. This colossal silver-mining center had a population of more than 100,000 in the Spanish colonial era. Profitable silver mining required costly capital equipment (like the huge hydraulic wheel which crushed the ore) and inexpensive forced labor (supplied by Indian workers). (The Hispanic Society of America)

In the highland areas of Spanish America, demographic disaster was almost as severe. For example, an estimated pre-Conquest population of between five and ten million in central Mexico dropped to about 1.4 million by the end of the sixteenth century.[1] The major cause of depopulation was a series of epidemics of European diseases to which the Indians lacked immunity. The hardships of forced labor and cultural shock contributed to the continuing decline in population, as Spanish colonists attempted to adjust to the reduction of their la-

bor force by a more intensive exploitation of the survivors. Then, at different times in the seventeenth and eighteenth centuries and in different regions, the population stabilized and resumed growth.

Spain created a vast empire that produced great wealth. Spain proved to be a failure at imperialism, however, unable to derive lasting benefits from the treasures of the New World. The aristocracy, bureaucracy, church, and military squandered much of the wealth acquired from the New World. Business played a lesser role in economic decision making in Spain than did these other groups. Much of the silver produced by forced labor in America paid for the importation of goods that Spain's economy was unable to produce. It also paid for the extensive wars waged by Spain in its effort to dominate Europe. Although trade with the colonies was closely controlled, it failed to prevent foreigners from participating in commerce with Spanish America. By the early eighteenth century, Spain was clearly an economic backwater of Europe, unable to fill the needs of its colonies or even to provide adequate protection for them. The economic expansion of eighteenth-century Spanish America served only to increase the attractiveness of that market to French and English business. Spain's stronger imperial rivals proved to be the ultimate beneficiaries of the integration of this large segment of the Western Hemisphere into a European-centered world economy.

Holland

The first nation to take advantage of the growing weakness of the Iberian powers was Holland, a province of Spain until its war of independence in the latter part of the sixteenth century. The Dutch held a position of leadership in the trade of northern Europe, based on their efficiency in commerce, shipping, and shipbuilding and on their central geographical location. They carried bulky commodities from the Baltic region to the Low Countries and much of the rest of Europe, returning salt, fish, wine, woolen textiles, and increasing amounts of Asian and American goods purchased in Lisbon and Seville. By the early years of the seventeenth century, Amsterdam had established itself as the major business metropolis of Europe—the principal commodity market, an important shipping point, and a leading banking center.

When continued warfare with Spain disrupted the commerce between Holland and the Iberian countries, the Dutch realized that they would have to develop their own trade with the new worlds in order to maintain distribution of Asian and American goods in Western Europe. After unsuccessful efforts to find a northeast passage around Russia, the Dutch government chartered the United East India Community. Its goal was to challenge the Portuguese directly in the Far East and along their southeast passage via the Cape of Good Hope. (From 1580 to 1640, Portugal was governed by the king of Spain.) This joint stock company applied its large amount of permanent capital to long-term investments in ships, warehouses, trading posts, and other commercial facilities as well as in large stocks of trading goods for voyages that lasted as long as five years. Naval power ousted the Portuguese from the Indonesian islands, enabling the Dutch East India Company to establish its own monopoly of the trade to Europe in spices and coffee as well as the sale of European goods in the East Indies.

While the East India Company was establishing a Dutch commercial empire in Asia, the West India Company, chartered in 1621, was conceived as an instrument to undermine the power of Holland's archenemy, Spain, in the Western Hemisphere. One of its notable achievements was the capture of the entire Mexican silver fleet in 1628. However, the company's major effort was directed toward the conquest of Portuguese Brazil. Since Dutch shippers controlled much of the transatlantic sugar trade, they were already familiar with this area. For a time in the 1630s and 1640s, the Dutch occupied a good portion of the sugar-producing region of Brazil. They also seized Portuguese strongholds in West Africa, gaining control of the trade in slaves to the Western Hemisphere, a commerce they dominated for several decades.

By comparison with the West India Company's enterprises in South America and Africa, the colony of New Netherlands, established in

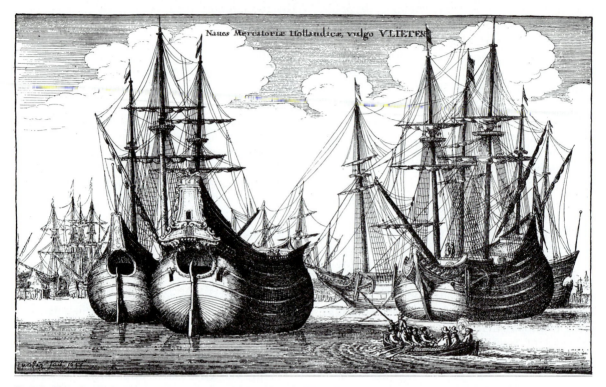

Naues Mercatoriæ Hollandicæ, vulgo VLIETEN

Dutch Merchant Ships.   The technical innovations of Dutch shipbuilders made their ships the most efficient of any in Europe. This contributed to Holland's ability to become Europe's leading merchant shipper and to make Amsterdam the world's most important business center for a time in the seventeenth century. (Historical Pictures/Stock Montage)

the Hudson River Valley in 1623, was of considerably less importance. While hope for profits in the fur trade induced the company to make the investment, the directors realized that only agricultural settlement would produce a population sufficiently large to defend Dutch claims to the territory. In order to minimize the commitment of its own resources in an area considered peripheral to its principal operations, in 1629 the company introduced the *patroonship system*, a way of delegating to private individuals much of the responsibility for organizing agricultural settlements. Using a semifeudal form for a modern purpose of capitalistic economic development, the West India Company made large grants of land to

patroons on the condition that they organize the settlement of families who would work as tenant farmers. However, life as a tenant in New Netherlands held little appeal; in 1638, the company began providing grants of land as well as the right to participate in the fur trade to individuals and families who settled in the colony. Although the company did not succeed in recruiting many settlers from Holland, the new policy did serve to attract groups of migrants from New England as well as from England.

In the 1660s, a majority of the population of about ten thousand was engaged in farming, but the fur trade continued as the economic mainstay of New Netherlands. By the middle

t' Fort nieúw Amsterdam op de Manhatans

A View of New Amsterdam, 1620s. This sketch, the first known view of what would become New York, was made about 1626 by an engineer to show the directors of the Dutch West India Company what his planned town and fort at the mouth of the Hudson River would look like. (Culver Pictures)

of the century, the Dutch in New Amsterdam (at the mouth of the Hudson River) had organized a large part of the carrying trade of the English colonies, which had been established in the Chesapeake and Caribbean earlier in the century. This was a major factor in England's decision in 1664 to take over the Dutch holdings in the Hudson Valley and along the Delaware, which the Dutch had seized from the Swedes in the 1650s. Despite the vast efforts undertaken by the West India Company, only Guiana in South America and a few Caribbean islands remained in Dutch control. Clearly Holland was far less successful as an imperialist in the Western Hemisphere than it was in the Far East.

In the mid-seventeenth century, Holland was the greatest trading nation of the world. It had commercial outposts in Asia, Africa, the Americas, and throughout Europe, all focused on a sophisticated system of exchange in Amsterdam. The nation had a productive agriculture and a diversified industry in addition to a highly efficient commercial sector. Economic energy and enterprise found a hospitable environment in Holland; in no other country at that time did business exercise more power, influence, and prestige. Indeed, the directors of the East India Company could write to the governing body of the Dutch Republic: "The colonies of the East Indies are not acquisitions made by the state, but by private traders who may sell them if they wish, even to the king of Spain or to any other enemy of the United Provinces."[2]

By the eighteenth century, however, Holland was no longer the economic leader of Europe. Competitive advantages in shipping, shipbuilding, and commerce once held by the Dutch were reduced as other maritime nations copied their methods. As a small country, Holland was unable to deal effectively with the economic threat posed by English and French mercantilistic measures. Equally serious was the military and naval strength that larger countries deployed against the Dutch in a series of wars between 1650 and 1680. Warfare undermined Amsterdam's entrepôt position and gave its maritime competitors a chance to take over a significant portion of the Dutch carrying trade. When larger national states developed ways to mobilize their own resources, Holland's population and resource base proved to be too small to support a worldwide imperialism.

France

With the decline of the Iberian powers and the inability of Holland to maintain its commercial supremacy, France and England emerged as the principal contenders in the struggle for imperial leadership. On the basis of explorations made in the sixteenth and seventeenth centuries, initially undertaken to discover a northwest passage to the Far East, France established claims to a large part of the North American continent—the St. Lawrence Valley, the Great Lakes region, and the Mississippi Valley.

The initial economic activity of the French in North America was in the fisheries of Newfoundland and the Grand Banks lying south of that island. This led to the discovery of an even more lucrative resource of the North American continent—furs, the demand for which was growing rapidly as beaver hats came into style in Western Europe. Like Europeans elsewhere dealing for other commodities, French fur traders for some decades dealt not with the producers, the Indian hunters, but with native traders who took European goods inland and brought furs to trading posts like Quebec (founded in 1608). After the 1670s, when the locus of hunting moved westward into the Great Lakes area and beyond, the French or-

ganized their own transport and distribution systems, bypassing Indian middlemen to make direct contact with the western tribes—the source of furs.

To protect the highly profitable fur trade, policymakers in Paris came to see the need for a larger population to hold the territory against encroachment by other European powers. For over a century and a half, the government of France searched for effective ways to organize settlement. Early efforts by chartered companies, starting in the 1620s, proved to be unsuccessful. Little more effective in luring settlers were the *seigneurs*, wealthy individuals who attempted to establish a semifeudal system in New France. Under any mode of settlement, the harsh climate and the limited amount of arable land along the St. Lawrence River would have discouraged settlement and limited the expansion of farming. And the fur trade was an ever-present attraction to labor and capital, offering the freedom of the wilderness and the possibility of becoming wealthy. The province's population of about 55,000 by the middle of the eighteenth century was no more than 5 percent of the total number of people in the English mainland colonies at that time. Some industry, chiefly centered around shipyards and ironworks, had developed, but fur remained the only important export. Because of its narrow economic base, New France did not become an important market for French manufactured goods, except those that entered the fur trade. New France was barely self-sufficient in its food supply.

Louisiana, including the entire Mississippi Valley, was even less developed; it had a population of about four thousand in the mid-eighteenth century. Exports of indigo, tobacco, and naval stores supported a small trade with France. New Orleans, founded in 1718, served intermittently as a base for an interloping trade with nearby Spanish colonies. In short, both Canada and Louisiana were parasites on the French economic body, kept alive by subsidies from the royal treasury.

France's major imperial success in the Western Hemisphere was in the Caribbean. Guadeloupe, Martinique, and Saint-Domingue produced wealth derived from the cultivation of coffee, chocolate, and cotton, as well as sugar, the principal commodity of all Europeans with colonies in the West Indies. The slave trade furnished a supply of labor from French trading posts in Africa. Colonial trade contributed to the growth of Bordeaux, Nantes, and other Atlantic ports in France. However, the expansion of the French West Indies paradoxically served as an engine of growth for England's mainland colonies, which furnished them with much of their foodstuffs and purchased some of their commodity output. The inability to develop an agriculture in Canada that could supply its West Indian possessions with foodstuffs thus encouraged migration to the colonies of France's principal imperial rival. This, in turn, helped to create the population pressure that eventually crushed New France.

Although then the largest national state of Western Europe, France was unable to create a viable overseas empire in the seventeenth and eighteenth centuries. As a continental power, France was heavily involved in land warfare and the struggle for territory in Europe, using resources that otherwise might have been invested in colonial development as well as in a larger navy to protect its lines of communication and supply with overseas possessions. While French businesspeople were more prominent than those in the Iberian powers, their influence in national decision making was more limited than in England and Holland. Regulation of almost every aspect of industry and commerce in this period restricted the mobility of labor and capital and stifled initiative and innovation in France. A basic problem in colony building was the inability of business and government in France to find a close identity of interest in promoting the nation's colonial expansion.

Toward a World Economy

Portugal, Spain, Holland, and France each contributed in its own way to the creation of a world economy centered on Europe. Portugal, the early leader, demonstrated the profitability of establishing direct commercial relations with non-European worlds in Africa and Asia. It also pioneered in Brazil the development of plantation export agriculture, using slave labor from Africa, thereby incorporating a distant region into the European economy. The Spanish created wealth by harnessing the labor of Amerindians and Africans to its mining and agricultural operations in the Western Hemisphere. Because of their economic backwardness, Portugal and Spain were unable to apply effectively the profits of imperialism to their own economic development. For Latin America, the productive systems developed by the Portuguese and Spanish left a heritage of economic colonialism, or dependence on economically more advanced areas—a pattern that would be difficult to change even after the achievement of political independence in the nineteenth century. Colonial rule left Brazil and Spanish America with business communities too weak to provide leadership in decision making or to deal with changing conditions.

The North American empires of both Holland and France rested on narrow economic and demographic bases. The developmental efforts of the Dutch and French powers ultimately benefited England, which took over most of the colonies established by them. As we will see, the English became the most successful European colonizers.

The Economic Expansion of England

Several factors contributed to England's rise to economic prominence. The nation's insular position conferred an initial advantage, enabling it to avoid heavy involvement in European wars and to concentrate on building the sea power essential to maintaining overseas possessions. England's small size facilitated the early development of a national state and thus a national market; at the same time, though, its resource base was broad enough to support a fairly wide range of economic activity. Significantly, in no other country (except Holland) did business attain the extent of power, influence, and market freedom—the ability to make and carry out decisions on the basis of anticipated profits—as in England. While the French government was expanding controls over industry and commerce, England was creating an institutional framework that enabled entrepreneurs to exploit economic opportunity with a minimum of restraint.

During the sixteenth century, the English economy changed at a fast pace. Manufacturing expanded and became more diversified. Woolen textiles, the leading export industry in the Middle Ages, grew not only in volume but also in the variety of cloths produced. Shipbuilding and metalworking increased in importance. The development of coal as a low-cost energy source led to the expansion of industries like soap making, brewing, and dyeing.

In agriculture, a reorganization of property rights accelerated a shift away from subsistence farming toward production for the market. Members of the village community, who held land under various forms of tenure, lost decision-making power to profit-oriented entrepreneurs, who could then adjust land use to the demands of the market. In the sixteenth century, opportunity for profit lay in producing wool for the growing textile industry; the landlord who found a way to turn tenants with small holdings off the land could then shift the land from cultivation to sheep pasture. In English society, land was increasingly perceived as not just a means of subsistence for the community but also as a form of capital investment. The modern institution of private property, including the concept of autonomy of

individual decision makers, was what most English settlers carried to America. Individual ownership and decision making were replacing a variety of legal relationships to the land that had long characterized the medieval open-field system and its communal organization of decision making.

Foreign Trade and Overseas Expansion

England's first contact with the Western Hemisphere came in 1497 as a result of the voyage of John Cabot, commissioned by English merchants to search for a northwest passage to the spice markets of Asia. On the basis of this and later explorations, England laid claim to much of the continent of North America. The most important immediate result of Cabot's enterprise was to draw attention to the treasure of the sea—the cod fisheries of Newfoundland—in which England developed a substantial interest.

During the first half of the sixteenth century, the buoyant European markets for woolen cloth, which could be reached through the exchange facilities at Antwerp, diverted the attention of English business away from the Western Hemisphere. The Merchant Adventurers, a regulated company, held a monopoly of the trade. It maintained a branch office in Antwerp staffed by young men who could take advantage of the opportunity to learn about the then most sophisticated ways of doing business. When this profitable trade tapered off, English merchants were stimulated to search for markets outside of their traditional pattern of commerce with the Low Countries.

The institution of the chartered company proved to be the most useful device in the development of new markets and trade routes. The pooling of capital and enterprise and a grant of a monopoly from the English government were of great advantage to a company that planned to carry on a commerce involving long voyages, heavy start-up expenses, no immediate profits, overhead costs (of operating warehouses and other facilities), and sometimes diplomatic negotiations with foreign rulers. Beginning in the 1550s, a series of such enterprises worked to open up new areas to English trade. The Eastland Company conducted most of the direct trade between England and the Baltic region, not only a valuable market for woolen cloth but also an important source of naval stores for England's shipbuilding industry. One objective of the Muscovy Company was to find a northeast passage across Asia to Far Eastern spice markets, but it was more successful in developing a fur trade with Russia. In the last quarter of the sixteenth century, the Levant Company captured from the Venetians the commerce to England from the long-established markets of the eastern Mediterranean. Then, with the chartering of the East India Company in 1600, England made a direct challenge to Portugal's monopoly position in the Far East itself.

Business and political leaders in England also looked for ways to gain access to the wealth of the Spanish empire in America. Although Spain prohibited other nations from trading with its colonies, the English turned to smuggling and privateering. Each year in the last decade of the sixteenth century, as many as two hundred English ships sailed to the Caribbean to extract what wealth they could from the Spanish Main, a profitable kind of enterprise for the "sea dogs" and their financial backers.

In the late sixteenth century, some English policymakers were urging the establishment of permanent settlements in the areas of North America not occupied by the Spanish. The first English attempt at colonization—Sir Humphrey Gilbert's venture in the 1580s to found a settlement in Newfoundland—grew out of a revived interest in finding a northwest passage to the Far East. A few years later, Sir Walter Raleigh organized an effort to plant a colony on Roanoke Island (in what is now North Carolina), designed primarily as a support base for English privateers operating in the Caribbean. These early, unsuccessful ventures were followed by a much greater effort toward colony building in North America in the seventeenth century.

The Essential Elements of English Colonization

When the English began to organize settlements in North America in the early seventeenth century, there was little precedent for them to follow. Earlier colonization undertaken in Ireland had not been entirely successful. The experience of Spain did not furnish a useful model, since the Spanish had attained their greatest profits in areas where they found a combination of silver mines and a native population that could be utilized as a labor force. It was not certain that the English would find such a combination of resources and labor in the regions of the Western Hemisphere that they claimed. However, England was able to furnish the necessary elements of colonization that involved settlement of Europeans: organizational methods and funds of capital, people to migrate, a favorable governmental policy, and a flow of information about opportunities.

Trade—The Keystone of Colonization

Profits from trade furnished much of the capital for colonization, while prospects of expanded commerce created an incentive for investment in overseas expansion. Many of the same British businesspeople who led the way in opening commercial relations with Russia, the eastern Mediterranean, the Baltic, and the Far East were searching in the early seventeenth century for new investment opportunities in the Western Hemisphere. They applied the organizational method they had earlier used—the chartered company—to develop new markets and trade routes. Wealthy landowners also made substantial financial investments in these early colonial ventures. Drawing on profits derived from market-oriented agricultural enterprise, nobles and gentry perceived their participation in large-scale trading and colonizing companies as a means to advance national goals as well as a source of personal gain.

Migration to the Colonies

England contributed more migrants—individuals, families, and groups—to its colonies than did any other national state. An intensification of middle-class values and a growing emphasis on individual achievement, material success, and upward mobility contributed to the willingness of large numbers of English people to migrate. To some families that felt blocked by the high price of land needed to establish or expand farming operations in England, and to others who experienced difficulty in gaining a foothold in the urban business community, America appeared to be a place of opportunity.

Another important factor was the Reformation settlement in England, which left two dissatisfied groups: Roman Catholics and Puritans (Calvinists). These minorities were too large and too tenacious to be suppressed, but in an era of close association of church and state, governmental authorities regarded religious freedom as subversive to the state. Political leaders looked with increasing favor on colonization as a way to relieve them of the necessity of dealing with minority problems at home; the prospect was particularly attractive because many members of both religious groups had sufficient funds to finance their own migration. (Later, other persecuted religious minorities, like the Quakers, also sought refuge in the New World.)

Finally, the reorganization of agricultural production and other economic changes in the sixteenth century contributed to demographic dislocation and a belief that England was overpopulated. Colonization was seen as a way to relieve the nation of its surplus work force at home and to resolve what seemed to be a shortage of labor in the colonies. A system of indentured servitude was organized to allow people to pay for their passage to America with their own labor.

Government Policy

The colonization of English America was accomplished largely by individuals and groups in the private sector. However, each project required a charter or grant from the monarch, conferring not only a wide range of economic rights (such as land titles and trading monopolies) but also extensive political and judicial authority. The English government lacked the ability to organize and finance settlements overseas, but it did have the power to influence the course of colonization through the distribution of privileges. Organizers of each colonizing venture bargained with the crown over the specific mix of privileges to be conferred in the charter. In each case, though, the set of rights granted to a private individual or group had to be justified in broad social, economic, and political terms. Because mercantilistic ideas provided a rationale for the extensive exercise of power by private individuals and groups, projectors of colonies had to show how their ventures would contribute to an increase in the economic strength of the nation.

Flow of Information

Decisions about how to invest money and human capital in colonization rested on the information (or often misinformation) available about potential opportunities, circulated at the time through the printed word. In the late sixteenth and early seventeenth centuries, proponents of English expansion such as the Richard Hakluyts (cousins) collected and published accounts of explorations and settlements in order to excite broad interest. They then added arguments that would make colonization attractive to potential investors, traders, settlers, and government policymakers. Appeals were made along several lines: business profits, national glory and prestige, religion, and the ability of individuals to improve their social and economic position. In addition to the general literature promoting colonization, founders of colonies, needing to attract recruits, issued pamphlets extolling the virtues of their own particular settlements.

Summary

The creation of a world economy, within which English colonization took place, can best be viewed as an outgrowth of the long-term expansion of the European economy, highlighted by a shift in emphasis from subsistence to market orientation and profit making. Business played a central role in developing the economic institutions, practices, and concepts that were so important to Europeans' conquest of large parts of the non-European world. These institutions, practices, and concepts were carried to America by settlers and became part of the basic outlook on economic affairs held in each nation's colonies. The leading national states first emphasized the establishment by their own traders of links with existing commercial systems as the means by which non-European areas would be integrated into the European economy. Early in the history of imperialism, however, decision makers came to recognize the importance of European production systems specifically oriented to furnish supplies of raw materials for the European market, which would, in turn, involve overseas settlement by Europeans. To become the leader in overseas expansion, England proved to be better able than any other national state to supply the needed organization, capital, and work force for colony building.

Endnotes

1. Rudolph A. Zambardino, "Mexico's Population in the Sixteenth Century: Demographic Anomaly or Mathematical Illusion?" *Journal of Interdisciplinary History*, 11 (1980), p. 25. Other estimates of the pre-Conquest population of central Mexico range as high as 25.2 million. John D. Daniels, "The Indian Population of North America in 1492," *William and Mary Quarterly*, 49 (1992), concludes: "More than a century of debate has produced neither generally accepted population estimates nor consensus on the methods of obtaining them." (p. 320) This generalization, made for North America, applies also to other parts of the Western Hemisphere.
2. E. E. Rich and C. H. Wilson, eds., in *Cambridge Economic History of Europe*, vol. 4, *The Economy of Expanding Europe in the Sixteenth and Seventeenth Centuries* (Cambridge: Cambridge University Press, 1967), p. 249.

Suggested Readings

Robert S. Lopez, *The Commercial Revolution of the Middle Ages, 950–1350* (Englewood Cliffs, N.J.: Prentice-Hall, 1971), and Harry A. Miskimin, *The Economy of Early Renaissance Europe, 1300–1460* (Englewood Cliffs, N.J.: Prentice-Hall, 1960), contain readable accounts of changes in the European medieval economy. Carlo M. Cipolla, ed., *The Fontana Economic History of Europe*, vol. 1, *The Middle Ages* (London: Collins-Fontana, 1972), is a comprehensive survey.

Students interested in specific topics dealing with the economic history of medieval Europe can consult the following collections: M. M. Postan and E. E. Rich, eds., *Cambridge Economic History of Europe*, vol. 2, *Trade and Industry in the Middle Ages* (Cambridge: Cambridge University Press, 1952), and M. M. Postan, E. E. Rich, and Edward Miller, eds., *Cambridge Economic History of Europe*, vol. 3, *Economic Organization and Policies in the Middle Ages* (Cambridge: Cambridge University Press, 1963). See also Fernand Braudel, *Civilization and Capitalism*, vol. 2, *The Wheels of Commerce* (New York: Harper & Row, 1982), and vol. 3, *The Perspective of the World* (New York: Harper & Row, 1984) (translated by Sian Reynolds). The following works offer useful interpretative frameworks: Douglass C. North and Robert P. Thomas, *The Rise of the Western World: A New Economic History* (Cambridge: Cambridge University Press, 1973); E. L. Jones, 2nd edition, *The European Miracle: Environments, Economies and Geopolitics in the History of Europe and Asia* (New York: Cambridge University Press, 1987); and Nathan Rosenberg and L. E. Birdzell, Jr., *How the West Grew Rich: The Economic Transformation of the Industrial World* (New York: Basic Books, 1986). Rondo Cameron, *A Concise Economic History of the World: From Paleolithic Times to the Present* (Oxford: Oxford University Press, 1989), places European developments in the perspective of world economic history. Felipe Fernandez-Armesto, *Before Columbus: Exploration and Colonization from the Mediterranean to the Atlantic, 1229–1492* (New York: Macmillan, 1987), surveys the early phases of European overseas expansion. Philip D. Curtin, *Cross-Cultural Trade in World History* (Cambridge: Cambridge University Press, 1984), is a broad study of early commercial contacts between Europeans and non-Europeans. A three-volume work, Immanuel Wallerstein, *The Modern World-System*, vol. 1, *Capitalist Agriculture and the Origins of the European World-Economy in the Sixteenth Century* (New York: Academic Press, 1974), vol. 2, *Mercantilism and the Consolidation of the European World-Economy, 1600–1750* (New York: Academic Press, 1980); and vol. 3, *The Second Era of Great Expansion of the Capitalist World-Economy, 1730–1840s* (New York: Academic Press, 1989), offers a challenging interpretation of European economic history, useful for its perspectives on expansion. D. C. Coleman, ed., *Revisions in Mercantilism* (London: Methuen, 1969), and W. E. Minchinton, ed., *Mercantilism: System or Expediency?* (Lexington, Mass.: D. C. Heath, 1969), contain essays that cover a range of interpretations of mercantilism.

The following are notable for their comparative approach to the development of colonial empires: Ralph Davis, *The Rise of the Atlantic Economies* (London: Weidenfeld & Nicolson, 1973); K. G. Davies, *The North Atlantic World in the Seventeenth Century* (Minneapolis: University of Minnesota Press, 1974); and Max Savelle, *Empires to Nations: Expansion in America, 1713–1824* (Minneapolis: University of Minnesota Press, 1974). Chapters in E. E. Rich and C. H. Wilson, eds., *Cambridge Economic History of Europe*, vol. 4, *The Economy of Expanding Europe in the Sixteenth and Seventeenth Centuries* (Cambridge: Cambridge University

Press, 1967), furnish information on specialized topics. Essays in James D. Tracy, ed., *The Rise of Merchant Empires: Long-Distance Trade in the Early Modern World, 1350–1750* (Cambridge: Cambridge University Press, 1990), deal with various aspects of the early expansion of Europe. Ida Altman and James Horn (eds.), *"To Make America": European Emigration in the Early Modern Period* (Berkeley: University of California Press, 1991), compares settlers of various nationalities.

Leslie Bethell, ed., *The Cambridge History of Latin America*, vols. 1 and 2, *Colonial Latin America* (Cambridge: Cambridge University Press, 1984), explores various topics dealing with the economic history of the Iberian empires in the Western Hemisphere. For the significance of the colonial experience for Latin America's later economic fate, see Stanley Stein and Barbara H. Stein, *The Colonial Heritage of Latin America: Essays on Economic Dependence* (New York: Oxford University Press, 1970). The articles in *William and Mary Quarterly*, 49, 2 (April 1992), explore various facets of the "Columbian Encounters." Jonathan I. Israel, *Dutch Primacy in World Trade, 1585–1740* (Oxford: Oxford University Press, 1989), surveys the commercial empire created by Holland. Van Cleaf Bachman, *Peltries or Plantations: The Economic Policies of the Dutch West India Company in New Netherland, 1623–1639* (Baltimore: Johns Hopkins University Press, 1969), focuses on decision making by managers of the West India Company. Harold A. Innis, *The Fur Trade in Canada*, rev. ed. (New Haven: Yale University Press, 1962), is a classic work that analyzes the influence of the fur trade on Canadian history. Still useful is Sigmund Diamond, "An Experiment in 'Feudalism': French Canada in the Seventeenth Century," *William and Mary Quarterly*, 18 (1961). John G. Clark, *New Orleans, 1718–1812: An Economic History* (Baton Rouge: Louisiana State University Press, 1970), explores French efforts to organize economic activity in the lower Mississippi Valley.

For a comprehensive synthesis that incorporates recent scholarly research, see C. G. A. Clay, *Economic Expansion and Social Change: England, 1500–1700*, 2 vols. (Cambridge: Cambridge University Press, 1984). Kenneth R. Andrews, *Trade, Plunder and Settlement: Maritime Enterprise and the Genesis of the British Empire, 1480–1630* (Cambridge: Cambridge University Press, 1984), and David B. Quinn and A. N. Ryan, *England's Sea Empire, 1550–1642* (Winchester, Mass.: Allen & Unwin, 1983), provide excellent surveys of England's early overseas efforts. Essays in W. E. Minchinton, ed., *The Growth of English Overseas Trade in the Seventeenth and Eighteenth Centuries* (London: Methuen, 1969), explore various aspects of foreign commerce, while Ralph Davis, *English Overseas Trade, 1500–1700* (London: Macmillan, 1973), presents a good overview. Theodore K. Rabb, *Enterprise and Empire: Merchant and Gentry Investment in the Expansion of England, 1575–1630* (Cambridge: Harvard University Press, 1967), is a quantitative study of investment in English trading and colonizing companies, while Ann M. Carlos and Stephen Nicholas, " 'Giants of an Earlier Capitalism': The Chartered Trading Companies as Modern Multinationals," *Business History Review* 62 (1988), analyzes the development of managerial hierarchies in the large trading companies of the sixteenth and seventeenth centuries. David B. Quinn, *England and the Discovery of America, 1481–1620* (New York: Knopf, 1974), traces England's changing interest in North America. Joyce Appleby, "Modernization Theory and the Formation of Modern Social Theories in England and America," *Comparative Studies in Society and History*, 20 (1978), contains an analysis of economic concepts formed in sixteenth- and seventeenth-century England.

Chapter 2

Regional Patterns of Colonial Development

B
Y THE MIDDLE OF THE EIGHTEENTH CENTURY, Britain had created a worldwide empire, including colonies along the eastern coast of North America and on islands in the Caribbean. Early English efforts to establish a foothold in the Western Hemisphere had been inspired by the hope of finding precious metals or of expanding the nation's foreign trade. But England's major discovery in North America was an abundance of natural resources, particularly a seemingly unlimited supply of fertile land. With it came a growing realization of what could be gained by exploiting that base for the production of staple commodities for the European segment of the world economy. At first joint stock companies and later individuals or groups known as proprietors arranged the planning, management, and financing of colonial ventures. The settlers, coming from a society with a strong commercial orientation, organized productive efforts in each colony; they directed their efforts not only toward their own subsistence but also toward the development of an export base resting on one or more staple commodities. Integration of the North American settlements into a commercial empire then required the creation of transatlantic channels of commerce that could handle the export of colonial commodities and the import of a wide range of goods.

The early settlements throughout British America were a classic model of *economic colonialism*—a strong orientation toward extractive industry and dependence on a more advanced economy for commercial services and manufactured goods. However, by the middle of the eighteenth century, the colonies' efforts in finding suitable staples led to the emergence of distinctive regional patterns of economic development. The West Indian and southern mainland provinces found success in plantation capitalism—a system that produced staple commodities for the European segment of the world economy. At the same time, the New England and Middle Colonies were evolving

(though not entirely by choice) a system of merchant capitalism—a more complex economy that later enabled economic decision makers in that region to assume leadership in the long process that transformed America into a leading industrial nation.

Planting the English Colonies

Joint Stock Companies

The Jamestown Colony. England's first permanent settlement in America was initially planned and undertaken by the Virginia Company as a business enterprise. London merchants who had assumed leadership in organizing large-scale trading companies to Russia and the eastern Mediterranean secured a charter for the company in 1606, authorizing the company to plant a settlement and hold a monopoly of its trade. From the colony initiated at Jamestown in 1607, the company planned to search for a northwest passage to the Far East, look for precious metals, trade with the natives, and organize a support base for continued economic penetration of Spanish America. On the basis of their projections of profitable activity, the promoters sold shares of the Virginia Company to a wide range of investors, including nobles and gentry as well as merchants. With nearly seventeen hundred members, the company was for a time the most popular venture for those attracted by the potential profits in overseas enterprise.

The Virginia Company soon learned that profitable colonization required long-term economic development and the investment of far larger amounts of capital than was originally anticipated. The inability of the company to produce a profit quickly, however, resulted in a sharp decline in investors' interest. Subscribers, receiving no dividends, refused to make further payments on installments due on their purchases of shares. A lottery run by the Virginia Company provided the funds needed to maintain the Jamestown Colony; it supplied almost one-third of the total funds raised by the company during its eighteen years of operation.

No less perplexing than the problem of raising money was that of determining what could be profitably produced for export. Hopes centered at various times on a wide variety of products, including wine, silk, iron, glass, oranges, and pineapples. Success in the search for a staple to support the new colony came with the discovery of a variety of tobacco suitable for European tastes and cultivation in Virginia. A market in Europe already existed for the commodity, supplied largely by imports from the Spanish West Indies.

Intertwined with the problems of securing adequate financial support and of finding an export staple was the need to organize a productive effort in Jamestown. Since the promoters in London lacked the funds to pay the "planters" or settlers, whom they sent to the colony at company expense to work on company projects and property, they instead promised each settler a share in the enterprise's profits and a tract of land after seven years of service. However, the strategy was unsuccessful in that the company did not earn a profit and the paramilitary organization employed to impose strict discipline was largely ineffective. In 1618 the Virginia Company developed a new policy that gave individual planters a major share of the responsibility for managing production in the Jamestown colony. Settlers who came at their own expense received fifty acres of land as well as a like amount of land for each additional person they brought along. This marked the beginning of the *headright system* of land distribution in Virginia, which continued even after the Virginia Company's charter was revoked in 1624. Individuals and groups who transported their own work forces were authorized to organize new plantations or new settlements. Only after a

decade of effort did the promoters realize that land hunger would provide the motive to develop Virginia. Yet it was not merely land ownership that attracted settlers to America; also important was the lure of profits to be made from growing and selling tobacco for export to England. As a result, Jamestown in the 1620s acquired the characteristics of a boom town.

The Massachusetts Bay Colony. The joint stock company was employed in several other efforts to establish colonies, but, as in Virginia, without financial success for investors. However, in one case a religious group used this form of business organization as a device to facilitate the migration of its own members from England to America. The Puritan promoters of the Massachusetts Bay Company, chartered in 1629, sought to establish in the New World a community organized on Calvinist socio-religious principles. As a result, their experiences were markedly different from those of the Jamestown colonists. By taking the government of the company with them to America, settlers in Massachusetts Bay assured themselves of considerable autonomy in making decisions about religious, political, and social affairs. Moreover, their English business backers made minimal economic demands, so the Puritans did not feel the pressure to export as did the settlers in Virginia.

Financing the initial settlement of the Massachusetts Bay colony was not as difficult as it had been in early Virginia. Most Puritan settlers financed their own migration and that of their families, using proceeds from the sale of their property in England. Although the immigrants came from many different occupational backgrounds, most became farmers, a calling that met the economic need of a pioneer country. Since the Puritans constituted a tightly knit group whose settlement in Massachusetts was motivated largely by religious considerations, they attempted to re-create in the colony the old-style *open-field system* (a system of communal farming) that still survived in parts of England. Provincial authorities granted land to town founders, who, in turn, distributed strips of land to the families settling there. Inhabitants resided in houses along the streets or around the commons of a village, rather than on scattered farms, and they worked their strips of land in large open fields. The open-field method of farming required common decisions by the group to determine what would be produced. Of basic economic significance right from the start, however, was private land ownership. The ability to buy, sell, and trade land made possible the accumulation of strips of land by individuals, which undermined the communal system of farm operations.

Other colonies were established in the New England region as offshoots of Massachusetts Bay. Corporate bodies of religious dissenters created communities in what became Rhode Island, Connecticut, New Hampshire, and Maine; they organized these communities according to their own particular variety of Calvinist principles. The seventeenth-century Puritan emphasis on orthodoxy had the unplanned economic result of stimulating settlement over a wider area of New England than was anticipated by the original founders of the Massachusetts Bay Colony.

Proprietors

After colonization companies lost favor as a way to finance and organize settlement in North America, English government policy came to rely on proprietors—wealthy individuals or groups—to develop colonies. With a charter conferred by the king, a proprietor or a group of proprietors received title to a large tract of land as well as extensive political authority. Some proprietors had a particular objective, such as enabling members of a religious minority to establish their own community. Most proprietors planned to create an orderly society in the New World by strengthening the older, hierarchical values that were diminishing in influence in England. However, many proprietors also had a more modern economic purpose in projecting colonies—a hope to increase their own fortunes. The proprietors of seventeenth-century colonies were the first great real estate developers in American history. Pennsylvania, Maryland, the Carolinas, New Jersey, and several West Indian colonies were among the ventures undertaken by proprietors.

The experience of William Penn illustrates the methods used by seventeenth-century proprietors to establish colonies. A charter granted in 1681 enabled Penn to undertake his plan to establish in America a "Holy Experiment"—a community satisfying to Quakers (members of the Society of Friends), who were being persecuted in England. He initially contemplated an orderly kind of settlement in Pennsylvania, where people would live in agricultural villages built around their meetinghouses. But Penn was a realistic colony builder. Like other proprietors, he knew that he could not provide all of the capital himself, though he was prepared to make a substantial investment. Penn's greatest appeal was to ordinary people, and he reached them through the wide distribution of tracts among Quakers and other disaffected groups that explained the advantages of settlement in Pennsylvania. Significantly, Penn offered a variety of terms that appeared attractive to a broad range of prospective settlers. The moderately well-to-do, for example, could buy land at the rate of £100 for five thousand acres. To those without command of much capital, Penn agreed to rent land at a low rate. Even those unable to pay rent could seek an assignment of land and a stake of tools, seed, and the right to work the tract for seven years, at which time they would have an option to buy. To encourage the migration of those unable to pay the cost of passage, Penn made a grant of fifty acres to the person financing the transportation of a servant and another

The Port of Philadelphia, ca 1720.   Philadelphia along with New York and Boston became not only busy shipping ports but also major commercial centers with strong business communities. This view was painted by a contemporary signboard artist. (The Library Company of America)

fifty acres to the servant on expiration of the agreed-upon term. He promised large blocks of land to religious and other groups of people migrating to the colony. As in the other proprietary colonies, Penn received a return on his investment of capital and entrepreneurial activity by collecting an annual quitrent (more like a tax than a rent) on land that he sold or granted. The proprietor also retained ownership of as much as one-tenth of the land in each area as it was settled, property that he believed would increase in value with the demographic and economic growth of the colony.

Instead of following Penn's plan of settlement in agricultural villages, however, the settlers turned the Holy Experiment into a major real estate speculation. Penn's liberal land policies and the Quaker toleration of other religious faiths and ethnic groups appealed not only to large numbers of English men and women but, from the early years of the eighteenth century, to other Europeans as well, especially Germans and Scotch-Irish (people of Scottish origin who lived in Ireland). Those who came to farm wanted to adopt the most up-to-date kind of agricultural organization existing in England rather than outmoded communal farming. They wanted to live on their own farms, in line with the growing emphasis on individual achievement. This desire, in turn, encouraged a dispersion of rural settle-

ment, the opposite of Penn's initial hope for compactness.

Proprietors, like investors in joint stock companies, received small financial rewards for their developmental efforts in British North America. Of all of the proprietors involved in colonization, only the Penns and the Calverts (of Maryland) retained ownership until the American Revolution. Yet even members of the Penn family, the most successful colonizing proprietors, earned from their investment in Pennsylvania no more than they would have received from a similar investment in government bonds.

Euro-Americans

The major contribution of joint stock companies and proprietors to colonization was the creation of a framework within which the initial settlement of an area could be organized, including a method of establishing title to the land. However, it was the productive effort of the settlers that made growth of these settlements possible within the orbit of the European-centered world economy.

What distinguished English colony building from that of other national states was the readiness of large numbers of men and women to invest themselves and whatever funds they possessed in the development of overseas colonies. A substantial number of those who migrated were of middle-class status in England; they had sufficient capital for their own transportation and for the establishment of a plantation, farm, or other productive enterprise in the New World. They hoped to produce a surplus beyond their subsistence needs for sale to the market, making it possible for them to improve their material position.

Indentured Servants

There were others in the British Isles in the seventeenth and eighteenth centuries, and in Germany in the eighteenth century, looking to improve their lot in life but who lacked funds to migrate to America. Many of these men and women chose to become indentured servants, agreeing to work for a specified period in return for their passage as well as food, clothing, and shelter during the term of service, and often freedom dues afterwards. Most were in their late teens or early twenties. Males outnumbered females by about three to one in the seventeenth century, but men constituted perhaps nine-tenths of indentured servants in the eighteenth century.

The standard length of service was four years, although there was some room for bargaining, the terms depending upon the individual's level of skills, the market conditions for labor in the colonies, and the colonial region to which the person was willing to go. The hope of land ownership or operation of an independent economic enterprise after completion of the term of service outweighed the temporary restrictions imposed on the personal freedom of the migrant. Throughout the colonial period, indentured servitude worked as a kind of credit system by which young people could borrow what they needed to position themselves in an area of greater perceived opportunity.

Another group of indentured servants, increasingly important in the eighteenth century, consisted of convicts transported to the colonies. They worked for a term of seven to fourteen years and had no choice about the kind of work they would do or the location to which they would be sent. The British government considered this method of dealing with convicts a low-cost alternative to maintaining prisons.

An estimated 350,000 European men and women came to British America in the seventeenth and eighteenth centuries as indentured servants. They accounted for at least one-half of all European migrants to the colonies. Most of them came willingly, though some (about one-seventh) arrived unwillingly. The labor of indentured servants met the needs of settlers, who found that an abundance of land in the New World and its low cost made wage labor scarce and expensive. Over a century and a half, the institution of indentured servitude displayed considerable flexibility. It evolved from primarily a source of unskilled labor for plantation agriculture to one of **supplying** workers with a wide range of differnt kinds of skills for many of the colonies. Throughout the colonial period, the shipment of indentured servants was a highly organized business, as ship captains recruited candidates for indenture and transported them for sale to planters, farmers, and other entrepreneurs in America.

The economic concepts and practices carried to America by the English settlers were predominant in the American colonies. But other peoples also played an important role in the creation of the economy, including both the native population and the unwilling migrants brought from Africa. In contrast to the economic benefits that could be gained by a large majority of the migrants from Europe and their descendants, American Indians and African-Americans paid a high price in the process of integrating North America into a European-oriented world economy. To the

Life in an Indian Village.   By 1200 A.D., Etowah, located in what is now northwestern Georgia, was an important cultural center, containing temples, plazas, and a defensive palisade around the town.

Euro-Americans, the former were compelled to surrender their land, the latter the fruits of their labor.

American Indians

Historians once conveyed the impression that the eastern seaboard of the North American continent settled by the English was a forested wilderness inhabited by only a few nomads. Actually, the region had a considerable population. Though scholars continue to differ over the precise number of people residing in North America when the Europeans arrived, recently formulated estimates of a total population of 10 to 12 million in present-day United States and Canada have found good support.[1] Belonging

to many nations or tribes, the aboriginal population lived in small semipermanent villages and carried on an economy that combined hunting and gathering with agriculture, notably the cultivation of maize (Indian corn). But the native culture lacked some of the basic elements of European culture, such as writing, the wheel, the plow, livestock, iron implements, and firearms.

The first to establish contact with the native peoples of the eastern seaboard were the traders. They sought, as did other Europeans on other continents, to integrate the region into the world economy through trade. American Indians became increasingly dependent on English and other European traders for iron goods, textiles, and other articles, integrating these goods into their own culture in novel ways. Liquor also played an important role in this commerce. Firearms and ammunition were crucial, since American Indian nations without access to this form of European technology were at the mercy of those with it. Furs were the only surplus commodity that the native economy could offer in exchange. From the point of view of traders, the American Indian economy could furnish a valuable export and provide a profitable market for imported goods. However, while the interest of English traders lay in preserving the general shape of the American Indian economic system, trade tended to disrupt the traditional native economic life-style. It also encouraged intertribal warfare, as groups of American Indians sought to expand their production of furs by devoting more time to trapping and moving into hunting grounds claimed by other tribes.

Unlike the traders, the settlers who came to America to engage in agriculture had a somewhat different attitude toward American Indian society. In the early stages of settlement, the newcomers were introduced by the natives to many new crops, including maize and tobacco, and taught how to clear land and cultivate the crops. It soon became clear, though, that the land uses of the colonists were incompatible with those of the American Indians. Thus, everywhere that the English settled, the American Indians came to be regarded as an obstacle to be removed so that their land could be taken. Some colony builders, like Roger Williams of Rhode Island and William Penn of Pennsylvania, tried to develop fair methods for the purchase of land claimed by native groups. But too often the pressures generated by land hunger led settlers to extinguish American Indian titles by fraud or force.

In addition to a technological superiority and a more sophisticated political organization, Europeans carried with them to North America many organisms that proved to be even more devastating to the native population. Isolated from Europe for thousands of years, American Indians lacked immunity to

many common European diseases, including smallpox, measles, influenza, and tuberculosis. Contact with European disease thereby set in motion a long process of native depopulation. Between 1492 and 1900, the native population of the present-day United States declined from an estimated 10 to 12 million to fewer than 500,000. While the American Indians were declining in numbers, the English demographic base was growing.

Disagreements and friction between the two groups over land use and other issues eventually led to open and bloody war. The English settlers, including rival groups, united long enough to triumph over the natives, who were not able to develop an effective resistance. Many native survivors retreated to the West; those who stayed sought to eke out a living on the margins of the white-controlled economy.

African-Americans

From the beginning of settlement, a major problem facing agricultural entrepreneurs in America was how to secure an adequate supply of labor in order to expand the production of low-cost staple commodities for the European market. American Indians were enslaved throughout the colonies; in South Carolina, an extensive slave trade developed late in the seventeenth century. But the devastating effects of European disease as well as the cultural shock associated with a different way of life and harsh discipline made the American Indian population an unsatisfactory source of labor supply. Unlike the Spanish in Mexico and Peru, English colonists did not succeed in turning the native peoples into an effective labor force.

As noted previously, the settlers had early turned to indentured servants from England as one form of forced labor. However, a major shift, from white indentured servants to black slaves from Africa, got under way in agriculture in the West Indies and the southern mainland colonies during the latter half of the seventeenth century. It was encouraged by the changing relative costs of the two forms of labor. A combination of factors caused the cost of European servants to rise as an increasing supply of slaves from Africa became available. The planters soon realized that, for a somewhat higher initial price, they could purchase a slave's labor for life, rather than a servant's labor for only a few years, as well as gain ownership of the offspring of female slaves. In addition, the planters were in a position to impose lower living standards on Africans than on European servants, resulting in reduced maintenance costs. Furthermore, use of black slaves from Africa rather than white servants from England avoided the threat to social stability sometimes created by dissatisfied, freed indentured servants, especially those who faced limited opportunity if they completed their terms of service during an economic depression. African-Americans were by no means willing workers in American agriculture, but planters used both the carrot and the stick to organize them into an effective labor force. Thus, forced migrants from Africa and their descendants came to form the bulk of the labor force in the West Indies and the southern mainland colonies, first in unskilled agricultural work and later in a variety of skilled craft occupations as well.

One problem facing the colonists was how to create a legal status for slavery, which did not exist in English law. At first, African-Americans in Virginia, who had begun to arrive in small numbers as early as 1619, were regarded as servants. Some of them served for life and their children inherited the same obligations. In the 1670s and 1680s, the colonies worked out legal codes to create the status of slavery for blacks. These codes denied to black slaves the basic elements of humanity, including personal rights and liberty, and treated them as chattel property. At the same time, racist assumptions led whites to believe that blacks were inferior, supposedly justifying to the former the enslavement of the latter. Control was facilitated by racial differentiation, since the physical characteristics of the black person could be easily distinguished from those of the white European person.

Nearly 1.5 million blacks were transported from Africa to England's colonies in the Western Hemisphere, with over 80 percent going to the West Indies and another 16 percent to the southern mainland provinces. Since most slaves were purchased by Europeans from African traders, an efficient system of middlemen developed in Africa not only to gather slaves in the interior and deliver them to the coast but also to distribute European imported goods (such as firearms, liquor, textiles, and a variety of metal products). Available evidence indicates that in the eighteenth century, about one-half of the slaves gathered by the middlemen were prisoners of war and about one-quarter were enslaved in small-scale operations of slave raiders. It is likely that the demand for slaves induced Africans to alter their military strategy so as to maximize the number of prisoners taken in battle without actually increasing the incidence of warfare.

Slave trading was open to any citizen of the British empire (except for a short time late in the seventeenth century, when it was a monopoly of the Royal African Company). As a result, many colonial and English merchants participated in some aspect of that commerce. Slavers from many other nations of Western Europe also participated in the slave trade, seeking supplies of labor for their own colonies. At the same time, a substantial number of Africans organized the sale of slaves to Europeans. The existence of so many European buyers and African sellers contributed to the highly competitive market for slaves, whose prices reflected conditions of supply and demand.

The transatlantic slave trade was a speculative as well as competitive business, with some individual ventures extremely profitable and others recording financial losses for British or colonial shippers. However, the risk to the African slave being carried away involved not money but life—his or her own. It is estimated that 12 percent of the slaves carried from Africa to the southern colonies died in transit during the latter half of the eighteenth century. (This represents a somewhat lower figure than that which prevailed a century earlier, due primarily to a reduction in the average time of passage.) Contributing to the high rate of mortality in the transatlantic slave trade were inadequate supplies of food and water, especially when bad weather lengthened the voyage; diseases that spread quickly among the men and women on overcrowded ships; the harsh suppression of attempted slave revolts; and suicide as a way to escape an unknown fate.

Slavery and the slave trade supplied what seemed like a never-ending stream of labor to produce staple commodities in the tropical and semitropical regions of the Western Hemisphere. Expanding the low-cost production of these commodities inevitably drove down their prices, creating in Europe a mass market for what had once been luxuries. But this was accomplished at high costs—in human life and in dignity for the forced African immigrants who composed the labor force.

Plantation Capitalism

The simplest way for early Americans to satisfy their desire for goods they could not produce themselves was to exchange the products of their agricultural economy for those made in England. This is essentially what colonists achieved in the West Indies and the southern mainland colonies. Here the efficient application of enterprise, capital, and labor to the resource base (soil and climate) resulted in a system of *plantation capitalism*—organizing the production of staple commodities (like sugar, tobacco, rice, and indigo) for export, usually on a large unit known as a plantation and using slave labor. This broad region was integrated into the European economy as a supply area for tropical and semitropical products. As the following survey of the West Indies, the Lower South, and the Chesapeake shows, the production of staple commodities for export to Europe generated both wealth and population in these provinces. However, it also threatened future economic development in those regions, especially after the conditions that had made plantation capitalism so profitable changed.

The West Indies

Of all their American possessions, the English regarded their West Indian provinces most highly. Jamaica, Barbados, and several smaller islands occupied a land area no larger than present-day New Jersey and contained, in the mid-eighteenth century, a white population of a little more than one-tenth the size of the European population of the mainland colonies. Yet the value of the Sugar Islands' commerce with England was greater than the combined trade carried on by the thirteen mainland colonies.

In the early years of English settlement in the West Indies, tobacco was the chief cash crop, produced mainly by small farmers using their own labor and occasionally that of a few indentured servants. A sharp drop in tobacco prices around the mid-seventeenth century stimulated a shift to sugar, a commodity for which the tropical climate of the Caribbean was well suited. A Golden Age was ushered in, first for Barbados and later for the other West Indian islands, based on a combination of the low cost, high yield, and good price of sugar. Although sugar prices declined from the peak experienced at the beginning of the sugar boom, the drop was moderate and served to broaden the market.

With the shift to sugar, black slaves soon became the principal element in the labor force. The same factors that made the forced migrant from Africa a desirable source of labor in other colonies—cost and discipline—were also apparent to decision makers in the Caribbean. In contrast to the mainland colonies, where the slave population grew by natural increase as well as by importations, underfeeding and overworking in the West Indies resulted in a natural decrease—an excess of deaths over births—so that the slave supply had to be constantly replenished by imports. Demographic data reflect the close relationship between sugar and slavery. As early as 1660, the number of blacks surpassed the number of whites on Barbados. By the mid-eighteenth century, slaves accounted for about 90 percent of the total population of England's Caribbean colonies.

The sugar revolution created opportunities for aggressive entrepreneurs with access to capital to increase significantly their economic distance from those with slender financial resources. The purchase of slaves required a larger investment in labor than had been the case with indentured servants. More important, though, sugar processing involved the use of expensive equipment, so the competitive advantage was held by the planters who owned their own machinery. In Barbados in 1680, only 175 planters (comprising 7 percent of all property holders) owned 54 percent of the slave labor force. The situation was similar elsewhere in the Caribbean where sugar was dominant. A large sugar plantation was a complex agro-industrial operation, with the greatest financial rewards going to the owner-managers who paid the most diligent attention to business. Despite the system of large estates, there continued to be opportunities for

enterprising newcomers to enter sugar production by purchasing a plantation with capital accumulated through a commercial or professional activity. Some small producers on the islands were more likely to gain success in minor tropical commodities, such as ginger, coffee, cocoa, or cotton. Unlike the mainland colonies, where production of a staple for export was combined with the tillage of food crops, the high returns from sugar and the limited amount of arable land encouraged the West Indies to rely on imports from England, Ireland, and mainland North America to provide much of the food for both planters and slaves. (As we will see later in the chapter, the West Indies thereby played an important role in the economic development of the northern mainland colonies.)

In the late seventeenth and early eighteenth centuries, much of the sugar shipped to England was reexported to continental Europe. However, by the 1730s, the home market had expanded to absorb almost the entire production of the British West Indies, except what was exported to Britain's colonies in North America. Insulation of the British market by tariff protection served to maintain sugar prices at a higher level than on the continent. Most planters consigned their sugar to merchants in London, who arranged its sale and then purchased goods to the order of the planter. The consignment merchant also performed an essential financial function—selling goods on credit and making long-term loans secured by mortgages.

From Britain's point of view, the West Indian provinces constituted an almost perfect colony—they supplied tropical commodities to England and used British commercial services and manufactured goods. In addition, their highly commercial agriculture produced profits for both planters and merchants. Satisfying the sweet tooth of Europeans, however, took its toll on both human and natural resources—the lives and freedom of African-Americans and the exhaustion of the soil. Despite the presence of vigorous and aggressive entrepreneurs among the planter-businesspeople in the colonies, developmental activity took place almost entirely within the limits of staple production for export, with crucial control of foreign trade remaining in the hands of British business. With sugar so profitable, there was little encouragement for development along other lines that might have resulted in greater economic diversity. In short, the West Indian provinces remained economically dependent on Britain's more highly developed economy. Historians have long argued about the role of West Indian sugar profits in financing Britain's Industrial Revolution. More significant, though, is that no such economic transformation ever occurred in the Caribbean.

The Lower South

Another region of plantation capitalism was the Lower South, consisting of the coastal areas of South Carolina, Georgia, and the southern part of North Carolina. No other region of British mainland colonies developed an economic and social structure that more closely resembled that of the West Indies. The major staple commodities that the Lower South produced for the European market differed from those of the West Indies—rice and indigo instead of sugar. But specialization on these commodities had similar economic results to those associated with sugar production.

Charleston, the center of settlement, was founded in 1670. The early settlers, many of whom migrated from Barbados and other British West Indian colonies, made slow progress for several decades in their search for an economic base. They achieved some success in producing foodstuffs and timber products for export to the West Indies, and found a European market for the deerskins they obtained in trade with Native Americans. For a time in the early eighteenth century, South Carolina had a flourishing trade with England in naval stores—tar, pitch, turpentine, and other products of the forest.

During the late years of the seventeenth century, South Carolina discovered a variety of rice suitable for cultivation in the colony's subtropical climate and inland swamps fed by freshwater streams. Black slaves, who had been a part of the labor force almost from the time the colony was founded, played an essential role in the establishment of rice as a major staple by supplying from their African experience a knowledge of its cultivation and processing as well as serving as a low-cost labor force. By the 1720s, rice had become the colony's leading staple commodity. Over the ensuring half-century, rice exports grew more than tenfold, accounting for between 50 percent and 60 percent of the Lower South's exports (see Figure 2–1).

In the 1740s, the South Carolina planter Eliza Lucas Pinckney successfully introduced indigo production, which quickly became the region's second staple. Indigo found a ready market in England as a dye stuff for the important woolen cloth industry. Needing better drainage than rice and soil of a different composition, indigo was produced on lands up the rivers and streams from the rice fields. Also, slaves could be employed in indigo cultivation during slack seasons in rice production. Exports grew rapidly after 1750, with indigo accounting for about one-fifth of the value of commodity exports from the Lower South on the eve of the American Revolution.

Rice and indigo transformed the Carolina Low Country in much the same way that sugar had led to basic changes in the West Indies. White workers would not willingly endure the hard and disagreeable labor involved in the production of rice and indigo. As one contemporary observer commented: "No work can be imagined more pernicious to health than for men to stand in water mid-leg high, and often above it, planting and weeding rice."[2] During

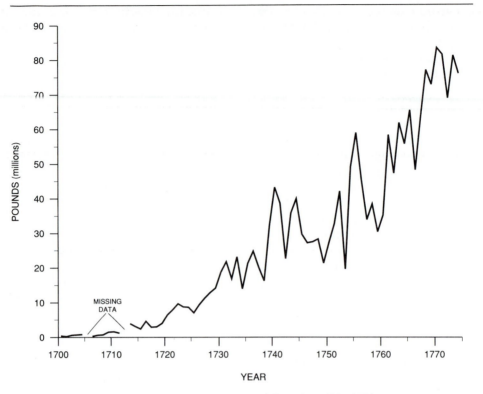

Figure 2–1 *Rice exported from South Carolina and Georgia, 1699–1774*

Source: Data from U.S. Bureau of the Census, *Historical Statistics of the United States, Colonial Times To 1970* (Washington, D.C.: GPO, 1975), p. 1192.

the two decades after rice cultivation took permanent hold, the black population drew equal to and then surpassed the white population. By 1730, African-Americans comprised two-thirds of the total population of the province, a majority that they continued to hold in the lowland area of South Carolina and attained in Georgia after slavery was established there. That black slaves rather than white servants became the labor force in the Lower South was not due to any inherent characteristic of black people enabling them to perform difficult labor under conditions hazardous to the physical well-being of humans; rather, it resulted from the ability of most whites to exercise choices to migrate to colonies with healthier work envi-

ronments, thereby avoiding the dangerous conditions associated with rice and indigo cultivation.

Along with the growth of slavery as a labor force came an increase in the size of the production unit, as large plantations specializing in rice production came to dominate the colony's economy. As in other regions characterized by plantation capitalism, aggressive planter-entrepreneurs took the leadership in the developmental activities that created wealth by organizing the production of a staple commodity for the European market.

British law required that rice be exported to England, though after 1731 shipments could be made directly from the colonies to southern

Europe. However, most of the rice shipped from the Lower South to British ports was re-exported to the European continent, with Germany becoming a leading consumer of the commodity. Growing demand for indigo stemmed from the expansion of the textile industry in Britain. A bounty was paid by the British government to encourage colonial production, and even though Carolina indigo was deemed inferior in quality to that of the French West Indies, a high tariff on foreign indigo served to protect the market for American planters.

Some planters shipped their rice and indigo to British merchants on consignment, whereas others sold their crops to merchants in Charleston, accounting for much of the foreign trade of the region. However, even the larger export firms located in Charleston were in effect branches of houses in London or another British port. In short, dominance by British business of the export of rice and indigo was nearly complete. On the eve of the American Revolution, Charleston was the fourth-largest city in British America, a busy port, and a center of the retail and service trades. Even so, it did not develop into the kind of commercial center that was evolving in Philadelphia, New York, and Boston (as we will see later in the chapter). London business actually performed much of the entrepôt function for the staple economy of the Lower South. According to the economic historian Jacob Price, "entrepreneurial decisions were made in Britain, capital was raised there, ships were built or chartered there, insurance was made there—all for the South Carolina trade."[3]

Beginning in the 1730s, a back-country sector grew vigorously in South Carolina, Georgia, and North Carolina, where settlers engaged in mixed farming, the raising of cattle and hogs, hunting and fishing, and lumbering. Most holdings were small and worked by family members. Initially, the settlers displayed considerable self-sufficiency, but once transportation and marketing channels were available, it was usual for farmers to sell a portion of their output. In small urban centers throughout this back-country area, storekeepers sold imported goods and purchased local produce for shipment to Charleston by either inland waterways or wagon roads. Economic development of a back-country sector based on mixed farming opened up opportunities for indigenous business; however, much of the export of wheat, corn, meat, and other foodstuffs was likely handled by the merchants of northern colonial cities.

The inland area of the Lower South developed a different type of economy from that of the coastal area, based on its distinct resource base. It also had a different racial composition, since few slaves were employed in general farming. But with the nineteenth-century discovery that the soil and climate of the uplands could be exploited in the cultivation of cotton, plantation capitalism (production of staple commodities for export, using slave labor) became relevant to the back country of the Lower South.

The Upper South

On the eve of Independence, Virginia and Maryland together contained nearly one-third of the total population of the mainland colonies and accounted for 60 percent of the value of exports to Britain from the thirteen provinces. Here was a region of plantation capitalism literally built on smoke, as the economic health of the two provinces rested on one great staple export—tobacco.

Economic leadership in the early years was assumed by aggressive planters, whose principal talent was the application of brute force and shrewd manipulation to produce as much tobacco as possible. When expanding tobacco exports from the Caribbean as well as from the Chesapeake caused a glut in the English market in the 1640s, Virginia and Maryland pro-

A Tobacco Warehouse, Chesapeake Bay Region, ca 1750. In Virginia and Maryland, tobacco, the major export, was shipped from many small trading centers that sprang up around public tobacco warehouses. (Historical Pictures/Stock Montage)

ducers, unlike the West Indian planters who faced the same situation, did not change their basic staple crop. Although some older planters sought to deal with low prices by restricting production, younger planters devised ways to expand their activities, sensing that the lower price of tobacco would broaden the market.

In the late seventeenth and early eighteenth centuries, leading planters in Virginia and Maryland discovered that the way to wealth lay in combining merchandising, shipping, moneylending, and land speculation with volume production of tobacco. Moreover, they took the lead in shifting from English indentured servants to African slaves as a labor force

in plantation agriculture. The career of Robert "King" Carter, whose extensive operations made him something of an embryonic tycoon, shows how one large planter-businessman of the Chesapeake could thrive in a highly competitive system based on low and fluctuating tobacco prices. The youngest son of a middling planter who had migrated to Virginia in the mid-seventeenth century, Carter at the time of his death in 1732 owned 300,000 acres of land, operated 44 plantations in 12 counties, possessed over 1,000 slaves, ran a store system that bought tobacco and sold goods to small planters, and lent money like a banking firm.

Slavery was a major force in widening the gap between large and small producers of tobacco. It was easier for planters with enough capital to buy even a few slaves to expand their volume and earn enough to purchase several more slaves than it was for those working the fields themselves to save enough to purchase one slave. However, tobacco culture did not provide economies of scale (or decreasing unit costs with rising output), so the older structure that had been dominated by yeomen farmers survived alongside the large plantations worked by slaves. At the end of the colonial period, whites still accounted for a majority of the total population of the tobacco colonies, despite the importation of substantial numbers of black slaves.

After a period of rapid growth between the 1620s and early 1670s, tobacco exports experienced a slower increase in the last quarter of the seventeenth century and then leveled off for another quarter-century. From the 1720s to the eve of the American Revolution, exports of tobacco from the Chesapeake colonies grew steadily (see Figure 2–2). While British law from 1660 required that all tobacco not consumed in the colonies be exported to England (including Scotland after 1707), the home market accounted for a decreasing part of tobacco consumption. Reexport markets in Europe absorbed nearly two-thirds of English tobacco imports by the end of the seventeenth century,

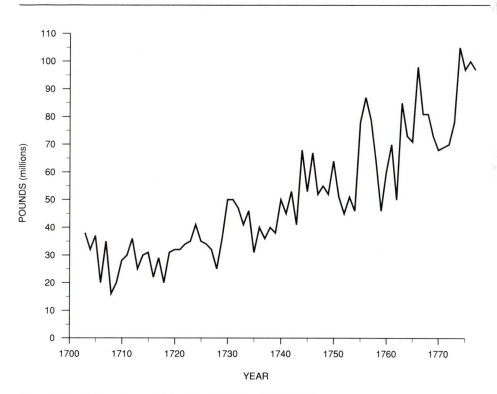

Figure 2–2 *Tobacco Imported by Great Britain, 1700–1775*

SOURCE: Data from U.S. Bureau of the Census, *Historical Statistics of the United States,* (Washington, D.C.: GPO, 1975), p. 1190.

and as much as 85 percent in the eighteenth century. From an early date, the Netherlands and Germany provided a strong market for the tobacco produced in Virginia and Maryland; then, in the 1720s, France emerged as a major market. To meet the expanding demand, large planters and small farmers alike, faced with soil exhaustion in the older tidewater area, took up fresh lands in the Piedmont region west of the fall line.

For a half-century or so after the beginning of tobacco production, many small English traders, attracted by high returns, participated in the trade by selling manufactured goods to Chesapeake planters and buying their tobacco. Starting in the 1680s, larger merchants came increasingly to dominate the tobacco trade. Some operated under a *consignment system*, by which colonial planters consigned their tobacco to a merchant in London or an outport, who sold it at the best market price and received a commission for the service. The consignment merchant also purchased goods ordered by the planter and attended to other needs, including the extension of credit. Smaller planters and farmers usually sold their tobacco outright in their own communities, at stores run by agents or employees of British firms. There they also bought imported goods, usually on credit. Several Scottish houses operated chains of stores; in the 1770s, one Glasgow firm owned seven stores in Maryland and fourteen in Virginia.

The eighteenth century witnessed a notable move toward a diversification of exports from the Chesapeake colonies. This diversification, mainly into grain production, initially represented efforts by planters to cushion the effects of volatility in the tobacco market by producing more of the goods and commodities which they needed for their own consumption, rather than directing all of their resources and efforts toward production for the market. Soon grain production not only met the region's own food needs but also provided a surplus

for export. In contrast to the tobacco trade, which was dominated by British business, provincial merchants handled much of the export of grain and other foodstuffs from Virginia and Maryland. On the eve of the Revolution, the "stinking weed" still accounted for almost three-quarters of the value of the exports of Virginia and Maryland; but this was down from 95 percent in the early years of the century. And grain and grain products stood at nearly one-fifth of the total between 1768 and 1772.

Urban development in Virginia and Maryland was limited. Since the tributaries of Chesapeake Bay were accessible for long distances to oceangoing vessels, exports could be shipped directly from many points (rather than being channeled through a single port serving a large region, as in other colonies). Then, too, tobacco, requiring little processing, did not serve to stimulate the growth of towns around an industrial base. Through much of the seventeenth century, English ships loaded tobacco and discharged imported goods at the wharves of individual planters. By the mid-eighteenth century, small urban centers in all parts of Virginia and Maryland were performing most of the business of their immediate localities. The provincial capitals of Williamsburg and Annapolis took on special significance in certain kinds of business, including the buying and selling of foreign exchange and the retail and service trades. Norfolk and Baltimore were beginning to assume importance as entrepôts in the years just prior to the revolution. Still, each of the many parts of the Chesapeake region maintained direct economic communications with Britain.

In spite of a promising trend toward diversification and the resulting expansion of opportunities for indigenous independent business firms by the time of the American Revolution, the economy of the Chesapeake evolved through the colonial period within the framework created in the early phases of its development. Even though the leading tobacco planters have sometimes been portrayed as agrarian gentlemen who frowned upon engagement in business, they typically acted as aggressive entrepreneurs. The result of their activities in economic development was to strengthen, not challenge, the basic pattern of staple production for the European market, with foreign trade controlled by British business.

Merchant Capitalism

While the West Indian and southern mainland colonies developed staple crops suited to the European market, settlers in colonies with more temperate climates—from Pennsylvania to New Hampshire—found that the commodities they could produce most effectively largely duplicated rather than supplemented those of England. Only by seeking outlets for their surplus outside of the normal, or bilateral, pattern of trade between a European country and its dependencies could the New England and Middle Colonies obtain the means to pay for desired imports. Significantly, in contrast to the experience of the plantation colonies, where British merchants and their agents maintained control of foreign commerce, trade outside of the ordinary colonial pattern created opportunities for American business to manage a large portion of the export trade of these provinces. In the process of integrating their regions into the world economy in a novel way, American merchants in the Middle and New England colonies assumed many of the business functions usually performed for colonial areas by the merchants of the imperial power. This led to a development unusual in the history of colonialism: the growth within a colonial area of strong centers of entrepreneurial decision making, creating the basic conditions necessary for the later evolution of a diversified economy less dependent on the export of staple commodities.

The New England Colonies

Throughout the colonial period, farming supported a large majority of the population of New England, a region comprising the colonies of Massachusetts Bay (including what is now Maine), Connecticut, Rhode Island, and New Hampshire. However, unlike the fertile land and hospitable climate that made possible an abundant agriculture in the southern and West Indian colonies, mediocre soils and a severe climate limited the ability of settlers in New England to develop a crop that would form an export base. Only in a few areas of New England were colonizers able to find a profitable form of specialized agricultural production for export markets, such as horses and cattle in Rhode Island and livestock, dairy products, and flax in parts of Connecticut. Most of the region's farmers grew maize and other foodstuffs primarily for themselves and their families. They earned enough for a frugal living, made somewhat more comfortable if they were able to supplement their income by other activities (like the operation of a sawmill or gristmill, tavern keeping, small-scale retailing, or simply hiring out for wages). During the early decades of the eighteenth century, Boston and other towns became dependent on imports of foodstuffs from the Chesapeake and Middle Colonies, as the farm production of the region did not expand sufficiently to feed the growing urban population.

When agriculture did not provide a way to wealth, as it did in most other colonies, settlers in New England looked elsewhere—to the sea. Fishermen—from Boston and the smaller ports along the Massachusetts coast as well as from New Hampshire—worked the shores of New England. By the 1660s, they went as far north as Nova Scotia and Newfoundland. However, unlike the sugar of the Caribbean, the tobacco of the Chesapeake, and the rice and indigo of the Lower South, the treasures of the sea did not provide New England colonies a basis for a bilateral trading system with England, the typical colonial relationship. Because English markets were served by England's own fishing fleets, New Englanders had to find other outlets for their fish in order to pay for imports from England. This they did by selling the better grades of fish to Spain and Portugal and their island possessions in the Atlantic. The poorer grades of fish went to feed the slaves in the expanding sugar economy of the West Indies. In both markets, fish was exchanged for cash, credits, or commodities that could be sold in England (such as Caribbean sugar products or Iberian wine and salt). The fisheries led to the development of a more general commerce as well as to the emergence of Boston as one of the major commercial centers of the Atlantic world. Merchants reached out to organize the collection of a variety of commodities from other English settlements along the Atlantic Coast, to which they distributed European goods shipped from England and West Indian tropical commodities. In short, Boston became the hub of a complex system of exchange of goods, credits, and cash; and in all of this trading, fish was a central element. The fisheries and shipping also fostered a shipbuilding industry in New England, which first involved the construction of small vessels used for fishing and the coastwide trade and then large ships for the transatlantic traffic.

By the middle of the eighteenth century, however, Boston had lost its position as the major trade center for all of British America. As we will see later in the chapter, merchants in Philadelphia and New York took advantage of the growing population and economic activity in the Middle Colonies to create their own domains of commerce. Boston remained the most important commercial center in New England, though a number of smaller ports in the region also participated in the West Indian trade.

Aside from Boston, only Newport, Rhode Island, conducted a direct trade with England; and because of geographical factors, it drew upon a limited hinterland.

The Middle Colonies

Climate and soil made possible a bountiful agriculture in the Middle Colonies of Pennsylvania, New York, New Jersey, and Delaware. Wheat was the most important crop grown in what were sometimes called the "Bread Colonies," but most farms also raised corn, flax, hemp, fruit, vegetables, cattle, hogs, and poultry. The typical unit of production in the region was the family farm, where the labor of family members was sometimes supplemented by that of one or two indentured servants.

The farmers of the Middle Colonies grew a surplus of agricultural commodities well beyond the needs of the region's population; still, their production largely paralleled that of Western Europe. Unlike the staples of the southern mainland and West Indian colonies, wheat and other foodstuffs from the Middle Colonies were not in demand in northern Europe until near the end of the colonial era. Thus, the commodities produced most efficiently in this region had to find markets outside of the usual colonial pattern of bilateral trade ties to England.

Merchants in Philadelphia and New York, the ports through which most of the trade of the Middle Colonies flowed, developed a growing market for food in England's West Indian colonies, where planters concentrated their efforts on the production of sugar. Because France failed to develop export agriculture in the St. Lawrence Valley, the English mainland colonies became the principal suppliers of foodstuffs to the French West Indies as well as to the British sugar colonies. Beginning in the 1730s, commerce with southern Europe, especially with Spain and Portugal, assumed growing significance. Trade with these

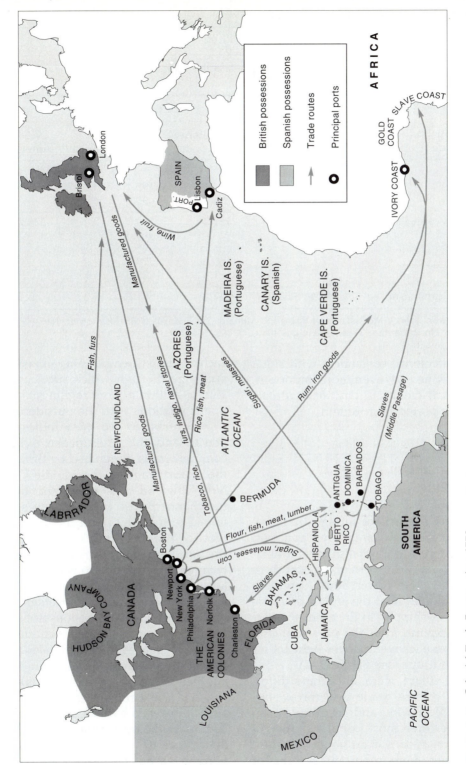

Figure 2–3. *Colonial Trade Routes, circa 1770.*

Source: Adapted from Martin Gilbert, *British History Atlas* (London: Macmillan, 1968).

Table 2–1   *Average Annual Value and Destinations of Commodity Exports, by Region, 1768–1772 (in pounds sterling)*

Colonial Region	Great Britain	Ireland	Southern Europe	West Indies	Africa	North America	Total
West Indies	£3383.9					£526.7	£3910.6
Lower South	394.0	£1.3	£54.1	£102.1	£0.3		551.9
Upper South	827.1	28.9	99.2	91.8			1046.9
Total: Plantation capitalism	4605.0	30.2	153.3	193.9	0.3	526.7	5509.4
New England	77.0	1.3	65.6	278.1	17.2		439.1
Middle Colonies	68.4	51.7	181.8	223.6	1.1		526.5
Total: Merchant capitalism	145.4	53.0	247.4	501.7	18.3	0.0	965.6

SOURCE: Adapted from John J. McCusker and Russell R. Menard, *The Economy of British America, 1607–1789* (Chapel Hill: University of North Carolina Press, 1985), pp. 108, 130, 160, 174, 199.

areas supplied colonial consumers with sugar products and wine and, even more important, earned cash and credits to pay for manufactured goods imported from Britain.

Toward Autonomy in Economic Decision Making

The contrasting patterns of foreign trade between the colonies of Plantation Capitalism and those of Merchant Capitalism are summarized in Table 2–1. While most of the exports of the West Indies, the Lower South, and the Chesapeake colonies near the end of the colonial period were shipped to England, the majority of the exports from the New England and Middle Colonies went to the West Indies and southern Europe (see Figure 3–2).

In addition, there were important differences in how colonial trade was carried on. Philadelphia, New York, and Boston were, in that order, the three most populous cities of British America. Each was an important shipping point. Even more important in terms of long-run economic development, merchants in each of these three cities organized a system of exchange through which producers and consumers within a large region maintained economic relations with the outside world.

In contrast to the West Indies, the Lower South, and the Chesapeake, where foreign commerce was dominated by British business, the export trade of the Middle Colonies and New England was organized by American merchants. British trading houses were accustomed to thinking in terms of recognized staples for European markets, but exports from the northern colonies involved a variety of commodities shipped to widely scattered markets, many of them relatively small. The American merchant was in a strategic position to make many crucial decisions about the selection of commodities, destination (or destinations) of voyages, terms of sale, and disposition of the proceeds (whether in cash, credits, another cargo, or some combination of all three). Each merchant relied on a network of agents that had to be given considerable discretion in doing business in distant places. Sometimes it was the ship captain or the supercargo (a business agent who accompanied the shipment) who had responsibility for selling the cargo and investing the proceeds. More often, though, the cargo was consigned to a resident merchant, who transacted business for a commission. Kinship formed an important element in creating a network of correspondents, as several family-run business groups spread through the Atlantic world during the seventeenth and eighteenth centuries.

No less important than the establishment of market relations overseas was the growth of a network of marketplace communities in the hinterlands for the collection of commodities and the distribution of goods. There emerged in each region a complex of urban places, varying in size and importance from small cities like Lancaster (which prided itself on being a little Philadelphia) to hamlets built around flour mills and taverns. Storekeepers in these places sold goods to farmers in the neighborhood and purchased local produce, usually serving as agents for merchants in the major business center of the region. Much of the inland trade moved by natural waterways, transported on small, open boats that could carry as much as thirty-five tons while drawing only four or five feet of water. Although more expensive than water travel, overland transport was also important, with wagons moving over road systems that had Philadelphia, New York, or Boston as their hub.

In the eighteenth century, the leading businesspeople of the three metropolitan centers were more than exporters and importers; as unspecialized merchants, they carried out many business functions that later became the province of specialized branches of business in the nineteenth century. Often in partnership with others, the merchants owned the vessels that carried their cargoes to and from the West Indies, Southern Europe, and, to a lesser extent, the British Isles. By the 1770s, Philadelphia merchants had accumulated an investment of £500,000 in oceangoing ships. In the conduct of their business, merchants performed financial functions: They dealt in foreign exchange, borrowed from British exporters, extended credit to inland traders and retailers (who then extended credit to consumers), and arranged for insurance of ships and cargoes. In the absence of an adequate supply of currency in the colonies, they helped to clear payments for transactions through bookkeeping techniques. In addition, the merchants promoted and financed manufacturing activities, many of them ancillary to foreign commerce and shipping: shipyards (with ships becoming an important export), rope walks, cooperage establishments, sail lofts, flour mills (usually located in the countryside at water-power sites), rum distilleries, sugar refineries, and iron furnaces (hardware for ships constituted one of the most important end products of iron).

Entrepreneurs in Philadelphia, New York, and Boston succeeded in organizing the economic activity of their regions within, but partially autonomous from, the British commercial system. The three great port cities provided services for their hinterlands of a kind supplied directly by British business to the plantation colonies. The extensive and complex commercial life of these regional centers mirrored London but on a smaller scale.

Summary

The economy of the Atlantic world in the seventeenth and eighteenth centuries contained many challenges and opportunities for business-minded people who possessed energy, vision, and access to capital. Whether they went to the Caribbean, South Carolina, or the Chesapeake, to Boston, Philadelphia, or New York, entrepreneurs who organized the economies of their colonies possessed enormous ambition as well as an ability to find the most appropriate "way to wealth" for the economic environment in which they operated. For some, that environment centered around producing sugar, rice and indigo, or tobacco with slave labor; for others, it was organizing a trade in fish or merchandising foodstuffs to producers of tropical commodities.

All thirteen mainland colonies as well as the West Indies participated in what historian Jacob Price calls a "quasi common market" with the British Isles and benefited from being in a free-trade zone.[4] However, when viewed from the perspective of long-term development, the colonies characterized by plantation capitalism played an adaptive and passive role in that their economies evolved within the limits of the structure created in the initial phases of colony building. London and other business centers from outside the region continued to dominate the trade in export staples. The basic relationship of such regions with the outside world did not change significantly in the nineteenth century, even with the development of a new staple (cotton) and the growth of new centers of initiative (New York and Boston) to which plantation capitalism responded.

Where merchant capitalism prevailed, new centers of entrepreneurial initiative were emerging to modify the pattern of economic colonialism. With increasing ability to challenge the dominance of London and other British centers, Americans became better able to achieve a measure of economic autonomy, even before political independence was gained. The commercial dynamism of eighteenth-century Philadelphia, New York, and Boston left as its heritage an infrastructure that comprised not only physical facilities but, even more important, a set of business institutions, skills, and attitudes that would later serve other economic purposes as well. Merchant capitalism was building in the Middle Colonies and New England colonies, what W. T. Easterbrook calls a "transformation area," where responses to the technological and economic changes of the nineteenth century would result in a basic change in the structure of economic life.[5] In short, the region was moving toward greater economic autonomy, an accomplishment achieved by few colonies.

Endnotes

1. See John D. Daniels, "The Indian Population of North America in 1492," *William and Mary Quarterly*, 49 (April 1992), pp. 298–320, for a discussion of the methods used by scholars to calculate the native American population.

2. Quoted in Russell R. Menard, "Slavery Economic Growth, and Revolutionary Ideology in the South Carolina Lowcountry," in Ronald Hoffman et al, eds. *The Economy of Early America: The Revolutionary Period, 1763–1790* (Charlottesville: University Press of Virginia, 1988), p. 261.

3. Jacob Price, "Economic Function and the Growth of American Port Towns in the Eighteenth Century," *Perspectives in American History*, 8 (1974), p. 163.

4. Jacob Price, "What Did Merchants Do? Reflections on British Overseas Trade, 1660–1790," *Journal of Economic History*, 49 (1989), p. 270.

5. W. T. Easterbrook, "The Entrepreneurial Function in Relation to Technology and Economic Change," in Bert F. Hoselitz, ed., *Industrialization and Society* (Paris: UNESCO, 1963).

Suggested Readings

The most useful starting point for students interested in the topics covered in Chapter 2 (as well as those in Chapters 3 and 4) is John J. McCusker and Russell R. Menard, *The Economy of British America, 1607–1789* (Chapel Hill: University of North Carolina Press, 1985). The essays contained in Jack P. Greene and J. R. Pole, eds., *Colonial British America: Essays in the New History of the Early Modern Era* (Baltimore: Johns Hopkins Press, 1984), supply valuable reviews of the state of the art in various fields of research. Edwin J. Perkins, *The Economy of Colonial America*, 2nd ed. (New York: Columbia University Press, 1988); Gary M. Walton and James F. Shepherd, *The Economic Rise of Early America* (Cambridge: Cambridge University Press, 1979); and the first four chapters of Stuart Bruchey, *Enterprise: The Dynamic Economy of a Free People* (Cambridge: Harvard University Press, 1990), are important surveys of the economic history of the colonial era. The books by Davis, Davies, and Savelle cited in the Suggested Readings in Chapter 1 place the economic development of England's North American colonies in a broad context. Melville H. Watkins, "A Staple Theory of Economic Growth," *Canadian Journal of Economics and Political Science*, 29 (1963), provides a useful theoretical orientation. W. T. Easterbrook, "The Entrepreneurial Function in Relation to Technology and Economic Change," in Bert F. Hoselitz, ed., *Industrialization and Society* (Paris: UNESCO, 1963), suggests a way to analyze contrasting patterns of colonial regional development.

David Galenson, *White Servitude in Colonial America: An Economic Analysis* (New York: Cambridge University Press, 1981), is the most important work on this topic. Also valuable are A. Roger Ekirch, *Bound for America: The Transportation of British Convicts to the Colonies, 1718–1775* (New York: Oxford University Press, 1987), and several articles by Farley Grubb: "The Market for Indentured Immigrants: Evi-

dence on the Efficiency of Forward-Labor Contracting in Philadelphia, 1745–1773," *Journal of Economic History*, 45 (1985); "Redemptioner Immigration to Pennsylvania: Evidence on Contract Choice and Profitability," *Journal of Economic History*, 46 (1986); and "The Auction of Redemptioner Servants, Philadelphia, 1771–1804: An Economic Analysis," *Journal of Economic History*, 48 (1988).

William Cronon, *Changes in the Land: Indians, Colonists, and the Ecology of New England* (New York: Hill and Wang, 1983), and Timothy Silver, *A New Face on the Countryside: Indians, Colonists, and Slaves in South Atlantic Forests, 1500–1800* (New York: Cambridge University Press, 1990), contain useful accounts of the economic life of the native population. *Handbook of North American Indians*, edited by William C. Sturtevant, vol. 4: *History of Indian-White Relations*, edited by Wilcomb E. Washburn (Washington, D.C.: Smithsonian Institution, 1988), includes sections on economic relations. Other works on this subject include Bruce G. Trigger, "Early Native Responses to European Contact: Romantic Versus Rationalistic Interpretations," *Journal of American History*, 77 (1991); James H. Merrell, *The Indians' New World: Catawbas and Their Neighbors from European Contact Through the Era of Removal* (Chapel Hill: University of North Carolina Press, 1989); Russell Thornton, *American Indian Holocaust and Survival: A Population History Since 1492* (Norman: University of Oklahoma Press, 1987); and Gary B. Nash, *Red, White, and Black: The Peoples of Early America* (Englewood Cliffs, NJ: Prentice-Hall, 1974).

Philip D. Curtin, *The Atlantic Slave Trade: A Census* (Madison: University of Wisconsin Press, 1969), is still basic to this subject. Several more recent additions to the literature are James A. Rawley, *The Transatlantic Slave Trade: A History* (New York: W. W. Norton, 1980); Jay Coughtry, *Notorious Triangle: Rhode Island and the African Slave Trade, 1700–1807* (Philadelphia: Temple University Press, 1981); Henry A. Gemery and Jan S. Hogendorn, "The African Slave Trade: A Tentative Model," *Journal of African History,* 15 (1974); Robert P. Thomas and Richard N. Bean, "The Fishers of Men: The Profits of the Slave Trade," *Journal of Economic History,* 34 (1974); Herbert S. Klein, "Economic Aspects of the Eighteenth-Century Atlantic Slave Trade," in James D. Tracy, ed., *The Rise of Merchant Empires: Long-Distance Trade in the Early Modern World,* 1350–1750 (New York: Cambridge University Press, 1990); and Joseph C. Miller, "Mortality in the Atlantic Slave Trade: Statistical Evidence on Causality," *Journal of Interdisciplinary History,* 11 (1981). Works on slavery in the Chesapeake colonies include Edmund S. Morgan, *American Slavery, American Freedom: The Ordeal of Colonial Virginia* (New York: W. W. Norton, 1975); Gerald W. Mullin, *Flight and Rebellion: Slave Resistance in Eighteenth-Century Virginia* (New York: Oxford University Press, 1972); and Russell R. Menard, "From Servants to Slaves: The Transformation of the Chesapeake Labor System," *Southern Studies,* 16 (1977). For slavery in the Lower South, see Peter H. Wood, *Black Majority: Negroes in Colonial South Carolina from 1670 Through the Stone Rebellion* (New York: Knopf, 1972), and Daniel C. Littlefield, *Rice and Slaves: Ethnicity and the Slave Trade in Colonial South Carolina* (Baton Rouge: Louisiana State University Press, 1981).

Philip D. Curtin, *The Rise and Fall of the Plantation Complex: Essays in Atlantic History* (Cambridge: Cambridge University Press, 1990), places the development of this system of agricultural enterprise within the context of European economic expansion. The most valuable discussions of economic and social developments in the West Indies are contained in Richard B. Sheridan, *Sugar and Slavery: An Economic History of the British West Indies, 1623–1775* (Baltimore: John Hopkins University Press, 1974), and Richard S. Dunn, *Sugar and Slaves: The Rise of the Planter Class in the English*

West Indies, 1624–1713 (Chapel Hill: University of North Carolina Press, 1972).

Lewis C. Gray, *History of Agriculture in the Southern United States to 1860,* vol. 1 (Gloucester, Mass.: Peter Smith, 1958), is still the standard account of the agricultural sector in the southern mainland colonies. Peter A. Coclanis, *The Shadow of a Dream: Economic Life and Death in the South Carolina Low Country, 1670–1920* (New York: Oxford University Press, 1989), analyzes the impact of staple production on long-run economic development. On the introduction of rice cultivation, see the two works by Wood and Littlefield cited earlier. On the beginning of indigo production, see David L. Coon, "Eliza Lucas Pinckney and the Reintroduction of Indigo Culture in South Carolina," *Journal of Southern History,* 42 (1976).

Among the large number of works dealing with the evolution of plantation capitalism in the Chesapeake, the following afford several useful perspectives: Russell R. Menard, "The Tobacco Industry in the Chesapeake Colonies, 1617–1730: An Interpretation," *Research in Economic History,* 5 (1980); Jacob M. Price, *France and the Chesapeake: A History of the French Tobacco Monopoly, 1674–1791, and of its Relationship to the British and American Tobacco Trades,* 2 vols. (Ann Arbor: University of Michigan Press, 1973); Jacob M. Price, *Capital and Credit in British Overseas Trade: The View from the Chesapeake, 1700–1776* (Cambridge: Harvard University Press, 1980); Jacob M. Price and Paul G. E. Clemens, "A Revolution of Scale in Overseas Trade: British Firms in the Chesapeake Trade, 1675–1775," *Journal of Economic History,* 47 (1987); Lois Carr et al., eds., *Colonial Chesapeake Society* (Chapel Hill: University of North Carolina Press, 1988); Gloria L. Main, *Tobacco Colony: Life in Early Maryland, 1650–1720* (Princeton: Princeton University Press, 1982); Allan L. Kulikoff, "The Economic Growth of the Eighteenth-Century Chesapeake Colonies," *Journal of Economic History,* 39 (1979); David C. Klingaman, "The Significance of Grain in the Development of the Tobacco Colonies," *Journal* of Economic History, 29 (1969); Harold B. Gill, Jr., "Wheat Culture in Colonial Virginia," *Agricultural History*, 52 (1978); P. G. E. Clemens, *The Atlantic Economy and Colonial Maryland's Eastern Shore: From Tobacco to Grain* (Ithaca, N.Y.: Cornell University Press, 1980); Carville E. Earle, *The Evolution of a Tidewater Settlement: All Hallow's Parish, Maryland, 1650–1783* (Chicago: University of Chicago Department of Geography, 1975); Robert D. Mitchell, *Commercialism and Frontier: Perspectives on the Early Shenandoah Valley* (Charlottesville: University Press of Virginia, 1977); and Carville V. Earle and Ronald Hoffman, "Urban Development in the Eighteenth-Century South," *Perspectives in American History*, 10 (1976).

Percy W. Bidwell and John I. Falconer, *History of Agriculture in the Northern United States, 1620–1860* (Gloucester, Mass.: Peter Smith, 1941), is outdated but not yet replaced. Douglas R. McManis, *Colonial New England: A Historical Geography* (New York: Oxford University Press, 1975), includes a brief survey of economic activities. The following works deal with various aspects of the economic history of colonial New England: Philip J. Greven, Jr., *Four Generations: Population, Land, and Family in Colonial Andover, Massachusetts* (Ithaca, N.Y.: Cornell University Press, 1970); Stephen Innes, *Labor in a New Land: Economy and Society in Seventeenth-Century Springfield* (Princeton: Princeton University Press, 1983); and Bruce C. Daniels, "Economic Development in Colonial and Revolutionary Connecticut: An Overview," *William and Mary Quarterly*, 37 (1980). For the Middle Colonies, see James T. Lemon, *The Best Poor Man's Country: A Geographical Study of Early Southeastern Pennsylvania* (Baltimore: John Hopkins University Press, 1972); Stephanie G. Wolf, *Urban Village: Population, Community, and Family Structure in Germantown, Pennsylvania, 1683–1800* (Princeton: Princeton University Press, 1976); and Sung Bok Kim, *Landlord and Tenant in Colonial New York Manorial Society, 1664–1775* (Chapel Hill: University of North Carolina Press, 1978).

Jacob M. Price, "Economic Function and the Growth of American Port Towns in the Eighteenth Century," *Perspectives in American History*, 8 (1974), is basic to understanding the development of merchant capitalism in the New England and Middle colonies. Harold A. Innis, *The Cod Fisheries: The History of an International Economy* (New Haven: Yale University Press, 1940), is still essential reading on New England's staple export. Bernard Bailyn, *The New England Merchants in the Seventeenth Century* (Cambridge: Harvard University Press, 1955), is a classic account of the role of business in organizing the region's commercial relationships with other parts of the Atlantic world. Richard Pares, *Yankees and Creoles: The Trade Between North America and the West Indies Before the American Revolution* (London: Longmans, Green, 1956), is still the most useful survey of this commerce. The following works contain discussions of various aspects of commercial development in the New England and Middle Colonies: Darrett B. Rutman, *Winthrop's Boston: Portrait of a Puritan Town, 1630–1649* (Chapel Hill: University of North Carolina Press, 1965); W. T. Baxter, *The House of Hancock: Business in Boston, 1724–1775* (Cambridge: Harvard University Press, 1945); Lynne Withey, *Urban Growth in Colonial Rhode Island: Newport and Providence in the Eighteenth Century* (Albany: State University of New York Press, 1983); James B. Hedges, *The Browns of Providence Plantation: The Colonial Years* (Cambridge: Harvard University Press, 1952); Gregory Nobles, "The Rise of Merchants in Rural Market Towns: A Case Study of Eighteenth-Century Northampton, Massachusetts," *Journal of Social History*, 24 (1990); and Thomas M. Doerflinger, *A Vigorous Spirit of Enterprise: Merchants and Economic Development in Revolutionary Philadelphia* (Chapel Hill: University of North Carolina Press, 1986). Jacob M. Price, "What Did Merchants Do? Reflections on British Overseas Trade, 1660–1790," *Journal of Economic History*, 49 (1989), provides a good understanding of contemporary practices in British business.

Chapter 3

Growth and Welfare in the Colonies

GRICULTURE WAS THE BASIC INDUSTRY OF COLO-
nial America. Much of the market-
oriented activity of the colonists was
connected to the production of agricultural
commodities for export. In looking at this
agrarian world, one might be impressed by its
simple character, compared to the highly developed industrial economy of the United
States today. Yet, at the time of Independence,
Americans lived and worked in a dynamic
economy in relation to the rest of the Western
world at that time. One reflection of that dynamic character was the rapid growth of population and production in the colonies. Regulations imposed by the British were intended
to channel the economic evolution of the colonies along lines that would perpetuate their
dependence on England for manufactured
goods and commercial services. Despite those
regulations, however, striking developments
occurred in eighteenth-century America: the
expansion of the nonagricultural sector—
commerce and manufacturing—as well as the
exercise of considerable ingenuity in adapting
and devising financial instruments to use in
making transactions. While wealth was not
equally distributed, there was ample opportunity for members of colonial society to improve
their position and quality of life. Middle-class
Americans, working in the context of the
family enterprise, participated in a consumer
revolution that swept through much of the
Western world in the seventeenth century.
Nevertheless, there remained pockets of poverty with which society had to deal.

Demographic Trends

Since there exists no general census of the
American people for the period before 1790,
our knowledge of the size of the colonial population must be based on estimates prepared
by historical demographers from data in tax

lists, militia rolls, and other surviving records.
From these sources, however, it is clear that
the population of the colonies grew rapidly by
European standards. Between 1650 and 1770,
the number of inhabitants of European and African origin in the mainland colonies grew
from almost 40,000 to over 2 million, representing an average annual growth rate of 3
percent for slightly more than a doubling of
the population every twenty-five years—see
Figure 3–1. As Table 3–1 shows, though, the
various colonial regions experienced different
rates of population growth—ranging from 2.5
percent per annum in the New England colonies to 4.3 percent in the Lower South.

For the mainland colonies as a whole, the
dynamic force behind demographic growth
was a high rate of natural increase. America
experienced a high birthrate, one that was
somewhat higher than that for Europe. Although teenage marriage was unusual in colonial America, women tended to marry at an
earlier age than in England, by four or five
years. (In America, as compared to the Old
World, greater economic opportunity for
young people enabled them to assume the
economic responsibilities associated with family formation at an earlier age.) Colonial families did not deliberately limit their size, so
most women spent a longer portion of their
lives bearing and rearing children. A lower
level of infant mortality in America than in
England also contributed to the larger American family. A more-than-adequate supply of
food contributed to the good health of most
Americans. This was especially important for
women of childbearing age, whose children
were better able to survive the hazards of
infancy and early childhood. In view of the
chronic shortage of labor in most parts of
America, it is not surprising that a large family was usually perceived as a blessing, since
young children were put to work in the family
enterprise as soon as they could make a contribution.

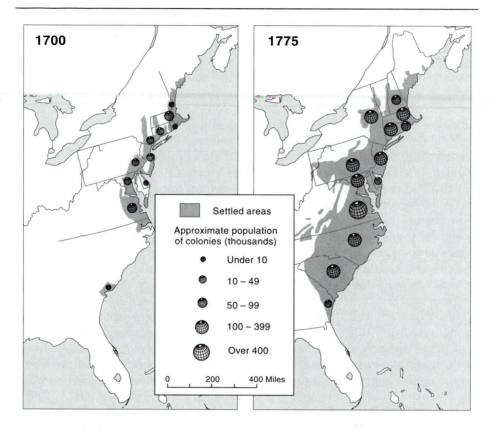

Figure 3–1. *Settled Areas and Population*
SOURCE: Adapted from Charles O. Paullin, *Atlas of the Historical Geography of the United States* (Washington, D.C.: Carnegie Institution, 1932).

Furthermore, immigration augmented colonial population. Attracted by economic opportunity in America, or repelled by social and economic circumstances in their homeland, Europeans crossed the Atlantic; most came from the British Isles, with a large minority from Germany. While a high rate of natural increase contributed to population growth in most regions during the eighteenth century, immigration did not augment the growth of population evenly across the colonies. Rather, immigrants from Europe were drawn to regions perceived to hold unusual economic opportunity for them, especially

the Middle Colonies and the interior of the southern colonies.

The importation of slaves also contributed to population growth in colonial America. An estimated 257,000 Africans were unwilling migrants to the mainland provinces. At the time of the American Revolution, African-Americans, most of them slaves, accounted for over one-fifth of the total population of the mainland colonies. Moreover, about 90 percent of the black population lived and worked in the southern colonies, primarily in the tobacco-growing areas of the Chesapeake and in the rice- and indigo-producing areas of the Lower South.

Table 3–1 *Estimated Population of the British Colonies by Region, 1650–1770 (in thousands)*

Region	Population			
	1650	1700	1750	1770
Lower South	—	16.4	142.2	344.8
Upper South	12.7	98.1	377.8	649.6
Middle Colonies	4.3	53.5	296.5	555.9
New England	22.9	92.4	360.0	581.1
Total	39.9	260.4	1,176.5	2,131.4

SOURCE: John J. McCusker and Russell R. Menard, *The Economy of British America, 1607–1789* (Chapel Hill: University of North Carolina Press, 1985), pages 103, 136, 172, 203.

The growth of the black population of the mainland colonies resulted not only from slave importations but also from natural increase. Unlike the experience of the West Indian slave population, which had an excess of deaths over births, the healthier environment of the Upper South and the more northerly colonies reduced the incidence of disease among the slaves. In addition, there was a better food supply because of the abundance of land on the mainland. This encouraged slave-holders to permit slaves to produce much of their own food, in contrast to the West Indian colonies, where much of the food supply was imported. The exception to this pattern was the Lower South, where demographic conditions more nearly resembled those in the West Indies. The unhealthy conditions of labor in the rice fields resulted in a net natural decline of the black population, which increased only as a result of large importations of slaves from Africa.

Patterns of Economic Growth

Since interest developed several decades ago in measuring the overall performance of national economies, historians have sought ways to calculate the rate of economic growth for the thirteen mainland colonies. Shortages of data and methodological problems remain. Yet there is widespread agreement that the national product of the colonies grew faster than the colonial population. Thus, some economic growth—that is, a rise in product per capita—did occur.

According to historians John McCusker and Russell Menard, there was an average annual rate of growth of gross national product (GNP) per capita of between 0.3 and 0.6 percent between 1650 and 1774.[1] Although this represents a growth rate considerably lower than the 1.6 percent per annum experienced in the United States after 1840—the so-called modern economic growth rate—it is clear that free white Americans of the revolutionary generation were well off by eighteenth-century standards. On the basis of an extensive analysis of the wealth held by a large sample of the colonial population, Alice Hanson Jones estimates that the average net worth of a free American on the eve of the revolution was £74, equivalent to about $7800 in terms of the purchasing power of the 1989 U.S. dollar.[2] In terms of the standard of living, the per capita wealth of colonial Americans compared favorably with that of eighteenth-century Europeans and even with people in some parts of the world today. As Table 3–2 indicates, land was the most valuable component of the economy, not sur-

Table 3–2 *Components of Private Wealth per Free Capita in Colonial America, by Region, 1774 (in pounds sterling)*[a]

Type of Wealth	Thirteen Colonies	New England Colonies	Middle Colonies	Southern Colonies
Net worth	£74.1	£32.7	£51.3	£131.9
Physical wealth	76.0	38.2	46.0	136.8
Land	37.7	27.3	27.8	55.4
Servants and slaves	21.3	0.2	1.9	57.7
Producers goods	10.4	5.1	9.6	16.2
Consumer goods	5.3	4.5	4.2	7.0
Miscellaneous	1.2	1.2	2.4	0.3
Financial assets	12.3	6.8	16.0	14.0
Financial liabilities	14.2	12.2	10.6	18.8

[a]Figures are average per capita, excluding slaves and indentured servants. Also, one pound sterling in 1774 = U.S. $105.74 in 1989.

Source: Data from U.S. Bureau of the Census, *Historical Statistics of the United States*, (Washington, D.C.: GPO, 1975), p. 1175. Data calculated by Alice Hanson Jones.

prising since a large majority earned a living in agriculture.

However accurate the estimated colonial growth rate of 0.3 percent to 0.6 percent may be, it represents an average of the widely divergent experiences of different regions at different times. McCusker and Menard point to two surges of growth—the first occurring during the settlement of each region and the second taking place between 1740 and the American Revolution—with a long period of relative stagnation in between.[3] Within these long secular trends of economic activity were cyclical fluctuations marking shorter periods of expansion and contraction for the colonies as a whole or for individual regions and provinces. Data in Table 3–2 show that the average wealth per free white person of £74 on the eve of the Revolution masks significant differences among regions—ranging from £33 for New England and £51 for the Middle Colonies to £132 for the South. (Over 40 percent of the wealth of the South consisted of the value of slaves and servants, compared to less than 4 percent in the Middle Colonies and under 1 percent in

New England.) Furthermore, as we will see later in the chapter, not all Americans in the same region, even among the free population, participated equally as individuals or families in the distribution of the fruits of economic growth.

Sources of Economic Growth

Despite the scarce available data about the workings of the aggregate economy in colonial times, historians are able to identify some of the conditions that contributed to the economic growth achieved by early Americans. On one point, there is widespread agreement: Unlike modern economic growth, technological change contributed little to the rise in average per capita income and product in colonial America. The underlying development that made economic growth possible in the colonies was a shift away from self-sufficiency toward a market-oriented economy.

A progressive capitalization of agriculture as well as improved farming techniques contributed to greater productivity of the land and of the labor employed to work the land. For example, the average real value of agricultural equipment per farm in one Pennsylvania county nearly doubled from the early eighteenth century to the revolution, according to a study made by D. E. Ball and G. M. Walton.[4] Individual farmers in settled communities u‚ually owned their plows, hoes, rakes, sickles, wagons, and other capital equipment, so that they no longer needed to share the use of implements as they did in the initial phase of settlement. Throughout the colonial period, increased use was made of horse power, even though assuring an adequate supply of fuel (hay) was sometimes a problem. Control of the flow of water was achieved by the construction of dikes and irrigation ditches.

A study conducted by historian Peter Coclanis argues that improvements in productivity resulted from changes in rice production in the South Carolina Low Country (from higher lands to inland swamps and then to tidal swamps) as well as from a change in the organization of the slave labor force (from the gang system to the task system). However, Coclanis admits the difficulty of separating gains generated by these innovative practices from those resulting from increased inputs of capital, labor, and land.[5] Another study, by Lois Carr and Russell Menard, reveals how Chesapeake planters in the early eighteenth century found ways to introduce wheat production at the same time that they augmented corn production and maintained the level of tobacco production, without increasing their labor requirements. This they did by changing from hoes to plows in the preparation of land as well as by stretching out the workweek that accompanied the shift from white indentured servants to black slaves.[6]

Historians James Shepherd and Gary Walton emphasize the significance of a decline in distribution costs as a source of rising productivity. A reduction of piracy and privateering meant that merchant ships without armament could sail with smaller crews and carry more cargo in proportion to the size of the vessel. Greater security also translated into lower insurance costs. Improvements in commercial organization reduced the turnaround time of ships in port (thereby increasing the number of sailings each ship could make during a season) and enabled buyers and sellers to find markets and make transactions more quickly and economically.[7] Better bookkeeping methods and the appearance of specialized agents like marine insurance brokers helped to lower transaction costs. So too did the improvement in communication that resulted from the organization of a postal service and the foundation of newspapers. Travel time for the Philadelphia–New York post, for example, declined from three days to one day between 1720 and 1764; the frequency of service increased from once a week to every other day during that same period. The timeliness of sending and receiving commercial information—on which crucial decisions were based—served to improve its quality.

Although the domestic market did not become the major interest of American business until the nineteenth century, the expansion of intercolonial trade in the decades prior to the Revolution foreshadowed that development. Data on ship clearances provide dramatic evidence of the growth of domestic trade. For example, in 1772, nearly one-third of the tonnage shipped from New York was destined for ports in the mainland colonies, compared to less than one-fifth a century earlier. In 1768 to 1772, the value of commodities involved in the coastal trade represented an estimated 20 percent of that in overseas commerce. Bread and flour alone constituted nearly one-fifth of this trade, reflecting to a considerable extent New England's dependence on the Middle Colonies and the Upper South for its food supply. The evidence suggests that a large proportion of commodities shipped from one province to another was destined for consumption in the colonies, rather than for reshipment overseas, which represents an increasing specialization of production by region.

British Mercantilism and American Economic Growth

Starting in the middle of the seventeenth century, England passed the Navigation Acts and other statutes designed to promote its own economic welfare at the expense of its European rivals. What effect did the resulting pattern of mercantilistic regulation have on economic growth in America? Granted that government regulation, whatever its purpose, imposed some distortions on the pattern of economic activity and thereby encouraged inefficient use of resources, how serious was the effect of these distortions? Mercantilism applied a set of specific rules to the economic life of the colonies that can be summarized and evaluated to determine the nature of their impact.

1. The Navigation Acts restricted the carrying trade of the colonies to English-built, English-owned, and English-manned ships. Since this legislation accorded to shipbuilders and shipowners in the colonies the same legal rights as those possessed by their counterparts in England, colonial businessmen participated in an empire-wide monopoly. Indeed, evidence points to the ability of colonial shipowners to increase their share of the shipping business of the eighteenth-century British Empire. On the eve of the American Revolution, only tobacco exceeded in value the earnings generated by the sale of shipping services, according to the findings of James Shepherd and Gary Walton.[8] Shipbuilding became an important industry in the colonies, and ships became a significant export.

2. British regulation required that certain commodities be exported only to England; the most important of these enumerated commodities were sugar, tobacco, rice, indigo, and na-val stores. When large amounts of commodities like tobacco and rice were reexported from Britain to continental Europe, indirect routing imposed extra costs, such as port charges, commissions, and customs duties. Planters, supported by some later historians, argued that American producers would have earned more with direct routing. However, it cannot be assumed that distribution costs would have been substantially lower if the Navigation Acts had not existed. In the case of tobacco, for example, British business provided marketing services and developed commercial connections with the purchasers who bought in large volume for the French tobacco monopoly and the many importers and wholesalers who handled distribution in Holland and Germany. Within the framework of enumeration, British business introduced significant economies into the marketing system of the mid-eighteenth century, some of which were passed along to planters because of the vigorous competition that existed among buyers.

3. Another provision of the Navigation Acts stipulated that all goods of European origin destined for the colonies had to be shipped through England, with the exception of certain products of southern Europe. This was intended to encourage the colonials to purchase British manufactured goods, since foreign wares would be more expensive because of trans-shipment costs. Yet it is likely that Britain would in any event have been the principal supplier of manufactured goods for the colonies, due to its industrial lead over France and other potential European rivals. As François Crouzet, a leading French historian, concludes, "British superiority [over France] in the eighteenth century was in the manufacture of good quality products suitable for middle-class consumption"[9]—the kind of goods most appropriate for the colonial market.

4. The British government extended subsidies and tariff protection in the British market to encourage increased production of certain

colonial commodities such as naval stores (tar, pitch, and turpentine) essential to shipbuilding and ship repair, and indigo, a raw material used by the textile industry. However rewarding such governmental favors might have been to individual producers, they did not represent a clear gain to the colonies. As Robert Thomas notes, "Part of the bounty was a payment for the inefficient allocation of colonial resources." Yet it is impossible to measure exactly the extent to which resources were diverted "from more efficient uses into industries where they were employed less efficiently."[10] For example, the production of naval stores provided part-time employment for farmers. And indigo was generally grown on South Carolina soils not suitable for rice cultivation, using slaves at times of the year when they were not needed in the production of the major staple.

5. In order to preserve the provincial market for the products of British industry, Parliament imposed various kinds of restrictions on manufacturing in the colonies. No kind of manufacturing was ever forbidden. Rather, the expansion of colonial industry was discouraged through statutes restricting the size of the market (for woolen goods and hats), prohibiting the erection of new facilities (for making finished iron goods), or levying a prohibitive duty on raw material (molasses used in distilling rum). (This last regulation was intended to protect the sugar planters of the British West Indies.) In no case did the restrictive legislation have much practical significance, since little attempt was made to enforce the laws. This is not to say that British policy was purposely benign. If the policymakers in London had possessed more accurate information about the extent of manufacturing in the colonies, they perhaps would have created effective regulations to restrict industrial growth.

It should be emphasized that the colonials were in no way opposed to the basic assumption of mercantilism—that the powers of government should be actively used to shape economic development toward desired goals. Provincial legislatures, whose members were elected by colonial property owners, enacted a variety of measures to encourage economic development. They created inspection systems for their major exports, usually to promote the exports by improving their reputation for quality in foreign markets. For instance, Pennsylvania officials inspected flour, meat, and lumber products destined for export, while those in Virginia and Maryland required tobacco to be of a minimum quality. To encourage production of certain commodities, most colonies provided bounties. The items most commonly subsidized were hemp and flax, but Virginia and South Carolina also tried to promote shipbuilding by granting bounties. Some colonies experimented with tonnage duties as a device to favor local shippers. Everywhere, provincial legislatures sought to improve internal communication by financing roads and authorizing ferries. Finally, colonial governments assumed responsibility for furnishing a supply of money, an essential element in a market-oriented economy (as we will see later in the chapter).

Thus, a century of British mercantilistic regulation did little to alter the overall pattern of economic development in the colonies; that is, providing raw materials for a more advanced economy and, in turn, using that economy's manufactured goods and commercial services. For many decades, the colonials were unable to provide a full range of goods and services for their own use. The Navigation Acts meant that most of the goods and services that the colonials could not efficiently provide for themselves were supplied by British business, with business firms of other European powers legally excluded. Within the framework of regulation, Americans organized an extensive and highly profitable legal trade outside of the usual patterns of economic relationships between a colony and the imperial power, particularly in commerce with the West Indies and southern Europe.

A Blacksmith at Work, Mid-Eighteenth Century. Blacksmiths produced a variety of metal products for colonial consumers and businesses. (Historical Pictures/Stock Montage)

British government regulations imposed only a light economic burden on the colonials. Thomas calculates the annual net cost to America of membership in the British Empire for the decade following 1763 at twenty-six cents per capita. (This takes into account the value of defense provided by the British armed forces.)[11] However, as we will see in Chapter 4, new regulations and new perceptions of the impact of British mercantilism on American economic life contributed to the revolutionary crisis of the 1760s and 1770s.

The Industrial Sector

Handicraft Manufactures

As in Europe, the typical manufacturer in colonial America was an artisan whose industrial activity rested on skill in the use of hand tools and who principally served a local market, often producing individual items to the order of specific customers. Every town and village had its complement of artisans to provide basic services for the community—carpenter, blacksmith, tanner, shoemaker, wheelwright, and stonemason. In rural areas, itinerant artisans traveled from farmhouse to farmhouse to perform skilled work that farmers themselves were unable to do. In the southern colonies, slaves were trained to perform most kinds of skilled work.

However, it was in the cities, where the largest populations and the greatest amounts of wealth were concentrated, that the crafts flourished. The great commercial centers of Philadelphia, New York, and Boston, and even somewhat smaller cities like Charleston and Newport, contained almost all the kinds of handicraft manufacturers to be found in European cities, supplying not only the basic needs of the population but a variety of luxury goods as well. In Philadelphia, for example, artisans accounted for slightly over one-half of the tax-assessed population in 1774, and included 713 people engaged in making clothing, 522 in construction trades and furniture manufacture, 361 in producing transportation equipment, 246 in food processing and preparation, and 103 in metal work ranging from guns to silverware.

Artisans usually financed their entry into independent business with savings earned during a relatively short period of work in a certain trade. But the ease of entry into most crafts, due to the small investment required, often limited the ability of individual craft manufacturers to expand their operations by hiring other workers. The failure of guilds to control industry as they did in Europe, as well as the ability of relatively large numbers of people to acquire skills through apprenticeship, made competition intense. Individual artisans attempted through advertising to establish product differentiation based on their reputation for producing quality work and the originality of their design. Immigrant mechanics continually introduced new techniques that had been developed in Europe, and the force of competition encouraged members of the trade to adopt these new ways. The craft form of industrial production contributed to a widespread diffusion of business skills as well as technical knowledge, since most artisans were self-employed and thus had to have at least a rudimentary knowledge of business methods.

Mill Industries

Alongside handicraft manufactures, which primarily depended on manual dexterity, there developed in colonial America a variety of mill industries that applied water power to process raw materials. Flour mills were located everywhere that grain was produced. In a newly settled community, the custom miller, often a farmer who occupied a water-power site, met local needs by processing the grain of fellow farmers in return for a share of the material. Merchant millers, whose activities became increasingly important, purchased grain and produced flour on their own account more and more to meet the growing export demand for American foodstuffs. As the potential of the export market grew, flour millers sought to establish operations at locations that combined ample and reliable water power with river and ocean transportation. Thus, starting in the 1740s, Wilmington, Delaware, possessing these location factors, became an important center of flour milling, foreshadowing the industrial town of the nineteenth century.

The sawmill appeared almost as early as the grain mill and its operations were nearly as widespread. Wood was the indispensable raw material for dwellings and other buildings, transportation equipment (both land and water), packaging (casks, barrels, and the like), and consumer durable goods like furniture. Timber was abundant and labor was scarce. Water mills made possible not only greater economy in production but also a superior quality of material over what was possible using hand methods.

Shipbuilding and Ironworks

Shipbuilding and iron manufacture became two of the most important industries of the eighteenth century in applying industrial skills that capitalized on American's comparative advantage in raw materials. Ships were constructed in the early settlements to meet the needs of colonists for local transport. Some builders soon turned to the production of vessels for the coastal and West Indian trades. Later, American yards made some of the large ships employed in the transatlantic trade. America's competitive advantage in shipbuilding lay in the cost of the principal raw material, wood, which outweighed the higher wages paid to colonial workers. Shipyards were located in all of the mainland colonies, but output was concentrated in New England; it accounted for nearly two-thirds of the tonnage built in the early 1770s. By the eve of the American Revolution, shipbuilding had become an important export industry, as nearly one-half of the total output was sold abroad. Although ships do not appear in the customs records, they were perhaps the fourth most valuable export of the colonies.

With the advantage of cheap fuel—charcoal from the forests—and ores available close to the surface, the colonial iron industry expanded rapidly in the half-century prior to the Revolution, primarily to meet the needs of the growing American economy for a wide range of metal products. By 1775, the colonies had more blast furnaces and forges than did England and Wales, and they produced nearly one-seventh of the world output of iron (a relative position not again gained by America until the 1860s). Ironworks were located in nearly every colony, with Pennsylvania the leader in this activity from the 1750s. Iron plantations were established in rural areas at sites of water power and adjacent to supplies of ore and wood for charcoal. Because ironmaking required a relatively large amount of capital in addition to technical skill, the typical firm was a joint venture between a merchant, who supplied funds and developed marketing channels, and an ironmaster, who organized production. Although little technological change occurred in the colonial iron industry, owners learned by experience how to increase their managerial efficiency and thereby achieve productivity gains, as Paul Paskoff's study of the industry shows. The labor-intensive character of the industry, with wages accounting for 70 percent of total production costs for pig iron and 40 percent for bar iron, focused attention on the need to minimize the use of labor. Reducing the amount of waste in the production of charcoal, for example, enabled the owner to

cut back on the number of workers without decreasing the amount of total output of iron. In the running of pig and the drawing of bar, paying wages only for work that met stipulated standards helped to keep costs in line. This form of quality control also gave a competitive market edge to producers whose iron met high quality standards.[12] The British government, seeking to ensure a supply of material for its own manufacturers of metal goods, passed the Iron Act of 1750. It included a tariff that encouraged the colonies to export semi-finished iron to Britain. However, neither this provision, nor another that prohibited the erection in the colonies of new mills to make finished iron goods, proved to be effective. Some colonial producers shipped their semi-finished iron to England, but by 1775 most ironmasters found the domestic market more attractive than overseas trade, especially as increasing numbers of skilled colonial artisans purchased iron to make the tools, implements, hardware, and other metal products used by Americans.

Other Activities

While the colonies made greatest manufacturing progress in industries in which they held an advantage in raw materials—like flour milling, shipbuilding, and ironmaking—they also achieved considerable success in certain activities involving the conversion of imported raw materials into finished products. Colonial traders early discovered that opportunity existed in distilling West Indian molasses into rum, a cheap substitute for costly imported brandy. By the eve of the Revolution, American merchants had organized over 140 rum distilleries, a great many of them in Philadelphia, New York, Boston, and Newport, which together supplied about 60 percent of the colonial market for the product. Similarly, colonial merchants developed a sugar-refining industry, making white sugar out of imported muscavado sugar to meet

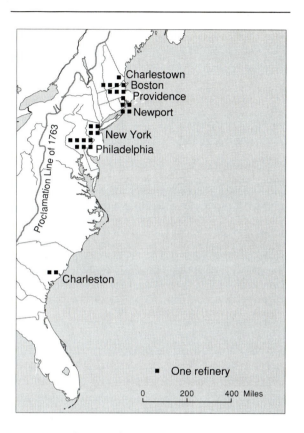

Figure 3–2 *Sugar Refineries, 1770.*
SOURCE: Adapted from Lester J. Cappon, *Altas of Early American History: The Revolutionary Era, 1760–1790.* (Princeton: Princeton University Press, 1976).

ganizing textile manufactories, or workshops, where they assembled implements and gathered a number of workers in one building. The societies that operated these establishments, organized for philanthropic and patriotic reasons as often as for commercial purposes, foreshadowed the later manufacturing corporation. And adoption of labor-saving machinery, which would become a widely recognized characteristic of American manufacturing industry in the nineteenth century, was a tradition already established in certain colonial industries like flour milling.

Despite the high cost of labor and capital in an area with an abundance of land, and despite British efforts to discourage some kinds of manufacturing, industrial development in America did not lag far behind that of Europe in the eighteenth century. Merchants, the most important economic decision makers in colonial America, were already turning their attention to manufacturing, which often complemented their commercial activities. Some, like the Browns of Rhode Island, were beginning to think of themselves primarily as industrialists; they increasingly conducted their foreign and domestic trade to meet the needs of their candle-making and iron-manufacturing businesses.

The Financial Sector

As participants in a market-oriented economy, the colonials recognized the inherent efficiency of money in the exchange process. However, in their view, they did not have enough money to conduct their business. By this, they meant that there was an insufficient amount of specie—gold and silver, which they regarded as the only "real" money. The scarcity of specie was due basically to an adverse balance of trade. Since the colonists consumed imported goods having greater value than the commodities they exported, a considerable portion of

a growing American demand for sweeteners— see Figure 3–2.

Although the modern factory system was just being created in England toward the end of the American colonial period, some of the elements of that method of industrial organization were being introduced in the colonies. In some lines of manufacture, like gun making, a considerable number of hand-workers came together in one establishment, each performing a specialized function as a part of "a continuous and reciprocally adjusted process" of production.[13] Other entrepreneurs were or-the specie that they gained in trade with areas like the West Indies was drained out to pay for imports.

To overcome what they perceived to be constraints on economic development imposed by existing monetary practices, Americans introduced a variety of innovations through both the public and private sectors to settle transactions with the use of a minimum of real money: overvalued foreign coins, monetized commodities, paper currency, commercial instruments like bills of exchange, and mercantile bookkeeping devices. One result was a separation of two of the principal functions of money: As a *standard of value,* all colonies used a variant of the English monetary system of pounds, shillings, and pence. However, they employed as a *medium of exchange* several different kinds of money, principally non-English, and nonmoney, or as some called it in the eighteenth century, "imaginary money," the most important of which consisted of paper notes. In turn, British authorities sought to impose regulations designed to deal with what they perceived to be defects in colonial monetary innovations.

Public Sector Responses

Due largely to a shortage of hard money in England itself, English law prohibited the export of English coins to the colonies, though some coins were carried there by travelers. Since provincial governments were forbidden to mint their own coins, Spanish and Portuguese gold and silver coins, obtained through trade with the West Indies, provided most of the real money in circulation in the colonies. These pieces of eight (or milled dollars), johannes, and coins of other denominations were valued in terms of the English monetary system. For example, the Spanish piece of eight, on the basis of its silver content, was equivalent to four shillings six pence in sterling. However, each colony, looking to dis-

The Spanish Peso or Piece of Eight. This coin, also known as the dollar, served in the seventeenth and eighteenth centuries as a kind of "universal money" for much of Europe and the Western Hemisphere. It accounted for perhaps as many as one-half of all the coins circulating in the British colonies. Because it was so familiar to Americans, the dollar was later defined as the basic monetary unit of the United States. (From Thomas Snelling, *A View of the Coins at this Current Throughout Europe* [London, 1766]. Courtesy of The Baker Library, Harvard Business School)

courage a drain on its supply of coins because of the adverse balance of trade with England, overvalued these coins by raising their value as legal tender in terms of the colony's own provincial currency. Although the British government prevented further inflation of the value of foreign coins from the early eighteenth century, at least five different valuations of pounds, shillings, and pence prevailed among the mainland colonies. The value of a piece of eight ranged from four shillings eight pence in South Carolina to eight shillings in New York. This colonial action did not alter the sterling value of gold and silver coins. What it did mean, however, was that a given number of pounds in colonial currency purchased fewer pounds in English currency; for example, £156 in New York currency was equivalent to £100 sterling.

Commodity money provided a second kind of currency for the colonies. The use of commodities as money differed from simple barter. A provincial legislature would decree that a certain product of that province would be accepted at a stipulated rate, in payment of taxes and other public debts. In other words, the commodity—whether it was tobacco, wheat, or lumber—was denominated in terms of pounds, shillings, and pence, and carried an element of legal tender. However, commodity money posed several serious problems: transporting and storing bulky goods, assessing the quality of the commodities tendered, and fluctuations in price. The Chesapeake colonies developed in the eighteenth century a variant of commodity money that dealt with the first two of these deficiencies. After inspection systems were organized in Virginia (1730) and Maryland (1747), tobacco notes—receipts issued to owners of tobacco deposited in public warehouses—were accepted in payment of provincial taxes and thus became a form of money. But fluctuations in the price of tobacco continued to create difficulties; a currency increasing in value worked hardships on debtors, as did a depreciating currency on creditors.

Paper money was issued by all of the colonies in varying amounts. It served not only to supplement the currency supply; also it met the fiscal needs of government and provided credit, with the objective of stimulating agricultural expansion. To finance military operations, provincial governments issued bills of credit, or treasury notes, with the understanding that they would be retired out of future tax receipts—a practice called *currency finance.* Since bills of credit were accepted in payment of taxes and other government obligations, they were used to settle private transactions as well and thus became part of the currency.

Another form of paper money consisted of notes issued by land banks, agencies created by the provincial governments to lend at low interest rates on the security of real estate. These notes also could be used to pay taxes, were accepted in private transactions, and formed part of the money supply.

When large amounts of paper currency issued by some colonies created an inflation of the price level, undermining the value of debts

Colonial Paper Currency. Notes like this were issued by all of the provincial governments. The colonies were innovators in creating the Western world's first fiat paper moneys.

owed to creditors (in America as well as in Britain), the British government attempted to develop a control mechanism. After efforts to limit the volume of paper money by administrative means failed, Parliament passed the Currency Act of 1751. The act prohibited the issue of paper money in the New England colonies, where the most serious inflation had occurred. Then the Currency Act of 1764 extended the prohibition to the rest of the mainland colonies. Some easing of the restrictions was contained in the Currency Act of 1773, which permitted the colonies to make paper money legal tender in payments to provincial governments but not in private transactions. At the same time, serious consideration was given to the establishment of a continental land bank with a branch office in each province, to be centrally managed from London. But by the 1770s, monetary problems had become too entangled in the conflict over taxes and trade regulation to be considered as a separate issue.

Business and the Money Problem

An expansion of the use of financial instruments allowed business to carry on an enlarged trade without a proportionate increase of money holdings. These devices, generated in the course of private business, served as a functional equivalent of money in providing a medium of exchange.

The financial instrument most familiar to colonial merchants was the *bill of exchange,* which had originated in medieval Europe as a means of settling international transactions. American importers making payments for goods purchased from British exporters normally used bills of exchange rather than shipping specie. When an importer found another American business firm holding credits on the books of a British firm, usually representing the proceeds from the sale of a shipment, the importer might purchase from the colonial colleague an order directing the British firm to pay a specified sum of money. The American firm used colonial currency to purchase the bill, which it then endorsed and sent to creditors in Britain; the latter presented it for payment in British currency. In this simplified exchange transaction, the seller of the bill had in effect transferred funds from Britain to America; the buyer had transferred funds from America to Britain.

A bill of exchange was negotiable when it was endorsed by the person to whose order it was drawn. Bills could be endorsed as many times as desired, and thus could be used as a form of payment among businesses either in the colonies or in England. In eighteenth-century London, specialized business firms discounted bills of exchange, not only those that originated in transatlantic trade but also inland bills arising out of transactions between London and the provinces. In the colonies, the market for bills developed in a less formal manner. Merchants in the larger port towns met daily in a designated place, where they made known their wishes to buy or sell bills on London, the most useful form of sterling exchange. In a colony like Virginia, where no one urban center dominated trade, merchants and planters bought and sold bills of exchange in the provincial capital at periodic meetings that coincided with the quarterly sessions of the courts.

In conducting business within a colony, urban merchants and country storekeepers used a variety of techniques to buy and sell without actually using money. Even though no cash actually changed hands, all transactions were calculated in money values. The most sophisticated of several methods was the *triangular transfer of credits,* by which bookkeeping entries made it possible to settle debts among several parties. For example, those without cash or goods on hand to pay a sum owed to a creditor might direct a merchant or storekeeper on whose books they had a cash balance to transfer funds from that account to the account of the creditor. If the order was written, it could be made "to order," endorsed by the payee, and then circulated as a form of money until presented for payment. It resembled a modern bank check in that it could be endorsed and transferred from party to party.

Adequacy of the Monetary System

The expedients devised by decision makers in both the public and private sectors were successful in providing a supply of money for the rapidly expanding market-oriented economy. The colonies did not experience a long-run deflation or a decline in the price level that would

A Bill of Exchange, 1742. In this typical exchange transaction, Philadelphia merchant John Reynell drew the bill on the Bristol merchant firm of Michael Atkins, Richard Farr, and Son (who held funds belonging to Reynell) for payment to Michael Lee Dicker, another Philadelphian who presumably needed to remit funds to England in settlement of a transaction. (The Historical Society of Pennsylvania)

have indicated an insufficient supply of money. The record of the various colonies, however, was uneven with respect to controlling inflation or a rise in the price level. On the one hand, in Pennsylvania, where the paper money supply was well managed, prices rose by 57 percent between 1720 and 1774, an annual rate of 0.8 percent. On the other hand, large volumes of paper currency were issued by the New England colonies, particularly Massachusetts and Rhode Island. It is not surprising that prices in Boston rose 4.5 times higher than did those of Philadelphia in the half-century prior to the American Revolution.

That the colonial monetary systems worked does not imply the absence of several serious inadequacies. In the first place, supplying a medium of exchange was often only a secondary function of issues of paper money. War finance was usually the occasion for the emission of bills of credit, with provision for retirement when peace returned. Thus, an important component of the money supply expanded and contracted not with the changing level of economic activity but in response to the fiscal needs of provincial governments. Even the paper money issues made by land banks in connection with agricultural development were not managed with a view to keeping a specified amount of currency in circulation. In Pennsylvania, for example, year-to-year fluctuations of 10 percent to 67 percent in the stock of paper money outstanding were not uncommon.

Another weakness of the monetary systems was related to the significant role that trade credit, an inherently unstable element, played in the financial mechanism of the colonies. The ability of British merchants to extend credit to Americans depended on the working of the financial system in Britain. Thus, when problems in the London money market caused contraction by bankers there, British merchants had to reduce the amount of credit outstanding in the colonies by collecting old debts and refusing new credit. A credit crunch in Britain meant a serious decline in colonial purchasing power because of the withdrawal of trade credit, a drain of available hard money to settle balances, and a reduction in the amount of sterling bills of exchange. This process had potentially severe effects on the well-being of any American who participated in the market economy. In this setting of adversity, colonials might have sought to offset decreases in certain kinds of money with increases in local paper currency. However, after 1751 in New England and after 1764 in the rest of the colonies, the colonists were blocked by British restrictions on the issue of paper money designed primarily to protect British investments in America. Perhaps the nub of the currency problem was the inadequacy of the imperial system to resolve conflicts between British and American interests. American business could view lack of effective control of monetary policy as a serious impediment to achieving economic autonomy.

Wealth Distribution in Colonial America

It is clear that colonial America was not a land of equality, or near equality, of property ownership, even among the members of the free population. On the eve of the Revolution, the top 20 percent of wealth holders owned about two-thirds of the total physical wealth of colonial America, while the lowest 20 percent held less than 1 percent.[14] However, it should be kept in mind that this "snapshot" reflects the experience of a group of people at different stages of the life cycle. Wealth held by an individual at a given time represents property accumulated during a working life up to that time. As Jackson Turner Main explains in his study of the distribution of wealth in Connecticut, a young man living at home with his parents might own little property besides the shirt on his back but still enjoy a comfortable level of living. Main concludes that a given cohort (including many men poor in property when they were young, just embarking on a career) contained fewer than 8 percent poor men by the time it reached its forties and fewer still a decade later. The wealthy did not constitute a closed circle, since a growing population and an expanding economy continually provided room at the top for newcomers.[15] Based on his analysis of landholdings in a North Carolina county, Robert Gallman concludes that while old families achieving early success held important advantages in the competition to keep ahead, families new to the community in later years also had a good chance to succeed.[16]

Family Enterprise and the Market

In spite of the prominent position of a small wealthy class, most distinctive about the society of colonial America in the perspective of the eighteenth-century Western world was its large proportion of middle-class property owners. Most numerous among the middle class were property-owning farmers. While some historians argue that most colonial farm families were self-sufficient and that a system of communal *mentalité* prevailed in rural areas, recent research conducted by economic historians shows clearly that a commercial *mentalité* made farmers almost everywhere aware that they were participating directly or indirectly in the larger Atlantic economy. Even if they were not single-minded profit maximizers, most farmers were utility maximizers who desired a comfortable subsistence beyond a bare sufficiency. This required that they gear their work routines toward market-oriented production in order to provide the means to acquire the goods and services they could not themselves produce.[17]

On family farms throughout the colonies, there existed a clearly defined division of labor by gender. While the husband labored in the fields to produce commodities for subsistence and market, the wife devoted herself to filling the needs of the family. The core of the woman's role as homemaker was the bearing and rearing of children. But homemaking also involved a variety of other responsibilities, including preparing meals, nursing the family in illness, caring for livestock (such as milking cows) and poultry, making prepared foods (like butter and cheese), growing vegetables, cleaning, and sometimes the making of cloth and clothing for members of the family. Many of the duties that women performed as homemaker were not for the weak; for example, cooking was usually done over an open fire, using heavy kettles and other containers and clumsy utensils. Increasingly through the eighteenth century, more women were participating directly in market activity through the small-scale home manufacture of items ranging from cheese to woolen cloth, which they exchanged with their neighbors or carried to urban markets.

Within the colonial family enterprise, the husband was regarded as the head of the household. He controlled all property, even what the wife brought into the marriage, and assumed authority over the work of the wife and children. However, the husband, in exercising his household governance authority, was expected to incorporate his wife's opinions and interest into his decisions. Furthermore, the wife, in addition to exercising her specialized homemaking skills, regularly served as a "deputy husband" in carrying out the husband's responsibilities in case of his absence or incapacity. Indeed, almost any task, including work in the fields during harvest,

was suitable for women as long as it contributed to the family enterprise.

Children also formed an important part of the labor unit in the family agricultural enterprise. Children were regarded as "producer goods" whose labor was a necessary contribution to the process of capital formation. From an early age, "little men" and "little women" were instructed in the work appropriate to their sex. In an era when work was central to life, success required a high level of economic discipline. Sometimes, if parents believed that leniency with their own children would not provide them with the best training, they bound out their sons and daughters at age ten or eleven to neighboring families for as long as seven years to learn farming or a trade. At the same time, they would assume responsibility for training someone else's children. Sons and daughters continued to labor on their parents' farm until they were ready to form their own family enterprise, usually when they were in their mid- or late twenties in the case of males and in their early twenties for females. This was a system that paid off for both generations. In return for their contribution to creating the wealth of their family of orientation, young men and women drew on this wealth when establishing their own family enterprise. If the farm was not large enough to support more than one family, younger sons who wanted to continue a career in farming migrated to the frontier, often to land previously purchased by their fathers. Other sons might elect to follow nonagricultural pursuits in their communities—as, for example, blacksmiths, carpenters, tanners, millers, or distillers—often starting with a stake from their families. Upon marriage, a daughter expected her family to provide a dowry in the form of some kind of property for the family farm enterprise that she and her husband would establish.

The growth of urban communities furnished an abundance of opportunities for middle-class family enterprise in handicraft manufacture, retail trade, and service establishments. Most types of craft manufacture were considered to be "men's work." However, while the woman held responsibility for homemaking, she also usually assisted her husband in the shop, typically located adjacent to the home. Like farming, urban children worked in the family craft enterprise. They were trained formally through apprenticeship or informally to the tasks ordinarily performed by adult members of their sex.

Acquisition of a thorough knowledge of the husband's business served as a kind of life insurance for women married to artisans or tradesmen. In the event of the death or disability of the husband, the wife could run the family enterprise, even if it was considered a "man's business." Alternative self-employment possibilities for widows and other unmarried women included the establishment of businesses that commercialized traditional women's work. Thus, women were often found as tavern keepers, where they generated income by applying inherited physical capital (such as a house) in combination with their human capital (housekeeping skills). Other resourceful women developed businesses making and selling baked goods or other types of prepared foodstuffs. Still others operated boarding schools, did nursing and midwifery, or took in washing and mending work.

As a result of their extensive market-oriented economic activity in the family enterprise, women and children made a substantial direct contribution to the growth of the national product of the colonies. In an era of high fertility, married women could participate effectively in market activity only if the home and the workplace were unified, as they were in the family enterprise that was prevalent in both town and country during the colonial era. Historian Claudia Goldin contends that the labor participation rate of married women over the long run of American history has been "U-shaped," with the left peak of the "U" located in the late eigh-

teenth century. As home and workplace became separated during industrialization in the nineteenth century, the labor participation rate of married women experienced a long-run decline to the end of the century, not to rise again to its eighteenth-century level until the second half of the twentieth century.[18]

Toward a Consumer Society

Except for the early settlers at Jamestown, securing an adequate supply of food was never a problem for colonial communities, in contrast to the experience of large numbers of people in many other parts of the world. Generous amounts of pork, beef, dairy products, and poultry, supplemented by hunting, yielded a high level of protein in the diet of most colonials. An important reflection of colonial nutritional well-being was the stature of adult males. A study of Revolutionary War soldiers conducted by Robert Fogel reveals that native-born American troops were an average height of five feet eight inches, an inch or more taller than their fellow troops who were foreign-born and two inches taller than British troops. As Fogel concludes, "The evidence both on stature and on food allotments suggests that Americans achieved an average level of meat consumption by the middle of the eighteenth century that was not reached in Europe until well into the twentieth century."[19]

In the early stages of colony building, colonial Americans put much of the surplus that they produced beyond subsistence needs (which included a plain but wholesome diet) into capital formation—the acquisition of equipment, livestock, and the like. Middle-class landowning families typically lived in one- or two-room dwellings. Under a system of household manufactures, widespread in rural areas throughout the colonies, members of the family produced a variety of goods for their own use, including clothing, furniture, eating utensils, and most other items needed for daily living. Made with limited skills, many of these goods were necessarily crude. For some time after the founding of a colony, even wealthy Americans pursued a relatively simple life-style.

A Consumer Revolution

By the late seventeenth and early eighteenth centuries, however, Americans were beginning to benefit from the market availability of a greater variety of personal and household goods, a development that would eventually reach almost all levels of colonial society. The ability of large numbers of ordinary people to consume many of the amenities of life beyond the elements of basic subsistence was a significant development throughout much of the Western world during this period. This development could be characterized as a consumer revolution, foreshadowing an even greater proliferation of consumer goods generated by nineteenth-century industrialization.

More and more people in the colonies as well as in Western Europe were becoming consumers of tobacco, sugar, tea, and coffee—the so-called "fancy groceries" of the seventeenth and eighteenth centuries. The same tobacco-smoking craze that had spread over Europe extended to the colonies as well. Caffeine drinks like tea and coffee gained in popularity, as did confections and sugar (though tastes shifted from the cheaper muscavado sugar toward the more costly white refined product). Sugar was also consumed as molasses, but much of that commodity was further processed into rum.

The eighteenth century also witnessed a proliferation of consumer semidurable goods, particularly those associated with eating and drinking—knives and forks, glassware, ceramic dishes, tea equipment, and napkins and tablecloths. To some extent, the expanding

consumption of tobacco and caffeinated drinks appears to have stimulated changes in eating and drinking utensils. For example, tobacco was usually smoked in clay pipes mass produced by British ceramic manufacturers; those manufacturers soon began to make stoneware dishes out of the white clay they used for pipe making. For colonial families, the substitution of easier-to-clean ceramic tableware for wooden plates made possible an improvement in sanitation. Furthermore, the experience of people who imbibed tea and coffee showed that ceramic drinking vessels were the most appropriate way to consume those drinks. Other popular amenities were related to sleeping, with increasing numbers of consumers using better mattresses, sheets, pillows and pillow cases, blankets, and bed curtains. (The latter made possible some element of privacy in the small dwellings where most ordinary families continued to live.) Also among the wide variety of goods offered by storekeepers and peddlers were woolen, linen, cotton, and silk fabrics, in many different colors, patterns, weights, and weaves, and a variety of ornaments like ribbon, buttons, and buckles—all reflecting a taste for luxury on the part of rural people.

The diffusion of new consumer goods through different categories of the population of southern New England has been traced by Gloria L. Main and Jackson T. Main, using household inventories. Amenities were adopted initially by members of the elite, first in Boston in the late seventeenth century, then in towns close to the principal waterways of the region, and finally in the older towns of the interior by the second quarter of the eighteenth century. Middle-class householders in each area quickly followed the elite of their communities in adopting as many elements of the new life-style as they could afford. According to the Mains, "By the final years of the colonial period, many of the most ordinary households deep in the interior were using such new goods as forks at tables laid with tablecloths and napkins."[20] Historian Lorena Walsh discovered a similar pattern of diffusion in the Chesapeake colonies: acquisition of a greater array of consumer goods by the tidewater elite starting about 1715, reaching middling families by the 1730s, and even poorer households by the 1750s.[21]

Thus, the new consumer goods appealed to a broad range of colonial society. Most remarkable is that this consumer revolution was largely accomplished without families having to make significant increases in the proportion of their incomes allocated to consumption. That they were able to do so was in part due to an improvement in the terms of trade between the colonies and Britain: The prices of American export commodities rose relative to those of imported manufactured goods. This reflected a strong European demand for many of the raw materials of the Western Hemisphere—tobacco, sugar, rice, indigo, wheat, and other products. Furthermore, many of the manufactured goods of the early consumer society in America represented the first fruits of the economic advances being made in England; those advances resulted in the production and distribution of a great variety of inexpensive and plentiful consumer goods that often substituted for more expensive handmade items. Historian Marc Egnal calculates the gain that the colonial consumer received from these developments: "The 100 bushels of wheat produced by a small farm in the mid-1740s could command 150 yards of woolen cloth, [whereas] the same 100 bushels could be traded for over 250 yards of cloth in the early 1760s."[22]

The Paradox of Poverty

The Poor Laws

In spite of the wealth of colonial America, poverty existed. The poor were regarded as part of the order of things, so each colony early in its history enacted legislation assigning to local governments the responsibility for caring for those unable to support themselves. County or town officials levied taxes on residents to provide a minimum level of living for those entitled to seek relief by virtue of their birthright, or residence in the community for a stipulated period. The Poor Laws not only established but also limited responsibility, as nonresidents were not eligible for relief and thus could be "warned out" of the community. Much of the assistance consisted of outdoor relief—funds allocated by overseers of the poor to provide for a particular need of an individual, such as an item of clothing or a pair of shoes, a specified amount of firewood, funeral expenses, or medical care. By the 1730s, some of the larger towns had built almshouses where the poor were housed and required to perform useful work for the community. In addition to the Poor Laws, efforts were made in the private sector to deal with the problems of poverty. Churches mobilized support for their less fortunate members as did societies formed by immigrant groups and organizations created by artisans.

Characteristics of Poverty in Colonial America

Who were "the Proper Objects of Publick Charity"? Unfortunately, colonial records do not permit us to classify the sources of poverty, since colonial Americans tended to define the poor by their needs, not by a process. However, it is clear that four groups of people made up the bulk of the "unfortunates" who were unable to support themselves: (1) women and children left widowed and orphaned (as a result of the death of the husband at sea, by epidemic, or from an accident); (2) the sick and injured suffering a long-term disability; (3) the physically and mentally handicapped; and (4) the aged. When war touched colonial America during eighteen of the twenty-four years between 1739 and 1763, the Overseers of the Poor assumed responsibility for administering aid to disabled veterans as well as to the widows and orphans of deceased troops. Individuals or families who experienced temporary misfortune—victims of fire or other disasters, war refugees from frontier areas, or newly arrived immigrants too ill to work because of the atrocious conditions they had experienced on shipboard—also received relief.

Evidence indicates that the amount expended for relief of the poor by public bodies and voluntary organizations increased in the half-century prior to the American Revolution. These rising outlays reflected in part a growing humanitarian concern. Moreover, the increasing size and complexity of communities may have encouraged a rationalization of poor relief, as society sought to dispense a greater proportion of its help to the poor through formal institutions rather than individual giving, whether to neighbors in need or to beggars.

But increasing resources allocated to poor relief also resulted in part from the growth in the number of the poor in America in the years just prior to the Revolution. There were in the larger cities a number of industrious, able-bodied persons, ordinarily self-supporting, who needed public assistance as a result of their unemployment during an economic downturn. For example, high wages during a war boom from 1754 to 1763 drew large numbers of semiskilled workers to Philadelphia. A postwar depression left many of these workers unemployed. As a result of cuts in wages, even employed workers found their earnings no longer sufficient to cover family living costs, requiring wives and children to seek paid work. However, we do not know why some able-bodied people exercised the option of moving on to other places where the supply of labor was scarce and jobs were available, while other able-bodied people remained in Philadelphia living in poverty.

Some recent research suggests that a permanent underclass was forming in large cities like Philadelphia.[23] The main characteristic of these unskilled urban workers with little chance for advancement anywhere in America was their lack of the right kind of marketable skill. In spite of widespread opportunity and strong inducements in America, there were young people who did not become apprentices to a craft or choose a trade that provided opportunity for a measure of economic security through property ownership. We do not know why some individuals were unable to find the first rung on the economic ladder or even whether their reasons were personal or societal. Nor do we know whether their economic plight was more or less serious than that of their counterparts in European society.

Whatever conclusions future historical research may support regarding the extent and sources of poverty in colonial America, it is significant that provincial society developed a set of standards for making decisions about the care of its economically less fortunate members—standards that were operative for several generations. In an age when the wealth of society was still low by modern standards, and so the ability to abolish poverty, colonials accepted the inevitability of economic deprivation but determined that its most extreme forms were intolerable. Borrowing both from tradition and ongoing developments in England, colonial Americans developed a set of attitudes and institutions in both the public and private sectors to carry out the responsibilities that had been defined for the relief of the poor. These attitudes and institutions survived until the twentieth century, when larger amounts of wealth generated by the Industrial Revolution made possible new approaches for dealing with poverty.

Summary

The American population nearly doubled every twenty-five years after 1700, the result of immigration, slave importations, and, most significantly, a high rate of natural increase compared to that of the Old World. Because the national product of the colonies grew even more rapidly than population, free white Americans were relatively well off on the eve of the Revolution. Advances in technology were of minimal importance in the colonial advance of product per capita. However, Americans did benefit from the technical improvements in British industry that made a greater variety of consumer goods available at low prices, contributing in some ways to a more comfortable life-style. An increase in the amount of human capital—that is, the skills of the labor force—occurred as a result of learning by doing, primarily in agriculture, and by the transfer of craft skills from Europe. As historians McCusker and Menard note, "improvements in economic organization, specifically shifts away from self-sufficiency and toward production for exchange and the development of more efficient markets, were the principal sources of growth in the colonies of British America."[24]

British regulation, as it was implemented before 1763, did not prevent the growth of commerce outside of the British Empire nor the expansion of a manufacturing sector. Although colonials experienced what they perceived to be a shortage of money or specie, they developed substitutes like government-issued paper currency with which to carry on their business. On the eve of the Revolution, wealth was highly concentrated in the hands of a few segments of the population. However, the larger proportion of middle-class farmers, artisans, and traders in America as compared to Europe reflected the numerous opportunities that were available to ordinary colonials in the growing economy.

Endnotes

1. John J. McCusker and Russell R. Menard, *The Economy of British America, 1607–1789* (Chapel Hill: University of North Carolina Press, 1985), chapter 3.
2. U.S. Bureau of the Census, *Historical Statistics of the United States: Colonial Times to 1970* (Washington D.C.: Government Printing Office, 1975), series 169, p. 1175. The data were calculated by Alice Hanson Jones. For further details, see Alice Hanson Jones, *Wealth of a Nation to Be: The American Colonies on the Eve of the Revolution* (New York: Columbia University Press, 1980), and her *American Colonial Wealth: Documents and Methods*, 2d ed., 3 vols. (New York: Arno Press, 1978).
3. McCusker and Menard, *Economy of British America*, p. 60.
4. D. E. Ball and G. M. Walton, "Agricultural Productivity Changes in Eighteenth-Century Pennsylvania," *Journal of Economic History*, 36 (1976).
5. Peter A. Coclanis, *The Shadow of a Dream: Economic Life and Death in the South Carolina Low Country, 1670–1920* (New York: Oxford University Press, 1989).
6. Lois G. Carr and Russell R. Menard, "Land, Labor, and Economies of Scale in Early Maryland: Some Limits to Growth in the Chesapeake System of Husbandry," *Journal of Economic History*, 49 (1989).
7. James F. Shepherd and Gary M. Walton, *Shipping, Maritime Trade, and the Economic Development of Colonial North America* (Cambridge: Cambridge University Press, 1972).

8. Ibid., p. 116.

9. F. Crouzet, "England and France in the Eighteenth Century: A Comparative Analysis of Two Economic Growths," in R. M. Hartwell, ed., *The Causes of the Industrial Revolution in England* (London: Methuen & Co., 1967), p. 165.

10. Robert Paul Thomas, "A Quantitative Approach to the Study of the Effects of British Imperial Policy upon Colonial Welfare: Some Preliminary Findings," *Journal of Economic History*, 25 (1965), p. 627.

11. Ibid., p. 637.

12. Paul F. Paskoff, *Industrial Evolution: Organization, Structure, and Growth of the Pennsylvania Iron Industry, 1750–1860* (Baltimore: John Hopkins University Press, 1983).

13. Victor S. Clark, *History of Manufactures in the United States*, 3 vols., reprinted (New York: Peter Smith, 1949), vol. 1, p. 193.

14. Edwin J. Perkins, *The Economy of Colonial America*, 2nd ed. (New York: Columbia University Press, 1988), p. 219. The calculations are based on data in Jones, *American Colonial Wealth: Documents and Methods*.

15. Jackson Turner Main, *Society and Economy in Colonial Connecticut* (Princeton: Princeton University Press, 1985), pp. 374–375.

16. Robert E. Gallman, "Influences on the Distribution of Landholdings in Early Colonial North Carolina," *Journal of Economic History*, 42 (1982), p. 573.

17. For an assessment of the literature dealing with the economic *mentalité* of colonial Americans, see Edwin J. Perkins, "The Entrepreneurial Spirit in Colonial America: The Foundations of Modern Business History," *Business History Review*, 63 (1989), pp. 160–186.

18. Claudia Goldin, *Understanding the Gender Gap: An Economic History of American Women* (New York: Oxford University Press, 1990), pp. 11–12, 46–50, 55–57.

19. Robert W. Fogel et al, "Secular Changes in American and British Stature and Nutrition," *Journal of Interdisciplinary History*, 14 (1983), p. 464.

20. Gloria L. Main and Jackson T. Main, "Economic Growth and the Standard of Living in Southern New England, 1640–1774," *Journal of Economic History*, 48 (1988), p. 41.

21. Lorena S. Walsh, "Urban Amenities and Rural Sufficiency: Living Standards and Consumer Behavior in the Colonial Chesapeake, 1643–1777," *Journal of Economic History*, 43 (1983).

22. Marc M. Egnal, "The Economic Development of the Thirteen Continental Colonies, 1720 to 1775," *William and Mary Quarterly*, 32 (1975), p. 205.

23. See, for example, Billy G. Smith, *The "Lower Sort": Philadelphia's Laboring People, 1750–1800* (Ithaca: Cornell University Press, 1990).

24. McCusker and Menard, *Economy of British America*, p. 270.

Suggested Readings

The starting point for students interested in the population of early America is Jim Potter, "Demographic Development and Family Structure," in Jack P. Greene and J. R. Pole, eds., *Colonial British America: Essays in the New History of the Early Modern Era* (Baltimore: John Hopkins University Press, 1984). Robert V. Wells, *The Population of the British Colonies in North America Before 1776* (Princeton: Princeton University Press, 1975), summarizes the results of various demographic surveys conducted at different times by provincial governments. Aspects of early and late migration to the colonies are discussed in Russell R. Menard, "British Migration to the Chesapeake Colonies in the Seventeenth Century," in Lois G. Carr, Philip D. Morgan, and Jean B. Russo, eds., *Colonial Chesapeake Society* (Chapel Hill: University of North Carolina Press, 1988), and Bernard Bailyn, *Voyagers to the West: A Passage in the Peopling of America on the Eve of the Revolution* (New York: Knopf, 1986).

Economic growth and its sources in the colonial era are analyzed in Robert E. Gallman, "The Pace and Pattern of American Economic Growth," in Lance E. Davis et al., eds., *American Economic Growth: An Economist's History of the United States* (New York: Harper & Row, 1972); Stuart Bruchey, *The Roots of American Economic Growth, 1607–1861: An Essay in Social Causation* (New York: Harper & Row, 1965); Marc Egnal, "The Economic Development of the Thirteen Continental Colonies, 1720 to 1775," *William and Mary Quarterly*, 32 (1975); Gary M. Walton and James F. Shepherd, *The Economic Rise of Early America* (Cambridge: Cambridge University Press, 1979); D. E. Ball and G. M. Walton, "Agricultural Productivity Changes in Eighteenth-Century Pennsylvania," *Journal of Economic History*, 36 (1976); and Lois G. Carr and Russell R. Menard, "Land, Labor, and Economies of Scale in Early Maryland: Some Limits to Growth in the Chesapeake System of Husbandry," *Journal of Economic History*, 49 (1989). Many of the works listed in the Suggested Readings for Chapter 2 also contain important information on economic growth in the colonies.

Developments in overseas and intercolonial trade, as they relate to the growth of the colonial economy, are covered in James F. Shepherd and Gary M. Walton, *Shipping, Maritime Trade, and the Economic Development of Colonial North America* (Cambridge: Cambridge University Press, 1972), and James F. Shepherd and Samuel H. Williamson, "The Coastal Trade of the British North American Colonies, 1768–1772," *Journal of Economic History*, 32 (1972). The following materials provide a history of the on-going controversy among scholars over the impact of British mercantilistic regulation of the American economy: Lawrence A. Harper, "The Effect of the Navigation Acts on the Thirteen Colonies," in Richard B. Morris, ed., *The Era of the American Revolution* (New York: Columbia University Press, 1939); Robert P. Thomas, "A Quantitative Approach to the Study of the Effects of British Imperial Policy on Colonial Welfare," *Journal of Economic History*, 25 (1965); Gary M. Walton, "The New Economic History and the Burdens of the Navigation Acts," *Economic History Review,* 2nd ser., 24 (1971); and Larry Sawers, "The Navigation Acts Revisited," *Economic History Review*, 45 (1992).

Victor S. Clark, *History of Manufactures in the United States, 1607–1860*, vol. 1 reprinted (New York: Peter Smith, 1949), is still the only general history of manufacturing in the colonial period. Carl Bridenbaugh, *The Colonial Craftsman* (New York: New York University Press, 1950), is the only comprehensive survey of the subject. Works dealing with the history of individual industries include Paul F. Paskoff, *Industrial Evolution: Organization, Structure, and Growth of the Pennsylvania Iron Industry, 1750–1860* (Baltimore: John Hopkins University Press, 1983) and Joseph A. Goldenberg, *Shipbuilding in Colonial America* (Charlottesville: University Press of Virginia, 1976).

The following deal with various aspects of colonial monetary practices: Leslie V. Brock, *The Currency of the American Colonies, 1700–1764* (New York: Arno Press, 1975); John J. McCusker, *Money and Exchange in Europe and America, 1600–1775: A Handbook* (Chapel Hill: University of North Carolina Press, 1977); Richard Sylla, "Monetary Innovation in America," *Journal of Economic History*, 42 (1982); Roger W. Weiss, "The Issue of Paper Money in the American Colonies, 1720–1774" *Journal of Economic History*, 30 (1970); and Elmus Wicker, "Colonial Monetary Standards Contrasted: Evidence from the Seven Years' War," *Journal of*

Economic History, 45 (1985). Mary M. Schweitzer, *Custom and Contract: Household, Government, and the Economy in Colonial Pennsylvania* (New York: Columbia University Press, 1987), discusses paper money issues of that province as well as other aspects of government economic activity. Joseph A. Ernst, *Money and Politics in America, 1755–1775* (Chapel Hill: University of North Carolina Press, 1973), focuses on the interaction between American monetary innovation (in the form of paper money) and British efforts to impose regulation of colonial monetary practices.

Alice Hanson Jones, *Wealth of a Nation to Be: The American Colonies on the Eve of the Revolution* (New York: Columbia University Press, 1980), is a comprehensive analysis of wealth and wealth holding; the same author's *American Colonial Wealth: Documents and Methods*, 2nd ed., 3 vols. (New York: Arno Press, 1978), supplies data for the study of living standards and property ownership. Jeffrey G. Williamson and Peter H. Lindert, *American Inequality: A Macroeconomic History* (New York: Academic Press, 1980), puts the colonial experience in long-term historical perspective. Jackson Turner Main, *Society and Economy in Colonial Connecticut*, is an important in-depth study (Princeton: Princeton University Press, 1985) of property ownership and social mobility. Several studies of wealth distribution are included in Gary B. Nash, ed., *Class and Society in Early America* (Englewood Cliffs, N.J.: Prentice-Hall, 1970); see also Gloria L. Main, "Inequality in Early America: The Evidence from Probate Records of Massachusetts and Maryland," *Journal of Interdisciplinary History*, 7 (1977).

On the debate over whether early America was "capitalist" or "precapitalist," Edwin J. Perkins, "The Entrepreneurial Spirit in Colonial America: The Foundations of Modern Business History," *Business History Review*, 63 (1989), emphasizes in a review of the literature the strength of market values held by most segments of provincial society. Winifred B. Rothenberg, "The Market and Massachusetts Farmers, 1750–1855," *Journal of Economic History*, 41 (1981), brings statistical analysis to this question. For other perspectives, see James Henretta, *The Origins of American Capitalism: Collected Essays* (Boston: Northeastern University Press, 1991), which includes his noted "Families and Farms: *Mentalité* in Preindustrial America"; Daniel Vickers, "Competency and Competition: Economic Culture in Early America," *William and Mary Quarterly*, 47 (1990); and Allan Kulikoff, "The Transition to Capitalism in Rural America," *William and Mary Quarterly*, 46 (1989). On the economic role of women, Julie A. Matthaei, *An Economic History of Women in America: Women's Work, the Sexual Division of Labor, and the Development of Capitalism* (New York: Schocken, 1982), provides a general interpretation. Marylynn Salmon, *Women and the Law of Property in Early America* (Chapel Hill: University of North Carolina Press, 1986) is the basic work on this subject. Mary Beth Norton, "The Evolution of White Women's Experience in Early America," *American Historical Review*, 89 (1984), surveys a growing body of literature. Laurel Thatcher Ulrich, *Good Wives: Image and Reality in the Lives of Women in Northern New England, 1650–1750* (New York: Knopf, 1982), and Joan M. Jensen, *Loosening the Bonds: Mid-Atlantic Farm Women, 1750–1850* (New Haven: Yale University Press, 1986), are valuable regional studies, while Carole Shammas, "The Female Social Structure of Philadelphia in 1774," *Pennsylvania Magazine of History and Biography*, 107 (1987), is a useful case study of one city. Authors of the essays in Stephen Innes, ed., *Work and Labor in Early America* (Chapel Hill: University of North Carolina Press, 1988), analyze the experience of various segments of the colonial labor force. On the issue of growing urban poverty, see Gary B. Nash, *The Urban Crucible: Social Change, Political Consciousness, and the American Revolution* (Cambridge: Harvard University Press, 1979), and Billy G. Smith, *The "Lower Sort": Philadel-*

phia's Laboring People, 1750–1800 (Ithaca, N.Y.: Cornell University Press, 1990).

Carole Shammas, *The Preindustrial Consumer in England and America* (Oxford: Clarendon Press, 1990), explores major elements of the transatlantic changes in consumption patterns during the seventeenth and eighteenth centuries. T. H. Breen, "An Empire of Goods: The Anglicization of Colonial America, 1690–1776," *Journal of British Studies,* 25 (1986), presents a useful interpretation. Regional studies of the dimensions of this consumer revolution include Gloria L. Main and Jackson T. Main, "Economic Growth and the Standard of Living in Southern New England, 1640–1774," *Journal of Economic History,* 48 (1988), and Lorena S. Walsh, "Urban Amenities and Rural Sufficiency: Living Standards and Consumer Behavior in the Colonial Chesapeake, 1643–

1777," *Journal of Economic History,* 43 (1983). Important studies of nutrition among the colonial population include Robert W. Fogel et al., "Secular Changes in American and British Stature and Nutrition," *Journal of Interdisciplinary History,* 14 (1983); Kenneth Sokoloff and Georgia Villaflor, "The Early Achievement of Modern Stature in America," *Social Science History,* 6 (1982); Sarah F. McMahon, "A Comfortable Subsistence: The Changing Composition of Diet in Rural New England, 1620–1840," *William and Mary Quarterly,* 40 (1985); and Henry M. Miller, "An Archaeological Perspective on the Evolution of Diet in the Colonial Chesapeake, 1620–1745," in Lois G. Carr, Philip D. Morgan, and Jean B. Russo, eds., *Colonial Chesapeake Society* (Chapel Hill: University of North Carolina Press, 1988).

Chapter 4

Foundations of Economic Independence

LTHOUGH AMERICANS HAD FARED WELL WITHIN the London-centered commercial empire of the Atlantic, economic and political developments after 1763 brought the problem of colonial status to the fore: The colonies lacked control over the decision-making system that affected them in so many ways. When political means failed to change British policy, Americans mobilized their economic resources to support a prolonged military operation. Attaining political independence released their entrepreneurial energies into new channels and made possible the use of government policy to stimulate economic development. However, independence coincided with a period of difficult economic readjustment and confronted the new nation's leaders with the problem of establishing the authority to cope with it through a new national government. The Constitution that they adopted both provided the political stability necessary for economic growth and furnished the legal framework for the establishment of a nationwide market economy.

The Breakdown of the Imperial-Colonial Structure

In 1763, the British government needed more revenue to retire the large debt it had incurred during the Seven Years' War (known in America as the French and Indian War) as well as to support the military defense of its American colonies. The government was also concerned with what it had come to perceive as inadequate enforcement of its regulations regarding colonial economic activity; even while England was fighting France, some American colonials had persisted in trade with the enemy. To secure a source of revenue in the colonies, the British attempted in the decade after 1763 to impose a tax on newspapers and legal documents and to levy import duties on a series of items. To improve the customs service (its ef-

ficiency was at such a low level that the amount it collected was only one-fourth of the cost of administration), the British government tried to impose stricter discipline on appointed officials in America and to tighten the enforcement of regulations. More colonial commodities were placed on the enumerated list, and Americans were prohibited from exporting nonenumerated items to northern Europe. The Tea Act of 1773, which authorized the East India Company to set up a system of direct distribution of tea in the colonies, showed that British business would use political influence to penetrate colonial markets. Under the provisions of the Tea Act, the East India Company could undersell American merchants, whether they imported tea legally from Britain or smuggled it from Holland.

As a result of the broadened scope and closer enforcement of trade regulation, as well as the efforts to collect taxes in the colonies to support the royal government, it seemed to colonials that American economic interests would always be subordinated to those of British business and other interest groups. Americans thus organized political opposition and formed nonimportation agreements to apply pressure on British merchants and the British government. The experience of the 1760s and 1770s raised questions concerning the ability of Americans to control their own economic affairs. As noted in Chapter 2, the growth of strong merchant communities and regional economies focused in Philadelphia, Boston, and New York meant that the New England and Middle Colonies had achieved more autonomy in economic decision making than was typical of a colony; it was an autonomy that they wanted to maintain. Although production of staple commodities for export stimulated the growth of the southern colonies, some planters were concerned about problems like indebtedness, which they perceived to be the result of dependence on British business. Mercantilistic regulation may have imposed

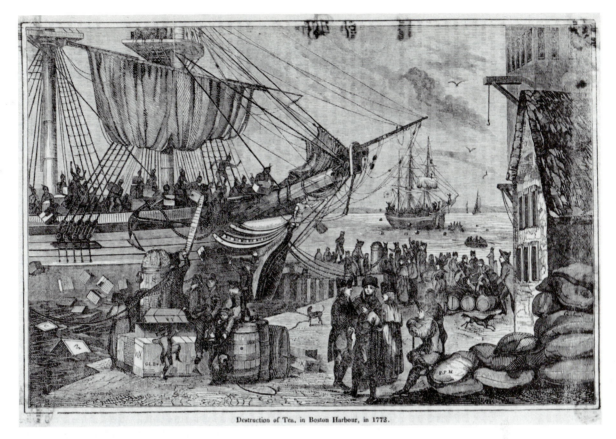

Destruction of Tea, in Boston Harbour, in 1773.

The Boston Tea Party, 1773. The Tea Act, passed by Parliament in 1773, enabled the British East India Company to sell directly to retailers in the colonies, thereby undermining the position of American merchants. Destruction of tea on a British ship in Boston harbor was part of the American protest against the act. (Photo Researchers/Mary Evans Picture Library)

only a light economic burden on Americans; but in the 1760s and 1770s, it appeared to interfere with their goal of managing their own economic destiny.

The Economics of War

Troops and Materials

The outbreak of armed conflict in the spring of 1775 required the Continental Congress, occupied up to this time with political strategy, to organize a major military effort for a period of eight years (the longest American war before the Vietnam conflict). Its economic task was to provide the troops, materials, money, and management to support military operations against one of the most powerful nations in Europe.

The size of the Continental Army was never large by modern standards. The peak number of soldiers serving under George Washington's command at any one time was sixteen to eighteen thousand; more often the commander-in-chief had a force of five to ten thousand troops.

The armed forces were recruited by voluntary enlistment at first and then by conscription. As in other wars, the well-to-do could avoid military service by hiring a substitute. In the last years of the struggle, the military burden fell heavily on the low income segment of the community.

When the men went off to war, wives could elect to go with their husbands. Most, however, found military life unattractive, where they served as cooks, nurses, or laundry workers. Thus, women who joined the army generally did so only if they lacked other means of support. Most women stayed at home, serving as deputy husbands in managing the family enterprise. Here they not only had to perform their traditional duties as homemaker; they also had to carry out what was considered "men's work" on the farm or plantation or in the shop.

The interruption of foreign trade by the war stimulated the growth of manufacturing in order to produce substitutes for goods previously imported. Domestic production of linen and woolen cloth had to expand to meet the need for both military and civilian goods. Much of the increased production of "homespun" was undertaken by rural and urban people working in their homes. To provide arms and ammunition for the armed forces, Congress and several states established armories for the manufacture of rifles and muskets and also offered subsidies to encourage munitions makers to expand their facilities. To mobilize a work force for war production, the government provided exemption from military service for those working in establishments producing munitions and tried to encourage the immigration of skilled workers from Europe.

However, since Americans were not able to produce enough military supplies for the Continental armies and the militias, foreign aid was indispensable. Over the course of the war, 60 percent of all the gunpowder used by the revolutionary forces came from Europe. Even many of the uniforms worn by American troops had to be imported from abroad. France was the most important foreign supplier, providing not only material for American troops but also (after 1778) military and naval support. Other aid was secured from Spain and Holland. The enemy also became an important, although unwilling, supplier, when American forces captured British arms and equipment as well as consumer goods. (During the course of the war, American privateers captured about two thousand British vessels, worth, together with their cargoes, an estimated £18,000,000 sterling.)

A continuing problem for the Americans was how to fashion an adequate administrative structure to oversee the war effort. Congress supervised the operation of the Continental Army through subcommittees; it also designated a commissary general of stores and purchases as well as a quartermaster general to secure the necessary food, feed, equipment, and services. Lack of experience in managing such a large effort caused repeated breakdowns; these led to frequent administrative reorganizations, changes in leadership, and experimentation with new procedures of collecting supplies and distributing them to troops in the field. But whatever the political leaders tried, certain problems of procurement continued to plague the war effort: rivalry between purchasing agents of Congress and the states (each state had a committee to purchase supplies for its own militia); lack of cooperation between the commissary and the quartermaster; inaccurate bookkeeping leading to overcharges, graft, and corruption among minor employees; and delivery of goods of inferior quality.

What made the system work at all was the development of a *military-mercantile complex*, an informal network of leading merchants. While various structural reorganizations and shuffles in top-level governmental positions went on, merchants occupied key positions in

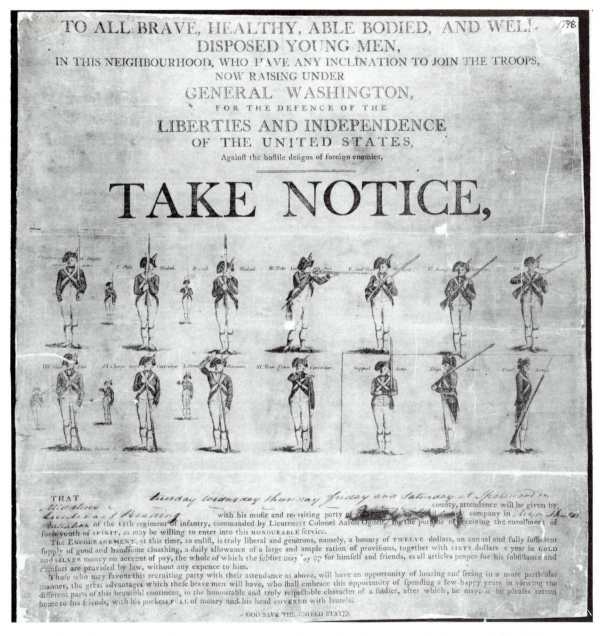

A Recruiting Poster. Recruits were promised an enlistment bonus, ample clothing and food, and generous pay in return for "spending a few happy years in viewing the different parts of this beautiful continent." (The Historical Society of Pennsylvania)

Destruction of the Statue of King George III.   This print is actually a fictitious view of an event that really happened in New York on July 9, 1776. It symbolized the removal of British restraints upon American economic enterprise. (Line engraving by Francis X. Habermann, Museum of the City of New York)

the procurement services. These merchants continued in their private businesses while performing their public functions and dealt with fellow traders on both public and private accounts simultaneously. While they sometimes financed their own private businesses with funds advanced by the government, they also applied their own money for public purposes when necessary. Although Congress eventually created an imposing bureaucratic structure, with almost three thousand employees in the quartermaster department alone, the merchants' better knowledge of the commer-

cial world enabled them to carry out the business of supply to meet the needs of the war effort.

Financing the War Effort

One of the most perplexing problems for the political leaders of the new nation was how to pay for the military operations and other costs of government. Loans and subsidies furnished by France, Spain, and Holland were used primarily to finance the American purchase of weapons, gunpowder, and other supplies in Europe. Only a promise of a high rate of interest to be paid in scarce specie enticed U.S. citizens to make voluntary loans to the new government. Foreign and domestic loans together accounted for less than one-fifth of the cost of the war.

Without the power to tax, the Continental Congress had to make estimates of its revenue needs annually and then levy a requisition on the states, which held the power to tax, each for its share. During the colonial era, provincial legislatures had regularly imposed only a low level of taxes per capita on average. In the years just prior to the war, American taxpayers probably paid in taxes no more than one-third as much per capita than did their counterparts in England. In spite of war needs, state legislative bodies were understandably reluctant to levy taxes on their citizens. Levies by Congress on states accounted for only a bit more than 6 percent of the total revenues of the U.S. government during the Revolutionary War years. Thus, Congress resorted to financing the war by issues of fiat money, a form of involuntary loans made to the government by the people of the United States.

In the summer of 1775, Congress began to issue noninterest-bearing notes to pay troops and military suppliers, who used the notes as currency to settle transactions they had made. By the end of 1779, Congress had authorized emissions of over $225 million. States and sometimes even counties issued their own bills of credit, which became a part of the money supply. Quartermaster and commissary certificates also served as money when they were used by military purchasing agents for impressment, a process that forced owners of goods to sell at prices stipulated by government buyers, even if below market level.

The result of the monetary practices used to finance much of the war effort was hyperinflation. For example, an index of wholesale prices of key commodities on the Philadelphia market more than doubled in 1776, in 1777, and in 1778, and then advanced almost tenfold

from the spring of 1779 to the spring of 1781 (see Table 4–1). To describe the impact of inflation in another way, the £100 of currency that in 1776 bought over fourteen thousand pounds of flour or five thousand pounds of beef commanded considerably less than one hundred pounds of either commodity in 1781. Although shortages of certain goods at different times contributed to the problem, the method of war finance employed by Congress and the states was the dominant influence in the dramatic price rise. Inflation resulted not only from putting into circulation such a huge amount of money; it also reflected the public's skepticism about the ability of the U.S. government eventually to redeem the notes.

When depreciation of the currency seriously threatened to undermine the war effort, some political leaders called for price controls, arguing that speculators and monopolists were to

Table 4–1 *Index of Estimated Wholesale Prices,*
1775–1789

Year	Index (1850–59 = 100)[a]
1775	78.0
1776	108.0
1777	329.6
1778	598.1
1779	2,969.1
1780	10,544.1
1781	5,085.8
1782	139.6
1783	119.1
1784	112.7
1785	105.0
1786	105.1
1787	103.9
1788	97.4
1789	94.0

[a]Index for Philadelphia

Source: Data from U.S. Bureau of the Census, *Historical Statistics of the United States: Colonel Times to 1970* (Washington, D.C.: U.S. GPO, 1975), p. 1196.

blame for inflation. Some states enacted price-fixing laws and placed embargoes on the export of key commodities; they then attempted to formulate regional agreements to regulate economic transactions. However, state restrictions proved ineffective in holding down prices. Farmers refused to sell in the regulated markets, and merchants found ways to evade the rules. Some critics argued that regulation contributed to price increases by encouraging the hoarding of commodities. Even if eighteenth-century governments had possessed the capacity to administer effective price controls, such regulation would not have dealt with the real source of inflation—the large increase in purchasing power that resulted from the issue of paper money to finance the war. At best, such controls would have only postponed a rise in prices until after the conflict (as occurred, for example, after World War II).

In 1780, the Continental Congress attempted to halt the spiraling inflation by revaluing outstanding notes at one-fortieth of their face value. The notes continued to depreciate and, by a year later, had disappeared from circulation. The government eventually redeemed the bills at a penny on the dollar, thereby repudiating a substantial portion of the huge debt it had incurred to fight the war and giving rise to the popular expression "Not worth a continental."

Upon becoming superintendent of finance in 1781, Robert Morris, a leading Philadelphia businessman and member of Congress, imposed budgetary controls, attempted to maximize the flow of revenue from requisitions on the states, and called for a national bank to serve as the government's fiscal agent. The Bank of North America, chartered by Congress in 1781, became the nation's first commercial bank. In connection with its loans to the government and private business, the bank issued notes that became part of the country's circulating currency. However, Morris's principal fi-

nancial objective—to secure taxing power for the national government—became a victim of politics when the issue of taxation turned into a power struggle between centralists, who wanted to strengthen the central government, and localists, who stood for preservation of state sovereignty.

Inflation as a way to pay for the war effort imposed a heavy economic burden on the American people. In addition, it had disruptive effects on the operation of the economy. When money no longer served as a reasonable standard of value, individuals and groups arranged among themselves how to carry out transactions at prewar price and wage levels and to make payments in kind when possible. As Anne Bezanson points out in a study of prices in Pennsylvania, throughout the war period all groups "searched for means of shifting part of the impact of inflation" away from themselves.[1] Despite the inefficiencies in making transactions because of the hyperinflation, America's ability to mobilize the resources for a long war demonstrated the productive strength of the economy and a sophistication of the business structure that kept channels open for the flow of goods and materials from abroad and within the country.

Impact of the War and Independence on the Economy

Although the political result of the American Revolution—independence from Britain—was highly visible, the economic effects were not so obvious. The American economy still displayed an important characteristic of colonialism: an emphasis on the production of raw materials for export. The country continued to operate within the orbit of London's business and financial system. Yet the war experience and the new political status of the United Sates accelerated a trend already under way toward

greater autonomy for American economic decision makers.

Economic Trends

The war brought to a temporary halt the growth that had characterized the economy of the colonies during much of the half-century prior to 1775. The economic cost of freedom was high. On the basis of the data available, it is almost certain that the gross national product (GNP) actually declined during the years of hostilities, and possibly rather severely. In the last years of the war, plantations and farms in many parts of the southern states suffered extensive damage at the hands of British troops. Production was further curtailed when the British carried away large numbers of slaves from Virginia and South Carolina. Trade was disrupted, for varying lengths of time, by a British blockade and enemy occupation of major port cities—New York, Philadelphia, Newport, and Charleston. Curtailment of immigration contributed to labor shortages, and in some areas the mobilization of farmers into the armed forces may have reduced the acreage that was planted. Many farm producers experienced prosperity from sales to the military (both American and British), and some industries like gunmaking expanded to meet the demand for equipment. But iron, a leading industry before the war, does not appear to have fared well. According to a recent study, the Revolution disrupted and retarded the growth of the iron industry rather than stimulate it.[2] Military technology did not then involve the large-scale commitment of economic resources that is associated with total war in the twentieth century.

In the decade after the war, the economy achieved some measure of recovery. According to data compiled by James Shepherd, the average annual value of exports from the United States in the early 1790s was 34 percent above that of the thirteen colonies in 1768 to 1772; however, since the population had grown by over 50 percent, the per capita value of exports declined by 24 percent during this period[3] (see Table 4–2). Less is known about how much growth occurred in the domestic sectors of the economy. Historian Jacob Price suggests that gross national product per capita may have recovered to the prewar level only after the onset of the boom touched off by the outbreak of war in Europe in 1793.[4]

Aside from the overall performance of the American economy, there were significant differences in the experience of the regions of the country. According to Shepherd's data, New England's per capita exports in 1791 to 1792 stood at a slightly higher level than in 1768 to 1772.[5] Based on strong foreign markets for its foodstuffs, the Middle Atlantic states' exports per capita made a strong recovery, showing an increase of 10 percent over the prewar level; while Pennsylvania lost some ground, New York gained due to a more rapid growth of its back-country agriculture. The traditional southern staples did not fare so well. Tobacco exports stood at an all-time high in the early 1790s, but this level was only moderately above that set before the war. The Upper

Table 4–2 *Average Annual Exports per Capita, by Region: The Thirteen Colonies (1768–1772) and the United States (1791–1792) (pounds sterling, 1768–1772 prices)*

Origin	Per Capita Exports	
	1768–1772	1791–1792
New England	0.82	0.83
Middle Atlantic	1.01	1.11
Upper South	1.79	1.09
Lower South	1.75	0.88
Total	1.31	0.99

SOURCE: Adapted from James F. Shepherd, "British America and the Atlantic Economy," in *The Economy of Early America: The Revolutionary Period, 1763–1790,* ed. Ronald Hoffman et al. (Charlottesville: University Press of Virginia, 1988), p. 28.

South lost 39 percent in the value of its per capita exports. Rice and indigo did even less well. Without a British subsidy and tariff protection, production of indigo ceased. Exports per capita from the Lower South declined by almost 50 percent from before the war. There was little evidence that plantation capitalism in that region was on the threshold of an enormous expansion to be based on cotton production and slave labor.

New Lines of Enterprise

The attainment of political sovereignty made possible the expansion of American business along new lines. As noted in Chapter 2, even before Independence merchants in the major commercial centers performed functions of a kind that British business firms carried out for the plantation colonies. During the war, merchants from Philadelphia, New York, Boston, and a few smaller centers—not all of them from the top level of the prewar business community—attained wealth and prestige by organizing military supply and taking advantage of other war-related opportunities. They then played key roles in developing a new worldwide commerce legalized by the Revolution. During and after the war, American business found commercial outlets in France and Holland, as well as in Germany, Sweden, and Russia. Trade with the West Indies and southern Europe resumed its growth. Although the ships of U.S. traders were legally excluded from the British West Indies, American merchants expanded their markets in the Caribbean colonies of other powers, continuing a prewar trend. The slave trade was renewed, though commerce with Africa accounted for only a minute percentage of total American foreign trade. The most striking new direction of trade was the opening of commercial relations with the Far East, previously a monopolistic preserve of the British East India Company. Initiated by a voyage from New York to

Canton in 1784, within half a decade this unusually profitable branch of trade became a complex one involving not only China but also India and the East Indies (now Indonesia).

Britain remained the single most important trading partner of the United States. Immediately after the war, it seemed that American economic ties to Britain would become stronger than ever. British exporters, offering generous credit terms, earnestly solicited orders from importers in the United States. But adjustments in commercial patterns made by American merchants resulted in a significant overall reduction in American dependence on the British market and marketing system. By the early 1790s, Great Britain was the destination of fewer American exports than before the war, accounting for less than one-third of the total (compared to nearly 60 percent before Independence).

Significant developments in the 1780s foreshadowed a business revolution that would reach full flower in the nineteenth century. Its principal elements included the creation of new mechanisms to facilitate investment, the development of greater specialization of business units by function, and improvements in transportation and communication. The use of the corporation was a major organizational innovation by which government delegated much of the responsibility for economic development to private business groups. The corporate form gave greater flexibility than a partnership owned by many individuals, ensured continuity of the firm apart from the biological lives of its members, and sometimes limited the financial liability of owners. Thus, the corporation facilitated the mobilization of larger amounts of capital from a greater number of investors than could a proprietorship or partnership. Only a few corporations had been chartered in the colonial period, and those for activities that met a strict definition of the general welfare. By the end of the eighteenth century, however, state governments had conferred corporate charters on over three hundred enterprises. In contrast, fewer than a score of business corporations existed in either England or France. The more extensive use of the corporation in America reflected the willingness of the new nation to define general welfare broadly to include most kinds of enterprises that promised to generate economic growth. The most frequent uses of the corporation before 1800 were in transportation, banking, and insurance.

Through much of the colonial era, the predominant figure in the business world had been the unspecialized merchant, who traded many products to a number of geographical areas and performed a variety of functions. By the 1780s, a clear trend toward specialization had emerged in the mercantile communities of Philadelphia and New York, the country's largest business centers. More traders were becoming geographically specialized, carrying on commerce with one or two areas, and beginning to concentrate on one type of commodity, such as dry goods or provisions.

The decade of the 1780s also witnessed the development of specialized financial institutions—commercial banks. As noted earlier in the chapter, the founding of the Bank of North America was part of Robert Morris's wartime program to revive government finance. After the war, the bank was rechartered as a Pennsylvania corporation; it concentrated on developing a commercial banking business to serve Philadelphia merchants. Similar institutions were chartered in Boston and New York in 1784. Each bank accepted deposits, usually from wealthy mercantile customers. But a more important activity was discounting—that is, making short-term loans to finance commercial transactions. As N. S. B. Gras has written of the bank formed in Boston: "Discounting was to the Massachusetts Bank what teaching is to a college, playing to an orchestra, and moving to a train. It was not everything, but it was the chief function."[6] For the bank as a business enterprise, lending was the principal way to make profits. The founders of many banks were merchants, and one of their ma-

jor motivations was to secure a source of loans to finance their own commercial operations. In connection with their lending operations, the banks issued notes redeemable in specie; thus the notes became an increasingly important part of the nation's money supply as more banks were organized in ensuing decades. From the beginning, bank organizers launched their enterprises as corporations, securing charters from the states in which they operated. The role of chartered commercial banks in accepting deposits, making loans, and issuing private paper that circulated as money contributed to a more effective mobilization of financial resources to support the economic growth of the nation.

The formation of commercial banks that could issue securities as well as perform financial functions was an important element of emerging regional capital markets. Through these markets agricultural savings could be mobilized and channeled toward new and growing forms of economic enterprise. Winifred Rothenberg's careful study of Boston and its agricultural hinterlands shows that this trend was well under way in the 1780s, building on the growth of wealth in the colonial era and stimulated by the events of the war and postwar years. One basic ingredient was the growing acceptance of the concept of interest as a price for money, to be set by the market according to the return on investment and replacing the traditional limits imposed by usury laws. Lending was becoming less personal and local in nature; credit markets were thickening and widening, as more farmers in the hinterlands searched for increased returns to their capital by lending to a greater number of borrowers located over a wider area. Over the decades after Independence, financial assets (loans and mortgages, securities, and cash) grew faster than real estate and other physical assets in the wealth held by farmers, thereby enhancing the liquidity of asset holdings. Thus, the greater liquidity of rural wealth meant that capital would not be embedded in declining economic activities but could be effectively transferred to sectors of potential growth made possible by new technology.[7]

When the war was over, Americans turned their attention to transportation—to the improvement of turnpikes and other roads, canals, and toll bridges. State governments chartered seventeen corporations for this purpose before 1790. The corporate form was used here for the same reason it had been applied in banking—its facility in collecting large amounts of capital. Yet many smaller projects were organized and financed by individual entrepreneurs.

The flow of communication was as important to business operations as was the movement of goods and materials. Thus, the Continental Congress sought to improve the postal service, which was used mainly by business because of its high cost. In 1786, the postmaster general negotiated contracts for thrice-weekly transportation of mail along the main route between Portsmouth, New Hampshire, and Savannah, Georgia. In the following year, service was extended to the interior of the country, where regular routes were set up as far west as Pittsburgh. Postal contracts encouraged private carriers to build and improve roads in the areas where they carried the mail.

The most important function of newspapers at the time was to supply business information in the form of commercial news and advertising. The number of newspapers increased from thirty-seven on the eve of the Revolution (none of which appeared more than once a week) to ninety-two in 1790 (including eight daily papers).

Industrial development continued in the postwar decade, encouraged to a considerable extent by Americans' patriotic desire to achieve economic as well as political independence from Britain. Necessity was also a factor, since a trade depression required a reduction in imports. Societies were organized in several cities to promote "useful manufactures,"

which employed fairly sizable work forces in manufactories using hand methods to make cloth. American entrepreneurs were already alert to the economic potential of the textile-making machinery recently introduced in English factories. An American inventor, Oliver Evans, designed a fully automated water-powered flour mill that greatly reduced labor inputs and improved the quality of the finished product. This foreshadowed the spread of mass-production methods throughout American industry in the nineteenth century.

Land Policies: Speculation and Settlement

Land had always been a major interest of Americans, and mobility, in the form of migration to new areas, was one of their leading characteristics. Business firms often participated in the organization of settlements, seeking profits through land speculation and other enterprises associated with the development of a new region. Beginning in the mid-eighteenth century, increasing numbers of potential settlers and speculators looked to the territory west of the Appalachian Mountains. In this area, there were few Europeans, most of them engaged in the fur trade. Rival business groups attempted to secure grants of land and created plans for settlement and agricultural development of large parts of the West. But the British government blocked expansion into the area by issuing the Proclamation of 1763, which prohibited colonization west of the mountains.

Independence ended British control of land-disposal policy. State governments, by confiscation as well as by forced purchase, took over title to lands formerly held by the king and various proprietors (such as the descendants of William Penn and Lord Baltimore). States also seized the estates of loyalists. At the same time, the last vestiges of feudalism,

Figure 4–1 *United States After the Treaty of 1783.* Adapted from R. R. Palmer, ed., *Atlas of World History* (Chicago: Rand McNally & Co., 1957), p. 151.

such as quit rents, were eliminated from the land system.

Government Policies for Disposal of the Public Domain

The Treaty of Paris (1783), in which Britain formally recognized American independence, established the boundaries of the new nation, as shown in Figure 4–1. As states ceded to the federal government their land claims based on colonial charters, the United States became the owner of vast tracts of western land in the 1780s. The concept of public domain was firmly held, but it was not envisioned that the land would be held in common forever. Rather, it was assumed that the land would be privately owned, not used for government-operated activity. Government revenues from the public domain would be derived from the proceeds of land sales as well as from taxes generated by private use of the land for market-oriented economic pursuits.

The major problem for political decision makers, therefore, was how to transfer the land from government to private ownership. Congress contributed to a solution through two major statutes. The first, the Land Ordinance of 1785, created a mechanism for the survey and orderly disposal of land to which the U.S. government held title. Tiers of townships of six square miles were opened to settlement; land sales were made by auction of tracts of not less than 640 acres at a minimum price of one dollar per acre. The second statute, the Northwest Ordinance of 1787, provided for newly settled areas to be admitted into the Union as states in full partnership with the existing states. This represented a replay of the actions of the English founders of the colonies, who had also encouraged economic development by granting political rights to settlers.

Organizing Settlement in the West

Turning to the economic dimension of land disposal, Congress expected land companies to play an important role in managing the settlement of the West (a policy similar to the earlier reliance of the English government on joint stock companies and proprietors as agents of colonization). The policy enabled Congress to make sales in large tracts, thereby relieving the national government of the responsibility of dealing directly with many small buyers. Also, middlemen could provide the credit needed by many of the settlers.

Thus, in 1787, Congress granted one million acres of land in what is now northern Ohio to the Ohio Company, a land company that was originally formed by army veterans planning to migrate west but that came to involve leading eastern business interests as well. The company paid for the tract in depreciated government paper, making the effective price eight or nine cents an acre. A smaller grant was made on similar terms to the Miami Reserved Land Associates, which was also backed by eastern investors. These and other ventures developed as part of the surge in speculative interest in land promotion during the postwar period. Unincorporated joint stock companies, partnerships, and individuals negotiated with both the states and Congress to gain control over large tracts of land. However, few speculative ventures yielded the high profits anticipated by the original promoters, and many suffered losses. It soon became apparent that migrants to the West, would assume the major responsibility for settlement. Individuals, families, and small groups migrated to the West in increasing numbers, many of them already acquainted with the potential of the new areas through their service in the military. Some purchased land from speculators; others acquired land directly from the government. But many disregarded the legalities of land disposal to "squat" on the land; some moved in even before American Indian titles had been legally extinguished. By the end of the 1780s, over 100,000 people of European origin had settled in the area between the Appalachians and the Mississippi River.

Changes in Social Structure

The American Revolution did not bring revolutionary results in terms of social structure. Anthony Trollope, a nineteenth-century English novelist and commentator on political affairs, later remarked: "This new people, when they had it in their power to change all their laws, to throw themselves upon any Utopian theory that the folly of a wild philanthropy could devise . . . did not do so."[8] While studies of wealth distribution are not entirely in agreement regarding the precise effects of war and independence, they do indicate that there was probably only a slight shift toward greater or lesser equality from the structure of the late colonial era, when the top 20 percent of wealth holders had owned about two-thirds of the total physical wealth of the thirteen colonies.

American ideology continued to emphasize economic opportunity and social mobility. During the war and the postwar years, some individuals and families gained and others lost as a result of the ways in which events affected their particular fortunes. Some of the merchants who capitalized on wartime opportunities and the new lines of enterprise that came with independence gained entry into the top level of the mercantile community; but others, particularly those who remained loyal to Britain, lost most of their fortunes. For middle-class Americans, the majority of whom were farmers, the resumption of the westward movement meant cheap land and the possibility of economic advancement.

The Status of Minority Groups and Women

Slaves.   The 1780s marked the beginning of a change in the legal status of slavery in the northern states. In two states—Massachusetts and New Hampshire—slavery was ended; in three other states—Pennsylvania, Connecticut, and Rhode Island—laws were enacted providing for the emancipation of the children of slaves. But in New York and New Jersey even gradual emancipation did not commence until the turn of the century. In addition, by the terms of the Northwest Ordinance of 1787, slavery was prohibited in the territory of the United States west of the Appalachians and north of the Ohio River. However, in the southern states, where nearly 90 percent of the U.S. slave population lived, there was no move to emancipate the black population beyond some encouragement to individual slaveholders to grant freedom to their slaves.

Thus, the abolitionist movement of the Revolutionary period had extremely limited effects: Only small numbers of blacks were freed, and their freedom did not include political rights or an improved social or economic standing. The African-American, whether slave or free, remained for all intents and purposes an outcast of American society.

Indentured Servants.   While chattel slavery continued for a large majority of the black population, white bound labor tended to disappear in the decades following the Revolution. The war had put a halt to traffic in indentured servants; when it resumed in the 1780s, it was in reduced numbers. Independence also meant a stop to the shipping of convicts, who had constituted one source of labor supply. The British government further discouraged the migration of individuals under indenture by prohibiting the use of English ships for that purpose.

Women.   There appeared to be little discernible alteration in the female economic role in the new United States. However, because of the disruptions occasioned by the war, argues Mary Beth Norton, there undoubtedly occurred a "partial breakdown and reinterpretation of the gender roles that had hitherto remained unexamined." As Norton points out, "Increasing numbers of American families no longer conformed to the previously dominant patriarchal style."[9] The decades immediately after the Revolution marked the beginning of important changes in the legal status of women, particularly with respect to property rights. Most states now gave divorced women, when they were the innocent party, control over their own property. The end of primogeniture, which had favored the oldest son in the partition of the family estate, meant that females had become the equal of males with respect to inheriting property.

Economic Forces and the U.S. Constitution

Articles of Confederation

The first constitution of the United States, the Articles of Confederation, adopted in 1781, assigned most of the decision-making powers of government to the thirteen states. However, it soon became apparent that this arrangement left the central government with little ability to carry out many of its responsibilities. There was widespread concern about the inability of the government to deal effectively with encroachments on the nation's sovereignty; the United States apparently could neither remove British troops from the forts in the northwestern part of the country nor counter Spanish opposition to American frontier expansion into the Southwest. Many people were alarmed about the threat posed by local insurrections. In one such event, Shays's Rebellion in Massachusetts in 1786, a band of armed farmers had closed the courts to prevent foreclosures on farms and the imprisonment of debtors and had even appeared to threaten a federal arsenal.

The Constitutional Convention of 1787

Delegates from each of the thirteen states met in 1787 to determine how they could strengthen the central government through amendments to the Articles of Confederation. After surveying the nation's economic and political problems, the delegates concluded that their objective could best be attained by replacing the Articles with an entirely new document of government—the U.S. Constitution.

A majority of the delegates to the Constitutional Convention were nationalists, who through war service had acquired a continental as opposed to a provincial perception of political problems. They emphasized the impor-tance of a strong economic base for the development of a powerful nation. The most obvious need was the power to tax, essential to the ability of the U.S. government to meet external and internal challenges to its independence and unity. Honoring the nation's debt was crucial to establishing a credit standing that would enable the country to meet future financial emergencies. This required payment of interest and eventual redemption of securities. While advocates of a strong government recognized that "windfall" profits would be gained by some investors who had purchased bonds at discounted prices, they regarded this as a small price to be paid to attain more authority for the central government. Nationalists also argued that government should actively promote the economic growth essential to an increase of national power. As early as 1782, Robert Morris had advocated a protective tariff to promote domestic manufacturing as well as government construction of transportation improvements, needed to encourage rapid development of the West. Significantly, nationalists assumed that successful operation of the kind of government they were seeking would require the attachment to that government of the business community—the principal economic decision makers in America.

Assessments of the effectiveness of government under the Articles of Confederation were taking place in the context of a serious economic depression. After the termination of hostilities, a decline in government expenditures had created deflationary pressures. In response, states pursued a variety of antidepression policies: tariffs to protect local industries, navigation acts to penalize British shippers (whose own Navigation Acts now discriminated against American shippers), and issues of paper money to provide a circulating medium and ease deflationary pressures. However, these state government actions to combat the depression seemed inadequate to many.

Manufacturers quickly saw the limited effectiveness of the tariff laws passed by states with industrial establishments; the laws did not afford protection against cheap English imports in the states without industry, where tariffs were not enacted. Shippers found fault with the navigation laws of the states because of their lack of uniformity and the possibility that such legislation would be used as a weapon against the shipping of rival states. Above all, serious depreciation of paper money in Rhode Island and North Carolina revived memories of the recent wartime inflation. Paper money was particularly upsetting to creditors, since state laws often required its acceptance at face value in the settlement of debts. Compounding the problem of dealing with the depression was the apparent failure of the national government in its efforts to expand foreign markets for American goods and commercial services. Negotiations with Britain and Spain failed to gain any substantial trade concessions.

Even though the government, with all of its political defects, had not produced the economic difficulties and could not reasonably be expected to remove them, Americans blamed the Confederation for the hard times and for the failure of depression remedies to work. In other words, the depression had raised the level of public dissatisfaction with the political system and thereby created a favorable climate for making changes to its basic structure. Steady improvement of American trade relations with the rest of the world, achieved in large part without government action, provided the basis for the return of more prosperous times even before the establishment of a new government. In looking at the relationship between economic conditions and politics in the 1780s, economist Guy S. Callender observed many years ago: "Just as hard times had brought failure to the old Confederation, so prosperity, it if did not actually cause the success of the new

government, greatly simplified the problem of its establishment."[10]

Economic Provisions of the Constitution

Although the U.S. Constitution had little immediate economic impact, the new system of government it created would have important long-term effects on the nation's economy. The federal system furnished a framework for containing the political controversy between centralism and localism and created the stability essential to economic growth. Beyond this, specific provisions of the Constitution provided basic rules for many aspects of economic life.

With the authorization to levy import duties, the government of the United States for the first time acquired a basic attribute of sovereignty—the power to tax. This assured a source of financial support; in addition, tariff duties could be used to protect domestic industry. Congress was empowered to assume and redeem the debt incurred by the old national government and states as well as to borrow money in the future. (Government securities would play a key role in the development of a capital market.) In order to assure a single national monetary system, Congress was given exclusive power to coin money and issue paper currency. (However, states retained the right to charter banking corporations authorized to issue bank notes that circulated as money.) The national government had sole authority over foreign affairs. With the power to adjust import duties, the hand of the United States was strengthened in negotiating commercial treaties. This source of revenue also enabled the national government to develop military forces and thereby reinforce its diplomatic efforts. Shipping was encouraged by the passage of navigation acts. And Congress, using its constitutional powers to regulate territory in the West, manage American Indian affairs, and employ force against the native population, was able to accelerate the pace of settlement in the West.

In addition, the Constitution furnished the legal underpinnings for a national market. It gave Congress the exclusive power to regulate interstate commerce, and thus to minimize legal barriers to trade within the country's boundaries. Congress was also empowered to maintain a postal system, basic to the flow of communication; to pass patent and copyright laws to promote invention; to establish rules for the naturalization of immigrants; and to create bankruptcy laws that would be applied uniformly throughout the states. One constitutional provision prohibited states from enacting laws that might impair the obligation of contracts; this provision was to be enforced in federal courts.

As legal historian James Willard Hurst points out, "Federal protection would [come to] embrace all the conditions important to the existence of broad markets."[11] In particular, "the federal Constitution sanctioned and pro-

tected the play of supply and demand in sectional or national markets, including the free movement of labor and investment money wherever they might find profitable employment."[12] In short, a legal framework of contracts and property rights established by the Constitution contributed to the creation of the market system; through that system entrepreneurs in nineteenth-century America would make and carry out the decisions that would transform the economy. Americans of the Revolutionary generation did not discover for the first time the concept of the market. Indeed, almost from the beginning of colonization, Americans had looked to the market as a guide for deciding how to use and allocate resources. But the existence of a large body of law concerning property and contract, resting on basic rules contained in the supreme law of the land, encouraged Americans "to think of market processes as the normal mode of ordering the economy."[13]

Summary

The American colonists pursued a strategy that would eventually lead to Independence once they came to perceive that the policies of the British government after 1763 imposed limitations on their economic and political autonomy. Despite shortcomings in the arrangements made to supply the troops and finance the war, the new United States achieved victory in a military struggle against the imperial leader of Europe. Political sovereignty was achieved, and Americans moved toward expansion of their economic autonomy. Development of trade with new partners reduced American economic dependence on England,

while the use of the corporation, the beginning of greater specialization in business, the chartering of commercial banks, the emergence of regional capital markets, and improvements in transportation and communication together enhanced the growth potential of the economy. The ineffectiveness of the new U.S. government led to the adoption of the Constitution. It not only provided the political stability necessary for economic growth but also furnished the legal underpinnings for a market economy that could operate on a national scale.

Endnotes

1. Anne Bezanson et al., *Prices and Inflation During the American Revolution, 1770–1790* (Philadelphia: University of Pennsylvania Press, 1951), pp. 312, 316.
2. Paul F. Paskoff, *Industrial Evolution: Organization, Structure, and Growth of the Pennsylvania Iron Industry, 1750–1860* (Baltimore: Johns Hopkins University Press, 1983), pp. 71–72. However, the industry made a rapid recovery after the war.
3. Percentages are calculated from data in James F. Shepherd, "British America and the Atlantic Economy," in Ronald Hoffman et al., eds., *The Economy of Early America: The Revolutionary Period, 1763–1790* (Charlottesville: University Press of Virginia, 1988), table 2, p. 28.
4. Jacob M. Price, "Reflections on the Economy of Revolutionary America," in Ronald Hoffman et al., eds., *The Economy of Early America: The Revolutionary Period, 1763 to 1790* (Charlottesville: University Press of Virginia, 1988), pp. 321–322.
5. Shephard, "British America," p. 28.
6. N. S. B. Gras, *The Massachusetts First National Bank of Boston 1784–1934* (Cambridge: Harvard University Press, 1937), p. 45.
7. Winifred B. Rothenberg, "The Emergence of a Capital Market in Rural Massachusetts, 1730–1838," *Journal of Economic History*, 45 (1985).
8. Quoted in Samuel Mencher, *Poor Law to Poverty Program* (Pittsburgh: University of Pittsburgh Press, 1967), p. 147.
9. Mary Beth Norton, *Liberty's Daughters: The Revolutionary Experience of American Women, 1750–1800* (Boston: Little, Brown, 1980), pp. 224, 229.
10. Guy Stevens Callender, ed., *Selections from the Economic History of the United States, 1765–1860* (Boston: Ginn, 1909), p. 182.
11. James Willard Hurst, *Law and the Conditions of Freedom in the Nineteenth-Century United States* (Madison: University of Wisconsin Press, 1956), p. 45.
12. James Willard Hurst, *Law and Economic Growth: The Legal History of the Lumber Industry in Wisconsin, 1836–1915* (Cambridge: Harvard University Press, 1964), p. 53.
13. Ibid., p. 53.

Suggested Readings

Marc Egnal and Joseph A. Ernst, "An Economic Interpretation of the American Revolution," *William and Mary Quarterly*, 29 (1972), emphasizes economic autonomy as a major objective of the revolutionary movement. Arthur M. Schlesinger, *The Colonial Merchants and the American Revolution, 1763–1775* (New York: Columbia University Press, 1918) is still a classic account of the responses of American business to British legislation after 1763. Joseph D. Reid, Jr., "Economic Burden: Spark to the American Revolution?" *Journal of Economic History*, 38 (1978), suggests directions that economic analysis of Revolutionary political activity might follow.

Curtis P. Nettels, *The Emergence of a National Economy, 1775–1815: (The Economic History of the United States, vol. 2)* (New York: Holt, 1962), remains the best overview of the principal economic events during this period. The essays contained in Ronald Hoffman et al., eds., *The Economy of Early America: The Revolu-*

tionary Period, 1763–1790 (Charlottesville: University Press of Virginia, 1988), emphasize the regional diversity that characterized these years. Military supply is the subject of Victor L. Johnson, *The Administration of the American Commissariat During the Revolutionary War* (Philadelphia: University of Pennsylvania Press, 1941), and R. Arthur Bowler, *Logistics and the Failure of the British Army in America, 1775–1783* (Princeton: Princeton University Press, 1975).

E. James Ferguson, *The Power of the Purse: A History of American Public Finance, 1776–1790* (Chapel Hill: University of North Carolina Press, 1961), is the standard account of war finance, but it is well supplemented by Charles W. Calomiris, "Institutional Failure, Monetary Scarcity, and the Depreciation of the Continental," *Journal of Economic History*, 48 (1988). Robert A. Becker, *Revolution, Reform, and the Politics of American Taxation, 1763–1783* (Baton Rouge: Louisiana State University Press, 1980), discusses provincial and state taxation during these years. Clarence L. Ver Steeg, *Robert Morris, Revolutionary Financier* (Philadelphia: University of Pennsylvania Press, 1954), is still the most useful study of the financial role played by this leading businessman-politician. Anne Bezanson et al., *Prices and Inflation During the American Revolution: Pennsylvania, 1770–1790* (Philadelphia: University of Pennsylvania Press, 1951), is the most valuable study available of the course of wartime inflation. The social and economic effects of the larger events of the revolutionary period are seen from the vantage point of the ordinary people of a New England community in Robert A. Gross, *The Minutemen and Their World* (New York: Hill & Wang, 1976).

James F. Shepherd and Gary M. Walton, "Economic Change After the American Revolution: Pre-and Post-War Comparisons of Maritime Shipping and Trade," *Explorations in Economic History*, 8 (1976) analyzes the changing pattern of American foreign trade. Neil Long-

ley York, *Mechanical Metamorphosis: Technological Change in Revolutionary America* (Greenwood, CT: Greenwood Press, 1985) surveys the forces influencing technological change during this period, while James Willard Hurst in *The Legitimacy of the Business Corporation in the Law of the United States, 1780–1970* (Charlottesville: University Press of Virginia, 1970) is important to an understanding of the emergence of this form of business organization. Important recent studies of local or provincial developments include Thomas M. Doerflinger, *A Vigorous Spirit of Enterprise: Merchants and Economic Development in Revolutionary Philadelphia* (Chapel Hill: University of North Carolina Press, 1986); Edward C. Papenfuse, *In Pursuit of Profit: The Annapolis Merchants in the Era of the American Revolution* (Baltimore: Johns Hopkins University Press, 1975); and Ronald Hoffman, *A Spirit of Dissenion: Economics, Politics, and the Revolution in Maryland* (Baltimore: Johns Hopkins University Press, 1973). Several older works have not been superseded in tracing the changes in business leadership and the development of new institutions during these years: Robert A. East, *Business Enterprise in the American Revolutionary Era* (New York: Columbia University Press, 1938); James B. Hedges, *The Browns of Providence Plantations: The Colonial Years* (Cambridge: Harvard University Press, 1952); Joseph S. Davis, *Essays in the Earlier History of American Corporations*, 2 vols. (Cambridge: Harvard University Press, 1917); Fritz Redlich, *The Molding of American Banking: Men and Ideas* (New York: Johnson Reprint Corporation, 1968); and N. S. B. Gras, *The Massachusetts First National Bank of Boston, 1784–1934* (Cambridge: Harvard University Press, 1937).

Jackson Turner Main, *The Social Structure of Revolutionary America* (Princeton: Princeton University Press, 1965) and the same author's *The Sovereign States, 1775–1783* (New York: Franklin Watts, 1973) contain analyses of social and political changes of the Revolutionary era. Mary Beth Norton, *Liberty's Daughters: The Rev-*

olutionary Experience of American Women, 1750–1800 (Boston: Little, Brown and Company, 1980), and the essays contained in Ronald Hoffman and Peter J. Albert, eds., *Women in the Age of the American Revolution* (Charlottesville: University Press of Virginia, 1989), discuss the impact of the war and the economic and political changes of the period upon the role and status of women. Joyce E. Chaplin, "Tidal Rice Cultivation and the Problem of Slavery in South Carolina and Georgia, 1760–1815," *William and Mary Quarterly* 49 (1992), provides a case study of the experience of slaves and slave owners in a staple-producing region.

The publication of Charles A. Beard, *An Economic Interpretation of the Constitution of the United States* (New York: Macmillan, 1913), touched off an ongoing controversy among historians about the precise nature of the relationship between economic forces and the political movement to strengthen the central government in the 1780s. Among important works challenging Beard's conclusion that economic self-interest motivated the framers of the Constitution are Robert E. Brown, *Charles Beard and the Constitution: A Critical Analysis of "An Economic Interpretation of the Constitution"* (Princeton: Princeton University Press, 1956), and Forrest McDonald, *We the People: The Economic Origins of the Constitution* (Chicago: University of Chicago Press, 1958). Recent contributions to the debate include Richard H. Steckel and Richard A. Jensen, "An Economic Model of Voting Behavior over Specific Issues at the Constitutional Convention of 1787," *Journal of Economic History*, 46 (1986), and Mary M. Schweitzer, "State-Issued Currency and the Ratification of the U.S. Constitution," *Journal of Economic History*, 49 (1989). For the role that the Constitution played in furnishing a legal framework for a market economy, the works of James Willard Hurst are indispensable; see especially, *Law and the Conditions of Freedom in the Nineteenth-Century United States* (Madison: University of Wisconsin Press, 1967). See Sidney Ratner, *Taxation and Democracy in America* (New York: Octagon, 1980), for a long-range study of taxation in the United States.

Part II

The Agricultural Era and Emerging Industrialism

1790–1860

D
URING THE SEVEN DECADES FROM 1790 TO 1860, industrialization and sustained increases in real production and income per capita were the key economic developments in the United States. These developments marked the beginning of a process of modernization that before the end of the nineteenth century would propel the American economy to the first rank. The theme of Part II, *economic modernization*, involved much more than industrialization and higher rates of economic growth. Modernization's important antecedents and accompaniments included revolutions in internal transportation and communication, transcontinental territorial expansion, the transfer of huge amounts of land from public to private ownership, the dynamic expansion of commercial agriculture, the mushroomlike growth of banks, and increasingly specialized commerce in both foreign and domestic markets. In the long run, however, industrialization sustained the high rate of economic growth that differentiates the modern from the premodern economy. Industrialization also transformed America from the simple agrarian economy of colonial times to the complex, highly specialized, and interdependent economy and society of today.

As the process of economic modernization took hold, the territorial and human resources of the United States were greatly enlarged. By 1860, the geographical area of the nation was more than three times larger than it had been in 1790; the Republic stretched from sea to sea.

The growth of human resources was both a cause and a result of economic modernization. Between 1790 and 1860, the population of the United States increased at a high rate by historical standards—3 percent per year—and was fairly uniform—doubling every twenty-three years, from 3.9 million in 1790 to 31.5 million in 1860. Although immigrants contributed much to the drama of American history, they were not the major source of population growth. That source was a high rate of natural increase—both before and after the Civil War. Annual birthrates of about fifty per one thousand people combined with death rates of about twenty per thousand to produce a rate of natural increase of roughly 3 percent, which prevailed from colonial times to about 1830. Before the 1830s, the contribution of immigrants to population growth averaged only about 3 or 4 percent of the total increase. In the following decades, however, immigration became more important. The number of immigrants averaged about 13,000 per year in the 1820s, 54,000 in the 1830s, 143,000 in the 1840s, and 281,000 in the 1850s. The arrival of greater numbers of immigrants offset a declining rate of natural increase and helped to maintain a 3 percent rate of population growth until the Civil War. But even in the 1850s, more than two-thirds of the population growth derived from natural increase.

The economic significance of the immigrants in both antebellum and later decades was disproportionate to their numbers. Immigrants were more concentrated in the fifteen-to-forty age group than was the population as a whole. This meant that the labor force grew faster than did the population. The elasticity that immigrants thus gave to the labor force likely made an important contribution to the expansion of economic activity.

In terms of the American economy, immigrants were something of a gift of human capital. American resources were not expended on their early upbringing and training; instead, the costs of creating an enlarged labor force were borne by others. It is also possible that many immigrants were especially energetic and talented. Whether their main incentive was the attraction of economic opportunity in America or to escape unfavorable economic, political, or social conditions in their country of origin, a certain boldness was required on the part of immigrants to undergo the hardships of migration and the uncertainties surrounding life and work in a new land. Ultimately, though, the many dimensions of American life were enriched by the flow of human resources from overseas.

Chapter 5

Revolutions in Transportation and Communications

ELIABLE, LOW-COST TRANSPORTATION AND A
rapid flow of information are crucial to
economic development. Economic his-
tory offers no better illustration of this principle
than the experience of the United States between 1790 and 1860. After nearly two centuries
of colonization and settlement, most of the 3.9
million Americans in the United States in 1790
still lived within a hundred miles or so of the Atlantic Coast. The high cost of internal transportation was chiefly responsible for this situation.
The young nation was extremely well endowed
with land and other natural resources, but high
internal transport costs, particularly for products of the land that were bulky in relation to
their value, constituted a great barrier to turning
those endowments of nature into economic resources. The Americans of 1790, therefore,
tended to live and work in proximity to navigable waters. Numerous rivers and bays connecting with the Atlantic Ocean provided them with
a means of reaching larger domestic and overseas markets.

The lure of untapped resources farther inland was nonetheless strong for a people
whose numbers continued to grow at a rapid
rate. By 1790, there were 109,000 settlers in
Kentucky and Tennessee, with perhaps an
equal number west of the mountains in Pennsylvania and Virginia. It is estimated that, at
the outbreak of the War of 1812, at least 1.5
million people out of a total population of 8
million had moved westward across the Appalachians. Many of these pioneers could find
only local markets for their resource-intensive
products, which could not compete in other
more distant markets because of high transportation costs. What the pioneers needed was
improved means of internal transportation and
communication to help them get their products to the markets in the East and overseas.

A revolution in transportation and communication thus began. It included the improvement of roads, the construction of canals, and
the introduction of steam railroads and steam
navigation on rivers, providing a solution to the
problem of high inland transport costs. (Overseas transport costs also fell a great deal in these
decades; see Chapter 9.) At the same time, information gathering and communications—
two essential ingredients for effective economic
decision making—improved significantly with
advances in newspaper publishing and in the
Postal Service, and with the introduction of the
electromagnetic telegraph. By 1860, Americans, with the help of these revolutionary developments, had settled half a continent. And
in the process, the vastly enlarged economic resources of the United States were turned toward specialized, market-oriented production.

Transportation Costs and Economic Development

Why is costly transportation a barrier to economic development? Improvements in transportation were so critical to America's economic progress in the early decades of the
nation's history that it is worth devoting attention to some theoretical aspects of this question. In his classic work *The Wealth of Nations*
(1776), the great Scottish economist Adam
Smith wrote: "The division of labor is limited
by the extent of the market."[1] A progressing
division of labor and the specialization of economic activity were the keys to increased productivity. The essence of Smith's insight is that
increased specialization leads to economies of
larger-scale production; or, in other words, as
the size of a producing unit grows, the output
produced grows more rapidly than the productive inputs of labor, land, and capital. In
the early nineteenth century, another great
economist, the Englishman David Ricardo,
amplified and extended Smith's argument
with his theory of comparative advantage. It
suggests that nations, regions, and even indi-

viduals can increase their standards of material well-being by specializing in the kind of economic activity in which they have the greatest capabilities, both natural and acquired.[2]

To reap the great advantages of specialization, as analyzed by Smith and Ricardo, it is necessary to have markets large enough to absorb the increased production derived from specialization. This is where the cost of transportation becomes important. If high transportation costs double or triple the price of a commodity when it is sold more than a few miles away from where it is produced, then most of that commodity has to be sold locally. But a group of people residing in a given location will demand a variety of goods and services, not merely the one or two goods that they are best able to produce. High transportation costs therefore dictate that most of the items demanded be produced in that local area. The high costs of moving goods to market limit the possibilities for greater specialization and the exploitation of comparative advantages in production. Persons who live and work in an economy of small, local markets tend to be jacks of all (or several) trades and masters of none, not by choice but rather of necessity.

Many aspects of economic life in the United States before the transportation revolution of the early 1800s are illuminated by the foregoing analysis. Food, fuel, and construction materials for cities and towns on or near the Atlantic seaboard were obtained either from nearby agricultural areas or from more distant areas within reach of navigable water; freight rates over water were much lower than those over land. Most of the manufactured articles of that era were simple and produced locally, many of them at home. The first settlers of fertile western lands marketed their products outside their own locales only to a limited extent. They converted their bulky crops into livestock, which often could walk to distant markets. Or, they turned crops into whiskey and other products that had greater value in relation to their bulk and thus could be marketed over greater distances than the crops from which they were made. With limited markets in which to sell, there were inevitably limited markets in which to buy. Settlers made for themselves most of what they needed, or they traded for them with their neighbors. Decisions to produce and market in these ways reflected the economic realities of high-cost transportation.

The people who moved west in the decades after the revolution were more disturbed than other Americans by the implications for market development of high transportation costs. Congressman Peter B. Porter from western New York State spoke for them in 1810:

The great evil, and it is a serious one indeed, under which the inhabitants of the western country labor, arises from the want of a market. There is no place where the great staple articles for the use of civilized life can be produced in greater abundance or with greater ease, and yet as respects most of the luxuries and many of the conveniences of life the people are poor. They have no vent for their produce at home, and, being all agriculturalists, they produce alike all the same article with the same facility; and such is the present difficulty and expense of transporting their produce to an Atlantic port that little benefit is realized from that quarter. The single circumstance of want of a market is already beginning to produce the most disastrous effect, not only on the industry, but on the morals of the inhabitants. Such is the fertility of their land that one-half their time spent in labor is sufficient to produce every article which their farms are capable of yielding, in sufficient quantities for their own consumption, and there is nothing to incite them to produce more. They are, therefore, naturally led to spend the other part of their time in idleness and dissipation.[3]

Very soon, however, the "great evil" described by Porter would be dissipated by revolutionary changes in American internal transportation.

Gallatin's Report on Roads and Canals

In April of 1808, Treasury Secretary Albert Gallatin delivered to Congress a voluminous report on roads and canals. The report contained a sophisticated discussion of the benefits to be derived from improved transportation, a consideration of the difficulties that stood in the way of improving transportation, and a comprehensive ten-year plan for a governmental solution to America's transportation problems. In the United States, Gallatin argued, "a great demand for capital" and the "extent of territory compared with population" had prevented improvements or rendered them unprofitable. The prosperity of foreign trade from 1793 to 1807, which was largely induced by wars in Europe, had caused the demand for capital to grow rapidly in the United States. High interest rates militated against internal transportation improvements, "which offer[ed] only the prospect of remote and moderate profit." Also, the low density of the American population did not, "except in the vicinity of seaports, admit that extensive commercial intercourse within short distances, which, in England and some other countries, form[ed] the principal support of artificial roads and canals." From his observations, Gallatin drew a sweeping conclusion: "The General Government can alone remove these obstacles."[4]

Gallatin's program called for a ten-year expenditure of $20 million, either in the form of federal construction of internal transportation improvements or of federal aid through stock subscriptions or loans to specially chartered private corporations. His proposals included (1) canals and a turnpike road along the Atlantic Coast; (2) canals, roads, and river improvements from the east across the Appalachians to the Mississippi Valley; and (3) canals and river improvements to connect the Atlantic Coast with the Great Lakes and the St. Lawrence River. Of the $20 million projected expenditures, $16.6 million was to be allocated to Gallatin's specified projects and $3.4 million to unspecified local improvements designed to fit in with the overall system.

However, Gallatin's farsighted proposals for a federally sponsored transportation system were not carried out in a way that even remotely corresponded to his plan. Only a section of the previously planned national road from Cumberland, Maryland, to Wheeling (then in Virginia) on the Ohio River, was completed by 1818. A number of factors caused this early failure of federal decision making on transportation. Fiscal problems were the immediate source of difficulty. Federal revenues came mostly from duties levied on imports, but these fell as a result of the Jeffersonian embargo and Madisonian nonintercourse policies of 1807 to 1809, as well as the trade derangements resulting from the War of 1812. Also, in 1808 and later years, domestic political debates impeded federal action. President Thomas Jefferson had strong misgivings about the constitutionality of federally aided improvements, believing that a constitutional amendment was necessary before a program like Gallatin's could be undertaken. This strict constructionist view of the constitutional powers of the federal government led to vetoes of internal improvement bills by Presidents Madison, Monroe, and Jackson in 1817, 1822, and 1830, respectively. Finally, the local and sectional interests that Gallatin had foreseen in 1808 proved difficult to harmonize on the national level. The South in particular, since its economy was based on exports, grew increasingly hostile to the import tariffs that could have provided much of the federal revenue for financing transportation improvements on the comprehensive scale of Gallatin's plan. Indeed, the South opposed any extension of federal powers that might set precedents for later federal interference with its slave labor system.

Before 1860, then, the federal government's role in internal transportation improvement remained largely passive. The national road was extended to Illinois by the 1850s, and further aid was given via congressional appropriations of revenues from land sales, subscriptions to the stock of corporations constructing improvements, and land grants to states for improvements. But the bold and imaginative federal program suggested first by Gallatin and later by such leaders as John C. Calhoun, Henry Clay, and John Quincy Adams did not come to fruition.

Although the failure of federal transportation policy probably delayed the economic development of the United States, it was not crippling. Private enterprise and state and local governments, sometimes working separately but more often in close cooperation, moved in to fill the void left by the federal government. When Gallatin wrote his report, the country was in the midst of a road-improvement boom, and soon there were other developments: the application of steam power to water transportation, a canal-building era, and the railroad age. By the time of the Civil War, the objective of improved transportation was largely realized. Still, it had come about through decentralized decision making, not through the central government planning that Gallatin and others had envisioned.

The Building of Turnpikes and Other Roads

The early United States, in addition to having rivers and coastal waters as avenues of transportation, was served by a lengthy network of local country and post roads. However, most of these roads were little more than widened dirt paths over which horses and horse- or ox-drawn wagons and carriages could travel in good weather only. Constructing and maintaining the roads were community responsibilities in settled areas, financed largely by taxes in kind (that is, by the labor services of able-bodied citizens during the slack season for agricultural work). In general, though, the roads were poorly designed and poorly maintained. Local interest did not call for great expenditures of effort or funds to ease the way for nonlocal users. The techniques used to build and repair the roads were essentially those used in Europe during the Middle Ages.

Toward the end of the eighteenth century, Americans became aware of the British use of turnpike roads. At the time of the American Revolution, for example, a turnpike cut the travel time between Edinburgh and London, a distance of four hundred miles, from about two weeks to three days. Americans seized upon the concept, and the result was a boom in turnpike construction from the 1790s to the 1820s. Turnpike roads were built primarily to connect the larger towns to the settled rural areas in the New England and the Middle Atlantic states. A few turnpikes, such as the federally constructed national road, provided routes to the trans-Appalachian West. Of the more than eleven thousand miles of turnpikes in existence by 1830, most had been planned and built in the two decades from 1800 to 1820. Four states—New York, Pennsylvania, Connecticut, and Massachusetts—contained 80 percent of the mileage, with New York accounting for nearly 40 percent of the national total.

The typical turnpike road was built and operated by a corporation that received from a state legislature a special charter outlining its rights and obligations. Important aspects of the turnpike movement may be seen in the history of the first turnpike—Pennsylvania's sixty-two-mile Philadelphia–Lancaster route. In 1733, an ordinary road between Philadelphia and Lancaster had been laid out, but like other colonial roads it was not very good. The Philadelphia and Lancaster Turnpike Road, as the company was called, was incorporated in April 1792. The charter called for the issuance of one thousand shares of stock at $300 per share; the issue was sold immediately. Construction began in the fall of 1792 and the road completed two years later at a cost of $465,000, or $7,500 per mile. Construction costs were well in excess of the projected $300,000, a common fate of later turnpikes as well. Paved with stone overlaid with gravel and well drained, the Lancaster Pike was built to last, which it did as a corporate entity until late into the nineteenth century (long after most early nineteenth century turnpikes had been abandoned or turned over to the states). However, the tolls did not produce large dividends for the Lancaster Pike's stockholders; Gallatin's report of 1808 quotes a rate of 2.5 percent.[5] Primarily responsible for the low return were unexpectedly large costs of construction, maintenance, and operation, coupled with smaller gains in efficiency than those resulting from subsequent transportation technologies. Another reason was the willingness of some turnpike users to evade tolls by bypassing the toll houses on hastily developed "shunpikes."

Despite low returns, the turnpike movement flourished in the first two decades of the nineteenth century, in part because stockholders were often interested in other businesses located along or near the roads. Returns from these businesses were increased by the greater volume of economic activity arising from road improvements. Early American decision makers were well aware of the modern economic distinction between private and social returns on investment, and in the turnpike movement they showed that government planning and finance of transportation improvements were not necessary to bring about an adequate level of investment. Thus, by 1820, private enterprise, acting through the medium of turnpike companies, furnished the settled areas of the

northeastern United States with a network of improved roads.

The Canal Era (1817–1844)

In the era of canal building from 1817 to 1844, the role of state governments in planning, building, and financing was much greater than for turnpikes. What motivated canal building? And why did governmental decisions play a major role in it? The answer to the first question again involves England as a model. The success of canals had clearly been demonstrated in that country during the latter half of the eighteenth century. Americans began trying to emulate England's canals in the 1790s but had little success until 1815; only some one hundred miles of canals were constructed in that quarter-century. Again, America's orientation toward foreign commerce delayed progress in internal economic development. Also contributing to America's interest in canals was the relatively high cost of turnpikes as a means of transportation. Moving goods over water—the ancient means of city and commercial development—involved less friction than movement over roads and therefore required lower inputs of energy.

Large-scale government involvement in canal building came about because of the high cost of the undertaking and the important role canals played in opening up and developing new areas and resources. While turnpike construction costs could be measured in the thousands or hundreds of thousands of dollars, the major canals cost in the millions to build. Accumulations of wealth were limited and capital markets were primitive in the new nation. In the case of canals, the need for the government to sponsor the investment was obvious.

Early Canals

Of course, not all American canal building was aimed at opening up newly settled or unsettled areas to market development. The major projects of the period before the War of 1812—the Middlesex Canal in Massachusetts, the Santee and Cooper Canal in South Carolina, and the Dismal Swamp between Norfolk, Virginia, and North Carolina's Albemarle Sound—provided more efficient connections between developed trading areas. Many later canals, such as the Delaware and Raritan connecting Philadelphia and New York City, served the same purpose. Because these canals were relatively short and oriented toward existing commerce, they were often built by private enterprise, as were the canals that helped to develop the anthracite coal area of eastern Pennsylvania.

Other American canal projects were far larger and more significant. A number of these canals joined Atlantic tidewater areas with the eastern upcountry and the growing settlements of the trans-Appalachian West: New York's Erie Canal; Pennsylvania's Mainline Canal; the Chesapeake and Ohio Canal serving Maryland, Virginia, and the District of Columbia; and Virginia's James River and Kanawha Canal. Other major canals provided direct water routes from the West to eastern population centers: those of Ohio, Indiana, and Illinois accomplished this by connecting the Ohio and Mississippi river valleys with the Great Lakes. (See Figure 5–1.)

The Erie Canal

The earliest and most successful of the great canals was New York's Erie, built from 1817 to 1825 between the Hudson River above Albany and Buffalo on Lake Erie. Although the idea of a canal project across New York State had been in the air since the 1790s, the stimulus for building the Erie Canal was the fear of New Yorkers (especially the City and port of New York at the mouth of the Hudson River) that the federal government's National Road and Pennsylvania's east-west turnpike (developed under private auspices) would deny New York

a proper share of the developing western trade. New York's decision to compete for the trade paid off: The Erie Canal, 40 feet wide and 4 feet deep with 84 locks covering the rise of some 650 feet between the Hudson River and Buffalo, built at a cost of $7.1 million, collected nearly $1 million in toll revenue even before its completion. Between 1826 and 1835, when some three thousand canal boats operated on the Erie and an adjoining canal connecting the Hudson with Lake Champlain, New York State earned a rate of return of nearly 8 percent on its cost of building the canals.

Other Canal-Building Ventures

With the success of the Erie Canal, New York had outflanked its commercial rivals to the north and south. More important, though, the City and port of New York quickly became the nation's largest in population and commercial activity. Rival states and cities attempted to remain competitive by imitating the Erie, but their endeavors were largely unsuccessful. Between 1826 and 1834, Pennsylvania completed its Mainline Canal between Philadelphia and Pittsburgh—a conglomeration of canal and railroad with 174 locks and a rise over the mountains much higher than that of the Erie, resulting in costly trans-shipment problems. Although the Mainline had some advantages over the Erie—a longer operating season and a direct connection with the Ohio River Valley—it was more costly to construct and earned a far lower return than its New York competitor.

Farther south, in 1828, the Chesapeake and Ohio Canal Company began construction of a canal along the Potomac—from the District of Columbia westward toward Cumberland, Maryland—with the goal of reaching the Ohio River. Despite generous financial support from Maryland, Virginia, Washington city, and the federal government, construction costs far exceeded estimates, and construction proceeded slowly; Cumberland was not reached until 1850. This disappointing experience, combined

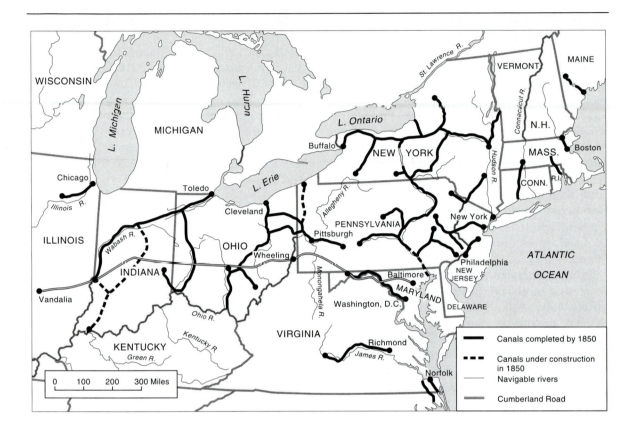

Figure 5–1 *Canals and the Cumberland Road, 1785–1850*
SOURCE: Adapted from Martin Gilbert, *American History Atlas* (New York: Macmillan, 1969).

with the emerging competition of the Baltimore and Ohio Railroad, resulted in the shelving of the plan to extend the canal farther. In a like fashion, the James River and Kanawha Canal, extending west from Richmond, never reached its goal of the Kanawha River across the Appalachians in western Virginia.

The artificial waterways built in imitation of the Erie Canal failed to open up various regions to the trans-Appalachian West for several reasons. That their construction began as improvements in the railroad were being made may in part explain the failure. Perhaps even more important were improvements in west-

ern river transportation, which occurred well before the railroad era. These improvements, as we will see later in the chapter, provided an effective river and sea alternative to waterway trade over the mountains. Finally, the terrain surrounding the Erie was far better suited for a canal than any of the other canal routes.

For all of its early success, even the Erie did not immediately accomplish a revolution in interregional trade. Until 1830, most of its west–east shipments originated in western New York, and only small amounts of grain came to it from northern Ohio via Lake Erie. The products of the more densely settled Ohio River

Valley moved down river toward New Orleans. Nevertheless, the potential for development in Ohio resulting from the Erie Canal was recognized very early. While the Erie was still in the planning stage, Ohio Governor Thomas Worthington urged the Ohio legislature to contribute financial support to the New York project. The support was not given, but before the Erie was completed Ohio had embarked on a program of its own that resulted in the construction of two great north–south canals joining the Ohio River Valley with Lake Erie. The first canal, the Ohio and Erie (completed in 1833) between Cleveland and Portsmouth, traversed the central and eastern parts of the state. Farther west, the Miami and Erie Canal moved north from Cincinnati and reached Dayton in 1832; but it was not until 1845 that the through route to Toledo on Lake Erie opened.

Ohio's canal system, consisting of over eight hundred miles of canal and slack-water navigation, never generated enough toll revenue to pay back the $16 million cost. Even in its best years, the more successful eastern branch did not yield an annual direct return on the state's investment of more than 4 percent. However, the social rate of return, which included rising land values and increased production due to lower costs of transportation, ranged from 6 percent to more than 12 percent between 1836 and 1853. The social returns help to explain Americans' enthusiasm for canals. But that enthusiasm may have been carried too far; an excessive number of short feeder canals which seldom carried enough traffic to be economical were constructed by virtually all the major canal-building states, thereby reducing substantially the direct return on their investments.

Just as the Erie Canal found imitators in the East, Indiana and Illinois followed Ohio's lead in the West. Both states received federal land grants in 1827 to aid their canal-building endeavors. Construction of Indiana's Wabash and Erie Canal, joining Lake Erie in Ohio to

Evansville, Indiana, on the Ohio River, began in 1832 but was not completed until 1853. Although it was America's longest single canal, it was also one of the least successful. A good part of the canal's revenue came from land sales rather than from tolls, and its total revenue represented only a fraction of the total cost.

Illinois began construction in 1836 of its Illinois and Michigan Canal connecting Chicago with the Illinois River, a tributary of the Mississippi. The nationwide financial crises and economic depressions of the late 1830s and early 1840s increased construction costs and delayed competition until 1848. As a result, the financial success of the canal was limited. Whatever social returns it created for Chicago and north central Illinois were soon dwarfed by improvements in the railroad (as we will see later in the chapter).

Three Cycles of Canal Construction

Table 5–1 summarizes some important features of antebellum canal construction from 1815 to 1860. Canal building was neither a steady activity nor a wholly unpatterned one, as the table shows. Rather, it developed in three stages or cycles: (1) 1815 to 1834, (2) 1834 to 1844, and (3) 1844 to 1860. The first two cycles were of special significance in terms of mileage completed, resources expended, and the relative role of public investment. The third cycle was less significant on all three counts as well as in its economic impact. To a large extent, the third cycle was marked by the carrying out or completion of canal projects planned earlier; by this time almost all the canals were facing the competitive pressure of the railroads.

Nearly three-quarters of the total investment in canals during all three cycles came from public agencies, though most of the funds were borrowed from private investors rather than derived from taxation. Significantly, about one-third of the loans came from foreign countries,

Table 5–1 *Cycles of Canal Construction, 1815–1860*

Cycle	Peak Year	Completed Mileage	Investment (in $ millions)	Public investment (as a percentage of total investment)
First cycle, 1815–34	1828	2,188	$ 58.6	70.3%
Second cycle, 1834–44	1840	1,172	72.2	79.4
Third cycle, 1844–60	1855	894	57.4	66.3
Total		4,254	$188.2	73.4%

SOURCE: Harvey H. Segal, "Cycles of Canal Construction," in Carter Goodrich, ed., *Canals and American Economic Development* (New York: Columbia University Press, 1961), pp. 172, 215.

chiefly Great Britain. Overseas investors had developed a confidence in and appetite for the securities of American governments—federal, state, and municipal—in these decades of rapid economic growth and grand improvement projects. When some of the states defaulted on, even repudiated, their debts in the depression of the early 1840s, American credit was damaged but not irreparably. Despite the brief setback, the marketing of government securities helped to develop the investment banking institutions and capital markets that later played crucial roles in financing American railroads and industrial development.

The Steamboat

As the turnpike era gave way to canal building in the eastern part of the United States, an equally significant development in transportation—the steamboat—was taking place in the West. The steamboat was important for three reasons. First, it represented the earliest large-scale application of steam power to transportation, a prime feature of the emerging industrial age. Turnpikes and canals, in contrast, relied on the ancient animate converters of energy, primarily horses, for their motive power. Second, the steamboat vastly increased the transportation capacity of the great river sys-

tem of the American heartland—from the Appalachians to the Rockies and from Canada to the Gulf of Mexico. The earliest and greatest development of this river system occurred along the Mississippi and its eastern tributary, the Ohio. But numerous other tributaries were also opened up to regional, interregional, and international trade by the steamboat. Finally, steamboating from all indications was a competitive business par excellence. As such, it proved extremely flexible and responsive in meeting the growing and changing transportation needs of the western areas it served.

The successful commercial application of steam power to water transportation did not originate on western rivers but on the Hudson, when in 1807 Robert Fulton's *Clermont* made its historic voyage from New York to Albany. Fulton and his partner, Robert Livingston, secured a monopoly right to steam navigation in New York waters from the New York legislature, a tactic that they attempted, without much success, to extend to other areas of the country such as the lower Mississippi. A landmark Supreme Court decision in 1824, *Gibbons v. Ogden*, ruled against the monopoly, insofar as it attempted to control interstate steam transportation, on the grounds that the Constitution grants Congress, not state legislatures, the right to oversee interstate commerce. Thus, constitutional law allowed the new technology of the steamboat to become a

The *Clermont*. The first commercially successful steamboat was built by the engineer Robert Fulton (1765–1815) and launched on the Hudson River in 1807. Powered by a 28-horsepower steam engine from James Watt's firm in England, the *Clermont* soon "sailed" from New York City to Albany in thirty-two hours. Fulton also designed the first steamboat to operate on the Mississippi; it was there and on other western rivers that steamboats made their greatest contribution to American economic growth. (Brown Brothers)

On these waters, flatboats and keelboats, relying primarily on river currents and human strength, provided a slow but moderately effective means of moving products downstream. Keelboats were an especially slow, strenuous, and costly means of moving merchandise upstream. The first steamboat, built at Pittsburgh in 1811, made the down-river trip to New Orleans in about two and a half months, and it continued to operate on the lower Mississippi for several years. It was not until 1815 that a steamboat made a round trip between Louisiana and Pennsylvania. Between then and the Civil War, the western steamboat business expanded rapidly, as Table 5–2 indicates, in terms of the number of steamboats and their tonnage (a measure of capacity by volume rather than weight). The greatest economic impact of the steamboat was the reduction of upriver freight rates, which caused a rapid decline in the keelboat business during the 1820s. Flatboats, however, continued to operate throughout the antebellum era for two reasons: (1) the volume of bulky agricultural produce moving down river was greater than that of the merchandise carried upstream, and (2) the steamboat provided an efficient means of transporting the flatboat workers back upstream. The young Abraham Lincoln, after serving as a flatboat crew member from Illinois to New Orleans via the Mississippi, took advantage of this opportunity.

The significance of the competitive nature of steamboating is also indicated by the data in Table 5–2 on the industry's rapid expansion and growth in productivity. Profits generated by the quantum jump in transport efficiency generated a competitive expansion that quickly reduced freight rates. Moreover, the cost of constructing a steamboat was not large, so most were owned and operated by an individual or a small group of partners. The decentralized nature of ownership and decision making led to considerable experimentation and innovation in steamboat design and operation.

competitive enterprise. In eastern and coastal waters, as well as on the Great Lakes, steamboats became important supplements to sailing vessels, particularly in carrying passenger traffic. Steamboats were also used as tows for canal boats on the Hudson River between Albany and New York.

Western River Steamboat Expansion

Far more important to American development because of the lack of a viable alternative, particularly in upriver navigation, was the application of steam power on the western rivers.

Table 5–2   *Western River Steamboat Progress, 1815–1860*

Year	Number of Steamboats in Operation	Operating Tonnage (in thousands)	Productivity Index (1815 = 100)
1815	7	1.5	100
1820	69	14.2	180
1825	80	12.5	203
1830	151	24.6	290
1835	324	50.1	441
1840	494	82.6	514
1845	538	96.2	710
1850	638	134.6	722
1855	696	172.7	732
1860	817	195.0	655

SOURCES: Steamboat counts and tonnage data are from Erik Haites and James Mak, "The Decline of Steamboating on the Antebellum Western Rivers: Some New Evidence and an Alternative Hypothesis," *Explorations in Economic History*, 11 (Fall 1973): 35–36; productivity index is calculated from the Louisville–New Orleans route and is adapted from James Mak and Gary Walton, "Steamboats and the Great Productivity Surge in River Transportation," *Journal of Economic History*, 32 (Sept. 1972): 639.

The long, narrow, and prominently keeled design of eastern steamboats soon gave way to the wider, relatively flat-bottomed, and ornately superstructured vessel so admirably suited to the natural and social realities of river life, as Mark Twain later recorded in his *Life on the Mississippi*. The size of the steamboat also increased, particularly for those traveling the major routes, and the ratio of carrying capacity to measured tonnage rose by a factor of three to four between 1820 and the 1840s. The speed of the steamboat as well as the length of the navigation season increased, while more efficient operations in the river ports reduced cargo-collection times. Between 1820 and 1860, a roughly fourfold increase in productivity applied to a thirteenfold increase of measured tonnage in operation yielded a greater than fiftyfold increase in the amount of transport capacity supplied by western steamboats.

Virtually all improvements to productivity in river steamboating occurred before 1845. While tonnage doubled over the next fifteen years, productivity gains ceased and railway competition appeared. The era of the western river steamboat did not last much beyond the Civil War. Still, the steamboat had made a crucial contribution to economic development, not only in the West but throughout the rest of the nation as well. On the eve of the Civil War, the lower Mississippi Valley with its great port at New Orleans, the focal point of steamboat navigation, was likely the most prosperous region in the United States.

The Early Railroad Age (1828–1860)

Just as American canal-building and steamboating developments were getting into high gear, a new transportation technology—the railroad—arrived to challenge them. Ultimately, the railroad prevailed. In a way, the railroad combined the basic principles of earlier technologies: From the steamboat it inherited the idea of steam as the motive power for a carrier of passengers and freight, while the

The "Best Friend," the First Locomotive built in the United States for actual service on a Railroad.

The "Best Friend" was built at the West Point Foundery Shops, in New York City, for the South Carolina Railroad, arrived in Charleston by ship Niagara October 23d, and after several experimental trials, in November and December, 1830, made the first excursion trip, as above, on Saturday, 15th January, 1831, being the anniversary of the commencement of the road. (See extract from *Charleston Courier*, page 152.)

The *Best Friend* of Charleston. One of the first U.S. locomotives, the *Best Friend* here is pulling South Carolinians on an excursion to celebrate the first anniversary of their railroad in 1831. The locomotive was built in New York City and carried to Charleston by ship in 1830. An African-American, more than likely a slave, is stoking the boiler. (The Bettmann Archive)

canal furnished a compelling model of the benefits of a low-friction, artificially constructed route of commerce. The railroad's inherent advantages over both the canal and steamboat included its greater speed, its ability to serve areas away from natural waterways (where high costs made canal building prohibitive), and its all-season operation.

The railroad's advantages over other means of transportation were not obvious at first. The first application of the railroad to public transportation occurred almost simultaneously in England and the United States in the late 1820s. This meant that Americans did not have with the railroad, as they did with canals, successful and long-existing precedents from abroad on which to base their own planning. And this explains why, for example, Pennsylvanians debated vigorously the merits of canals and railroads and chose a curious and rather unsuccessful amalgam of both in the state's Mainline system. However, the merits of Americans' dedication to decentralized decision making and their willingness to experiment with new technologies were most evident in the rapid progress of the railroad in the

1830s. By 1840, when the railroad was barely a decade old, American railroad mileage virtually equalled that of its canals. Two decades later, on the eve of the Civil War, some thirty thousand miles of track had been put into operation, and railroad mileage was over seven times canal mileage (see Figure 5–2).

Why was the unproven technology of the steam-powered railroad seized upon so boldly by American decision makers? The initial impetus was the old but rapidly changing commercial rivalry among eastern seaport cities for trade with the interior. When the first general-purpose American railroad, the Baltimore and Ohio, was chartered in 1828, Baltimore businesspeople feared that the projected Chesapeake and Ohio Canal, which ran roughly parallel, would divert inland trade to Virginia ports. Similarly, in South Carolina, the business interests of Charleston hoped to cut into Savannah's trade by building a railroad inland to Hamburg on the Savannah River. When completed in 1833, the 136-mile-long railroad was the longest anywhere in the world. In other states along the Atlantic seaboard, the examples set by Baltimore and Charleston

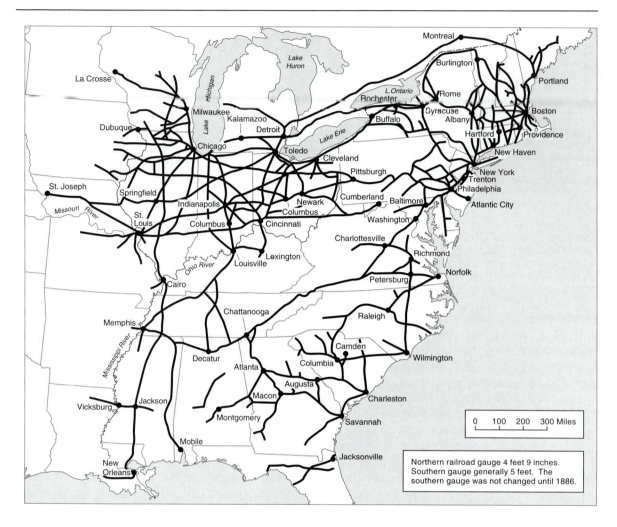

Figure 5–2 *Railroads in 1860*

SOURCE: Adapted from George Rogers Taylor, *The Transportation Revolution 1815–1860* (New York: Holt, 1951), p. 87.

were soon imitated. The railroad quickly proved itself an effective competitor to other modes of transportation, especially in the carrying of people.

From the beginning, most American railroads were organized as corporations chartered by state governments. In this regard they followed the pattern used by the turnpike

companies and by a few short canals, not the method employed by the major canals and steamboat enterprises. It is interesting to ask why different forms of organization were chosen. One reason may have been the advantages of the corporate form of organization in raising large amounts of capital. Since steamboats could be built inexpensively, individual enterprises and small partnerships were feasible forms of organization. Turnpikes, in contrast, were more costly to construct and canals even more so. Unlike the great canals, turnpikes were not near to being statewide in length. Moreover, local interests along the roadways received enough indirect benefits from them to induce private stock subscriptions sufficient to finance construction even when the direct return from tolls was not as high as the return from other investments. The relatively small turnpike corporation thus provided an efficient middle ground between individual or partnership organization, which was unfeasible, and state planning and ownership, which was unnecessary because inland economic activity was still essentially local rather than statewide.

Even more perplexing in terms of capital requirements is the comparison of railroads with the great canals. Since both were devourers of capital as compared with turnpikes and steamboats, why were corporations dominant in railroads and state ownership in canals? Timing may explain part of the answer. The railroad era began somewhat later than the canal era, so wealth had increased to an extent that made private financing more likely for railroads. Also, in terms of their length in miles, many of the earliest railroads were more like turnpikes than statewide canals. However, another factor may have been more important than timing: Of all the transport innovations of the early nineteenth century, only the railroad was able to build the fixed facilities that carried goods and people and to operate the means of conveyance itself. For turnpikes, canals, and steamboats, these two functions were organized separately. The complexity of building and operating the railways lent itself to private, decentralized decision making.

Although most early railroads were organized as private corporations, they still received significant financial and other types of support from all government levels. State charters granted them rights of eminent domain and, in some cases, tax exemptions, banking privileges, and monopoly rights. In the South and West, when private capital and entrepreneurship did not meet transportation needs of the people, railroads were sometimes built and operated by state governments. Eventually—and in some cases, rather quickly—most of these state-built railroads were transferred to private ownership and operation. More frequently, state and local governments provided financial assistance to railroad corporations, often in the form of loans but sometimes through stock subscriptions and guarantees of railroad securities. While state aid was greatest in the South, it was not as important to railway progress in the less developed West, partly because of the timing of regional railway developments. By the 1850s, the decade of greatest antebellum railway expansion, eastern and foreign sources of private capital were available to the West, where most of the expansion took place. In addition, the West pressured the federal government to aid railroad development; the government responded in 1850 by granting several million acres of land to the states of Illinois, Alabama, and Mississippi to be used for construction of a north–south railroad from Illinois to the Gulf of Mexico. The land was turned over to the Illinois Central Railroad Company, which then mortgaged or sold parcels of it to obtain the funds needed to build the railroad. Completed in 1856, the railroad set a precedent for the massive land grants made by the federal government to western and transcontinental railroads during the following two decades.

Despite the large amount of government assistance, private capital supplied about three-fourths of the more than $1 billion invested in American railroads between 1828 and 1860. In contrast, only about one-fourth of the $188 million cost of antebellum canals came directly from private sources, the rest from public investment. The comparison is somewhat biased in that locomotives and rolling stock are included in the railroad figure, whereas canal boats and horses are excluded from canal costs. Nonetheless, the differences in railway and canal investment before the Civil War are obvious. Even in its infancy in 1860, the railroad had demonstrated a much wider range of application. The ultimate triumph of the railroad over other means of internal transportation was achieved largely because of its greater flexibility and efficiency.

The Decline of Transport Costs

Our survey of the early nineteenth century's transportation innovations thus far has emphasized technological and organizational characteristics. From it we have learned something of the ways in which Americans of the early national period approached problems of economic development. During the first decades of the new nation's history, the artificial stimulus of European wars served to focus much of the country's attention on foreign commerce rather than on internal market growth. There were constitutional debates and the emergence of clashing sectional interests on the subject of transportation improvements. People pointed to the drawbacks of a federal system of government and questioned Gallatin's view that only the central government could effectively mount an attack on the nation's transport problems. Out of this milieu there came a more decentralized approach to transportation problems, one that promoted progress through a pragmatic pursuit of local and regional interests. A pragmatism appeared in the varied roles assumed by governments and private enterprises in the development of turnpikes, canals, steamboats, and railroads. Ideologies of laissez-faire and government intervention had little or no influence on the organization of the rapidly expanding transportation sector. The mix of public and private decision making was determined by

the technical characteristics of each innovation as well as by the economic conditions of the states or regions involved.

Although the technologies and organizational forms of American transportation innovations were varied, their effects on transport costs were similar and usually quite dramatic (see Figure 5–3). Over the course of the nineteenth century, inland freight rates fell, roughly to less than one-fiftieth of their level in the late eighteenth century. Transport costs decreased because of the widespread application of new technologies and the resulting competition among sellers of the major transport services. For example, wagon freight rates fell when improved turnpike roads led to greater competition among wagon haulers and again when the water-transport alternatives of steamboats and canals came along.

The greatest reduction in inland freight rates, as Figure 5–3 indicates, occurred between 1815 and the 1850s, primarily due to steamboats and canals. The fall in upstream river rates is especially noteworthy both for its rapidity and for the fact that it was virtually complete before 1830. Freight rates on the earliest railroads were five to ten times higher than those on rivers and canals. It is not surprising that, in the first two decades of railway development, the railroads earned more than half of their total revenues in the passenger business since it was their major advantage over alternative carriers. By the 1850s, however, the growth and improvement of rail transport led to its effective, and sometimes devastating, competition for freight with water carriers (even though railroad rates, on a ton-mile basis, remained well above water-transport rates). Rail transport was faster and more direct than shipping by water. Moreover, unlike canals and steamboats, railroads operated throughout the year and reached places where water transport was unavailable.

These various developments in the railroad and other services represented a transporta-

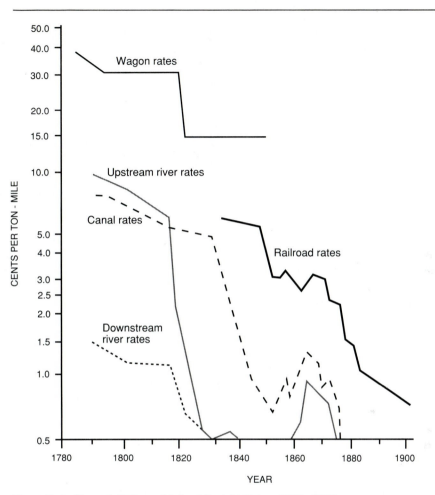

Figure 5-3 *General Pattern of Inland Freight Rates, 1780–1900*

SOURCE: Douglass C. North, "The Role of Transportation in the Economic Development of North America," in *Les grandes voies maritimes dans le monde XV–XIX Siècles* (Paris: SEVPEN, 1965), p. 222.

tion revolution. At the start of the nineteenth century, the internal markets of the United States were largely scattered and local affairs. By the 1850s, and in many cases as early as the 1820s, this was no longer the case. The products of the farm, the forest, the mine, and the factory—as well as people themselves—moved more quickly and at greatly reduced costs in regional and interregional trade. Pro-

ducers received higher real prices for their goods and services and saw the value of their resources increase. Consumers witnessed declines in the prices they paid for goods and services. And greater specialization in production—based on individual, local, and regional comparative advantages—was encouraged and even demanded by the increased competition of distant producers as markets were extended by improved transportation. The Constitution had created the possibility of a great common market throughout the United States; the transportation revolution made it a reality.

Information and Communications

Improved transportation in antebellum America also facilitated increases in the flow and dissemination of information. Unlike the exchange of commodities, the exchange of information has received relatively little attention from economic historians. This is surprising because information is a fundamental factor of production in an economy based on decentralized decision making and the coordination of economic activity through prices and markets. In other words, a decision is no better than the information on which it is based.

Information reduces the boundaries of uncertainty faced by economic decision makers. It also plays a key role in the efficient allocation of scarce resources. Suppose, for example, a commodity is being produced and sold in two different places at prices that differ by more than the cost of transporting the commodity between them. In such a case, scarce resources are being allocated in an inefficient manner. Someone who had price information from both markets could profit by buying low and selling high. This commercial activity, in addition to being profitable, serves the social function of improving resource allocation because it tends to equalize prices in the two markets. The orders placed in the low-price market draw more resources into producing the commodity where it can be made more efficiently. Shipments to the high-price market then release resources from producing the commodity, which now can be used in more productive activities. This illustrates the relationship between specialization and comparative advantage.

New Transportation and Communication Technologies.   The canal, the steam railroad, and telegraph poles and wires are featured in this fascinating old photo. Note the motive power for the canal boat: a team of horses connected to the boat by a tow line proceeds along the tow path next to the canal. The railroad won out in this head-to-head competition; it was faster and continued to operate when the canal froze in cold weather. (Brown Brothers)

In the antebellum era, the single greatest innovation in information transmission was the electromagnetic telegraph. It appeared relatively late in the period, with its first practical demonstration taking place in 1844. Before the telegraph, the volume and speed of the flow of information depended heavily on the means of moving people and goods from place to place. As a result, communications and transportation improvements went hand in hand. While improvements in communications prior to the telegraph involved roads, canals, steamboats, and railroads, also important were advances in ocean transport (see Chapter 9), the growth of newspapers, more efficient postal services, and the development of commercial practices.[6]

By modern standards, the flow of information in early America was very slow indeed, as the following examples illustrate; improvements in transportation helped reduce the time involved. In 1799, for instance, it took a week for the news of George Washington's death to travel from Alexandria, Virginia, to New York City. By 1831, in contrast, relay expresses traveling over improved roads carried the news of President Jackson's State of the Union address from Washington, D.C. (near Alexandria), to New York in about fifteen hours. The Battle of New Orleans, on January 8, 1815, took place about two weeks after the peace treaty ("ending" the second war with Britain) had been signed in Europe. New York City did not receive news of the battle until February 6, twenty-eight days later, or of the treaty until February 11, or forty-nine days after its signing. By 1841, however, news traveled between New York and New Orleans in nine days, three times faster than in 1815. By the late 1830s, steamships had begun to cross the Atlantic in two to three weeks. Finally, while in the 1790s it had taken some twenty days for information to move between New York and a distant city such as Cincinnati, Detroit, or Charleston, by 1840 the time had been reduced to about five days, and even less when express mail was used. Although by today's standards the pretelegraphic communication times were slow, there were substantial improvements in the flow of information, particularly between 1815 and 1840.

Of course, communication is much more complicated than the mere transmission of information. It also involves gathering and processing information as well as making decisions about what information to gather, process, and transmit. Insight into these activities can be gained by examining the development of three important institutions: newspapers, postal services, and common carriers.

Newspapers

The American newspaper business developed rapidly between 1790 and 1840 (see Table 5–3). During this half-century, the annual circulation of newspapers increased by a factor of 37, and per capita newspaper consumption grew by a factor of almost 9. These data represent compounded annual rates of increase of 7.2 percent and 4.3 percent, respectively; the rates were well in excess of those of population and per capita income.

Newspaper publishing, like other types of information enterprises, was a growing industry in the early United States for many reasons— relatively high levels of literacy, growing urban populations, and Americans' democratic interest in international and domestic politics. But newspapers also served important economic functions. They published advertising, shipping intelligence, current price lists, and other commercial information. In a period when markets were expanding geographically, such information was important for producers, consumers, and the various agents of commerce. Their daily decision making depended on their having the best information available, and newspapers often provided that information.

Table 5–3 *Growth of U.S. Newspaper Publishing, 1790–1840*

	1790	1800	1810	1820	1828	1835	1840
Number of newspapers published	92	235	371	512	861	1,258	1,404
Annual circulation (in millions)	4.0	12–13	24.6	50.0	68.1	90.4	147.5
Annual newspaper copies per capita	1.0	2.4	3.4	5.2	5.6	6.0	8.6

SOURCE: Adapted from Alan R. Pred, *Urban Growth and the Circulation of Information* (Cambridge, Mass.: Harvard University Press, 1973), p. 21.

Newspapers flourished in commercially oriented cities, especially New York, and from these papers many other city and town papers cribbed their news. The frontier was also served, largely through the agency of postal services.

Postal Services

During his visit to America in 1831 to 1832, Alexis de Tocqueville wrote of Kentucky and Tennessee:

There is an astonishing circulation of letters and newspapers among these savage woods. We travelled with the mail. From time to time we stopped at what is called the post office; almost always it was an isolated house in the depths of a wood. There we dropped a large parcel from which no doubt each inhabitant of the neighborhood came to take his share. I do not think that in the most enlightened rural districts of France there is an intellectual movement either so rapid or on such a scale as in this wilderness.[7]

As Tocqueville's comments imply, a major agency for the diffusion of newspaper information was the U.S. Post Office, which also transmitted information in the form of business and personal correspondence. Between 1790 and 1860, the number of post offices increased greatly, from 75 to 28,498 (see Table 5–4). In addition, aggregate postal revenues and revenues per capita expanded at compound annual rates of 9.6 percent and 6.6 percent, respectively, even though postage rates did not change appreciably. From 1840 to 1860, rates of growth of total and per capita revenues fell, but this was due more to a dramatic reduction in postage charges in 1845 than to a slower growth in the volume of mail carried.

The Post Office improved the quality of its services in many ways over the antebellum period. Easier access to post offices, as a result of the sharp increase in the number of post offices, was only one aspect of improved quality. In the 1830s, express mails and the use of railroads as mail carriers speeded up deliveries and made them more regular and reliable. The introduction of postage stamps in 1847 allowed people to mail letters at times when local post offices were closed. And throughout the period, federal government policy resulted in an extension of service that kept up with the westward movement of the population.

With the 1845 Postal Act came large reductions in the rates charged for transmitting cor-

Table 5–4 *Growth of U.S. Postal Services, 1790–1860*

	1790	1800	1810	1820	1830	1840	1850	1860
Number of post offices	75	903	2,300	4,500	8,450	13,468	18,417	28,498
Population per post office (in thousands)	52.4	5.9	3.1	2.1	1.5	1.3	1.3	1.1
Postal revenues (in $ thousands)	$38	$281	$552	$1,112	$1,185	$4,543	$5,500	$8,518
Postal revenue per capita (in $)	$0.01	$0.05	$0.08	$0.12	$0.14	$0.27	$0.30	$0.27

SOURCES: 1790–1840 data are from Alan R. Pred, *Urban Growth and the Circulation of Information* (Cambridge, Mass.: Harvard University Press, 1973), p. 80; 1850 and 1860 data are from U.S. Bureau of the Census, *Historical Statistics of the United States* (Washington, D.C.: GPO, 1960), pp. 7, 497.

respondence. The act also marked the acceptance of a policy decision that had long been debated in government circles: because the Post Office served an important public function, it did not have to make a profit or even cover all of its costs. The idea was that, even if the Post Office lost money, the social benefit to the nation from more extensive information flows would easily outweigh the loss of federal revenue.

Common Carriers

Also aiding the flow of information, particularly before the telegraph, were improvements in common-carrier passenger transportation. These developments facilitated the spread of information from one place to another by word of mouth. In the early days of the Republic, passenger travel over land by stagecoach was slow, costly, and exceedingly uncomfortable. Travelers had to add to their stagecoach fare the cost of meals and lodging at the inns that dotted the landscape. As roads were improved and steam was applied to the movement of people over water and land, both fares and journey times fell sharply. Total costs of travel were therefore greatly reduced by the antebellum transportation revolution.

The chief result of reduced travel costs was an increased intensity of travel, particularly between growing urban centers. Consequently, the flow of information via the movement of people became more intense. Regularly scheduled passenger services were expanded and improved. The passengers were predominantly businesspeople. Retailers from all over the country made seasonal or annual trips to eastern cities to place orders for their stores. This was especially common in the earlier decades, when the spatial dispersion of retail markets made it too expensive for agents to seek out retailers. As transportation improved in the 1820s and 1830s, however, inland cities began to develop into wholesale markets, and whole-sale merchants and sales agents of manufacturers swelled the ranks of business travelers on the common carriers.

The Telegraph

In the developing U.S. economy of the antebellum decades, there was a growing demand for faster and more reliable means of transmitting information and economic intelligence. There was also a variety of supply responses on the part of both public and private parties, often acting as competitors. Before the 1840s, though, information transmission did not come close to the ideal of nearly instantaneous communication. The invention and application of the telegraph changed this situation and in the process had great economic and social effects.

Inventor Samuel F. B. Morse developed the idea of the telegraph and made limited experiments with it in the 1830s. However, in order to present convincing demonstrations of his invention's uses, he required substantial financial backing. After private sources turned him down, Morse sought the aid of the federal government. In 1843, Congress appropriated $30,000 for the construction of a telegraph line between Washington, D.C., and Baltimore. The pilot project, completed in 1844, was a technical success, and private investors soon became interested in the new innovation. Several telegraph companies were formed and the mileage of telegraph lines in operation grew rapidly—some 40 miles of line in 1846 grew to 2,000 miles by 1848, to 12,000 miles by 1850, and to 23,000 miles by 1852. By this time, the major cities of the Northeast and Middle West were connected by telegraph. Competition among the telegraph companies led to rate wars that bankrupted some of them and caused others to merge or consolidate their operations. By the eve of the Civil War, only three telegraph companies had survived, but together they operated fifty thousand miles of telegraph line. In addition, an undersea cable for transmitting messages across the Atlantic was completed in 1858; however, it ran into technical problems that were not solved until after the war.

The Western Union Company was by far the most successful of the early telegraph firms. Its organizers and managers were skilled businesspeople whose acumen produced the profits that soon allowed the company to absorb many of its weaker competitors and thus tap the capital markets for more funds for expansion. Western Union's patents and demonstrated abilities were also instrumental in obtaining government subsidies for an east–west transcontinental line, which the company completed in 1861. Another key factor in Western Union's success was its relationship with the railroads; it was the first company to convince the railroads that the telegraph could be complementary to railway operations. As a result, Western Union cut its construction and operating costs by utilizing railroad rights-of-way and by teaching railroad workers how to operate and maintain telegraph equipment. In return, the railroads gained access to a means of transmitting information that allowed them to coordinate and follow traffic movements more effectively.

Summary

The transportation and communications revolutions of early U.S. economic history were crucial to developments in other sectors of the economy. As a result of these revolutionary improvements, vast acreages of land were settled and specialized commercial agriculture emerged. Commerce and industry enjoyed expanding markets that promoted specialization, economies of scale, and the incentive to develop and use new technologies. Demands for money, bank credit, and an integrated financial system expanded. Without rapid, low-cost transportation and communication these economic developments could not have evolved as they did. The slower pace of seventeenth- and eighteenth-century economic development in all sectors demonstrates how important the transportation and communications revolutions were to economic modernization in the nineteenth century.

Endnotes

1. Adam Smith, *An Inquiry into the Nature and Causes of the Wealth of Nations* [1776], Modern Library (New York: Random House; 1937), p. 17.
2. David Ricardo, *The Principles of Political Economy and Taxation* [1817], Everyman's Library (London: Dent, 1933).
3. Quoted in G. S. Callender, "The Early Transportation and Banking Enterprises of the States in Relation to the Growth of Corporations," *Quarterly Journal of Economics*, 27 (1902): 123.
4. Albert Gallatin, "Reports on Roads and Canals," document no. 250, 10th Congress, 1st session, reprinted in *New American State Papers—Transportation*, vol. 1 (Wilmington, Del.: Scholarly Resources, 1972).
5. Ibid.
6. The following discussion is based on information in Allan R. Pred, *Urban Growth and the Circulation of Information: The United States System of Cities, 1790–1840* (Cambridge, Mass.: Harvard University Press, 1973).
7. Alexis de Tocqueville, *Journey to America*, J. P. Mayer, ed. (New York: Doubleday, 1971), p. 283.

Suggested Readings

For a general survey of the development of the antebellum economy with an emphasis on transportation, see George R. Taylor, *The Transportation Revolution, 1815–1860* (New York: Holt, 1961). Chapter 13 of Lance Davis et al., *American Economic Growth: An Economist's History of the United States* (New York: Harper & Row, 1972), "Internal Transportation" by Albert Fishlow, is a masterful treatment of the subject in its command of the historical facts and of their meaning in terms of economic analysis. A basic source of data on the remarkable decline of transport costs is Douglass C. North, "The Role of Transportation in the Economic Development of North America," *Les grandes voies maritimes dans le monde XV–XIX Siecles* (Paris: Sevpen, 1965). The revolutionary character of nineteenth-century transportation improvements is reaffirmed in an article that surveys much of the technical work done by economic historians: Robert W. Fogel, "Notes on the Social Saving Controversy," *Journal of Economic History,* 39 (March 1979).

Studies of specific transportation technologies and facilities are numerous. On turnpikes, see Joseph A. Durrenberger, *Turnpikes: A Study of the Toll Road Movement in the Middle Atlantic States and Maryland* (Cos Cob, Conn.: John E. Edwards, 1968). The canal era is surveyed and analyzed in Carter Goodrich, ed., *Canals and American Economic Development* (New York: Columbia University Press, 1961). For case studies, see Ronald E. Shaw, *Erie Water West: A History of the Erie Canal, 1792–1854* (Lexington: University of Kentucky Press, 1966), and Harry Scheiber, *Ohio Canal Era: A Case Study of Government and the Economy, 1820–1861* (Athens: Ohio University Press, 1969). Economic issues pertaining to the contributions of canals are covered in Roger L. Ransom, "Social Returns from Public Transport Investment: A Case Study of the Ohio Canal," *Journal of Political Economy,* 78 (Sept.–Oct. 1970), and Ronald W. Filante, "A Note on the Economic Viability of the Erie Canal," *Business History Review,* 48 (Spring 1974).

The classic study of steamboating is Louis C. Hunter, *Steamboats on the Western Rivers* (Cambridge, Mass.: Harvard University Press, 1949), but the economic analysis of the contribution of this technology is well set out in Eric F. Haites, James Mak, and Gary M. Walton, *Western River Transportation: The Era of Early Internal Development, 1810–1860* (Baltimore: Johns Hopkins University Press, 1975).

The economic impact of early railroads is analyzed in considerable detail in Albert Fishlow, *American Railroads and the Transformation of the Antebellum Economy* (Cambridge, Mass.: Harvard University Press, 1965). For both more general questions and an emphasis on the path-breaking influence of railroads on business organization and management, see the following two works of Alfred D. Chandler, Jr., *The Railroads: The Nation's First Big Business* (New York: Harcourt, 1965), and *The Visible Hand* (Cambridge, Mass.: Harvard University Press, 1977). For the impact of one of the earliest land-grant railroads, consult Paul W. Gates, *The Illinois Central Railroad and Its Colonization Work* (Cambridge, Mass.: Harvard University Press, 1934).

Governmental concerns with and activities in early transportation improvements are an important part of the story. One can still gain a valuable perspective on the dimensions of America's transportation problems circa 1808 by reading the reprinted work of Albert Gallatin, "Report on Roads and Canals," document No. 250, 10th Congress, 1st session, in *The New American State Papers—Transportation,* vol. 1 (Wilmington, Del.: Scholarly Resources, 1972). Another classic work discussing forms of governmental aid is Guy S. Callender, "The

Early Transportation and Banking Enterprises of the States in Relation to the Growth of Corporations," *Quarterly Journal of Economics,* 27 (Nov. 1902). Also see two studies by Carter Goodrich, *Government Promotion of American Canals and Railroads, 1800–1890* (New York: Columbia University Press, 1960), and "Internal Improvements Reconsidered," *Journal of Economic History,* 30 (June 1970).

Information and communications improvements have received much less attention from economic historians than improvements in transportation. However, two valuable studies relating to the antebellum years are Allan R. Pred, *Urban Growth and the Circulation of Information: The United States System of Cities, 1790–1840* (Cambridge, Mass.: Harvard University Press, 1973), and Robert L. Thompson, *Wiring a Continent, The History of the Telegraph Industry in the United States, 1832–1866* (Princeton, N.J.: Princeton University Press, 1947).

Chapter 6

Land Policy, Agricultural Expansion, and the Political Economy of Slavery

T HE MOST ABUNDANT RESOURCE OF THE YOUNG United States was land, and its primary use was in agricultural production. At the close of the War of Independence, however, most of the new nation's land was not being used as an economic resource. The lands extending westward from the Appalachians to the Mississippi were scarcely used at all except occasionally by Native American and other hunters and trappers. Although it was unclear at the time who controlled or owned these lands, Americans' interest in acquiring and utilizing them was great. They thus saw a need for making fundamental decisions about such matters as who owned the unsettled land or who should own it, the terms and conditions for converting it from a natural to an economic resource, and the public and private aspirations that could be achieved by various land policy options. Some of these issues were resolved by policy decisions of the 1780s; others were dealt with over time as the nation grew in population and production and as it acquired new territories. In general, the result was a transfer of vast acreages of public lands through market mechanisms to numerous private owners (mostly farmers).

U.S. Land Policies Before the Civil War

In 1783, as a result of the Treaty of Paris that formally ended the American Revolution, the original territory of the United States consisted of some 889,000 square miles of land. This territory extended from the Atlantic Coast westward to the Mississippi River, and from the Great Lakes and Maine in the North to a rough line stretching westward from the southern boundary of Georgia in the South. During the half-century from 1803 to 1853, the territory of the nation expanded to more than three times its original size and covered slightly more than three million square miles—all the land now occupied by the forty-eight contiguous states.

The territorial acquisitions of 1803 to 1853 emphasized in bold strokes the acquisitive and expansionist goals of the young Republic (see Figure 6–1). President Thomas Jefferson had hoped in 1803 to secure American control of the mouth of the Mississippi, but when Napoleon offered not only to fulfill that limited objective but also to give Jefferson a chance to double the size of the United States with one move, Jefferson quickly set aside his fondness for constitutional procedures and accepted. The Louisiana Purchase thus added 827 thousand square miles to the United States at a cost of $15 million. Much of the purchase price was borrowed from European lenders who, in contrast with their attitudes barely a decade earlier, had great confidence in the credit of the U.S. government (see Chapter 7). Florida, a territory of 72,000 square miles, was annexed by treaty with Spain in 1819.

From 1845 to 1848, under President James K. Polk, one of the great imperialists in U.S. history, territories larger in their aggregate than the Louisiana Purchase were added. The United States in 1845 annexed the 390,000 square miles of the independent Republic of Texas, which had been set up by American settlers in 1836 after their celebrated battles with Mexican armies at the Alamo and San Jacinto. In 1846, conflicting claims to the northwestern Oregon territory were settled by a treaty with Great Britain that added 286,000 square miles. U.S. victory in a war with Mexico resulted in 1848 in the Mexican government's cession of 529,000 square miles of what is now the American Southwest. A small additional area of 30,000 square miles in southern New Mexico and Arizona was acquired from Mexico in the Gadsden Purchase of 1853; it was thought to contain the best southern route for a future east–west railroad.

Early Land Policy (1781–1802)

The early land policy of the United States was directed toward acquiring a national public do-

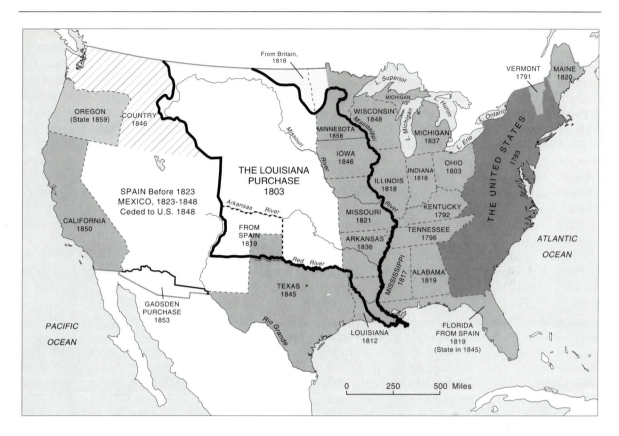

Figure 6-1 *The Expanding Frontier, 1783-1860*
SOURCE: Adapted from Martin Gilbert, *American History Atlas* (New York: Macmillan, 1969), p. 39.

main, setting the conditions under which it would be utilized economically, and determining the political position of the new territories. The problem of acquisition was complicated by the claims of several of the original states, dating from their colonial charters, to lands lying beyond their borders. States without such claims wanted the landed states to be stripped of their holdings, which would then pass into the national domain. The alliance of states under the Articles of Confederation was fragile, however, and delicate political maneuvering was needed to persuade the claimant states to cede their western lands to the federal government. New York began the process in 1781. By

1790, Virginia, Massachusetts, Connecticut, and the Carolinas had relinquished most of their western claims; and in 1802, Georgia ceded to the United States its western lands that covered most of what is now Alabama and Mississippi. The pre-Louisiana Purchase national domain then consisted of this southern area and the lands north and west of the Ohio River.

In the earliest stages of the national domain's formation, the basic pattern for transferring public land to private ownership and utilization was established by the Land Ordinance of 1785, which was patterned in part after an earlier plan of Thomas Jefferson's.

Systematic land division into townships followed the orderly pattern of colonial New England, rather than the haphazard method of locating practiced in much of the South. Rectangular surveys established the boundaries of each township, 6 miles on a side, and divided it into 36 sections, each measuring one square mile or 640 acres. The lots thus surveyed were to be sold for cash but for not less than $1 per acre. Hence, a minimum of $640 —a substantial sum with the per capita income level at roughly $100 —was required initially to purchase a tract of the minimum size set by the U.S. government. In each township, four sections were retained by the government and one section was reserved to support public schools.

The first surveys commenced in 1785 in southeastern Ohio. But little land was sold by the U.S. government in the early years. The original states still possessed land within and without their borders, and they could offer prospective buyers better financial terms and more immediate economic opportunity. The states, in fact, were much more innovative and flexible in land policy than the national government. They took the lead in abolishing the feudal obligations attached to land use that had migrated to the American colonies from Europe and instead sold or granted land on the basis of freehold tenure. Although the widespread practice among the states of paying or rewarding soldiers with land grants was feudal in origin, in the American context it can be viewed as a decision based on economic and political realities: The states' economies were underdeveloped, a popular antipathy to taxation limited public revenues, and land thus became the greatest disposable resource available to state governments. Particularly in the South, the states also pioneered the practice of granting preemptive rights to land to those who had settled on it in advance of survey and sale. These state policies, many developed during the colonial era, provided a wealth of experience on which the U.S. government could later draw.

With national land sales proceeding slowly and the confederation government pressed for funds, the United States in 1786 and 1788 sold million-acre tracts of Ohio lands to two eastern groups—the Ohio Company and John Symmes and his associates. This was an attempt to decentralize the sale of national lands so to raise revenue and encourage more rapid settlement. The plan, however, was not very successful on either count. The companies were permitted to tender depreciated government debt certificates and soldiers' warrants rather than cash for the lands, but even with this concession, which amounted to a price reduction, they were not able to make full payment. The companies faced the same problem that plagued the central government: land at better locations was still available in large quantities from the states.

While national land sales remained modest for a decade under the Ordinance of 1785, a significant piece of related legislation came in 1787. The Northwest Ordinance of that year provided for the political organization of the Northwest Territory, the area north of the Ohio River between Pennsylvania and the Mississippi River. In addition to forbidding the extension of slavery to the territory, the ordinance granted specific rights to territorial inhabitants and established the steps to be taken for subdivisions to become states with powers and privileges equal to those of the existing states. The territory eventually became five states: Ohio, Indiana, Illinois, Michigan, and Wisconsin. In rejecting the mercantilist concept of metropolis–colony relationships—the idea against which the American colonies had rebelled—the Northwest Ordinance marked a far-reaching decision about the basic pattern that the constituent units of the United States were to follow in their political development.

The Land Act of 1796, the first under the new federal government, reaffirmed the rectangular survey principle of the 1785 Ordinance. The minimum price was doubled to $2 per acre, where it remained until 1820, but the minimum tract was kept at 640 acres. Although raising the price of an item that is not selling well is not usually recommended, Congress had political motives for setting the higher price for public land. It sought to discourage the large, speculative purchases that had resulted in scandals and caused both federal and state governments embarrassment in the preceding years. (It actually discouraged other potential purchasers as well.) In addition, some members of the dominant Federalist party of the 1790s were opposed to cheap land, arguing that high-priced land would encourage commerce and manufacturing. Finally, the existing states and other land sellers desired to keep the price of federal land noncompetitive with their own properties.

Two provisions of the 1796 Land Act, however, worked to stimulate sales because of certain precedents they set, which were followed and liberalized up until 1820. The first provision allowed land to be bought on credit with a small down payment (half of the purchase price had to be paid within thirty days and the remainder within one year). The other provision established auction sales at specific locations, initially in the settled areas of the East.

Federal land sales continued to be sluggish until 1800, when, at the behest of William Henry Harrison (a future president but then a delegate from the Northwest Territory), the land laws were modified in three important ways to encourage sales and settlement: (1) the minimum purchasable tract was reduced to 320 acres, (2) credit terms were liberalized to provide for installment payments spread over four years, and (3) land offices were located more conveniently in the vicinity of the lands offered for sale. Thereafter, federal land sales picked up significantly.

Public Policy and the Land Market (1800–1860)

The federal land acts of the late eighteenth century established the essential principles and mechanics of land sale in later years without actually selling much land. After 1800 and until the Civil War, the annual rate of disposal of the public domain was typically in the hundreds of thousands of acres up to the 1830s and in the millions of acres thereafter (see Figure 6–2). Three periods of rapidly rising and ultimately frenzied sales occurred from 1814 to 1819, from 1833 to 1836, and from 1854 to 1855. The rising trend of federal land sales reflected a growing population, transportation improvements that extended the markets for the products of the land, and increasingly liberal disposal policies. The three periods of peak sales, though often attributed to irrational speculation, were actually rational responses to generally rising price levels (see Chapter 7 for explanations of these inflations) as well as to some relative price increases for products of the land. Such price movements increased the value of land at a time when federal policies, by making vast quantities of land available for sale, held land prices relatively constant. Demand for land, in other words, shifted outward along an elastic supply curve. Predictably, sales of land soared.

The increasingly liberal character of antebellum public land policy is evident in the reduction of prices and of the minimum acreage that could be purchased, in the recognition of squatters' rights to preemption, in the adoption of graduated price reductions for offered but unsold lands, and in the growing use of grants of land to promote public purposes. The minimum acreage offered for sale, set at 320 acres in 1800, was reduced to 160 acres in 1804, to 80 acres in 1820, and to 40 acres in 1832. Throughout the period from 1796 to 1820, the federal government financed sales by granting credit to buyers at the set price of $2 per acre. Although a discounted price of $1.64 per acre was offered for cash sales in 1804, a great many private purchasers availed themselves of federal credit, especially during the boom sales period of 1814 to 1819. This was not surprising,

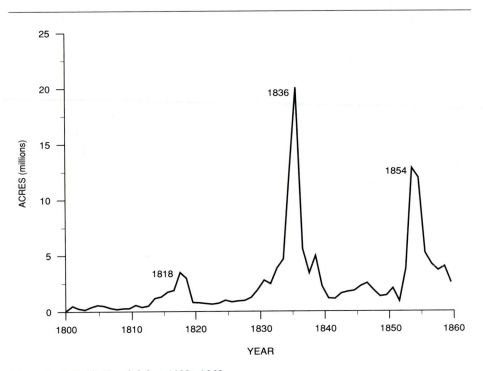

Figure 6–2 *Public Land Sales, 1800–1860*
Source: Data from U.S. Bureau of the Census, *Historical Statistics of the United States, Colonial Times to 1957* (Washington, D.C.: GPO, 1960), p. 239.

for the 6 percent interest charge was generally well below what private credit institutions, insofar as they existed at all in frontier areas, were charging.

Before 1820, however, the limited extent of western markets, plus the time involved in bringing virgin land into production, made it difficult for settlers to pay their debts to the government when they fell due. Although numerous relief and credit extension acts were passed in response to the settlers' plight, over one-third of the lands sold between 1787 and 1820 had reverted to the federal government by 1820. Faced with these reversions as well as an outstanding amount of over $20 million due on land sales, the federal government in 1820 abolished the credit system and reduced the minimum price of land to $1.25 per acre, pay-

able in cash only. This policy remained in effect until the Homestead Act of 1862, which belatedly fulfilled the fond hope of many people by providing for free land. Most sales after 1820 were also financed by credit, but from private sources rather than from the federal government. The government's abandonment of credit sales marked a recognition that it had discharged an early developmental function. From then on, the finance of land purchases could be handled by private credit-granting enterprises and individual lenders.

Throughout the antebellum era, federal land policy operated to keep the supply of land extremely elastic at the minimum price. The pace of surveying and offering land for sale continually outpaced demand, with the result that average prices received were, with few exceptions, close to the minimum price asked. Nonetheless, a good many people settled and improved western lands in advance of government sale. These squatters, as they were called, constituted a potent political force in favor of the granting of liberal preemption rights. Before 1830, a number of special acts recognized their claims, but in 1830, the first general preemption act was passed. It provided that settlers who were living on public land they had improved as of 1829 had the right to purchase it, up to a maximum of 160 acres, at the minimum price of $1.25 per acre. This policy was renewed periodically in the 1830s, but the preemption rights remained retrospective rather than prospective. A family of squatters thus faced some risk that "their" land could eventually be sold out from under them. Finally, in 1841, the right of prospective preemption was enacted into law. From then until the Homestead Law achieved the goal of free land, anyone could go out and settle on unsold public land and gain the right to buy it later at the minimum price. It was one example of the democratic tendency to transform privileges into rights.

Since parcels of land vary greatly in their physical and economic attributes, the federal government, before 1854, exhibited inflexibility in setting a single minimum price for all land. Substantial acreages of public land remained unsold behind the westward-moving frontier. As early as 1824, Senator Thomas Hart Benton of Missouri called for graduated price reductions for unsold land. Congress did not act positively until three decades later, when the Graduation Act of 1854 reduced prices to $1 per acre for land offered but not sold for ten years. The price fell to 12.5 cents per acre for land that remained unsold for thirty years after it had been offered. Graduated prices proved very successful in promoting land sales. Until it was repealed in 1862, the 1854 Graduation Act resulted in over seventy million acres being sold at the reduced

prices. Congress had finally discovered the law of demand.

The use of grants was another significant aspect of federal land policy in the antebellum era. The major beneficiaries of land grants were the veterans of military campaigns and the states. The purposes of federal land grants were to reward veterans for their service to the nation and to promote useful public functions by the states, chiefly education, internal improvements in transportation, and land reclamation. Granting land warrants to veterans dated back to the revolution and was based on colonial, even ancient, precedents. From the earliest years, the ex-soldiers often disposed of these rights without ever claiming or setting foot on the lands to which they represented a claim. This practice became institutionalized in the 1850s, when an active market in warrants developed. Warrants selling at prices below $1.25 per acre became an important land-office currency. They were attractive to that sort of person who—ever the enemy of business stability—resists paying full price when a discount is available. In some years the acreage purchased with warrants actually exceeded the amount of land bought for cash.

The practice of granting federal lands for educational purposes originated with the ordinances of 1785 and 1787; grants for improvements began with the 1802 act enabling Ohio to become a state. Five percent of the proceeds of federal land sales in Ohio were set aside for road building under both state and federal auspices. This precedent was followed in other states, culminating before the Civil War in grants to states to aid railroad construction. The Illinois Central railroad was the most prominent example. Other large grants were donations of swamp lands to states in the 1850s; the states were to sell these inferior lands and use the proceeds for reclamation.

Before the Civil War, the federal government thus gave away some sixty-eight million acres of the public domain for military support

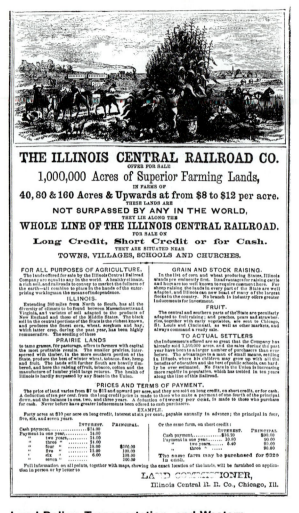

Land Policy, Transportation, and Western Settlement. In the 1850s, the Illinois Central Railroad Co. received large grants of land from the federal government. The company then advertised and sold the land to farmers, using the proceeds to finance the building of the railroad. Note the advertising techniques and terms of payment. (Historical Pictures/Stock Montage)

purposes and twice that quantity to the states. The grants added up to an area larger than the state of Texas. Yet the most significant aspect of federal land policy was the creation and nurturing of a great land market through which the public domain passed into private ownership and utilization. Both publicly and privately, Americans looked on their vast land endowment as a resource to be applied toward material ends. The quickest way to realize that goal was to turn the resource over to widespread private ownership and decentralized decision making. The evolution of American land policy is best understood by recognizing the pervasiveness of these attitudes over the course of the nineteenth century. The young United States was a country splendidly endowed with land and other natural resources. Equally if not more important for long-term economic growth, it fashioned a set of institutions designed to encourage development and use of its natural resources. In modern economic history, not all resource-rich economies have been as successful as the United States. Others less well endowed with natural resources have done quite well. The lesson appears to be that the institutions that organize and use available resources are at least as important as the resource endowments of nature.

Sectional Politics and Land Economics

The increasingly liberal terms on which the federal government disposed of the public domain between the 1780s and the 1860s reflected both economic rationality and the rising political power of the western states and territories. One basic principle of economics is that increased use of productive resources gives rise to greater production. In the American context, more land also contributed to rising levels of per capita output and to material welfare. This occurred for two reasons. First, the ratio of land per worker increased, promoting a rise in output per worker. Second, the western lands settled and brought into production before the Civil War were more productive than the lands east of the Appalachians that had been settled earlier. These two factors, along with the growth of markets, go a long way toward explaining the magnetic attractiveness of the West to nineteenth-century Americans.

Indeed, these economic arguments are sufficiently compelling to cause one to ask why the decision to have a liberal land-disposal policy was adopted only gradually and not at the very beginning of the period. The underdeveloped state of early transportation, discussed in Chapter 5, no doubt mitigated the appeal of the economic argument. But it is also important to recognize that politico-economic factors of a sectional nature operated to protract the movement toward a more liberal land policy. Many advocates of manufacturing, who lived primarily in the Northeast, feared that the availability of cheap land in the West would raise the wages of industrial labor by drawing actual and potential workers into western agriculture. The advocates of manufacturing therefore favored a policy of high land prices. But they also favored protection of domestic manufactures by means of tariffs on imported goods. Since both customs duties levied on imports and land sales were sources of government revenue, policies calling for both high land prices and high tariffs might have furnished more revenue than the federal government required to carry out its functions. In the earlier decades, reducing the national debt provided a convenient outlet for surplus revenues (see Chapter 7). As the debt shrank, the manufacturing interests found a way out of their dilemma by advocating that further surplus revenues be turned over to the states for financing internal improvements and other state purposes. (Such a policy also appealed to those who on principle were against a direct federal role in internal improvements.)

The farming interests of the South, in contrast, were very much opposed to high tariffs on manufactures because they were primarily consumers rather than producers of manufactured goods. Also, since they relied on export markets for selling their agricultural products, southerners in general were opposed to restrictions on international trade. Relatively well endowed with natural routes of water transportation as well as a passion for states' rights, southerners took a dim view of internal improvements financed by federal tariff revenues. The South's views on land policy were initially ambiguous. Cheap and more productive land in the Southwest would undercut land values in the older South Atlantic states, but opening up the southwestern lands to plantation agriculture would also serve to increase the value of slave labor. Because planters and their slaves were quite mobile, and because the dominant slaveholding interests felt a political need to extend their slave system as it became a subject of growing opposition both within and outside the South, southerners tended over time to favor cheap land policies. Their perceived interests were therefore diametrically opposed to those of the manufacturers in the Northeast.

Westerners desired expansion of both their political and economic power through low land prices. Less wealthy than the plantation South and not as well endowed with natural navigable waterways, they were less opposed to tariffs that could provide federal revenues for internal improvements. As the West grew in population in both its northern and southern sections and developed economically, a shift in the sectional balance of power in the country operated to reinforce the economic argument for greater exploitation of the nation's land resources, and federal land policy became increasingly liberal. Tariffs on manufactures were not, however, eliminated.

The clashing and shifting of sectional interests over land policy undeniably contributed to the pattern of policy evolution in the antebellum years. But it should not be concluded that sectional interests as perceived at the time were necessarily correct. Alexander Hamilton, the architect of many of the new nation's economic policies and an ardent advocate of tariffs and subsidies to aid manufacturers, saw that manufacturing development and agricultural development were complementary, not opposed. Hamilton, in fact, recommended in 1790 that federal lands be sold to the public at the low price of thirty cents per acre. He foresaw what was later to become fact—a prosperous and growing agriculture that served as a source of abundant food and raw materials for the manufacturing sector and as a great market for manufactured products. For example, much of the benefit to the United States of increasing cotton production on new lands in the South was reaped by northeastern manufacturers in the form of lower raw cotton prices. And the farmers and their families engaged in the more specialized agriculture that was emerging in the South and the West soon furnished an important component of the demand for factory-produced cloth.

What is to be made of the fear of manufacturers that cheap land would harm manufacturing by raising wages? It was largely ungrounded for two reasons. In the first place, tariff protection was granted and remained in effect at varying levels from 1789 on. By allowing American manufacturers to charge higher prices, the tariff provided a cushion against wage pressures. Second, labor supplies available to manufacturers increased sufficiently to prevent wages from becoming high enough to be a drawback to manufacturing growth. Indeed, agricultural expansion was partially responsible for the increased labor supply, for as the West developed on better and more abundant land, farms in the Northeast were abandoned and many farm workers took jobs in manufacturing. Also, while the free flow of manufactured goods to America from abroad was interfered with by tariff policies, the flow of immigrant labor was encouraged by America's liberal immigration policies. Immigrant workers swelled the supply of industrial labor. Thus, in conjunction with federal tariff and immigration policies, Hamilton's broad view of

the national interest in cheap land was vindicated in the notable antebellum progress made by both agriculture and manufacturing. In economic theory, a cheapening of land, by attracting labor into agriculture, raises manufacturing wage levels provided everything else remains constant. In economic history, however, everything else constantly changes.

Agricultural Development: Abundant Land, Growing Markets, and Slave Labor

Although America's increasingly liberal land policies were controversial in many respects, there is little reason for doubting that the policies favored the growth of agriculture. As with most of the world's people two centuries ago, the experience and skills of Americans were overwhelmingly those of the farmer. The availability of land on progressively easier terms would have been expected to draw an ever-increasing number of Americans into agriculture as a traditional and appealing way of life. With the coming of the industrial and transportation revolutions, however, agriculture began to become less a highly individualistic and independent way of life and more an increasingly specialized and market-oriented business.

Agriculture was far and away the dominant economic activity in the United States before the Civil War, and in absolute terms the expansion of agriculture was remarkable. The number of farms and total farm output are estimated to have increased sixfold between 1800 and 1860. During these same decades, the agricultural labor force quadrupled. On the eve of the Civil War, agriculture accounted for about three-fifths of the nation's total production of commodities. In terms of value added (the measure of a sector's contribution to the national product), the agricultural sector was nearly twice as large as the manufacturing sector in 1859.

Equally significant to an understanding of the nature of antebellum economic development, however, is agriculture's relative decline. At the beginning of the nineteenth century, approximately five out of every six American workers labored in agriculture. By 1860, this proportion had fallen to just over one out of two. And while the value added by agricultural commodity production in 1859 was still nearly twice that of manufacturing, just two decades earlier it had been about three times larger.

In this context of absolute expansion and relative decline, America's farmers made a great contribution to the nation's early economic development. They provided increasing supplies of food and raw material to themselves and, more important, to the nation's growing nonagricultural sectors and foreign customers. Agricultural expansion also provided a major source of demand for the products of other sectors, notably transportation services and manufactured goods. Last, but by no means less important, increases in the productivity of agriculture meant that an expanding proportion of the nation's labor force could be released from agricultural pursuits to find employment in nonagricultural activities. The antebellum release of labor from agriculture (in relative terms) was particularly pronounced during the three decades from 1820 to 1850, when agriculture's share of the nation's labor force declined from 79 percent to 55 percent. This momentous shift toward economic diversification reflected the youthful vigor of an economy just entering modernization.

Agriculture in the 1790s

In the last decade of the eighteenth century, American agriculture was similar to what it had been in colonial times. In the South, tobacco continued as the major cash crop, while in the Middle Atlantic and New England states, general grain and livestock farming pre-

dominated. To a great extent, agricultural production was destined for on-farm consumption or for sale in local or nearby markets. Production for larger markets was confined to areas in the vicinity of coastal port cities and to the export-oriented, staple-producing areas of the South. The latter included the Chesapeake Bay area, which produced exportable surpluses of tobacco and grain, and the Atlantic coastal area from southern North Carolina to the Sea Islands of Georgia, where rice and long-staple cotton were the important cash crops.

Already in the 1790s, however, two forces were at work that would soon alter the pattern of American agriculture. One was Eli Whitney's invention of the cotton gin in 1793; it overcame a technical barrier to extensive and specialized production of short-staple upland cotton. Whitney's invention laid the foundation for the cotton kingdom of the antebellum South. The other impetus for agricultural change in the 1790s involved the New England and Middle Atlantic regions, where large numbers of people began to move out to the settlements on the western and northern frontiers of the original states and to the territories beyond. A combination of factors contributed to this movement: population growth in the settled eastern areas, the availability of cheap and fertile land on the frontier, and a striving for the cherished independence of family farming. These factors, along with the cotton gin and improved transportation, were the proximate causes of the great northern and southern migrations to the West that shaped the development of American agriculture in the following decades.

The Cotton Economy of the South (1793–1860)

When Whitney solved the problem of removing the seeds from short-staple cotton plants, virtually all the conditions were present in the

American South for one of the greatest expansions of specialized agriculture in recorded history. In the three decades from 1763 to 1793, a series of remarkable English inventions for the spinning of cotton yarn by means of power-driven machinery in centralized factories created the first great manufacturing industry of the Industrial Revolution. At that time, much of the world's production and consumption of cotton took place in Asia, particularly in India. The expansion of English cotton mills created a new demand for raw cotton and resulted in sharply rising cotton prices. Before Whitney's invention, American participation in the growing international cotton market had been limited to production of the high-quality, long-staple cotton that could be grown along the coasts of Georgia and South Carolina. It was not difficult to remove the smooth seeds from this variety of cotton,

COTTON-GIN.

The Cotton Gin.   Eli Whitney's (1765–1825) invention in 1793 provided the solution to removing seeds from cotton lint at a time when the demand for raw cotton was growing rapidly because of British breakthroughs in textile manufacturing. The invention changed cotton from a minor U.S. crop into the nation's leading export, and it breathed new life into the institution of slavery. (Culver Pictures)

but the area in which it could be produced was small. Short-staple cotton, however, could be grown in a much larger area, extending from southern Virginia through the Carolinas, Georgia, Tennessee, Alabama, Mississippi, and into the later acquisitions of Louisiana, Arkansas, and Texas.

In addition to an expanding market for cotton, the South was favored with numerous navigable rivers that, although not ideal avenues of transportation, were more than adequate for moving cotton, a crop that had a relatively high value in relation to its bulk. The situation with regard to the traditional economic factors of production—land, labor, and capital—was equally propitious. Cotton could be grown over an extensive area—land that was still largely unsettled at the end of the eighteenth century. A slave labor force easily adaptable to cotton culture was already present in the South, and the declining attractiveness of the tobacco, rice, and indigo cultures made the use of slaves in cotton cultivation both feasible and profitable. Finally, the fact that cotton was a major cash crop meant that its growers would be able to accumulate the capital and have access to the credit they would need to carry on an expanding agricultural operation.

The cotton kingdom of the South expanded by leaps and bounds. In 1793, the year Whitney unveiled his gin, American cotton production was about five million pounds, mostly of the long-staple or Sea Island variety, and amounted to less than 1 percent of the world's production. By the first years of the nineteenth century, it had increased to over forty million pounds, about half of which was exported, mainly to Great Britain. Thereafter, production approximately doubled each decade until 1860, reaching some two billion pounds by the close of the antebellum era (see Figure 6–3; a bale of cotton weighed about four hundred pounds). By 1830, the southern United States produced about one-half of the world's supply of cotton; by the 1850s, this fraction had risen to two-

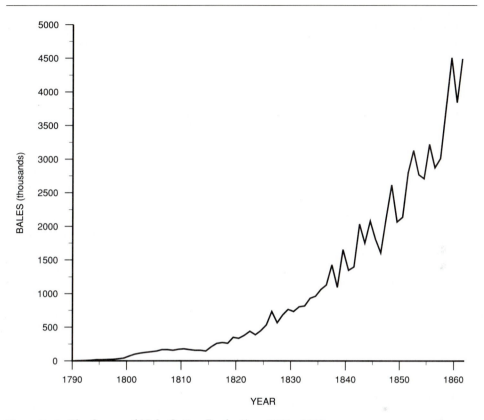

Figure 6–3 *The Course of U.S. Cotton Production, 1791–1861*
SOURCE: Data from U.S. Bureau of the Census, *Historical Statistics of the United States,*
Bicentennial Edition (Washington, D.C.: GPO, 1975).

thirds. After the War of 1812, exports typically absorbed at least 75 percent of the crop. Cotton became the nation's dominant export, often accounting for over half the value of all American exports.

The growing worldwide demand for cotton and the seemingly limitless supply of land on which it could be grown contributed to a pattern of intensive land use by continuous cropping and, as soil fertility declined in the older states, to a westward shift of production. Antebellum writers as well as latter-day historians often comment unfavorably on this pattern of land use, but given the abundance of land and the mobility of the southern population, it

likely was a wise decision at the time. Thomas Jefferson, a paragon of rational thinking, remarked that it was usually cheaper and more efficient to buy new land than to restore depleted soils with fertilizer.[1] His fellow southerners generally followed his advice, as can be seen in the westward movement of the cotton kingdom. South Carolina was the leading producer into the 1820s; then Georgia assumed the mantle. By the 1830s, Alabama and Mississippi were the leading producers, a position they kept until the Civil War. Tennessee had been one of the four leading cotton producers in the 1820s, but gave way to Louisiana in subsequent decades. Although the center of production gradually moved west, the antebellum cotton kingdom essentially consisted of the five states of South Carolina, Georgia, Alabama, Mississippi, and Louisiana. Throughout the period, these five states of the Lower South accounted for over three-fourths of total American cotton production.

The Diversity of Southern Agriculture

Although cotton was the leading cash crop of the Lower South and at times an important source of income in some areas of the Upper South, the southern agricultural economy was far larger, more complex, and more diversified than is implied by the term *cotton economy.* There were two broad aspects of the South's agricultural diversity. First, a number of cash crops besides cotton were produced in sufficient quantity to make foreign markets and domestic markets outside of the South important to southern farmers. Second, the South produced large quantities of products like corn, wheat, livestock, vegetables, and fruits for home consumption on the farm or for sale at local markets within the South. Recent scholarship has demonstrated that, contrary to earlier assumptions, the antebellum South was largely self-sufficient in food production despite its emphasis on producing cash crops for sale in distant markets.[2]

Southern cash crops, in addition to cotton, included tobacco, rice, sugar, hemp, flax, and even wheat until the 1840s and 1850s, when the center of wheat production shifted to the states of the old Northwest. Unlike cotton, which could be grown over a large area of the South and planted in millions of acres, the other cash crops were grown in limited areas where climate and soil made their culture feasible. Tobacco, along with rice a major market crop of the colonial era, originally had been cultivated intensively in the tidewater area of the Chesapeake Bay in Virginia and Maryland. However, it had taken a heavy toll from the

soil, and this led to a shift of tobacco production into the Piedmont region of Virginia and North Carolina. The development of a mild, bright-leaf variety of tobacco and of the process of flue curing in the late antebellum years helped to revive a tobacco culture that had been stagnating since the American Revolution. Across the Appalachians, Kentucky and Tennessee also became leading tobacco producers before the Civil War.

From colonial times through the antebellum period, rice production was concentrated in a small area within a few miles of the Atlantic Coast in South Carolina and Georgia. The crop was grown on large plantations that made intensive use of slave labor. Much of the American rice crop was exported to West Indian and European markets.

After the American Revolution, French settlers in Louisiana developed economical processes for making sugar from the sugar cane plant, which grew well along the Mississippi River near New Orleans. The Louisiana Purchase in 1803 created a favored American market. There ensued a rapid growth of sugar production in southern Louisiana. Because expensive equipment was required for refining sugar, large plantations using slave labor tended to dominate the business, but many smaller planters also participated. Most of the sugar produced found its way into the domestic American market. This domestic-market orientation, along with the large capital investment needed to produce sugar, perhaps explains why sugar was one of the few agricultural products favored with tariff protection. (Wool, produced chiefly in the North for domestic consumption, was another.)

Wheat, not usually thought of as a southern cash crop, was actually quite important to the states of the Upper South right up to the Civil War. Virginia, for example, was the nation's fourth-largest producer in 1839, following Ohio, Pennsylvania, and New York. By 1859, Virginia had even passed New York and Pennsylvania in wheat output, although in that year the western states of Illinois, Indiana, and Wisconsin had assumed leadership. The emergence of wheat as a major crop in Virginia, Maryland, and, to some extent, North Carolina was in part a response to problems with tobacco: soil exhaustion and stagnant demand. Wheat represented a move toward diversification and mixed farming. Major markets for southern wheat were in the Northeast. Small amounts were sent to the Lower South, although it appears that these areas, usually identified with cotton specialization, were able to meet a large part of their own needs for wheat and flour. Kentucky and Tennessee also produced wheat surpluses, and it is likely that this wheat, rather than wheat from the Northwest, satisfied the remaining needs of the cotton and sugar areas of the lower Southwest.

Even more important to the diversified nature of antebellum southern agriculture was corn production. Corn was grown nearly everywhere in the United States—North and South—and in 1849, for example, a southern corn planting of some eighteen million acres was far in excess of the five million acres planted to cotton. In some antebellum years, moreover, the value of the southern corn crop exceeded the combined values of the South's cotton, tobacco, sugar, and rice crops. Unlike these crops, corn was not often sold for cash or shipped in large quantities to distant markets. Rather, it was a principal food for slaves and livestock and was largely consumed where it was produced.

Economic historians once argued that specialization on staple crops for export led to the South becoming a food-deficit area, and that the newer states of the Northwest developed agriculturally and commercially in order to supply the South's food requirements.[3] This view no longer is tenable, for the South's plantations and farms largely met their own needs and supplied food to the southern nonagricultural population. However, this does not imply that the South's degree of agricultural specialization was less complete or efficient than it might have been. The nature of agricultural production in the South made food self-sufficiency a rational choice. The South's cash crops required relatively great amounts of labor at concentrated times in the production cycle, usually at the harvest. During other times of the year, the labor of free farmers or slaves would have been underemployed if it had not been engaged in growing corn and other foods or in tending livestock. In other words, it would have been wasteful for the South not to have grown its own food supplies.

Slavery: Economics and Morality

No single aspect of American economic history has given rise to more controversy than the antebellum South's "peculiar institution" of black slavery. And none has been more altered in its interpretation by the scholarship of recent decades. Older interpretations of the southern slave economy often emphasized its inefficiency and economic irrationality. Planters' investments in slaves were thought to be unprofitable or, if profitable, only within the context of a stagnant southern economy that could barely overcome the poor work incentives of slaves by treating them in a harsh and degrading manner. These past contentions have been refuted by more recent interpretations.[4] The southern economy was not stagnant in the antebellum years, and its slave labor system, however deplorable on other grounds, apparently contributed to the South's overall economic prosperity. It was a prosperity, however, that was much less evenly shared than it would have been without slavery.

In thinking about southern slavery it is important to recognize that until about two centuries ago, with certain important exceptions, slavery was not thought of as an abnormal or illegitimate institution. Its roots were ancient and it had existed over wide areas of the world. Europeans introduced African slaves into the New World at the beginning of the sixteenth century, primarily to work on sugar plantations. The relative insignificance of sugar production in the North American colonies and in the United States in its early years explains why this area received only a small fraction, about one in sixteen, of the millions of Africans brought to the New World during the three and one-half centuries after 1500. Before the 1790s, most of the slaves in North America (about 90 percent of the total) were concentrated near the Atlantic tidewater from Maryland to Georgia and worked on plantations where tobacco, rice, and indigo were the major cash crops. In the first years of the United States, markets for these crops were not expanding and southern planters on the whole showed no great and irrevocable attachment to the institution of slavery. At the Constitutional Convention of 1787, slavery was an issue open to compromise. In the northern states, which had about 10 percent of the slave population in 1780, schemes providing for gradual emancipation were enacted into law before 1805.

Then came the cotton gin. The rapidly expanding market for American cotton that it helped to create injected new vigor into the institution of slavery. Thus, in the same era that the ideals of political liberty and individual freedom were translated into action through great revolutions and the beginnings of the slave emancipation movement, slavery was becoming more entrenched in the American South. Through the constitutional compromise of 1787, the import of slaves into the United States could be—and was by later legislation—made illegal after 1807. Nonetheless, the American slave population grew steadily, mostly through natural increase, from about one million in 1800 to two million in 1830 and to nearly four million in 1860. Paralleling

Plantation Slavery. This early photo shows a gang of slave workers in South Carolina returning from the cotton fields with their pickings. Evident here are signs of labor regimentation, which possibly contributed to the relatively high productivity of plantation agriculture. Note also the nearly equal number of men and women in the picking gang, as well as the presence of children and at least one infant-in-arms. (Photograph by B.N. Barnard, The New York Historical Society)

the westward migration in the North, southern planters and their slaves moved west in these years in response to the expanding demand for cotton and the availability of land.

The vigorous expansion of the slave economy along with a growing anti-slavery movement complicated the politics of land at the federal level. There were eleven slave states and eleven free states in the Union as of 1819. To maintain this balance of interests in the U.S. Senate, slave and free states were admitted in pairs, starting with the Missouri Compromise of 1820, when Missouri (a slave state) was paired with Maine (a free state). By 1850, there were fifteen slave states and fifteen free states. The huge territorial acquisitions of 1845 to 1848 increased the conflict between those who sought to maintain and extend slavery and those who desired to abolish it everywhere. A decade later, Americans in both the North and South decided that slavery was an issue that would no longer permit a peaceful compromise.

The nearly four million slaves of 1860 were owned by fewer than 400,000 persons. Less than one-third of southern families, in fact, held slaves. The slaveholders were greatly outnumbered by small, nonslaveholding planters and yeoman farmers. Slaveholders nevertheless dominated the economic, political, and social life of the South and exercised great power in national affairs. This resulted from their inherited wealth, social position, and control of southern policies, but it was also based on incomes and wealth that continued to increase throughout the antebellum years as the result of a cotton boom unique in history.

Slave agriculture appears to have been more efficient than free agriculture in the sense that slave farms on the average produced more output (in value terms) with given inputs of land, labor, and capital than did free farms. What was the secret of this efficiency? A clue is provided in the finding that the most efficient of all American farms were the larger plantations utilizing great numbers of slaves. In short, there were economies of large-scale production in southern agriculture, although their extent is still debated by economic historians. These economies resulted from the high degree of specialization that large-scale production facilitated as well as from the management practices that coordinated it. On plantations, slaves specialized in a great variety of agricultural tasks (e.g., plowing, hoeing, seeding, ginning) and nonagricultural jobs (e.g., carpentry, blacksmithing, cooking, child care). Field labor was performed by groups of specialized gangs, particularly in planting and cultivating operations, which worked with a rhythm and intensity that made them highly

interdependent. This specialization and intensity of work, along with managerial coordination, apparently explains the finding that slave agriculture on plantations was relatively efficient compared to nonslave agriculture in the South and North. Figure 6–4 shows the antebellum course of cotton and slave prices and of slave productivity, i.e., cotton output per slave. The similarities of trends and fluctuations indicate market mechanisms at work.

The efficiency of large-scale slave agriculture raises the important question of why free farmers did not strive for similar efficiency by organizing their production in the same way. The answer appears to be that the gains in efficiency and output were not sufficient to compensate free people for the drudgery and intensity of effort required to achieve them. Slaves, in contrast, had no real choice but to do what the slaveholders required. This does not necessarily mean that the material conditions of life for slaves were exceptionally harsh or cruel. Indeed, some scholars contend that the food, clothing, and shelter accorded adult working slaves, while lacking the variety free people chose, did not differ much in terms of basic necessities (e.g., nutrition) from that of free workers—at least the poorer ones—of the same era.[5] These findings are not especially surprising. Slaveholders had a substantial portion of their capital invested in slave workers, so it was to their economic advantage to see that this capital was well maintained. Exceptions to such rational behavior have, of course, been documented. A most important recent finding is that slave children tended to have low weights at birth and high infant mortality. Evidence on the stature of slave children who survived infancy suggests that they were malnourished. The likely explanation is that slave mothers were overworked both before and after they gave birth.[6]

Who benefited from the efficiency gains created by the denial of freedom to the black population of the South? The planter slaveholders

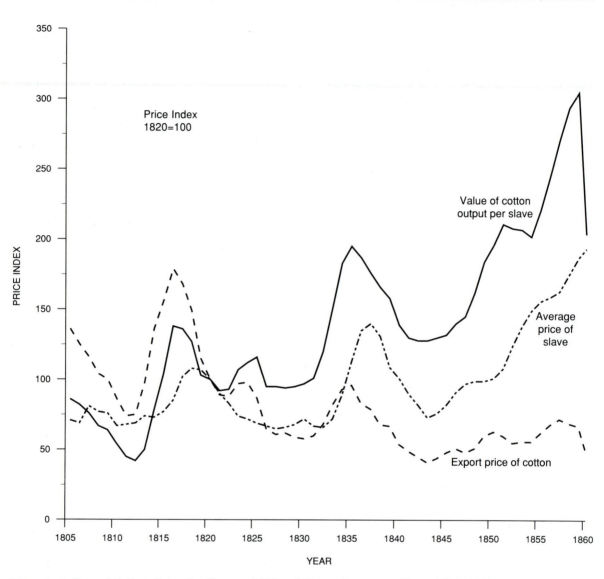

Figure 6–4 *Price of Cotton, Price of a Slave, and Value of Cotton Output per Slave, 1805–1860*
SOURCE: Adapted from Roger Ransom, *Conflict and Compromise* (Cambridge: Cambridge University Press, 1989), p. 56.

reaped some of the gains but apparently not the major part of them. Agricultural production was a competitive business, and competition in both slave and product markets appears to have led to competitive returns of about 10 percent throughout the South on slave investments. Those families owning slaves in the period before slaves increased greatly in value (as slave imports were restricted and cotton demand grew) did better because they reaped capital gains on their slave assets. The major beneficiaries of slave exploitation were American and foreign consumers of the products produced by slave labor. The greater efficiency and larger output of slave plantations increased supplies and reduced prices for products like cotton to less than what they would have been without slavery. However, as indicated by the earlier discussion of why free farmers did not organize themselves on large-scale plantations, what the slaveholders and consumers of slave-produced products gained was more than offset by what the slaves lost in not having freedom to choose their own working conditions.

Although slavery was efficient in a narrow, economic productivity sense, it was less than optimal from the point of view of overall economic welfare. Free people could always produce more material goods by working under unpleasant conditions, but they chose not to. Slaves did not have that choice. In this sense, slavery represented a violation of America's professed ideals of individual liberty and equality of opportunity; it was, therefore, a fundamentally immoral inconsistency of early U.S. history. Both economic and moral arguments provided rationales for the ending of slavery. Unfortunately for the United States, valid economic arguments against slavery were not well understood in 1860, and in any case would not have appealed to those who considered slavery a legitimate institution. Their abolitionist opponents deemed slavery illegitimate, period. Consequently, the issue of slavery was resolved in a bloody civil war that set back for decades the once-prosperous agrarian economy of the South. The immoral slave labor system was ended, obtaining for African-Americans what has been called "one kind of freedom." Other kinds of freedom, from racial discrimination and poverty, for example, would prove more elusive.

Northern Agricultural Development

During the pre-Civil War period, agricultural progress in the northern states was more grad-ual and less dramatic than in the southern cotton economy. The reasons for the contrast follow from our discussion earlier in the chapter of the South's extremely fortunate situation following the invention of the cotton gin in 1793. No invention of similar economic impact was brought forward to release the latent productivity of northern soils. Also, northern inland transportation facilities, particularly for bulky, low-value agricultural commodities, were slow to develop in the early years of the Republic. Largely as a result of inadequate transportation, markets for northern farm products were rather limited in comparison with the international markets enjoyed by southern staples. Indeed, self-sufficiency and lack of specialization characterized much of northern farming, although even in the colonial era local and regional markets were features of farm life in areas of early settlement.

The contrast with the South should, therefore, not be overdone. As in the South, abundant virgin land lay within the borders of the original states and just beyond them. The North, even more than the South, possessed a population of energetic and individualistic agriculturalists who were willing to undertake the arduous task of pioneering settlement on this western land. And, perhaps because of necessity in the face of greater natural and economic obstacles, the North developed a greater sense of community will in tackling, for example, its problems of transportation.

The earliest pioneering in the northern area of the new nation occurred in northern New England and in western Pennsylvania and New York. After 1800, the turnpike movement encouraged the settlement process by providing improved facilities for moving settlers west and their surplus commodities east. A more significant impact of turnpikes, however, was in encouraging greater agricultural specialization and production for market in the settled eastern areas. The improved roads enlarged the agricultural areas that could supply growing cities and towns in the Northeast.

The overriding importance of transportation facilities in stimulating western agricultural development is clearly evident in the early settlement of the Ohio River Valley. This occurred while substantial acreages of unsettled land still remained in northwestern Pennsylvania and western New York. The reason was the advantage of water over land transportation. Even with primitive flatboat and keelboat technologies, the advantage of water travel was so great that it was more efficient to move most western agricultural products to eastern markets over several thousand miles of water than over a few hundred miles of land. The relative efficiency of waterway transport was very much on the minds of proponents of steamboating and canal building.

The gradual development of transportation and markets for northern farmers led to an equally gradual movement toward greater specialization. For much of the antebellum period, agricultural production on many northern farms in both the East and West was nonspecialized. Individual farmers grew several different crops and raised a number of varieties of animals. While such diversification perhaps reduced risks and was attuned to the farm family's manifold needs, it did not promote productivity by economizing on the range of knowledge needed to farm efficiently. The process of becoming a farmer was in many ways more complicated in the North than in the South. A young man, for example, might work for a time as a farm laborer, perhaps on his parents' farm, and accumulate as best he could the range of knowledge and the funds required to obtain his own farm. Then he would face the choice of buying a developed farm in the East, a partially developed farm near the frontier, or virgin land on the frontier. Growing numbers of farmers often chose one of the two latter alternatives; among the reasons were the facts that the soil improved and the costs of land fell as one moved westward.

After 1820, eighty acres of land in the West could be purchased for as little as $100 from the federal government. The estimated total cost of establishing a farm was from five to ten times the cost of acquiring the land. A good part of this expense, especially in the forested areas east of the Illinois prairie, represented the value of a settler's own labor employed in clearing and fencing the land and erecting buildings on it. Farmers' direct labor investment economized on cash outlays in an era when credit facilities were underdeveloped, but it also meant that several years passed before as much land was cleared as could profitably be tilled. Prairie farming required more cash for breaking the tougher soils and purchasing fencing materials; developed at a later time, it gained feasibility from the establishment of better-organized product and credit markets. The railroad, which penetrated the prairies in the 1850s, played a large role in this development.

The influence of transportation improvements on northern agriculture between 1790 and 1860 was also evident in the changing location of production centers and in greater specialization. Wheat, the leading breadstuff and chief cash crop of the northern states, was produced nearly everywhere in the earliest decades, mostly for farm consumption and local marketing. Improved roads and, especially, the completion of the Erie Canal caused wheat production to become concentrated in the western sections of New York and Pennsylvania as well as in Ohio during the 1820s and 1830s. In 1839, these three states produced about one-half of the nation's wheat crop of eighty-five million bushels. Two decades later, the extension of railroads into the West led to another major shift: In 1859, the wheat crop was over twice as large as it had been in 1839, and Illinois, Indiana, and Wisconsin were now its leading producers, together accounting for one-third of the total national production. The combined share of Ohio, Pennsylvania, and

New York fell to 22 percent. (The decline was not merely relative, for each state produced fewer bushels in 1859 than it had in 1839.)

Although wheat in the North and cotton in the South were the nation's leading market crops, corn was actually the nation's greatest crop and was grown practically everywhere. In 1859, the corn crop in bushels was nearly five times that of wheat. Used mostly as animal feed, corn was also an important part of the diet of farmers, both slave and free. The pattern of shifting corn production was somewhat different from that of wheat, but the direction was the same. The first reliable data, for 1839, reveal that the leading corn-producing states were not in the North but rather in the upper tier of the South—Tennessee, Kentucky, and Virginia. Ten years later, Ohio assumed leadership, and by 1860 the center of corn production had shifted to Illinois.

The ubiquity of corn production as well as the production of grasses and other forage materials meant that livestock raising was feasible in nearly all agricultural areas. Nonetheless, specialized producing areas developed quite early. Cattle and hogs raised in the Ohio Valley were driven overland to eastern seaboard cities well before the canal era. In this period, Cincinnati emerged as a leading center of pork packing, with the meat products moving to market down the Ohio and Mississippi rivers. Under the pervading influence of transportation improvements, a gradual westward shift of livestock production followed. Chicago, on the basis of its growing rail connections, developed into a leading shipping point for livestock and meat products in the 1850s. The greatest gains in western livestock production and meat packing, however, occurred after the Civil War under the influence of further railroad extensions and the invention of the refrigerated freight car. In the antebellum years, most of the meat consumed in a given region was also produced in that region.

Recognition that livestock and meat production did not shift westward as rapidly as grain production, or with quite the force, provides insight into how the older farming areas of the Northeast responded to western agricultural growth. Their loss of comparative advantage in grain did not entail a corresponding loss in the raising of cattle and hogs for consumers of fresh meat. As the grain belt moved farther west, sheep raising (mainly for wool but also for meat) provided another outlet for the farmers left behind, particularly in the hilly areas of New England and New York but also in Ohio. Eastern dairy farming also expanded in response to lost grain markets. Initially, butter and cheese were the main marketable products, with fresh milk and the by-products of butter and cheese making consumed by the farm family and its hogs. The spreading network of eastern railroads in the 1830s and 1840s, however, created the possibility of shipping fresh milk from farms to cities located some distance away; the result was a substantial boost to dairy farming. Growing fresh fruits and vegetables for urban markets was also stimulated by rail transportation. A diversified and market-oriented agriculture thus developed in the older states to help solve the problems created by the agricultural progress of the West. Mixed farming represented a creative response to changing market conditions.

Agricultural Technology and Productivity

Between 1790 and 1860, improvements in transportation and the consequent growth of markets wrought a revolution in American agriculture. Farming changed from a way of life for most of the American people to an increasingly specialized business for about half of them. The sheer magnitude and diversity of the nation's agricultural enterprise, along with its highly decentralized organizational structure, make the task of generalizing about technological progress and agricultural productivity both difficult and important. The overall impression one gains is that of substantial progress in output, techniques, and productivity as markets grew. Because of the highly competitive nature and rapid expansion of agricultural production in these decades, the major beneficiaries of agricultural progress may not have been the farmers but the growing numbers of nonfarm people who obtained cheap food and raw materials from the farms and sold back to them much of their output of nonagricultural goods and services.

The antebellum era is often viewed by agricultural historians as setting the stage for an agricultural revolution marked by the widespread application of horse-powered machinery during the two or three decades after 1860. There is validity in this view, but it has had the unfortunate effect of leading many scholars to disregard or play down the significant technological progress made in earlier decades. In a few cases, this progress was quite dramatic. The cotton gin revolutionized southern agriculture as early as the 1790s. Steam power was introduced on the plantation sugar mills of Louisiana in the 1820s, and in short order most of the cane crop was processed with the aid of steam engines. The horse-drawn reaper for harvesting wheat and small grain crops was applied on a large scale during the 1850s. In each of these cases, an existing or rapidly emerging market played a crucial role in the widespread adoption of an impressive new technique.

The more gradual widening of markets for other agricultural products was marked by less dramatic but nonetheless effective technical advances. For much of the antebellum period, hand tools—hoes, forks, rakes, scythes, and axes, for example—were major implements, and they were continually improved through better designs and the use of new materials. The nation's abundance of land, however, exerted a powerful influence on the development of animal-powered implements and machines

that could till more acres with fewer laborers. In preharvest operations as well—soil preparation, seeding, and cultivating—significant inventive and innovative progress was made. Plows were transformed from crude, multipurpose tools to specialized implements for different types of plowing and varied soil conditions. Wooden plows with a few iron parts gave way to cast-iron plows and then to steel plows by the late 1830s; they allowed more land to be plowed with less effort. Horse-drawn cultivators and seeding machines were developed, although not widely applied, before 1840.

In harvesting operations, similar sequences emerged. Grain cradles supplanted sickles and scythes and in turn gave way to the horse-powered rakes in haymaking. In the earlier decades, limited markets and the availability to farmers of free time during the winter months made threshing with simple flails and corn shelling by hand feasible postharvest activities. But from the 1830s onward, machines of varying complexity began to take over these tasks.

While the greatest development of organized science and education in the service of agriculture came later, the antebellum years witnessed a growth of technical and economic informational channels commensurate with the importance of agriculture in the economy. The ubiquitous general newspaper often devoted space to agricultural topics and market conditions. From the 1820s on, this role was more and more fulfilled by specialized agricultural periodicals (which grew to have a combined circulation of about 350,000 by 1860). Agricultural societies and fairs also spread information and encouraged improved farming practices. Starting in the 1830s, the federal Patent Office began to collect and distribute both seeds and general agricultural information. By the 1850s, its annual reports on agriculture received wide distribution.

Improved transportation and wider markets encouraged westward movement onto more fertile lands. This, along with better techniques and information flows, led to increased agricultural specialization and growth in productivity. Significant progress was made before 1840, even though mechanization and the widespread use of animal power were still in their infancy. A study of labor productivity in the major crops—wheat, corn, and cotton—indicates steady gains between 1800 and 1840, even under the assumption that crop yields per acre did not improve during these four decades. In wheat production, for instance, hours of labor per 100 bushels are estimated to have fallen from 373 hours in 1800 to 233 hours in 1840, an improvement of 38 percent. Much of the gain was due to more efficient harvesting, where hours of labor per acre fell from 40 hours to 23 hours. Over the same four decades, hours of labor per 100 bushels of corn declined from 344 hours to 276 hours, a 20 percent gain in labor productivity. Finally, hours of labor per bale of cotton declined from 601 hours to 439 hours; most of this 27 percent productivity gain was the result of a drop—from 135 hours to 90 hours of labor per acre—in the time required for preharvesting (i.e., plowing, planting, and cultivating).[7]

With land and capital inputs expanding faster than the farm labor-force input, one would expect to find similar increases in agricultural labor productivity. However, one study of *total* factor productivity—a measure of output per weighted unit of all three inputs—indicates notable efficiency gains before 1840.[8] The average rates of total productivity growth

for the 1820s and 1830s were estimated at over 1 percent per year. These rates are at best only suggestive because of measurement problems and the lack of adjustment for relatively good or poor crops in the decade years surveyed, but they do indicate that improvements in agricultural efficiency between 1820 and 1840 compare favorably with those for other decades of the century. Coming largely before the advent of widespread mechanization, the gains are testimony to the substantial effects of transport improvements and market growth in bringing about a more intensive application and efficient allocation of resources in agriculture.

Early gains in agricultural efficiency were instrumental in promoting the increasingly diversified nature of economic activity in antebellum America as well as in bringing about sustained increases in incomes and material welfare. In these years, agriculture was the nation's biggest business, the major supplier of food and raw materials, and the chief market for a wide range of nonagricultural goods and services. Agriculture's absolute expansion increased greatly these sources of both supply and demand. If agriculture had merely expanded without becoming more efficient, however, it is clear that economic development would have proceeded much more slowly than it actually did. Gains in agricultural efficiency were among the major forces that allowed forty-five out of one hundred American workers to labor outside of agriculture in 1850, whereas just three decades earlier, in 1820, only twenty-one out of one hundred workers were in nonagricultural employments.

Summary

In the land policy and agricultural developments of the young United States, different levels of decision making complemented one another. Decisions to acquire a public domain and to set the terms for disposing of it, thereby encouraging its use as an economic resource, were centralized at the national governmental level. In these fundamental decisions, there was a preference for uniform national policies in regard to the nation's most abundant resource. After the basic centralized decisions were made, however, other issues (such as land ownership and use) were left to competitive markets and individuals to resolve through decentralized decision making. The centralized decisions helped Americans avoid such problems as differing concepts of owner-

ship and land tenure and such uncertainties as the terms under which land might be acquired and used. The scope of decentralized decision making allowed for individuals' specialized knowledge of time and place to guide the nation's land resources into economically efficient uses. As a result of these decision-making approaches, the United States did not experience many of the disincentives that hindered agricultural development elsewhere in the world.

Endnotes

1. Cited in Paul W. Gates, *The Farmer's Age: 1815–1860* (New York: Holt, 1960), p. 101.
2. See the discussions of self-sufficiency in Gavin Wright, *Political Economy of the Cotton South*, and Robert Fogel, *Without Consent or Contract* (full citations in *Suggested Readings* at end of this chapter).
3. See Douglass C. North, *The Economic Growth of the United States, 1790–1860* (Englewood Cliffs, NJ: Prentice-Hall, 1961).
4. The old and new interpretations are discussed at length in Robert W. Fogel and Stanley Engerman, *Time on the Cross*, and Robert W. Fogel, *Without Consent or Contract* (full citations in *Suggested Readings* at end of this chapter).
5. See Fogel and Engerman, *Time on the Cross*, Chapter 4.
6. See Richard H. Steckel, "A Peculiar Population: The Nutrition, Health, and Mortality of American Slaves from Childhood to Maturity," *Journal of Economic History* 46 (September 1976), and Steckel, "Birth Weights and Infant Mortality Among American Slaves," *Explorations in Economic History* 23 (April 1986).
7. See U.S. Department of Agriculture, *Progress of Farm Mechanization*, Miscellaneous Publication No. 630 (October 1947).
8. Robert E. Gallman, "Changes in Total U.S. Agricultural Factor Productivity in the Nineteenth Century," *Agricultural History*, 46 (January 1972): table 8, p. 208.

Suggested Readings

On land policy, two general works are Benjamin H. Hibbard, *A History of the Public Land Policies* (New York: Macmillan, 1924), and Roy M. Robbins, *Our Landed Heritage: The Public Domain, 1776–1936* (Princeton, N.J.: Princeton University Press, 1942). An incisive shorter treatment of the major issues is found in Lance Davis et al., "The Land, Minerals, Water, and Forests," in *American Economic Growth: An Economist's History of the United States* (New York: Harper & Row, 1972), chap. 4; chap. 11 of this work, "Agriculture," is also useful. More specialized studies on land include Vernon Carstensen, ed., *The Public Lands: Studies in the History of the Public Domain* (Madison: University of Wisconsin Press, 1963), and Malcolm J.

Rohrbough, *The Land Office Business: The Settlement and Administration of American Public Lands, 1789–1837* (New York: Oxford University Press, 1968). For formal economic analyses of the impacts of abundant land on the antebellum economy, see Peter Passell, "The Impact of Cotton Land Distribution on the Antebellum Economy," *Journal of Economic History,* 21 (Dec. 1971); Peter Passell and Maria Schmundt, "Pre-Civil War Land Policy and the Growth of Manufacturing," *Explorations in Economic History,* 9 (Fall 1971); and Peter Passell and Gavin Wright, "The Effects of Pre-Civil War Territorial Expansion on the Price of Slaves," *Journal of Political Economy,* 80 (Nov.–Dec. 1972).

A valuable survey of antebellum agricultural developments is Paul W. Gates, *The Farmer's Age: Agriculture, 1815–1860* (New York: Holt, 1960). See also Darwin P. Kelsey, ed., *Farming in the New Nation: Interpreting American Agriculture* (Washington, D.C.: Agricultural History Society, 1972). On northern agriculture in these decades, see Clarence H. Danhof, *Change in Agriculture: The Northern United States, 1820–1870* (Cambridge, Mass.: Harvard University Press, 1969), James W. Whitaker, ed., *Farming in the Midwest, 1840–1900* (Washington, D.C.: Agricultural History Society, 1974), and Jeremy Atack and Fred Bateman, *To Their Own Soil: Agriculture in the Antebellum North* (Ames: Iowa State University Press, 1987). The market orientation of American farmers during colonial times and after independence is documented by Winifred B. Rothenberg, "The Market and Massachusetts Farmers, 1750–1855," *Journal of Economic History,* 41 (June 1981).

Antebellum southern agriculture and slavery have attracted generations of economic historians. A comprehensive classic is Lewis C. Gray, *History of Agriculture in the Southern United States to 1860,* 2 vols. (Washington, D.C.: Carnegie Institution, 1933). Other useful works include Stuart Bruchey, *Cotton and the Growth of the American Economy* (New York: Harcourt, 1967), and William N. Parker, ed., *The Structure of the Cotton Economy of the Antebellum South* (Washington, D.C.: Agricultural History Society, 1970). An important and controversial work on slavery is Robert W. Fogel and Stanley L. Engerman, *Time on the Cross: The Economics of American Negro Slavery* (Boston: Little, Brown, 1974); to see why it is controversial, see Paul A. David et al., *Reckoning with Slavery* (New York: Oxford University Press, 1978). A thoughtful and provocative analysis is Gavin Wright, *The Political Economy of the Cotton South* (New York: W. W. Norton, 1978). Wright's more recent book, *Old South, New South* (New York: Basic Books, 1986), discusses the impacts of the slave economy on later southern economic developments. Robert W. Fogel, in *Without Consent or Contract: The Rise and Fall of American Slavery* (New York: W. W. Norton, 1989), summarizes the protracted debate over slavery as an economic and social system, explores at length the antislavery movement that in the end prevailed, and provides a lengthy bibliography for further reading. Also helpful in tying together many of the complex issues that surrounded slavery is Roger L. Ransom, *Conflict and Compromise: The Political Economy of Slavery, Emancipation, and the American Civil War* (Cambridge: Cambridge University Press, 1989).

On agricultural technology and productivity, see especially Paul A. David, "The Mechanization of Reaping in the Antebellum Midwest," in Henry Rosovsky, ed., *Industrialization in Two Systems: Essays in Honor of Alexander Gerschenkron* (New York: Wiley, 1966); Robert E. Gallman, "Changes in Total U.S. Agricultural Factor Productivity in the Nineteenth Century," *Agricultural History,* 46 (Jan. 1972); and U.S. Department of Agriculture, *Progress of Farm Mechanization,* Miscellaneous Publication No. 630 (Oct. 1947).

Chapter 7

Critical Changes in the Financial System

158

O
F ALL THE POLITICO-ECONOMIC DECISIONS THAT had to be made to create a truly independent United States, none were more crucial than those regarding (1) the nation's public finances and debts, (2) its monetary system, and (3) the role of government in the new and controversial activity of banking. Few areas of modern economic organization are more closely interrelated than these three, and in no other ones are the effects of governmental decisions on private economic activities more apparent and critical. Early American leaders, most notably Alexander Hamilton, understood these points; they proceeded to build a remarkably solid, though far from perfect, financial underpinning for the new nation. As financial problems arose in subsequent years, the interdependencies were less appreciated, and the United States proceeded in money, banking, and finance more by trial and error than by comprehensive reasoning and action. Fortunately for the nation, though, later experiments were predicated on the firm financial foundation laid during the first federal administration of 1789 to 1793. The debates and decisions of this creative period set the tone of American political economy for decades to come.

Early Federalist and Republican Financial Policies

The initial business of the First Congress, which met in the spring of 1789, was implementing its constitutional power so "to lay and collect taxes, duties, imports, and excises, to pay the debts and provide for the common defense and general welfare of the United States." After three months of deliberation, the Tariff Act of 1789 was passed and signed into law by President George Washington on July 4. Significantly, its stated objectives were not only to support the government and help pay its debts but also to encourage and protect manufactures. In addition, the Tariff Act favored U.S. shipping interests with a reduction of duties on goods imported on American vessels. The Tonnage Act, also passed in July 1789, extended this concept by calling for differentially high fees on foreign ships entering American ports. In effect, it restricted the fishing business and coastal trade of the United States to Americans.

The decision to make import duties the primary source of federal revenue initiated a policy that remained in effect for well over a century. Running counter to the powerful argument advanced by Adam Smith in 1776 that tariffs interfere with specialization and the division of labor, the tariff of 1789, even though its protectionist features were modest, opened up a veritable Pandora's box of politico-economic problems that preoccupied Americans for decades. Nonetheless, at the time the choice made sense. Internal taxes were politically unpopular and would have been difficult to collect, because the country was so large and thinly populated and because a market economy with widespread money transactions had not yet developed at most places within it. Tariffs, in contrast, were directed toward market transactions and could be collected at a relatively small number of seaports. In addition, they had the advantage of appearing to be taxes on foreign producers, though in reality they also were taxes on American consumers.

Origins of the National Debt

With a revenue provided for, the First Congress turned next to establishing a treasury department. A bill was drafted by Alexander Hamilton, who then became the first secretary of the treasury. Hamilton's first task as secretary was to report on and see through to enactment provisions for the support of the public credit of the United States. During the 1780s, the new nation's credit was poor indeed. A host of financial claims against both national and state governments remained after the American Revolution. They were a part of the price of independence that had not been paid, either to domestic or to foreign creditors. The confederation government in place before adoption of the Constitution was so strapped for funds that it often could not meet interest due on its debts, much less redeem any of the principal.

Hamilton's celebrated *Report on the Public Credit* of January 1790 estimated the nominal value of the national debt, including arrears of interest, at $54.1 million and of state debts at $15 million. Hamilton proposed that all of these obligations, incurred largely to finance the Revolution, be funded into long-term federal bonds with principal and interest guaranteed in specie—that is, metallic money. To do this, Hamilton argued, would make the federal government's credit so secure that money could easily be raised in case of future national emergencies. And, he continued, it would have the immediate effect of augmenting the nation's purchasing power with debt instruments that would be close substitutes for money.

After much debate, Hamilton's proposals were adopted in the Funding Act of August 1790. The federal government's proposed assumption of state debts was a particularly knotty issue in the debate. Some states had already discharged portions of their revolutionary war obligations and felt it unfair to be asked to pay, indirectly through federal revenues, the debts of others. To gain their assent, Hamilton struck a famous bargain with Thomas Jefferson and other southern leaders: In return for their support of the funding proposals, the nation's permanent capital would be located in the South—in a new federal capital on the banks of the Potomac River (rather than in New York or Philadelphia, the first and second federal capitals). More important in the short run, assumption relieved the states of

Alexander Hamilton (1755–1804). As first Secretary of the Treasury, 1789–1795, Hamilton in a few years transformed the new nation's finances from chaos to stability and strength. His vision of a strong federal government aiding the growth of a powerful and diversified economy was not shared by such eminent contemporaries and colleagues as Thomas Jefferson and James Madison, but most of his policies were adopted and proved successful. The description on this statue in front of the Treasury Department in Washington, D.C., reads: Soldier, orator, statesman, champion of constitutional union, representative government, and national integrity. (The Bettmann Archive)

heavy financial burdens and led to a wide diffusion of federal bonds, thereby strengthening the Union. However, it also required more revenue to pay interest than had been provided for in the Tariff Act. Hamilton's powers of persuasion again prevailed. In his *Report on the*

Public Credit, he recommended that additional revenue be raised by excise taxes on distilled spirits. His proposals were embodied in the Excise Act of March 1791, the first internal tax of the new government.

The Bank of the United States

Hamilton's first *Report on the Public Credit* hinted he would soon recommend that Congress establish a national bank. A report on that subject came in December 1790. At the time, there were only four state-chartered commercial banks in the United States. The bank proposed by Hamilton would be empowered to engage in the same lines of business as the other banks—discounting the bills of exchange and promissory notes of merchants, accepting deposits, and issuing bank notes that would serve as paper currency. But it was to be much larger than other banks and obligated to serve the federal government, which would own part of its capital stock. Hamilton stressed the bank's public functions: It would augment the nation's money supply by issuing several dollars of bank notes for each dollar of specie it held, serve as a source of short-term loans to the government, receive deposits of government funds and transfer them to places where they were to be expended, and support the public credit by increasing the value of the government's newly funded debt (since in Hamilton's comprehensive plan these securities could be used by private investors to subscribe for a large part of the bank's stock).

A controversial bill embodying Hamilton's bank proposal was passed by Congress in February 1791. The Bank of the United States was to be chartered for twenty years with a capital of $10 million, more than twice the combined capital of the several existing banks. The federal government would subscribe one-fifth of the capital, and the $8 million of private capital could be subscribed one-fourth in specie and three-fourths in government bonds. Passage of the bill did not, however, imply enactment. In the congressional debate, serious questions were raised as to the constitutionality of Hamilton's bank. When President Washington asked the secretary of state, Jefferson, and the attorney general, Edmund Randolph, for their advice, both were of the opinion that the bank was unconstitutional. In defense of the bank, Hamilton summoned all of his resourcefulness. His eleventh-hour opinion, upholding the bank's constitutionality, developed the doctrine of implied powers, holding that the federal government could implement measures not specifically forbidden by the Constitution in pursuance of that document's explicit objectives. Jefferson, in contrast, subscribed to the strict constructionist position, holding that the government could not take such an action unless it was specifically authorized by the Constitution. Washington was persuaded by Hamilton's argument and signed the bank bill into law. The bank controversy marked the beginning of a constitutional debate between strict and broad constructionists that has continued for two centuries.

The Dollar and Coinage

In the midst of congressional deliberations over the bank, Hamilton submitted the *Report on the Establishment of a Mint,* which, when embodied in the Coinage Act of 1792, defined the basic monetary unit of the United States and made provision for its supply. This was the least original of Hamilton's proposals in that it was based to a large extent on Jefferson's earlier recommendations adopted by the Confederation government. These had specified the dollar, a coin similar to the Spanish silver dollars widely circulating in America, as the unit of account, and had called for a decimal coinage including a $10 gold piece and small coins (cents and half-cents) of copper. The 1792 Coinage Act defined the dollar as containing 371.25 grains of pure silver and a $10 gold coin as containing 247.50 grains of pure gold. Smaller silver and gold coins as well as copper cents and half-cents were defined. The act established a mint that would coin gold and silver presented to it without charge and in unlimited quantities. Following provisions of the Constitution, gold and silver coins were made the only legal tender for all debts in the United States. The mint, located in Philadelphia, commenced operations in 1794.

The bimetallic coinage system thus adopted was to create many difficulties for the United States during the next century. Hamilton personally favored a monometallic system based on gold, but perhaps because of the Jeffersonian precedent and his own desire to increase the American money supply, he recommended bimetallism. The coinage ratio adopted by the United States implied that a dollar contained fifteen times as much silver as gold, which was very close to the market price ratio of the early 1790s. Had this parity of mint and market price ratios continued, bimetallism would have worked. But it was most unlikely to continue. Indeed, the price of silver in terms of gold soon fell, making it profitable for individuals to sell gold on world markets instead of bringing it to the U.S. mint. Few gold coins were in fact minted. Moreover, another tactical error made the U.S. silver dollar slightly lighter than the Spanish dollar. As a result, many of the newly minted American dollars were exported and exchanged at par for Spanish dollars that were then reminted into more American dollars, from whence this profitable operation could begin anew. Not wishing to supply everyone but Americans with U.S. silver dollars, President Jefferson in 1806 suspended their coinage. Americans rather paradoxically were forced to rely for many years on foreign coins and bank notes because of defects in their coinage laws.

The later history of American coinage is replete with attempts to cope with the nagging problems of bimetallism. In 1834 and 1837, the gold content of a dollar was reduced from one-fifteenth to about one-sixteenth of its silver content in an attempt to have both metals circulate in coined form. As the market ratio was in between these mint ratios, silver coins then became undervalued at the mint and soon began to disappear from the money stock. A de facto gold standard replaced the de facto silver standard of 1792 to 1834. This shift of policy had negative effects because a shortage of silver coins created real problems in small retail transactions. In 1853, Congress finally solved the problem by reducing the silver content of coins under a dollar, thereby creating a subsidiary or token coinage (i.e., a coinage worth less intrinsically than the value stamped on it by the government). The Coinage Act of 1853 effectively abolished bimetallism in the United States by withdrawing the right of citizens to unlimited coinage of silver and by restricting the legal tender of subsidiary silver coins to debts not exceeding $5. Foreign coins, which had possessed legal tender status from the earliest days of the Republic, lost this status in 1857.

A Solid Financial Underpinning for the United States

While Hamilton and his contemporaries failed to provide a lasting solution to coinage problems, in most other respects the Federalist financial policies were successful. The tariff, though modified on numerous occasions (most importantly by a temporary doubling of rates during the War of 1812), remained essentially a revenue measure until 1816. Its moderate rates, together with the remarkable growth of the nation's foreign commerce between 1793 and 1808, supplied the greater part of early federal revenue requirements. The funded debt appeared to have the immediate effect, predicted by Hamilton, of raising prices and stimulating commercial activity. And well it might, for it increased current wealth by creating credible drafts on the future. The Bank of the United States, with its home office in Philadelphia and branches in four, and later eight, major cities, proved quite useful to the government and the country. Besides performing fiscal functions for the Treasury Department, it supplied the country with a large quantity of paper currency redeemable in hard money and it acted to strengthen the nation's other banks and their note issues in a manner that had some aspects of modern central banking. Internal taxes—the excise on distilled liquors was supplemented by additional excise, documentary, and direct taxes in 1794, 1796, and 1798 — remained unpopular, but they helped to avoid complete reliance on tariffs in a period when land sales produced little revenue.

Perhaps the greatest tribute to the wisdom of the Federalist financial policies came from the Jeffersonian Republicans who had vigorously opposed them when they were first introduced. This political party, formed during the period of opposition to the Federalists, gained the presidency in 1801 and held it for a quarter-century. In office, the Republicans either continued Hamiltonian and Federalist policies or, when they did not, came to regret it. The claims of public creditors were honored, and in consequence Jefferson's government found it easy to borrow from overseas the money necessary to purchase the Louisiana Territory in 1803. Trade prosperity swelled the Treasury coffers and allowed Secretary Albert Gallatin to reduce an $86 million debt to $45 million between 1803 and 1812.

Soaring revenues from duties on imported goods also allowed President Jefferson to fulfill his campaign promise to eliminate all internal taxes. This was to prove a mistake, however, for the taxes had to be reinstated during the War of 1812, at which time their effectiveness was greatly reduced by the necessity of rebuilding the machinery of collection. A similar error was the failure to recharter the federal bank when its original charter ran out in 1811.

President Madison and Secretary Gallatin had come to realize the usefulness of the bank to the government and they supported its rechartering. But some Republicans revived the controversy over its constitutionality, and others resented the competition and control it created for the growing numbers of state-chartered banks. This coalition of principle and interest defeated the recharter bill. The bank was sorely missed in the War of 1812 emergency that soon followed, and creating a similar institution became one of the first tasks of postwar legislation. As for the tariff, the postwar Jeffersonian Republicans became as enamored of the protective concept as Hamilton had been.

The U.S. Monetary System

Specie Money and Bank Money

The comprehensive financial program of Alexander Hamilton demonstrated an uncommon understanding of the interrelationships among money, banking, and public finance. The history of money, banks, and public finance up to the Civil War is replete with further illustrations of the interaction of private and public decision making. To examine them, we need first to develop some basic theoretical ideas about the nature of the early U.S. monetary system.

Throughout its history, two essentially different types of money have made up the U.S. money supply: money supplied by the government and money supplied by banks. The first type of money is defined, and often created and managed, by the federal government for public or social purposes. Providing for an adequate supply of money is an important function of government. Money transactions are far more efficient than barter transactions, and money as a unit of account aids economic decison making at all levels by minimizing the costs of acquiring information about relative values of goods, services, and factors of production. Up until the Civil War, with few and temporary exceptions, this government-supplied money consisted of metallic coins in multiples and fractions of the basic monetary unit—the dollar. Gold and silver coins and their equivalent in bullion thus made up the governmentally sanctioned monetary base of the antebellum American money supply. Furthermore, only gold and silver coins were recognized in American law as legal tender for all private and public debts.

The other type of money in the U.S. money supply—bank money—was and is a product created by private banking institutions for profit-making purposes. Before the Civil War, bank money consisted of paper bank notes and bank deposits transferable by check. Bank notes and deposits were created in the process of carrying out the ordinary banking functions of making loans and discounting promissory notes and bills of exchange for customers. To illustrate the process of bank money creation suppose, for example, that an antebellum storekeeper in Ohio wanted to stock pots and pans and sell them to retail customers over the following six months. To buy the pans from a wholesaler, the storekeeper might give a note promising to pay $500 six months hence to the local banker. If the interest rate or discount rate was 6 percent per annum (equivalent to 3 percent for six months), the banker would take the note and hand the storekeeper $485 in bank notes. The storekeeper would use the bank notes to buy the pots and pans. As they were sold to retail customers in the following months, the storekeeper would accumulate enough funds to pay the banker $500 as well as to earn a profit as reward for mercantile effort. Less commonly in antebellum times, except in large cities, the storekeeper would use the loan as a bank deposit on which to write a check for the pots and pans.

Once the paper bank notes were used to buy the storekeeper's stock of pots and pans, they would begin to circulate as money. The wholesaler would use some of the notes to pay workers and suppliers and keep the rest as profit. Workers and suppliers, in turn, would respend them to purchase other goods and services. So why was the bank necessary at all? Why didn't the storekeeper just give the wholesaler a personal note of debt? The answers to these questions hinge on the division of labor and growing specialization encountered so often in economic history. The bank was a specialized institution for supplying credit. By specializing on credit and developing modes of behavior consistent with performing its business efficiently, the bank developed a standing that made its notes more widely acceptable to sellers of goods and services than the notes of nonbank institutions and individuals. This is what made the bank's paper notes and checks a generally acceptable means of exchange or, in short, money.

Recalling that only the gold and silver money specified by the federal government was legal tender, it is easy to deduce what modes of behavior were consistent with performing individual banking functions effectively. The keys to having its notes and checks accepted as money were the bank's willingness and ability to pay the gold and silver base money whenever the holder of a note or check of the bank presented it for payment. Maintaining the convertibility of notes and deposits into specie was, therefore, basic to effective bank operations.

To maintain convertibility a bank did not require a dollar of metallic specie money for every dollar of bank-note or deposit money. In a given period of days or weeks, payments of specie by the bank in exchange for its own notes or checks were balanced by receipts of specie. Banks were, among other things, storehouses and safe depositories for specie. The public usually preferred to use paper bank notes and checks to make payments, since

Pre-1860s State Bank Notes. Paper currency before the Civil War was issued not by the government but by banks operating under state—and, in a few cases, federal—charters of incorporation. The five and ten dollar notes of the Bank of the Republic promised to pay those amounts in "hard" money on demand at the bank's Washington, D.C., office. The notes portrayed were never issued: they are unnumbered and unsigned by the bank's cashier—and one wonders whether the bank's president was really "G. Washington." (Culver Pictures)

they were easier than specie to carry around and to transport from place to place in more distant transactions. Consequently, banks could usually issue several dollars of notes and deposits subject to check for each dollar of specie they held. This is the principle of *fractional reserve banking*. It was of great private advantage to the banks because they could make more loans and discounts, and thus earn more interest income, than would have been possible with 100 percent rather than fractional specie reserves. And it had a social advantage as well. In addition to being more convenient for the public, paper money was far less costly to create than specie money, which had to be mined, refined, assayed, and minted.

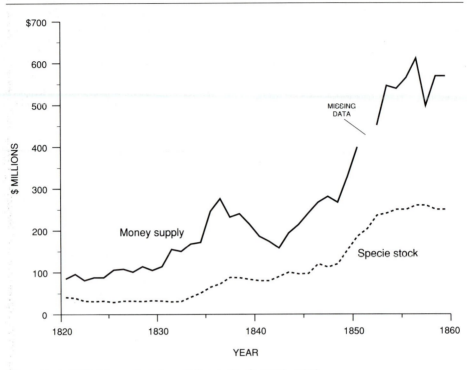

Figure 7–1 *U.S. Money Supply and Specie Stock, 1820–1858*
SOURCE: Peter Temin, *The Jacksonian Economy* (New York: W. W. Norton, 1969), pp. 71, 159.

Thus, the pre–Civil War money supply in the United States consisted of two types of money: a base of specie money, as defined by the government in terms of gold and silver coins, and bank money—bank notes and deposits—created in the process of ordinary banking operations and usually convertible into specie. Specie in banks thus served as bank reserves. Unfortunately, banking and monetary data for the antebellum years are notably sketchy and incomplete, but a few scholars have attempted to cull from them estimates of the money supply and its components. Some of the most reliable estimates, compiled by Peter Temin, cover the period 1820 to 1858 (see Figure 7–1). The overall trend during this period was strongly upward, at a rate of 5 per-

cent per year. It largely reflected the real growth of the country, because price levels in the late 1850s were not very different from those of the early 1820s. The only major exception of the money supply's strong upward trend came in the years of the late 1830s to the early 1840s, one of the few periods in American history when the money supply trended downward for a period of several years.[1]

Trends in the specie stock, the monetary base of the United States in these years, are also shown in Figure 7–1. Largely in the form of gold and silver coins, specie served as hand-to-hand currency and as reserves for bank notes and deposits. In fulfilling these monetary functions, the specie stock was the primary determinant of the money supply. Indeed, the broad correspondence of the two series is evident in Figure 7–1. Specie, like the money supply, grew at approximately 5 percent per year between 1820 and 1858. The only major divergence of the two series occurred during the decade of 1822 to 1832, when the stock of specie remained relatively unchanged but the money supply nearly doubled. Interestingly, it was during these years that the second Bank of the United States and its president, Nicholas Biddle, exercised a powerful and politically controversial influence on the nation's monetary and financial affairs. That bank's activities appear to have increased the public's confidence in all U.S. banks, allowing bank money to become a much greater part of the total money supply.

The Money Supply and Price Levels

The expansion of the money supply, and of bank money in particular, played a role in the real growth of the American economy during the antebellum decades. Although some Americans living in those decades, and later, many writers on the period as well, thought that the process of creating bank money by monetizing private debts (i.e., by issuing bank notes and deposits in return for promises to repay the loans later) was highly inflationary, there is little evidence to support that view. Looking at the behavior of the general price level shown in Figure 7–2, it is apparent that from the mid-1790s to 1860 the overall trend was downward, implying that the money supply did not increase fast enough to maintain a stable price level. In other words, the supply of goods and services exchanged for money grew faster than did the supply of money.

It is also clear from Figure 7–2 that there were a number of departures from the trend of falling prices. Some scholars argue that the departures were the result of excessive monetization of private debt by banks.[2] However, a very different reason for the trends is indicated

by a close examination of the four major upward movements in the price level that occurred, respectively, in the mid-1790s, during the War of 1812, in the mid-1830s, and in the early 1850s. In each of these inflationary periods, the chief impetus for rising prices did not come from overissues of bank money by reckless bankers responding to the loan demands of speculators and entrepreneurs; rather, they resulted from increases in the base of specie money or, in one instance, from paper money issued by the federal government.

For the 1790s period, monetary and banking data are too limited to give a precise answer to the question of why prices rose. However, there were only a few banks operating in these years and most of them were just getting organized. The major causes of rising prices were likely the great foreign demand for American exports, American reexports of West Indian products, and American shipping services as a result of wars between England and France. The wars interfered with both the production and commerce of those two European powers, and the United States stood ready to take up the slack. Sales of American goods and services to foreigners generated an inflow of specie and foreign capital to the United States, and prices rose. After the initial rise peaked in 1796, American prices fluctuated up and down for the next fifteen years with the ebb and flow of European warfare. If there was a trend in these years, it appears to have been slightly downward despite the growth of American banks, whose numbers increased from three in 1790 to about thirty in 1800 and about one hundred in 1810.

The explanation of the inflationary periods of the 1830s and 1850s is much the same. In the 1830s, imports of silver, primarily from Mexico, swelled the specie base of the American money supply and caused it to expand rapidly. Ordinarily, the rise of American prices would have led to exports of specie as foreigners stopped buying more expensive American

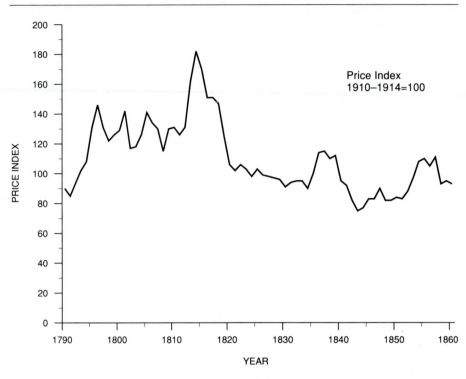

Figure 7–2 *U.S. Wholesale Price Index, 1790–1860*
SOURCE: U.S. Bureau of the Census, *Historical Statistics of the United States: Colonial Times to 1957* (Washington, D.C.: GPO, 1960), pp. 115–16.

products and Americans themselves sought cheaper imports. In the mid-1830s, however, the United States accomplished the rare historical feat of paying off its entire national debt; in turn, foreigners had such great confidence in the American credit that they were willing to finance rising U.S. imports by lending rather than demanding specie. The granting of loans by foreigners to Americans allowed the specie imported from Mexico to remain in the U.S. money supply. An increased use of foreign bills of exchange to finance imports had the same effect. Americans earned these bills of exchange when they exported commodities such as cotton.

In the 1850s, the chief cause of rising prices was the expansion of specie money resulting from the discovery of gold in California. Much of the gold was exported to pay for imports, but enough remained in the United States to increase the specie base from $120 million to $260 million between 1848 and 1856. The fraction of bank money in the total money supply was roughly constant during this period of inflation.

The sharpest inflation of the whole antebellum period came during the War of 1812. In this case, government borrowing to finance the war, not a growth in specie, was the major cause of inflation. The federal debt rose from

$45 million to $127 million between 1812 and 1816. Part of the increase was in the form of short-term Treasury notes, which were for all practical purposes a paper money issue. Though bearing interest and redeemable in one year, Treasury notes were receivable in payment of all duties, taxes, and debts of the federal government until redeemed. In all, some $37 million of Treasury notes were issued during the war, with about $17 million as the maximum outstanding at one time. This was a substantial addition to the American money supply. Some small denominations circulated as hand-to-hand currency. Most of the Treasury notes, however, were in large denominations that, in combination with their legal-tender status in government transactions and their short maturity, made them an ideal form of bank reserves. Aided by these paper reserves, bank credit expanded, largely to accommodate the government. The money supply increased and prices rose. Late in the war, the government's voracious demands for credit and the resulting swollen credit structure forced all banks except those in New England to suspend specie payments. The suspension of convertibility between bank money and specie happened after, not before, the worst of the inflation.

The preceding survey of major antebellum price trends may serve as a useful antidote to the all-too-common view that reckless, inflationary, wildcat banking practices were endemic to the early history of the United States. In the 1790s, there were few banks, and in the 1850s, perceptive observers realized that increases in monetary gold, not bank money, were the source of rising prices. Although many contemporaries and later writers contended that the price-level inflations that had occurred during the War of 1812 and again in the 1830s were caused by large increases in the number of banks and the amount of bank-created money, this was not the case. Increases in the monetary base of specie (and, in the case

of the War of 1812, government paper money) were at the heart of the inflations.

Banks and Politics

Lack of a historical foundation for the long-accepted view that early American banks were engines of inflation does not imply that their numerous critics were unjustified in all of their charges. The business of banking was new to Americans, in part because the British had not looked with favor on the attempts of colonists in North America to engage in it. When in 1784 some merchants of Boston obtained a charter from the Massachusetts legislature to form the second incorporated bank in the newly independent country, they wrote to the first—the Bank of North America founded at Philadelphia in 1781—requesting advice on how to proceed. Thomas Willing, president of the Philadelphia bank and later president of the Bank of the United States, responded:

> *When the bank first opened here, the business was as much a novelty to us . . . as it can possibly be to you. It was a pathless wilderness, ground but little known to this side of the Atlantic. No book then spoke of the interior arrangements or rules observed in Europe— accident alone threw in our way even the form of an English bank bill. All was to us a mystery.*[3]

In such circumstances, it is not surprising that banks sometimes made mistakes.

Problems with the Banking System

In addition to lack of experience and formal guides concerning bank management, early American bankers were hampered by the system under which they operated. Two related aspects of that system remained problematic until the early twentieth century: the absence of a central bank and the metallic monetary standard. Under fractional reserve banking, in normal times a bank could issue bank note and deposit liabilities in amounts several times greater than its reserves of specie into which these liabilities were supposed to be convertible. Unfortunately, not all times were normal. An abnormal time for bankers could well be defined as one in which holders of notes and deposits attempted to convert them into specie on such a scale that there were not enough reserves of specie in banks to meet the demands. No matter how well managed a bank might have been, if it could not borrow specie at such a time of panic it would be forced to suspend convertibility. Typically, the problem would not be that of just one bank but of a great many banks all at once. Thus, it happened that in 1814, and again in 1837 and 1857, large numbers of American banks temporarily suspended convertibility of their liabilities into specie. This smacked of dishonesty to many, but in the particular circumstances it was a constructive decision. When the banks did not have to redeem their own liabilities in specie, they could be more lenient in demanding it from their borrowers. This leniency prevented some business failures that might otherwise have occurred and therefore hastened recovery from financial panics.

One of the functions of a central bank in the modern economy is to act as a lender of last resort to temporarily illiquid banks. This was not a recognized function in nineteenth-century America, though on a few occasions the banks of the United States and the U.S. Treasury did come to the aid of commercial banks. If a central bank had held large reserves of the base money—specie before the Civil War—it could have lent to banks under pressure to redeem large amounts of their note and deposit liabilities in specie. Had such an institution been present and the lender-of-last-resort function recognized, the probability of temporary panics involving individual

banks or the whole system of banks would have been reduced substantially. The problems of panics and widespread suspensions of convertibility that did occur, however, were problems of institutional organization, not of poor bank management.

The metallic monetary standard was another institutional factor that presented problems for price-level and banking stability. For one thing, even if a central bank had been present, its own reserves of specie might have been severely strained in a major convertibility panic. Today's central bank—the Federal Reserve System—does not labor under such a disadvantage, since it can create bank reserves and paper currency with, as is sometimes said, "a stroke of its pen." But when the United States had a metallic monetary standard, banking and price stability depended on the flow of specie into and out of the economy. Such specie flows arose from imports and exports of existing stocks, from discoveries of gold and silver deposits in the earth, and from improved technologies for extracting the monetary metals from their ores. At times, such flows could be price stabilizing, but often they were not. The inflations of the 1830s and 1850s are examples of the latter. Inflows of specie stimulated rising prices, which were then expected by borrowers and lenders. When prices failed to continue rising because specie inflows tapered off or turned into outflows, Americans' inflationary expectations were jolted and financial panic resulted. In principle, if not so clearly in practice, the managed paper monetary standard of today is more capable of promoting price-level stability than its metallic predecessors.

Thus, both an absence of experience and an imperfect institutional environment created problems for early American bankers. The same was true for many other businesses in the developing U.S. economy. In one respect, however, banks were different. The bankers' stock in trade—bank notes and deposits—

were owned by other people, and they circulated as a large component of the nation's money supply. Attempts to regulate bank behavior therefore arose. Monetization of debt through creating note and deposit liabilities several times larger than specie reserves was a profitable activity and carried with it a temptation to excess, particularly since a bank itself would bear only a part of the costs of the failure that might result, with holders of its liabilities bearing the remainder. State legislatures and Congress, in chartering the earliest banks, attempted to address this problem by specifying the amount of equity capital to be paid into a bank before operations could commence and by limiting bank note issues to some stated multiple of capital. Although sketchy and often misdirected, such regulations furnished guidelines to inexperienced bankers and reminded them of their public responsibilities.

Continuing restraint on the temptation of bankers to overissue their monetary liabilities was accomplished by some large banks. The first and second Banks of the United States, operating under federal charters from 1791 to 1811 and from 1816 to 1836 respectively, were notable examples of nationwide regulation in this respect. These large and prestigious institutions with branches in the leading cities of the country received payments due the government and generally followed conservative lending policies. Therefore, they tended to accumulate net balances of notes and checks issued by other banks. By promptly returning the liabilities to the issuing banks for conversion into specie, the Banks of the United States could and sometimes did restrain the expansion of money and credit by the state-chartered banks.

The Results of the Bank War

The credit-restraining activities of the Banks of the United States were unpopular both with bankers and entrepreneurs who desired more

and cheaper credit. Still other factions were against banking and paper money in general and against large federal banks in particular, which they viewed as bastions of privilege with dubious constitutionality. As noted earlier in the chapter, these groups coalesced in 1811 to defeat the attempt in Congress to recharter the first Bank of the United States. The second federal bank, chartered for twenty years in 1816, ran into similar political difficulties in the early 1830s. Its friends in Congress succeeded in passing a recharter bill in 1832, but President Andrew Jackson's veto of the measure was sustained. The contest, or "Bank War" as it came to be known, pitted the strong-willed, antibank Jackson against an able but rather arrogant Philadelphian, Nicholas Biddle, president of the bank. Jackson was victorious when attempts in Congress to recharter the bank ended in failure.

One result of the Bank War was that the federal government, beginning in 1833, transferred its banking business to state banks. In addition, the Bank of the United States redeemed its stock held by the federal government and was reorganized as a Pennsylvania corporation. These new arrangements were short-lived, however. The reorganized bank failed in 1841, after ill-timed speculations in the international cotton market. And the federal government, growing increasingly wary of its new relations with state banks, moved to isolate its fiscal affairs from the nation's banking system by creating the so-called Independent Treasury. Instituted for a year in 1840 to 1841 and then reestablished in 1846, the Independent Treasury accepted payments due the government only in specie or Treasury notes. Government funds were held in subtreasuries scattered throughout the nation rather than in banks.

Private Regulation: The Suffolk Bank System

In New England during the four decades before the Civil War, the Suffolk Bank of Boston

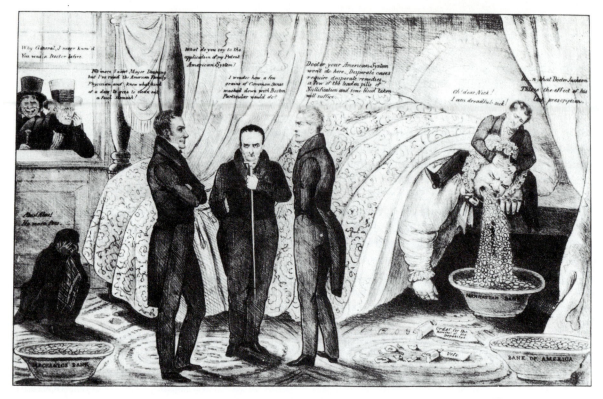

THE DOCTORS PUZZLED OR THE DESPERATE CASE OF MOTHER U.S BANK.

The Bank War.   Whether the federal charter of the Second Bank of the United States was to be renewed or allowed to lapse was the greatest U.S. political issue of the 1830s. President Andrew Jackson in 1832 vetoed Congress's bill to renew the charter, and Treasury Secretary Roger Taney in 1833 began to drain the bank of its U.S. government deposits. In this contemporary political cartoon, the bloated bank from its sickbed disgorges money into bowls labeled with the names of state banks friendly to Jackson while "Nick" Biddle, the bank's president, attempts to control the flow. At the window, "Doctor" Jackson says that he has administered a dose of medicine to "clean out a foul stomach," while bank defenders Henry Clay, John Quincy Adams, and John C. Calhoun propose their own cures for the patient. (Brown Brothers)

exerted control over money and credit on a regional basis in much the same way as the two Banks of the United States had done nationally during their years of existence. Cooperating with other Boston banks, which in the normal course of trade received net balances of New England country bank notes, the Suffolk Bank pressured the country banks into maintaining with it deposits for redemption of their notes. If they did not, the Suffolk threatened to embarrass the smaller banks by suddenly presenting large amounts of their notes for redemption. In the face of this threat, the country banks agreed to the Suffolk's terms. Under this private regulatory scheme, the New England states enjoyed a stable paper currency with bank notes exchanging at par throughout the region for much of the antebellum period.

Outside New England, bank notes commonly were received at a discount from par whenever they were presented away from the locale of the issuing bank. The discount, which varied with the distance from the issuing bank, was not a sign of excessive note issuing by banks. Rather, it reflected the real costs of returning notes for redemption in an era of slow communication. Only when the issuing banks refused to convert their liabilities into specie were the discounts more than a few percent.

The Safety Fund

The note-redemption operations of the Banks of the United States and the Suffolk Bank, along with similar efforts on the part of numerous note and exchange brokers, represented the activities of private institutions pursuing essentially private ends while also promoting the public goal of a more reliable money supply. Direct regulation by government agencies was slower in coming. When it did, the state of New York was in the forefront.

In 1829, the New York legislature instituted the Safety Fund system, a scheme for insuring the note issues of its member banks. New York banks chartered by the legislature were required to contribute a small percentage of their capital to a safety fund and to submit to periodic inspection by state-appointed bank examiners. If a member bank of the system failed, the holders of its outstanding notes were reimbursed from the Safety Fund. The New York Safety Fund foreshadowed bank deposit insurance, one of the more significant innovations of twentieth-century American banking. And like the later deposit insurance funds, the Safety Fund was not always able to meet the claims made upon it.

Free Banking

New York State was also in the forefront of the movement to free the business of banking from the vagaries of politics. From their beginnings in the 1780s, American banks had been incorporated by special charters of legislative bodies. Banking was a new and often very

profitable business. When the privilege of entering into it with corporate charters was in the hands of politicians and legislators on a case-by-case basis, bribery and corruption inevitably resulted. Moreover, deposits of public funds could be used by politicians to assist friendly banks and to punish those less friendly. This attitude was so widespread that even President Jefferson wrote in 1803 to his treasury secretary, Albert Gallatin, that "I am decidedly in favor of making all the banks Republican, by sharing deposits among them in proportion to the dispositions they show."[4] Three decades later, President Jackson followed in his illustrious predecessor's footsteps by authorizing the funds of the United States to be deposited in so-called "pet banks"; that is, banks friendly to the Jacksonians.

New York's solution to the problems created by too close a nesting of banks and politics was the Free Banking Act of 1838. It made the granting of corporate charters to engage in banking a routine function of an administrative office of state government, instead of one that involved special acts of the state legislature. Banking was made free in the sense that any person or group of associates could obtain a bank charter by complying with the conditions and regulations specified in the Free Banking Act. As such, the act reflected the ascendent idea that free competition in banking as well as other businesses was the best guarantee of effective economic performance.

In addition to reflecting the growing laissez-faire trend in American economic thinking, the New York Free Banking Act instituted a notable innovation in banking—a bank-note currency backed by specified types of bonds and mortgages, including state and federal bonds and mortgages on New York land. A free bank could purchase the allowable securities and deposit them with an agency of the state government, which could then issue to the bank notes equal to the amount of pledged bonds or to half the amount of pledged real estate mortgages. Like the Safety Fund, this was an attempt to provide insurance to holders of bank notes. If a bank failed outright, or failed to redeem its notes when they were presented, the state comptroller could liquidate the securities pledged by the bank and use the proceeds to redeem its notes. The system worked fairly well in New York. Between its adoption there in 1838 and the Civil War, it gradually spread throughout the United States and by 1863 became the model for the National Banking System. The free banking system, while popular, was hardly foolproof. Events in other states demonstrated its drawbacks when securities of dubious value were allowed to serve as backing for bank notes. The desire of state governments to expand the market for their own bonds was often as much a motive for free banking legislation as was the desire to make bank notes safer.

As free banking spread to more and more states in the 1840s and 1850s, it helped to reduce the deleterious effects of politics on banking development. The struggle for free banking was not an easy one, however, and its widespread institution came only after other possibilities were tried. A few states owned and operated their own banks, sometimes as monopolies or in competition with privately owned banks. Some of these state operations were among the best of antebellum banks, and others were among the worst. Certain states, disgusted with their own banking experiences or with those that cropped up elsewhere, experimented with the extreme policy of prohibiting incorporated banking within their borders. The policy was usually abandoned in favor of free banking, though, because it merely served to encourage banks in other states to send their notes to the "bankless" states.

Patterns of Private Banking

In reality, few states were ever bankless even when they tried to be. European and English common law traditions recognized the legal right of anyone to engage in banking operations without having to obtain the permission of the government. These traditions migrated to the United States in the form of private unincorporated banks, which often grew out of or were carried on along with other types of business. Hundreds of private banks were in business during the late antebellum years. However, except for a few of the larger and more famous ones, little is known about the nature and scope of their operations because private banks did not have to file reports with public authorities. Nonetheless, two patterns of private banking are discernible. First, in the larger cities, private banks often specialized in the domestic and foreign exchange operations that financed interregional and international trade as well as in marketing securities for both government bodies and business corporations. The latter activity foreshadowed specialized investment banking. This type of private banking increasingly came to be centered in New York City, where Wall Street already contained the nation's largest banks, brokers, other financial firms, and organized exchanges. Second, private banks of a different sort operated in many smaller cities and towns, especially in the newer areas of settlement. Here they served as substitutes for incorporated banks that were either slow to develop or prohibited by law. Generally, private banks were forbidden by law from circulating their own bank notes, but they could accept deposits and extend credit in other ways.

The heterogeneous American banking system of the antebellum decades had a number of bad features, but it also had some good ones for an expanding and developing economy. A more uniform national currency of the type promoted (but not altogether achieved) by the Banks of the United States would have constituted a better medium of exchange and store of value than the thousands of varieties of bank notes that actually circulated. The diversity of bank notes—some of failed banks and some counterfeit—undoubtedly hindered smooth and efficient transactions; it also caused resources to be expended on the flourishing business of producing and distributing bank note reporters and counterfeit detectors. Such costs could have been avoided with better institutional arrangements. However, even if such "better" arrangements had been accompanied by more centralized and restrictive controls over bank operations and money creation, it is still not clear whether the overall result would have been preferable to the dynamic and variegated bank-financed economic development of the period.

It should be remembered that in these years the American economy was expanding over a great geographical area and bringing previously dormant resources into use. Communication and transportation, though advancing with the westward movement, were nonetheless rather primitive during most of the antebellum period. Wealth that had accumulated in Europe and in the older, settled eastern states exhibited a reluctance to migrate to the newer areas of settlement even though there is evidence that it could have earned higher returns there. In these circumstances, entrepreneurs on the scene, and hence more aware than others of the productive potential of the nation's expanding resources, turned to local banks for the supplies of money and credit needed to realize that potential. Had the spread of such local banking been restricted or disallowed by uninformed prejudice against banks, the United States might well have advanced more slowly in settlement, economic growth, and financial development before 1860.

Government-Sponsored Economic Activity (1790–1860)

Whether measured in terms of dollar amounts or in relation to the national income, the government's participation in economic activities between 1790 and 1860 was limited by modern-day standards. Total federal expenditures during these seven decades amounted to about $2 billion, or what the federal government now spends in less than one day. The present-day United States, of course, is much larger in population and income, and the purchasing power of the dollar (in terms of comparable goods and services) is much less than it was in the antebellum years. Nonetheless, these factors account for only a part of the historical difference. Federal spending before the Civil War typically was only 1 percent to 2 percent of the national income, or less than one-tenth of its percentage share in today's economy. The spending of state and local governments was also small by twentieth-century standards, totaling for the states about $3 billion from 1790 to 1860. On the whole, government spending on all levels likely amounted to 5 percent to 10 percent of the nation's income, with the former figure prevailing most of the time.

The absolute and relative levels of government spending, however, provide a misleading indication of the role of government in antebellum economic development. While Americans in general tended to agree with Adam Smith's view—that government activity ought properly to be limited to such matters as defense, justice, and a few "public" works—they gave it a broad construction consistent with the expansion of a relatively undeveloped economy. Directly and indirectly, government decisions attempted, with substantial success, to augment the nation's resources of land, capital, and labor, as well as their efficient combination in the production of material wealth and welfare.

Federal Financial and Tariff Policies

Before the Civil War, the federal government's revenue came essentially from three sources—

customs duties, land sales, and internal taxes. Internal taxes were the least important of the revenue sources, accounting for about 2 percent of total receipts. Taxes were levied in only sixteen years, the last time in 1817. Land sales provided about 10 percent of federal revenues between 1790 and 1860; with the exception of the land boom of the mid-1830s, their contribution seldom rose much above this percentage. Moreover, after accounting for the costs of acquiring, surveying, and marketing the public lands, the actual net federal revenue from land sales was much less. Customs duties provided the largest source of federal revenue, comprising some seven-eighths of the total.

The original Tariff Act of 1789 stated that import duties were "necessary for the support of government, for the discharge of the debts of the United States, and the encouragement and protection of manufactures." In varying degrees, these three aims provided the rationale for all later tariff measures. Revenue was the dominant purpose from 1789 to 1816. Duties averaged less than 10 percent of the value of imports, except when they were temporarily doubled for revenue purposes during the War of 1812. The Tariff Act of 1816, though reducing average duties slightly from their temporarily high wartime levels, made protection of domestic producers the primary object of American tariff policy. This was a response to the wave of nationalism that swept through the country as a result of the war; it also was a response to special pleading by the manufacturing interests that had grown up under hothouse conditions of restricted foreign trade after 1808. Duties moved upward, reaching average levels of about 50 percent in the 1828 Tariff of Abominations. Thereafter, the rates were reduced periodically up to the Civil War, except for a brief revival of protectionist spirit in 1842.

Protective tariff policies undoubtedly led to greater production and higher profits in the industries protected, but it is far from clear that the nation as a whole benefited from the differential protection accorded to some producers. Protection may have allowed firms in a few industries to reap economies of scale and to engage in the process of learning how to employ the developing technologies of large-scale factory manufacturing. But protection often continued long after these benefits were reaped. It thus constituted more a means of transferring income to the protected industries from the users of their products than one of creating wholly new productive activities. To the extent that protected industries engaged in the production of consumer goods such as textiles, these continuing income transfers may well have led to higher levels of capital formation as profits were reinvested. But producer goods such as iron were also protected; in such cases, the higher profits of some manufacturers were obtained at the expense of raising costs to other industries.

Considered as a whole, however, the tariff policies of the United States likely did increase the overall rate of capital formation. To understand why, it is necessary to examine how the federal government used the revenues it derived almost entirely from customs duties. One major use of tariff revenues throughout the nineteenth century was to pay interest on, and the principal of, the public debt of the United States. The time path of the federal debt in the antebellum decades is shown in Figure 7–3. In the 1790s, the debt was more or less constant. However, already at that time its value represented a huge capital gain to investors because Hamilton's funding scheme had raised the credit of the United States and consequently the value of government bonds. From 1800 to 1812, the conservative fiscal policies of Gallatin reduced the debt in every year save one, 1803, when funds were borrowed for the Louisiana Purchase. During the War of 1812, the debt rose sharply to its antebellum peak as the government borrowed heavily to prosecute the war at inflated prices. Then, in

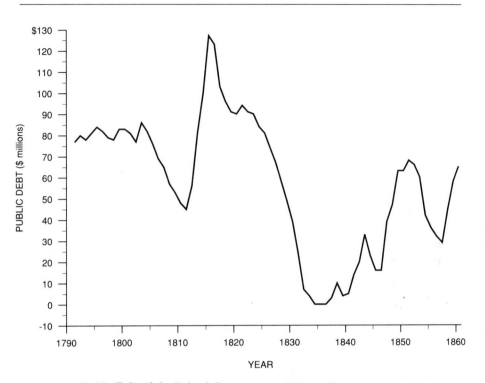

Figure 7–3 *Public Debt of the Federal Government, 1791–1860*

Source: U.S. Bureau of the Census, *Historical Statistics of the United States: Colonial Times to 1957* (Washington, D.C.: GPO, 1960), p. 721.

the two decades after 1816, the debt was virtually extinguished by payments made in dollars more valuable than the ones that had been borrowed earlier. The debt rose again on three occasions before the Civil War—in the two depressions that followed financial panics during the late 1830s and 1850s, when lower imports combined with reduced tariff rates led to a falling off of federal revenues, and in the late 1840s as a result of increased spending for the Mexican War. From 1843 to 1846, and again from 1851 to 1857, the federal debt was substantially reduced.

In short, the federal government borrowed when it had to but viewed the normal condi-

tion as one in which surplus revenues were desirable in order to reduce the public debt. This policy favored capital formation in two ways. First, the direct transfer of funds from import taxes to public creditors on balance taxed consumers to provide funds for investors. The dollar amount of these transfers understated the actual transfer of purchasing power because the government generally borrowed cheaper dollars (e.g., during wartime inflations) than it paid back (in peacetime years). Second, government debt retirement reduced the supply of bonds, thereby raising bond prices and reducing interest yields. To the extent that government bonds were viewed by investors as substitutes for other public and private investments, this tended to reduce the interest costs of other borrowers. Federal debt policy thus increased the availability and reduced the supply price of capital funds to private investors. In the decades after the Civil War, federal debt policies continued to promote private capital formation but on an even greater scale (see Chapter 15).

Tariff and debt policies were only a few of many economically significant federal activities during the period. Expenditures on general government—the legislative, executive, and judicial branches—implemented a framework of law that protected individual and property rights and carried out the Constitution's mandate for a nationwide free-trade area. That area was extended by expenditures for the acquisition, protection, and distribution of new territories; much of the spending on defense and Native American affairs, as well as on land management and aids to internal transportation, was for these purposes. Foreign commerce was promoted by favored treatment to American shipping interests and by expenditures on navigation improvements and the navy, which helped to suppress piracy. Subsidies to the Post Office and to the first telegraph line represented a recognition of the social nature and utility of information and communications. While the federal government limited the scope of its operations, most of what it did do had strong economic significance for the nation.

State and Local Government Activity

For at least a quarter-century after 1790, state and local financial activities were rather unimportant. Hamilton's funding scheme freed the states of most of their debts. An aversion to taxes and fondness for limited government led a number of states to obtain the bulk of their revenues from land sales and interest on federal securities (which they had received as a part of Hamilton's program). One economically significant state policy in this early period was the incorporation, and in some cases partial financing, of banking and transportation companies. Dividends, especially on bank stock, were a good source of revenue and allowed state taxes to be kept low. Other states, notably Massachusetts, received large revenues from taxes on the banks they had chartered. Still others demanded lump-sum bonuses from banks in return for corporate charters, and a few states required banks to invest in worthy projects that otherwise might have required tax revenues. The interrelations of public and private finance are again illustrated by these policies.

After the War of 1812, wider appreciation of the need for transportation improvements, coupled with federal reluctance to assume a major role in providing them, led to a much more active economic role for the states. The great success of federal credit policies and a continuing aversion to taxes were important in determining how state activities were financed. Chief reliance was placed on borrowing, and many states hoped to pay the interest and principal of their bonded debts with earnings from their investments in banking and transportation facilities rather than from general tax revenues. The early and great success of the Erie Canal showed that this might indeed be possible. Eventually, however, many of the states failed in their attempts to operate as business enterprises rather than as governments. During the 1830s, all sorts of enterprises were launched with funds borrowed on state credit, often from foreigners. But the earnings of many of these ventures proved disappointing; when credit tightened in the late 1830s, many of the states were in trouble. In the ensuing depression, some defaulted on their debt obligations and a few actually repudiated their debts. State interest in improvement projects declined thereafter, and greater reliance was placed on taxation rather than on borrowing. General property and poll levies were the mainstays of state (and county) taxation throughout these decades. As the economy grew in complexity, however, a variety of new taxes was introduced. The reorganization of state finances with a greater emphasis on taxation led to a sounder expansion of state borrowing in the 1850s; on the eve of the Civil War, the gross debt of the states was more than four times that of the federal government.

Although local government economic activity was less innovative than that of the states, after 1820 it increased rapidly because of growing urbanization. Most of the public services of modern urban entities were introduced or expanded during this period, including water and sewer systems, improved and lighted streets and sidewalks, police and fire protection, health services, and public education. Municipalities also aided transportation companies. Property taxes and license fees financed much of the public activity, but borrowing was utilized to finance larger capital investment projects. Local government indebtedness increased from $27 million in 1843 to $200 million by 1860, when it was some three times the federal debt.

Summary

By 1860, after some seven decades of experimentation, the financial system of the United States had reached a high level of development. The most durable achievement was the establishment of public credit. With Hamilton as the architect, Federalist policies in the 1790s put the credit of American governments on a very high level. Even debacles like the repudiation of debts by some states in the 1840s were discounted by most American and overseas lenders as temporary deviations from normal practices. Domestic credit markets and foreign borrowing revived quickly after these disturbances. In the monetary area by 1860, the United States had achieved a gold-based currency, dispensing with the assorted foreign coins and tokens that had been used for many years. And, on the eve of the Civil War, the utility of banks was no longer a highly charged issue in the political economy; by then, thousands of American banks were furnishing a low-cost medium of exchange as well as loans for commercial, agricultural, and industrial development. When one considers that the national government of the 1780s was virtually bankrupt, that currency systems varied from state to state, and that only three banks conducted their business in isolation (not only from most Americans but also from one another), the financial progress of United States in the following seven decades was great indeed.

Yet problems remained. Federal revenue gathering continued to place too heavy a reliance on customs duties, a form of taxation molded and remolded by special-interest politics. The metallic base of the monetary system was capricious, expanding with new ore discoveries, being abandoned during financial panics and war, and varying in the short run with changes in international trade and capital movements. The paper bank-note currency, with its thousands of varieties of notes, lacked the uniformity needed to reduce the information and transaction costs of exchanging goods and services. The banking system, moreover, lacked the central leadership that to some extent had been given by the abandoned Banks of the United States. And the federal government, through its Independent Treasury, had isolated itself as much as possible from the financial system in a marked departure from the vision of Hamilton.

The next generation of financial decision makers had to deal with these problems. As it turned out, events impending in 1860 did not allow them much time to prepare for the task. The Civil War created massive financial stresses that led to fundamental changes in the U.S. financial system (see Chapter 15).

Endnotes

1. Peter Temin, *The Jacksonian Economy* (New York: W. W. Norton, 1969), pp. 71, 159.
2. For example, see Bray Hammond, *Banks and Politics in America from the Revolution to the Civil War* (Princeton: Princeton University Press, 1957; reissued as a paperback in 1991).
3. Quoted in Bray Hammond, *Banks and Politics in America from the Revolution to the Civil War,* p. 66.
4. Quoted in Henry Adams, ed., *Writings of Albert Gallatin,* vol. 1 (Philadelphia, 1879), p. 129.

Suggested Readings

Federalist and Republican financial policies are set forth in some detail by Curtis P. Nettels, *The Emergence of a National Economy, 1775–1915* (New York: Holt, 1962), and are interpreted by Stuart Bruchey, *The Roots of American Economic Growth, 1607–1861* (New York: Harper Torchbooks, 1968). Also valuable on these and other financial policies is Paul Studenski and Herman E. Krooss, *Financial History of the United States* (New York: McGraw-Hill, 1963).

For longer-term analyses of government revenue, spending, and debts, see Sidney Ratner, *The Tariff in American History* (New York: Van Nostrand, 1972); Ratner's *Taxation and Democracy in America* (New York: Wiley Science, 1967); Paul B. Trescott, "The United States Government and National Income, 1790–1860," in National Bureau of Economic Research, *Trends in the American Economy in the Nineteenth Century, Studies in Income and Wealth,* vol. 24 (Princeton, N.J.: Princeton University Press, 1960); Lance Davis and John Legler, "The Government in the American Economy: A Quantitative Study," *Journal of Economic History,* 26 (Dec. 1966); and B. U. Ratchford, *American State Debts* (Durham: Duke University Press, 1941). For the ways in which U.S. states used banks as sources of public revenue, see Richard Sylla, John B. Legler, and John J. Wallis, "Banks and State Public Finance in the New Republic: The United States, 1790–1860," *Journal of Economic History,* 47 (June 1987).

The development and diversity of banking institutions are the subjects of Fritz Redlich, *The Molding of American Banking: Men and Ideas* (New York: Johnson Reprint Corp., 1968); J. Van Fenstermaker, *The Development of American Commercial Banking, 1782–1837* (Kent, Ohio: Kent State University Press, 1965); and several articles by Richard Sylla, "American Banking and Growth in the Nineteenth Century: A Partial View of the Terrain," *Explorations in Economic History,* 9 (Winter 1971–72); "Forgotten Men of Money: Private Bankers in Early U.S. History," *Journal of Economic History,* 36 (March 1976); and "Early American Banking: The Significance of the Corporate Form," *Business and Economic History,* 14 (1985).

Benjamin Klebaner's *American Commercial Banking: A History* (Boston: Twayne Publishers, 1990) offers a compact survey of all the eras of U.S. banking history, while Larry Schweikart, *Banking in the American South from the Age of Jackson to Reconstruction* (Baton Rouge: Louisiana State University Press, 1987) provides a provocative analysis of antebellum banking in one U.S. region. The origins of the dollar as the American monetary unit are traced by Arthur Nussbaum, *A History of the Dollar* (New York: Columbia University Press, 1957). Issues in control of the money supply and banks are the subjects of Bray Hammond, *Banks and Politics in America from the Revolution to the Civil War* (Princeton, N.J.: Princeton University Press, 1957; reissued in paperback, 1991); Hugh Rockoff, *The Free Banking Era: A Re-Examination* (New York: Arno Press, 1975); Walter B. Smith, *Economic Aspects of the Second Bank of the United States* (Cambridge: Harvard University Press, 1953); Peter Temin, *The Jacksonian Economy* (New York: W. W. Norton, 1969); and Richard H. Timberlake, Jr., *The Origins of Central Banking in the United States* (Cambridge: Harvard University Press, 1978).

Chapter 8

Beginnings of the Industrial Revolution in America

Obstacles to U.S. Industrialization

"Manufacturing" in the Early United States

The Industrial Revolution

The Spread of Antebellum Manufacturing

Antebellum Technological Developments

Government Assistance to Manufacturing

Rudimentary Labor Organization

Education and Human Capital

INDUSTRIALIZATION IS THE GREAT WATERSHED OF modern economic history. Dating from the eighteenth century, industrialization reduced the real cost (that is, in terms of labor and natural resources) of producing goods and services to such a degree that the resulting levels of material welfare for the average person came to vastly exceed those reached by premodern and nonindustrial economies. In the United States, the process of industrialization began late in the eighteenth century and was firmly established by the early decades of the nineteenth century. By the late nineteenth century, the United States became the leading nation in industrial production, a position it has now maintained for more than a century.

Obstacles to U.S. Industrialization

That the United States would become one of the first nations to embark on industrialization was far from obvious at the end of the eighteenth century. Favoring such an outcome were America's close ties with Great Britain (home of the first Industrial Revolution) and the vicissitudes of the Napoleonic War era, which both stimulated economic activity in the United States and at times interfered with the flow of manufactured goods from Britain and Europe. The obstacles standing in the way of industrialization in the United States were much greater, however. A population smaller than Britain's was scattered over a massive geographical area, and internal transportation costs were high. Together these factors limited the markets for mass-produced industrial goods. The accumulation of capital and facilities for mobilizing funds for investment were also limited. But the greatest obstacle, somewhat paradoxically, was America's abundance of land and natural resources. This abundance meant that the return to labor applied in activities such as farming, forest products, and

maritime trades was high enough to work against the formations of a concentrated labor force and a highly interdependent urban lifestyle typical of modern industrial economies. Later generations would view Thomas Jefferson's urgings that Americans follow an independent, uncomplicated existence in a simple, agrarian republic as old-fashioned. In truth, there was economic logic in the great Virginian's views at the time he formulated them. Soon, however, the machine appeared in the garden.

Industrialization in the American context therefore meant a number of things. It meant that cost-reducing manufacturing technologies borrowed from overseas pioneers had to be adapted to America's different circumstances. It also meant that new technologies developed by Americans would have to emphasize principles different from the technologies developed abroad. And it meant that internal markets had to be opened up to absorb the enlarged flow of manufactured goods produced at new centers of production. Because of the attractions of agriculture, industrialization meant that American manufacturing had to depend in a crucial way on agricultural raw materials and farmers' needs for nonfarm products. In addition, the effects of abundant land on labor returns meant that American manufacturers had to experiment in forming reliable industrial labor forces, and that they favored tariff protection for their products but desired a free flow of labor and capital from overseas. Finally, industrialization meant that American workers had to search for methods of protecting and advancing their interests in new situations of increased economic interdependence.

"Manufacturing" in the Early United States

The term *manufacturing* today is defined as the mass production of goods from raw materials in factories owned by large enterprises that employ wage laborers and salaried managerial staffs and that use large inputs of power-driven machinery embodying sophisticated technologies. Yet the etymology of *manufacture*—that is, its Latin roots—has the rather simple connotation of making things by hand. In the United States, the years from 1790 to 1860 marked the transition from the Latin meaning of *manufacture* to the new and more complex definition. The shift in meaning reflected dramatic changes in the progress of economic development.

What manufacturing meant to Americans around 1790 is well illustrated by the following account of Lancaster, Pennsylvania. It is from *A View of the United States of America* by Tench Coxe, an advocate of American manufacturing in the early days of the Republic:

> *In the midland counties of Pennsylvania, many precious manufactures have resulted from a flourishing agriculture, and immediately on their birth, have contributed to the prosperity of the cultivators. The borough of Lancaster, which is the largest inland town in the United States, is sixty-six miles from a seaport, and ten from any practiced boat navigation. The number of families was in 1786, about 700, of whom 234 were manufacturers. The following is a list of them. Fourteen hatters, thirty-six shoemakers, four tanners, seventeen saddlers, twenty-five tailors, twenty-five weavers of woolen, linen, and cotton cloth, three stocking weavers, twenty-five white and black smiths, six wheel wrights, eleven coopers, six clock and watchmakers, six tobacco and snuff manufacturers, four dyers, seven gun smiths, five rope makers, four tinners, two brass founders, three skin dressers, one brush maker, seven turners, seven nail makers, five silver smiths, three potters, three brewers, three copper smiths, and two printers in English and German. There were in 1786 also, within thirty-nine miles of the town, seventeen*

> *furnaces, forges, rolling mills and slitting mills, and within ten miles of it, eighteen grain mills, sixteen saw mills, one fulling mill, four oil mills, five hemp mills, two boring and grinding mills for gun barrels, and eight tanneries. . . . It may be safely affirmed, that the counties of Lancaster (in which the borough is), York and Berks are among the most vigorous in Pennsylvania, perhaps in the Union, and that there are none in the state in which there are more manufactures, is beyond all question. They are all fifty miles or more from the nearest seaport.*[1]

Coxe's sketch of a progressive manufacturing area depicts the chief manufacturing unit as the family, not the specialized shop or factory. A good many of the manufacturing families were probably also farm families engaged in the production of simple manufactures during slack agricultural times and seasons. The markets, although competitive as evidenced by the number of manufacturers in each category, were highly localized. The primitive state of transportation was a boon to small-scale manufacturing, not a drawback; it acted like a high tariff on imported articles. Thus, comparatively rural areas such as Lancaster were centers of manufacturing, whereas the larger seaport cities specialized in trade and imported most of their manufactured goods from overseas. American manufacturing was located in and served local markets that were not near the seaports.

Two decades after Coxe published his *A View of the United States of America*, he was employed by the federal government to compile the *Digest of Manufactures of the United States* based on returns gathered under government instructions by the marshals of the 1810 Census.[2] Coxe's *Digest* was the first extensive and tolerably systematic study of American manufacturing. It reported the value of U.S. manufactured products as $127.7 million. However, Coxe added $45.1 million to this total to make up for undercounting and included $25.9 million for activities he termed of a "doubtful or agricultural" nature (such as flour and grist milling, saw milling, and brick making). The estimated gross value of American manufactures in 1810, then, was just under $200 million. Since the country's population was about 7.25 million, per capita production of manufactured goods was approximately $27 in 1810 values.

The leading manufactures specifically enumerated in the $127.7 million total for 1810 were textiles ($41.5 million), hides and skins ($17.9 million), distilled and fermented liquors ($16.5 million), iron ($14.4 million), machinery ($6.1 million), wood products ($5.6 million), and cables and cordage ($4.2 million). The widespread businesses of grain milling and lumber production were excluded from the totals because they were considered agricultural, not manufacturing, activities. Most of the manufactured products of 1810 were produced in much the same ways as they had been produced in Lancaster, Pennsylvania, in the 1780s. For example, the 1810 Census returns showed that over 90 percent of textile products, then the leading industry, were made in homes, not in shops or factories. In other industries, two slightly more specialized types of productive organization were more common: (1) in artisan shops craftspeople labored with journeymen and apprentices; and (2) in the merchant-employer system, a merchant supplied raw materials to a craftsperson who produced the product at home and later turned it over to the merchant for sale. The latter type of manufacturing was more common in 1810 than in 1790, and it became still more widespread in later decades as production for distant markets expanded under the influence of improved methods of transportation and communication. Nonetheless, the household, shop, and merchant-employer methods of manufacturing represented the traditional way of making things by hand that had persisted for centuries.

The Industrial Revolution

The late eighteenth century witnessed a political revolution in America that resulted in an independent United States. Although Britain opposed the revolution, it was in the midst of revolutionary changes of a different nature—in manufacturing. Unlike a political revolution, the Industrial Revolution in Britain did not have exact beginning and end points. Indeed, industrialization continues today. The persistent nature of the Industrial Revolution as well as the difficulties of determining when it began have led some scholars to question whether it was a revolution at all.[3] However, the way of life and the standard of material welfare of the average British or American person two hundred years ago were very different from what they are for the average person in an industrially developed country today. Whether revolutionary or evolutionary, modern industry has greatly advanced the productivity and value of human labor in a fairly brief period of time in human history. Enormous economic, political, and social changes came with sustained industrial progress, beginning in eighteenth-century England and spreading in greater or lesser degrees throughout much of the world. The United States was among the first nations to follow England's lead in developing a modern industrial sector.

Core Principles and Innovations

The early Industrial Revolution of the eighteenth and nineteenth centuries consisted of several major changes in the way goods were produced. Each change was first introduced in a particular line of production. Later, as its efficacy became clear, the principles involved were applied to more and more lines of production until virtually all manufacturing fell under its sway. One such change was the substitution of power-driven machines for human labor, most evident in British cotton textile manufacturing. Another change was the substitution of inanimate for animate converters of energy; here the classic example is the steam engine, which converted the heat energy of fuels into mechanical power. The Industrial Revolution also brought the large-scale substitution of new raw materials and fuels (such as iron and coal) for vegetable and animal materials.

Each major innovation of the Industrial Revolution in England interacted with the others. For example, steam engines were built of iron and burned coal; they were also used to pump water from mines so that more coal could be produced. Later, steam engines came to be a primary source of power for a wide range of transportation and manufacturing technologies, including those of the textile and iron industries. Iron was used in textile machines as well as in steam engines; soon iron and its derivative products found so many uses that they became the chief raw materials and symbols of the new industrial age. The principles involved in the core innovations of the Industrial Revolution were extended to more and more lines of economic activity. The result was a rather steady expansion of the output of manufactured goods at rates substantially in excess of population growth.

The Early Cotton Textile Industry

The first great factory industry of the Industrial Revolution in England was cotton textiles. Cotton cloth imported from India became popular with English consumers in the early eighteenth century, but it was understandably less popular with the large numbers of English producers of wool and woolen cloth. The wool interests succeeded in obtaining restrictions on imports of Indian cotton goods. Nonetheless, the existence of a wide market for cotton textiles has been demonstrated, encouraging the English to find ways to produce cotton goods.

From the 1740s to the 1780s, English inventors created a remarkable series of textile machines that greatly increased the productivity of labor in textile production. The chief inventions in yarn spinning and, somewhat later, in cloth weaving were large machines requiring water power. As a result, textile production shifted out of homes and small shops and into factories located at sites where water power was available.

Americans in the 1780s were aware of the English inventions in textile production and sought to imitate them. However, the English tried to reserve the inventions for their own use by passing laws forbidding the export of the new machines and making it illegal for persons knowledgeable in the technology to leave the country. Nonetheless, one such person, Samuel Slater, migrated to America in 1789. One year later, in partnership with two Rhode Island merchants, William Almy and Moses Brown, Slater established a cotton factory on the Blackstone River at Pawtucket, Rhode Island. The partners utilized the water-frame spinning machine developed by the English inventor Richard Arkwright in 1769. Their business prospered, and in the next quarter-century, particularly after 1807 when Jefferson's embargo cut off imports from England, a number of similar ventures were founded. Cotton textile production was centered in southern New England.

The major product of the new American cotton factories was yarn, the output of the spinning machines. Although the yarn factories made great strides in supplanting household spinning, cloth, the product of weaving, continued for the most part to be produced in households and shops on handlooms. As noted earlier in the chapter, Coxe's *Digest* indicated that in 1810 over 90 percent of American "products of the loom" were still produced in homes.

Credit for initiating the complete transfer of cotton cloth production into factories goes to

Samuel Slater's Cotton Spinning Factory.   Erected at Pawtucket, Rhode Island, in the early 1790s, this "first American factory" is seen in a photo taken about a century later. The falling water of the Blackstone River turned a waterwheel in the mill; shafts and belts transferred the power to the spinning machinery. Two centuries on, the "Old Slater Mill," looking better than here, still stands on its original site as a component of a museum of industrial history. (Brown Brothers)

Francis Cabot Lowell, a Boston merchant. Lowell went to England from 1810 to 1812 to learn the secrets, still jealously guarded by the English, of constructing and operating power-driven looms. In this he was successful, but Lowell's contributions to American industrial development went well beyond the transfer of new technologies to the United States. Unlike many other manufacturers of the time, Lowell realized that the improved technology was a complex and roundabout method of production requiring time and money to implement. Upon returning to the United States, he persuaded a group of Boston merchants to invest $100,000 in the stock of the Boston Manufacturing Company, which he used to finance the development and implementation of the new techniques. The company was founded in 1813, and late in the following year Lowell and his co-worker, skilled mechanic Paul Moody, constructed their first power loom.

The Boston Manufacturing Company built the first vertically integrated textile factory in the United States, on the Charles River at Waltham, Massachusetts, near Boston. In the Waltham factory, the various steps in textile manufacturing—from processing the raw cotton to producing the finished cloth—were carried out in one place under a single management. The new techniques and organizational methods were quickly imitated; large, integrated cotton factories were established along a number of rivers in New England, New York, and Pennsylvania. Lowell, Massachusetts, located on the Merrimack River north of Boston and named after Francis Cabot Lowell,

Power Loom Weaving *circa* **1820.** By that date the power looms introduced to the United States in 1814 by Francis Cabot Lowell were multiplying rapidly. Note the great preponderance of female workers and also the overhead shafts and belts that transferred power from waterwheels to the looms. (Historical Pictures/ Stock Montage)

rapidly became the leading center of the new industry in the 1820s. It was also the first urban area in the United States to be founded around an industry.

Cotton textile production in American factories increased rapidly in the two decades following the introduction of the power loom. Between 1815 and 1833, output of all cotton goods grew at a compound rate of over 16 percent per year, and cloth output alone grew at 29 percent per year as production shifted out of homes and into factories. Prices of cotton cloth declined because the new technology was vastly more efficient in using resources than were the handicraft methods of earlier years. However, the supply factors of improved manufacturing techniques and falling raw cotton prices accounted for only part of the expansion of textile output. On the de-

mand side, population and income were expanding and would have led to larger output even if prices had not declined. Transportation improvements also helped to widen the market for cloth that was mass-produced at centralized locations. Tariffs on textile imports after 1816 also expanded the markets of the new factories by reducing cloth imports. All in all, the expanding demand for American factory cloth may have outweighed the contribution of improved technology in this first great expansion of industrial output in the United States.

One reason demand was so important in the early expansion of the cotton textile industry is that it took time to learn how to build and operate the new machines on an extended scale. In the earliest years of the industrial age, only a limited number of people had this knowledge, and they earned substantial profits or, more properly, rents, because the supply of their talents was limited. Only after machine making and managerial skills became more widely diffused throughout industry did textile prices fall to near the cost of production, as is the tendency of prices in a competitive market economy. In the interim, the leaders of the new industry reaped substantial fortunes.

The Spread of Antebellum Manufacturing

Cotton textile manufacturing, with water-powered machinery and a large labor force centralized in factories, was the first truly modern industry to develop in the United States. The *McLane Report,* an 1832 U.S. Treasury survey of American manufacturing, showed that 88 of 106 manufacturing enterprises with invested capital of $100,000 or more were textile companies. Most of these were producers of cotton cloth. The report also showed that 31 of 36 enterprises employing

250 or more workers were textile producers.[4] The leading role of cotton manufacturing continued up to the eve of the Civil War. According to the 1860 Census, the cotton industry led all others in terms of value added—value of products less cost of raw materials—which is a measure of an industry's contribution to the total national product for any given year.

Moreover, in terms of the factory organization of production, textile making far outdistanced other major industries. The average cotton factory in 1860 employed 143 wage laborers. In contrast, woolen goods production, the next leading industry, averaged only thirty-three workers per establishment.

Leading American Industries

The leading U.S. industries in 1860, ranked by value added, are shown in Table 8–1. Census information is useful in clarifying the dual nature of American manufacturing in 1860. As noted earlier in the chapter, most manufacturing in the young Republic was carried out in

Table 8–1   *The Leading U.S. Industries in 1860*[a]

	Value Added (in $ millions)	Number of Establishments (in thousands)	Workers Employed (in thousands)	Workers per Establishment
1. Cotton goods	$ 55	0.8	115	143
2. Lumber	54	20.2	76	4
3. Boots and shoes	49	12.5	123	10
4. Iron	46	2.3	68	30
5. Clothing	41	4.2	121	29
6. Flour and meal	40	13.9	28	2
7. Machinery	33	1.4	41	30
8. Leather	26	5.2	26	5
9. Woolen goods	25	1.2	41	33
All manufactures[b]	$854	140.4	1,311	9

[a] Ranked by value added (i.e., value of products less cost of raw materials).
[b] Includes some mining activities.
Source: Calculated from data in U.S. Bureau of the Census, *Eighth Census of the United States, 1860*, vol. 3, *Manufactures* (Washington, D.C.: GPO, 1865), pp. 733–42.

VIEW OF THE BOOTT COTTON MILLS, AT LOWELL, MASS.

The Boott Cotton Mills at Lowell, Massachusetts *circa* **1852.** By the 1850s, the United States had many factories as well as a number of industrial cites. It was established as an industrial nation. (Culver Pictures)

homes or small shops and most products were destined for consumption in nearby markets. Although specialization had increased substantially by 1860, even then a number of the leading industries were still organized on the basis of small-scale production units. Lumber, boots and shoes, flour and meal, and leather production fall into this category. Lumber and flour were used throughout the country, the former as a construction material and the latter as a basic element of nearly everyone's diet. Because both products were derived from the ubiquitous forests and farms and were rather bulky in relation to their value, it was still efficient in 1860 to produce them near where they were to be consumed. Leather and its related products (such as boots and shoes) were more valuable in relation to their bulk, so they could bear the cost of shipping from more centralized producing areas. The boot and shoe industry was concentrated to a great extent in New England; but before the Civil War, production in relatively small shops continued to predominate over factory production. In contrast, the factory by 1860 had made greater inroads in other leading industries, especially textiles and clothing, and iron and machinery.

Textiles and Clothing. Cotton and woolen cloth produced in factories supplanted home textile production in the decades after 1815. Since a major use of cloth was to make garments, the development of specialized clothing manufacturers soon followed and was hastened by the invention of the sewing machine in the 1840s. Production of ready-made clothing, however, was not based on dramatic technological improvements such as those of textile production. Although clothing manufacture had become a leading industry in 1860, a great deal of it, especially the making of women's clothing, continued to occur in the home or in small shops.

Ironworks. Iron, iron products, and machinery are widely and properly considered basic

heavy industries in industrial economies. It is somewhat surprising, therefore, that as late as 1860 the average employment in individual iron-producing enterprises was far smaller than that in cotton textiles and on a par with woolen goods and clothing manufacturers (see Table 8–1). To some extent the figure of thirty employees per ironworks establishment in 1860 is misleading because the category lumps together a number of lines of manufacture. Two subcategories—pig iron production, and forged, rolled, and wrought iron products—for example, employed fifty-six and fifty-five persons per establishment, respectively, whereas in the production of castings the average was nineteen persons per establishment. Even so, much progress toward a larger scale of iron production in the individual firm was made in the last decade before the Civil War. Data from the 1850 Census indicate that there were about two and a half times as many iron enterprises in 1850 as there were in 1860, and the average employment in these firms included only ten people in 1850 but thirty workers in 1860. The amount of capital invested in the average iron enterprise nearly quadrupled in the 1850s, though in 1860 it was still less than one-third of the capital invested in the average cotton mill.

The late antebellum transformation of the American iron industry to larger-scale production by individual firms is especially interesting because it was so different from the experience of the British iron industry during the first Industrial Revolution. While the U.S. cotton industry generally followed the pattern of its English predecessor, American iron making did not. Rather, it followed a different path and experienced slower development, both in total production and in the scale of productive organization. As we will see, the differences explain how technology interacts with resources in an economy.

Fuels. Factors related to the fuels used in iron processing account for much of the difference in the early histories of the British and American iron industries. Before the Industrial Revolution, pig iron was produced by smelting iron ore in charcoal-fueled furnaces. Charcoal was also widely used in refining pig iron into wrought iron, a more malleable form suited to making many iron products. During the seventeenth and eighteenth centuries, however, wood for making charcoal became scarce in England. In response to rising fuel costs, eighteenth-century British inventors laid the basis for the modern iron industry by perfecting the methods of making iron and iron products with coal, an abundant resource. The English innovations that allowed iron production to be concentrated in larger units included (1) the use of coke (derived from coal) as the fuel for smelting ore in blast furnaces to make pig iron and (2) the puddling process for refining pig iron into wrought iron.

In the United States, charcoal continued to be the major fuel used in iron production during the early decades of the nineteenth century. Wood was widely available in the forested eastern United States, and small iron deposits were numerous. The result was scattered, small-scale iron production by many firms (often called plantations rather than factories or mills because of their rural locations). Bituminous coal for coking was available west of the Appalachian Mountains, particularly in western Pennsylvania. But the earliest deposits exploited contained impurities that resulted in low-grade iron. In addition, the coal deposits were located far from the major markets for iron in the East. By the 1850s, however, the American population had shifted westward and better grades of bituminous coking coal were discovered, explaining in part the growing scale of iron-producing units in the 1850s. After the Civil War, western coals and ores led to a tremendous expansion of the American iron and steel industry along the lines pioneered by the British.

More significant for antebellum industrial development, in iron as well as in a broad range of other industries, was the exploitation of the hard anthracite coal found on the eastern slope of the Alleghenies, primarily in Pennsylvania. Although geographically closer to potential markets, the anthracite fields were isolated in an economic sense until canals reached them in the 1820s and 1830s. Shortly thereafter the use of anthracite coal was adopted in all of the several stages of eastern iron production—from reheating wrought iron bars in order to fashion products, to refining pig iron into wrought iron, to producing pig iron from ore in blast furnaces. In making pig iron, the required technique for using anthracite—the hot blast method—was patented by an Englishman only in 1828, more than a century after the discovery of the bituminous coke-smelting process.

Although anthracite coal production was insignificant in the early 1820s, it rose to a million tons per year by the late 1830s and to nearly four million tons by the end of the 1840s. Anthracite provided the first cheap source of mineral fuel for eastern manufacturers and urban dwellers. Makers of cast and wrought iron products were the major beneficiaries of anthracite development, but other industries requiring substantial inputs of heat in their production processes were also aided. Anthracite thus became an important fuel for eastern steam engines, with far-reaching effects. Up until about 1840, most factory production in the United States (except in textiles) was limited to water-powered sites away from the major cities. After 1840, however, the new mineral fuels allowed heat and power to be brought to population centers, contributing significantly to the growth of factories in a wide range of industries as well as to the industrialization of American cities.

Centers of Manufacturing. American manufacturing in 1860 was heavily concentrated in the Northeast. The three leading states—New York, Pennsylvania, and Massachusetts—contained about one-fourth of the 1860 population and accounted for approximately one-half of the value added by all manufacturing. Massachusetts dominated the textiles and boots and shoes industries, whereas Pennsylvania was the leader in iron and machinery. New York possessed a more diversified industrial base, but it was the dominant producer in the expanding ready-made clothing industry. Following the three leaders in the Northeast were Ohio, Connecticut, and New Jersey. However, the total value added by manufacturing in these states barely exceeded that of Massachusetts alone and was less than that of either New York or Pennsylvania. The six leaders were contiguous states, and it is evident that antebellum America had a manufacturing belt as real as the Cotton Belt across the Deep South and the Corn Belt emerging in the Midwest. All three belts shifted to the West after 1860, but they remained important parts of the economic landscape in the United States.

Increased Economic Share of Manufacturing.

How significant was manufacturing in the economy of 1860? Early historians often viewed the antebellum years as an agrarian period with industrialization taking hold after the Civil War. While it is true that as late as 1880 more than half of the American labor force was still engaged in agricultural pursuits, the decline in the percentage of agricultural workers in the total labor force was rapid in earlier decades, falling from 84 percent to 55 percent between 1810 and 1850. During that same period, moreover, the percentage of American workers engaged in manufacturing on a full-time basis rose from 3 percent to 15 percent. Thus around two-fifths of the decline in agriculture's share of the labor force resulted as workers shifted to full-time manufacturing pursuits. This shift into manufacturing was robust by later standards as well: The share of American

workers in manufacturing increased to a peak of 27 percent in 1920 and declined thereafter. Clearly, then, manufacturing was growing well before the Civil War.

Yet the contribution of manufacturing to the total national product was even greater than its share of the country's labor force. This contribution can be measured by the value added to raw materials by manufacturing processes, whereas the national product is the sum of value added by every sector of the economy. In both 1850 and 1860, the value added by manufacturing was about 20 percent of the national product.

This comparison—of manufacturing's share of the labor force with its contribution to the national product—provides important insights into why the manufacturing sector grew so rapidly during the antebellum years. The average American worker engaged in manufacturing was able to produce goods that had a greater value than the goods produced by a worker in the nonmanufacturing sectors. Well before 1860, the relatively greater productivity of manufacturing labor, as reflected in prices, wages, and profits, favored American industrial development by encouraging increasing numbers of entrepreneurs and workers to engage in manufacturing pursuits.

Antebellum Technological Developments

The great technological advances of the nineteenth century were centered on the development of machinery, power, and the use of new materials, especially metals and mineral fuels. England's Industrial Revolution forcefully demonstrated the substantial advantages of new techniques of production in textiles, iron, and power. Americans were among the first of many to benefit from the English techniques. However, several original contributions to modern technology were also made by antebellum Americans. These led, even before the Civil War, to a reverse flow of productive knowledge across the Atlantic.

Borrowed Technologies

As noted earlier in the chapter, American technical development came about in part as a result of British innovations in textile manufacturing (such as spinning and power-weaving methods) during the late eighteenth and early nineteenth centuries. James Watt's steam engine also migrated from England to the New World. Robert Fulton's *Clermont,* the first steamboat introduced on the Hudson in 1807, was powered by a low-pressure steam engine constructed by the British firm of Boulton and Watt. Americans, however, pioneered in the development and application of high-pressure steam engines; because of their comparatively light weight, they were better suited than low-pressure engines for river steamboats. They also required more fuel than Watt's engine, but fuel—especially wood fuel—was abundant in the United States. Early American technologists learned that a technology transferred from one set of economic circumstances to another often requires modifications for maximum economic efficiency.

In the United States, steam found its greatest application in transportation. An 1838 report of the federal government on the scope of steam-engine use indicated that 60 percent of steam power was devoted to propelling steamboats at a time when the railroad was just beginning to exert its demand for steam as a source of tractive power.[5] Yet stationary industrial uses of steam power were also widespread. Steam engines, introduced in textile manufacture by Samuel Slater in 1828, furnished the power for an estimated 15 percent of textile production a decade later. Steam power was also employed extensively in iron making and in sugar and lumber mills during the late 1830s, when some fourteen hundred to

sixteen hundred stationary steam engines were already in use. Thereafter, the greater availability of anthracite coal and the full exploitation of better water-power sites encouraged rapid growth in the use of steam power in northeastern manufacturing. Water, nonetheless, remained the chief source of industrial power up to the Civil War.

Only in the smelting of iron did American producers lag well behind their British counterparts. As noted earlier in the chapter, American smelters relied almost completely on charcoal before 1840 because of the nature and the location of demand in relation to that of coking coal. The American iron industry much earlier had adopted British techniques of puddling and rolling at the refining and shaping stages of iron manufacture.

Original Technologies

America's early and original contributions to technology came not in the great industries of the English Industrial Revolution but rather in a group of smaller and lighter industries as well as in methods of material handling. The industries affected were primarily those concerned with light metal products and woodworking.

Gun making and Interchangeable Parts.   Gun making—where the important technical principle of interchangeable parts was introduced— was one of the earliest industries. Connecticut gun makers, including Eli Whitney, took the first steps in the early nineteenth century to make by hand uniform parts for the weapons they produced. The great advantage of standardization was that the finished product could be assembled by relatively unskilled labor instead of a skilled gunsmith. Also, worn or defective parts could be replaced easily with others of the same specifications. The following decades thus witnessed the development of sophisticated machinery for parts making. The machines were more precise than was handworking and they could be run by non-human power sources, greatly extending the scope and efficiency of gun-making operations. By 1820, the metal and wooden parts of the gun, including even the irregularly shaped gunstock, were being made almost entirely by machine.

The principle of manufacturing goods with interchangeable parts made by sophisticated, power-driven machinery spread from gun making to a number of other industries, including watches and clocks, locks, simple fasteners (such as nails, screws, nuts, and bolts), sewing machines, and agricultural implements. By the mid-nineteenth century, Americans were showing their wares at European exhibitions and Europeans were forming committees to cross the Atlantic and visit the workshops of America. Soon Europeans were looking to purchase not only American goods but also the highly specialized machines that made them.

Machinery and Machine Tools. American ingenuity in the development of complex machinery was critical to implementing the principle of interchangeability. The antebellum decades saw specialized machine and machine-tool makers develop out of earlier, more general operations. The textile industry played an important role. During the early phases of the industry's expansion, textile companies established their own machine shops to build and repair both textile machines and the power apparatus. As the demand for textile machinery increased, some of these shops separated from their mills and joined other machine shops to form an industry of specialized machine makers. The machine shops also branched out into making nontextile equipment, including not only machine tools but steam engines and railway locomotives as well. The growth of markets led to further economies as still more specialized firms emerged in each of these lines of activity.

Machine making thus started as an adjunct of other industrial operations in the early nineteenth century, emerged as a separate industry before the Civil War, and went on to become the leading American industry in the twentieth century.

Origins of the Assembly Line. Another antebellum technical development was related to the handling of materials. The origin of the assembly line—where a product moves through stages of manufacture and assembly while workers remain relatively stationary—was in the automated flour mill constructed by Oliver Evans, a Philadelphia inventor, in the 1780s. Grain entered the mill at one end, went through milling processes, and emerged as flour at the other end without the direct use of any labor in the intervening stages. However, Evans's mill did not enjoy much success, possibly because at that early date ingenuity and capital, the chief factors in such an operation, were more scarce than labor. The idea of moving products automatically through processing stages reemerged in the pork-packing plants of Cincinnati during the two or three decades before the Civil War. Hog carcasses were suspended from an overhead rail and moved at a steady rate past a line of workers, each performing one small specialized task in the packing process. The assembly line and the principle of interchangeable parts, two early American contributions to technology, were later combined with dramatic effect in such twentieth-century industries as automobile and airplane manufacturing.

Explaining U.S. Technological Developments

What explains early Americans' success in adapting technologies invented by the British and in perfecting potent and original techniques of their own? Because technological change and its diffusion have played a major role in shaping the modern world and America's role within it, this question has long fascinated scholars. Some emphasize economic factors; others place more stress on social or political characteristics of early American society. In practice, of course, it is difficult to separate such influences. The standardization of products and their mass production, for example, may have been effective because the population had fairly homogeneous tastes or because of the substantially lower product prices generated by cost economies and market competition.

Recognizing the interpretative problem, there were a few broad characteristics of antebellum America that did exert powerful influences on the direction of technological change. Foremost among these was the nation's great endowment of natural resources in relation to its population size and accumulated savings. Contemporary Europeans viewed American production methods in agriculture and manufacturing as wasteful of land, wood, and mineral resources. Today, it is widely recognized that such methods were a rational response to relative resource endowments. Cheap natural resources were rationally substituted for more expensive capital and labor. American techniques often reflected capital scarcity as much as labor scarcity. Early American textile machines were flimsily constructed of much more wood and much less metal than their English counterparts. Within the United States, there were regional variations on the same theme. Stationary steam engines were relatively more important than water power in the West for several reasons: The rivers and streams in the West fell less rapidly than in New England, steam was a more labor-intensive, less capital-using form of power than falling water, and capital was scarcer in the West than in New England.

Antebellum Americans were thus sensitive to the relative prices of productive factors. But why they were that way was more than simple cost minimization. During the last two centuries, large areas of the world have at one time or another been in a similar position with respect to factor endowments but produced fewer advances in technological and economic development than the United States. The level and timing of patenting activity in the early nineteenth century provide additional clues. The large numbers of patents filed and granted at this time suggests that American inventors were active in part because they could secure property rights in their inventions. Moreover, according to economic historian Kenneth Sokoloff, the surges in patenting activity from 1808 to 1812, when imports were interrupted by the fallout of the Napoleonic Wars, and from 1823 to 1836, when tariffs became more protective and internal transportation breakthroughs occurred, suggest that rapidly expanding domestic markets also contributed to high rates of technological progress.[6]

Government Assistance to Manufacturing

In the early United States, direct governmental aid in the form of investment in manufacturing facilities or in the training of labor was uncommon, though not altogether insignificant. The federal government underwrote part of the early development of gun making, a pioneering industry in the application of the principle of interchangeable parts. Later, the government operated arsenals that manufactured weapons on that principle. Such policies were limited in scope, however, and not confined to the manufacturing sector. A few direct investments were made in transportation enterprises, and federal funds financed the first successful telegraph line in the 1840s. In transportation, communication, and banking, the direct role of state governments was much more extensive than the federal role. State and local participation in manufacturing, however, was negligible. Most of the benefits obtained from government by the manufacturing sector were therefore indirect: Governments promoted institutions and activities that, while apart from manufacturing, were very useful to it. An example is the government-established patent system, which gave inventors property rights in their inventions.

Tariff Protection

In one area, however, government policy seemed directly attuned to the aspirations of manufacturers: the protective tariff. Alexander Hamilton's classic *Report on Manufactures* (1791) proposed to Congress an extensive program—of which the tariff was only one aspect—to aid the development of manufacturing.[7] One rationale for protection to manufactures—not clearly formulated by Hamilton but consistent with the tone of his report—was the so-called infant industry argument, which contends that a new or young industry needs protection if it is to develop in a world where industries in other countries have already perfected modern techniques of manufacturing, management, raw material supply, and so on. Without protection, the argument holds, competition from the more mature industries of other countries (like Great Britain) would stifle and perhaps destroy the native infant industry. When the industry eventually matures enough to compete on its own, presumably protection could be withdrawn.

American tariff policy became purposely protective in 1816. At this time, British manufacturers with backlogs of goods built up during the years when war interrupted their foreign trade were underselling many of the products of domestic manufacturers. The Tariff of 1816 and its successors clearly alleviated some of the problems of American manufacturers, both by giving them a greater share of the domestic market and by acting to raise the prices they received. Less clear, though, is whether the very existence of the protected industries depended on the tariff. An infant industry as vigorous as cotton textiles, which expanded its output from 1815 to 1833 at a compound rate of 16 percent per year, probably did not need the tariff for its survival. Indeed, painstaking analysis of its early growth indicates that the tariff made almost no difference. Frank Taussig, a leading student of American tariff history, argues that by 1824 the textile industry was well able to stand on its own feet.[8] More recent research conducted by Paul David demonstrates that, while productive efficiency in textiles increased over time through a process of learning by doing, the tariff on imported textiles nonetheless played a largely redundant role. The important learning effects were related to perfecting the new technology; once this was done—and it could have been accomplished by a free-trade policy accompanied by subsidies to a few pilot plants—the technology could be transferred to other producers.[9] Such a decision on the part of the federal government was far from unthinkable; by 1816, it had already subsidized gun making and later would aid the initial development of the telegraph. In both cases, the technologies perfected in the subsidized pilot projects were quickly adopted by other producers.

In the case of pig iron production, however, there are indications that reductions in tariff rates beginning in 1846, from the high levels of the 1842 tariff, did reduce American output significantly by stimulating increased imports. Although many of the old charcoal smelters ceased operations, the newer anthracite smelters were much less harmed by the lower duties. These results, inconsistent with the infant industry argument for protection, are accounted for by changes in the composition of American iron demand (such as an increased demand for rails made from lower-grade iron smelted with coal and a stagnant demand for the more refined iron products that used charcoal-smelted pig iron as a raw material).

In two major industries, then, protective tariffs were far from critical in allowing them to mature to the point where they could survive in competition with foreign producers. In addition, tariffs did not likely mean survival for most other industries. This, of course, does not imply that tariffs had no effect on industrial growth. Tariffs increased the prices of protected goods as well as the market shares of domestic producers. As producers' profits were raised, greater savings and capital formation in the protected industries were encouraged. However, this represented income redistribution from consumers to producers. In order to determine fairly the tariff's impact on aggregate capital formation, one would need to know how the savings and capital-forming activities of those who bought the higher-priced protected products were affected.

Rudimentary Labor Organization

On the eve of the Civil War, over one-half of the total American labor force was engaged in farming and many of the remaining workers were self-employed. Approximately 70 percent of all workers worked for themselves rather than as employees of others. At the beginning of the nineteenth century, the percentage of self-employed workers was even greater—about nine in ten. The antebellum economy was thus very different from that of later decades, when a far greater percentage of the labor force came to be employees.

The preponderance of self-employment in an essentially competitive economy of numerous small-scale producers meant that problems of labor organization were both less significant in an aggregate sense and of a different character than in later decades. Nonetheless, as the American economy became more diversified and production increasingly specialized, the labor problems of particular sectors demanded innovative solutions. The emergence of the factory system in textile manufacturing furnishes the clearest example.

Forming a Labor Force: Textiles

The great advantage of textile making in factories was the availability of sophisticated machinery, which allowed workers to produce substantially greater quantities of yarn and cloth in a given time than was possible with the older handicraft methods. But factories required power to run their machinery, and for much of the antebellum period water was the primary power source. As a result, factory locations were restricted to sites where water power was available, and the rivers of New England provided many of the sites for the early factories. The labor supply was a problem for the factories because many of them were in rural areas, where the population was spread out and largely engaged in farming. Early American manufacturers faced labor-supply problems more serious than those of the manufacturers in more densely populated Europe.

The Family System. Textile manufacturers sought two solutions to their labor-supply dilemma. In southern New England and the Middle states, the early use of child labor evolved into a system in which whole families were hired to work in textile factories. When Slater opened his first cotton-spinning mill in Rhode Island in 1790, for example, he followed the familiar British practice of employing children from the surrounding area to operate the new machinery. Adult overseers were employed to supervise the children in the relatively simple tasks of tending to the power-driven machinery. With their background in farming, the new industrial workers were already accustomed to long hours of work for low remuneration. As the number of textile factories in southern New England grew, however, there were not enough children in nearby areas to staff them. Slater and other mill owners therefore turned to hiring whole families to work in the factories, inducing them to relocate to the burgeoning mill towns.

Female Labor. Farther north, Francis Cabot Lowell and other early textile manufacturers faced a similar labor-supply problem but sought a different solution, in part because of their aversion to replicating the industrial labor conditions in Britain. They hired young women, primarily from farms, to work in the mills. The young women were induced to accept the offer of mill employment—and their parents were persuaded to allow it—by promises of cash wages and the assurances that their living conditions away from home would be pleasant and instructive, and that their behavior would be carefully supervised by mature factory overseers as well as upright boardinghouse "mothers" in the mill towns. Most of the young women viewed the opportunity as a temporary situation that would allow them to earn some money before settling down into married life.

Evolution of the Industrial Labor Market

By 1820, the family and boardinghouse system of factory labor recruitment were well established in America's first modern industry. Both worked well and were widely regarded as more advanced and humane than the European factory labor systems. From a modern perspective, however, they represented only a temporary solution to industrial labor recruitment resulting from the unique circumstances of the early United States. By the late 1830s, the extremely buoyant conditions of initial industrial development in textiles settled down to a more normal pattern of gradual expansion. Then the innovative labor systems of the earlier years quickly evolved into systems that more nearly resembled those in Europe. With a fairly permanent labor force, mill owners were now able to abandon many of their earlier concerns for the social conditions of workers and to concentrate instead on increasing productive efficiency. Workers sought to return to the slower-paced and more humane industrial life created by earlier practices and conditions, but their efforts were unsuccessful.

Trends in the real wages of workers in manufacturing mirrored the changes taking place in the labor market. In the 1820s, during the initial burst of industrial growth, real wages of northeastern manufacturing workers are estimated by Kenneth Sokoloff and Georgia Villaflor to have increased by rates that ranged from 2.2 percent to 3.7 percent per year. In the 1830s and 1840s, the gains ranged from 1.1 to 1.5 percent per year. In the 1850s, money wages and consumer prices rose at similar rates, implying little change in real wages during that decade. Changes in both product and labor markets account for the real-wage trends. In the leading antebellum industries (textiles, for example, after factory-made products had supplanted home production), demand growth settled down to normal rates based on such factors as population growth. More important, by the 1840s and 1850s the supply of labor to textile and other manufacturing industries became much more elastic than it had been in previous decades.[10]

Two competitive developments in the industrial labor market undercut the earlier, more favorable position of factory workers. The growth of regional and interregional trade in agricultural products, coupled with the opening up of new and fertile lands in the West, subjected farmers in the older settled areas of New England and the Middle states to increased competition. One option in responding to the new competition was to take up farming in the West; a less costly option was to abandon full-time farming and move into manufacturing employment. Also increasing the supply of industrial labor was the growth of immigration after the third decade of the nineteenth century. Large numbers of antebellum immigrants, particularly those of Irish, German, or British origin, arrived in the northeastern states and swelled the region's pool of industrial workers.

Increased competition for factory jobs militated against the development of an organized labor movement for industrial workers. Also, because most of the jobs available required relatively few skills, many were filled by women and children. In 1860, cotton textiles—then the nation's leading and most factory-organized industry—employed 72,000 female hands and 43,000 male hands (many of them young boys). Women were also the dominant employee group in clothing manufacturing and supplied a significant part of the labor used in footwear and woolen manufacturing. The importance of women and children in the leading industries that were organized along factory lines helps to explain why industrial workers' organizations made little progress before the Civil War and for many years after it. Women and children were encouraged to view their jobs as temporary and less critical to family welfare than were males. They therefore were given fewer incentives to attempt to gain better working conditions and wages through organization. Employers and social norms encouraged women and children workers to accept their situation. Nonetheless, as Claudia Goldin's research demonstrates, the gender gap—the ratio of female to male earnings—was substantially reduced between 1820 and 1850 by the competition of manufacturers for female labor.[11] In industries such as textiles, mechanization and increased specialization of labor increased women's productivity relative to that of men.

The Struggles of Organized Labor

The failure of labor organizations to develop among the largely unskilled or low-skilled factory workers contrasts with the emergence of such forces at earlier dates in the traditional craft trades carried out in small shops. In these lines of activity, skills learned over long periods of apprenticeship represented a larger and more specific investment in human capital than the simpler knowledge necessary for factory employment. In the early days of the United States, these trades (a number of which are outlined by Tench Coxe in the excerpt cited earlier in the chapter) were carried on for local

markets. As the economy grew and markets widened, craft production became less personalized and custom work gave way to more standardized production for distant markets. The result, of course, was increased competition and less certain income and employment; craft workers responded in time-honored fashion by attempting through organized efforts to restrict production and limit employment to members of their labor organizations.

Legal tradition frowned on such worker efforts to restrict competition. In the first decades of the United States, employers were often successful in having labor unions declared unlawful conspiracies or illegal combinations against the public interest. Court hostility to craft workers' unions continued into the 1820s and 1830s, with a special emphasis on preventing craftspeople from enforcing, by strikes or other means, their goal of a closed shop (that is, a shop that hires only union members). During the same period, however, the political power of laboring groups was extended by the relaxation of property requirements for voting in the chief manufacturing states. Juries, moreover, began to return not-guilty verdicts in a few labor-conspiracy cases. In 1842, a Massachusetts court decision in a precedent-setting case, *Commonwealth v. Hunt,* declared that workers had the right to organize trade unions and that unions were not to be regarded as illegal.

Shorter Hours and Other Goals of Labor.   Craft labor organizations of the 1820s and 1830s pursued both direct economic objectives and indirect political goals. They were less successful in obtaining the economic objectives, which included not only the closed shop but also higher wages, apprenticeship regulations, and shorter working hours. The craft unions' lack of success in these areas was due in part to the hostility of the courts and the general public's aversion to strikes. In addition, the growing competition in the product and labor markets likely played a significant role in undermining the direct economic efforts of the unions (just as competition had earlier given rise to the movement). The early craft union movement was largely confined to cities, mostly in the East, at a time when trade was becoming less local. Thus, if members of a craft union in one city went on strike for one or more objectives, their goods could be brought in by someone else from another place. Recognizing the competitive threat, some craft unions attempted in the mid-1830s to develop wider regional or national organization, but without much success. Depressed economic conditions in the late 1830s and early 1840s not only put an end to such efforts but also undermined the effectiveness of local unions, causing many of them to disappear from the industries.

After the depression of 1839 to 1843, the trade union movement resurfaced during periods of prosperity before the Civil War but then declined when panic and depressed economic conditions returned. Craft workers, who had formed the earliest labor organizations, were becoming a smaller part of the labor force. Industrial labor—in factories, mills, and the scattered workshops of the putting-out system—became much more important in terms of numbers. Although the two groups of workers were very different in their ways of work and in organization, together they were partially successful in achieving one common economic objective: reduction in hours of work. The more organized craft unions led the way by negotiating or by striking for a ten-hour workday in many places before 1860. The federal government provided an important fillip to the movement for reduced work hours in 1840, when President Martin Van Buren put into effect the ten-hour workday for federal employees. In the late 1840s and early 1850s, some states passed ten-hour laws applying to industrial labor, although all contained loopholes. Nonetheless, work hours were gradually reduced from the sunrise-to-sunset system of earlier years; by 1860, an eleven-hour workday was in effect at many factories. Interestingly, workers sometimes willingly accepted wage reductions in or-der to gain shorter hours, an early illustration of the pervasive, long-term tendency of labor to value increments of leisure more highly than increments of goods as incomes rise in a growing economy.

The early labor movement enjoyed more success in its political objectives even though relatively few labor candidates were elected to important offices. Rather, success came when workers added their organized voices to those of reform-minded groups seeking to implement or extend free public education, abolish imprisonment for failure to pay debts punctually, protect workers against employers who defaulted on wages due, and find solutions to other problems facing the laboring class. Among these reform movements, increasing workers' educational opportunities was especially important to progress in wealth and welfare.

Education and Human Capital

Studies of modern economic growth show that substantial fractions of the growth in total national product cannot be accounted for by growth in conventionally measured inputs of the traditional productive factors—labor, capital, and land. That is, the growth in labor-hours or labor-years, in real capital stocks, and in acres of land used in production, when analyzed in the context of the economic theory of production, does not explain all of the growth of total output. The unexplained residual in measured economic growth, sometimes referred to as *productivity* or *technical progress,* is in part the result of growing specialization and efficiency of economic organization, as improvements in transportation, communication,and information extend markets and make them more competitive. But the growth in productivity also derives from improvements in the quality of the productive factors, as labor forces gain more knowledge and as capital equipment increasingly embodies the most up-to-date advances in technology.

Since labor is an economy's most important factor of production—returns to labor typically make up two-thirds to three-fourths of an economy's total income—special attention is often given to the conditions that make labor more productive, such as the quantity and quality of the tools, or capital equipment, with which labor works. A major reason why workers in developed economies are more productive than their counterparts in underdeveloped economies is that the former have more and better tools. It is also apparent, however, that the quality of an economy's tools as well as the efficiency with which those tools are employed in productive processes depend in an important way on the quality of the labor force itself.

Antebellum Schooling Levels

It is widely recognized that the skills and level of education of the American labor force today are high compared to those of most other countries. But did these characteristics apply to the labor force in the early American economy? In terms of both literacy and school enrollment rates (the percentage of student-age people actually attending school), the United States ranked close to the top of all nations surveyed during the years before the Civil War. And this was true despite the institutional barrier of slavery that kept most black children from enjoying the benefits of formal schooling. Concentrating on the white population alone usually raises the United States to the first rank among nations in terms of literacy and schooling. The Census of 1850, for example, showed that only 10 percent of the U.S. white population was illiterate and that over half of the school-age white population attended school. Only Germany and Denmark were at approximately the same levels of literacy and school enrollment. In contrast, Britain and France, two of the most highly developed of the world's economies in the mid-nineteenth century, lagged well behind the United States in terms of educational opportunities for the masses.

However, it should be noted that the provision of education varied substantially among the various sections of the United States in the nineteenth century. In terms of enrollment rates, New England was the leader, with 75 percent to 80 percent of its student-age population attending school between 1840 and 1860. Next came the Middle states, though by 1860 the states of the North Central region had caught up with the Middle Atlantic section. The southern section lagged behind, even when the slave population was excluded, but it exhibited large increases in enrollment rates in the last two antebellum decades.

According to economist Albert Fishlow, before the Civil War, "the United States probably was the most literate and education conscious country in the world."[12] Still, by modern standards, the level of educational attainment was low: school attendance by white school-age persons averaged only forty days a year, less than one-third of modern-day levels. It is important to note, however, that the standard was only twenty days in 1840 and only fourteen days in 1800.

As the American economy became more complex and lost its early agricultural orientation, the need for a more highly educated populace emerged. The northeastern states, the first to industrialize, were foremost in extending general educational opportunity. As English observers sent in the 1850s to study American technology noted:

The compulsory educational clauses adopted in the laws of most of the states, and especially those of New England, by which some three months of every year must be spent at school by the young operative under 14 or 15 years of age, secure every child from the cupidity of the parent, or the neglect of the manufacturer. . . . This lays the foundation for that wide-spread intelligence which prevails amongst the factory operatives of the United States. . . . The skill of hand which comes of experience is, notwithstanding present defects, rapidly following the perceptive power so keenly awakened by early intellectual training.[13]

Education increasingly became a public concern and, at the elementary-school level, compulsory. By 1860, over one-half of the expenditures on formal education were public. The public stake in education reflected the recognition that its benefits extended beyond those reaped by the individual student: economically, politically, and socially, the return to society from an investment in education exceeded the private return to individuals.

Hence, the decision was made for greater public involvement in providing formal schooling. Manufacturers, mindful of the industrial economy's need for adaptable and reliable workers, were often at the forefront of the movement for public education. To its credit, the early labor movement in the United States also was an important force in giving expression and political backing to the education movement.

Summary

The beginnings of industrialization in the early nineteenth-century United States altered the pattern of American economic development that had prevailed during the first two centuries of European settlement. Foreign commerce, including trade in the products of commercial agriculture, gave way to factory industry as the driving force of economic development. Mechanical, chemical, and power-driven technologies began to produce more manufactured goods at declining real costs. Women and children found new employment opportunities in factories. Urban manufacturing centers emerged and began to sprawl, as both employers and workers realized the advantages of locating near other firms and industries. The new urban-industrial way of life led to institutional innovations that helped to sustain it. Among these innovations, mass public education was the most important—in the short run, it inculcated basic skills and served to socialize future workers (both native and foreign-born) to industrial society; in the long run, it laid the groundwork for continuing advances in science, technology, and organization as applied to production. By 1860, industrialization was well established in the United States. Its greatest progress, however, was yet to come.

Endnotes

1. Tench Coxe, *A View of the United States of America* (Philadelphia, 1794), pp. 312–13.
2. *A Statement of the Arts and Manufactures of the United States of America, for the year 1810: Digested and Prepared by Tench Coxe, Esquire, of Philadelphia* (Philadelphia, 1814).
3. See Abbott Payson Usher, *An Introduction to the Industrial History of England* (Boston: Houghton Mifflin, 1920), and Rondo Cameron, *A Concise Economic History of the World from Paleolithic Times to the Present* (New York: Oxford University Press, 1989; 2nd ed., 1992).
4. U.S. Treasury, *McLane Report [Documents Relative to the Manufactures in the United States],* Washington, D.C., 1833.
5. House of Representatives, 25th Cong., 3rd sess., *Steam Engines,* House Executive Document 21 (Washington, D.C., 1839).
6. Kenneth Sokoloff, "Inventive Activity in Early Industrial America: Evidence from Patent Records," *Journal of Economic History* 48 (Dec. 1988), pp. 813–50.
7. Alexander Hamilton, *Report of the Secretary of the Treasury of the United States, on the*

Subject of manufactures, Presented to the House of Representatives, December 5, 1791 (Philadelphia, 1791).

8. Frank W. Taussig, *The Tariff History of the United States*, 8th ed. (New York: G. P. Putnam's Sons, 1931).

9. Paul A. David, *Technical Choice, Innovation, and Economic Growth: Essays on American and British Experience in the Nineteenth Century* (Cambridge, Engl.: Cambridge University Press, 1975), Chap. 2.

10. Kenneth L. Sokoloff and Georgia C. Villaflor, "The Market for Manufacturing Workers during Early Industrialization: The American Northeast, 1820 to 1860," in Claudia Goldin and Hugh Rockoff, eds., *Strategic Factors in Nineteenth Century American Economic History* (Chicago: University of Chicago Press, 1992), pp. 43–44.

11. Claudia Goldin, *Understanding the Gender Gap: An Economic History of American Women* (New York: Oxford University Press, 1990).

12. Albert Fishlow, "The American Common School Revival: Fact or Fancy?" in Henry Rosovsky, ed., *Industrialization in Two Systems* (New York: Wiley, 1966), p. 49.

13. Quoted in Stuart Bruchey, *The Roots of American Economic Growth, 1607–1861* (New York: Harper & Row, 1968), p. 179.

Suggested Readings

The most comprehensive discussion of American manufacturing before the Civil War is Victor S. Clark, *History of Manufactures in the United States, 1607–1850* (Washington, D.C.: Carnegie Institution, 1916). Insights into premodern manufacturing can be gained from Rolla M. Tryon, *Household Manufactures in the United States, 1640–1860* (Chicago: University of Chicago Press, 1917); and Tench Coxe "Digest of Manufactures," vol. 1, 13th Congress, 2nd session (Jan. 1814), in *The New American State Papers—Manufactures*, vol. 1 (Wilmington, Del.: Scholarly Resources, 1972). Cotton textiles, iron, and steam engineering are often considered the core industries of the Industrial Revolution. For early American developments in cotton manufacturing, see Caroline F. Ware, *The Early New England Cotton Manufacture* (Boston: Houghton Mifflin, 1931); for economic analyses, see Robert Brooke Zevin, "The Growth of Cotton Textile Production After 1815," in Robert William Fogel and Stanley L. Engerman, eds., *The Reinterpretation of American Economic History* (New York: Harper & Row, 1971). On iron, see Peter Temin, *Iron and Steel in Nineteenth-Century America: An Economic Inquiry* (Cambridge, Mass.: M.I.T. Press, 1964), and Robert W. Fogel and Stanley L. Engerman, "A Model for the Explanation of Industrial Expansion During the Nineteenth Century: With an Application to the American Iron Industry," *Journal of Political Economy*, 77 (May–June 1969). On steam power, see Peter Temin, "Steam and Waterpower in the Early Nineteenth Century," *Journal of Economic History*, 26 (June 1966). The paper by Alfred D. Chandler, Jr., "Anthracite Coal and the Beginnings of the Industrial Revolution in the United States," *Business History Review*, 46 (Summer 1972), provides a valuable analysis of the impact of a new energy source on manufacturing. Locational aspects of manufacturing development are treated by the geographer Allan R. Pred, *The Spatial Dynamics of United States Urban-Industrial Growth, 1800–1914: Interpretive and Theoretical Essays* (Cambridge, Mass.: M.I.T. Press, 1966). For an excellent short survey of developments in cotton, iron, and manufacturing in general, see the chapter entitled "Manufacturing" in Lance Davis et al., *American Economic Growth: An Economist's History of the United States* (New York: Harper & Row, 1972).

Several important articles that discuss why U.S. industrialization occurred mainly in the Northeast and why women and children were major components of the early industrial labor force are: Kenneth L. Sokoloff, "Was the Transition from the Artisanal Shop to the Non-mechanized Factory Associated with Gains in Efficiency? Evidence from the U.S. Manufacturing Censuses of 1820 and 1850," *Explorations in Economic History,* 21 (Oct. 1984); Claudia Goldin and Kenneth Sokoloff, "The Relative Productivity Hypothesis of Industrialization: The American Case, 1820–1850," *Quarterly Journal of Economics,* 69 (Aug. 1984); and Claudia Goldin and Kenneth Sokoloff, "Women, Children, and Industrialization in the Early Republic: Evidence from the Manufacturing Censuses," *Journal of Economic History,* 52 (Dec. 1982). The effects of industrialization on wages and employment opportunities of women are discussed in Claudia Dale Goldin, *Understanding the Gender Gap: An Economic History of American Women* (New York: Oxford University Press, 1990). Wage trends and other characteristics of the pre-1860 labor markets are studied in two recent essays: Kenneth L. Sokoloff and Georgia C. Villaflor, "The Market for Manufacturing Workers during Early Industrialization: The American Northeast, 1820 to 1860," and Claudia Goldin and Robert A. Margo, "Wages, Prices, and Labor Markets before the Civil War," both in Claudia Goldin and Hugh Rockoff, eds., *Strategic Factors in Nineteenth Century American Economic History* (Chicago: University of Chicago Press, 1992), pp. 29–65, 67–104.

A valuable and readable introduction to the role of technology is Nathan Rosenberg, *Technology and American Economic Growth* (New York: Harper & Row, 1972). More advanced analytical studies, including evaluations of the effects of tariffs on manufacturing development, may be found in Paul David, *Technical Choice, Innovation, and Economic Growth: Essays on American and British Experience in the Nineteenth Century* (Cambridge, Engl.: Cambridge

University Press, 1975). Merritt Roe Smith, *Harpers Ferry Armory and the New Technology* (Ithaca, N.Y.: Cornell University Press, 1972), offers interesting insights into both economic and social aspects of the introduction of new techniques. Long-term implications of early industrial technologies are discussed by David Hounshell, *From the American System to Mass Production, 1800–1932: The Development of Manufacturing Technology in the United States* (Baltimore: Johns Hopkins University Press, 1984). F. W. Taussig, *The Tariff History of the United States,* 8th ed. (New York: G. P. Putnam's Sons, 1931), remains a valuable study of a particular form of government aid to manufacturing. Two studies of the relationship of patent activity to market growth are Kenneth L. Sokoloff, "Inventive Activity in Early Industrial America: Evidence from Patent Records," *Journal of Economic History,* 48 (Dec. 1988); and Kenneth L. Sokoloff and B. Zorina Khan, "The Democratization of Invention During Early Industrialization: Evidence from the United States, 1790–1846," *Journal of Economic History,* 50 (June 1990).

On the role of education in improving the quality of the American labor force, see Douglass C. North, "Capital Formation in the United States During the Early Period of Industrialization: A Reexamination of the Issues," in Robert William Fogel and Stanley L. Engerman, eds., *The Reinterpretation of American Economic History* (New York: Harper & Row, 1971); and two papers by Albert Fishlow, "The Common School Revival: Fact or Fancy," in Henry Rosovsky, ed., *Industrialization in Two Systems: Essays in Honor of Alexander Gerschenkron* (New York: Wiley, 1966), and "Levels of Nineteenth-Century American Investment in Education," *Journal of Economic History,* 26 (Dec. 1966). Findings on the early motives behind mass public education are given by Alexander J. Field, "Educational Reform and Manufacturing Development in Mid-Nineteenth-Century Massachusetts," *Journal of Economic History,* 36 (March 1976).

Chapter 9

Growth and Change in Domestic and Foreign Markets

Foreign Commerce

Exports, Imports, and the Balance of Payments

Foreign Investment in the United States

Domestic Commerce

Specialization in Marketing and Commercial Information

FOR THE YOUNG UNITED STATES OF 1790 TO 1860, the transportation revolution and increased specialization in agriculture, finance, and manufacturing were part and parcel of a great economic historical theme—the growth of markets. These developments bear witness to the simple but profound truth of Adam Smith's dictum that the division of labor is limited by the extent of the market. In this chapter, we turn to a closer examination of markets themselves; for example, how commercial activity in the United States evolved over the first seven decades of government under the Constitution, the major types of goods in trade and how they were marketed, and what commerce contributed to economic growth during these decades.

Foreign trade was the dynamic factor in the economy of the colonial era and it continued in this role for nearly two decades after 1790. After the embargo and nonintercourse policies employed during the War of 1812 crippled foreign commerce, this element of the nation's economic activity revived and resumed expansion, with some interruptions, up to the Civil War. But after the return of peace to America and Europe in 1815, the dynamic economic role played earlier by foreign trade increasingly shifted toward domestic commerce. Barriers to domestic trade were progressively overcome, domestic markets for all types of American products were widened and deepened, and trade itself became more specialized. We must first look closely at this process of extending domestic markets and trade specialization in order to find the origins of modern economic growth in the United States.

Foreign Commerce

Comparative Advantages of the United States

Virtually all trade—whether between individuals, regions, or nations—is based on the principle of *comparative advantage,* or *relative cost.* If individual or nation A can produce and market good X (or service X) at a lower relative cost than individual or nation B, then it is to B's advantage to cease producing X and to buy it from A. Since the principle is based on relative cost, there must be some good or service (Y) that B can produce and market at a lower cost than A. If A desires to have some Y, it is to A's advantage to buy it from B. These circumstances establish the basis for trade between A and B, and with trade each can specialize in making and selling the good for which it has the lower relative cost. The economic theory of markets and trade shows that both A and B will be better off with trade than without it.

What determines whether A or B has the lower relative cost of producing and marketing a particular good? In general, relative cost is based on a combination of innate and acquired characteristics of the respective producers. In the case of individuals, it is well established that both heredity and environment (e.g., upbringing, formal education, and on-the-job experience) lead to differences in qualitative and quantitative production capabilities. Nations do not differ much from individuals in this respect. They are endowed with different combinations of economic resources, and they make decisions on how to allocate those resources. The resource endowments of nations in this sense are similar to the hereditary characteristics of individuals, while allocative decisions in historical time correspond to the individual's response to the environment. For both individuals and nations it is a difficult task to disentangle the hereditary and the environmental factors and to attribute to each a certain share of whatever success, economic or other, they enjoy. But tentative generalizations are possible.

In the case of the early United States, resource endowments played a major role in shaping the nation's trade with other countries. In terms of the classic economic resources—land, labor, and capital—the United States was well endowed with the first resource and relatively much less well endowed with the latter two. Consequently, the United States had low costs, relative to its foreign trading partners, in the making and the selling of products that were intense in their use of natural resources. These included the great staple crops of agriculture as well as the products of the forest and the ocean. In an era of wooden sailing ships when the seas were primary avenues of commerce, this happy conjunction of farm, forest, and ocean resources made the United States one of the world's great maritime nations.

Although an understanding of American resource endowments can bring important insights to the study of foreign trade in the early United States, resources cannot explain all of the features of commercial evolution. In spite of favorable natural resource endowments, the United States around 1790 was in the doldrums with respect to foreign commerce. Then a protracted period of trading prosperity set in and carried the nation to undreamed-of heights of economic well-being in the first decade of the nineteenth century. To understand this sequence of events, we must look at changes in the young nation's environment rather than at its resource endowments.

Trade and Prosperity (1793–1807)

After the revolution, an independent United States lost the trading advantages enjoyed in colonial times. Great Britain was the chief buyer of American products, but the annual value of U.S. exports to Britain was lower throughout the 1780s and early 1790s than it had been prior to the Revolution. British bounties and trade preferences, the pleasant features of colonial commerce, had disappeared, and the restrictive navigation policies of the colonial era, which continued after the revolution, were even less pleasant when the nation

was no longer a member of the British Empire. Moreover, other European nations followed the British lead in limiting American access to their markets at home and in their colonies. Independent Americans thus found that political situations not within their control restricted the new nation's ability to pursue its comparative economic advantages in producing land-intensive commodities and carrying the trade of other nations in American ships.

1793: A Crucial Year.   The dim economic prospects facing Americans during President George Washington's first administration were altered in 1793 by two important events, one foreign and the other domestic. In Europe, war broke out between Great Britain and revolutionary France; and in the United States, Eli Whitney invented the cotton gin. Warfare between the two great powers of Europe lasted, with brief interludes, for more than two decades. It involved most of the countries of Europe and ultimately the United States. But between 1793 and the embargo year of 1808, the European wars created a great demand for traditional goods and services in international commerce that the United States, as a neutral country, was in a unique position to supply. The cotton gin came at a time when the demand for cotton, as a result of England's Industrial Revolution, was growing by leaps and bounds. Again, the United States, with its great southern territory suitable for growing cotton, was in an excellent position to meet the demand.

An Export Boom.   The sudden and favorable changes in the economic prospects of the United States are reflected in data on the quantity, value, and composition of American exports of goods and services. The total value of all exports of goods from the United States increased from about $20 million in the early 1790s to $108 million in the peak year of 1807. On average, exports grew at a rate of about 10 percent per year in value terms. The gain derived from both increased quantities and rising prices.

Rapid growth in the demand for U.S. exports should be placed in the perspective of the size of the American economy at the time. Although estimates of the economy's gross product during the two decades from 1790 to 1810 are rather rough, exports were likely in the range of 10 percent to 15 percent of gross national product. Such a level may not seem of especially great economic importance, but there are at least two reasons for suspecting that it was. First, better data on the American national product in other periods—beginning in the late 1830s—imply that exports were a significantly smaller fraction, some 6 percent to 7 percent, of total national product. Second, the most numerous contributors to the national product in the 1790 to 1810 period were self-subsisting farmers who seldom engaged in monetary transactions. Therefore, in relation to the part of the national product that passed through markets, exports bulked much larger than 10 percent to 15 percent.

Composition of Exports and Re-Exports.   What goods did the United States export in this period, when foreign commerce played the dynamic role in the economy? Goods produced in the United States were of somewhat less importance than goods such as sugar, coffee, cocoa, and pepper gathered from other places and then reexported from the United States. Re-exports grew from an inconsequential three-tenths of $1 million in 1790 to nearly $60 million in 1807. The re-export trade loomed so large because the ships of warring European nations, save for Britain, were removed from foreign commerce. By first carrying goods from all over the world to the United States and then re-exporting them, American merchants turned the products into the exports of a neutral country and were thus less liable to seizure on the high seas by European belligerents.

Exports of products produced within the United States grew from $20 million in 1790 to $49 million in 1807. Only half of the increase consisted of exports of the traditional products of American farms and forests: foodstuffs, tobacco, lumber, and naval stores. The other half, cotton, was new. In 1790, the United States exported only 189,000 pounds of cotton; in 1807, cotton exports of 66 million pounds were valued at more than $14 million.

Imports and the Merchandise Trade Deficit. Prosperity generated by the booming export sector led Americans to increase their imports of foreign goods dramatically. The value of imports destined for American consumption (rather than for reexport) rose from $24 million in 1790 to $82 million in 1807. Imported goods consisted largely of the same products imported in colonial times, namely manufactured goods from Europe and tropical and subtropical foodstuffs and beverages. Innovative Yankee traders also opened up a lucrative trade with the Far East during these years. In each of these cases, the United States was consuming foreign products that it could not produce at all or could produce only at substantially greater costs than those of foreign sellers.

Data on the value of domestically produced exports and on imports destined for domestic consumption in 1790 and 1807 show that the balance of merchandise trade was, in mercantilist terms, unfavorable to the United States. In other words, the value of imports consumed by Americans exceeded the value of exports produced by Americans. Indeed, an unfavorable balance of merchandise trade was typical in these years, as it had been in colonial times and would continue to be for much of the nineteenth century.

There are a number of ways that such an unfavorable merchandise balance can be financed. An important source of finance in the years 1790 to 1807 was the net income Americans gained by providing shipping services to foreigners. From 1800 to 1812, American net shipping earnings from the freight charges paid by foreign shippers ranged from $18 million to $42 million per year, with the peak coming in 1807. Such levels of net shipping earnings were not characteristic of earlier years (in 1790, for example, they were less than $6 million), and they were seldom seen again until the Civil War despite further growth in the nation's foreign trade. The high level of shipping earnings reflected in part an increase in shipping capacity: The total tonnage of American ships engaged in foreign trade increased from 346,000 in 1790 to 981,000 in 1810. Also important were rises in ocean freight rates and a more intense utilization of existing tonnage. Earnings from shipping thus allowed Americans to import and consume substantially more goods, in value terms, than they themselves could produce and export.

Business Leaders: The All-Purpose Merchants.

American merchants led the way in the commercial expansion of 1793 to 1807, and they were its prime beneficiaries. The merchants, located mainly in the great port cities of Boston, New York, Philadelphia, Baltimore, and Charleston, were much less specialized than were later merchants. This was perhaps an advantage in that it gave the merchants the experience and flexibility to adapt to rapid changes in the environment of foreign and domestic commerce. In addition to dealing in both exports and imports and handling both wholesale and retail trade, many of the diversified merchants engaged in commercial credit and insurance activities as well as shipping and shipowning. The port-city merchants, strategically located at the centers of commercial activity, were the chief decision makers and risk takers of the early American economy. Their ingenuity, together with the boom in foreign trade between 1793 and 1807, allowed many of them—persons such as John Jacob As-

tor of New York and Stephen Girard of Philadelphia—to accumulate great wealth.

American Merchant Shipping

Wood and Sail vs. Iron and Steam. Most Americans today are not aware that in the decades before the Civil War the United States was a leading maritime nation of the world. The nation's prominent position on the seas resulted from its comparative advantage in building and operating wooden sailing ships and from the rapid growth of its domestic and foreign commerce. Around the time of the Civil War, however, American merchant shipping began to decline both absolutely (in terms of tonnage) and relatively with respect to other nations, especially Great Britain. From 1800 to 1840, between 80 percent and 90 percent of U.S. exports and imports were carried by American ships; by 1860, the proportion had declined to less than 70 percent.

There were two basic reasons for the downward turn of American maritime fortunes. First, the British developed a technological superiority and comparative advantage in building and operating both sailing and steam-powered ships made of iron and steel. The new ships were more efficient economically than the old wooden ships and began in rapid fashion to replace them on the seas. Second, within the United States, domestic commerce had grown rapidly relative to foreign trade, and a newer and far more adaptable means of moving goods and people—the railroad—eroded the former superiority of water transportation on ocean, river, and canal.

Composition and Growth of the Merchant Fleet.

Some trends in the structure of the American merchant fleet in its heyday before the Civil War are shown in Table 9–1. Total tonnage and tonnage of vessels engaged in foreign trade increased at annual rates of 5 percent to 6 per-

Table 9–1 *Merchant Fleet of the United States, 1790–1860 (in thousands of tons)*

Year	Tonnage of Ships by Type		Tonnage of Ships by Trade			Total Tonnage
	Steam	Sailing	Foreign	Coastal and Internal	Fisheries	
1790	—	478	346	104	28	478
1800	—	972	667	272	32	972
1810	1	1,424	981	405	39	1,425
1820	22	1,258	584	588	108	1,280
1830	64	1,127	538	517	138	1,192
1840	202	1,978	763	1,177	241	2,181
1850	526	3,010	1,440	1,798	298	3,535
1860	868	4,486	2,379	2,645	330	5,354

SOURCE: Adapted from data in U.S. Bureau of the Census, *Historical Statistics of the United States, Colonial Times to 1957* (Washington, D.C.: GPO, 1960), p. 445.

cent between 1790 and 1810 under the stimulus of booming foreign trade. Then a period of moderate decline in total tonnage set in for two decades. The reason for this decline is apparent in the drop of foreign-trade tonnage from 1810 to 1820. Carrying capacity built up before 1810 was underutilized during the embargo and war years of 1807 to 1815. After the war, freight rates fell sharply and discouraged shipbuilding. By 1830, freight rates were only about one-third of their level fifteen years earlier. Declining freight rates resulted primarily from greater competition, as the ships of European maritime nations returned to the seas after peace was restored there in 1815.

Within the United States, tonnage of vessels engaged in coastwise and internal trade increased right on through the troubled decade of 1810 to 1820; in both 1820 and 1830, domestic tonnage was on a par with that engaged in foreign trade. From 1830 on, coastwise and internal tonnage (excluding the tonnage in fishing and whaling) surpassed foreign-trade tonnage. The tonnage data thus reflect rather clearly the rising relative importance of domestic trade in the commercial activity of the country.

In 1860, despite the inroads of steam, the total sailing-ship tonnage of the American fleet

was still over five times the steam tonnage. Most American vessels, whether sail or steam-powered, used wood as their primary construction material. The iron horse and the iron ship dealt this great American merchant fleet of wood and sail a devastating blow in subsequent decades.

Productivity in Shipping. Yet tonnage data by themselves do not adequately describe the capacity of a fleet. The productivity of the antebellum merchant fleet grew much more rapidly than its tonnage for several reasons. Suppression of piracy reduced both gunnery and worker requirements on existing ships and thus increased cargo-carrying capacity. Through better hull and rigging design, ships increased in both size and speed. A famous example of improved design in this period was the clipper ship, the fastest large sailing vessel that had ever been built. Between the 1830s and 1860s, clippers dominated shipping on long-haul routes where time was of the essence—for example, in the China trade and in the California trade during the gold rush. The clipper's speed, however, came by limiting its cargo capacity compared to ordinary ships.

The Clipper Ship *Flying Cloud* in 1851.   The United States had a comparative advantage in building wooden sailing ships, and the clippers were the ultimate of that ship-type in graceful design and speed. Building for speed sacrificed carrying capacity, however, rather like the supersonic airplanes of our era. Hence, clippers specialized in transporting high-value cargoes and people in a hurry, such as California goldseekers. After the middle of the nineteenth century, iron steamships made wooden sailing ships uncompetitive in most markets. (The Bettmann Archive)

Also important in improving shipping productivity were growing markets and trade. Larger markets meant that ships spent less time gathering and unloading cargoes in ports. They therefore could make more voyages per year. In addition, the growing volume of trade led to better load factors for ships, as did increases in immigration to the United States. In earlier days of smaller markets and low immigration, ships carrying the bulky primary products of the New World to the Old World often returned largely in ballast.

Ocean trade before 1815 was not sufficiently great to encourage the development of regularly scheduled sailings by specialized shippers; instead, merchant-owned and tramp ships moved irregularly in whatever directions seemed to promise the greatest trading profits.

After 1815, shipping lines were formed to offer regularly scheduled sailings on major routes. Wooden packet ships dominated this business for some two decades but then began to give way to more efficient steamships.

The Decline of Ocean Freight Rates.   The most important result of shipping productivity gains was a drop in freight rates. As noted earlier in the chapter, increased competition in shipping after 1815 reduced freight rates to about one-third of their 1815 levels by 1830. Freight rates on U.S. exports continued to fall after 1830. Because of its great economic importance to the United States, cotton furnishes a good example of the effect of falling freight rates. During the 1820s, some 10 percent of the delivered price of American cotton in England was a freight charge; by the 1850s, this freight factor was reduced to less than 3 percent. Falling ocean freight rates thus increased market efficiency and stimulated greater production by making the prices that consumers paid more nearly equal to the prices that producers received. Although not as dramatic as the drop in freight rates over land during this period, the drop in ocean rates was nonetheless substantial.

Exports, Imports, and the Balance of Payments

The year 1815 marked the end of a quarter-century during which international political conditions first created a boom for American trade and shipping and then a depression. From 1815 until 1860, the foreign trade of the United States was carried on in a more peaceful atmosphere, where economic rather than geopolitical factors exerted the major influence. Reexport trade declined substantially from the lofty levels reached in the years before 1808. American traders increasingly concentrated on exporting products of U.S. origin and importing products destined for consumption in the United States. What American products did foreigners buy in these years? Who were the chief customers? And what were the origins and nature of imports from abroad?

Export Markets

The comparative advantage of the young United States in agricultural products is clear from data on exports. Cotton was by far the leading export commodity. It accounted for 39 percent of the value of commodity exports as early as the years 1816 to 1820. After rising to 63 percent in 1836 to 1840, cotton's share fell to 54 percent in 1856 to 1860. For these same five-year periods, the combined export shares of several agricultural products—cotton, tobacco, wheat and flour, corn and cornmeal, rice, and beef and pork products—totaled 78 percent in 1816 to 1820, 81 percent in 1836 to 1840, and 80 percent in 1856 to 1860. Exports of domestic manufacturers, in contrast, were only 7 percent, 9 percent, and 12 percent, respectively, of total merchandise exports in the three periods. Throughout the antebellum years, then, agriculture was the economy's largest source of exports.

The nation's chief foreign customers from 1815 to 1860 were Britain and France. Britain alone, with its great cotton textile industry exerting the major demand, absorbed about one-half of all American exports, and France took about one-seventh. The West Indies and South America were important customers, especially in the earlier part of the period when they bought about a quarter of U.S. exports. By the 1850s, however, the shares of these countries were much reduced. Exports to Canada and to European countries other than England and France rose to offset most of the relative decline in demand from Latin America.

Imports and a Continuing Trade Deficit

The geographical pattern, though not the content, of American imports was similar to that of exports. From 1815 to 1860, Britain and France together supplied over one-half of U.S. imports. The West Indies and Brazil on average supplied another 20 percent. From the Europeans the United States obtained a variety of manufactured goods; textiles alone (cotton, wool, linen, and silk goods) represented a significant portion of products imported from Europe and, in a smaller amount of trade, from the Orient. Sugar and coffee were the chief imports from Latin America. It is apparent that the import emphasis of antebellum Americans was on consumer goods.

Americans' tastes for imported products outran their ability to pay for them by exporting American goods in most of the years between 1790 and 1860. The exceptions occurred primarily during periods of domestic economic depression, when falling American incomes reduced import demand sharply and commodity exports remained relatively stable. The relationship between exports and imports of merchandise, shown in Figure 9–1, indicates the prevailing unfavorable balance of trade. The trade deficits were financed in some periods by special circumstances that arose. Before 1815, for example, political conditions in Europe threw much of the world's carrying trade into the ships of American merchants and shippers. Shipping earnings were so great in the early years of the Republic that they allowed the United States not only to cover its

Figure 9–1 *Merchandise Exports and Imports of the United States, 1790–1860*

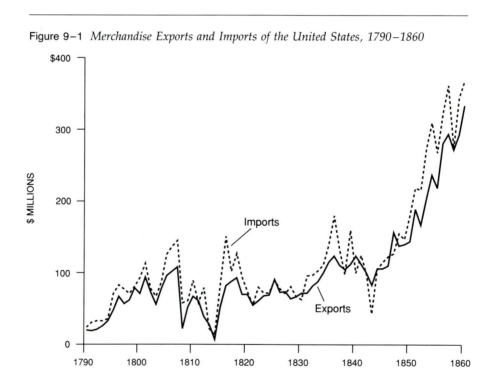

Source: Adapted from Douglass C. North, "The United States Balance of Payments, 1790–1860," in National Bureau of Economic Research, *Trends in the American Economy in the Nineteenth Century* (Princeton: Princeton University Press, 1960), pp. 577, 605.

merchandise trade deficit but also to pay interest on the country's debts to foreigners and even reduce the debts moderately. Another factor became important during the 1850s: Exports of California gold covered over three-fourths of the merchandise trade deficit.

During most of the years from 1790 to 1860, however, earnings from shipping and from exports of gold and silver were not sufficient to offset the American trade deficit with respect to the rest of the world. In addition to importing more merchandise than they exported, Americans owed money to foreigners for other reasons. Expenditures of Americans traveling abroad often exceeded those of foreigners who came to the United States, either temporarily or to stay. And in every year of these seven decades, Americans were committed to paying net amounts of interest and dividends to foreigners who had invested in U.S. enterprises and governments. The resulting payments deficits with respect to the rest of the world were made up by a flow of capital from abroad to the United States. This important aspect of the nation's early economic history merits separate treatment.

Foreign Investment in the United States

Between 1790 and 1860, the net foreign capital invested in the United States grew from about $70 million to over $380 million. However, these figures were low in comparison with the investments that Americans made in their own country during these decades. The flow of foreign capital to the United States, moreover, was not uniform over time. In some periods, the flow was small or even negative; in others, it played an important role in underwriting geographic and economic expansion. The motives of foreign investors were diverse, but for the most part they were responding to the higher investment return that was offered by

the young and developing nation deficient in capital resources. The United States, simply put, was a good place to invest.

Short- and Long-term Credit from Europe

British investors were by far the most important foreign creditors of Americans. There were two basic reasons for their interest in the United States. First, throughout the antebellum era, Britain was the preeminent trading partner of the United States, and with trade goes finance. In the earliest days of the Republic, domestic financial institutions were relatively undeveloped; American merchants dealing in exports and imports relied to a great extent on British merchants and bankers to finance their trade. Of the $70 million estimated indebtedness of Americans to foreigners in 1790, probably the greatest part took the form of these mercantile credits. Supplied by the British to American importers and exporters, mercantile credit continued to play an important role in the foreign trade of the United States even as the young nation developed an independent banking and financial system.

The second reason for the British interest in American investments has more to do with Britain's own economic history. The industrial and agricultural revolutions that swept across the British landscape in the late eighteenth and early nineteenth centuries created a tremendous amount of private wealth. Capital accumulation in Britain drove down domestic investment returns and spurred wealthy Britons to search for higher returns abroad. The nineteenth-century United States was just one among many foreign lands to benefit from their quest. British investors sought both steady incomes and capital gains from long-term securities or portfolio investments. Mercantile credit, in contrast, was short term in nature and designed to facilitate trade.

While American merchants were the primary beneficiaries of foreign short-term credits in the antebellum decades, the focus of foreign long-term investments varied. In the first decades, issues of the federal government attracted most of the foreign funds. Alexander Hamilton's provision for funding the national debt impressed foreign investors, and U.S. bonds began to move overseas. Dutch bankers played a leading role in floating the government's debt in 1791, and in 1803 when funds were raised to purchase the Louisiana Territory from France. But these federal securities, together with much of the stock of the Bank of the United States, soon found their way to Britain. By 1805, the famed British banking house of Baring handled the payment of interest and dividends on some $28 million of federal securities and bank stock. Most of these payments were to English investors. At the time they represented the return on about one-third of all the indebtedness of Americans to foreigners. Other estimates for the years 1803 and 1807 show foreigners owning over one-half of the entire debt of the federal government.

Aggregate indebtedness of Americans to foreigners declined in the years just prior to the War of 1812 but then rose from $63 million to $100 million in the postwar trade boom of 1815 to 1819. Much of the increase was in mercantile credit. Foreign capitalists also invested heavily in the stock of the second Bank of the United States and in New York State bonds issued to build the Erie Canal. But federal securities continued to be favored by foreign investors. In 1828, British and other continental investors held some $19 million of federal bonds, about one-third of the $58 million outstanding at the end of that year.

Boom-and-Bust Cycle of the 1830s and 1840s

The success of both the Erie Canal and the federal government's efforts to retire the national debt conjoined in the 1830s to produce an unparalleled episode in the annals of foreign investment in the United States. The Erie demonstrated to foreigners the favorable economic prospects of the country, while the unprecedented act of paying off the national debt created both euphoria about American creditworthiness and cash for reinvesting. In this propitious environment, foreign loans to and investment in the United States grew from $75 million in 1830 to almost $300 million in 1839. Much of the capital inflow from abroad went into transportation improvements and banking enterprises sponsored by state governments.

The newer canals were much less successful as investments than the Erie, and several state governments were fiscally less responsible than the federal government. When the bubble burst, first in 1837 and then again in 1839, foreign investors began to take a ferocious beating. In 1841 and 1842, nine American states ceased paying interest on their debts, large amounts of which were foreign-held. A few states, including Florida, Mississippi, and Michigan, even repudiated some or all of their debts. Moreover, the Bank of the United States, reconstituted under a Pennsylvania charter after 1836 and then turned into a speculative commercial and investment bank, failed in 1841, at a time when nearly $20 million of its $38 million of stock was in the hands of European investors. The image of America was tarnished. During the 1840s, the nation's foreign indebtedness fell from $297 million to $193 million. Loans were not renewed and American securities were sent back across the Atlantic to be liquidated.

Renewed Capital Inflow During the 1850s.

Then, in the 1850s, the inflow of capital began again. A number of factors renewed the earlier confidence of foreign investors. Discovery of gold in California was one. It stimulated a great interest in America's natural wealth. States resumed borrowing for improvement projects. In addition, the railroads, with their voracious appetite for capital, had begun to demonstrate their worth as investments. English ironmasters exported great quantities of rails to America in the 1850s and often accepted railway securities as payment. Increasing urbanization created a further demand for investment in capital improvements and corresponding supplies of municipal bonds. The sectoral distribution of foreign holdings of U.S. securities in 1853 is shown in Table 9–2; in that year, nearly 20 percent of all U.S. securities outstanding were in foreign hands. Moreover, as gold flowed into the money stocks of the United States and other nations, prices rose and trade expanded, creating further demands for mercantile credits. With so many factors turning favorable, it is not surprising that foreign capital flowed again to the United States in large amounts. Overall, America's net overseas indebtedness doubled from $193 million in 1849 to $387 million in 1859.

The flow of foreign capital to the United States in the antebellum years was of great significance to the growth of the economy. In the earliest years, confidence in the new nation exhibited by foreign investors helped to place its public credit on a firm footing. In later decades, loans from abroad allowed Americans to live beyond their current means while at the same time providing funds for enlarging those means in the future. Transportation improvements—first canals and later railroads—benefited disproportionately from the investment decisions of foreign wealth holders. These improvements were major instruments for extending the markets and trade of the United States. Complementing the facilities constructed with foreign funds were the flows of information, techniques, and ideas that accompanied them. Foreigners, especially the British, had much to teach American merchants, financiers, managers, and engineers. These lessons were important byproducts of the flow of foreign capital.

Domestic Commerce

Although commercial activity between Americans and foreigners continued to be an impor-

Table 9–2 *Foreign Investments in the United States, 1853*

Type of Security	Value Held by Foreigners (in $ millions)	Percentage of Total Securities Outstanding Held by Foreigners
U.S. government stock (mainly bonds)	$ 27.0	46%
State stock (mainly bonds)	111.0	58
113 cities and towns (bonds)	16.5	21
347 counties (mainly bonds)	5.0	36
985 banks (stock)	6.7	3
75 insurance companies (stock)	0.4	3
244 railroad companies (stock)	8.2	3
244 railroad companies (bonds)	43.9	26
16 canal and navigation companies (stock)	0.5	2
16 canal and navigation companies (bonds)	2.0	9
15 miscellaneous companies (stock)	0.8	5
15 miscellaneous companies (bonds)	0.3	11
Total	$222.2	19%

SOURCE: Adapted from Mira Wilkins, *The History of Foreign Investment in the United States to 1914* (Cambridge, Mass.: Harvard University Press, 1989), p. 76.

tant element of economic life in the decades before 1860, the truly significant development of this period was the growth of economic exchange among Americans. In these years, Americans were said to have turned their backs on European and other overseas markets in order to concentrate on the settlement and economic development of their own country, a country that had taken on the dimensions of a continent. However, this was an exaggeration, as a glance back at Figure 9–1 will confirm. Foreign commerce in the 1840s and 1850s was increasing about as rapidly as it did in any other period of comparable length after 1790. Nonetheless, the early nineteenth century marks the beginning of a long trend toward the expansion of domestic relative to foreign commerce.

Growth of Internal Markets

There were several factors that led to the absolute and relative expansion of American domestic commerce after 1800. Fundamental was the economic principle of comparative advantage (or relative cost) discussed earlier in the chapter. In the world economy, the young United States specialized in making resource-intensive products because, given its resource endowments, the relative cost of these products was lower than in other countries. Similarly, U.S. regions and cities specialized in commodities that gave them comparative cost advantages over other regions and cities. However, comparative cost advantages in production, fundamental in determining the location of various economic activities, depend for the degree of their exploitation on the costs of transporting and marketing commodities to their users. Hence, another major factor in the great expansion of domestic commerce was the dramatic decline in internal transportation costs (discussed at length in Chapter 5). Although both internal and overseas transport costs fell, by far the greatest impact of the

transportation revolution was on the former. Thus, the transportation revolution did not lead Americans to turn their backs on foreigners so much as it led them—in an economic sense—to discover each other.

Also important to the expansion of domestic commerce during the early 1800s was the relative absence of artificial restrictions on trade within the United States. In trading with foreigners, Americans of necessity had to conform to the taxes, tariffs, and other restrictive commercial regulations of sovereign nations. Within the United States, in contrast, the transportation revolution as well as judicial interpretations of the Constitution that eroded artificial barriers to domestic commerce together created a massive geographic area open to unrestricted trade.

Along with the increased emphasis by Americans on domestic markets came an even more basic change. Reasonably accurate estimates of the U.S. national product for the two decades before the Civil War (see Chapter 10) indicate that the American economy was then expanding at the high and sustained rates of per capita product growth that characterize modern economies. It is likely that these growth characteristics emerged in the quarter-century before 1840, and that they were predicated upon the expansion of domestic markets. How the expansion of domestic markets led to modern economic growth is a controversial issue among economic historians.

Markets and Economic Development

The Cotton Thesis and Its Problems.   The traditional explanation of the expansion of domestic markets and the emergence of modern economic growth might succinctly be termed the "cotton thesis." During the first seven decades of the twentieth century, a number of scholars argued that the dynamic factor in the economy of the United States in its earliest years, but especially after 1815, was the growing world demand for American cotton. From a negligible share of world cotton output in 1790, U.S. cotton production rose to 9 percent by 1801, to 16 percent by 1811, to about 50 percent by 1831, and to 66 percent by 1860. American cotton production grew at an average rate of almost 7 percent per year in the first three decades of the nineteenth century, and at 5 percent per year during the following three decades. The rate was close to 8 percent per year between 1811 and 1831. These rates of growth in output, sustained over such lengthy periods, are impressive by both historical and modern standards. Clearly, the American South's antebellum cotton kingdom was a potent and dynamic economic entity.

Proponents of the cotton thesis argued that extreme specialization in cotton production led the South to spend its growing income from cotton sales in other regions of the United States. Southern expenditures in the Northeast stimulated the growth of northern manufacturing, commerce, and finance. Southern expenditures in the West stimulated the growth of specialized grain and meat production in that region. Moreover, as the West specialized in production of agricultural goods, it in turn demanded manufactured goods and commercial services from the Northeast and supplied it with foodstuffs. The direct and indirect disposition of the South's growing cotton income was thus viewed as the force that expanded American domestic markets and promoted continuing gains from specialization and interregional trade.

Based on the powerful facts of cotton production and the appealing implications of interregional trade, the cotton thesis offered an understandable and attractive model of how sustained economic growth began in the United States after 1815. However, subsequent analysis of evidence pertinent to the cotton thesis casts doubt on its intersectional trade emphasis.[1] Consider first the West–South link.

A basic tenet of the cotton thesis was that food products moved from the West to the South to supply specialized cotton plantations. But analysis of products traveling down the Mississippi indicates that most of these products were shipped out of the South, either to the Northeast or to foreign markets. Moreover, the notion that substantial quantities of Western foodstuffs moved to the South over other river routes or by wagon and rail has also been deflated. Most damaging of all to the cotton thesis, however, are studies showing that southern cotton growers were largely self-sufficient in food and that southern agriculture was even capable of producing food surpluses for sale outside of the South (see Chapter 6).

Consider next the Northeast–South link. The cotton thesis envisioned the Northeast supplying the South with a variety of goods and services but emphasized the effect of southern demand on northern manufacturing. Most of the trade from the Northeast to the South was carried in ships engaged in the coastal trade. A study of this trade shows that it did in fact grow at fairly rapid rates between 1824 and 1839, but that even in the later year less than one-sixth of northern manufacturing output moved to the South.[2] And since cotton income was but one-eighth of the value of all southern production in that year, only a tiny fraction of northern manufacturing output could be said to have been directly stimulated by the demand of cotton growers for manufactures.

Finally, consider the trade between the Northeast and the West. Some western foodstuffs undoubtedly reached the Northeast via the Mississippi River and coastal trades between 1815 and 1840, just as imported and domestic manufactured goods returned by these routes. This water route to the West was, however, circuitous and costly. And, in terms of both population and per capita income, the West lagged behind the South in 1840. The West was unlikely, therefore, to have furnished the Northeast with a better market for manufactures than did the South. An analysis of Erie Canal toll revenues bears out this contention. The Erie, completed in 1825, is often thought to have stimulated agricultural development and population growth in the West, and it undoubtedly did. But when? From 1829 to 1835, toll revenues from western shipments over the Erie were only 7 percent of total revenues, while shipments from tidewater to the West were only 10 percent. Most of the revenues generated by the Erie in these years were derived from shipments within New York State, from its interior to tidewater and vice versa. Indeed, not until 1846 did toll revenue from western shipments over the Erie surpass revenue from shipments from the interior of New York to tidewater. Thus, before the 1840s, the West was neither a major supplier of food to the Northeast nor a major consumer of northeastern manufactures.

Market Growth Within Regions: Cities and Their Hinterlands.

If growing trade between the three great economic regions of the United States between 1815 and 1840 cannot account for the expansion of domestic markets and the beginnings of sustained growth in these years, then what can? An alternative to the cotton thesis contends that the initial stimulus to growth came from a widening and deepening of markets within regions of the country, especially within the Northeast. It is unlikely, for example, that Americans in the Northeast began to specialize in trading their manufactured goods over great distances in return for food before they began trading those goods among themselves. Great quantities of food and raw materials were in fact produced within the Northeast, and most of the region's inhabitants were still farmers in 1815.

Furthermore, analysis of Erie Canal toll revenues supports the more recent view that intraregional rather than interregional trade was the initiating force for greater specialization in the domestic economy. In the years from 1829 to 1835, shipments from the interior of New York State to tidewater accounted for almost one-half of the Erie Canal's revenues, and shipments from tidewater to the state's interior made up nearly 30 percent. When local shipments along the Erie Canal are added in, the result is impressive: More than 80 percent of the total revenue was derived from New Yorkers trading with other New Yorkers.

A careful study of Philadelphia's economic development and trade between 1815 and 1840 makes much the same point.[3] In this quarter-century, Philadelphia changed from a major port city of the country's foreign commerce to a leading center of domestic manufacturing. Much of the impetus for the shift came from a demand for manufactured goods in the city's own hinterland as well as in the coastal trading areas of Pennsylvania, New Jersey, Delaware, and Maryland. Trade in manufactures with other regions of the Northeast, the South, the West, and foreigners was of comparatively much less significance. In earlier years, Philadelphia's merchants had thrived on importing both European manufactures and tropical goods for distribution within the Philadelphia region and to southern and western markets. From the 1820s on, however, New York City gained a progressively greater share of the American import trade as Philadelphia declined as a foreign trade center and turned to manufacturing. The city continued to receive and to ship out agricultural commodities and extractive products (notably anthracite coal) gathered from its hinterland, but the major markets for these shipments were in the Northeast—in growing cities, such as New York, Boston, and Baltimore—rather than in the South and West. Hinterland incomes derived from these northeastern shipments of farm products and coal, and from Philadelphian's own consumption of these goods, created an expanding market for Philadelphia's manufactures. Thus, trade within the Philadelphia region and with other emerging urban areas of the Northeast stimulated to a great extent the city's market growth and increased specialization before 1840.

Much the same can be said about other parts of the Northeast in the nineteenth century. Increased specialization was promoted not so much by distant demands as by a growing volume of trade between urban areas and their hinterlands. Gradually, interregional demands became more important, but this happened largely after 1840. In the West, a similar story, albeit on a lesser scale, unfolded. Active trade developed first within city-hinterland areas and then spread throughout the western region. The importance of interregional and international trade came later. Thus, the river-connected cities of Pittsburgh, Cincinnati, Louisville, and St. Louis grew first through trade with their hinterlands and with each other. Detroit, Cleveland, and Buffalo on the Great Lakes also traded extensively among themselves, and Chicago's first external market was its hinterland area.[4] Only the South failed to develop an active internal trade between city and countryside. The South's lag in urbanization, manufacturing, and trade stemmed from its great comparative advantage in specialized agriculture, its orientation toward international markets, and its devotion to slavery. These features of its economy led the South to rely heavily on outsiders for commercial and financial services as well as on foreigners for many manufactured goods.

Urbanization and Economic Specialization. The newer view of the beginnings of modern economic growth in the quarter-century before 1840, with its emphasis on trade and specialization within regions, particularly in the Northeast, is consistent with our knowledge of urbanization and income trends for the period. The fraction of Americans living in urban places (that is, areas with 2500 or more people) rose from 5.1 percent to 7.2 percent between 1790 and 1820. Then urbanization picked up

speed, with the percentage living in urban places rising to 8.8 percent and 10.8 percent, respectively, in 1830 and 1840 and to 19.8 percent in 1860.

In 1840, almost half the urban population lived in just five cities: New York, Philadelphia, Boston, and Baltimore in the Northeast and New Orleans in the South. Personal incomes on a per capita basis were highest in the regions containing these cities: Estimates of this measure for 1840 show that the Northeast was 35 percent above the national average and the West–South Central region (containing both New Orleans and the best cotton lands) was 44 percent above the national average. Other regions of the South and the West were below the national average. Economic specialization reached its highest levels in cities, and through its effects on incomes it drew greater numbers of people to urban areas.

The appearance of New Orleans on the list of largest cities and highest income areas in 1840 reinforces the point that internal commerce, perhaps more than industrialization, was the important factor in the emergence of modern economic growth in the United States. New Orleans was not a manufacturing center, but it served as the focal point of the great hinterland of the Mississippi Valley with its increasingly specialized agriculture. Commercial activity also outweighed manufacturing activity in the major Northeastern cities before 1840. Goods manufactured in the smaller cities and towns of that section were distributed through the great commercial cities. In the Northeast, domestic commerce increasingly assumed the form of trade of manufactured goods for agricultural products and the exchange of some manufactures for others. Home production of cloth, for example, fell precipitously in the 1820s and 1830s as rural producers turned to specialized farming and to purchasing cloth from distributors of the factory-manufactured product.

Finally, the newer view of the origins of modern economic growth in the United States should bring about a reevaluation of the role of improvements in transportation and communications after 1815. The initial significance of these improvements was not so much in opening up interregional trade as in extending the hinterland markets and the producing areas of cities. As the city-hinterland markets grew, they began to overlap and the trading areas within regions began to widen. Ultimately, the process of market widening brought interregional trade into prominence and caused readjustments toward a greater degree of specialization within the Northeast, the South, and the West. The process was gradual, however, and far from complete by the time of the Civil War. Distinct regional economies still existed in 1860; their integration into a national economy was in its early stages.

Specialization in Marketing and Commercial Information

Before a nation made up overwhelmingly of farmers could obtain the income necessary to promote progressively greater economic diversification and specialization, ways had to be found to market more efficiently both agricultural commodities and manufactured goods. This called for greater specialization in marketing and for improved transportation facilities. Since marketing and transportation were so intimately related before 1860, it is not surprising that merchants often were the prime movers and key decision makers in the transportation revolution. As transportation improvements extended marketing areas, marketing itself became more specialized.

The Marketing of Cotton

Cotton, antebellum America's preeminent cash crop, provides one example of the trend to-

ward specialized marketing. In the earliest years of the rise of cotton, planters often marketed the crop themselves by hauling it over land or water to southern coastal ports and selling it to port merchants and shippers. This form of unspecialized marketing became less and less feasible as the cotton kingdom moved farther inland. Marketing specialists then appeared in the South. Most of them were so-called "cotton factors"—brokers who received cotton shipments from farmers and planters and who supervised their sale to buyers in Europe or the Northeast in return for a commission. The cotton factors located themselves in southern port cities and in the inland towns that grew up in the cotton belt. They acted as agents for cotton growers and dealt with the buying agents of distant merchants and manufacturers. They also relieved the growers of the burden of marketing their crop. The cotton factor had a comparative advantage in marketing, while the cotton grower had a comparative advantage in production.

However, the cotton factor was not completely specialized. In addition to arranging for the storing, selling, insuring, and forwarding of the crop, the cotton factor often acted as a purchasing agent and banker for the grower. The grower then relied on the cotton factor both for credit and for supplies of products imported into the South from abroad or from the Northeast—or both, since most foreign imported goods came first to northeastern port merchants for distribution to the rest of the country. The southern cotton factor was not a totally specialized agent, in part because the southern planter was an extremely specialized agriculturalist. In the South, agricultural specialization and an orientation toward export markets, rather than toward local or regional sales, worked against the tide of urbanization prevalent elsewhere in the United States. Cotton had a high value in relation to its weight and could be harvested, ginned, baled, and shipped efficiently from large plantations.

LOADING COTTON ON THE ALABAMA RIVER.

COTTON-SHOOT ON THE ALABAMA.

Cotton Marketing. Here we see the first step in moving cotton from plantation to textile mill. Bales of ginned cotton slide down a "cotton-shoot" (chute) from the plantation above and are loaded on a steamboat, the *Magnolia*, on the Alabama River. The next stop was a port city—Mobile, in this case—for transfer to larger, ocean-going vessels. (Culver Pictures)

223

Moreover, it did not have to be further processed until it arrived at faraway textile mills.

Northern Agricultural Marketing

Bulky grain, perishable livestock, and dairy products were another matter. Flour-milling, meat-processing, and dairy facilities were developed near the places of grain, livestock, and dairy production as a means of reducing transport costs. Many of the notable antebellum differences in town development between the Northeast and West, on the one hand, and the South, on the other, can be attributed to these agricultural product differences. Because the South developed fewer towns per unit of area, southern growers usually relied for supplies and credit on cotton factors rather than on local merchants and bankers.

Agricultural marketing in the West began much as it had in the South—with farmers performing much of their own marketing. As western populations grew and towns sprang up to act as processing centers for grain and meat, local merchants assumed a larger role in agricultural marketing. The local merchants traded their stocks of manufactured goods for crops and then acted as intermediaries for selling the aggregated surpluses of a number of farmers to more distant buyers. In earlier years, this sometimes required shipping the products all the way to New Orleans; as the cities of the Ohio and Mississippi valleys emerged, however, grain elevator operators, specialized brokers, and forwarding agents began to participate in marketing intermediation. Thus, the West, and even earlier the Northeast, developed a higher degree of agricultural marketing specialization than did the South.

Marketing Manufactured Products

Product and market differences go a long way toward explaining the evolution of decisions on how to market manufactured as well as agricultural goods between 1790 and 1860. Manufacturers had even more incentives than agriculturists for specialization because of the greater variety of manufactured products and because the markets for manufactured goods grew more rapidly than those for most agricultural commodities. Before 1815, the marketing of most goods was handled by the great merchants of the nation's leading port cities. The activities of these early merchants—exporting and importing, wholesaling and retailing, shipping and ship-owning, as well as commercial intelligence, insurance, and finance—were relatively unspecialized because the merchants dealt in numerous small and widely dispersed markets.

The growth of domestic commerce after 1815 led to progressively greater specialization in marketing. Larger markets for manufactured goods, of foreign and domestic origin, created opportunities for merchants to specialize both by function (e.g., exporting or importing, wholesaling or retailing) and product line (e.g., textiles or dry goods, hardware, drugs). The marketing of textiles, America's first modern factory-manufactured product, furnishes a good example of the growing specialization in commerce during this period. Before 1815, early spinning mills sold small lots to nearby weavers and storekeepers. Soon, though, as production exceeded local demand, yarn began to be marketed through more distant outlets, often on consignment. Under this arrangement, the producer retained ownership and received payment for the goods once they had been sold by the consignee. After 1815, with the introduction of mechanized weaving followed by an extended period of remarkable growth in textile production, two new and still more specialized marketing agencies appeared: the commission wholesaler of the large city, who purchased products from a number of mills, and the selling house, a wholesaling unit that handled the initial distribution of a given mill's entire production. These marketing specialists handled product distribution and furnished information to manufacturers about which goods were most in demand. They also provided the manufacturers with credit on goods produced but not yet sold to consumers. Freed from these credit and marketing concerns, manufacturers of textiles were able to specialize in producing their products more efficiently.

Commission wholesalers and textile selling houses dealt in volume sales. Located in large cities, they sold some of their stocks of goods to urban retailers. But the spatial expansion of the domestic market called forth still another type of specialized wholesaler—the jobber—who dealt in smaller lots with scattered retailers around the country. In textiles, the jobber's main function was to purchase fairly large stocks of yarn and cloth products from commission wholesalers and selling houses, and then to break these up into smaller and more variegated lots for the nation's retailers. Jobbers played an important role in the auction system of distribution that was common, especially for imported goods, before the 1830s. Ships carrying imported textiles could not possibly wait for the goods to be sold to retailers far inland, so they turned their cargoes over to port-city auctioneers. The jobber was a frequent auction buyer. Later, as goods of domestic manufacture increased in volume and as auction sales declined, jobbers turned to larger wholesalers and selling houses for their stocks. The big-city jobber was an important agent in the flow of economic information and credit. Retailers from around the nation visited the jobber periodically to place their orders, which allowed the jobber to gather information on consumer preferences around the country. Access to city bank credit allowed the jobber to provide the out-of-town retailers with trade credit.

Merchants and Manufacturers

The patterns of marketing change and specialization that prevailed in textiles extended to many other products in the years after 1815. Moreover, the importance of specialized marketing went beyond increased efficiency of distribution. Marketing specialists often played a dominant role in manufacturing development as well, primarily because established merchants had better access than new manufacturers to a major requirement of modern industrial development—capital. Trade credit and commercial banking long antedated the appearance of factory industry in both Europe and the United States. These institutions were developed initially to finance the movement of goods from small-scale producers to scattered consumers, rather than to meet the working capital and long-term investment needs of modern industry. But they were applied easily to the developing problems of industrial finance. As a result, the merchant's access to capital (in the form of bank credit and as part of personal wealth accumulation from trading activity) often became instrumental in financing early industrial enterprises. Many manufacturing firms in the antebellum United States were either founded by merchants or closely allied with them. In either case, merchants' access to capital put them in a position to exert substantial control over manufacturing enterprises. Moreover, merchants' knowledge of buyers' preferences served as useful information for manufacturers in their decisions about what goods to produce.

Even before the Civil War, however, the dominance of the merchant over the manufacturer was on the wane in some industries. Railroad equipment provides a good example. In the 1830s, the first railroads were small enterprises relative to what they were to become, and their worth as investments was largely untested. The railroad-equipment industry was also new and consisted of a number of relatively small and capital-hungry firms. In these circumstances, independent wholesalers with both more knowledge of the conditions of railroads and more capital than the equipment manufacturers became merchant-agents in their dealings with manufacturers and railroad customers. But railroad equipment was technically more sophisticated than most consumer and producer goods. Moreover, by the 1840s, many railroads had proven themselves as viable economic entities and the equipment industry had become more concentrated into larger-scale producing units. Hence, equipment manufacturers and railroads found it more convenient to deal with each other directly rather than through the merchant-agents. This marked the beginning of a long-term trend toward a reduced role for the merchant in American economic development.

Commercial Credit Reporting

The decreasing importance of the merchant–manufacturer relationship in some industries did not mark the end of increasing specialization in commercial activity. Rather, the nationwide market that was emerging for many products during the last antebellum decades stimulated still more specialization. Two examples from the area of information, the key ingredient to decision making, illustrate the continuing progress of specialization in commerce. Wholesale merchants had been so important to domestic economic development after 1815 in part because they took on the role and assumed much of the risk of providing credit to both retailers and manufacturers. The merchants were in a good position to undertake these functions because their day-to-day dealings generated the information necessary to make credit decisions. However, as the number of retail customers and suppliers grew and as trade became much less personal than in earlier years, it became difficult for individual wholesalers to gather all the credit information they needed. And expanding their information bases would have involved much duplication of effort. But in 1841, Lewis Tappan, a New York dry-goods wholesaler, established the Mercantile Agency,

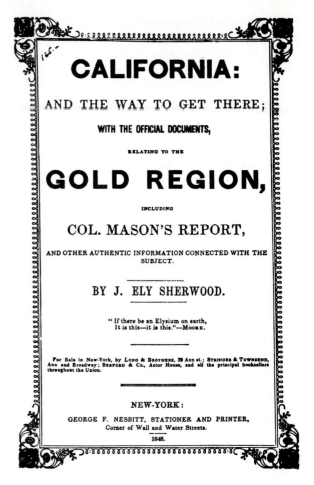

The California Gold Rush.   The title page of an 1848 book shows that the next year's "Forty-niners" were not uninformed when they set out for the goldfields. California's population (not counting American Indians) rose from about 14,000 in 1848 to more than 250,000 by 1852. The initial gold discovery was in January 1848, and it did not become widely known in the East until September of that year. Instant publishing is not a recent innovation. (The Bettmann Archive)

a firm that specialized in gathering commercial credit information from all over the country and disseminating it to subscribing clients. Its business grew rapidly. Branches of the Mercantile Agency were organized in Boston (1843), Philadelphia (1845), Baltimore (1846), Cincinnati

(1849), New Orleans (1851), and eleven other cities by 1858. Tappan's Mercantile Agency is the lineal ancestor of the present-day Dun & Bradstreet, a leading commercial information firm.

Bank-note Reporters

Another example of commercial specialization is the bank-note reporter. Hundreds of independent commercial banks, each issuing its own handsomely engraved notes that served as a part of the nation's paper currency, emerged in the antebellum decades. Not all of the banks were well managed. In addition, the great number of differing bank notes encouraged counterfeiting. As domestic trade expanded and spread over greater distances, the bank notes increasingly came to be presented to merchants far away from their place of origin. How was a merchant to know whether or not the notes presented were worth the nominal values printed on them? The answers were provided by bank-note reporters and counterfeit detectors, publications that presented information on the conditions of the banks and the prices at which their notes were being traded in major money markets. Bank-note reporters were popular from the 1820s to the end of the Civil War, reaching their peak of importance during the 1840s and 1850s. In 1855, the most prominent publication, *Thompson's Bank Note and Commercial Reporter*, had 100,000 subscribers from all over the country. The note reporters ceased publication after the Civil War, when federal banking legislation finally brought a uniform paper currency to the United States. But their earlier business success, like that of the Mercantile Agency, strongly indicated that a nationwide market for many goods and services was developing well before 1860.

Summary

Improvements in internal transportation and communications were the basic ingredients of the expansion of domestic commerce in the United States after 1800. The improvements allowed the interior resources of America to be exploited along lines of comparative cost advantage, just as the availability of cheap ocean transportation had promoted specialized production for overseas markets in the New England, Middle, and South Atlantic regions during the colonial era. A relative absence of artificial barriers to trade within and between regions also favored trade expansion as markets widened under the influence of ever-lower transport costs.

The expansion of domestic commerce created conditions favorable to still further expansion. The growth of domestic markets prompted an increasing division of labor and specialization in commercial activity and marketing organization. Transactions costs—the costs of moving products from producer to consumer—were reduced further by the more specialized and efficient merchant-agents. Thus, the expansion of domestic markets became self-sustaining. The United States entered the era of modern economic growth with its continued increases in productivity per capita during the first half of the nineteenth century. In crossing this historical divide, the growth of markets and the developments in commercial activity may have been less dramatic than the breakthroughs in manufacturing industry, but they were likely just as important in promoting self-sustained economic growth in the United States.

Endnotes

1. See, for example, Albert Fishlow, "Antebellum Interregional Trade Reconsidered," *American Economic Review,* 59 (May 1964), pp. 352–64, reprinted in Ralph Andreano, ed., *New Views on American Economic Development* (Cambridge, Mass.: Schenkman Publishing Co., 1965), pp. 187–200; and also the Herbst and Lindstrom citations below.
2. Lawrence A. Herbst, "Interregional Commodity Trade from the North to the South and American Economic Development in the Antebellum Period," *Journal of Economic History,* 35 (March 1975): 264–70.
3. Diane Lindstrom, *Economic Development in the Philadelphia Region, 1810–1850* (New York: Columbia University Press, 1978).
4. See, for example, William Cronon, *Nature's Metropolis: Chicago and the Great West* (New York: Norton, 1991).

Suggested Readings

Although somewhat dated, the most comprehensive work on the early domestic and foreign markets of the United States is still Emory R. Johnson et al., *History of Domestic and Foreign Commerce of the United States,* 2 vols. (Washington, D.C.: Carnegie Institution, 1915). A concise yet broad view of foreign commerce in American history is given in Robert E. Lipsey, "Foreign Trade," in Lance Davis et al., eds., *American Economic Growth: An Economist's History of the United States* (New York: Harper & Row, 1972). The standard quantitative reference for this period on exports, imports, and the balance of payments is Douglass C. North, "The United States Balance of Payments, 1790–1860," in National Bureau of Economic Research, *Trends in the American Economy in the Nineteenth Century: Studies in Income and Wealth,* vol. 24 (Princeton: Princeton University Press, 1960). North also provides a sophisticated analysis of the forces making for reduced transport costs in ocean shipping in his paper, "Sources of Productivity Change in Ocean Shipping, 1600–1850," *Journal of Political Economy,* 76 (Sept.–Oct. 1968). The effects of the Napoleonic Wars on the U.S. economy are discussed by Claudia D. Goldin and Frank D. Lewis, "The Role of Exports in American Economic Growth During the Napoleonic Wars, 1793–1807," *Explorations in Economic History,* 17 (1980). Aspects of the American shipping industry in its antebellum golden age are illuminated in two works of the noted maritime historian, Robert G. Albion, *The Rise of the Port of New York, 1815–1860* (New York: Scribner's, 1939); and *Square Riggers on Schedule: The New York Sailing Packets to England, France and the Cotton Ports* (Princeton: Princeton University Press, 1938).

On the organization and finance of foreign trade, see Norman Sydney Buck, *The Development of the Organization of Anglo-American Trade, 1800–1850* (New Haven: Yale University Press, 1925); Ralph Hidy, *The House of Baring in American Trade and Finance* (Cambridge, Mass.: Harvard University Press, 1949); and Edwin J. Perkins, *Financing Anglo-American Trade: The House of Brown, 1800–1880* (Cambridge, Mass.: Harvard University Press, 1975). Foreign investment in the United States from colonial times to the Civil War era is treated in part 1 of Mira Wilkins's encyclopedic study, *The History of*

Foreign Investment in the United States to 1914 (Cambridge, Mass.: Harvard University Press, 1989). Still useful on some specific aspects of foreign investment is Leland H. Jenks, *The Migration of British Capital to 1875* (New York: Knopf, 1927).

The rise of internal commerce in the antebellum years is a subject of much interest among scholars because of its relation to the origins of modern economic growth. See Albert Fishlow, "Antebellum Interregional Trade Reconsidered," *American Economic Review,* 59 (May 1964); Lawrence A. Herbst, "Interregional Commodity Trade from the North to the South and American Economic Development in the Antebellum Period," *Journal of Economic History,* 35 (March 1975); Diane Lindstrom, *Economic Development in the Philadelphia Region, 1810–1850* (New York: Columbia University Press, 1978); Diane Lindstrom, "American Economic Growth Before 1840: New Evidence and New Directions," *Journal of Economic History,* 39 (March 1979), and William Cronon, *Nature's Metropolis: Chicago and the Great West* (New York: Norton, 1991).

For insights into the changing nature of antebellum commerce and marketing organization, the following works are valuable: Lewis E. Atherton, *The Frontier Merchant in Mid-America* (Columbia: University of Missouri Press, 1971); Stuart Bruchey, "The Business Economy of Marketing Change, 1790–1840: A Study of Sources of Efficiency," *Agricultural History,* 46 (Jan. 1972); Glenn Porter and Harold C. Livesay, *Merchants and Manufacturers: Studies in the Changing Structure of Nineteenth-Century Marketing* (Baltimore: Johns Hopkins University Press, 1971); and Harold D. Woodman, *King Cotton and His Retainers* (Lexington: University of Kentucky Press, 1968). On the emergence of specialized commercial information services that accompanied the expansion of long-distance trade, see William H. Dillistin, *Bank Note Reporters and Counterfeit Detectors, 1826–1866* (New York: American Numismatic Society, 1949); James H. Madison, "The Evolution of Commercial Credit-Reporting Agencies in Nineteenth-Century America," *Business History Review,* 48 (Summer 1974); and James D. Norris, *R. G. Dun Co., 1841–1900: The Development of Credit Reporting in the Nineteenth Century* (Westport, Conn.: Greenwood Press, 1978).

Chapter 10

Economic Growth and Social Welfare

The Economic Transformation in Perspective

The Emergence of Modern Economic Growth

Regional Differences

Economic Welfare: Distributing the Gains from Growth

URING THE SEVEN DECADES FROM 1790 TO 1860, the United States made the transition from a premodern to a modern economy. Considerable self-sufficiency and slow rates of economic change gave way to a new order in which individuals, enterprises, and governments became specialized and interdependent, and change was accepted as part of the system. In Chapters 5 to 9 of Part II, we examined the key changes and critical decisions that brought about this epochal transformation. The shift from handicraft manufacturing to mechanized, factory industry was of the greatest long-term significance because it embodied the forces that propelled later economic development. During the transformation itself, however, other changes—territorial and population growth, the transportation and communications revolutions, the rise of the cotton belt, and the emergence of specialized commercial institutions such as banks—were also significant in terms of economic growth. Together, the key economic changes of 1790 to 1860 were of great historical significance, for they laid the foundation for the leadership role that the United States would later play in the international economy and world politics.

This chapter begins with a brief summary of the economic changes of the antebellum era and then turns to some important questions about what the transformation meant in terms of trends in economic growth and social welfare: When did the rate of economic growth change from a premodern to a modern level? How were regional economies within the United States affected by the forces propelling economic growth? Were increases in aggregate income and wealth widely shared? Although much has been done by economic historians to address these and other questions, problems of interpretation remain.

The Economic Transformation in Perspective

Major Developments

Population Growth. Expansion in the resources of the American economy between 1790 and 1860 is evident in terms of territory and population. The nation's land area more than tripled during the seven decades and reached its present-day continental proportions. Land resources utilized for economic purposes increased even more rapidly as a result of population expansion and redistribution. In 1790, the U.S. population of 3.9 million represented about 40 percent of Great Britain's estimated 10 million; in 1860, it was 31.5 million, a figure nearly 40 percent greater than Britain's 23 million. Over these seven decades, then, the U.S. population grew at a high rate of 3 percent per year.[1] And while doing so, it spread out from its initial concentration in a relatively narrow strip along the Atlantic seaboard to nearly full settlement of the eastern half of the nation's continental territory as well as in thriving pockets of settlement from there to the Pacific.

Economic Diversification and Specialization. Territorial and population expansion say little, however, about the movement toward economic modernity that took place between the administrations of George Washington and Abraham Lincoln. The contrasts between 1790 and 1860 in this regard are addressed in Chapters 5 to 9. In 1790, for example, there were few good roads, no canals, no steamboats, no steamships, and no railroads; by 1860, however, relatively few Americans were without access to one or more of the improved facilities for transporting goods and people. The communication and information flows in 1790, even between major cities along the Atlantic Coast, were limited and very slow; by 1860, in contrast, some fifty thousand miles of telegraph line furnished nearly instantaneous communication between widely separated points throughout the nation. In agriculture, the most dramatic change was the rise of cotton: From negligible U.S. production in 1790, its output increased steadily to an estimated two-thirds of the entire world's production of cotton by 1860. Progress in other dimensions of the nation's agricultural enterprise was also great, particularly in agricultural technology: By 1860, the age-old hand tools and simple implements of former years were giving way to sophisticated machinery and nonhuman power sources (animate and inanimate).

In commerce and manufacturing, the contrasts between 1790 and 1860 are even more striking. For instance, there were in 1790 only four commercial banks in the United States, one each in Philadelphia, New York, Boston, and Baltimore. None had existed a decade before. By 1860, there were 1600 state-chartered commercial banks and hundreds more unincorporated merchants, bankers, and brokers who performed banking functions. These banking institutions emerged in all areas of the young nation. In manufacturing, few Americans in 1790 would have listed their major occupation or employment as being in manufacturing; most of them—approximately nine in ten—were farmers, and the nation's manufacturing at that time was usually carried out as a simple handicraft adjunct to farming and rural life. By 1860, in contrast, some 15 percent of the nation's workers were employed in manufacturing on a relatively full-time basis. A manufacturing labor force had been formed. Large-scale factory production was present in some industries and dominant in a few. Technological change was beginning to become institutionalized. Urbanization and manufacturing

Urban Change: New York City's Wall Street in the 1790s and the 1860s.   The modest wood and brick structures of the earlier era gave way to the stone temples of finance by the Civil War period. Stocks and bonds were just beginning to be traded in 1790, in and outside of the coffee houses. By the 1860s, activity had clearly picked up on "the Street." Trinity Church, then the tallest structure in the city, still stands on Broadway at the head of Wall Street, but today it is dwarfed by the modern temples of finance. (Both prints: Historical Pictures/Stock Montage)

were reinforcing each other and breaking the path toward more complex forms of social and economic organization.

Internal Market Growth. Common among the many different transformations of American economic life were the emergence, expansion, and intensification of internal market activity. Around 1790, the important markets of the United States were abroad, and a relatively small proportion of Americans were involved with them. Internally, the great majority of Americans were independent and self-sufficient farmers, though they sometimes traded agricultural products and handcrafted items with their neighbors. By 1860, however, Americans in all lines of economic activity increasingly sold their products to distant consumers and purchased their own consumption and capital goods in equally impersonal markets. The great advantages of the impersonalization of economic life were, of course, specialization and the increased efficiency, wealth, and welfare that specialization promoted. Specialization was made possible by the extension of markets and of the information that the markets provided to economic decision makers. The growth of markets in the antebellum era fundamentally altered the context of decision making from one of independence to one of interdependence.

The Life of Roger Brooke Taney (1777–1864)

The great transformation of American economic life between 1790 and 1860 took place during the lifetime of many Americans. The life of Roger Brooke Taney, for example, who was born in 1777 during the American Revolution and who died in 1864 during the Civil War, reflected something of the "life" of the young American nation before 1860. The son of slaveholding planters, Taney was born and grew up on a tobacco plantation in southern Maryland. After graduating from Dickinson

College in 1795, he studied law and then entered upon a legal and political career. A Federalist, he was elected to the Maryland legislature in 1799 but was defeated for reelection in the Republican electoral tide of 1800. For the next three decades Taney practiced law, first in Frederick and later in Baltimore, but he continued to remain active in politics. Unlike many Federalists, he strongly supported the U.S. government during the War of 1812. From 1816 to 1820, he was a state senator and, in 1827, he became attorney general of Maryland.

In his early private and public life, Taney emphasized the needs for better currency and banking arrangements as well as improvements in the position and rights of blacks, both slave and free, in American society. A director of two Maryland banks at various times between 1810 and 1823, Taney was conversant with bank operations; during the 1820s, he developed misgivings about the power and dominance that the second Bank of the United States exerted over other American banks. Slavery he deemed an evil institution, one with which Americans had been saddled during their colonial dependency. Taney argued for an end to slavery, calling for a gradual freeing of slaves because of the problems that the long-deprived black minority would face in a predominantly white society. He also freed his own slaves around 1820, after ensuring that they would be able to cope on their own. On another occasion, Taney lent a talented young slave the money to purchase his freedom from his owner. The great issues of banking and slavery would later stamp Taney's name indelibly in the annals of American history.

Taney's rise to national prominence commenced in 1824 when, with the disappearance of the Federalist party, he became an active and avid supporter of Andrew Jackson for the presidency. Jackson lost in the so-called corrupt bargain after the election of 1824, but he and his supporters were successful in 1828. Jackson appointed Taney attorney general of the

Roger B. Taney, 1777–1864. Born during the Revolution, Taney (pronounced Tawney) was a Maryland slaveholder, a lawyer, a Federalist, a Jacksonian, an advocate of free competition in banking and business generally, Secretary of the Treasury, and the successor to John Marshall as Chief Justice of the United States from 1835 until his death in 1864, during the Civil War. Although Taney's opinions on the Court made constructive contributions to law and economic development, he is chiefly remembered for the 1857 *Dred Scott* decision, which held that black Americans—whether slave or free—were not citizens. The decision enraged abolitionists, fanning the flames of divisiveness that resulted in the Civil War. (Historical Pictures/Stock Montage)

States, and after the presidential veto was sustained, he supervised the transfer of federal monies from it to state-chartered banks. Taney advocated free competition in banking, a policy toward which America was fitfully moving at the time.

In 1836, Jackson appointed Taney to succeed John Marshall as Chief Justice of the United States. Taney served as Chief Justice until his death twenty-eight years later. On the Supreme Court, he was a proponent of the principle of divided sovereignty between the states and the federal government. This meant that the states could not hinder the execution of federal powers but that the federal government could not prevent the states from interfering with the rights of property or from regulating private activities within their borders as long as the public interest was served and the Constitution was not violated. A number of opinions of the Taney court effectively promoted the competitive development of corporate enterprise and thus generalized the Chief Justice's views on banking.

Taney's most noted opinion, however, came in the case of *Dred Scott v. Sanford* (1857). Scott, a black slave, sued his owner, claiming freedom and U.S. citizenship on the ground that he had been taken into "free" territory as defined in the Missouri Compromise of 1820. Taney's majority opinion, however, held that Congress had no constitutional power to exclude slavery from U.S. territories and that Scott had to remain a slave because he had no right to sue in a federal court. The opinion caused a bitter reaction among opponents of slavery and thereby contributed to the hostile climate that soon led to the Civil War.

Taney's long life thus illustrates the economic progress and problems, both resolved and unresolved, of the United States between 1790 and 1860. Economic development led people of agrarian origins to concern themselves with the emerging problems of law, banking, corporate rights and responsibilities,

United States in 1831 and secretary of the treasury in 1833. In both these roles, Taney was a key figure and ally of the president during Jackson's war with the Bank of the United States over the recharter of that institution. Taney advised Jackson to veto the congressional bill to recharter the Bank of the United and the framework of enterprise that would best promote increased wealth and social welfare. The solutions to most of these problems were largely effective; however, the issue of slavery continued to divide the nation as well as the consciences of Americans such as Taney.

The Emergence of Modern Economic Growth

Our knowledge of economic growth in pre-Civil War America has increased substantially since the 1950s. Scholars working with information from such sources as the decennial U.S. census and employing insights from economic theory and modern concepts of national income accounting have constructed measures of national income and product for the antebellum era. The results of these careful studies, even the tentative and conjectural ones, bring a fresh understanding of the overall performance of the early U.S. economy.

The studies that attempt to measure antebellum economic growth are not all equally well grounded in a firm base of quantitative evidence. The census material, for example, al-

lows one to measure the national product using the techniques of a modern economic statistician, but only for the years after the late 1830s. Some results of the measurements of economic growth are presented in Table 10–1. In prices current during the years listed in the table, the gross national product (GNP) increased from $1.54 billion in the 1839 Census year to $4.17 billion in 1859. Measured in prices of 1860, the economy's real GNP expanded less rapidly because prices in general rose somewhat over the two decades. Real GNP per capita—a better measure of economic growth because it adjusts for changes in both general price levels and population—is shown in column three of Table 10–1. Measured in 1860 prices, it rose from $95 in 1839 to $130 in 1859. Increases in real GNP per capita were greater, both relatively and absolutely, during the 1850s than in the 1840s. But it should be kept in mind that the nation's business was relatively prosperous in 1839 and then suffered one of the most severe depressions in U.S. history in the several years thereafter.

A number of historically important questions may be addressed to the data in Table 10–1: (1) What rates of economic growth do

Table 10–1 *Measures of Economic Growth, 1839–1859*

Year	GNP in Current Prices (in $ billions) (1)	GNP in 1860 Prices (in $ billions) (2)	Real GNP per Capita[a]($) (3)
1839	$1.54	$1.62	$ 95.00
1844	1.80	1.97	98.00
1849	2.32	2.43	104.00
1854	3.53	3.37	123.00
1859	4.17	4.10	130.00

[a]Calculated by dividing the figures in column 2 by total population.

SOURCES: Data in columns 1 and 2 are from Robert E. Gallman, "Gross National Product in the United States, 1834–1909," in National Bureau of Economic Research, *Output, Employment, and Productivity in the United States After 1800: Studies in Income and Wealth,* vol. 30 (New York: National Bureau of Economic Research, 1966), p. 26; population data for calculations in column 3 are from U.S. Bureau of the Census, *Historical Statistics of the United States* (Washington, D.C.: the GPO, 1960), p. 7.

the data indicate? (2) How do the rates compare with the subsequent American experience? And (3) where did the United States stand economically in the world community at the time? First, the indicated rate of growth of real GNP from 1839 to 1859 was approximately 4.6 percent per year, whereas that of GNP per capita was about 1.6 percent per year. The difference between the rates for those two years—3 percent—was the approximate rate of population growth.

Second, in evaluating how the rates of economic growth for 1839 to 1859 compared with those of the subsequent American experience, it should be noted that the long-term trend for the growth rate of real GNP per capita has been roughly 1.6 percent per year from the late 1830s to the present day. In other words, during the two decades prior to the Civil War (the period for which reasonably detailed and comprehensive estimates of national product first become possible), the U.S. economy was already expanding in terms of per capita GNP at a rate characteristic of modern economic growth. This is a significant finding because it challenges the views of earlier historians who emphasized either the post–Civil War decades or the period from 1843 to 1861 as marking the beginning of economic modernization in the United States.[2] Rather than beginning in the 1840s, though, the new findings indicate that the growth of the American economy was already at a high, modern level.[3]

Third, the question of the United States' economic position in relation to other countries in 1840 has a somewhat surprising answer. At that time, Great Britain and France were considered to have the most successful economies. They had been the leading political powers in colonial North America, and their long national histories of institutional, social, and industrial development had established them as economic powers. The United States, however, was a new nation with a predominantly agricultural economy. Nonetheless, international comparisons of national products indicate that the size of the American economy around 1840 was not very different from that of the two leading European nations. Various techniques of comparison show that the U.S. national product ranged from two-thirds to three-fourths of the roughly equal national products of Britain and of France. In 1840, though, Britain's population was somewhat greater and France's substantially greater than that of the United States. Hence, the U.S. national product per capita approached that of Great Britain and was somewhat greater than that of France.[4] In short, by 1840, the United States was already on a rough par in terms of per capita and total product with the leading nations of Europe.

It should be noted that the comparisons are based on modern concepts of national product, which exclude some economic activities important during earlier periods of U.S. history. In the early United States, for example, farmers invested their own labor and farm materials in constructing farm buildings and in the clearing, fencing, and draining of farmland. In addition, the manufacturing of products in the home largely for the family's own use is not accounted for in the modern calculations. Such activities today are not counted in the GNP because they do not involve flows of goods and services through markets. Moreover, they are no longer important in a quantitative sense. But estimates for 1840 show that they may have had a value equivalent to about 15 percent of the narrower, modern concept of American GNP for that year. Since it is likely that these activities were more important in the United States than in Britain or France, their inclusion in a more comprehensive measure of aggregate national product would make the U.S. level of product and product per capita around 1840 even larger relative to those of the other two countries.

The finding that the United States as early as 1840 was already among the world's leading nations in terms of product per capita, and that this measure of the American economy's productivity was already growing at a high rate, raises the question of when the process of modern growth began. It seems clear that a per capita product growth rate averaging 1.6 percent per year could not have been present for very many decades before 1840, for such a high rate of growth would imply ridiculously low levels of per capita product in the earlier years. Growing at 1.6 percent per year, real per capita product would double every 45 years. This roughly is what has happened in the U.S. economy since 1840. Had such a rate of growth characterized the American economy during the ninety years before 1840, real per capita product (in 1860 values) would have been only about $24 in 1750 and $48 in 1795. On the basis of a variety of other evidence, most American economic historians think that these hypothetical levels are unrealistically low. Accepting this manner of reasoning, one must conclude that the American economy's rate of growth accelerated and reached modern levels sometime during the four to five decades before 1840.

Nothing in the actual historical record of the American economy contradicts such a view. The preceding chapters reflect and analyze the economic transformation that took place in the United States before the Civil War. Economic measurement shows that expansion at modern rates of per capita product growth was established by 1840. Combining these insights points to the quarter-century before 1840 as the period when economic growth most likely accelerated and began to sustain itself. In that quarter-century, developments in transportation, agriculture, finance, industry, and commerce began strongly and simultaneously to reinforce one another. Internal markets grew rapidly and as a result the expanding resources of the young American nation began to be combined more effectively. Proceeding as it did on a number of fronts, the acceleration of

economic growth after the War of 1812 can be considered more gradual than abrupt, particularly when it is recognized that many of the elements contributing to it were present earlier in embryonic form. Nonetheless, a new and vibrant economic order emerged in the United States. The emphasis of economic decision making shifted from foreign trade to internal economic development as a rapidly growing percentage of Americans were drawn into market activity. And all of these developments came during a relatively brief period in the nation's history.

Regional Differences

The transition to modern economic growth during the early nineteenth century tended to accentuate regional differences within the United States. Because economic development promotes specialization along lines of comparative advantage as well as the exchange in markets of goods and services produced by specializing individuals and regions, increased regional differences were to be expected. Regional differences and disparities have arisen in virtually all nations that have modernized their economies during the past two centuries. In 1790, most Americans in the three large regions of the time—the Northeast, the South, and the sparsely settled West—were relatively unspecialized, self-sufficient farmers. Only near tidewater was there much specialized economic activity—in the differentiated occupations of the port cities and towns, in the hinterlands that supplied towns with food, and on the southern plantations that produced staple crops for export to distant markets. By 1860, the three regions were much more distinct as economic entities. Their differences were enhanced by the continuing presence of slavery in the South long after it had been abolished in the North and prohibited in the West.

The Northeast

The distinctiveness of the economies of the Northeast and the West between 1800 and 1860 is relatively easy to understand, though it did not last for long after 1860. The farmland of the Northeast, especially in rocky New England, was inferior to that of the West (today's Midwest). Thus, northeasterners from the first colonial settlements sought nonagricultural pursuits instead, such as domestic and overseas trade, artisanal manufacturing, shipping and shipbuilding, and using the products of the sea. These pursuits were a part of the European heritage brought to America and, as in Europe, they were carried on in towns and cities. Still, most people remained farmers.

When the industrial and transportation revolutions took hold in the decades after 1790, the options open to rural and urban northeasterners expanded. Jobs opened up in the new factories as well as in nonfactory employments in the towns and cities that serviced the manufacturing industries and their workers. For those who chose to remain in farming, the options were either to move to the fertile West to pursue grain farming or to stay in the Northeast and farm different products—fruits, vegetables, livestock, and dairy products—for urban consumers. Although many northeasterners attracted by cheap and fertile land moved to the West during the early nineteenth century, the potential loss of labor for the urbanizing, industrial economy they left behind did not materialize. At first, women and children with low opportunity costs supplied labor for factory industries; later, immigrants arriving and settling in the Northeast added to its labor supply.

The West

The West—the old Northwest—was thus settled primarily by people from the Northeast who for the most part continued as farmers. In due course, they built cities, towns and villages, schools, churches, and other institutions similar to those they had left behind. Although the two regions made up one economy, they were at different stages of development. Eventually, they came to be similar in development as well, once transportation improvements, banking institutions, factories, and immigrants moved into the West during the decades after the pioneer settlements. The only notable difference between the two regions was the Midwest's devotion of more of its resources to agriculture because of its abundant and fertile land.

The South

The antebellum South, however, had an economy fundamentally different from the economies of the Northeast and the West. The main form of wealth in the South was slaves, not land or factories. As economic historian Gavin Wright notes, southern planters were "labor-lords," not landlords, and their slave wealth, unlike land and factories, was very mobile.[5] Table 10–2 shows the great wealth differences in 1860 between slaveowning and free farmers, whether in the North or the South. In particular the table points out the preponderance of slaveowners' wealth in personal estate, mainly slaves. The value of slave wealth depended on the demand for slave labor in the whole slave economy, not on local conditions such as good transportation, thriving cities and towns, factories, or schools. Although these types of conditions attracted people and raised land values, slaveholders were more interested in raising the value of their slave labor. As a result, the slaveholders who were economically, politically, and socially dominant in the affairs of the South had little incentive to promote or pay for local improvements. Moreover, they had no reason to welcome immigrants, as northerners did, or to seek any increase in the labor supply other than the natural increase of the slaves they owned. The great demand for

Table 10–2   *Wealth of Farmers by Region, 1860*

Region[a]	Number of Farms Sampled	Total Reported Wealth (in $)	Value of Personal Estate (in $)	Value of Farm (in $)	Average Age of Farmer (in years)
North	1,050	$ 3,858	$ 834	$ 2,909	44.2
Northeast	3,599	4,620	1,104	3,694	46.9
Old Northwest	5,349	3,176	682	2,524	42.8
West	846	2,212	532	1,672	39.9
South	643	22,819	13,277	8,186	44.0
Slave farms	417	33,906	19,828	11,817	45.2
Free farms	226	2,362	1,188	1,568	41.8

[a]Northeast—Connecticut, Maine, New Hampshire, New Jersey, New York, Pennsylvania, Rhode Island, and Vermont; Old Northwest—Illinois, Indiana, Michigan, Ohio, and Wisconsin; West—Iowa, Kansas, and Minnesota; South—Alabama, Georgia, Louisiana, Mississippi, South Carolina, and Texas.
SOURCES: Samples drawn from the 1860 manuscript Census and adapted from Roger Ransom, *Conflict and Compromise* (Cambridge: Cambridge University Press, 1989), p. 63.

American cotton raised slave prices and made slaveholders wealthy. However, their wealth did not lead the South to increase its population or to develop roads, canals, railroads, towns, cities, factories, schools, and farm machines to any degree remotely resembling what was taking place in the Northeast and West. Between 1790 and 1860, the North and South thus followed separate paths to economic development.

Economic Welfare: Distributing the Gains from Growth

Economic growth refers to how certain factors—such as wealth, income, and production—change over time. To measure economic growth in real terms, adjustments are made to compensate for changes in the value of the measuring rod—usually a monetary unit such as the dollar. And since a nation with a rapidly growing population often has a more rapid growth of total wealth, income, and production than one whose population grows less rapidly, many analysts focus on real changes

per capita as the most meaningful indicators of economic growth.

Per capita measures of real product, income, and wealth, and their rates of growth over time, also reveal information about the levels of and changes in a nation's average economic welfare. Material welfare, for example, is considered greater in nations with higher levels of per capita product; it is thought to be increasing more rapidly when per capita product grows at faster rates. But discussions of economic welfare often move beyond these average measures of the levels and growth rates of production, income, and wealth into a consideration of how these magnitudes are distributed both across the population and by functional groupings. Two nations with equal populations and equal amounts of aggregate wealth and production would have the same per capita wealth and product. But the two nations might be viewed differently in terms of economic welfare if in one of them the leaders appropriated a large share of the wealth and product for personal use and kept the rest of the population at a subsistence level, while in the other nation wealth and production were distributed equally among the people.

An Egalitarian Nation?

Vigorous and sustained economic growth at the high rates characteristic of modern nations emerged in the United States between the Revolution and the Civil War. What happened in these years to economic welfare in terms of the distribution of the fruits of economic growth? There is little information available to answer that question and what is available does not lend itself to simple interpretations (although various interpretations are put forth by scholars even when they imply conflicting views of the underlying historical situation). One long-standing interpretation of the distribution of wealth and income in antebellum America is that of *egalitarianism.* Numerous foreign observers of American society, including the Frenchman Alexis de Tocqueville, as well as many native Americans, thought that in both political and economic affairs, power and opportunity were much more equally distributed among the population of free people in the United States than in the old societies of Europe. Later historians adopted this idea and referred to the antebellum period as the era of the "common man"—an era of relative equality between the more aristocratic colonial and federal periods and the post–Civil War gilded age of industrial expansion, which had highly visible inequalities of income and wealth. The egalitarian theory does not deny that disparities existed in the material welfare of individual free people; rather, it affirms that in the United States the disparities were relatively narrow compared to Europe's, that more opportunities were open for Americans of modest backgrounds to attain wealth, and that the well-to-do groups of the United States were composed primarily of active and self-made people rather than of idle beneficiaries of inherited wealth.[6]

Or a Land of Inequality?

Another interpretation is offered by revisionist historians. They argue that proponents of the egalitarian interpretation are taken in by the rhetoric of equality and of the common person in the antebellum era as well as by their own imaginations. In reality, the revisionists hold, wealth and economic opportunity were unequally distributed in the early United States, just as they were in Europe. Although the existence of slavery in the South resulted in marked inequality in the distribution of wealth and income in that section, neither the egalitarian interpreters nor the revisionists argue their point on that ground. The issue concerns the free population, and the revisionists hold that among free people there were wide economic disparities. Many of the wealthiest Americans, the revisionists continue, derived their positions from inheritance rather than from native ability, and well-to-do families tended to preserve their positions of wealth and influence over the decades.[7]

Evidence of Unequal Distribution

To assess the two positions, detailed and quantitative evidence on wealth and income distributions at various years throughout the antebellum era is needed. Evidence on income distribution is not available, but some records, though incomplete, are available for the distribution of wealth. The Census of 1860, for example, asked Americans to report the value of their personal and real properties, along with their ages, occupations, and places of birth. The original manuscript forms of the 1860 Census are preserved in the National Archives in Washington, D.C. They show, for example, that in Springfield, Illinois, there lived one Abraham Lincoln, aged fifty-one, a lawyer, born in Kentucky, the owner of $5,000 of personal property and $12,000 of real property; and that in Chicago, there lived one Cyrus McCormick, fifty-one years old, occupied in a reaper factory, a native of Virginia, the owner of $278,000 and $1,750,000 of personal and real property, respectively.

With such detailed information and statistical sampling procedures, economic statisticians are able to estimate with reasonable accuracy the distribution of wealth in the United States and its constituent parts for 1860. The results of their work indicate a high degree of inequality in wealth distribution. The richest 1 percent, 5 percent, and 30 percent of all families in 1860 are estimated to have held 24 percent, 54 percent, and 95 percent, respectively, of the reported wealth. On the other end of the wealth spectrum, one-half of American families in 1860 apparently had no wealth at all.

Variations on the theme of marked inequality of wealth are evident in subclasses of the manuscript census data. In the United States as a whole, 5.5 percent of free adult males possessed total estates (real and personal property) greater than $10,000, whereas 64 percent possessed property valued at $1,000 or less. In the South, the proportion of wealthy males was greater: 9.5 percent of Southern free adult males valued their property—which included slaves—at $10,000 or more, whereas 62 percent were at or below $1,000. Lesser, but still substantial, inequality was present in the wealth distribution of the young northern state of Wisconsin, where 1.9 percent of the adult males had property valued at over $10,000 and 64 percent under $1,000. Inequality of wealthholding apparently was greatest in urban areas. For example, in ten urban counties in 1860 (all of them in the North except for the District of Columbia), 4.8 percent of adult males owned property worth over $10,000, 80 percent owned property worth $100 or less, and over 50 percent reported no real or personal wealth at all. In contrast, only 29 percent of free adult males both in the South and in Wisconsin reported no wealth.[8] From the available evidence, then, it appears that urbanization in the modern industrial era promoted increased inequality in wealthholdings.

Trends of Inequality, 1774 to 1860. Thus, the finding that substantial inequality existed in the distribution of American wealth in 1860 seems to challenge the egalitarian theory and support the contrary historical interpretations of revisionist scholars. Before examining this issue more closely, however, we need to determine whether inequality of wealth increased, remained relatively constant, or decreased during the antebellum decades. The notion of a late eighteenth-century aristocratic society and economy, followed by the era of the "common man" after 1815, would lead to an expectation of increasing equality over time. However, recognition of industrial growth and the urbanization and commercialization of more and more economic activity favors the hypothesis of increased inequality in terms of wealth. Or, the two trends might have offset each other so that few changes in wealth distribution between early and late antebellum dates would be observed.

Evidence on the trend of wealth distribution from the late eighteenth century to the Civil War is much more restricted than for 1860 alone. But summary statistics computed from distributions of slaves among slaveholders and among families in 1790, 1830, 1850, and 1860 reveal that the concentration of this peculiar form of wealth changed little over time. Since in 1860 the inequality of total wealthholdings in the South and in the United States as a whole did not differ much, one might infer from the slave data that inequality in the United States also changed little over the seven decades. Further information on this point is now available. Comprehensive data on the wealthholdings of Americans in 1790 do not exist, but estimates of the distribution of wealth in the New England and Middle colonies for 1774 have been constructed from information contained in the probate records of the estates of persons who died in that year. There is also information from the first U.S. direct tax levied in 1798. The 1774 and 1798 estimates indicate that the richest one-fifth of the free adult population in 1774 possessed from 60 percent to 66 percent of colonial wealth, whereas the bottom half of wealthholders had approximately 8 percent. The estimates for 1798 are much the same. For 1860, the corresponding estimates are 88 percent and 12 percent.[9] The estimates of wealth distributions for 1774 and 1860 thus reveal a high degree of inequality but also a moderate tendency toward increased inequality over time. The underlying wealth data for 1774 and 1798 are, however, sketchier and less complete geographically than those for 1860. Therefore, the hypothesis of a relatively constant and high degree of inequality in the distribution of wealth between the revolutionary and Civil War eras cannot yet be rejected. But if a change did occur, it was likely in the direction of somewhat increased inequality in wealthholding. Using other information, such as wage data, some analysts argue that inequality may have increased substantially after 1820.[10]

Interpreting the Evidence on Distribution: The Life Cycle

What can be said, then, of the egalitarian interpretation? Surprising as it may seem, given the evidence on widespread inequalities in the distribution of antebellum wealth, there are reasons to believe in the validity of the egalitarian position. Adults in modern societies tend to move through life in a fairly typical pattern of income and saving and therefore of wealth accumulation. They tend to have low incomes and low or even negative savings and wealth when they are young; then their incomes, savings, and accumulations grow in the middle adult years before tapering off and, in the case of savings, becoming negative in the retirement years. Now, if every individual had exactly the same level and life-cycle pattern of income, saving, and wealth accumulation, it would follow that middle-age and older persons would possess most of the wealth and that young adults would have little of it. Moreover, if the young adults were far more numerous than the older adults, a very unequal distribution of wealth would be measured even

though each individual's life-cycle pattern of income and accumulation was, by assumption, exactly the same.[11] In short, a highly egalitarian society, when observed at any one point, could appear to have a very unequal distribution of wealth.

Age and Wealth.   What does this imply about antebellum America? In 1860, the median age of the American population was only 19.4 years as compared with more than 30 years today. In other words, only one-half of the 1860 population consisted of adults. Moreover, the adult group was comparatively youthful. Of adult males, over five million in 1860 were between ages twenty and thirty-nine and less than three million were aged forty and over; in the late twentieth century, by contrast, adult males over age forty and those between the ages of twenty and forty are more evenly balanced in numbers. In the antebellum era, therefore, a disproportionate number of adults compared to our own time were in the age groups where wealth accumulation would be expected to have been relatively small. This expectation is confirmed in the studies cited earlier, which find a strong and direct relationship between age and wealth in 1860. Consequently, the observed inequality of wealth distribution in 1860—and presumably in earlier years, when the American population was even younger in average age—cannot be taken as unqualified evidence against the egalitarian interpretation.

Effects of Urbanization and Mobility.   Increasing urbanization of the antebellum American population is another factor bearing on the interpretation of observed inequalities in wealth distribution at given points in time. Inequality appears to have been greater in urban areas; in particular, the proportions of people reporting no wealth or almost no wealth were noticeably larger in urban places than in nonurban areas. Growing immigration to the United States in

"The Spirit of Progress in the West." This 1872 allegorical painting by John Gast captures the ideas of progress and manifest destiny that gripped many Americans by the middle of the nineteenth century. Settlers in covered wagons, miners, and stage coaches—followed by railroads and telegraph lines—push west from the farms and cities of the East. In the painting the buffalo, other wildlife, and American Indian peoples are pushed back and out of the way in an uneven clash of numbers, cultures, and technologies. (Culver Pictures)

the late antebellum decades accounts for some of this difference. Immigrants tended disproportionately to settle in urban areas, and the studies of wealth distribution in 1860 indicate, as might be expected, that the foreign-born had accumulated less wealth on the average than native Americans. Expanding urban labor markets, moreover, attracted young native-born adults away from alternative rural employments. These Americans, as well as the immigrants, tended to be in the early, minimal-accumulation phases of their life cycles. In in-

creasing numbers, they chose to live and work in the seemingly less egalitarian cities because of the greater economic opportunities and advantages that these areas afforded them as compared with their prospects in rural areas.

Geographic and economic mobility thus characterized the American population before the Civil War. In 1860, well over one-third of the free population resided in states other than the ones in which they had been born. Such a high degree of mobility was surely a response to economic opportunity, and in this respect mobility has long played a role in the egalitarian interpretation. Mobility also sheds some light on the revisionist position that inherited wealth and privilege counted for more than ability and hard work in the distribution of wealth. The evidence for the revisionist view comes mostly from research into the defining characteristics of the rich living in the old and large cities of the Atlantic seaboard: they tended to come from the old, established families of these cities and to have substantial amounts of inherited wealth. However, evidence for the newer cities of the West and South indicates that the well-to-do were far more likely to have come from other places and to have built their fortunes from their own efforts rather than from inheritance. Throughout history, no doubt, being born into a wealthy family has had its advantages for maintaining a position of wealth during one's lifetime. But the evidence shows that, in the expanding American economy of the nineteenth century, these advantages hardly precluded other people of initially limited means from attaining wealth. The widespread availability and abundance of resources, together with a highly mobile and acquisitive population, encouraged this result. Thus, it was perhaps more on a basis of reason and observation than on myth that the United States impressed the egalitarian interpreters who contrasted it with the older societies of Europe.

Income Distribution and Wage Levels

With regard to the distribution of income in the antebellum economy, such impressionistic evidence and reasoning tend to take on greater weight in historical interpretations because in a quantitative sense much less is known about it than about wealth distribution. It is certain, however, that income was more equally distributed than wealth. In the first place, the distribution of the ability to earn income from one's labor was more equal than the distribution of wealth. While the census evidence argues that about one-half of all American families had essentially no wealth at all in 1860, it is inconceivable that more than a tiny fraction of these families earned no income by working. Furthermore, estimates of the division of the national income between labor income and property income indicate that labor's share was approximately two-thirds of the total. Since labor income was both the largest part of total income and almost certainly more equally distributed than wealth, it is safe to say that the income distribution, if it was known for the antebellum years, would show considerably less inequality. Indeed, comparisons of later income and wealth distribution invariably indicate this relationship.

Under the assumption that returns to labor made up about two-thirds of the national income in 1860, the average labor income per member of the labor force in that year was about $250 in 1860 values. Although less than one-half of the labor force was in the employee category—more than one-half of all workers were self-employed—independent estimates of wage levels are broadly consistent with this average annual wage figure. In 1860 farm laborers earned an average of $13 to $14 per month with board, whereas nonfarm common laborers earned just over $1 a day. Industrial wages on an annual basis ranged from about $200 per year in cotton manufacturing to $350 in iron making. Miners earned from $250 to $350 per year. The antebellum workweek was long by present standards: Eleven or twelve hours per day for six days was not uncommon, and labor organizations were still struggling for the ten-hour day in most industries.

Standard of Living

By themselves, the wage and income data mean little. A better idea of the standard of living in 1860 emerges when these data are related to prices of the necessities of life. Rents in the manufacturing towns of the Northeast averaged from $4.50 to $6.00 per month for four- to six-room tenements. In the food category, meats cost ten to fifteen cents per pound and bread seven to eight cents per loaf. Milk was around five cents a quart, while a bushel of potatoes could be had for anywhere between twenty cents and a dollar. Men's suits and overcoats ranged upward from $10 and $5, respectively. Detailed budget studies are not available for the period, but a few impressionistic estimates indicate that a typical working-class family of the 1850s spent about one-half of its income on food, one-fourth on shelter, and most of the remainder on clothing.[12] For the majority of Americans, then, there was neither much leisure nor, after providing for the basic necessities of life, much money to spend on leisure-time activities.

The standard of living of the typical person in the United States at the close of the antebellum era was thus not very high by modern standards. But this conclusion is to be expected. In a growing economy, each generation lives on average with more goods and services per person than were available to earlier generations, and six or seven generations have passed between the 1850s and the 1990s. Still, the economic growth process was under way during the antebellum years. Stanley Lebergott, for example, estimates from a wide range of painstakingly gathered evidence that real wages in the United States rose substantially in the decades before the Civil War. After remaining essentially level from 1800 to 1820, he argues that real wages rose about 25 percent between 1820 and 1832, another 25 percent between 1832 and 1850, and about 1 percent in the last antebellum decade, when immigration increased the competition for jobs.[13] If Lebergott's estimates are accurate, then real wages grew at nearly 1.5 percent per year from 1820 to 1850 and over 1.1 percent per year from 1820 to 1860. The laboring Americans of the antebellum United States were already experiencing the fruits of economic growth.

Slave "Incomes." However, the one glaring exception was the black slave, who was being exploited economically as well as in other ways. The basic annual per capita "income" of American slaves—that is, the value of their food, clothing, shelter, and medical care—was an estimated $34 in 1850 (approximately one-third of the American GNP per capita at the time). Adult male slaves had similar "incomes" of $50 to $60 per year, also about one-third or less of what they might have earned as free workers. Next to this one great inequality of welfare in the antebellum economy, the others were comparatively insignificant.

Summary

Americans of the first half of the nineteenth century lived in an age of transition to economic modernity. In their lifetimes were unleashed the forces that changed the old order of barely perceptible changes in long-run living standards to the new order of steady increases in the standard of living. Signs of economic progress were visible everywhere—in industry, agriculture, commerce, transportation, and communication. Economic progress was, of course, not an altogether new phenomenon. Earlier periods of history, both in America and elsewhere, had witnessed broad-based economic advances. But in nearly all such periods the elements making for progress had played themselves out or were reversed. The elements of economic progress that emerged in the United States during the early nineteenth century—technological change, specialization of activities, and market growth—were different in that they were capable of being expanded indefinitely. Economic growth, therefore, became self-sustaining, and continuing advances in production and incomes per worker and per person were translated into ever-rising standards of material welfare for most Americans.

Economic modernization was not without its drawbacks. Although the increasingly specialized and interdependent economic organization produced and distributed goods and services at ever-lower real costs in terms of resources, it also uprooted people from their traditional ways of economic existence and made them more liable to suffer from periodic instabilities of prices, production, and employment. Economic modernization prior to the Civil War also increased economic inequality in many ways, particularly in the persistence of slavery. The new economic world made less personal the relationships between employers and employees, between producers and consumers, and between decision makers and those affected by the decisions. In such ways, the economic progress of one generation often led to the problems of the next. However, the material advantages of the new order were so great that few people in America favored returning to the simpler economy of the past.

Endnotes

1. In addition to the comparison with Britain, some hypothetical calculations demonstrate why 3 percent was a high rate of growth by historical standards: If the U.S. population had continued to expand at 3 percent per year from 1860 to 1990, it would have had a population of 1.4 billion by that year, more than China's population in recent years and far above the 248.7 million Americans counted in the 1990 U.S. Census.

2. The post–Civil War period was emphasized by Charles A. and Mary R. Beard, *The Rise of American Civilization* (New York: Macmillan, 1930), and by Louis Hacker, *The Triumph of American Capitalism* (New York: Columbia University Press, 1940). The period from 1843 to 1861 was characterized as the economic "takeoff" of the United States by Walt W. Rostow, *The Stages of Economic Growth* (Cambridge, Engl.: Cambridge University Press, 1960).

3. See the chapters and articles of Robert Gallman, Paul David, and Thomas Weiss cited in Suggested Readings.

4. See the two chapters by Robert Gallman cited in the first paragraph of Suggested Readings.

5. Gavin Wright, *Old South, New South: Revolutions in the Southern Economy Since the Civil War* (New York: Basic Books, 1986). The antebellum southern economy is discussed in Wright's Chapter 2.

6. See Robert Gallman, "Professor Pessen on the 'Egalitarian Myth,'" *Social Science History* (Winter 1978).

7. See Edward Pessen, *Riches, Class, and Power Before the Civil War* (cited in Suggested Readings).

8. The data reported in this paragraph come from several studies by Lee Soltow: "Economic Inequality in the United States in the Period from 1790 to 1860," *Journal of Economic History*, 31 (Dec. 1971): 822–39; *Patterns of Wealthholding in Wisconsin Since 1850* (Madison: University of Wisconsin Press, 1971); and "The Wealth, Income, and Social Class of Men in Large Northern Cities of the United States in 1860," in

James D. Smith, ed., *The Personal Distribution of Income and Wealth* (New York: National Bureau of Economic Research, 1975), pp. 233–76.

9. On the distribution of slaves, see Soltow, "Economic Inequality," pp. 823–28; on the wealth distribution for 1774, see Alice Hanson Jones, "Wealth Estimates for the New England Colonies About 1770," *Journal of Economic History,* 32 (March 1971): 98–117.

10. See the references to the works of Peter Lindert and Jeffrey Williamson in Selected Readings.

11. See Robert E. Gallman, "Professor Pessen on the 'Egalitarian Myth,'" *Social Science History* (Winter 1978): 194–207.

12. See Edgar W. Martin, *The Standard of Living in 1860* (full citation in Suggested Readings).

13. Stanley Lebergott, *Manpower in Economic Growth,* p. 154 (full citation in Suggested Readings). Sokoloff and Villaflor (cited in Chapter 8 above) confirm Lebergott's findings.

Suggested Readings

A quantitative and analytic introduction to the emergence of modern economic growth in the United States is Robert Gallman, "The Pace and Pattern of American Economic Growth," in Lance Davis et al., eds., *American Economic Growth: An Economist's History of the United States* (New York: Harper & Row, 1972). The basic source of quantitative information on economic growth since the 1830s is Robert E. Gallman, "Gross National Product in the United States, 1834–1909," in National Bureau of Economic Research, *Output, Employment, and Productivity in the United States After 1800: Studies in Income and Wealth,* vol. 30 (New York: National Bureau of Economic Research, 1966).

The pattern of economic growth before the 1830s is a subject of much interest among economic historians for its bearing on the issue of when growth began; it is also rather intractable to the growth statistician. Both points are well illustrated in the following two papers, which should be read in conjunction: Paul David, "The Growth of Real Product in the United States Before 1840: New Evidence, Controlled Conjectures," *Journal of Economic History,* 27 (June 1967); and Robert Gallman, "The Statistical Approach: Fundamental Concepts as Applied to History," in George R. Taylor and Lucas F. Ellsworth, eds., *Approaches to American Economic History* (Charlottesville: University Press of Virginia, 1971). For a recent status report on this issue, see Thomas Weiss, "Economic Growth Before 1860: Revised Conjectures," in Donald Schaefer and Thomas Weiss, eds., *Economic Development in Historial Perspective* (Stanford: Stanford University Press, 1993).

Regional developments emphasizing the South but holding it up to a northern mirror are analyzed in Gavin Wright, *Old South, New South: Revolutions in the Southern Economy Since the Civil War* (New York: Basic Books, 1986), which follows up on and extends Wright's *The Political Economy of the Cotton South* (New York: Norton, 1978). Implications of slavery for industrialization are discussed in Fred Bateman and Thomas Weiss, *A Deplorable Scarcity: The Failure of Industrialization in the Slave Economy* (Chapel Hill: The University of North Carolina Press, 1981). Why slaves were little used in urban areas is the subject of Claudia Dale Goldin, *Urban Slavery in the American South, 1820–1860: A Quantitative History* (Chicago: University of Chicago Press, 1976). A recent and comprehensive study of slavery that integrates economics, politics, and history is Roger L. Ransom, *Conflict and Compromise: The Political Economy of Slavery, Emancipation, and the American Civil War* (Cambridge: Cambridge University Press, 1989). Interesting and informed speculations on how southern economic history would have unfolded had slaves been freed in 1790 are offered in Chapter 3 of William N. Parker, *Europe, America, and the Wider World: Essays on the Economic History of Western Capitalism,* vol. 2 (Cambridge: Cambridge University Press, 1991).

Economic welfare is a rather nebulous concept subject to many definitions and interpretations. Chapter 10 emphasizes aspects that are measurable, such as wealth and income distributions, and trends in wages and living standards. Basic sources of such information include Donald R. Adams, Jr., "Wage Rates in the Early National Period: Philadelphia 1785–1830," *Journal of Economic History,* 28 (Sept. 1968); Alice Hanson Jones, *Wealth of a Nation to Be: The American Colonies on the Eve of the Revolution* (New York: Columbia University Press, 1980); Robert E. Gallman, "Trends in the Size Distribution of Wealth in the Nineteenth Century: Some Speculations," in Lee Soltow, ed., *Six Papers on the Size Distribution of Wealth and Income* (New York: National Bureau of Economic Research, 1969); Stanley Lebergott, *Manpower in Economic Growth: The United States Record Since 1800* (New York: McGraw-Hill, 1964); Edgar W. Martin, *The Standard of Living in 1860: American Consumption Levels on the Eve of the Civil War* (Chicago: University of Chicago Press, 1942); Lee Soltow, "Economic Inequality in the United States in the Period from 1790 to 1860," *Journal of Economic History,* 31 (Dec. 1971); Lee Soltow, *Patterns of Wealthholding in Wisconsin Since 1850* (Madison: University of Wisconsin Press, 1971); Lee Soltow, "The Wealth, Income and Social Class of Men in Large Northern Cities of the United States in 1860," in James D. Smith, ed., *The Personal Distribution of Income and Wealth* (New York: National Bureau of Economic Research, 1975); Lee Soltow, *Men and Wealth in the United States, 1850–1870* (New Haven: Yale University Press, 1976); Lee Soltow, *Distribution of Wealth and Income in the United States in 1798* (Pittsburgh: University of Pittsburgh Press, 1989); Peter H. Lindert and Jeffrey G. Williamson, "Three Centuries of American Inequality," *Research in Economic History,* 1 (1976); and Jeffrey G. Williamson and Peter H. Lindert, *American Inequality: A Macroeconomic History* (New York: Academic Press, 1980). More interpretative in emphasis are Edward Pessen, *Riches, Class, and Power Before the Civil War* (Lexington, Mass.: D. C. Heath, 1973); and Robert Gallman, "Professor Pessen on the 'Egalitarian Myth,'" *Social Science History* (Winter 1978).

Because agriculture remained the largest sector of the American economy in 1860, the distribution of wealth among farmers is a topic of importance; on it, see Jeremy Atack and Fred Bateman, "Egalitarianism, Inequality, and Age: The Rural North in 1860," *Journal of Economic History,* 41 (March 1981), and Donghyu Yang, "Notes on the Wealth Distribution of Farm Households in the United States, 1860: A New Look at Two Manuscript Samples," *Explorations in Economic History,* 21 (January 1984). The value of human capital in farming, particularly that supplied by women and children, is studied by Lee A. Craig, "The Value of Household Labor in Antebellum Northern Agriculture," *Journal of Economic History,* 51 (March 1991).

Part III

The Transformation of the American Economy

1860–1914

THE 1860 TO 1914 PERIOD OPENED WITH THE TRAGIC Civil War, which resulted in an intact nation that was badly scarred by the great loss of life and property. Yet the gains from the war were impressive. Slavery was abolished and black Americans acquired new legal rights that, after bitter setbacks, formed the basis for the current thrust toward economic betterment. For the great majority of Americans, the preservation of the Union meant both political unity (one nation-state) and all the opportunities that a unified yet large and diversified economy afforded: Labor and capital had great mobility, natural resources could be exploited, and a nationwide market existed for the exchange of goods and services.

The economic growth of the United States advanced at a dramatic pace after the Civil War. Real GNP per capita grew at an average annual rate of 2 percent and, shortly before World War I, had reached about three times its 1865 level. An even better record was achieved for total output: Real GNP increased at an average annual rate of more than 4 percent—an eightfold advance. In no prior period of American history had economic growth been as rapid or persisted for so many years. Depressions created periodic setbacks, but the secular or long-term trend was upward.

By 1913, the United States had become a predominantly urban industrial economy with the largest manufacturing output of any country in the world. Agriculture had undergone a relative decline in economic importance as urban manufacturing, commerce, and the service industries had increased their share of the national labor force and the national income. This process of economic growth manifested itself in the agricultural sector through the closing of the frontier, an unprecedented expansion of commercial agriculture, and an immense transfer of public land to private ownership. Basic to all these changes was an increase in the numbers and varied abilities of the American people. Between 1860 and 1920, the population of the United States increased threefold, rising from 31.5 million to 106.5 million. Most of this great population expansion—about 60 percent of it—came from a high rate of natural increase, and the other 40 percent came from a gigantic flow of immigrants to the United States. Between 1801 and 1890, some 11.1 million immigrants came, mainly from western Europe. Then, from 1890 to 1920, an additional 18.2 million immigrants arrived, mostly from southern and eastern Europe.

The tidal wave of immigration occurred primarily because of the pull of economic opportunity in America and the push of adverse economic and social conditions in Europe. From this inflow of immigrants came an increase in the rate of per capita economic growth, due in part to the higher percentage of males between the ages of fourteen and forty-four among the immigrants than in the native population. Hence, the American labor force increased at a higher rate than did the population, and the level of per capita income rose in turn.

The contributions of immigrants to the American economy were many—a massive supply of different skills for industry and agriculture, scientific discoveries, works of art and literature. Since the cost of the immigrants' upbringing and education had been taken care of in their countries of origin, American resources were spared this expense. Immigration thereby provided a great net gain in human capital for the United States.

Chapter 11 is a study of agricultural expansion and the extensive exploitation of natural resources after the Civil War. Agricultural modernization was long delayed in the American South, and both there and in other farming regions the rapid growth of farm output led to low prices and agrarian protest movements. In manufacturing, the subject of Chapter 12, the key developments were mass production and mass distribution; together they resulted in the rise of big business in the form of the giant industrial corporation. Labor markets had to adjust both to large influxes of immigrants from overseas and to the rise of big business. In the process several types of labor organizations came forward to promote labor's economic and political goals, as discussed in Chapter 13. Giant corporations with market power also arose in the transportation (mainly railroad) and communications (telegraph and telephone) industries, prompting the appearance of new forms of governmental regulation of business; these developments are featured in Chapter 14. Chapter 15 studies the U.S. financial system as it was thoroughly revamped during and after the Civil War. As in other sectors of the economy, the gains that were made were tempered by remaining problems such as a proneness to banking panics followed by business depressions. The development of nationwide internal markets and the expansion of U.S. business interests in foreign markets are treated in Chapter 16; in the 1860 to 1914 period, protective tariffs, imperialistic territorial acquisitions, and so-called dollar diplomacy were important features of the emergence of the United States as the world's preeminent industrial power.

Chapter 11

Continental Expansion, Agricultural Modernization, and Southern Backwardness

Between the Civil War and World War I, America's farmers, ranchers, and miners expanded their use of the nation's landed resources on an unprecedented scale. Decision makers in the federal government encouraged expansion through policies designed to expedite the passing of public lands into individual ownership and use, through grants of land to railroads intended to bring Western resources into the national economy, and through a host of other measures—many directed against Native Americans—that cleared the way for pioneer settlers from the East. At the same time, the vast expansion of land use stimulated inventors and manufacturers to develop and diffuse improved farm implements, machinery, and other equipment and techniques that contributed to spectacular increases in the total output of the primary producing sector and its productive efficiency.

The consequences of expanded land use were momentous. In just a few decades, an enormous amount of land—comparable in size to all of Western Europe—was made available to farmers. The frontier (the western line of settlement that had been present from the earliest days of colonization in America) disappeared as a vast area from the Mississippi to the Pacific Ocean became dotted with pioneer communities. Improved transportation facilities, chiefly railroads, bound these communities into national and world markets for agricultural and natural resource products. The result was specialized, commercial production. And for the first time American farmers had to be concerned with both the market prices of the commodities they produced and the prices of the productive inputs and consumption goods they purchased.

The rapidity and magnitude of the changes caused major problems of adjustment for American farmers. The tremendous growth of agricultural production exerted a depressing effect on farm prices. Moreover, as this long-term trend was accentuated by general price-level deflation and periodic business depressions emanating from outside the agricultural sector, it was easy for farmers to conclude that they were being deprived unjustly of the fruits of their labor. Remedies were sought by the emerging farmers' organizations and coalitions that looked to use the political process to advance agrarian goals. The goal of higher prices for farm products was sought by calling for various measures to increase the money supply. The goal of lower prices for productive inputs—such as credit, transportation, marketing, and processing—led to calls for government regulation and other interventions in favor of the farmer. Some of these goals were achieved in the late nineteenth century. But the golden age of American farming during the two decades before World War I was at least as much the result of a slowing down in the rate of expansion of the agricultural sector relative to other economic sectors as from a partial achievement of the farmers' monetary and regulatory goals.

Southern Agriculture After the Civil War

The greatest problems of adjustment to changed economic circumstances, for both farmers and other Americans, arose in the South. As noted in Chapters 6 and 10, slavery had accentuated economic differences between the southern regional economy and those of the Northeast and Midwest. The end of slavery after the Civil War meant that in the long run the South's economy would have to become more similar to that of other U.S. regions, but the process of doing so encompassed an entire century. In the short run, the end of slavery turned the southern economic world upside down (much as recent events in Eastern Europe have affected economies there) and a new but still distinctly different economy emerged in the South.

Economic Reorganization of the Postbellum South

Four options were presented to southern agricultural decision makers after the Civil War. One option, given serious consideration by federal authorities, was to take over land in the South and give freed blacks and their families forty acres and a mule. In retrospect, this might have been the best option, but it was rejected as being too radical. Therefore, the planters who formerly had owned slaves still maintained ownership of their land in the postbellum era. Another option available to landowners was to attempt to reconstruct the old plantation system but with hired rather than slave labor. This system was tried in some cases immediately after the war, but it quickly broke down and was abandoned. The collapse of the southern monetary and banking systems caused problems in making wage payments, but more important was the reluctance of former slaves to work in the way they had been forced to work when they were slaves.

Tenancy: The Rise of Sharecropping. The two remaining options were forms of agricultural tenancy. The old plantation, with the owner's "big house" and slave quarters in close proximity, was now divided up into small, decentralized farms (see Figure 11–1). Under the new configurations, landlords could (1) rent their lands to former slaves for fixed cash rental payments or (2) enter into sharecropping agreements with the freed blacks, in which each party supplied some inputs and the output was shared between them according to their relative contributions. Landlords, of course, mainly supplied land and former slaves mainly supplied the labor, but the sharecropping system was capable of many adjustments in shares to reflect other resource contributions.

Although both tenancy systems existed in the postbellum South, sharecropping predominated. Why? Note that cash-renting places most of the risk on the tenant; the negotiated rent is due whether the crops are good or bad. Former slaves, who had been deprived of just about everything except subsistence under slavery, could hardly be expected to bear the risks of agricultural production in the postbellum South. Sharecropping, in contrast, divided these risks between landlord and tenant and gave the former an incentive to provide managerial inputs to go along with the tenant's agricultural skills. The market decision making that guided the organization of production once slavery was ended therefore pointed toward sharecropping.

Decline of Southern Output and Productivity. Although market decision making thus prevailed, the circumstances of the postbellum South were such that production and productivity fell sharply from prewar levels after the Civil War. Production recovered fairly soon, but productivity remained low for decades; the South became a backward economic region in an otherwise advancing U.S. economy. The physical destruction of the South's economic infrastructure and other forms of capital during the war played some role in reducing production in the short run. More important was the reduction in labor supply once slavery ended. Former slaves supplied less labor as tenant farmers than they had been forced to supply as slaves. In particular, the participation of women and children in field work was much reduced, though their economic contributions in the household likely increased. Nonetheless, both production and labor-force participation of the freed people recovered and reached prewar levels during the 1870s. But productivity— output per worker—was much lower in 1880 than it had been in 1860. Some historians attribute this change to the ending of the gang labor system under slavery and the intensity of labor that it was able to elicit. Whatever the explanation, though, the output per worker was

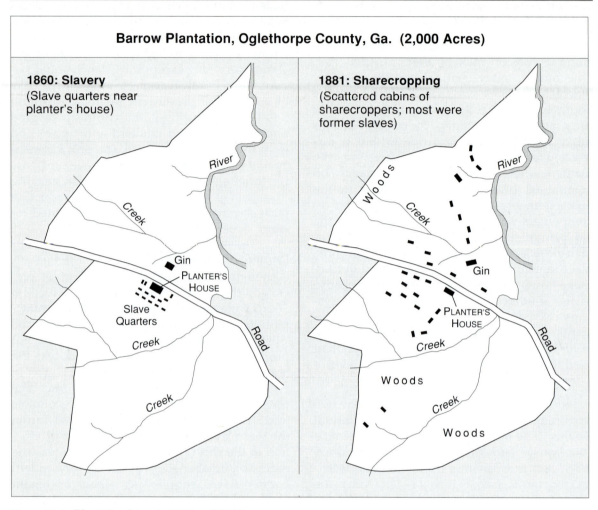

Figure 11-1 *Plantation Layout, 1860 and 1881*

Note how the compact living arrangements of 1860 — slave quarters in close proximity to planter's house — gave way by 1881 to sharecroppers' cabins scattered throughout the old plantation.

Source: David C. Barrow, Jr., "A Georgia Plantation," *Scribner's Monthly* 21 (1881): 832.

lower for former slaves than it had been for slaves. Still, free black farmers were better off than they had been when they were slaves because as free laborers they got to keep the fruits of their labor. The South as a whole was poorer than it had been, but its former slaves were better off economically than they had been in slave days. That was one kind of freedom.

Debt Peonage and Southern Backwardness

Other changes in the organization of southern agriculture also operated to keep the South

Southern Sharecroppers in the 1880s. An African-American family stands in a cotton field that surrounds the modest farmhouse. Note the white visitor with horse and buggy; possibly he was the landowner looking in on the tenant farmers. (Brown Brothers)

backward and poor. The antebellum system of factors and bank credit that had financed plantation production and cotton marketing gave way in postbellum times to a system of localized mercantile credit and marketing services supplied by country stores. Agricultural production involved a lot of work and waiting before crops could be sold at discrete—usually annual—intervals. In the interim, farmers required inputs, including agricultural inputs like fertilizer and seed as well as food and clothing for themselves and their families. The country stores that arose to supply tenant farmers in the South charged high prices for supplies on credit, with implicit rates of interest ranging from 40 percent to 70 percent per year. This meant that storekeepers, either because they were monopolists in the local credit market or just not very efficient as financial

intermediaries, drained off a good share of the poor tenant farmer's income.

Another aspect of the postwar southern financial and marketing system was the crop lien. To secure loans made by storekeepers, southern law gave them a lien on the farmer's crops. The storekeeper's interest was to assure loan repayment, which provided an incentive to encourage the farmers to produce cash crops (mainly cotton because it had a high value per acre grown and could be turned into cash to repay loans at the end of the year). Paradoxically, tenant farms thus often came to specialize in cotton to a greater extent than plantations had done in antebellum times. Under this system, sometimes called *debt peonage,* the South's cotton output grew far beyond antebellum levels. Production was aided by a high rate of population growth in the South, which meant more farmers. Labor productivity advanced as well between the 1870s and the early twentieth century but from levels that were much reduced compared to those of plantation days. World cotton demand, however, did not grow as rapidly as it had in the early decades of the Industrial Revolution, and cotton production in other countries increased. The results for southern farmers before 1914 were low prices and low incomes.

Although some poor southern farmers escaped to factories and cities in the South or North or to the Midwest and Far West in search of better farm and nonfarm opportunities, most continued farming in the South. As a result, the large gap in farm incomes and nonfarm wages that existed between the South and the rest of the country remained. The South persisted for decades as a low-wage, low-income regional economy in a high-wage, high-income country. Although in many cases small white farmers and urban workers were no better off economically than their black counterparts, racial divisiveness complicated most southern attempts at modernization. Discrimination against both former slaves and their descendants in the South and elsewhere contributed to the South's postbellum economic backwardness, which lasted well into the twentieth century.

Land Policy Decisions

During the antebellum years, the trend of U.S. land policy decisions, as shown in Chapter 6, was in the direction of making it easy for individual Americans to become owners of land. A fundamental reason for this policy was the large quantity of land available in relation to the nation's population. Coupled with internal transportation improvements and the development of wider markets for the products of land, the amount of land in the public domain created irresistible political and social pressures for easier terms of land acquisition by individuals. On the eve of the Civil War, one could have predicted with confidence a continuation of these pressures. During the two preceding decades, the United States had increased its territory almost 70 percent by annexing Texas, by clearing American claims to the Oregon Territory with Great Britain, and by acquiring California and the remainder of the Southwest from Mexico through war and purchase. In 1860, all of these areas were only sparsely populated.

The Homestead Act: Pitfalls of Free Land

Congress acted in 1862 by passing the Homestead Act and taking an entirely new direction in national land policy. With some exceptions, the principle of antebellum land policy had been that public land should be sold to private buyers to provide revenue for the federal government. The Homestead Act, however, embodied a new philosophy—public land should be given free of charge, subject to certain conditions, to citizens of the United States. Thus, a person could obtain ownership of 160 acres of the public domain by residing on his or her claimed land for five years and cultivating it. Or, a person could purchase the land after only six months of residence at the prevailing minimum price, usually $1.25 per acre.

Although the Homestead Act embodied the revolutionary concept of free land, some historians stress the weaknesses of the act and its amendments. The great bulk of the lands opened up to homesteading lay west of the ninety-ninth meridian, from the Great Plains to the Pacific Coast. In this semiarid and arid West, a homestead of 160 acres was usually too small to provide an adequate income for a family engaged in dry farming or livestock raising. The Homestead legislation was superimposed, moreover, on a public land system with which it was incongruous in many ways. The federal government continued until 1891 to sell land for cash, and in fact more land was sold this way than was homesteaded. In addition, Congress granted some 130 million acres of public land to railroads, about 140 million to new and old states, and 175 million acres to Native Americans for their reservations. Subsequent legislation opened up large tracts of Native American land for sale to settlers.

Therefore, the great bulk of land put into cultivation after 1865 was bought from federal and state governments and from land-grant railroads, whereas less than one-fifth of all the new land was homesteaded. These facts, along with the activities of large-scale land speculators and the use of fraudulent homestead entries made by individuals for the benefit of land, timber, and mining companies, lead many scholars to conclude that the Homestead Act was in large measure a failure. If by this it is meant that the act precluded individuals from obtaining farms of adequate size given the environmental conditions of the West, there are grounds for disagreement. Congress retained on the statute books the 1841 Preemption Act; combined with the Homestead law, it made possible farm units of 320 acres. Moreover, in passing the 1873 Timber Culture Act, the 1877 Desert Land Act, and the 1878 Timber and Stone Act, Congress enabled individuals to obtain still larger tracts on favorable terms. Together these land laws enabled settlers to acquire tracts as large as 1120 acres in the semi-arid high plains and in the desert and inter-mountain regions of the West.

However, the land policy measures were often poorly drafted from a legal point of view; hence, they were abused by individuals and corporations who obtained large tracts through fraudulent devices and unscrupulous intermediaries. These abuses and the ineptness of public land administration led Congress in 1889 to 1891 to adopt several measures that restricted individual acquisition of public land to 320 acres, encouraged sales to bona fide farmers rather than to speculators, and introduced a number of additional safeguards to earlier statutes that had been abused.

Ownership and Tenancy

Despite the limitations of the Homestead Act, the federal land system in the late nineteenth century worked well in terms of the progress made by owner-operated farms. Outside of the cotton-growing South, where tenancy and sharecropping prevailed after 1865, a great deal of public land was acquired by owner-operators and tenancy was less common. In the public land states outside of the South, a total of 1.7 million farms had been created by 1880. Of these, 1.3 million (roughly four-fifths) were owner-operated. In only four states in the West—California, Oregon, Colorado, and Nevada—did the farms average over 160 acres. Furthermore, much of the land granted to the railroads, given to the states, and purchased in quantity on speculation by absentee owners was eventually divided into single-family farms and sold to settlers. By 1900, the non-southern public land states contained 2.4 million farms; roughly 70 percent were owner-operated. Hence, the goal of disposing of the public domain in order to increase the class of small landowners had in good measure been achieved.

Patterns of Westward Movement

During the later decades of the nineteenth century, so many Americans moved to the West that the frontier—a clearly delineated line of settlement—ceased to exist. The population of the trans-Mississippi West increased from 4.5 million in 1860 to 16.4 million in 1900 and to 27.2 million in 1910. The migration of such large numbers of people in a relatively short period of time was the result of many changes

Western Plains Settlers Around 1890.   The pioneer farm family sits for the photo next to the well. Behind them is their sod house—wood was a scarce commodity on the plains—and two dogs, a rooster, and a carriage. Compare and contrast this setting with the earlier one in this chapter showing southern sharecroppers in the same era. (The Bettmann Archive)

in the American economy and society. Decisions to transfer great amounts of the public domain to private ownership through the systematic application of old and new public land legislation greatly facilitated the westward movement. But other factors were equally important. One was the great expansion of the nation's population, which nearly tripled from 31.5 million to 92.4 million between 1860 and 1910. Other factors included the great extension of existing technologies (e.g., the building of transcontinental railroads) and the development of new technologies (e.g., barbed wire, windmills, and farming and mining machinery).

Throughout American history the availability of natural resources had always attracted people to and beyond the westward-moving frontier well in advance of surveyors and public land sales. Hunters and trappers were among the earliest of these people. During the last half of the nineteenth century, mineral deposits and grasslands capable of sustaining large-scale livestock production drew pioneers to the West. More often than not, agricultural production on lands transferred from the public domain to private ownership was the last stage rather than an early stage of western settlement. Mining and cattle frontiers often preceded the farmers' frontier.

Mining Frontiers

Gold was discovered in the California foothills of the Sierra Nevada mountain range in 1848. The gold rush that followed drew thousands of wealth seekers to the West. The chance of making a fortune was small for any one prospector, but the rewards to the lucky few were high enough to make many Americans willing to take the risk of great losses in time and capital.

From the 1850s to the 1890s, other discoveries of valuable mineral deposits in the mountains and hills to the east of California led to the development of other mining frontiers. A succession of gold and silver discoveries between 1858 and 1876 caused swarms of miners to seek their fortunes in territories ranging from western Utah, Nevada, and Arizona to Idaho, Montana, the Dakotas, and Missouri. The most famous bonanzas were at Pike's Peak in Colorado and at the Comstock Lode in western Nevada.

Systematic Mineral Resource Exploitation. With the 1875 to 1876 Black Hills gold rush, the eastward advance from California of the mining frontier came to an end. At the same time, the era of the small-scale placer miner was drawing to a close and the period of the mining capitalist was beginning. With their crude techniques, the prospectors had only mined ore close to the surface; they had not been able to touch the far greater quantities of gold and silver contained in quartz lodes beneath the surface. After the pioneer miners revealed the potential mineral wealth of the Far West, eastern and British investors decided to invest in the financing of mine-shaft drilling, hydraulic and strip mining, quartz mills, and the numerous tunnels required for bringing the mineral deposits into production. These new sources of capital financed the extraordinary growth of copper, lead, and zinc mining—operations that proved to be more profitable in the long run, after 1875, than the more spectacular gold and silver rushes. By 1881, the center of mining-stock transactions had shifted from San Francisco to New York. Until then, more mines had been operated with locally contributed funds on an unincorporated basis or as closely held incorporations not subject to public sale of stock, than as joint stock companies. But the shift to New York indicated that the future of mining development lay with big corporations, and that mining was increasingly being integrated into the national economy on both a financial and a technological basis, rather than remaining a largely isolated western effort on a premodern technological level.

Natural Resources and U.S. Economic Development. The growing economic importance of the mining industries in the West was evident in the increasing value of all metal-mining products—rising from $29 million in 1870 to $131 million in 1890 and to $468 million in 1919. Western mineral development had important impacts on economic growth as well as on finance and national politics. The flow of copper, lead, zinc, and other metals from the trans-Mississippi region greatly contributed to developments in manufacturing, transportation, and communication by telephone and telegraph. Indeed, recent research findings strongly indicate that Americans' systematic search for intensive use of minerals and other natural resources were the key ingredients of U.S. industrial development between 1880 and 1940.[1] Moreover, the decline in gold production relative to silver production between 1860 and 1894 not only had significant effects on the composition of the U.S. money supply but also created a major politico-economic movement favoring free coinage of silver from the 1870s to the 1890s (see Chapter 15).

Although the various mining bonanzas in the West were picturesque, in most cases they were also short-lived events. Yet they had longer-term effects on western development because they stimulated an influx of tradespeople, artisans, and professionals (e.g., doctors, lawyers, engineers) to provide goods and services needed by the miners. Small farmers and ranchers also were attracted to the bonanzas; they raised crops and livestock in the valleys near the mining settlements and supplied the settlements with foodstuffs, animals, and feed. When the bonanza mines declined, some of the nearby communities had reached sufficient size to sustain themselves as viable local economies; others became ghost towns.

The Cattle Kingdom

Another natural resource that drew pioneers to the West was abundant grassland. From the Civil War until the 1880s, the range-cattle industry expanded from Texas and New Mexico into the central and northern plains. An old gold miner once said of western resources, "There's gold from the grass roots up." Those who saw an element of truth in this remark created the western cattle frontier that has became a legendary part of American history.

American Indians and the Buffalo. The emergence of the cattle frontier was facilitated by the removal, between 1867 and 1890, of American Indians from their hunting grounds on the Great Plains to the more restricted quarters of government reservations. This drastic change in the way of life of many American Indians was achieved through the use of military force and by the slaughter of millions of bison, or buffalo, by thousands of hunters. Often encouraged by the military (which operated under the doctrine that the best way to subdue an enemy was to destroy the enemy's commissary) and by land-hungry pioneers, the hunters were unconcerned about the importance of the bison to the Indians as the economic basis of their tribal way of life. The hunters sought to obtain cash for bison hides;

stripped of their hides, the bison carcasses were left to rot on the plains. In this manner, and largely because government failed to protect the bison or to extend property rights to the Indians, a once vast natural resource of potential value to later generations was virtually extinguished within only a few decades. The American Indians and their wild cattle were thus forced to give way to the pioneers of the cattle frontier.

The Open Range and Cattle Drives. Other conditions and developments also promoted the growth of the range-cattle industry. Among them, on the supply side, were the great extent of the open-range grasslands, stretching from Texas to Montana, and the discovery that Texas cattle (the first to be herded) could withstand being exposed to the severe winters on the northern plains. Texas longhorns, descendants of Spanish and Mexican breeds, had multiplied many fold when they were left untended during the Civil War. On the demand side, the late nineteenth century brought an expanding market for meat in the East (especially in the cities), western access to that market through rail connections, and the development of the meat-packing industry (particularly in the areas of refrigerated storage and shipping).

Between 1866 and 1885, over five million cattle were driven northward from Texas ranges to cattle markets in Kansas, Missouri, and Nebraska. At an average price of $20 per steer, the sale of cattle brought roughly $100 million of gross income to cattle ranchers. Many of the Texas cattle driven northward were not sold for immediate consumption but used to stock the northern ranges. Others were fattened on corn and grass before sale. As the range-cattle industry expanded, western meat-packing centers grew up in cities such as Chicago, St. Louis, Kansas City, and Omaha. By moving west, meat packers tended to minimize the cost of transporting cattle and meat products from the ranges to the consumers.

By the 1880s, the cattle kingdom encompassed the entire plains from the Rio Grande to the Canadian border and from the croplands west of the Mississippi River to the slopes of the Rocky Mountains. The number of cattle on the northern Great Plains increased from 130,000 in 1860 to 4.5 million in 1880. By the latter date, ranching had become a business with efficient methods of operation. Ranchers cooperated with one another, often through the formation of livestock associations that registered different ranchers' brands and enforced members' right to ranch even though they had simply appropriated a "range right" to public grazing land. As cattle prices and ranchers' profits rose in the early 1880s, capital from the eastern United States and Europe was invested in the range-cattle industry, leading to the formation of huge ranches. In 1884, some members of Congress pointed out that foreigners, mainly from Great Britain, had acquired more than twenty million acres of land, most of it in the range-cattle area. Many of the foreign-owned ranches were held by corporations, and their chief investors came to be known as cattle barons.

Ranchers, Farmers, Barbed Wire, and Windmills. The peak of the range-cattle boom was reached in 1884. After that year overstocking of the range and the marketing of cattle at a rate greater than the usual rate of consumption led to depressed cattle prices. Then climatic disasters—the harsh winter of 1885 to 1886 and the great blizzard of January 1887—hit the industry with large cattle losses and hastened the decline of open-range ranching. The era of longhorns grazing on the public domain gave way to one of stocking with improved European breeds (Herefords, Shorthorns, and Anguses), barbed-wire fencing, and winter feeding. Quality of product was increasingly emphasized in the cattle business.

Cattle were not the only livestock herded in the West. During the 1870s, many sheep raisers moved from Ohio to California, Colorado, or New Mexico. After achieving success there, they began in the 1880s to move on to the Great Plains. Despite several years of open warfare between sheep and cattle raisers, sheep raising soon became established as an important livestock industry in the West. By 1903, nearly one-half of the sixty-four million sheep in the United States were located on the plains and in the Rockies.

After the cattle and sheep ranchers came the farmer. During the late 1880s, pioneer farmers began to compete with the cattle ranchers for land on the Great Plains. Although farmers worried about the lack of timber and water on the plains, they overcame these obstacles through the use of barbed-wire fencing and windmills that pumped subsurface water for livestock and irrigation. Farm machinery was also utilized to allow mechanical cultivation of the large farms needed to support a family under semiarid conditions. By 1890, a farmer could independently plant, take care of, and harvest 135 acres of wheat, as compared to only seven acres before the new techniques.

Western Lands and U.S. Farm Output, 1870–1920. The new methods of ranching and farming were implemented on a massive scale in the American West. Between 1870 and 1900, millions of farmers occupied hitherto unexploited farmland in Kansas, Nebraska, the Dakotas, Wyoming, Montana, and Oklahoma. More land was settled in the last three decades of the nineteenth century than in all of America's past: 407 million acres were occupied and 189 million improved between 1607 and 1870, whereas 430 million acres were settled and 225 million placed under cultivation between 1870 and 1900. By 1900, this newly occupied western part of the United States raised nearly 50 percent of the nation's cattle, 56 percent of the sheep, about 25 percent of the hogs, and 32 percent of the cereal crop. Fifty-eight percent of the wheat was produced in the western states and territories.

Table 11−1 *Gross and Net Farm Output, 1869–1919*
(in millions of 1929 dollars)

Year	Gross Farm Output	Intermediate Products Consumed	Net Farm Output
1869	$ 3,950	$ 440	$3,510
1879	6,180	730	5,450
1889	7,820	1,000	6,820
1899	9,920	1,360	8,560
1909	10,770	1,620	9,150
1919	11,930	2,250	9,680

SOURCE: Adapted from John W. Kendrick, *Productivity Trends in the United States* (Princeton, N.J.: Princeton University Press, 1961), p. 347.

Agricultural expansion continued after the turn of the century but at a much subdued pace. Whereas the number of farms in the United States had more than doubled from 2.7 million to 5.7 million between 1870 and 1900, it increased to only 6.4 million in 1920. Data on real farm output, given in Table 11–1, reveal in still clearer terms the change that took place. From those data it can be calculated that gross farm output (which counts the value of corn fed to pigs and the value of pigs) grew at an annual compound rate of 3.1 percent from 1869 to 1899 and at 0.9 percent from 1899 to 1919. For the same two periods, net farm output (only the value of pigs and not the corn they ate) grew, at annual rates of 3 percent and 0.6 percent, respectively. The early twentieth-century deceleration of agricultural growth is important to an understanding of why agricultural prosperity followed the late nineteenth century's agrarian unrest. The disappearance of the frontier implied a reduction in the amount of previously unused land suitable for agriculture. Under this new condition, American farmers prospered as the growth of demand for their products exceeded the growth of supply.

Agricultural Productivity and Its Sources

Mechanization

As American agriculture expanded in the half-century after the Civil War, a number of significant changes took place in the nature of agricultural production. Of these changes by far the most important was mechanization—the substitution of machinery and equipment for labor. As shown in Table 11–2, the total amount of capital used in agriculture increased at a rate of 2 percent per year between 1869 and 1919, virtually the same rate at which net farm output grew during the same period (see Table 11–1). Most of the subcategories of agricultural capital grew at similar rates except for one—machinery and equipment—which grew almost twice as fast at a rate of 3.9 percent per year over the fifty-year period.

The significance of mechanization becomes clear when its effects on labor are considered. The agricultural labor force numbered approximately 6.8 million in 1870 and 10.8 million in 1920. These data imply that the farm labor force grew at 0.9 percent per year, or about one percentage point less than the rate of growth of output. In other words, output per worker in agriculture, largely as a result of mechanization, increased at a rate of approximately 1 percent per year. The substitution of capital for labor in agriculture also had a dramatic effect on the composition of the American labor force. Over one-half of American workers labored in agriculture in 1870, whereas by 1920 only about one-quarter did so.

The Civil War acted as a catalyst in farm mechanization. Between 1830 and 1860, various machines and implements—notably improved iron and steel plows, seed drills, cultivators, mechanical reapers, and threshing machines—were invented and came into use on American farms. When a million farmers were withdrawn from agricultural production

Table 11-2 *Material Capital Stocks in Agriculture, 1869–1919 (in millions of 1929 dollars)*

Year	Total Capital	Land	Structures	Machinery and Equipment	Work Stock	Inventories	
						Livestock	Crops
1869	$23,145	$13,836	$ 4,578	$ 564	$ 623	$2,697	$ 847
1879	32,941	19,643	6,367	828	906	3,643	1,554
1889	40,132	23,863	7,006	1,217	1,274	4,698	2,074
1899	48,004	29,107	8,057	1,900	1,504	4,770	2,666
1909	55,295	31,735	11,255	3,012	1,739	4,960	2,594
1919	62,600	34,254	13,671	3,984	1,906	5,745	3,040

SOURCE: Adapted from John W. Kendrick, *Productivity Trends in the United States* (Princeton, N.J.: Princeton University Press, 1961), p. 367.

to serve in the Union armies, the trend toward mechanization was given a powerful boost. The men and women left on the farms of the North and West turned to the new machinery, especially reapers and threshers, and succeeded in producing a wheat crop greater than those produced previously during peacetime.

Horse Power. With mechanization came a general displacement of humans by horses as the motive power for agricultural implements. After the war, the number of important horse-drawn implements were developed to complement or replace those innovated earlier. These included the Marsh harvester, the twine binder, the sulky, the gang plow, the spring-tooth and disc harrows, the self-binding reaper, and the combined reaper-thresher. The new machines created a large demand for horses, and in response to that demand the number of horses on American farms increased from 7.1 million in 1870 to 16.9 million in 1900. In 1920, there were 19.7 million farm horses, but by that time the horse had begun to be replaced by the gasoline tractor. Introduced in 1905, gas-powered tractors on American farms increased from 1000 in 1910 to 246,000 in 1920.

Analysis of Productivity Growth. The effect of mechanization on agricultural productivity shows up clearly in studies conducted on the production of wheat, corn, and oats.[2] The output per farm worker engaged in producing these crops increased between three and four times from 1840 to 1910, or at compound annual rates of 1.5 to 2 percent. About 60 percent of the observed increase in productivity was due to mechanization. Nearly all of the growth in productivity came about as a result of the combined effects of mechanization and the westward expansion of agriculture, two historical processes that interacted and reinforced one another. The West meant that great amounts of additional land were available, and the new machines meant that an individual farmer could plant and harvest many more acres and thresh many more bushels of grain than had previously been possible with hand implements.

A Case of Nonmechanization: Cotton

Mechanization was much more successful in some types of agriculture, such as grain production, than in others during the half-century before World War I. In this period, mechanization had little effect on the production of cotton, tobacco, sugar beets, and garden vegetables, or on the milking of cows. The problems of mechanization in these areas were more complex than in grain production. Nonetheless, a failure to mechanize did not prevent some great expansions of output in these areas. Cotton production, for example, increased from 2.5 million bales to 13.4 million bales in the half-century after 1869, and cotton during many of these years continued to be the nation's major export product as it had been in antebellum times. The output of cotton grew because of the abundant supply of unskilled farm labor in the Southeast, the increased use of fertilizer there, and the expansion of the cotton belt to the Southwest. But the inability or failure to mechanize did create large differences in the economic welfare of farmers and regions. In the absence of mechanization, output per farmer remained much lower in the South than in the rest of the country throughout the 1870 to 1920 period. During the same decades, mechanization raised farmer productivity in much of the rest of the country to considerably higher levels than had prevailed in 1870.

Regional Specialization in Agriculture

Between the end of the Civil War and the outbreak of World War I, American farmers developed the distinct patterns of farming in different regions of the United States that persist to the present day. A trend toward specialization in production, both on individual farms and in particular regions, occurred with an increase in the mechanization of agriculture and striking improvements in transportation and marketing facilities. An increasing number of farmers shifted from the small, diversified farm to the specialized, usually larger commercial farm as railroads expanded throughout the country

and as markets for farm products were extended or created by the spread of grain elevators, warehouses, stockyards, packing plants, and transport facilities. Among the important factors determining the location of farm production were variations in soil and climate from one area to another as well as the distance and transportation cost for specific commodities from the farms to the consuming centers.

Millions of farmers had to engage in decision making about which farm products they wanted to produce in any specific area. Their judgment in any particular case usually depended on applying the economic principle of comparative advantage. This principle, which we have encountered many times in earlier chapters, implies that an area tends to specialize in the production of those products for which the value of output per unit of input is highest relative to other areas. In other words, a region tends to specialize in those products for which its cost of production is lowest relative to other areas. Thus, comparative advantage explains why the Great Plains came to specialize in wheat production and cattle raising, the Corn Belt in corn production and livestock feeding, the Lake states and the Northeast in dairy production, and the South in cotton and tobacco production.

Transportation improvements and opportunities for mechanizing production were the major causes of changes in regional specialization to exploit comparative advantages after the Civil War. The shift of wheat production onto the Great Plains provides an instructive illustration of the decision-making process. When the railroad reached the plains and machinery made it possible for a farmer to plant and harvest large acreages, the center of wheat production moved to the plains even though wheat yields per acre were substantially greater in the midwestern Corn Belt and the East. This location decision may seem puzzling until one considers that the opportunity cost of growing wheat in the Corn Belt or the East would have involved the loss of valuable corn and dairy products that otherwise might have been produced. The plains, in contrast, were not suited for corn and dairy production; therefore, despite the relatively low yield per acre, the true cost of wheat production was lower there than on the more fertile lands to the east.

Agrarian Crises and Farmers' Welfare

Large and widespread increases in land ownership, capital goods, and output in American agriculture between the Civil War and World War I represented an unparalleled advance in the economic well-being of millions of Americans engaged in farming. Measured in terms of the wealth acquired by farmers who had little or no capital at the beginning of their careers, a greater number of poor and tenant farmers became members of the middle class than in any previous period in American history. During periods of prosperity, most farmers were reasonably content with their lot. But in periods of depression—especially in 1873 to 1879, 1882 to 1885, and 1893 to 1897—the discontent of many farmers, particularly in the Midwest and the South, became intense and inspired them to organize movements to protest against a variety of economic ills.

Grangers, Greenbackers, and Populists

The first powerful farm pressure group, the Grange, originated in 1867. It sought mainly to fight the excessively high railroad and grain elevator rates, to form cooperatives for the purpose of lowering the cost of the commodities the farmers bought, and to market more profitably the farmers' products. After achieving some notable successes in railroad and elevator-rate regulation in the early 1870s, the

Grange suffered a sudden decline in popularity in 1876 because of the failure of many of its cooperative enterprises. Many farmers then turned to the Greenback party, a movement that sought a great expansion in the supply of greenbacks (the paper money the U.S. government had first issued during the Civil War) in order to counteract the declining price trend and to bring about a rise in the general price level (see Chapter 15). When the efforts of the Greenback party failed after considerable political activity between 1876 and the mid-1880s, many farmers joined together to form new agrarian organizations. These farmers' alliances, wheels, unions, and clubs had widespread support in the cotton-growing South and in the wheatlands of the trans-Mississippi West. Although they had initially stressed issues such as education and self-help through agrarian cooperatives, by 1890 they had turned to politics. In 1892, farmers helped form the Populist or People's party, which advocated radical reforms of finance, transportation, and other aspects of the economy. Agrarians and others made support of the free coinage of silver the dominant plank of both the Populist and the Democratic party platforms in the presidential election of 1896. Although the Populists (along with the Democrats) were defeated and the Populists disappeared as an effective party, the silver issue put "fire into the belly" of many a champion—and many a critic—of their views. But the important question for economic historians is: How valid were the Grange and Populist complaints in light of statistical and theoretical analysis?

Agrarian Protest Issues

One major protest of American farmers was against the falling price level for farm products between 1867 and 1897. The wholesale price index for farm products fell from 133 in 1867 to 71 in 1890 and then to 40 in 1896. Many farmers felt that the falling prices unfairly increased

A Populist-Farmer Image of the American Economy in the 1890s.   Toiling farmers of the West and South produce to feed an elongated cow which is milked in Wall Street for the benefit of bankers and tariff-protected manufacturers. Agrarian movements protesting economic conditions and policies flourished from the 1870s through the 1890s. Although some of their favored policy measures were enacted, most were toned down or beaten back by conservative coalitions. (Brown Brothers)

the heavy burden of debt repayment on their mortgages. They also felt that the situation hurt their terms of trade—the prices they received compared to the prices they paid—when they sold in world competitive markets while buying goods and services in local or national markets, which were thought to be, and sometimes were, protected by tariffs and dominated by monopolies or oligopolies. Farmers often saw themselves as caught in a cost-price squeeze. Railroad freight rates were stressed as a specially grievous cost factor, as was the cost of borrowing money to finance the purchase of such inputs as land and machinery.

Railroad Freight Rates.   However, scholars' careful analysis of wholesale price indexes for farm and nonfarm products for the period 1867 to 1897 indicates that nonfarm prices fell as rapidly as farm prices in many cases, and in some cases they fell even more rapidly. Hence, the relative price position of farmers—of their terms of trade—was not impaired. On the subject of railroad freight rates, though, the farmers' claims were justified. A comparative study of railroad rates and farm prices demonstrates that railroad freight rates fell sharply and steadily from 1867 to 1897, but that farm prices for such major crops as corn, cotton, and wheat fell as much and in some years (e.g., the mid-1890s) even more drastically than did railroad rates.[3] Since transport charges constituted a major part of farmers' costs, particularly west of Chicago, many farmers felt that the decrease in railroad rates in the post–Civil

War period was not large enough to improve their economic position. In addition, farmers felt like victims of discrimination because rates per ton mile were often much higher from the farm to regional markets than for intercity and interregional shipments (see Chapter 14). In areas where transport charges represented a relatively high percentage of farm costs, the hostility of farmers toward the railroads was most intense; considerably less protest came from areas where transport charges were less onerous.

Deflation and the Burden of Debts. Another important complaint of farmers centered on the heavy burden of farm mortgages during periods of depression. In 1890, approximately 29 percent of all farms were mortgaged to 35 percent of their value. But in the North Central region, the center of the Populist party, almost 39 percent of the farms were mortgaged. A seeming safeguard against financial injury was the short life span of most mortgages, ranging from three and one-half to five years. Yet when substantial changes occurred in the price level, as happened in 1873 to 1879 and again in 1893 to 1897, farmers with mortgage debts based on higher price levels suffered financial loss (that is, they had to pay their debts with dollars that had more value than the ones they had borrowed).

Interest Rates. Meeting the interest payments on farm mortgages was also difficult for many farmers during periods of depression. In 1880, interest rates on farm mortgages in the Far West were almost twice as high as those in the Middle Atlantic region. During the next three decades, as the flow of investment funds from the Northeast to the West increased, this difference in interest rates gradually diminished. Between 1875 and 1900, interest rates dropped sharply in the Great Plains from a high of 16 percent or 17 percent to a low of 5 percent or 6 percent. But the prices received

for farm products also declined, so farmers with high debt-to-asset ratios encountered great hardships in making their interest payments. A substantial number of such debtor farmers lost their farms through foreclosures on their mortgages, especially in the North Central states. Western and southern debtor farmers were driven by fear of foreclosure to seeking remedies through the radical political programs of the Grangers and the Populists. Farmers' decisions to seek political action represented a rational response to economic distress, even though some of their proposed remedies were unrealistic.

Tenancy. Many Populists were convinced that strong economic pressures drove a large number of once independent farmers into becoming tenant farmers. The U.S. Census statistics show an increase in the percentage of all farms in the United States operated by tenants from 25.6 percent in 1880 to 35.3 percent in 1900 and to 38.1 percent in 1920. The basis for concern by the Populists was the fact that the percentage of farm tenancy was highest in the South and the Midwest, where the impact of debt burden was greatest; tenancy percentages were lower in New England, the Rocky Mountain states, and the Pacific Coast, as was Populist support.

For many American farm tenants, tenancy was a temporary condition, a way of stepping up on the agricultural ladder; young people from a locality and newcomers to an area could start out as farm laborers to gain experience and time before buying land for themselves. But some farmers remained permanently in the status of farm tenants; this was especially true in the South for both poor whites and poor blacks. Farm tenancy in the South, as noted earlier in the chapter, developed on a large scale after the breakup of the pre–Civil War plantations. Especially in the form of sharecropping, tenant farming was a method of reorganizing the South's agricultural production after slave labor was abolished. The sharecropper system was gradually extended to large numbers of poor white farmers. Nonetheless, the percentage of black farmers who were sharecroppers was twice as large in 1900 as that of white farmers: 38 percent versus 19.9 percent. The trend toward increased tenancy was intensified by the major depressions that began in 1873 and 1893 as well as the lesser depression of 1882.

Monetary Growth and the Price Level. One important factor in the post–Civil War agrarian unrest was the farmers' belief that the money supply had contracted. Actually, though, the money supply (coin and paper currency plus commercial bank deposits) expanded between 1867 and 1896 at a rate in excess of the growth of population and at about the same rate as that of total production. But price levels fell drastically in the United States and Europe. Hence, although the money supply did not actually contract in the long run, it clearly did not increase rapidly enough to maintain a stable price level. Farmers' organizations and other protest movements were aware both of the widespread demonetization of silver in Europe and America during the 1870s and of a slowing rate of worldwide gold production. This led to calls for more paper greenbacks and the free coinage of silver (see Chapter 15).

Overproduction. Since nonfarm prices fell as rapidly as farm prices, the proposed monetary solutions to farm problems probably would not have had much effect on the farmers' terms of trade, though they would have lightened farmers' real debt burdens. American farmers' problems in the last three decades of the nineteenth century resulted more from nonmonetary developments, in particular the rapid expansion of farm production, the competition of other farmers in new producing areas within and outside of the United States, and the difficulty in agriculture of quickly adjusting production decisions to changes in demand. As noted earlier in the chapter, net farm output increased at a rate of more than 3 percent per year between 1869 and 1899. This expansion of production substantially exceeded the growth of population and created supply-demand imbalances at critical phases of the business cycle that caused sharp farm-price fluctuations. When depressions occurred in the 1870s, the 1880s, and the 1890s, employment and income contraction in the manufacturing and service sectors contributed greatly to the hardships of farm producers, particularly those who produced staple crops (e.g., wheat, corn, cotton) and livestock. Farmers who turned to the production of dairy products, orchard and citrus fruits, or garden vegetables were more protected from the bad consequences of business fluctuations because of the rapidly increasing urban demand for those products.

Competition and Production Lags. Growing domestic and foreign competition also created difficulties for many farmers. As grain and livestock production expanded in the West, producers of these products in the Midwest and the East faced falling prices and incomes as well as a need to reorient their product mixes. Foreign competition was less directly perceived as a threat by American farmers, but in fact it may have exerted a more powerful influence than domestic competition. On the whole, American farmers benefited greatly from world demand (particularly in Europe) for their rising output of agricultural products. The share of U.S. gross farm output absorbed by Europe increased from one-eighth to one-quarter in the three decades after the Civil War. But the international market proved fickle in the short run. In the 1880s and 1890s, competition in grain production came from newly developed agricultural regions in Canada, Australia, New Zealand, Argentina, and South Africa, as well as from Russia and India. In the 1890s, growing competition in cotton came from Egypt and India. As a result, the American farmer was plagued by uncertainty and fluctuating prices. In some cases, good crops in the United States coincided with bad crops elsewhere, and so the American farmer profited. In other cases, bumper crops outside the United States led to falling prices and losses for American farmers. More and more, farmers found that they were operating in an international market where the prices of agricultural commodities fluctuated widely under changing conditions of world supply and demand.

A problem faced in greater measure by farmers than by other producers compounded the difficulty of adjusting to the rapid changes in supply and demand that were characteristic of the late nineteenth century. Agricultural production decisions—the choice of what commodities to produce and how much of each—had to be made many months in advance of the time when the commodities would be ready for marketing. Unlike nonfarm producers with shorter production cycles, farmers could not easily vary the flow of material inputs and labor in response to short-run shifts in market conditions. This vulnerability of farmers to forces over which they had little or no control goes far toward explaining their problems in coping with the dynamics of commercial agriculture in a period of rapid change. Later generations of American farmers sought to enlist still more aid in the form of government farm programs and regulations in their attempts to deal with ongoing problems of adjustment to change. In this endeavor, they were more successful than were the farmers of the late nineteenth century. But they were not successful in halting the relative decline of agriculture in the overall economy.

The Golden Age of Agriculture

During the 1897 to 1915 period, American agriculture enjoyed the greatest measure of sustained prosperity in its history. What happened was essentially a reversal of the pattern of the three decades before 1897. In this earlier period, the supply of farm products increased faster than demand; after 1897, the demand grew faster than the supply.

As noted earlier in the chapter, real farm output in either gross or net terms grew at less than one-third of its 1869 to 1899 rate between 1899 and 1919. The slowing of output growth was caused in part by the closing of the frontier, which implied a reduced availability of potential farmland, and in part by a shift of labor in relative terms away from agriculture. In 1900, almost 40 percent of American workers were employed in agriculture; fifteen years later, only 30 percent were in agricultural jobs. Workers were attracted to industry by higher industrial wages and incomes, but the rapidity of the shift during this period resulted in farm workers' wages and farmers' incomes rising relative to those in the nonfarm sector. During the years 1911 to 1915, the average annual net income for persons engaged in agriculture was about $370 compared to $495 per worker engaged in industry. Thus, farm incomes were about three-fourths of those in industry, an unusually favorable ratio for the farmers, whose costs of living historically were lower than those of urban workers.

While agricultural output growth slowed considerably from earlier rates, domestic and foreign demand for farm products continued to expand at high rates. In the domestic market, one factor of crucial significance was the rapid growth of industrial production. By 1915, industrial production was one and one-half times greater than it had been in 1895, whereas agricultural output rose only by one-half. Industrial expansion attracted a growing proportion of the population—including large numbers of immigrants—to urban areas, where they depended on farmers for supplies of food instead of competing with farmers on the land. As a result, the terms of exchange became increasingly favorable to agriculture, and the ratio of the prices paid for goods to the prices received by farmers remained unusually steady in the years 1910 to 1914 — the so-called "parity years" to which later farm groups would point in seeking government assistance to raise their incomes. These years truly were a golden age for agriculture, a time when there were more farmers than in any previous or subsequent period of American history and when the relative economic position of the farmer was extremely favorable by historical standards.

Summary

From the Civil War to World War I, American agriculture continued in the pattern of absolute expansion but relative decline that had begun in the antebellum period. Agriculture's growth was unusually high during the last three decades of the nineteenth century. Land policy decisions to continue the rapid transfer of the public domain to private ownership on liberal terms were important to the expansion. The natural resources of the West — minerals, grasslands, and farmlands — acted as magnets to easterners and migrants from overseas. At the same time, railroad building on a colossal scale opened up markets for western products, while mechanization allowed westerners to increase greatly the amount of land that could be farmed by an individual farmer.

The rapid growth of farm output and the extension of specialization and commercial agriculture to new areas created a number of economic problems for farmers and prompted the emergence of agrarian protest movements during the 1870s, 1880s, and 1890s. Even though these movements enjoyed limited success in obtaining their specific objectives, from the experience farmers learned political lessons that were helpful to them in subsequent decades. The farmer's need for protest organizations and political pressure groups declined rapidly after the end of the nineteenth century. In the early years of the twentieth century, farmers enjoyed a golden age of prosperity. It resulted from a sharp drop in the rate of growth in agricultural output at a time when the demand for farm products continued to expand at high rates because of rapid industrialization and urban development.

Endnotes

1. Gavin Wright, "The Origins of American Industrial Success, 1879–1940," *American Economic Review,* 80 (Dec. 1990): 651–68.
2. See William N. Parker and Judith L. V. Klein, "Productivity Growth in Grain Production in the United States, 1840–60 and 1900–10," in National Bureau of Economic Research, Conference on Income and Wealth, *Output, Employment, and Productivity in the United States After 1800,* Studies in Income and Wealth, 30 (New York: National Bureau of Economic Research, 1966). See also Parker's chapter in Lance Davis et al., eds., *American Economic Growth,* cited in Suggested Readings.
3. See Robert Higgs, *The Transformation of the American Economy, 1865–1914* (New York: John Wiley & Sons, 1971), pp. 87–90, and "Railroad Rates and the Populist Uprising," *Agricultural History,* 44 (July 1970).

Suggested Readings

The South's unique problems in and beyond agriculture after the Civil War were discussed at length in Roger Ransom and Richard Sutch, *One Kind of Freedom: The Economic Consequences of Emancipation* (Cambridge: Cambridge University Press, 1977); and Gavin Wright, *Old South, New South* (New York: Basic Books, 1986). Also of value on this topic are Robert Fogel, *Without Consent or Contract: The Rise and Fall of American Slavery* (New York: Norton, 1988): Robert Higgs, *Competition and Coercion: Blacks in the American Economy, 1865–1914* (Cambridge: Cambridge University Press, 1977); and Stephen J. DeCanio, *Agriculture in the Postbellum South* (Cambridge, Mass.: M.I.T. Press, 1974).

Among the most informative studies of post–Civil War frontiers and U.S. land policy are Ray Allen Billington, *Westward Expansion: A History of the American Frontier,* 4th ed. (New York: Macmillan, 1974); Gilbert C. Fite, *The Farmer's Frontier, 1865–1900* (New York: Holt, 1966); Paul Gates, *History of Public Land Law Development* (Washington, D.C.: GPO, 1968); Louis Pelzer, *The Cattlemen's Frontier* (Glendale, Calif.: Arthur H. Clark, 1936); Rodman W. Paul, *Mining Frontiers of the Far West* (New York: Holt, 1963); and Walter Prescott Webb, *The Great Plains* (Boston: Ginn, 1931).

For valuable analyses of the economics of mining and cattle raising, see Israel Borenstein, *Capital and Output Trends in Mining Industries, 1870–1948,* Occasional Paper 45 (New York: National Bureau of Economic Research, 1954); Orris Herfindahl, "Development of the Major Mining Industries: 1839 to 1909," in National Bureau of Economic Research, *Output, Employment, and Productivity in the United States After 1800: Studies in Income and Wealth,* vol. 30 (New York: Columbia University Press, 1966); and Gene M. Gressley, *Bankers and Cattlemen* (New York: Knopf, 1966). The great signifi-

cance of intensive natural resource use for America's remarkable industrial growth is established in Gavin Wright, "The Origins of American Industrial Success, 1879–1940," *American Economic Review,* 80 (Dec. 1990).

Among the vast literature on post–Civil War agriculture, the following works rank high for their illuminating treatment of controversial topics: Harold Barger and Hans Landsberg, *American Agriculture, 1899–1939* (New York: National Bureau of Economic Research, 1942); John W. Kendrick, *Productivity Trends in the United States* (Princeton: Princeton University Press, 1961); Ralph Loomis and Glen Barton, *Productivity of Agriculture: 1870–1958* (Washington, D.C.: U.S. Department of Agriculture, Technical Bulletin 1238, 1961); William Parker, "Agriculture," in Lance E. Davis et al., eds. *American Economic Growth* (New York: Harper & Row, 1972); Harvey S. Perloff et al., *Regions, Resources, and Economic Growth* (Baltimore: Johns Hopkins University Press, 1960); Nathan Rosenberg, *Technology and American Economic Growth* (New York: Harper & Row, 1972); James H. Shideler, ed., *Agriculture in the Development of the Far West* (Washington, D.C.: Agricultural History Society, 1975); Frederick Strauss and Louis Bean, *Gross Farm Income and Indices of Farm Production and Prices: 1864–1937* (Washington, D.C.: U.S. Department of Agriculture, Technical Bulletin 703, 1940); Alvin S. Tostlebe, *Capital in Agriculture Since 1870* (Princeton: Princeton University Press, 1957); James W. Whitaker, ed., *Farming in the Midwest, 1840–1900* (Washington, D.C.: Agricultural History Society, 1974); and Vivian Wiser, ed., *Two Centuries of American Agriculture* (Washington, D.C.: Agricultural History Society, 1978). A classic work of agriculture-industry relations from 1896 to 1914 is Theodore W. Schultz, *Agriculture in an Unstable Economy* (New York: McGraw-Hill, 1945).

On the causes and issues of the Grange and Populist revolts, the following are worth careful reading. For pro-Populist perspectives, see Lawrence Goodwyn, *Democratic Promise: The Populist Movement in America* (New York: Oxford University Press, 1976); John D. Hicks, *The Populist Revolt* (Minneapolis: University of Minnesota Press, 1931); Theodore Saloutos, *Farmer Movements in the South, 1865–1933* (Lincoln, Neb.: Bison Books, 1960); and Fred Shannon, *The Farmer's Last Frontier: Agriculture, 1865–1897* (New York: Farrar & Rinehart, 1945). For revisionist views, see Allan Bogue, *From Prairie to Corn Belt* (Chicago: University of Chicago Press, 1963); Allan Bogue, *Money at Interest* (Ithaca, N.Y.: Cornell University Press, 1963); John D. Bowman, "Midwestern Farm Land Values and Farm Land Income, 1860 to 1900," *Yale Economic Essays,* 5 (Fall 1965); Robert Higgs, *The Transformation of the American Economy, 1865–1914* (New York: Wiley, 1971); Anne Mayhew, "A Reappraisal of the Causes of Farm Protest, 1870–1900," *Journal of Economic History,* 32 (1972); and Morton Rothstein, "America in the International Rivalry for the British Wheat Market," *Mississippi Valley Historical Review,* 47 (Dec. 1960).

Chapter 12

Mass Production and the Advent of Big Business

SINCE THE UNITED STATES WAS ALREADY A LEADing industrial nation in 1860, it is useful to view the Industrial Revolution of 1865 to 1914 as a continuation of that industrialization process, temporarily slowed by the events of the Civil War. Between 1860 and 1920, the proportion of the U.S. labor force employed in manufacturing almost doubled, rising from 14 percent to 27 percent. Industrial output grew much faster, reflecting the mechanization of more manufacturing processes. By the eve of World War I, the United States was clearly the global leader, accounting for over one-third of the world's industrial production, greater than the combined share held by the next two im-

portant manufacturing nations of Great Britain and Germany (see Figure 12–1).

With the emergence of the large manufacturing corporation during this period, significant changes took place in the organization of economic decision making in many segments of American industry. During the first three-quarters of the nineteenth century, U.S. industrial growth was accomplished through a system of decentralized economic decision making. A multitude of entrepreneurs made decisions about investment, output, and price in relation to their perceptions of the market. Most manufacturing firms were small in size, were organized as proprietorships or partner-

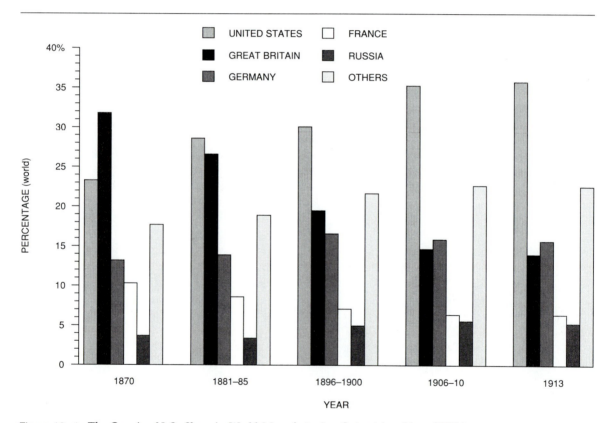

Figure 12–1 *The Growing U.S. Share in World Manufacturing Output (world = 100%)*
SOURCE: Adapted from Folke Hilgerdt, *Industrialization and Foreign Trade* (Geneva: League of Nations, 1945), p. 13.

ships, were managed by their owners, required relatively little capital, performed a single function and produced a single product, and served local markets. The few exceptions to this pattern of manufacturing existed mainly in the cotton-textile industry. By 1914, however, a new industrial structure was in place in the United States. A small number of large firms dominated many key industries, especially those that had spearheaded the growth that took place between the 1860s and World War I. These large companies used the corporate form of organization; applied large amounts of capital, particularly in the form of machinery and other fixed assets; performed several functions and often manufactured more than one product; and sold in national and increasingly in international markets. Whereas the individual was the owner and decision maker in the small business firm, many persons in the large corporation, where management was separated from the ownership function of property, participated in the making and carrying out of decisions within a bureaucratic hierarchy.

An Industrial Revolution

From the base established in the decades before the Civil War, manufacturing grew dramatically in the ensuing years. According to Edwin Frickey's widely accepted index, manufacturing production expanded by twelve times between 1860 and 1914. Similarly, Robert E. Gallman's data on value added by manufacture show a more than seven fold increase from 1859 to the end of the nineteenth century.[1] These figures imply an industrial growth rate of 5 percent to 7 percent per annum on average. Major advances were recorded in the late 1870s and early 1880s and again from the late 1890s into the early twentieth century. As Figure 12–2 shows, value added in the manufac-

turing sector grew from less than a third of value added in total commodity output in 1859 to more than one half in 1899.

Industrial development did not proceed evenly in all regions of the country, however. In 1860, a manufacturing belt already existed along the Atlantic Coast, from north of Boston to south of Philadelphia. New England and the Middle Atlantic states then accounted for almost three-quarters of the nation's industrial employment. A half-century later, the manufacturing belt extended westward to include the Middle West (see Figure 12–3). From 1870 to 1910, industry in the Middle West increased by over six times (as measured by value added), compared to a fourfold advance for the country as a whole. From almost the beginning of settlement west of the Appalachian Mountains, industry developed to process the region's agricultural commodities into flour, meat, beer, and whiskey. In addition, a highly diversified industrial sector was developing to provide the region's growing population with a wide range of manufactured goods. By the turn of the century, the Great Lakes region had become an "American Ruhr"—its vast metallurgical complex second to none in the world—based on its leadership in primary metals (especially steel), metal fabricating, machinery, and transportation equipment. The Northeast and Middle West constituted an industrial heartland, as establishments in the states east of the Mississippi and north of the Ohio employed 70 percent of U.S. industrial workers and accounted for 77 percent of the nation's value added by manufacture in 1910 (see Table 12–1). Outside the industrial heartland, smaller industrial advances were made in the South in the processing of raw materials and low-wage textile production, and in the Far West in the manufacturing of consumer and producer goods for a regional market that supplemented the processing of raw materials for the national market.

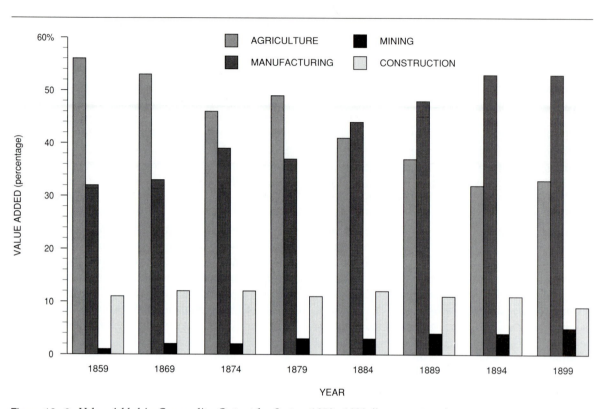

Figure 12–2 *Value Added in Commodity Output by Sector, 1859–1899 (in percentages)*
Source: Adapted from Robert E. Gallman, "Commodity Output, 1839–1899," in *Trends in the American Economy in the Nineteenth Century* (Princeton University Press, 1960), p. 26.

Manufacturing continued to be a largely urban phenomenon. According to the 1909 Census of Manufactures, there were 339 manufacturing cities, each with one thousand or more wage-earners, located in nine manufacturing districts within the industrial heartland. However, during these years, more industry was becoming concentrated in the nation's largest cities—New York, Boston, and Philadelphia in the Northeast, and Chicago, St. Louis, Detroit, and Cleveland in the Middle West.

Technology, the Market, and the Resource Base

The growth of manufacturing of the order experienced from 1865 to 1914 was based on a technological revolution. Discoveries in basic science were usually European in origin, but their application was often worked out by Americans who prided themselves on being practical, not theoretical. Most advances in manufacturing were made through empirical, trial-and-error methods. Perhaps a typical inventor of a manufacturing method was a mechanic or an engineer familiar with the problems of the particular industry. Development of a finished product for consumers was more likely to be the work of amateurs. Only toward the end of the nineteenth century did business begin to organize research laboratories for the systematic pursuit of scientific knowledge and its application to industry. Since the United States patent system encouraged invention by

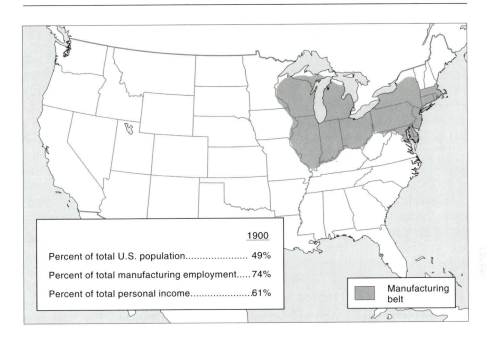

Figure 12–3. *The Manufacturing Belt, 1900.*
SOURCE: Adapted from Harvey S. Perloff, Edgar S. Dunn, Jr., Eric E. Lampard, and
Richard F. Muth, *Regions, Resources and Economic Growth*, (Baltimore: Johns Hopkins Press,
1960), p. 49.

Table 12–1. *Regional Distribution of U.S. Value Added by Manufacture in the Industrial Heartland, 1870 and 1910*

Region	1870 (percent)	1910	1870 ($ millions)	1910
New England	24%	14%	$ 378	$1,173
Middle Atlantic	42	37	665	3,022
Great Lakes	18	26	285	2,096
Total	84%	77%	$1,328	$6,290

SOURCE: Adapted from Harvey S. Perloff et al., *Regions, Resources, and Economic Growth* (Baltimore: Johns Hopkins
University Press, 1960), p. 153.

protecting the property rights of the inventor, the number of patents granted serves as a rough measure of the expanding interest in industrial novelty—patents increased from an annual average of twelve thousand in the 1860s to twenty-five thousand in the 1880s and to forty thousand in 1914. Generally, a correlation existed between the number of inventions of capital goods in an industry and the sales volume of capital goods to that industry, suggesting that inventors directed their talents toward areas of the economy in which they perceived growth and profit potential.

Even more important than the invention of new manufacturing techniques were their rapid adoption and diffusion, thereby minimizing the lag or differential between the best available practices (for example, the most efficient machines that had been invented for a particular purpose) and the average level of technique employed in the industry. The idea of progress in nineteenth-century American society encouraged acceptance of new products and new ways of doing things. Most industrialists took pride in using progressive methods in their factories. Through much of the nineteenth century, there was little to discourage or stop innovation. Opposition by workers to the introduction of labor-saving machinery was ineffective; employers had little difficulty in recruiting new workers on the relatively rare occasions when conflict did develop over this issue. Even a depression might encourage the spread of innovation in an industry, as manufacturers sought to reduce their costs to solve the problem of falling prices.

However, successful nineteenth-century industrialists were not gamblers. Typically, when they approached the possibilities of innovation, they sought ways to reduce the chance of loss that might result from change. But perhaps this caution contributed to the rapid rate of technological change, in that there were few spectacular failures to discour-

age entrepreneurs. Americans excelled in getting inventions into mass production. Unlike Europeans, who continued to emphasize finely crafted work, American industrialists were willing to accept products and methods that were less than perfect in quality if reduced costs resulted. As early as the 1870s, an observer used the contrast between a magnificent clock made for the cathedral at Beauvais in France and the pocket watch that was mass produced in an American factory to explain the difference between European and American industry:

> At Beauvais the ingenuity of lifetimes is wasted on a toy with ninety thousand wheels. Here mechanical genius devises machinery which puts into the pockets of people of moderate means a watch whose hands give all the really useful information supplied by the costly trifle in the Cathedral Tower at Beauvais.[2]

From the beginnings of American history, an abundance of natural resources had played a basic role in molding the course of economic development. This was no less true for the period of 1860 to 1914 than for earlier eras. The basic raw materials for industrial success at this time were at hand, especially copper, coal, zinc, iron ore, lead, and petroleum. In all of these, the United States was the world's leading producer. Even more important, no other nation possessed such a wide range of these resources so basic to the industrial growth of the period. Nor did any other nation develop its resource base as thoroughly as did the United States. While both capital intensity, in the form of application of technology, and an abundance of natural resources played key roles in American industrialization, more important was the link between them. As Gavin Wright argues, "Capital intensity derived not from economy-wide abundance of capital per se, but from specialization in an industrial technology in which capital was complementary to natural resources," especially the abundance of industrial

Table 12–2 *Net Output of Consumer- and Capital-Goods Industries, 1850–1914 (percentage of total industrial output)*[a]

Year	Consumer-Goods Industries	Capital-Goods Industries
1850	43.5%	18.2%
1870	38.6	23.3
1880	43.8	24.7
1890	35.6	23.6
1900	33.9	28.0
1914	31.1	34.3

[a]Balance of output is from "excluded industries," which cannot be clearly classified as consumer goods or capital goods.
SOURCE: Adapted from W. G. Hoffmann, *The Growth of Industrial Economies* (Manchester: Manchester University Press, 1958), p. 96.

minerals. Thus, the abundance of these resources encouraged resource-using technologies that were distinctively American.[3]

Capital Goods

Modern industrialization meant not just the expansion and proliferation of consumer goods. Also during this period, production of capital goods, or of goods used in the production of other goods, increased faster than consumer goods, so that by 1914 capital-goods industries accounted for a larger share of total manufacturing output than did consumer-goods industries (see Table 12–2). This reflected, of course, the continuing substitution of machine for hand labor, not only in manufactures but in other sectors as well. For the economy as a whole, the stock of capital increased in size almost fourteen times from 1860 to 1920, whereas the labor force grew by less than four times. In manufacturing alone, real capital per worker more than tripled between 1879 and 1914 (see Figure 12–4). An increasingly intricate nexus of industrial activities was inserting itself between the producer of raw materials and the consumer of final products. It is important to note that not only was more capital being applied to industrial processes to increase the productivity of labor but also the capital stock itself was being made more productive as the result of technological and organizational changes. The progress of consumer-goods industries thus rested on the advances made in the vigorous capital-goods sector. Americans were able to save, or abstain from consuming, a significant portion of current production to invest in capital; this was reflected in the rising rate of capital formation from about 15 percent in the 1850s to one-quarter or more of gross national product in the 1870s and 1880s.

Metallurgy

A key characteristic of the Industrial Revolution was the progressive but rapid replacement of wood by metal as the basic material of the economy. Iron was increasingly used in the early nineteenth century by railroads, machinery makers, and manufacturers of other goods. However, what was needed was a stronger and more durable metal that could be produced cheaply. The basic advance in this area was the introduction of the Bessemer process, a technology by which the age of steel began to replace the age of iron in the 1860s. Bessemer steel was not of the same high quality as the expensive steel used in cutlery and hand tools, but it had greater tensile strength and hardness than wrought iron and could be produced on a large scale at low cost. The principles embodied in the Bessemer process had been discovered through trial and error by an American inventor and a British inventor working independently. An alternative method, the open-hearth process, was developed shortly after in Germany. Although initially more expensive to operate, the open-hearth process made it possible to control the final product more closely. While both systems had their

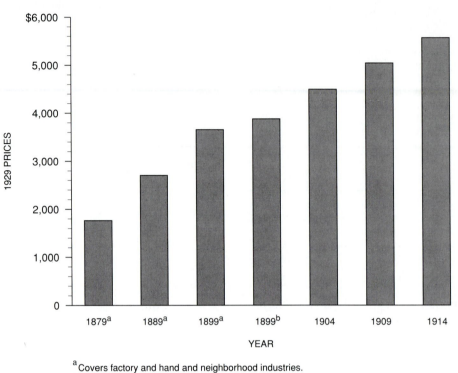

^{a}Covers factory and hand and neighborhood industries.

^{b}Covers factory with annual volume of production of $500 or more.

Figure 12–4 *Real Capital per Worker in Manufacturing, 1879–1914*
Source: Data from U.S. Bureau of the Census, *Historical Statistics of the United States, Colonial Times to 1970* (Washington, D.C.: GPO, 1975), pp. 666, 685.

proponents, the open-hearth technique gained steadily in favor and by 1900 was more widely used than the Bessemer process.

For a time, most Bessemer steel produced in the United States went into railroad rails. A group of industrialists associated with railroads, including Andrew Carnegie, who initially perceived a profitable use for cheap steel, purchased the patent rights to the new process and then organized production. From about 1880, however, more and more mass-produced steel was incorporated into other kinds of products: factory and office machinery, ships, construction and mining equipment, farm im-

plements, cans, wire, bicycles, girders for skyscrapers, and, after 1900, automobiles. Continuing improvements in steel making increased the range of applications where high speeds and close tolerances were involved.

Steel production expanded phenomenally, from under 1.25 million tons in 1880 to over 10 million tons in 1900 and to 26 million tons in 1910. By the turn of the century, the United States accounted for over one-third of the world's steel production. In this key industry, America clearly had great advantages due to its abundance of iron ore and coal. The fastest-growing segment of the steel industry in the

Bessemer Converter in Action.   Invention of the Bessemer process of steel making ushered in the modern era of metallurgy. (Historical Pictures/Stock Montage)

late nineteenth century was located in the Middle West, where an efficient organization of Great Lakes shipping tied together economically the sources of iron ore and fuel.

The Machine Age

As the Industrial Revolution metalized the economy, so too did it mechanize more and more manufacturing processes. As noted in Chapter 8, from the early decades of the nineteenth century, American industry held a lead over Europe in the use of specialized machinery. The scope of mechanization then widened

considerably in the decades after 1860. As one American engineer observed in 1899:

In America the tendency is to reduce all production to machine operations. In European countries, the tendency is to employ machinery as an assistant to production, and to rely on skillful hand labor to complete, and in some cases to produce outright, the highest grade of work. The consequence is that we find in America the highest skill and talent devoted to the production of machinery on which the article is made, and in Europe the highest skill devoted to the production of the article itself.[4]

In the United States, then, highly specialized firms not only produced machines and machine tools of the best quality and most approved design at the lowest price, but they also developed equipment adapted to the needs of particular sets of customers. The significant point, as Nathan Rosenberg stresses, is that "the machine tool industry was a center for the acquisition and diffusion of the skills and techniques uniquely required in a machinofacture type of economy."[5] Producers of specialized machinery acquired skills and techniques in solving the problems of specific customers, and these techniques were then transferred to other machine-using industries. The experience gained by sewing-machine manufacturers, for example, was transmitted to bicycle makers; their experience, in turn, was applied to the specific problems of automobile producers. Mechanization was applied most extensively to attain low unit costs when two preconditions were present: a large demand for the final product and sufficient standardization to permit use of special-purpose machinery.

Power Engines

Over the 1869 to 1914 period, the power employed in American manufacturing increased by more than nine times. Even more significant, the amount of power per production worker almost tripled.

While water power had been important in the early stages of industrialization, the latter third of the nineteenth century was the age of steam. With the development of anthracite coal mining and the organization of the distribution of coal throughout the Northeast, steam power became prevalent in factory industry by the 1850s. Steam had the advantage of freeing industry from needing to locate along streams, as areas with adequate power sites were becoming scarce. Also, steam raised dramatically the upper limits of power available to an individual establishment. Although steam accounted for just over one-half of total horsepower employed in manufacturing in 1869, by the end of the century, at its relative peak, steam supplied four-fifths of industrial power.

However, manufacturers in a variety of industries were turning in 1900 to electric power. The initial advantages of electric power included the savings achieved by powering each operation with an individual motor as well as the flexibility which made possible improved plant layout and organization of work flows. Furthermore, electricity facilitated the introduction of mechanization into an ever-wider range of operations. By 1919, purchased electricity accounted for almost one-third of the power capacity of the nation's industry.

In the preindustrial era, wood was a principal source of energy, providing heat and power for industrial purposes as well as domestic use. From the mid-nineteenth century, coal became closely associated with industrialization; its production nearly doubled almost every decade between 1850 and 1910. Coal came to account for three-quarters of the nation's total energy consumption in the first two decades of the twentieth century. However, by the time of World War I, petroleum was already well on the way to becoming an important fuel for industry (see Table 12–3).

Mass Production

Key elements of the system of mass production introduced into the automobile industry by Henry Ford in 1913 included, as he explained, "the planned orderly and continuous progression of the commodity through the shop" and "the delivery of work instead of leaving it to the workman's initiative to find it."[6] What Ford did was to put together several practices already used in industry. Mass production required standardization and inter-

---

Table 12–3 *Energy Consumption in the United States, 1860–1910*

Year	Total Consumption (in trillion BTUs)	Percentage of				
		Coal	Oil	Natural Gas	Hydro Power	Wood
1860	3,162	16.4%	0.1%	—	—	83.5%
1870	3,952	26.5	0.3	—	—	73.2
1880	5,001	41.1	1.9	—	—	57.0
1890	7,012	57.9	2.2	3.7%	0.3%	35.9
1900	9,587	71.4	2.4	2.6	2.6	21.0
1910	16,565	76.8	6.1	3.3	3.3	10.7

SOURCE: Adapted from Sam H. Schurr and Bruce C. Netschert, *Energy in the American Economy, 1850–1975* (Baltimore: Johns Hopkins University Press, 1960), pp. 35–36.

Moving Assembly Line, Ford Motor Company.   The popularity of the Model T required Henry Ford to expand production. This he did with the innovation in 1913 of the moving assembly line, which soon became a symbol of modern mass production. (Brown Brothers)

changeable parts, which had been developed in the making of firearms a century earlier and were employed in a number of industries in Ford's day. Automatic cutting tools built by machinery manufacturers made it possible for one man to operate a battery of drills or other tools. The concept of the moving assembly line could be seen in grain mills dating back to the 1780s, in slaughterhouses of the mid-nineteenth century (where it was actually a moving "disassembly line"), and in conveyers used by brewers after 1900 to wash, fill, cap, and label their product with automatic equipment. The scientific management of the late-nineteenth and early twentieth centuries, led by men like Frederick W. Taylor, put emphasis on organizing the individual worker's labor and on careful scheduling of the flow of materials—necessary prerequisites for a system employing minute division of labor. The productivity gains in Ford's factories were enormous, resulting in a sharp reduction in the worker-hours required to assemble a car. Similar results were achieved when mass production methods were applied in a wide variety of other industries.

Emergence of the Large Corporation

To some observers in the late nineteenth century and since, the business leaders who organized large sectors of the economy have been characterized as "semipiratical entrepreneurs who roamed the United States virtually unchecked." To others, what was most important about these same individuals was their constructive achievement.[7]

The generation of Americans born in the 1830s and 1840s assumed that progress came through competition and the survival of the fittest and that profit was the most reliable

incentive for actiohey were applying. This usually
who entered　　　　　　　　　　　nuch higher velocity of through-
kinds of oppor　　　　　　　　　of materials through the plant us-
Jay Gould, Da　　　　　　　　　capital-intensive processes, than
how the increa　　　　　　　　xperienced in manufacturing op-
ticularly by the　　　　　　　　cond, to assure that the increased
ity for large pr　　　　　　　　ild be sold and the larger amount
nipulating the　　　　　　　　cured, entrepreneurs had to inte-
and bonds). C　　　　　　　　operations forward and backward
and Andrew C　　　　　　　　nore effectively the marketing of
no-holds-barre　　　　　　　and the acquisition of components
great wealth o　　　　　　　ls. Finally, to administer and coor-
turing by usir　　　　　　　irger size of facilities and expanded
products, and　　　　　　　usiness functions, entrepreneurs
national mark　　　　　　　ion a management structure con-
telegraph; in s　　　　　　　veral levels.[8]
talents to buil　　　　　　　ess of the formation of large corpo-
　　　　　　　　　　　　king mass production and mass dis-
Vertical Grow　　　　　oegan in the 1880s along a broad
　　　　　　　　　　　　ong the makers of branded, pack-
The revoluti　　　　　　　s were manufacturers of cigarettes,
and commur　　　　　　　ods, and photographic materials.
nineteenth ce　　　　　　ited in new continuous-process ma-
potential of a　　　　　　hich resulted in large increases in
Constitution　　　　　　capacity, and soon found that inde-
ity and spee　　　　　　wholesalers could not move their
tion now ma　　　　　　ckly enough. Some products, like
of raw mate　　　　　　quired refrigeration for storage, which
products ou　　　　　　istributors could not provide. Manufac-
mass produ　　　　　　rs thus moved to set up their own net-
seminal work of Alfred D. Chandler, Jr., forcefully demonstrates, many of the new technologies being developed in the last quarter of the
nineteenth century yielded significant *economies of scale*—a decrease in cost per unit accompanying an increase in the number of units
produced—as well as *economies of scope*—a decrease in unit costs achieved by producing
more than one product within an establishment. However, to realize these economies to
sell in the national market, entrepreneurs had
to make substantial investments along three
lines. First, they had to create production facilities of an optimal size to take full advantage
of the scale and scope potentials of the new

works of wholesale sales offices and employed
aggressive marketing tactics. All of these manufacturers of branded, packaged goods found
advertising to be a particularly potent weapon
in reaching the mass of middle-class consumers. For most of these products, a low unit
price made it difficult to stimulate demand by
price reductions. Gaining the advantages of
the "first mover" in each of these industries
were James B. Duke (cigarettes), Henry Heinz
and Joseph Campbell (canned foods), and
George Eastman (photographic materials).
Companies that produced a variety of new
kinds of durable goods, for sale either to consumers or to producers, found the independent

wholesaler lacking in ability to perform essential functions, such as demonstration, providing credit to the buyer, installation, and repair. First movers in this type of industry included Singer (sewing machines), McCormick and Deere (agricultural implements), Remington (typewriters), Patterson (cash registers), General Electric and Westinghouse (electrical equipment), Otis (elevators), and Ford (automobiles). They created their own national and international marketing organizations; these included branch offices to supply not only a flow of products but also funds to extend credit for "big-ticket" items, spare parts, and specialized repair service. In some industries, franchised dealers performed the retailing function under the supervision of the manufacturer's branch office. In the early history of the automobile industry, for example, manufacturers sent their cars to wholesalers, who sold them to retailers in cities and towns in their regions. By the second decade of the twentieth century, the large companies set up factory branches to supply car dealers in major urban markets. Around 1915, Ford established regional assembly plants and eliminated all wholesalers.

Producers of perishable goods for the mass market—such as Armour and Swift (meat packing), Schlitz and Pabst (beer), and Preston (bananas)—also found it necessary to build marketing organizations. For instance, the new refrigerated railroad car used to supply fresh meat to eastern markets required refrigerated warehouses, a facility that local butchers were unwilling to provide.

Many of these firms integrated not only forward into marketing but also backward into purchasing in order to assure supplies for a large volume of production. Manufacturers of durable goods created purchasing organizations and sometimes bought or constructed factories to manufacture parts and materials. Producers of nondurable goods followed similar patterns. Meat packers, for example,

bought into stockyards along the cattle frontier, and cigarette makers built their own storing and curing facilities for the tobacco they purchased directly from farmers.

Horizontal Combinations

In some industries, the first movers had enough of a head start over potential rivals to establish a position of dominance, which was enforced when necessary by ruthless competitive tactics employed against potential challengers. However, in other sectors, manufacturers who invested in new technology to expand production found themselves in a bitter competitive battle with other members of their industry. Reduction of transportation costs increased the market area where manufacturers, who previously produced primarily for the local market, could now sell their expanded output, throwing them into competition with other producers whose previous markets also had been local in nature. Inevitably, in industry after industry, the result was a growth in the supply of even the "most useful and desirable things in excess of any demand at remunerative prices to the producer," as David Wells observed in the 1880s.[9] Since manufacturers had invested in specialized equipment that could be used only for limited purposes, it was impossible for them to withdraw from the market (i.e., to transfer capital) without incurring heavy losses. Thus, manufacturers were led to continue producing as long as the price they received exceeded their direct costs (labor and material). The best they could hope for by selling at a loss was that competitors would be driven out of business. But this was not an effective solution; the exit of one competitor through bankruptcy usually resulted in the entry of a new competitor who purchased at a bargain price the equipment of the bankrupt firm. Industrialists described the situation as "ruinous" or "destructive" competition. A few of the most efficient firms were able to make money even at low prices, but most were unsuccessful.

To meet the threat posed by falling prices and vanishing profits, industrialists formed national and regional trade associations, through which they entered into agreements to set minimum prices, limit total output, or divide markets. In most European countries, such cartel agreements were legally enforced and thereby helped to solve for industry there the same problems of overproduction faced by many American manufacturers. However, in the United States, these pooling agreements had no standing in courts of law. If participants broke the agreement by selling at a price below that established by the cartel, they could not be sued, even if the agreement was contained in a written contract. Thus, most pooling agreements lasted only a short period of time, followed by a quick return to price war. To John D. Rockefeller, head of the Petroleum Refiners Association, such groups were no more than "ropes of sand."

The problem was an obvious one: Manufacturers had to devise a more permanent form of combination. A major step was invention of the trust form by Rockefeller and his associates in Standard Oil in 1882. In an adaptation of an old legal device to meet the current needs of business, a board of trustees was empowered to manage the properties of the forty corporations joining the trust on behalf of the stockholders, the legal owners. The arrangement had the advantage of permanence, since the irrevocable deed of trust prevented withdrawal by any participant in the combination. Only eight combinations operating on a national scale utilized the trust form in the 1880s, and six of these were successful in controlling their industries—sugar, whiskey, lead, cottonseed oil, and linseed oil, in addition to petroleum. They were pioneers in creating the large industrial enterprise through *horizontal combination*—the process of joining together a number of firms operating at one

level or stage in the productive process. They not only found a legal form for big business, but, even more important, they also began to develop centralized managerial techniques, since the trustees were authorized to make all decisions for the members of the trust. When the trust form came under legal attack in the early 1890s, soon after New Jersey had changed its incorporation laws to authorize one corporation to own the stock of other corporations, these combinations and others formed in the ensuing years began to employ the holding company device. Large-scale activity appeared so striking in the 1880s, however, that the term trust continued to be applied to big business long after that legal form had been abandoned.

Rockefeller and the other leaders of Standard Oil moved to take full advantage of the trust form to establish and maintain their leadership in the petroleum industry. The trustees rationalized production through the closing of inefficient plants and the building of new facilities. Thus, they directed a reduction in the number of refineries from fifty-three in 1882 to twenty-two just four years later. Production of kerosene, the major product line, was soon concentrated in three giant refineries, providing nearly one-quarter of the world's supply. In order to coordinate operations more effectively, Standard Oil integrated vertically, with investments in crude oil production, pipelines, a fleet of railroad tank cars, and a national and an international marketing organization. As a result of the cost reduction achieved through rationalization and integration, Standard Oil's profit margins doubled.

Public Policy Toward the Giant Corporation

The emergence of giant corporations within a relatively short period of time resulted in a great deal of public concern and, in some quarters, alarm. However, the developing movement against the trusts, or big business, was not an attack on business or capitalism. Indeed, some of the strongest critics were small entrepreneurs who believed that they had been damaged by the aggressive behavior of large corporations. They could point to the old sentiment against monopoly, reflecting in turn a widely held belief in America about the virtue of freedom of opportunity. In short, big business appeared to be undermining the traditional business system, one that rested on a wide dispersion of economic decision making and economic power.

The problem was how to translate public concern into political action. In an era when the federal government still exercised relatively little regulatory power, it is not surprising that those who felt threatened by big business turned to their state governments to provide protection. Two cases illustrate how states sought to protect local business interests against an invasion of their turf by large national corporations. The first case followed the creation by the Singer Sewing Machine Company of its own marketing organization, primarily because the existing system of independent, local distributors was unable to provide the credit, make the demonstrations, and furnish the repair that the company needed to market its machines on a mass basis. Local interests, to protect their markets, applied peddler licensing and tax laws to members of Singer's organization. These laws discriminated against out-of-state products and against the traveling salespersons employed by the company. Singer stood to gain greatly if such statutes could be overturned and possessed the financial resources to fight protracted legal battles. Singer therefore appealed the convictions of its agents and employees all the way to the U.S. Supreme Court. The Court ruled in favor of Singer in 1876 *(Welton v. Missouri)*. Peddler licensing laws were found to be discriminatory taxes on out-of-state products. Members of the Court reasoned that such state laws, unless

voided, could even lead to tariff wars among the states.

The second case involved the mass producers and marketers of fresh meat, who found themselves the targets of local interests. The innovation of the refrigerated railroad car allowed the large packers to achieve economies of scale in processing meats at central locations like Chicago and then shipping it hundreds of miles for sale at prices below those charged by local butchers. With their market eroding, local butchers raised the red flag of monopoly and induced a number of states to pass inspection laws. If these laws were applied, they would destroy the ability of the large packing companies to compete effectively in local markets. When an agent of Armour was convicted under a Minnesota statute, the case was appealed to the U.S. Supreme Court. In *Minnesota v. Barber* (1890), the Court, ruling for the defendant, reasoned that under the guise of such inspection laws, a state could keep virtually any product of out-of-state manufacture from being sold within its borders.

As the preceding examples demonstrate, overcoming parochial interests sometimes required lengthy and expensive legal battles. Large business corporations had the incentive and financial resources to fight these battles. The U.S. Supreme Court showed an understanding of the larger legal issues involved in these cases.

The Sherman Antitrust Act (1890)

With the failure of state political action to halt the expansion of the giant corporation, critics turned increasingly to Congress to produce effective legislation. There was little doubt about the intensity of hostility concerning the ability of big business to drive out competitors. Yet many people saw some virtue in the combinations because they appeared to be efficient, a value almost as important as competition.

The result of debate about the trusts in and out of Congress was the Sherman Antitrust Act (1890), written in sweeping but somewhat vague terms in declaring illegal "every contract, combination in the form of trust or otherwise, or conspiracy in restraint of trade or commerce among the several states." There ensued over the next decade strenuous efforts to determine what the law really meant or should mean as it related to the evolving economic situation. Some critics blamed the Justice Department for not enforcing the law more strenuously, but this agency had only eighteen lawyers employed in Washington, and Congress did not appropriate funds to enlarge the staff. Others criticized the conservatism of the courts in interpreting the law in a narrow fashion, but antitrust cases produced volumes of records that had to be evaluated and involved an analysis of economic issues that even professional economists found complex.

Based on cases brought before the U.S. Supreme Court, the meaning of the Sherman Antitrust Act after a decade seemed to be this: (1) Pooling agreements, or cartels, were clearly illegal because they were contracts made by independent companies to restrain trade (*United States v. Addyston Pipe & Steel Company*, 1899); and (2) combinations or mergers of manufacturing companies seemed to escape the Sherman Act, as the Court ruled that a monopoly of manufacture only incidentally and indirectly affected commerce and that it therefore was not subject to a federal statute based on the commerce clause of the Constitution (*United States v. E. C. Knight Company*, 1895).

The Great Merger Movement (1897–1903)

At the turn of the century there occurred the most widespread merger movement in American history (see Table 12–4). In the space of a half-dozen years, over 2800 business firms en-

Table 12–4 *Number of Consolidations Formed per Year in Manufacturing, 1895–1904*

Year	Number of Consolidations[a]
1895	4
1896	3
1897	6
1898	16
1899	63
1900	21
1901	19
1902	17
1903	5
1904	3

[a]Includes only horizontal consolidations of at least 5 previously competing firms.

SOURCE: Adapted from Naomi R. Lamoreaux, *The Great Merger Movement in American Business, 1895–1904* (New York: Cambridge University Press, 1985), p. 2.

tered mergers, including over 1200 in 1899 alone. Paradoxically, the Sherman Antitrust Act encouraged the formation of large corporations. Industrialists and their lawyers, seeking ways to control their markets, believed that the Supreme Court's decisions in the 1890s implied that consolidation of competing firms was the only legal method to achieve stability. Consolidation seemed to be particularly appealing to members of industries characterized by high fixed costs, who had earlier expanded rapidly and who found themselves caught in vicious price wars during the severe depression of the 1890s. To many observers, the large combinations appeared to have fared rather well during the hard times.

The finance capitalist, or investment banker, played a leading role in the great merger movement; the development of a market for industrial securities proved to be a decisive factor. In the earlier growth of big business, the initiative had been taken by industrialists, who financed acquisitions and internal growth with prior earnings or bank loans, sometimes arranged through the commercial banks they controlled. Turn-of-the-century mergers, however, often involved far larger capitalizations. What particularly sparked the interest of investment bankers in creating combinations was the growing eagerness of investors to buy the stocks of industrial corporations, a type of security that only a few years earlier attracted little market attention. Finance capitalists had already gained experience in financing large corporations through their consolidation and reorganization of railroad companies in the 1880s and 1890s. J. Pierpont Morgan and other leading investment bankers of Wall Street controlled access to capital in large amounts through their ties with brokerage houses; they sold securities to wealthy individuals and institutional investors like life insurance companies and savings banks. Sometimes the investment banker took the initiative in seeking out firms to consolidate and industries to organize, as did Morgan in 1901 with the founding of the United States Steel Corporation, the first billion-dollar corporation in America. Even when industrialists conceived the idea of consolidating competing firms, they usually turned to Wall Street to arrange the raising of new capital through the issue of securities. The relationship was a continuing one, as investment bankers held positions on the board of directors of the industrial corporation, a practice introduced earlier by Morgan in the railroad field to give him some supervisory power over corporate financial affairs.

Big Business and the Law

After Theodore Roosevelt assumed the presidency in 1901, the legality of combination to control the market became less certain. Sensing a strong public concern about big business, Roosevelt pledged strict enforcement of the Sherman Antitrust Act and demanded that large corporations "subserve the public good." In his first action in this area, he ordered pros-

ecution of the Northern Securities Company, a railroad holding company formed by Morgan and other top business leaders, charging that it was an illegal combination. Conviction, upheld by the Supreme Court, lessened the confidence of lawyers that the use of the holding company shielded monopolistic combinations from the provisions of the Sherman Act. Furthermore, Congress in 1903 authorized establishment of the Bureau of Corporations with investigative powers.

President Roosevelt distinguished between "good" trusts, which he thought made for greater efficiency through rationalization, and "bad" trusts, which he believed to represent abuse of power. He thus directed his trust busting against the "bad" trusts, those, like Standard Oil and American Tobacco, that had

"President Theodore Roosevelt's Dream of a Successful Hunt," 1907. This cartoon illustrates Roosevelt's distinction between "good trusts," large corporations, which, if properly supervised by government, contributed to the nation's economic welfare, and "bad trusts," or predatory corporations, which should be destroyed. (The Library of Congress [LC-USZ62-10544])

gained notoriety with their predatory tactics toward competitors. The Justice Department instituted antitrust suits against the two giants, each of which was ordered by the Court to be dissolved into several separate corporations. The Supreme Court, in upholding these convictions in 1911, set forth the "rule of reason." The Sherman Act had outlawed all restraint of trade, but the Supreme Court now declared that only unreasonable restraint of trade was illegal. In other words, Standard Oil and American Tobacco were guilty not because of their large size but because of the ruthless methods they had used in earlier decades to eliminate competition. However, the Court did not provide a clear definition of what constituted unreasonableness in business behavior.

Legal problems ensued even for the "good" trusts, whose actions Roosevelt generally approved. For example, with the apparent endorsement of the White House during the Panic of 1907, the United States Steel Corporation acquired the Tennessee Coal and Iron Company, enabling the former to extend its dominance over the industry into the southern states. But the Taft administration later repudiated this understanding, or détente, when it filed an antitrust suit charging that the acquisition was a violation of the Sherman Act.

There continued into the second decade of the twentieth century controversy over an appropriate public policy for big business. On the one hand, critics of giant corporations argued that the Sherman Antitrust Act was ineffective in dealing with the problem of monopoly. There was a strong sentiment throughout the country that the power acquired by big business was undermining the foundations of democracy as well as restricting opportunity for small enterprise. In short, critics believed that the antitrust law should be strengthened. On the other hand, business leaders emphasized not only their own accomplishments in improving production but also the large area of uncertainty about the scope of governmental

authority in determining the boundaries of their decision-making power. With support from political leaders like former President Roosevelt, in 1912 some industrialists advocated the establishment of a government commission with power to define how the Sherman Act applied to specific business situations. Such a public agency, it was thought, might regulate prices, particularly those in a heavy industry like steel, where price competition was regarded as financially dangerous. Small business also hoped that a government commission would help its trade associations to stabilize competition in the sectors where small firms operated.

In response to these sometimes conflicting pressures, Congress in 1914 passed two statutes: the Clayton Act as an amendment to the Sherman Act and the Federal Trade Commission Act. The Clayton Act aimed to spell out the "rule of reason" by defining what constituted unreasonable restraint of trade. Certain practices—such as tying contracts, price discrimination, interlocking directorates, and even mergers—were prohibited, but only "where the effect [of these tactics] may be to substantially lessen competition or tend to create a monopoly." But there was no definition of "substantially" in the act. Thus, the power of the Clayton Act to police business relationships came to depend on administration by the executive branch and interpretation by the judiciary. Nevertheless, some held the hope that the law was a "sleeping giant" that might some day do battle with giant business.

The Federal Trade Commission Act established a commission; its members, appointed by the president, were given the power to investigate and to issue cease-and-desist orders, subject to judicial review. The law forcefully stated that "unfair methods of competition in commerce are hereby declared unlawful," reflecting a widespread assumption that giant corporations had gained their economic power through ruthless competition. But Congress did not define what constituted unfair competition, on the grounds that "there is no limit to human inventiveness in this field."[10] It became the task of the newly established Federal Trade Commission (FTC) to interpret the general rule.

During the first decade and a half of the twentieth century, the basis of a new relationship between business and government was developed. In the view of nineteenth-century businesspeople, government had no meaningful function in economic life unless called on by business to support specific efforts of the private sector. During that era, the workings of the competitive market protected society, to some extent at least, against the "fallout" from unrestrained economic individualism. When the structure of much of industry was altered from the competitive system of an earlier era, government regulation attempted to establish an element of social control over the economy. By 1914, business had to adjust to a new reality: Government would apply the antitrust laws not only to punish business for transgressions of what was regarded as the "public interest" but also to prevent business abuses. As Robert Wiebe describes it, executives of large corporations now had to accept "the government as a superior power with unquestioned rights to regulate business."[11]

Transition to Oligopoly

At the turn of the century, when the monopolistic combination of members of an industry appeared to be legal, many businesses regarded merger as a panacea to prevent expropriation of their property by the forces of competition. Industrialists often justified combinations as a device to achieve economies of scale, appealing to the national belief in the virtue of efficiency, even as they sometimes raised prices to increase their profit margins.

But not all combinations resulted in the cherished goal of high profits through elimination of competition. Some failed financially, especially when promoters had "watered the stock," or set an unreasonably high capitalization for the new corporation. In other cases, the unanticipated happened: the collapse of the market for the combination's products. For example, when the American Bicycle Company was formed in 1899, it controlled about two-thirds of its industry. Bicycles had constituted a great growth industry in the 1890s, but shortly after the combination's formation sales dropped abruptly as the market became saturated.

However, unusual success and high profit margins stemming from control of an industry sometimes attracted the competition of newcomers. The changing political and legal environment after 1900 made it impossible for the large combination to destroy its competitors and to "mop up" an industry, as Standard Oil and others had done in the 1880s and 1890s. The concern of the public and the response by government in effect imposed an upper limit, however ill defined, on the share of the market that any firm could control.

Successful challengers usually copied the leader's pattern of mass production, mass distribution, and a managerial hierarchy, thereby realizing the economies of scale and scope inherent in the new technology. Significantly, newcomers could concentrate their efforts on the most rapidly growing segments of an industry. Standard Oil, for instance, with large investments in kerosene refineries, found its share of the petroleum industry declining in the first decade of the twentieth century; other firms were bypassing the industry's "age of illumination" and moving directly into gasoline and industrial fuels. (Standard's control of U.S. refining capacity declined from 82 percent in 1899 to 64 percent on the eve of dissolution.) Dismemberment of Standard Oil in 1911, the result of its conviction under the Sherman Antitrust Act, served to accelerate this process.

What had emerged in mass production industries in 1914 was an industrial structure now familiar to us as oligopoly. Successful "new" firms in these areas in the early twentieth century were themselves large, they were vertically integrated, and they were small in number relative to the total business population. Where one firm had apparently established monopoly control of its market at some point during the combination movement, it usually found its dominance challenged. But this did not mean a return in these industries to the nineteenth-century pattern of many firms competing largely on a price basis.

Developments in the steel industry illustrate the kind of change taking place in mass-production sectors. At the time of its formation in 1901, the U.S. Steel Corporation controlled 44 percent of the industry's capacity and 66 percent of total steel production. In contrast to the aggressive pricing and investment policies of Andrew Carnegie, the early steel leader, Judge Elbert Gary and fellow managers believed that U.S. Steel had to build a reputation for good behavior toward competitors in order to avoid an antitrust suit. As the result of a policy of stable prices, which yielded high profit margins and dividends for stockholders, U.S. Steel in effect held an umbrella over the industry, allowing less efficient companies to remain in business and to expand their operations through acquisitions or internal growth. Most notable was U.S. Steel's failure to move aggressively into the most dynamic sectors of the steel market—those that provided material for the growing construction and transportation equipment industries. Gary's policies were successful to the extent that U.S. Steel was not convicted under the antitrust laws. At the same time, though, the giant of the industry lost market share. By the time of World War I, U.S. Steel accounted for just one-half of total production. (And by the 1930s, its share would further decline to just one-third of the industry.) But not all members of the steel industry benefited equally from U.S. Steel's "cooperative competition" that resulted in slower growth than was experienced by the industry and in narrowing profit margins. The eleven largest steel makers (including U.S. Steel) increased their share of the industry's capacity from 55 percent in 1904 to 63 percent in 1920, whereas U.S. Steel's share of capacity declined from 44 percent to 40 percent during those years. The other successful steel manufacturers, all of which were or became vertically integrated, gained ground by exploiting new processes, new products, and new sources of materials under aggressive entrepreneurial leadership (like that of Bethlehem's Charles Schwab, a former protégé of Carnegie).

Clearly, entry was not easy into industries characterized by mass production and mass distribution. The most important set of considerations centered around the substantial barriers to entry into oligopolistic sectors. Sometimes, the oligopolists controlled essential raw materials. In other cases, large manufacturers used patent controls to police their industries. More important as a barrier to entry was the organization by leading corporations of their own research and development facilities. As George Eastman explained: "If we can get out our improved goods every year, then nobody will be able to follow us and compete with us. The only way to compete with us will be [for competitors] to get out original goods the same as we do."[12]

In any event, newcomers seeking to enter industries characterized by oligopoly had to create not only large-scale manufacturing facilities but also distribution systems, purchasing organizations, and management structures to be able to compete effectively with established firms. An important oligopolistic tactic came to be product differentiation—the effort by a seller to use brand names, trademarks, and advertising to instill in consumers a preference for the

Table 12–5 *Largest U.S. Industrial Corporations Ranked by Assets, 1917*

Rank	Firm	Assets [$ million]
1	United States Steel Corp.	$2,449.5
2	Standard Oil Co. of New Jersey	574.1
3	Bethlehem Steel Corp.	381.5
4	Armour & Co.	314.1
5	Swift & Co.	306.3
6	Midvale Steel & Ordnance Co.	270.0
7	International Harvester Co.	264.7
8	E.I. du Pont de Nemours & Co.	263.3
9	United States Rubber Co.	257.5
10	Phelps Dodge Corp.	232.3
11	General Electric Co.	231.6
12	Anaconda Copper Corp.	225.8
13	American Smelting & Refining Co.	221.8
14	Standard Oil Co. of New York	204.3
15	Singer Manufacturing Co.	192.9
16	Ford Motor Co.	165.9
17	Westinghouse Electric & Manufacturing Co.	164.7
18	American Tobacco Co.	164.2
19	Jones & Laughlin Steel Co	159.6
20	Union Carbide & Carbon Corp.	155.9
21	Weyerhaeuser Timber Co.	153.2
22	B. F. Goodrich Co.	146.1
23	Central Leather Co.	145.3
24	Texas Co.	144.5
25	Pullman Co.	143.3

Source: Adapted from Alfred D. Chandler, Jr., *Scale and Scope: The Dynamics of Industrial Capitalism* (Cambridge: Harvard University Press, 1990), pp. 638–643.

seller's product over nearly identical products offered by others. (Table 12–5 lists the twenty-five largest manufacturing corporations in the United States by the time of World War I.)

Managerial Enterprise

The corporate revolution implied not only new industrial structures and changing relationships between business and government but also innovations in the machinery of decision making within the firm. Where ownership and management were separated, as they came to be in the large enterprise, honesty and efficiency could no longer be assumed. In the early history of the modern corporation, managers with little ownership interest saw nothing wrong in taking advantage of their positions as insiders to make private gains (e.g., as in selling supplies from companies they owned to companies they managed). Unscrupulous operators worked out a variety of ways to transfer corporate assets into their own pockets. During the last half of the nineteenth century, rules of conduct were worked out for managers of other people's property, stimulated by the growing awareness that an improvement in ethics contributed to the ability to attract capital to corporate enterprise—a practical application of Benjamin Franklin's dictum that "honesty is the best policy." While cooperation to advance the welfare of the company was expected of managers, competition for promotion within the hierarchy, on the basis of ability and merit, was assumed to stimulate the exercise of initiative, thereby overcoming the lack of direct economic incentives. For many individuals accustomed to the freedom of action characteristic of independent business, it was not easy to accept the discipline inherent in group effort and accountability to an organization.

In contrast to the one-person management and informal relationships characteristic of the small family firm, participation of many individuals in the making and carrying out of decisions in the large corporation required formalization of channels of communication and lines of authority. The problem was finding an appropriate structure that could be applied to the large manufacturing company. The pattern of organization earlier developed by the railroads was not especially well suited to the operation of the large industrial corporation because of its greater variety of activities carried on over a larger geographical area. While early combinations had improvised ways to delegate authority and share power, their successful functioning usually depended on personal leadership exerted by an unusually able entrepreneur rather than on the formally coordinated efforts of professional managers.

In the late nineteenth and early twentieth centuries, each large corporation was developing a unified structure of management through which to coordinate operations and allocate resources. The goal was to reorganize the facilities inherited from predecessor companies into departments, with each department manufacturing a different type of product or performing a specific function, such as sales, purchas-

ing, development, legal, or financial. At the same time, an executive committee composed of the president and the heads of major departments became the company's ruling body. Its jobs included appraising the performance of the departments, coordinating the flow of materials through the corporation's plants and warehouses, and planning the lines of future growth. Special attention was directed to improving accounting procedures in order to provide the information on which to base decisions.

Within only a quarter-century, large corporations had come to dominate a number of key manufacturing industries. By 1914, the evolution of rational bureaucratic structures made it possible for ordinary executives working in groups to manage these giant enterprises. The centralized administrative structure formed during the early history of big business, however, was but one stage in the evolution of modern managerial structures. By the 1920s, the continuing growth of giant enterprises made apparent the need for greater decentralization of corporate governance.

The Business System

The sudden appearance of big business caused widespread public concern in the late nineteenth and early twentieth centuries. However, the large enterprise appeared to be gaining ever-increasing acceptance in American society during the early years of the twentieth century. By 1900, business leaders were becoming more aware of the need to replace the old "public-be-damned" attitude with a more modern "public-be-pleased" posture. They were recognizing the merits of modern corporate public relations—especially that business executives should take into account in their decision making the advice of specialists in molding public attitudes toward their corporations.

By the time of World War I, some intellectuals were picturing the large business corporation as a socially desirable institution in that it represented a move away from the old order of individualism toward a new era of collectivism. More and more members of the old middle class of small business owners and farmers, convinced that the antitrust laws had imposed effective restraints on corporate power, found ways to accommodate themselves to big business. Perhaps the most important development of these years was the emergence of a new middle class that embraced a wide range of salaried occupations, including middle managers, engineers, salespeople, and eventually white-collar workers of all kinds. The growth of the large bureaucratic business corporation had indeed expanded the range of career opportunities, which in turn created satisfying work experiences and seemed to offer greater economic security than did the operation of a small firm.

Yet the rise of big business did not mean the extinction of small enterprise. There persisted a structure of small and medium-sized firms over which a layer of several hundred large corporations had become superimposed. In spite of the prophesies of doom pronounced on small-scale enterprise, the nonfarm business population (comprising mainly small firms) actually grew in the early years of the twentieth century at a slightly faster rate than the total population of the nation. New kinds of opportunities developed in trade and service. Even in manufacturing, alert entrepreneurs could find niches where a small firm could produce efficiently without direct competition from a giant enterprise. Although many observers stressed the importance of economic integration and large-scale production, some economists then and later, like Allyn A. Young in the 1920s, argued that "industrial differentiation has been and remains the type of change characteristically associated with the growth of production," pointing to "the increase in the diversification of intermediate products and of industries manufacturing special products or groups of products."[13] More capital was necessary for entry into many lines of business than had been the case in the mid-nineteenth century, but increased savings were available to finance the entry of entrepreneurs. In the same economic environment that encouraged the growth of the giant enterprise, small enterprises also multiplied in numbers.

Summary

The process of industrialization—the central element of modern economic growth—involved the widespread application of capital in the form of new technology to an abundance of natural resources, with an expanding market absorbing the ever-increasing output of goods. The age of wood gave way to the age of iron and then, with the invention of the Bessemer process, to the age of steel. Machinery came into use in more and more manufacturing processes, with machine tools playing a key role in the transmission of the technology of mass production. The latter part of the nineteenth century was the age of steam generated by coal; the use of electric power and petroleum spread rapidly through industry in the early decades of the twentieth century.

Accompanying the revolution in production was one in organization—the rise of big business. In order to take full advantage of the economies of scale and scope contained in many of the new technologies, entrepreneurs not only created large production facilities but also integrated vertically—forward by developing marketing channels and backward toward sources of materials. In addition, industrialists organized structures of management to administer and coordinate their giant enterprises. With the growth of the large corporation there emerged a new relationship between business and government. By 1914, the principle of government regulation of corporate behavior was firmly established even though public policy, as embodied in the antitrust laws, had not yet drawn the precise boundaries of legally permissible action by the large corporation. The structure that emerged from the experience of business fitted neither of the long-familiar models of competition and monopoly. Rather, oligopoly had come to characterize a number of key industries—the dominance of a set of economic activities by a relatively few large corporations that were usually vertically integrated. Although the giant corporation dominated a number of key industries, there still existed a structure of small and medium-sized firms, as the total nonfarm business population continued to grow by capitalizing on new opportunities in trade, service, and manufacturing.

Endnotes

1. Edwin Frickey, *Production in the United States, 1860–1914* (Cambridge: Harvard University Press, 1947), p. 54. Robert Gallman, "Commodity Output," in *Trends in the American Economy in the Nineteenth Century* (Princeton: Princeton University Press, 1960), p. 43.

2. Quoted in Donald Hoke, "British and American Horology: Time to Test Factor-Substitution Models," *Journal of Economic History,* 47 (1987): 327.

3. Gavin Wright, "The Origins of American Industrial Success, 1879–1940," *American Economic Review,* 80 (1990): 660, 666.

4. H. F. L. Orcutt, "Machine Shop Management in Europe and America." *Engineering Magazine,* 16 (1899).

5. Nathan Rosenberg, *Technology and American Economic Growth* (New York: Harper & Row, 1972), p. 98.

6. Henry Ford, "Mass Production," *Encyclopedia Britannica.* 22nd ed. Quoted in Rosenberg, *Technology and American Economic Growth,* pp. 112–113n.

7. The first evaluation is made by Chester M. Destler, "Entrepreneurial Leadership Among the 'Robber Barons': The Trial Balance," *Journal of Economic History,* suppl. 6 (1946): 28. An example of the second perspective is Allan Nevins, *Study in Power: John D. Rockefeller,* 2 vols. (New York: Scribner's, 1953).

8. Alfred D. Chandler, Jr., *Scale and Scope: The Dynamics of Industrial Capitalism* (Cambridge: Harvard University Press, 1990).

9. David A. Wells, *Recent Economic Changes* (New York: Appleton, 1889), p. 71.

10. Quoted in William Letwin, *Law and Economic Policy in America* (New York: Random House, 1965), p. 277.

11. Robert H. Wiebe, "The House of Morgan and the Executive, 1905–1913," *American Historical Review,* 65 (1959): 60.

12. Quoted in Alfred D. Chandler, Jr., *Scale and Scope: The Dynamics of Industrial Capitalism* (Cambridge: Harvard University Press, 1990), p. 228.

13. Allyn A. Young, "Increasing Returns and Economic Progress," *Economic Journal,* 38 (1928): 537.

Suggested Readings

Victor S. Clark, *History of Manufactures in the United States*, vols. 2 (1860–1893) and 3 (1893–1928) (New York: Peter Smith, 1949) is still the most comprehensive historical account of major industries in the United States. A concise analysis of industrial growth in the nineteenth and early twentieth centuries is contained in Chapter 12 of Lance E. Davis et al, *American Economic Growth: An Economist's History of the United States* (New York: Harper & Row, 1972). Readers may also consult the appropriate chapters in Harold F. Williamson, ed., *The Growth of the American Economy*, 2d ed. (Englewood Cliffs, N.J.: Prentice-Hall, 1951). Nathan Rosenberg, *Technology and American Economic Growth* (New York: Harper & Row, 1972) is the starting point for those interested in the history of technology. Gavin Wright, "The Origins of American Industrial Success, 1879–1940," *American Economic Review*, 80 (1990) focuses on the relationship between technology and the resource base. David C. Mowery and Nathan Rosenberg, *Technology and the Pursuit of Economic Growth* (New York: Cambridge University Press, 1989) explores the relationship between basic science and technology innovation. Paul Uselding, "Studies of Technology in Economic History," *Research in Economic History*, suppl. 1 (1977) reviews an extensive body of literature. David A. Hounshell, *From the American System to Mass Production, 1800–1932: The Development of Manufacturing Technology in the United States* (Baltimore: Johns Hopkins University Press, 1984) offers a fresh interpretation of the elements of American mass production. Thomas P. Hughes, *Networks of Power Electrification in Western Society, 1880–1930* (Baltimore: Johns Hopkins University Press, 1983) analyzes the evolution of electric supply systems in the United States, Germany, and Britain.

Material in Harvey S. Perloff, Edgar S. Dunn, Jr., Eric E. Lampard, and Richard F. Muth, *Regions, Resources and Economic Growth* (Baltimore: Johns Hopkins Press, 1960) is basic to an understanding of the regional dimension of industrial growth. This pioneering work is well supplemented by Allan R. Pred, *The Spatial Dynamics of U.S. Urban-Industrial Growth, 1800–1914* (Cambridge: M.I.T. Press, 1966); Edgar S. Dunn, Jr., *The Development of the U.S. Urban System* (Baltimore: Johns Hopkins Press, 1980); Gavin Wright, *Old South, New South: Revolutions in the Southern Economy Since the Civil War* (New York: Basic Books, 1986); and Albert W. Niemi, *State and Regional Patterns in American Manufacturing, 1860–1900* (Westport, Conn, Greenwood Press, 1974), the last named a statistical summary.

The following works present case studies of the growth of individual industries, demonstrating the changing relationships among technology, the market, and industrial structure: Harold F. Williamson and Arnold R. Daum, *The American Petroleum Industry: The Age of Illumination, 1859–1899* (Evanston: Northwestern University Press, 1963); Harold F. Williamson et al, *The American Petroleum Industry: The Age of Energy, 1899–1959* (Evanston: Northwestern University Press, 1963); Peter Temin, *Iron and Steel in Nineteenth-Century America: An Economic Inquiry* (Cambridge: M.I.T. Press, 1964); Gertrude G. Schroeder, *The Growth of Major Steel Companies, 1900–1950* (Baltimore: Johns Hopkins Press, 1953); John N. Ingham, *Making Iron and Steel: Independent Mills in Pittsburgh, 1820–1920* (Columbus: Ohio State University Press, 1991); Paul F. McGouldrick, *New England Textiles in the Nineteenth Century: Profits and Investment* (Cambridge: Harvard University Press, 1968); Philip Scranton, *Proprietary Capitalism: The Textile Manufacture at Philadelphia,*

1800–1885 (New York: Cambridge University Press, 1984); Philip Scranton, *Figured Tapestry: Production, Markets, and Power in Philadelphia Textiles, 1885–1941* (New York: Cambridge University Press, 1989); and Reese V. Jenkins, *Images and Enterprise: Technology and the American Photographic Industry, 1839 to 1925* (Baltimore: Johns Hopkins University Press, 1975).

The most comprehensive history of the large corporate sector is Alfred D. Chandler, Jr., *The Visible Hand: The Managerial Revolution in American Business* (Cambridge: Harvard University Press, 1977). Chandler's *Scale and Scope: The Dynamics of Industrial Capitalism* (Cambridge: Harvard University Press, 1990) discusses corporate developments in Great Britain and Germany as well as in the United States. Thomas C. Cochran, *American Business in the Twentieth Century* (Cambridge: Harvard University Press, 1972) relates the growth of large-scale enterprise to the business system of which it was a part. Glenn Porter, *The Rise of Big Business* (Arlington Heights, Il: AHM Publishing Co., 1973) serves as a guide to the literature in this area. Matthew Josephson, *The Robber Barons: The Great American Capitalists, 1861–1901* (New York: Harcourt, Brace, 1934) is a colorful account whose title reveals its bias. On the other hand, the following accounts emphasize the constructive achievements of their subjects: Ralph W. Hidy and Muriel E. Hidy, *Pioneering in Big Business, 1882–1911 [History of Standard Oil Company (New Jersey)]* (New York: Harper & Brothers, 1955); Joseph F. Wall, *Andrew Carnegie* (New York: Oxford University Press, 1970); Harold C. Livesay, *Andrew Carnegie and the Rise of Big Business* (Boston: Little, Brown, 1975); Robert N. Hessen, *Steel Titan: The Life of Charles W. Schwab* (New York: Oxford University Press, 1975). Harold C. Livesay, *American Made: Men Who Shaped the American Economy* (Boston: Little, Brown, 1979) provides good reading about the careers of several of the business leaders of this period. Glenn Porter and Harold C. Livesay, *Merchants and Man-* *ufacturers: Studies in the Changing Structure of 19th Century Marketing* (Baltimore: Johns Hopkins University Press, 1971) discusses the role of marketing in the growth of large manufacturing firms. Naomi R. Lamoreaux, *The Great Merger Movement in American Business, 1895–1904* (New York: Cambridge University Press, 1985) contains a detailed analysis; but Ralph L. Nelson, *Merger Movements in American Industry, 1895–1916* (Princeton: Princeton University Press, 1959) may also be usefully consulted. Arthur S. Dewing, *Corporate Promotions and Reorganizations* (Cambridge: Harvard University Press, 1914) is notable for its case studies of unsuccessful combinations. Barry E. Supple, ed., *The Rise of Big Business* (Brookfield, Vt: Edward Elgar Publishing Co., 1992) contains a collection of seminal journal articles on this topic.

William Letwin, *Law and Economic Policy in America* (New York: Random House, 1965) and Hans B. Thorelli, *The Federal Antitrust Policy: Origination of an American Tradition* (London: George Allen & Unwin, 1954) trace the early history of efforts to regulate big business. Alfred S. Eichner, *The Emergence of Oligopoly: Sugar Refining as a Case Study* (Baltimore: Johns Hopkins Press, 1969) and Charles W. McCurdy, "The *Knight* Sugar Decision of 1895 and the Modernization of American Corporation Law, 1869–1903," *Business History Review*, 53 (1979) point to the importance of the Knight case from the economic and legal perspectives, respectively. Gabriel Kolko, *The Triumph of Conservatism: A Reinterpretation of American History, 1900–1916* (Glencoe: Free Press, 1963); Martin J. Sklar, *The Corporate Reconstruction of American Capitalism, 1890–1916* (New York: Cambridge University Press, 1988), and Robert H. Wiebe, *Businessmen and Reform: A Study of the Progressive Movement* (Cambridge: Harvard University Press, 1962) discuss, from different perspectives, the politics of business regulation in the early twentieth century. For a penetrating study of the efforts of state governments to impose legal obstacles to the expansion of giant corporations, see Charles W. McCurdy, "American Law and the Marketing Structure of the Large Corporation, 1875–1890," *Journal of Economic History*, 38 (1978). Thomas K. McCraw and Forest Reinhardt, "Losing to Win: U.S. Steel's Pricing, Investment Decisions, and Market Share, 1901–1938," *Journal of Economic History*, 49 (1989) is a valuable study of the business behavior of this giant corporation. The first part of Louis Galambos and Joseph Pratt, *The Rise of the Corporate Commonwealth: United States Business and Public Policy in the Twentieth Century* (New York: Basic Books, 1988) provides a useful survey of business–government relations during this period. Giles H. Burgess, Jr., ed., *Antitrust and Regulation* (Brookfield, Vt: Edward Elgar Publishing Co., 1991) is a collection of the most important journal literature dealing with government regulation of business.

Louis Galambos, *The Public Image of Big Business in America, 1880–1940: A Quantitative Study in Social Image* (Baltimore: Johns Hopkins University Press, 1975) and James Gilbert, *Designing the Industrial State: The Intellectual Pursuit of Collectivism in America, 1880–1940* (Chicago: Quadrangle Books, 1972) discuss the response to big business of middle-class groups and intellectuals, respectively. Olivier Zunz, *Making America Corporate, 1870–1920* (Chicago: University of Chicago Press, 1990) traces the formation of a new middle class of corporate bureaucrats and the work culture that they created. On the experience of small business during the rise of the large corporation, see Mansel G. Blackford, *A History of Small Business in America* (New York: Twayne Publishers, 1991), and several of the essays in Stuart W. Bruchey, ed., *Small Business in American Life* (New York: Columbia University Press, 1980).

Chapter 13

Labor in the Industrializing Society

As THE UNITED STATES DEVELOPED INTO THE world's leading industrial nation between the mid-nineteenth and early twentieth centuries, the American labor force became caught up in many of the stresses and strains as well as the benefits of economic modernization. In terms of size, the U.S. labor force nearly quadrupled between 1860 and 1920, growing even more rapidly than the nation's population. In addition, the functional composition of the labor force changed as it shifted (in relative terms) away from agriculture and toward manufacturing. This change implied a locational shift of work (again, in relative terms) from the countryside and small towns to urban industrial centers.

Both the growing size and changing composition of the labor force in these decades were responses to employment opportunities created by industrialization. And a high degree of labor mobility made it possible for workers to take advantage of these opportunities. As new resources, industries, and markets were opened up by the driving forces of technological change and improved transportation, emerging wage and income differentials attracted workers away from less remunerative occupations and locations. In addition, millions of foreign workers migrated to America to take advantage of the relatively more attractive job opportunities that were developing in the United States. American wage levels and living standards were not only higher than anywhere else in the world, they were also increasing more rapidly than in most other countries.

Although the rapidity of change in the American economy created new opportunities, it also led to many new problems for the working population. At the heart of most of these problems were fundamental changes in the nature of work. In 1860, the United States was predominantly a nation of farmers and self-employed workers whose work habits, life-styles, and decisions were marked by a high degree of independence. By 1914, however, it had become a highly industrialized, urbanized nation in which the majority of workers were employees who depended on their employers—often large, impersonal businesses and corporations—for their livelihoods. Many American workers in 1914 had far less control over the types of jobs available and the conditions of work—wages, hours, security, safety, and so on—than workers of earlier generations had enjoyed.

To cope with these new problems and increase their bargaining power, workers began to join organizations that sought to advance their interests. These organizations adopted a wide range of approaches and tactics, which, in turn, were met by a wide range of responses from business and government—some favorable to labor and others unfavorable. Although greater recognition of organized labor's rights and responsibilities took decades to achieve, by the time of World War I national labor organizations were an accepted part of American economic life.

Immigration and the Size of the Labor Force

Between the Civil War and World War I, the American economy expanded at a faster rate than in any other period of comparable length in its entire history. This growth was the result of multiple factors, including abundant quantities of land and other natural resources and technological breakthroughs across a wide range of productive activities, as well as the rapid growth of the nation's labor force. Between 1860 and 1920, the population of the United States grew at a compound rate of 2 percent per year, while the labor force increased even more rapidly at 2.2 percent per year (see Table 13–1). Thus, for the population as a whole, the labor force participation rate—that is, the percentage of all Americans who

Table 13–1   *Population, Labor Force, and Participation Rate, 1860–1920*

Year	Population (in millions)	Labor Force (in millions)	Participation Rate (percent)
1860	31.5	11.1	35%
1870	39.9	12.9	32
1880	50.3	17.4	35
1890	63.1	23.3	37
1900	76.1	29.1	38
1910	92.4	37.5	41
1920	106.5	41.6	39

SOURCES: Population: U.S. Bureau of the Census, *Historical Statistics of the United States, Colonial Times to 1957* (Washington, D.C.: GPO, 1960), series A2, p. 7; Labor Force: Stanley Lebergott, "Labor Force and Employment, 1800–1960," In National Bureau of Economic Research, *Output, Employment, and Productivity in the United States After 1800* (New York: National Bureau of Economic Research, 1966), table 1, p. 118; Participation Rate: Labor force divided by population.

were in the labor force—rose over the entire period, with an especially marked expansion between 1870 and 1910.

Throughout most of American history, increases in population and the labor force have come primarily from natural increase—that is, from the excess of births over deaths of people living in the United States. This was true for the period from 1860 to 1920, when in every decade except 1901 to 1910 natural increase accounted for 60 percent to 72 percent of the population growth. But during these decades there was also another important factor at work: immigration. The flow of foreign-born immigrants to the United States assumed massive proportions during this period and had both immediate and long-run impacts on the nation's economy. Between 1861 and 1890, some 11.3 million immigrants arrived, mainly from the United Kingdom, Germany, and the Scandinavian countries. Then, from 1890 to 1920, another 18.2 million immigrants came, mostly from southern and eastern European

countries such as Italy, Austria-Hungary, and Russia (see Figure 13–1).

Decisions by foreigners to emigrate to the United States were based on economic conditions both in this country and in the lands of their birth. The pull of economic opportunities in the United States is evident in the time pattern of immigrant arrivals, which tended to increase during periods of U.S. prosperity and decrease during and after depressions. But foreign economic conditions also influenced the flow of migration. As the Industrial Revolution spread across Europe during the nineteenth century, it was accompanied by large increases in European populations. In many European countries, though, the initially high rates of industrial growth were not sustained and the resulting shortage of jobs and economic hardships prompted many Europeans to embark for America, the land of opportunity. Modern-day scholars believe that this sequence of events largely accounts for the changing origins of immigrants arriving in America during this period. Northern and western Europeans were predominant among immigrants before about 1890, whereas southern and eastern European nationality groups predominated after that date.

Although about one-third of the 29.5 million immigrants who came to the United States between 1860 and 1920 eventually returned to Europe, the 20 million who remained constituted over one-fourth of the total increase in the American population during this period. Whether one considers the gross number of immigrants who came or the net number who stayed, such large accretions to the U.S. population from overseas had important economic effects. Thus, it is highly probable that immigration made a positive contribution to the rate of economic growth per capita if for no other reason than that the structure of the immigrant population was very different from that of the native population. More than one-half of the immigrants were males between the ages of

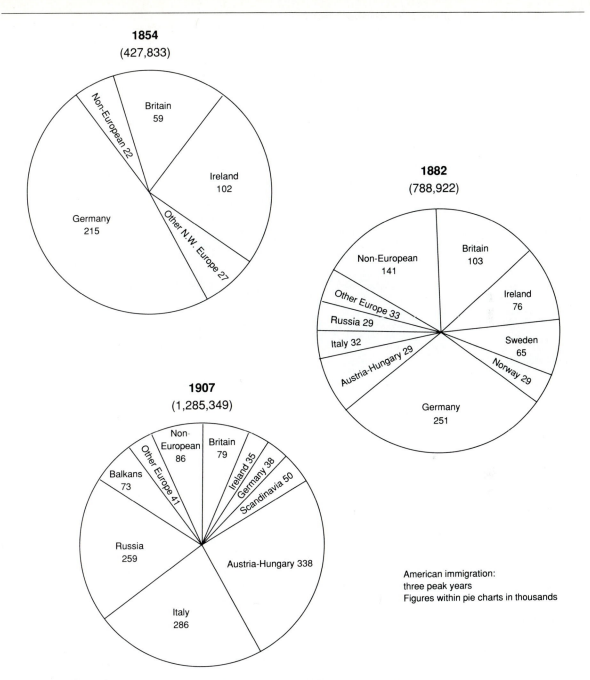

1854
(427,833)

Non-European 22
Britain 59
Ireland 102
Other N.W. Europe 27
Germany 215

1882
(788,922)

Non-European 141
Britain 103
Other Europe 33
Ireland 76
Russia 29
Italy 32
Sweden 65
Austria-Hungary 29
Norway 29
Germany 251

1907
(1,285,349)

Non-European 86
Britain 79
Other Europe 41
Ireland 35
Germany 38
Balkans 73
Scandinavia 50
Russia 259
Austria-Hungary 338
Italy 286

American immigration:
three peak years
Figures within pie charts in thousands

Figure 13–1 *Changing European Sources of American Immigration: Three Peak Years.*
Source: Adapted from Philip Taylor, *The Distant Magnet: European Emigration to the U.S.A.* (New York: Harper & Row, 1971), p. 63.

Immigrants from Europe.   These immigrants, arriving in New York in 1906, were among the many millions of Europeans who sought jobs and a better economic future in America. (The Library of Congress [LC-USZ62-11202])

fourteen and forty-four—a prime working-age group. However, the very young, the very old, and females—all groups less likely to work at the time—were underrepresented among immigrants in comparison with the native population. Hence, the rise in immigration during this period was likely an important reason for the rise in labor force participation rates noted earlier (refer again to Table 13–1). And, of course, the increase in labor force participation probably tended to raise the level and growth of per capita income.

Another related aspect of the immigrant contribution to the American economy is that the immigrants were raised and trained or educated in their countries of origin, thereby representing a net addition to the stock of human capital in the United States. If Americans had sought to have the same population without

allowing immigration, they would have had to devote vast additional resources to child rearing and education.

Immigrants came from, and entered into, all walks of life—from farming and the professions to highly skilled industrial work and domestic service. They furnished a large and continuous flow of workers, especially for the rapidly growing heavy industries as well as for textiles, clothing, mining, meat packing, and construction. Various ethnic groups were quite important in the labor forces of particular industries; for example, the Irish were leaders in heavy construction, Italians in the building trades, and Jews in the clothing industry. In agriculture, certain groups, notably the Italians and Japanese, drew on their previous experience to teach intensive farming methods to Americans. Individual immigrant inventors also made economically important contributions to major industries. In electricity, for example, the German inventor Charles Steinmetz was awarded some two hundred patents for electromagnetic ideas and devices. Similarly, Nikola Tesla, a Serbian, invented devices that made possible the long-distance telephone. All of the immigrant inventors came to America between the ages of fourteen and twenty-eight.

At one time, historians argued that the economic position of immigrants in America between 1860 and 1920 was substantially inferior to that of native workers; some go so far as to maintain that immigrants—particularly the "new" immigrants from southern and eastern Europe who arrived between 1890 and 1914—were grievously exploited both as workers and as consumers. More recent research, however, demonstrates that, although each new immigrant group tended to come in at the bottom of the economic ladder, as they acquired literacy, fluency in English, and other skills, their earnings rose to equal or nearly equal those of the native-born and the "old" immigrants from northern and western Europe. This does not mean that the "new" immigrants did not experience great hardships in finding employment, in locating places to live, or in avoiding discrimination in employment opportunities and job security. What it does mean, however, is that the old stereotype of the immigrant living on subsistence wages and with no opportunity to escape poverty is unfounded in light of recent findings. Immigrants and immigrant groups differed in social origin and economic background, but they were quite mobile, economically and socially, after they reached this country.[1]

Despite the undeniable contributions of immigrants to the American economy and to the enrichment of American life, they encountered much resentment from native-born Americans and "older" immigrant workers who, fearing the effects of cheap, abundant immigrant labor

on their own wages, opposed unlimited immigration. The Chinese were the first target of the movement to limit immigration. In 1882, Congress passed the Chinese Exclusion Act prohibiting the immigration of Chinese for ten years, and in 1902 this prohibition was made permanent. Then, in 1885, the Knights of Labor (a labor organization discussed in more detail later in the chapter) persuaded Congress to prohibit the importation of workers under contract, a practice that had been legalized as an emergency measure during the Civil War. Later, in an effort to stem the flow of Japanese labor to the United States that had begun in the 1890s, the United States and Japan in 1907 and 1908 reached an accord whereby Japan agreed to stop the emigration of some of its unskilled workers. Finally, in 1917, opponents of the "new" immigration succeeded in getting Congress to pass, over President Woodrow Wilson's veto, an act requiring a literacy test for every immigrant admitted to the United States. A few years later, quota laws ended the free flow of immigrants that for a century had been regarded as one of the strengths of the American democratic and economic system.

Labor Mobility Within the United States

The same economic forces that led overseas immigrants to the United States—greater job opportunities—also caused many American workers to move into different occupations and geographic areas. Between 1860 and 1920, the most important source of new jobs was the rapidly growing manufacturing sector. As Figure 13–2 demonstrates, in 1860 there were almost four workers in agriculture for every one in manufacturing; as late as 1900, agricultural workers still outnumbered workers in manufacturing by a ratio of two to one. By 1920, however, manufacturing had surpassed agriculture as the largest employment sector.

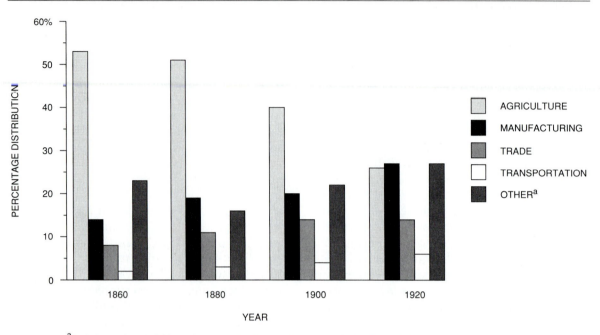

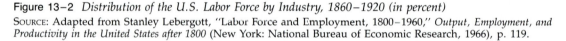

ᵃ Includes workers in fishing, mining, construction, professions, and domestic and other services.

Figure 13-2 *Distribution of the U.S. Labor Force by Industry, 1860–1920 (in percent)*
Source: Adapted from Stanley Lebergott, "Labor Force and Employment, 1800–1960," *Output, Employment, and Productivity in the United States after 1800* (New York: National Bureau of Economic Research, 1966), p. 119.

Other important developments during the period of 1860 to 1920 occurred in the trade and transportation sectors, which doubled their combined share of the labor force. The centers of American manufacturing and trade were in the cities of the Northeast and Great Lakes. Immigrants and domestic migrants settled in these centers in such large numbers that the urban proportion of the total population increased from 20 percent in 1860 to 51 percent in 1920.

One aspect of domestic labor mobility during this period, which would become even more significant after 1917, was the start of migration of African-Americans out of the South. At the outbreak of the Civil War, 92 percent of the black population lived in the South, and most of them were slaves working on planta-

tions or farms. By 1900, the proportion was still 90 percent. However, there were many reasons for African-Americans to want to leave the South, including low pay for farm labor, dissatisfaction with the sharecropping system, and racial discrimination in education, housing, voting rights, and justice. In these respects, black migration was similar to overseas migration: Both were inspired in part by unsatisfactory economic and social conditions at home. But the attraction of job opportunities outside the South was probably more important for blacks. Prior to World War I, most black migration had been to the West and Southwest, where agriculture was expanding and racial discrimination was somewhat less severe than in the older parts of the South. The North attracted relatively few black migrants from the South before World War I—that is, as long as the flow of unskilled immigrants was sufficient to satisfy the demand for low-skilled employment. But, as discussed in Chapter 17, the outbreak of World War I sharply cut down on the flow of unskilled, foreign-born workers to the United States at a time when the demand for labor increased because of war production. Thus began the Great Migration of large numbers of African-Americans from the rural South to the urban North, so that by the 1970s the black population of the United States was about evenly divided between the South and the rest of the country.

Although the centers of industry that attracted the new immigrants from overseas and the rest of the country were for the most part in the northeastern quadrant of the United States, the South also began to industrialize during the late nineteenth and early twentieth centuries. Southern industrial development was often characterized by the establishment of a paternalistic system of mill villages—reminiscent of the early textile industry in New England—where poor southern white farmers settled as a permanent working class. After 1900, however, a number of predominantly industrial cities—for example, Birmingham, Alabama (iron and steel); Greenville, South Carolina (textiles); and Gastonia (textiles) and Durham and Winston-Salem (tobacco), North Carolina—attracted large numbers of migrants from the countryside. But racism limited the opportunities for African-Americans in southern industry, and the presence of many low-skilled white workers in the South tended to discourage foreign-born immigrants from locating there.

Women in the Labor Force

Expanding employment opportunities associated with the shift in the nation's economic base from agriculture to manufacturing and service brought more women into the labor force during the late nineteenth and early twentieth centuries. Over the half-century after 1870, the number of female gainful workers grew by 4.7 times. In 1870, about one in seven females over the age of fourteen were gainful workers; fifty years later, almost one in four were counted as gainful workers.

In terms of marital status, there existed significant differences in the female labor participation rate. In 1890, the rates for single women (over the age of fourteen) and married women were 40.5 percent and 12.5 percent, respectively.[2] Since the "cult of domesticity" that then prevailed in American society dictated that the primary role of the wife was caring for children and maintaining the home, married women did not work outside of the home unless their husbands were incapacitated or otherwise unable to earn an income to support the family. This custom, widely held by working-class as well as middle-class families, was reinforced by the so-called "marriage bar"—formal policies, adopted by many business corporations and government agencies (especially school boards) in the late nineteenth and early twentieth centuries, that proscribed the hiring of married women and the retention of existing female employees when they married. Race was also an important determinant of female participation in the labor force. White women (both married and single) recorded in 1890 a labor participation rate of 16.3 percent, in contrast to 39.7 percent for nonwhite females. Three decades later, there were still substantial disparities in the labor participation rate between single and married women as well as between white and nonwhite females.

While some women workers could be found in almost all walks of life, the vast majority of female workers were confined to relatively few occupations (see Figure 13–3). In the traditional, agricultural, family enterprise, the woman's role as homemaker had been clearly

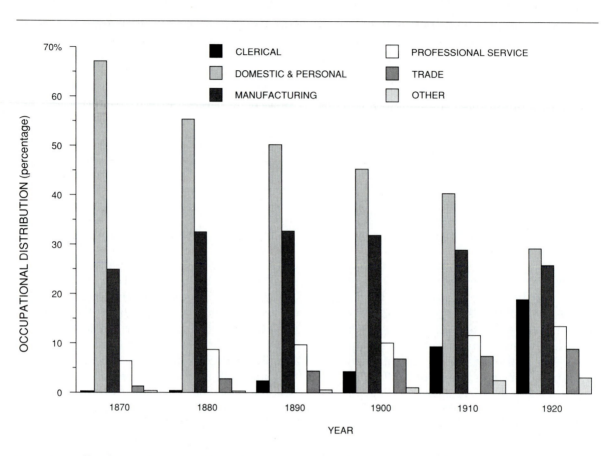

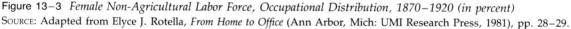

Figure 13–3 *Female Non-Agricultural Labor Force, Occupational Distribution, 1870–1920 (in percent)*
SOURCE: Adapted from Elyce J. Rotella, *From Home to Office* (Ann Arbor, Mich: UMI Research Press, 1981), pp. 28–29.

defined. Thus, it is not surprising that in 1870 two-thirds of all female gainful workers were employed in domestic and personal service, where they performed the homemaking role in other people's households. Despite the efforts of writers of the day to portray domestic service as the ideal form of preparation for a lifelong career as wife-homemaker, most young women regarded these unskilled, low-paying jobs as demeaning. When alternative opportunities developed for white women, their employment in domestic service declined over the next fifty years. However, the number of black

women in domestic service increased, as they shifted out of agriculture into this sector. A related activity of women during these years, particularly for married white women, was to take in roomers and boarders. There was much demand for these services in urban areas because many migrants from the countryside and overseas were unmarried males in need of housing.

Professional service accounted for 6.4 percent of the female labor force in 1870. School teachers accounted for 90 percent of this category. Despite the low pay, teaching was socially acceptable to middle-class families. Only 2.8 percent of female professional workers were physicians or surgeons in 1880, and there were only two hundred women lawyers in the entire United States a decade later. Many medical and law schools refused admission to women until well into the twentieth century. A few women pursued careers in the theater, music, and art; more achieved success as writers, particularly of fiction and nonfiction for the growing female middle-class market. Professional service grew to account for 13.6 percent of the female nonagricultural labor force by 1920, reflecting primarily an increase in the number of teachers due to the expansion of public education. There were also growing numbers of female nurses, librarians, and social workers, other professions that were considered acceptable for women.

The early nineteenth-century introduction of power machinery into industry gave large numbers of unskilled women with little formal education the opportunity to seek paid employment outside of the home. Although factory work was usually arduous, it allowed for more dignity than did domestic service; it also generally paid somewhat better. Manufacturing accounted for about one-quarter of all female gainful workers in 1870, slowly growing to about one-third in 1890 before declining to its earlier level of one-quarter in 1920. However, black women did not share this occupational experience; most of them were located in the South, the least industrialized region of the country. In 1890, only 6.4 percent of nonwhite female gainful workers were employed in manufacturing; there was little change in this percentage until after World War II.

About 70 percent of all female industrial workers in 1890 worked in just two industries—textiles and apparel—where they constituted 41 percent and 60 percent of the work force, respectively. By contrast, few or no women worked in a number of other industries, including primary metals, machinery,

lumber and wood, and transportation. Physical strength was a prerequisite for some of these industries or it had been at an earlier time; others required long training periods or formal apprenticeships from which females were barred, sometimes by union rules. However, men were now doing some kinds of jobs, such as baking and cheese making, that earlier had been considered women's work. In any event, an "aura of gender" came to characterize predominantly male occupations, with the development of a rhetoric that rationalized the exclusion of women from "men's work." Continuing technological change in the form of mechanization and specialization created new areas of employment for unskilled women in the late nineteenth and early twentieth centuries, such as making small metal parts, paper boxes, and a variety of other products. While broadening the range of industrial employment open to women, these jobs were likely to become categorized as female work, thereby helping to maintain in industry a high level of occupational segregation by gender. As it had been since the beginning of industrialization, most women continued to be concentrated in low-paying occupations that afforded little opportunity for advancement. Some contemporaries argued that women's lack of skills and their relatively short period of employment (typically, five to seven years prior to marriage) seemed to justify the assignment of the predominantly young and single female industrial labor force to tedious, low-paying jobs. However, one contemporary observer, Helen Sumner, pointed to the circularity of that argument: "In most cases, probably, woman's expectation of marriage is responsible for her lack of skill, but in some instances, doubtless, her enforced lack of skill is responsible for her longing for marriage as a relief from intolerable drudgery."[3]

The emergence of mass retailing in the decades after the Civil War provided a set of new employment opportunities for women (see

Chapter 16). The number of female sales clerks in department stores, chain stores, and other retail firms in the United States increased from just nine thousand in 1870 to over half a million in 1920. For many reasons, sales work appeared to be more attractive than factory labor or domestic service, especially to young women with limited education and little training. Generally, female store clerks earned less than male store clerks but more than their female counterparts in factory or service work, though the experience of women varied significantly among the different types of retailers. Earnings were significantly higher for the "Cinderella of occupations," the department store clerk, than for women working in five-and-ten-cent stores. Sales clerks experienced less seasonal and cyclical fluctuation in employment, though steady work for full-time employees was made possible by the practice of employing large numbers of part-time clerks to absorb the shocks of changes in the level of business. Retailers, especially the department stores, were more likely than were industrial companies to offer fringe benefits to their female employees during this period. There was generally a greater possibility of increasing one's salary as selling experience was gained, and, in some department stores, the potential of promotion to the position of buyer or floor-walker. A few firms, such as R. H. Macy of New York, offered almost unprecedented opportunities for women to advance to senior managerial positions.

The Emergence of the Clerical Sector

It was the development of white-collar clerical work from 1870 to 1920 that most dramatically altered the long-run employment picture for women. The growth of large industrial corporations, banks, insurance companies, and other kinds of business resulted in many more transactions, much more communication, and larger numbers of customers and suppliers to be serviced than could be handled by the traditional small office with its simple tools. Breaking the resulting paper bottleneck required technological and organizational innovations that amounted to a transformation of office work.

The key innovation was the typewriter, introduced in 1874 and advertised by its manufacturer as a device by which "one person can do the work of two, and in some kinds of work three to five."[4] The use of the typewriter spread rapidly and was followed during the next few decades by many other types of office equipment, including accounting and calculating devices. The new office machines not only mechanized clerical work but also made it possible to standardize tasks into routine operations. The office thus grew larger and more complex; in short, it became more like a factory.

At the same time, growing numbers of young women with an urban, middle-class background and a secondary education were beginning to seek employment opportunities. While employers considered these young women, without dependents, a source of low-cost labor, the women viewed the wages and working conditions associated with office work as better than those available in retail sales. The necessary training in basic skills quickly became widely available, at first through private commercial colleges and later in commercial courses given in public high schools. The earnings differential was sufficiently great to encourage families to invest in their daughters' education rather than to send them to work in retail stores.

From 1870 to 1920, the clerical labor force grew from about 74,000 to over 2.8 million—an increase of thirty-eight times. Female employment in the sector advanced from fewer than 2,000 to almost 1.4 million, constituting nearly one-half of the total persons engaged in clerical work. Almost one in five women in the nonagricultural labor force in 1920 worked in the office.

Dictaphone and Stenography Class, 1906.   High schools in major cities across the country, like this one in New York City, prepared students, mostly female, for work in the rapidly growing clerical sector. (Bryon Collection, Museum of the City of New York)

Women were performing a function that had once been an exclusive male preserve; however, because of the transformation of clerical work that had taken place, they were not replacing men. Only a part of the clerical function was to be performed by women. The office turned out to be just as segregated by gender as the factory, but in a somewhat different way. Men continued to play an important role in the office in jobs that were managerial and thus considered to be stepping stones to advancement. From these positions women were barred by personnel policies. Men were barred from the occupations that had been designed for women, like typing and filing—low-paying, routine, mechanized jobs. (For example, in 1920, about 40 percent of all female clerical workers were typists and stenographers, compared to just 3.5 percent of male clerical workers.) Because women as a

group were presumed to remain in the labor force for only a relatively short period of time (that is, until they married), the occupations into which they were channeled afforded only limited opportunities for advancement. While the difference in starting salaries, between unmarried male and female clerical workers was negligible, given education and prior work experience, the gender gap widened significantly in favor of the male with subsequent years of employment. Men and women began careers in clerical work with similar skills, but because men were placed on different tracks, their earnings rose more sharply. Many young females perceived employment in the office as only a temporary way station between completion of high school and marriage and may have been satisfied with jobs that carried little responsibility. But the women who suffered economically as a result of this form of discrimination were those seeking a lifetime career in an occupation that provided a ladder of opportunity.

An even more grievous discrimination was directed against black women, who, regardless of marital status or education, were generally barred from the office during this period. As late as 1940, nearly one-half of a group of business firms surveyed had personnel policies that specifically prohibited the hiring of black clerical workers; most of the remaining companies appear to have followed this practice: "No colored hired in office, no discrimination as to race."[5] Thus, in 1920, only 0.5 percent of all female clerical workers were nonwhite, a situation that did not change until the 1960s.

Changing Conditions of Employment

The American economy's increased emphasis on manufacturing and the declining importance of agriculture between 1860 and 1920 were accompanied by far-reaching changes in the conditions of labor. Most American farmers were independent businesspeople who engaged in a wide range of decision-making activities. Although guided by market demands and the productive resources at their disposal, individual farmers could still decide what commodities to produce, how to produce them, the amount of effort to devote to various farm activities, and the like. In contrast, the typical workers in manufacturing and increasingly in the trade, transportation, and service sectors were employees whose supervisors told them what to do, how to do it, how long to work, and how much they would earn. Employees' loss of control over many of the key decisions regarding their work was undoubtedly one of the major reasons for the growing worker discontent that invariably manifested itself during economic modernization.

Wages and Hours

Despite real difficulties, the statistical evidence contradicts the Marxian view that the American working class was doomed to increasing misery and lower living standards. Typical daily wages increased from $1.00 in 1860 to $1.50 in 1890. Since consumer prices were at the same level in both years, real wages as well as money wages advanced by about 50 percent, one of the highest percentage increases in American history. By 1880, according to a recent study made by Jeremy Atack and Fred Batemen, two-thirds of all industrial workers had achieved a ten-hour day. (This is "a decade earlier than the traditional dating.")[6] At least one-fifth of the increase in real wages was due to a relative shift in the composition of the work force—from soft goods industries (like cotton and woolen textiles) where wages were low, to hard goods industries (like iron and steel) where wages were high. Wage differences functioned to improve the allocation of labor within manufacturing, just as they drew workers from agriculture to industry.

At one time, it was thought that real wages did not rise after 1890 but stagnated between that year and 1914. According to research conducted by Albert Rees, however, the real earnings of manufacturing workers rose 37 percent during this time span, at an annual compound rate of 1.3 percent as against 1.6 percent compounded annually for the period 1860 to 1890. By 1914, real earnings had increased to around $580 and the workweek had fallen to between 50 and 55 hours.[7] Still, the rate of growth for real wages in manufacturing was less rapid than the increase in output per worker hour. The reason was that the cost of using more capital per unit of output had to be covered before real wages could rise if the flow of capital investment was to be sustained.

Working Conditions

Between 1860 and 1914, employment in manufacturing and construction tripled and the physical output of manufacturing rose six times. This great industrial expansion was accompanied by mechanization, which in many cases destroyed the need for special handicraft or artisan skills and increased the importance of less-skilled workers. In some cases, as in the clothing industry, managers subdivided a complex process that had been the responsibility of one skilled artisan into simple operations that were carried out by groups of unskilled workers. In most instances, though, as in the iron and steel industry, highly skilled workers were replaced by new machines that permitted a greater utilization of unskilled and semiskilled workers and thus enabled employers both to pay comparatively lower wages and secure a larger labor supply. For the workers, however, the shift to less skilled labor meant that they became more dependent on their employers and could more easily be replaced.

Workers in many trades fought tenaciously with managers for control of the pace of work. Artisans collectively tried to protect as much as possible of their technical knowledge from the "boss," so that, as one union leader put it, "The manager's brains are under the workmen's cap." In a broad range of industrial activities, workers followed the pattern of work collectively established by the members of the shop force. The most important pattern followed in the shop was the enforcement of the "stint"—the amount of output that workers believed constituted a fair day's work. Increased production beyond this amount, workers argued, would only lead to reduced piece rates and unemployment. The stint sometimes became institutionalized in the form of union work rules. For example, window-glass workers had sixty-six "Rules for Working," including the requirement that the "standard size of single strength rollers" should "be 40 by 58 to cut 38 by 56" and that blowers and gatherers should not "work faster than at the rate of nine rollers per hour." Not only did members of a particular trade stick

together; increasingly, they also came to support members of other crafts through sympathy strikes. As David Montgomery emphasizes, artisans did not envisage their work rules as devices to restrict production for "capitalistic" purposes (i.e., individual profit); rather, they sought to preserve a collective control of the workplace against efforts by managers to impose their own pace and pattern of work on shop workers.[8]

Job Security

In addition to the long hours of work and the real danger of injury or death from industrial accidents, job insecurity was a constant threat to working life. Depressions and recessions ushered in cyclical unemployment (see Table 13–2). Changes in weather and style brought seasonal unemployment. Novel machine practices rendered handicraft skills obsolete and caused structural unemployment.

The depressions that afflicted the United States in the years 1873 to 1878, 1883 to 1885, and 1893 to 1897 were particularly serious for workers. Even though the country embarked on a period of long-term business expansion in 1897, workers suffered from widespread unemployment during a brief depression in 1908 and 1909 and a relatively severe depression in 1913 and 1914, which ended only when the demands of World War I brought about an economic recovery. The percentage of unemployed workers varied from under 2 percent in the best of times to over 18 percent during the worst depression year.

Cyclical unemployment threatened economic security, but only temporarily. More serious perhaps were the problems of the many who were unable to work or unable to earn enough when they did work. According to surveys conducted by sociologists and social workers, many workers in key industrial cities (such as New York and Pittsburgh) as well as miners in West Virginia and Kentucky and migratory workers in California earned wages

Table 13–2. *Unemployment in the United States, 1890–1915*

Year	Number of Unemployed (in thousands)	Civilian Labor Force (percent)
1890	904	4.0%
1891	1,265	5.4
1892	728	3.0
1893	2,860	11.7
1894	4,612	18.4
1895	3,510	13.7
1896	3,782	14.4
1897	3,890	14.5
1898	3,351	12.4
1899	1,819	6.5
1900	1,420	5.0
1901	1,205	4.0
1902	1,097	3.7
1903	1,204	3.9
1904	1,691	5.4
1905	1,381	4.3
1906	574	1.7
1907	945	2.8
1908	2,780	8.0
1909	1,824	5.1
1910	2,150	5.9
1911	2,518	6.7
1912	1,759	4.6
1913	1,671	4.3
1914	3,120	7.9
1915	3,377	8.5

SOURCE: Data from U.S. Bureau of the Census, *Historical Statistics of the United States, Colonial Times to 1970,* series D-85 (Washington, D.C.: GPO, 1975), p. 135.

considerably below the minimal health and decency budgets drawn up by government and private social workers. Studies such as Robert Hunter's, conducted in 1904, suggest that in the industrial states of the United States, over one-fifth of the American people (more than six million) lived in poverty as a result of unemployment, old age, illness, dependent youth, or some other type of dependency.[9]

Industrial Discipline and Labor Relations

The spread of the factory system and the development of large corporations altered drastically the close relationship that had previously existed between employer and worker. Where once a few workers had labored in a shop under the direct supervision of one employer, by the late nineteenth century the labor forces of many enterprises numbered in the hundreds. In the 1879 to 1899 period, for instance, the average labor force in single steelworks and rolling mills rose from 220 to 412 workers; by the late 1880s, individual railroad companies had labor forces numbering in the tens of thousands. Large factories and plants tended to have an impersonal hierarchical structure, ranging from the factory and plant superintendents or managers and "overseers" of departments down to the supervisors and the workers they supervised at the machines. The control of time on the job, the flow of materials, the use of machines, and the transmission of orders all became systematized. Punctuality, following orders, and efficiency at work were highly valued, and violations of these requirements were penalized.

In some cases, owners or managers and workers continued to maintain close personal relations. (In the industrial South, the cotton mill owners or their agents assumed the responsibility for building mill villages, with houses, schools, and churches.) But regardless of how the problems of status and equality were resolved within an industrial plant, outside the plant most employers and managers did not have close relations with their workers. Class divisions developed in terms of housing, schools, clubs, and churches. The growing distinction between employers and employees, both on and off the job, contributed to class consciousness among workers and increased their interest in organizing to promote working-class interests.

The Course of Organized Labor

American labor unions developed alongside changes in technology, in market structures, in business organization, and in dominant social values. As far back as the 1850s, local unions in more than a dozen trades organized national craft unions to increase their bargaining power with individual employers and employers' associations. However, the depression of 1857 to 1861 brought about the collapse of the weakened national unions as well as many of the locals. Three national unions still in existence—those of the printers, the molders, and the machinists—managed to survive.

At the outbreak of the Civil War, fewer than 2 percent of the American labor force were union members, and these were mainly confined to trades outside the factories, since the labor force in the mills consisted for the most part of women, children, and recent immigrants. By 1862, however, rising living costs and labor shortages provided a powerful stimulus for labor organizations. Inflation, a product of wartime financing, caused real wages to fall by one-third between 1860 and 1865. Numerous strikes were called by workers to maintain their standard of living. In 1864, total union membership had risen to 200,000.

During the 1860s and early 1870s, many local unions were formed throughout the industrial areas of the country. A score or more of national craft unions were also organized; among them were locomotive engineers, cigar makers, tailors, carpenters, and bricklayers. A forerunner of the modern industrial union was the Knights of St. Crispin, a shoe workers' union founded in 1867 to protect the skilled workers against the introduction of new machinery and the influx of unskilled hands. By 1870, it was the largest national union in the country; within a decade though, it disintegrated owing to drastic wage cuts and the failure of the producers' cooperatives, which the union organized to counteract the new machinery. Two other unions powerful in the late 1860s—the iron molders and the anthracite coal miners, each at its peak claiming a membership of over 300,000—were weakened in the early 1870s.

The National Labor Union

In the 1860s, the successful formation of city central offices of all local unions and the national organization of all locals of a given craft inspired an attempt to establish a national body that would include all the national unions and the trade assemblies. In 1866, the National Labor Union (NLU) was formed with both national unions and city trade assemblies represented as well as farmers' societies and other political reform groups. The NLU concentrated its attention on the eight-hour day, producers' cooperatives, currency and land reform, and alien contract labor. In 1868, the NLU persuaded Congress to pass a law limiting the hours of federal employees (laborers and mechanics) to eight a day; but in 1872, after an unsuccessful effort to form a National Labor Reform party, the organization dissolved.

During the prolonged depression of the 1870's, many national trade unions disappeared. The whole movement was weakened by unemployment, lack of funds, the resort by employers to the blacklist and lockout, and their refusal to negotiate. As a result, labor organizations often became more or less secret societies. Many bitter strikes were called to protest against successive wage cuts, the introduction of labor-saving machinery, and other innovations that took away jobs or depressed working conditions. The railroad strikes of July 1877 against successive wage reductions led to nationwide rioting and bloodshed as well as the destruction of millions of dollars of railroad property; state and federal troops were called in to quell the disorders and thereby to break the strike.

The Knights of Labor

The depression of the 1870s convinced many workers of the necessity for a united labor organization. The Noble Order of the Knights of Labor, founded in 1869, was the most important attempt in the United States to unite the workers of all industries and occupations in one large general union, and it admitted to membership any person who worked or had worked for wages. At first the Knights of Labor was a small and secret organization, but under the leadership of Terence V. Powderly it developed into a spectacular mass movement. Its members included workers of all trades and degrees of skill, of both sexes, and of all races. The Knights aimed at the ultimate substitution of a cooperative society for the existing wage system. But the order also emphasized such trade-union demands as the eight-hour day, the prohibition of child labor, compulsory arbitration, health and safety laws, and a mechanics' lien law. In addition, the organization was interested in monetary reform, antimonopoly legislation, and land reform.

The structure of the Knights of Labor consisted of local assemblies, organized along either craft or mixed lines, that were combined into district assemblies with sole authority within their respective jurisdictions. The assemblies bargained with employers and conducted strikes, often calling out workers in various trades to aid strikers within a particular trade or plant. The membership of the Knights of Labor grew slowly at first, but the depression and wage cutting of 1884 began a rapid expansion. In 1885, spectacularly successful strikes against railroads controlled by Jay Gould and the occurrence of almost two hundred boycotts stimulated a sevenfold membership increase within one year. By the fall of 1886, there were over 700,000 members, almost 10 percent of the existing industrial wage earners. But it could not last. Many of the new members were unskilled and semiskilled workers, small-town merchants and mechanics, and farmers with little interest in the problems of urban wage earners. The result was disunity of purpose, internal conflict, and a decrease in effectiveness. A series of railroad strikes in 1886 almost completely eliminated the Knights from the western railroads and exposed serious weaknesses in its organizational structure. A mass movement for the eight-hour day led to a general strike in May 1886, which, after a few limited victories, ended essentially in failure.

The power of the Knights of Labor was further diminished by the general public's horrified reaction to the May 1886 bombing and rioting in Haymarket Square in Chicago. Although members of the Knights of Labor were not responsible, their reputation as a labor organization suffered greatly from unwarranted charges made against them. The greatest threat to the organization, however, came from the dissatisfaction of many skilled workers who were leaving it to form craft unions. The membership of the Knights fell to 100,000 in 1890; and by 1900, the organization had ceased to exist as a national movement.

The fate of the Knights of Labor demonstrated the difficulty of establishing in nineteenth-century America a strong, stable, nationwide labor organization for economic and political action. Skilled workers were persuaded only for a time to subordinate their craft interests to a program for helping the mass of unskilled workers. Nevertheless, the Knights of Labor was important in American labor history as a trailblazer for the idea of industrial unionism, which decades later was to find some realization in the CIO.

The American Federation of Labor

As early as 1881, the Federation of Organized Trades and Labor Unions of the United States and Canada had been formed by a group of national trade-union leaders, disaffected craft union groups from the Knights of Labor, and Socialists. But the new Federation could not compete effectively against the expanding Knights of Labor. In 1886, the hostile attitude of the Knights toward craft unions induced those favoring the craft method of organizing workers into unions to found the American Federation of Labor (AFL), which then united with the Federation of Organized Trades and Labor Unions. Samuel Gompers of the Cigar Makers' Union became the first president of the AFL and continued in that office, except for one year, until his death in 1924.

The basic units of the AFL were the national and international (i.e., North American) craft unions, each of which had complete autonomy. The new union philosophy put a high value on businesslike methods and centralization of authority and stressed trade organization, the control of jobs, and the negotiating of written agreements with employers. The AFL leaders, unlike those of the Knights of Labor, minimized or disparaged direct participation in political organizations and programs of radical and social reform. Instead, they concentrated on furthering the special interests and economic strength of each craft.

During its first decade, the AFL had to face and surmount some difficult circumstances. Although the national unions affiliated with the AFL grew in number, most of them were small and in a weak financial condition. The total membership of the AFL unions grew slowly until after the depression of the 1890s; then it rose at increasingly faster rates (see Table 13–3).

During the early 1890s, the AFL revived the strike for an eight-hour day and won some victories for the building and printing unions. One major setback, however, was the failure of the Homestead iron and steel strike in 1892. Another was the defeat of the American Railway Union in the Pullman strike of 1894.

The period from 1898 to 1904 was one of rising prices, prosperity, and comparative in-

Table 13–3. *American Federation of Labor Membership, 1897–1920*

Year	Number of Affiliated Unions	Memberships (in thousands)
1897	58	265
1898	67	278
1899	73	349
1900	82	548
1901	87	788
1902	97	1,024
1903	113	1,466
1904	120	1,676
1905	118	1,494
1906	119	1,454
1907	117	1,539
1908	116	1,587
1909	119	1,483
1910	120	1,562
1911	115	1,762
1912	112	1,770
1913	111	1,996
1914	110	2,021
1915	110	1,946
1916	111	2,073
1917	111	2,371
1918	111	2,726
1919	111	3,260
1920	110	4,079

SOURCE: Data from U.S. Bureau of the Census, *Historical Statistics of the United States, Colonial Times to 1970* (Washington, D.C.: GPO, 1975), p. 177.

dustrial peace. The AFL unions received wide recognition from employers and increased their membership considerably. They were aided by such business-dominated or middle-class organizations as the National Civic Federation, the National Consumers' League, and the National Child Labor Committee. Collective bargaining became more widely accepted. During the anthracite coal strike of 1902, President Theodore Roosevelt pressured the employers into accepting arbitration by a presidential commission. Thereafter, the United

The Pullman Strike, 1894.   Federal troops were sent to Chicago to protect the strikebreakers when the American Railway Union supported the strike by Pullman workers. Here was one of many examples of the intervention of government—federal, state, and local—on the side of management in labor disputes. (The Library of Congress [LC-USZ62- 3526])

Mine Workers (UMW) expanded into a large and well-organized affiliate of the AFL. During this period, a score of new national unions chartered by the AFL were established; among them perhaps the most notable was the International Ladies' Garment Workers Union (ILGWU), organized in 1900.

The very success of business unionism caused a stiffening of employer resistance to the AFL's organizing activities, with the result that total union membership remained almost stationary between 1904 and 1910. In the early 1900s, antiunion employers started a campaign of propaganda against the closed shop and unionism in general, with considerable suc-

cess, particularly in small towns. Then, around 1910, there was a renewed burst of activity among some unions, especially those in the coal-mining, building, clothing, and railroad industries. Successful strikes of coal miners occurred in 1910 and 1912, each of which strengthened the bargaining power of the miners. In the women's clothing industry, two major strikes in New York City in the 1900s increased the size and power of the International Ladies' Garment Workers Union. In the men's clothing industry, a group within the active United Garment Workers Union revolted against the AFL leadership and established a new industrial union, the Amalgamated Clothing Workers (ACW), which was independent of the AFL. Each of these unions was vigorous and grew in membership at a rapid rate.

The Industrial Workers of the World

The AFL's failure to organize semiskilled and unskilled workers was criticized by many groups. The most stringent attacks came from labor radicals, who in 1905 founded the Industrial Workers of the World (IWW), or the "Wobblies." The IWW was "one big union" made up of such diverse groups as the Western Federation of Miners and previously unorganized migratory workers in northwestern wheat fields and lumber camps. It appealed to all workers irrespective of skill level, nationality, race, or sex, and it attempted to organize the workers in different industries into large industrial unions. The philosophy embedded in the rhetoric of the IWW was that of revolutionary industrial unionism: The ultimate goal was to replace capitalistic society with an industrial democracy in which the unions would own and operate all industries. The major efforts of the IWW, however, were directed toward winning improvements in wages, hours, and working conditions for the hitherto unorganized workers. In these respects, the IWW and AFL shared a common objective, even though they differed on the craft versus the industrial union method of organization, on militant versus peaceful tactics, and on whether capitalism should be retained or supplanted by a workers' democracy.

In the West, the IWW organized the unskilled metal miners and migratory shipping and farm laborers. In the East, the "Wobblies" provided leadership for immigrant workers, especially those in the textile factories. The IWW's greatest strike success was at Lawrence, Massachusetts, in 1912. The membership of the IWW was very unstable and perhaps never exceeded sixty or seventy thousand members at its height before World War I. Yet between 1909 and 1918,

some two million to three million workers passed through its ranks, and millions more were influenced by its teachings and activities.

With the entry of the United States into World War I, which the leaders of the Wobblies had strongly opposed, the IWW went into a fatal decline. But this did not diminish the importance of the IWW as a protest against the AFL's claim to represent a working class that from 1890 to 1914 consisted to an increasing extent of unskilled workers, native and immigrant. The IWW proved that migratory, casual, and unskilled workers with varied languages, customs, religions, and antipathies could be organized. In addition, the campaigns and strikes of the Wobblies awakened various progressive and reform leaders of the 1900 to 1917 era to an awareness of the domination by industry of many local and state governments and to the use of government against strikers without regard to civil rights or to the deplorable living conditions of many working families. Thus, the IWW had a significant impact on the progressive movement and future social legislation.

Industrial Conflict and the Courts

Workers in different trades established labor unions as decision-making agencies to deal with employers on such vital subjects as wages, hours, and working conditions. In some cases, management and labor were able to negotiate mutually satisfactory agreements; in others, unions decided to use the strike as a means of settling disputes. Some strikes were notorious. Among the disastrous labor conflicts of the period were a national railroad strike in July 1877; the strikes leading to the Haymarket Affair in Chicago in May 1886; the iron and steel strike in Homestead, Pennsylvania, in 1892; and the Pullman strike in Chicago in 1894. The total number of strikes in the

United States rose from an annual average of 530 for the years 1881 to 1895 to a high of 3100 for the years 1911 to 1915. Between 1881 and 1903, in over 50 percent of the strikes the workers were successful; between 1904 and 1915, the success rate was only 36 percent. The record shows that, whereas strikes by unorganized workers almost always failed, unionized workers won from one-third to two-thirds of their strikes. The score of union successes was much higher in prosperity than in depression phases of the business cycle.

The efforts of unions to organize workers and to achieve their goals were often hindered by decisions of state and federal courts. Employers were usually able to persuade judges to issue injunctions against strikes, picketing, and the use of the boycott by organized labor. The U.S. Supreme Court in the Danbury Hatters' case—*Loewe v. Lawler* (1908)—declared that a secondary boycott conducted by a union against a business firm was a conspiracy in restraint of trade and thus a violation of the Sherman Antitrust Act. The United Hatters' Union (of the AFL) was held liable for triple damages because of a nationwide boycott against hats produced by a nonunion firm in Danbury, Connecticut. In the Bucks Stove and Range Case (1911), three AFL officers, including Samuel Gompers, were held guilty of contempt of court and sentenced to jail for not obeying an injunction forbidding the continuation of a union boycott against the company. The Clayton Antitrust Act of 1914, once widely hailed as organized labor's "Magna Carta," declared that unions were not to be construed as illegal combinations in restraint of trade under the antitrust laws; the law also limited the use of the injunction in labor disputes. However, this proved to be a hollow victory for Gompers and other union leaders, as the law's provisions regarding labor were subsequently weakened by court interpretation.

During this period, the courts consistently supported the use by employers of the "yellow-dog contract"—a requirement that the worker, as a condition of employment, not join a union. In *Adair v. United States* (1908), the Supreme Court struck down a provision of the Erdman Act (passed by Congress in 1908) that prohibited railroad companies from employing the yellow-dog contract. In *Coppage v. Kansas* (1911), the Court nullified a state law designed to achieve the same purpose. In both cases, a majority of the Court ruled that such laws violated the employer's freedom of contract and property rights. Before the 1930s, the balance of judicial powers in cases involving labor law and industrial relations usually favored employers over organized labor.

In addition to using the legal system to undermine the position of unions and their organizing efforts, employers were devising other methods to preserve the exclusive sphere of management in decision making about labor relations. Large corporations generally had little difficulty winning their own labor battles. However, smaller manufacturers from the 1880s on sought the help of regional and national employer associations to turn back unionization. As the AFL gained strength in the early twentieth century, the National Association of Manufacturers (NAM) coordinated the activities of local employer groups in the battle against unionization, especially the closed shop and the unions' efforts to establish their own work rules. The National Council for Industrial Democracy, an affiliate of the NAM, developed skillful lobbying tactics to defeat legislative programs backed by unions and reformers. Industrialists regarded as especially important the use of political means to influence local and state police and courts in applying the laws of trespass, traffic obstruction, and disorderly conduct against unions and their members.

Welfare Capitalism

In the 1880s and 1890s, a few industrialists were coming to believe that voluntary efforts by employers to improve the lot of workers would not only impede the spread of unionism but might also increase productivity in their plants. Welfare work, or *welfare capitalism*, embraced a number of practices. Companies tried to make their factories more habitable by stressing cleanliness, adequate lighting, and proper ventilation; some introduced suggestion boxes to encourage workers to submit their ideas about needed improvements in the production process. Some employers also installed cafeterias and adequate restroom facilities and implemented medical, insurance, and savings plans for employees. Several employers tried profit-sharing and company stock-ownership plans. Old-age pension programs, first adopted by railroad companies in the 1870s, were established by a few industrial corporations in the early years of the twentieth century, most notably by Carnegie Steel and Standard Oil. Employee-representation plans, work councils, or shop committees—company unions, as they later came to be known—were initiated and financed by a few employers during this period. By 1910, welfare work of some kind was being carried on in plants employing over 1.5 million workers. A greatly expanded welfare capitalism would become a basic instrument of labor-management relations in the 1920s, only to be submerged by the events of the Great Depression of the 1930s. After World War II, many of the elements of welfare capitalism would surface again as employee-benefit plans, often established in union contracts.

Social Legislation

While unions sought to improve the wages and working conditions of their members, social reformers urged legislation to deal with specific problems. From almost the beginning of factory industry in America, working children were the objects of special concern. By 1900, twenty-eight states had some kind of law prescribing maximum hours and requiring some school attendance for children, but the states generally lacked the machinery for effective enforcement. The laws applied only to manufacturing, even though only a small minority of working children labored in factories. Department stores, for example, employed numerous young "cash boys" and "cash girls" to carry money and receipted bills between sales clerks and the cashier's office. Many children worked in the "street trades"—selling newspapers and performing other tasks.

Over the first decade and a half of the twentieth century, legislation passed in most industrial states prohibited work by children in a wide range of occupations. Closely related to the movement to abolish child labor was the drive to establish effective compulsory school laws. Public school enrollments increased by almost 40 percent between 1900 and 1920, while high school enrollment alone grew even more dramatically. The requirement that children attend school through the elementary level served to place large numbers of them close to the next rung on the educational ladder, thereby encouraging more to continue with their schooling. High school enrollments quadrupled from 1900 to 1920; high school graduates increased from only 6 percent of all seventeen-year-olds in 1900 to 17 percent in 1920.

At the same time, a wide consensus was developing about the need for legislation to deal with the plight of working women—long hours, night shifts, low wages, and hazardous working conditions. Like children, women were regarded as dependents, easily exploited and unable to defend themselves through the law. Protective legislation for women received support from men. Some men believed that shorter hours for working women would lead to shorter hours for all working people, in spite of the widespread segregation by gender in industry. Other men sought to restrict the work hours of women so as to make them less employable, thereby reducing the possibility that women would take jobs that might otherwise go to men. This concern grew out of the widespread unemployment during the depression of the 1890s. The hostility of the courts to such state legislation was finally overcome with the decision in *Muller v. Oregon* (1908). The Supreme Court accepted the need for shorter work hours for women mainly because it believed long hours would adversely affect the ability of women to perform what was considered their primary child-bearing and maternal functions. By 1914, some form of regulation concerning the working hours for women was in effect in twenty-seven states, many of which also passed legislation to prohibit night work by women. Although reformers mounted a drive for legislation to establish minimum wages for women, by 1914 only one state had passed such a law—Massachusetts—and violators were threatened only by adverse publicity. Protective legislation for women was widely hailed then and later as beneficial to female workers, but, from the early 1920s, "protection" would be increasingly perceived as an obstacle to the achievement by women of true equality in the workplace.

The most controversial labor legislation of the early twentieth century involved maximum work hours for men. In 1898, the Supreme Court upheld the constitutionality of such a law applying to miners in the case of *Holden v. Hardy.* But in 1905, the Court ruled in *Lochner v. New York* that legislation regulating the work hours of bakers was unconstitutional. The pressure of public opinion gradually reached the Court, however, and in 1917 it upheld an Oregon law regulating hours of work in *Bunting v. Oregon,* paving the way for more state legislation in this area.

Among the consequences of the greater use of machines and the simplification of tasks was a rise in the number of industrial accidents. (Between 1880 and 1900, an average of over 570,000 work-related injuries occurred annu-

ally in the United States; 35,000 of them were fatal.) Where new technology contributed to improved labor productivity as well as safety for workers, employers quickly adopted it, as in the installation of airbrakes and automatic car couplers by railroad corporations. But for most industries some form of government action was needed to encourage employers to provide a safe working environment. Workers' compensation laws passed during the early years of the twentieth century were effective because they approached the problem from the point of view of financial burden. Under the then-prevailing legal concepts, the injured worker had to prove in a lawsuit that the accident was due to the negligence of the employer rather than that of the worker or a "fellow servant," to use the legal terminology for "co-worker." Usually the worker lost the suit, but occasionally a shrewd lawyer persuaded a jury to make a large financial award to an injured worker. Drawing on precedents established earlier in Europe, reformers successfully argued that it was equitable for the cost of an accident to be borne by the employer and passed along to consumers as a part of the cost of production. The early twentieth-century laws passed in most northern industrial states were beneficial to both parties: The injured worker was assured of medical expenses and a disability payment (usually fixed at one-half to two-thirds of previous pay), while the employer avoided the risk of a substantial court award that a jury might make to an accident victim. In other words, both the employer and the employee gained an element of predictability with respect to the financial burden of industrial accidents. Moreover, since the cost of insurance was based on the accident rate in the employer's factory, the laws also stimulated a strong movement by business to improve safety standards on the job.

With respect to another serious hazard to industrial workers—unemployment—little progress was made during this period. The private sector assumed much of the responsibility for dealing with the problems of the unemployed. Charitable organizations distributed food and other necessities to the unemployed and their families. A few trade unions provided small unemployment benefits for their members. During periods of depression, like those of 1894 to 1895 and 1914, local governments organized work-relief programs. Reformers advocated a system of public employment offices, with almost one hundred in operation by 1914. However, such agencies were better equipped to deal with frictional rather than cyclical unemployment.

Summary

In the late nineteenth and early twentieth centuries, the American labor force expanded more rapidly than did the nation's population, in part owing to the millions of immigrants that arrived from overseas. As the main source of employment shifted from agriculture to manufacturing and trade, workers were able to take advantage of the other opportunities afforded by the high rate of growth and changing sectors of production. But the drastically altered nature of work under conditions of mass production and the changed relationships between workers and employers created much discontent in the workplace.

Like immigrants, African-Americans and women were drawn into the paid labor force by industrial and commercial expansion and the growth of cities. Women participated most extensively in the rapidly growing clerical labor force, but discriminatory practices by employers limited their opportunity to pursue avenues of advancement. Blacks also suffered greatly from extensive discrimination during this period.

Industrial wage earners after the Civil War benefited greatly from increases in real wages and the standard of living. Nevertheless, workers were acutely concerned about improving their wages, hours, and working conditions and so experimented with different types of trade unions, some socially idealistic, others narrowly self-interested. The unions secured some improvements, especially for workers in the craft unions. But for decades organized labor encountered strong opposition on many issues from state and federal courts and thus was not able to emerge as a powerful force on the national level until the 1930s.

Industrialists sought to preserve the exclusive prerogative of management in labor relations by organizing vigorous opposition to unions and by adopting a program of welfare work designed to foster worker loyalty to the company. Social reformers in the early twentieth century achieved some success in lobbying for legislation to deal with specific problems associated with industrialism, primarily child labor and compulsory schooling, the hours and working conditions of women, and workers' compensation laws.

Endnotes

1. See Robert Higgs, "Race, Skill, and Earnings: American Immigrants in 1909," *Journal of Economic History,* 31 (1971); Peter J. Hill, "Relative Skill and Income Levels of Native and Foreign-Born Workers in the United States," *Explorations in Economic History,* 12

(1975); and Martha Norby Frauendorf, "Relative Earnings of Native and Foreign-Born Women," *Explorations in Economic History*, 15 (1978).

2. The discussion in this section owes much to the comprehensive analysis in Claudia Goldin, *Understanding the Gender Gap: An Economic History of American Women* (New York: Oxford University Press, 1990). The labor participation rate for married women cited here contains an adjustment to the census figures of gainful workers made by Goldin to take into account significant numbers of working married women not counted as having an occupation.

3. Helen Sumner's statement appeared in a U.S. Senate *Report on Condition of Woman and Child Wage-Earners in the U.S.* (1910–1911), quoted by Goldin, p. 95.

4. Quoted in Elyce J. Rotella, *From Home to Office: U.S. Women at Work, 1870–1930* (Ann Arbor, Mich.: UMI Research Press, 1981), p. 68.

5. Quoted in Goldin, *Understanding the Gender Gap*, p. 147.

6. Jeremy Atack and Fred Bateman, "How Long Was the Workday in 1880?" *Journal of Economic History*, 52 (1992).

7. Albert Rees, *Real Wages in Manufacturing, 1890–1914* (Princeton: Princeton University Press, 1961).

8. David Montgomery, *Workers' Control in America: Studies in the History of Work, Technology, and Labor Struggles* (New York: Cambridge University Press, 1979), Chapter 1. The quotations appear on pp. 9, 15.

9. Robert Hunter, *Poverty* (New York: Macmillan, 1904).

Suggested Readings

For informative studies on trends in U.S. population, immigration, and internal migration, see Richard A. Easterlin, *Population, Labor Force, and Long Swings in Economic Growth* (New York: Columbia University Press, 1968); Richard A. Easterlin, "The American Population," in Lance Davis et al, *American Economic Growth* (New York: Harper & Row, 1972); Peter J. Hill, *The Economic Impact of Immigration in the United States* (New York: Arno Press, 1975); Philip Taylor, *The Distant Magnet: European Migration to the U.S.A.* (New York: Harper & Row, 1971); Brinley Thomas, *Migration and Economic Growth*, 2d ed. (New York: Cambridge University Press, 1973); David Ward, *Cities and Immigrants: A Geography of Change in Nineteenth Century America* (New York: Oxford University Press, 1971); Virginia Yans-McLaughlin, ed., *Immigration Reconsidered: History, Sociology, and Politics* (New York: Oxford University Press, 1990); Dudley Baines, *Emigration from Europe from 1815 to the 1930s* (London: Macmillan Press and Economic History Society, 1991); John Bodnar, *The Transplanted: A History of Immigrants in Urban America* (Bloomington: Indiana University Press, 1985); James A. Dunlevy and Henry A. Gemery, "Economic Opportunity and the Responses of the 'Old' and 'New' Migrants to the United States," *Journal of Economic History*, 38 (1978); James A. Dunlevy and Richard P. Saba, "The Role of Nationality-Specific Characteristics on the Settlement Patterns of Late Nineteenth Century Immigrants," *Explorations in Economic History*, 29 (1992); Gordon W. Kirk and Carolyn J. Kirk, "The Immigrant, Economic Opportunity, and Type of Settlement in Nineteenth-Century America," *Journal of Economic History*, 38 (1978); and three articles by J. D. Gould: "European Inter-Continental Emigration 1815–1914: Patterns and Causes," *Journal of European Economic History*, 8 (1979); "European Inter-Continental

Emigration. The Road Home: Return Migration from the U.S.A.," ibid. 9 (1980); and "European International Emigration: The Role of 'Diffusion' and 'Feedback,'" ibid. 9, (1980).

On changes in the economic position of industrial workers, see Stanley Lebergott, *Manpower in Economic Growth* (New York: McGraw-Hill, 1964); Stanley Lebergott, *The American Economy* (Princeton: Princeton University Press, 1976); Clarence D. Long, *Wages and Earnings in the United States, 1860–1890* (Princeton: Princeton University Press, 1960); Albert Rees, *Real Wages in Manufacturing, 1890–1914* (Princeton: Princeton University Press, 1961); and Jeremy Atack and Fred Bateman, "How Long Was the Workday in 1880?" *Journal of Economic History,* 52 (1992).

The social life of industrial workers is explored by Melvyn Dubofsky, *Industrialism and the American Worker, 1865–1920* (New York: Crowell, 1975); and Herbert C. Gutman, *Work, Culture and Society in Industrializing America* (New York: Knopf, 1976). Richard B. Morris, ed., *The American Worker* (Washington: Government Printing Office, 1976) is a well-illustrated history. James R. Barrett, *Work and Community in the Jungle: Chicago's Packinghouse Workers, 1894–1922* (Champagne: University of Illinois Press, 1987); and Richard J. Oestreicher, *Solidarity and Fragmentation: Working People and Class Consciousness in Detroit, 1875–1900* (Champagne: University of Illinois Press, 1986) are useful case studies. Stuart M. Blumin, *The Emergence of the Middle Class: Social Experience in the American City, 1760–1900* (New York: Cambridge University Press, 1989) contains information on the growth of the white-collar labor force in the late nineteenth century.

William H. Harris, *The Harder We Run: Black Workers Since the Civil War* (New York: Oxford University Press, 1982) is a good survey. Robert Higgs, *Competition and Coercion: Blacks in the American Economy, 1865–1914* (New York: Cambridge University Press, 1977) contains a useful economic analysis. Claudia Goldin, *Understanding the Gender Gap: An Economic History of American Women* (Oxford: Oxford University Press, 1990) is a comprehensive quantitative analysis of women in the labor force and is basic to an understanding of the economic issues. Julie A. Matthaei, *An Economic History of Women in America* (New York: Schocken Books, 1982) and Alice Kessler-Harris, *Out to Work: A History of Wage-Earning Women in the United States* (New York: Oxford University Press, 1982) offer readable accounts of the historical experience of women in the economy. Elyce J. Rotella, *From Home to Office: U.S. Women at Work, 1870–1930* (Ann Arbor, Mich.: UMI Research Press, 1981) focuses on female participation in the clerical sector, and Susan Porter Benson, *Counter Cultures: Saleswomen, Managers, and Customers in American Department Stores, 1890–1940* (Urbana: University of Illinois Press, 1986) on women in retail selling. Martha Jane Soltow and Mary K. Wery, *American Women and the Labor Movement, 1825–1974: An Annotated Bibliography* (Metuchen, NJ: Scarecrow Press, 1976) is a valuable compilation of sources of information.

Daniel Nelson, *Managers and Workers: Origins of the New Factory System in the United States, 1880–1920* (Madison: University of Wisconsin Press, 1975) analyzes changes in the management of labor relations in American industry. John R. Commons et al, *History of Labour in the United States,* vols. 2–4 (New York: Macmillan, 1918–1935), the pioneering work in the field of labor history, is still an important source. The following works deal with varied developments in trade union history: David Montgomery, *Workers' Control in America: Studies in the History of Work, Technology, and Labor Struggles* (New York: Cambridge University Press, 1979); David Montgomery, *The Fall of the House of Labor: The Workplace, the State, and American Labor Activism, 1865–1925* (New York: Cambridge University Press, 1987); Melvyn Dubofsky, *We Shall Be All: A History of the Industrial Workers of the World* (New York: Quadrangle

Books, 1969); Anne Huber Tripp, *The I.W.W. and the Paterson Silk Strike of 1913* (Champagne: University of Illinois Press, 1987); Lloyd Ulman, *The Rise of the National Trade Union* (Cambridge: Harvard University Press, 1955); Leon Fink, *Workingmen's Democracy: The Knights of Labor and American Politics* (Urbana: University of Illinois Press, 1983); John H. M. Laslett, *Labor and the Left, 1881–1924* (New York: Basic Books, 1970); Harold Livesay, *Samuel Gompers and Organized Labor in America* (Boston: Little, Brown, 1978); and Stuart B. Kaufman, *Samuel Gompers and the Origins of the American Federation of Labor, 1848–1896* (Westport, Conn.: Greenwood Press, 1973).

The following works deal with different aspects of social legislation passed during this period: Lawrence M. Friedman and Jack Ladinsky, "Social Change and the Law of Industrial Accidents," *Columbia Law Review*, 67 (1967); Robert Asher, "Business and Workers' Welfare in the Progressive Era: Workmen's Compensation Reform in Massachusetts, 1880–1911," *Business History Review*, 43 (1969); Jeremy P. Felt, *Hostages of Fortune: Child Labor Reform in New York State* (Syracuse: Syracuse University Press, 1965); Moses Stambler, "The Effect of Compulsory Education and Child Labor Laws on High School Attendance in New York City, 1898–1917," *History of Education Quarterly*, 8 (1968); and Ronnie Steinberg, *Wages and Hours: Labor and Reform in Twentieth-Century America* (New Brunswick: Rutgers University Press, 1982). For reference to sources of information about welfare capitalism, see Martha Jane Soltow and Susan Gravelle, *Worker Benefits: Industrial Welfare in America, 1900–1935* (Metuchen, NJ: Scarecrow Press, 1983).

Chapter 14

Building Nationwide Railroad and Communication Networks

T HE REVOLUTIONARY DEVELOPMENTS IN TRANS-
portation and communication that began in the quarter-century after 1815
reached full flower in the decades following
the Civil War. To the railroads in transportation
and to the telegraph (and later the telephone)
in communication fell the Herculean labor of
unifying America economically and turning it
into one great marketplace. These technologies
were equal to the task. By the first years of the
twentieth century, the products of the land
and factory, as well as the American people,
moved quickly and freely throughout the continental United States over a vast network of
steel rails. Information flowed even faster as
messages were carried instantaneously over
millions of miles of telegraph and telephone
wire. The railroads especially, but also the wire
communication enterprises, were great industries in their own right; the demands they generated as they grew stimulated expansion in
numerous other activities. Their true significance, however, lay in the fact that the services
they provided were critical inputs into virtually all types of economic activity and processes of decision making. Amazing as it may
seem, many people living in 1900 could re-
member when neither railroads nor telegraphs
nor telephones existed. In a sense, such people
were older than the American economy, a
phrase that had seldom been used at the time
they were born because it lacked content when
economies were local and regional in nature.

The expansion of the key technologies of
transportation and communications during the
late nineteenth century was stupendous. Although the thirty thousand miles of railroad
operated in the United States in 1860 represented about one-half the mileage in the entire
world at that date, this achievement pales in
the light of subsequent growth. Main track
mileage of American railroads nearly quadrupled in the two decades after the Civil War and
then doubled between the mid-1880s and 1914,
when 289,000 miles were in operation. In the

case of the telegraph, in 1866 some two thousand offices transmitted roughly five million
messages over 76,000 miles of wire. By 1912,
the number of telegraph offices had increased
to 31,000; they handled 109 million messages
sent over 1.8 million miles of wire. Railway
mileage grew at a continuously compounded
rate of 4.3 percent per year over the period
1865 to 1914, and at 6.5 percent per year between 1865 and 1885. Mileage of telegraph
wire operated grew even faster, at 6.9 percent
per year compounded from 1866 to 1912. Neither the railroad nor the telegraph were new in
the 1860s. By that time they had already
passed through very rapid growth stages, yet
they remained important growth industries for
decades. In the case of the telephone, which
was not patented until 1876, growth was phenomenal. After a rather subdued beginning
during the initial seventeen years of patent
monopoly, the number of telephones in the
United States grew at a rate of 17 percent per
year between 1893 and 1914. In the latter year,
over ten million telephones were in operation,
one for every ten Americans, and calls averaged forty million per day in local exchanges
and a million per day in toll service.

Such data alone reveal little about the
decision-making processes that gave form to
transportation and communication expansion.
Nor do they say much about the impact of
such expansion on the American economy,
polity, and society. These subjects are worth
further investigation as a way of understanding the past as well as the present. The railroad
and telegraph, for example, represent the beginnings of the gigantic business enterprise in
U.S. history. The huge capital investment requirements and the scale of operation of these
enterprises gave rise to new forms of business
management and organizational structures.
And the nature of the technologies they utilized dictated that there would be only one or
a few suppliers of their services in any given
market area; competition for sales among sup-

pliers of railroad and telegraph services was therefore much more limited than in most markets. Moreover, the operations of these enterprises did not stop at local or state boundaries. As national transportation and communication networks were formed in the context of monopolistic and oligopolistic market structures (one or a few sellers), problems of intrastate and interstate commerce arose that called forth state and federal regulatory institutions. This marked the beginning of a significant long-term development in American political economy.

Railway Expansion Under Corporate Organization

Corporate Charters

American railroads were private enterprises organized as corporations under governmental charters. A corporate charter made a company a legal "person" that could own property, sue and be sued, and so on. As such, railroads differed from most earlier modes of transportation. The great canals of the early nineteenth century were developed and owned primarily by state governments, whereas the steamboats that revolutionized internal waterway transportation were for the most part individual proprietorships and partnerships. Unlike canals and steamboats, the railroads combined two transportation functions: They built their roadways and then moved the traffic of freight and passengers. These functions required building complex organizations, gaining access to large amounts of capital, and continuing administrative coordination and decision making on many levels. Neither the limited governments nor the small-scale family and partnership enterprises—the characteristic forms of public and private economic organization for much of the nineteenth century—

were suitable to the performance of these tasks. But governments could help. The corporate charters they conferred enlisted the right of eminent domain to secure routes for the corporations and brought them the limited liability so useful in attracting private capital funds to finance investment. Governments, moreover, could use their own resources to subsidize railway development in instances where they perceived the social returns from improved transport as exceeding the private returns that railroad corporations themselves could capture through their charges.

Completing the Rail Network

The corporate forms of organization and decision making proved to be remarkably flexible and dynamic methods for linking together a continent's resources, producers, and consumers in a network of rails in the half-century from 1865 to 1914. Figure 14–1 diagrams the railway expansion that occurred before, during, and after these years in terms of main-track mileage. The rate of expansion was very high in the 1850s, but at the end of that decade most of the mileage was still in the northeastern quarter of the United States. The Civil War markedly slowed the expansion, but after the war the work of covering the entire nation with a network of dependable rail facilities began in earnest. Mileage doubled between 1865 and 1873; the highlight of this boom came when the first transcontinental route was completed with the driving of the famed golden spike near Ogden, Utah, in 1869. After the deep and widespread business depression of the mid-1870s, two more booms in railway building followed in close succession during the years 1878 to 1883 and 1885 to 1893. These booms carried the main tracks to 181,000 miles, a sixfold increase over 1860. By the early 1890s, the national network was virtually complete. The substantial additions from 1900 to 1914 represented the filling out and further

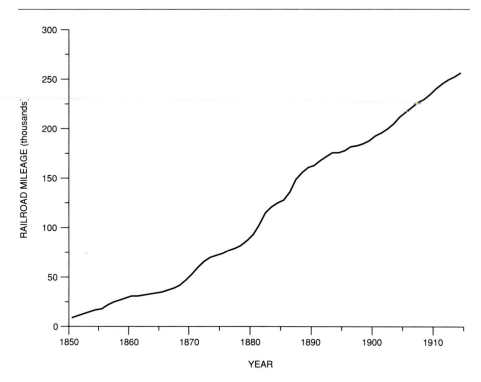

Figure 14-1 *U.S. Railway Mileage: Main Track Operated, 1850–1914*
Source: Data from U.S. Bureau of the Census, *Historical Statistics of the United States, Colonial Times to 1970, Bicentennial Edition,* part 2 (Washington, D.C.: GPO, 1975), pp. 728, 731.

equipping of an American rail system whose outline had been set earlier.

Railroads: The First Big Businesses

While the tremendous post–Civil War expansion of railroading was taking place, the strategies of railroad leaders and their companies as well as the scale of their operations were transformed in dramatic ways. Antebellum railroad corporations were large enterprises in their time, but even the largest ones owned tracks of only a few hundred miles in length; in their limited extent, they were like the earlier great canals with which they first competed and then made obsolete. Just after the Civil

War, for example, the Pennsylvania Railroad—considered one of the largest and best-managed of all American roads at the time—operated slightly fewer than five hundred miles of track, or less than 2 percent of the nation's total track. There were hundreds of smaller roads but few that were larger. By the early 1870s, however, the Pennsylvania Railroad led the way to the future by growing into a line that owned or controlled through leases nearly six thousand miles of track, some 8 percent of the national total. It then was a corporation with assets of nearly $400 million, representing just under 13 percent of all U.S. railroad investment. This was at a time when non-railroad enterprises with assets of $1 million were considered large.

Jay Gould's Competitive Challenge. What had happened to cause the railroad decision makers such as those of the Pennsylvania Railroad to transform their already large corporation into a gigantic one? Essentially, it was competition, a phenomenon that often presents special problems for enterprises with large amounts of fixed capital investment. Competition had not been much of a problem for antebellum railroads. Where it had been present—in the form of wagons on the roads and boats on the canals and rivers—railroads prevailed because they were faster, more flexible, and more reliable than their competitors. But in most cases the numerous, small lines of the early railroad era did not face much competition. They were built to facilitate trade between established population centers along their routes. Neither the corporate charters offered by governments nor the economic incentives offered by the size of markets were conducive to the construction of directly competing lines. When the volume of interregional trade in the United States later became more important, however, actual and potential competition became more of a threat to small, regional railroads. The threat could arise, for example, when an eastern road negotiated agreements with, or otherwise gained control over, roads farther west so to divert western traffic from other eastern roads to its own line. This type of situation was faced by the Pennsylvania Railroad in the late 1860s and by the Baltimore and Ohio and the New York Central a little later, after the noted financier Jay Gould gained control of the Erie Railroad in 1868. In order to increase the traffic and hence the earnings and securities values of the Erie, Gould moved quickly in an attempt to gain control of midwestern lines that could connect the Erie with Chicago, St. Louis, and other midwestern centers. In the end, Gould failed in his effort—perhaps because his attention was diverted to other nonrailroad speculations, such as trying to corner the American gold market in 1869—

but the threat he posed toward the other big eastern roads forced them to expand their regional lines into interregional systems. Leaders of the larger eastern railroads knew, of course, that a steady, high volume of through traffic was essential to the operating and financial health of their capital-intensive companies. Gould had demonstrated to them that with competition they could not take such a volume of traffic for granted. Their responses took the form of decisions to increase the scale of their companies many times over, either by buying or leasing existing roads or by constructing new lines to round out their systems.

The Response: Railroad Systems. The irrepressible Gould, having taught his competitive lessons in the Northeast, next turned to instructing the newer western roads. The Union Pacific Railroad, one of two lines that had formed the first transcontinental, had been rocked by both scandal and the general business depression that began in 1873. Gould bought enough of its stock at low prices to gain control by 1874. The Union Pacific tracks extended westward from Omaha, and so traffic between Omaha and cities in the East used other railroads. Gould attempted to assure favorable eastern connections through agreements with these roads—the Northwestern, Rock Island, and Burlington—but they resisted his overtures. Gould therefore embarked on a campaign to build his own system by using his considerable stock-market skills to gain control of other companies. By 1881, Gould's roads comprised nearly sixteen thousand miles of track, some 15 percent of the nation's total, and reached from Boston and New York in the East to New Orleans, El Paso, Denver, and Omaha in the South and West. Other western roads as well as eastern holdouts got the message from Gould's actions. Either they had to build extensive interterritorial systems of their own or risk losing traffic to other systems and eventually being absorbed by them. Thus, by the early 1890s, gigantic railroad systems came to dominate a transportation arena that earlier had been made up of numerous small companies. In 1893, the thirty-three railroad corporations with at least $100 million in assets operated nearly 70 percent of total U.S. railway mileage; by 1900, the mileage had risen to 80 percent of the total.

Bankruptcies and Reorganizations. Building large railroad systems did not guarantee profitable operations. The rush to systems that was generated by competition resulted in over-building during the 1880s, and once the systems had been built they in turn competed with one another. These problems came to a head in the depression of the mid-1890s, when many roads, including some systems, could not cover their bond interest charges. Track miles numbering in the tens of thousands passed into the hands of receivers. These defaults and the ensuing bankruptcies of large rail corporations brought investment bankers such as J. P. Morgan into the railroad reorganization and management picture. The bankers at first attempted to reduce the riskiness of railroading in two ways: They increased the ratio of equity to debt in the railroads' capital structures to reduce the risk of bankruptcy, and they negotiated cartel arrangements between competing roads with a view to sharing traffic and revenues in "orderly" ways. The financial strategy bore some fruit, but the cartel agreements proved less effective. Cartels tended to be unstable because individual cartel members as well as outsiders had an incentive to increase profits by undercutting the cartel price and taking business away from those who were faithful to the cartel agreement. American railroad cartels exposed this Achilles heel with great frequency.

Communities of Interest and Regulation. The final resolution of the competitive problems of railroads came shortly after the turn of the century. Bankers and railway managers further

J(ohn) Pierpont Morgan, 1837–1913. As head of J.P. Morgan & Company, private international bankers headquartered in Wall Street, Pierpont Morgan was the dominant figure in American finance as the United States became an economic colossus during the quarter century before World War I. Morgan financed trade, underwrote bond and stock issues, reorganized bankrupt railroads, organized corporations such as General Electric, International Harvester, and United States Steel, and on more than one occasion performed the functions of a central bank in an era when the United States lacked one. From the photo one can almost sense the conservatism, wealth, power, integrity, and dominating personality that were evident to contemporaries of this greatest of bankers. (Brown Brothers)

consolidated existing systems and developed communities of interest by having competitive systems invest in the stock of their competitors. These enlarged systems and communities of interest acted to discourage both rate cutting and the competitive construction activities of earlier years. At about the same time, federal regulation was strengthened to the point where tendencies toward "destructive" competition were curbed by law. Hence, by the first decade of the twentieth century, just seven groups or coordinated communities of interest exercised control of two-thirds of America's rail mileage. The age of railroad expansion and competition was over.

Railroad Investment and Finance

Magnitude of Investment

The construction and equipping of railroads devoured the capital funds available for investment after the Civil War. The net capital stock of U.S. railroads, amounting to about $1.06 billion on the eve of the Civil War, rose to $10.5 billion by 1909 (the data represent track and equipment valued in 1909 dollars). Gross investment, which does not adjust for the depreciation or wearing out of track and equipment, was, of course, much larger. Estimates show that gross investment (also in 1909 dollars) was nearly $1 billion in the 1860s, $2 billion in the 1870s, $4 billion in the 1880s, $2.5 billion in the 1890s, and almost $5 billion in the first decade of the twentieth century. Some rough calculations of the ratio of railroad gross investment to all gross investment puts these data in perspective. For example, the figures indicate that railroads accounted for 12 percent to 16 percent of all investment in the 1870s and 1880s, and for 7 percent to 8 percent of all investment in the 1890s and 1900s. These are impressive ratios for but one component of the economy's transportation sector, and they came in an era when the proportion of all investment (all plant, equipment, and residential construction) to GNP was rising to record heights.

Sources of Funds

The flow of funds into railroad investment between 1860 and 1910 is estimated at between $9 billion and $16 billion. These figures are of the same magnitude as the total of the gross investment figures cited earlier, though there are some important conceptual differences. The funds figures, for example, are in terms of dollars that varied in purchasing power over time rather than in 1909 dollars. Also, in many cases, the prices at which securities were actually sold to initial investors by railroad companies differed from their nominal or stated values. Bonds, for instance, were often sold at discounts from the stated par value; the advantage to newly projected railroads was a reduced current interest cost, to be made up later when the bonds matured and the bondholders were paid off at par from the income of going concern. Moreover, stock was sometimes "watered"; that is, the par or market value or both of the shares was in excess of the funds actually raised by the railroad company when it issued the stock. While some stock-watering practices were questionable, the phenomenon itself is not as mysterious or unethical as contemporaries assumed. Equity shares tend to obtain their market value from the prospective future earnings and the dividends of the assets they represent, not from the historical cost of these assets to the shareholders who first financed railroad investment by purchasing them.

Case Study: The Union Pacific Railroad. Who furnished the billions of dollars of funds that built America's railroads? For the most part, the funds were raised from private investors, though government aid in a variety of forms was also instrumental in financing a number of roads. The nature of government involvement as well as of other significant features of railway finance are highlighted by the experience of the first transcontinental road—the Union Pacific–Central Pacific link, completed in 1869. The notion of a railroad to the Pacific Coast had been suggested to Congress as early as 1845, but local and sectional bickering over the proposed route delayed passage of the Pacific Railroad Act until 1862, with revisions coming in

1864. The acts authorized private enterprise to build the railroad with government aid, on the ground that unaided private enterprise would not risk such a huge project through largely empty terrain. Aid came in two forms. One was a loan of federal government bonds in amounts from $16,000 to $48,000 per mile constructed, depending on the terrain. Once some mileage had been built, the company could collect the bonds due from the government and sell them on the market to raise funds for further construction. In this manner, the first transcontinental was lent some $65 million in U.S. bonds. The other form of aid to the Union Pacific–Central Pacific project came in the form of grants of public land. For every mile of track laid, the railroad company received twenty sections or square miles of public land—every other section in a forty-mile-wide strip of land centered on the railroad. Because of the way public lands were surveyed, this meant that the forty-mile strip took the form of a checkerboard, with the federal government retaining the black squares and the railroad being granted the reds. There were several motives behind this decision. One was that the land grants would give the railroad companies an asset base that would induce private investors to invest in railroad securities. Another was that the railroad itself would make the land more valuable so that it could be sold at a higher price to raise funds. Finally, the government would benefit to the extent that the railroad increased the value of the alternate sections of land that it retained for itself.

Despite the promise of government loans and land grants, the promoters of the Union Pacific Railroad had considerable difficulty raising enough cash from private investors to begin construction. The solution to the problem, later adopted by other railroads, took the form of a company—the Credit Mobilier—created and controlled by the Union Pacific's private promoters to act as a general contractor for the railroad's construction. The construc-tion company supplied limited amounts of its owner's funds to the railroad, and it received from the railroad large amounts of bonds and stocks at a discount, which it then retained, used as collateral for loans, or resold at a profit to other investors. Some, but not all, of the proceeds were spent on building the railroad. In the end, the Union Pacific issued some $93.5 million in securities to finance a railroad on which only $57 million was actually expended. Its promoters, through the Credit Mobilier, owned most of the stock of the railroad even though they had to put up very little cash. Their profit has been estimated at from $13 million to $16.5 million on an initial investment of about $3.9 million.

Considering the risks perceived by private investors (evident in their reluctance to buy the Union Pacific's securities except at substantial discounts from their nominal par values), scholars argue that the profit reaped by the promoters was not far out of line with what was reasonably justified. In the early 1870s, however, the company had difficulty earning enough from its operations to pay the interest charges on its large bonded debt. Government officials and others then seized on exaggerated calculations of the promoters' profits to argue that both the railroad and the public had been robbed by a small group of profiteers. This turn of events—the so-called Credit Mobilier scandal—was instrumental in causing the federal government to cease its policy of land grants and financial aid for railroad construction. It also depressed the value of Union Pacific stock to the point where Jay Gould, as noted earlier, was able to move in and gain control of the company. Financial scandals and corporate takeovers thus have a long history in the United States.

Land Grants to U.S. Railroads.   Between 1862 and 1871, however, the federal government did grant 200 million acres of public land to railroads; failures to meet construction time

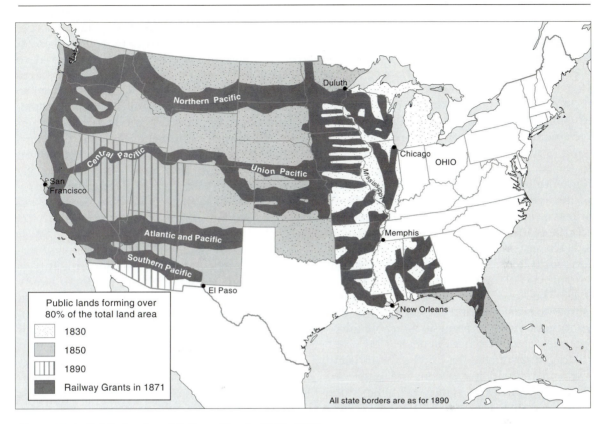

Figure 14–2 *Public Lands and Railway Grants, 1796–1890*
Source: Adapted from Martin Gilbert, *American History Atlas* (New York: Macmillan, 1969), p. 61.

limitations imposed along with these grants reduced the actual total amount of land claimed to 131 million acres. Figure 14-2 indicates the magnitude and location of the federal grants. Some states also made grants of land as well as cash subsidies. But even with generous valuations of the public lands donated, public aid financed less than 10 percent of the total investment in U.S. railroads between 1860 and 1910. Most of the resources used to build America's railroads were financed by private investors.

Foreign Investment in Railroads.   A significant portion of the private investment in railroads came from abroad. Foreigners made their decisions to invest in the United States by comparing the yields they could obtain on American securities with those available at home. Because the American economy was growing more rapidly than the economies of Europe and because wealth had not accumulated to the same extent in the United States as in Europe, the yield differential was in favor of the United States. This had been true for decades and had in fact led to earlier flows of federal, state, local, and private securities to Europe. After the Civil War, however, both economic interests and developments in technology and institutions combined to increase dramatically the flow of European funds into American railroads. The railways moved the cheap foodstuffs of the American heartlands to tidewater for export to an industrializing Europe. At the same time, the information flows necessary for efficient decision making (in the context of international markets for basic commodities and investments) were greatly improved by the laying of underseas cable to carry telegraphic messages. And investment banking houses, often with branches or affiliated firms in both Europe and the United States, perfected techniques for marketing large issues of American securities to Europeans. What became the fabled House of Morgan, for example, was founded in London in 1838 by Americans for the purpose of specializing in American finance. The New York affiliate, J. P. Morgan & Company, was founded in 1861 by its then twenty-four-year-old namesake, who later became America's greatest financier.

Estimates of the flow of European funds into American railroad investment are imprecise, but they suggest that some $2.5 billion to $3 billion migrated across the Atlantic between 1865 and the turn of the century. If these figures are accurate, they imply that European investors supplied over one-third of the financing for American railroad building during these years. The British undoubtedly accounted for the major portion. An 1898 estimate, derived from British tax records, of the value of British investment in American railways places the total at £400 million, or nearly $2 billion at the prevailing rate of exchange between the pound sterling and the dollar.

Yet the decision of foreigners to invest on such a scale in U.S. railroads was more than a mere investment decision on the part of passive rentiers. Some foreign investors had entrepreneurial ambitions, seeking to exploit America's undeveloped resources and to open up new markets. They looked after their investments by gaining control of the railroads

and becoming involved in management. The United States benefited from their activities because European expertise in technology, finance, and management was transferred to America. For example, British engineers came over to inspect and offer technical advice to railroads in which the British had invested; their firms undertook various types of construction, such as tunneling, in which the British had expertise. Through their interest in railroads, the British also introduced to the United States new types of financial instruments; for example, convertible securities as well as advanced accounting practices.

American Investors.   The contributions of foreign investors and American governments to the railroads were important, but the majority of funds for railroad building were raised from American private investors. Some of the investors were wealthy citizens who had accumulated or inherited their assets from earlier ventures in other lines of economic activity. The capitalists of Boston, for instance, had accumulated fortunes in foreign commerce and textile manufacturing in the eighteenth and early-nineteenth centuries; after the Civil War, they became heavily involved in western railroad development and management. New Yorker Cornelius Vanderbilt's stake had come in shipping before he and his son parlayed it into a fortune while building the New York Central system. But it is doubtful that the level of investment would have reached the heights that it did without the participation of hundreds of thousands of smaller investors. These persons had learned of the nature of bond investments during Jay Cooke's mass marketings of federal securities in the Civil War years (see Chapter 15). Improvements in communication kept them aware of developments in the emerging national capital market. With the economic benefits of rail transportation a matter of everyday observation, and with the techniques of financial investment increasingly understood, the stage was set for the widespread involvement of ordinary Americans in the myriad investment decisions that financed the railroads.

Railroad Productivity and Its Sources

Cost and convenience persuaded Americans of the enormous economic benefit of rail transportation, as is evident in the sheer size of the national railway system as it developed in the decades before World War I when it approached its all-time peak mileage. American railroads in 1859 carried 2.6 billion ton-miles of freight and 1.9 billion passenger miles. In 1910, the corresponding figures rose to 255 billion ton-miles and 32.5 billion passenger miles. Thus, freight output increased nearly one-hundredfold and passenger output over sixteenfold.

Competition and Technological Changes

The rapidly growing volume of transportation services was supplied at falling costs. The average passenger-mile rate was 2.44 cents in 1859 and 1.94 cents in 1910. Freight rates fell even more rapidly: In 1859, the average rate to carry one ton one mile was 2.58 cents; in 1910, it was 0.75 cents, or less than one-third of the charge fifty years earlier. These cost reductions, large as they are, do not reveal the true gains of consumers in rail service. In 1910, service was much more reliable and speedier than it had been on the eve of the Civil War.

Competition among railroads had much to do with the falling prices and improved service to consumers. Competition for control of railroads and for the traffic they carried was intense and was carried on from Main Street to Wall Street. Perhaps the best testimony to the strength of competition were the efforts devoted by the railroads to circumventing it.

These ranged from pooling of traffic and earnings to the building of large, interterritorial systems under unified control, and ultimately to support of government regulation—the erstwhile enemy of "destructive" and "disorderly" competition.

Steel Rails.   Competition itself, of course, will not lead to reduced prices unless more fundamental technological and organizational developments act to bring about cost reductions. Where such developments occur, competition serves to secure their rapid implementation. In the case of railroads, consider the substitution of steel for iron rails. Cheap steel first became available with the development of the Bessemer process in Britain at the end of the 1850s. In 1862, steel rails were introduced on the Pennsylvania Railroad; the head of that railroad, J. Edgar Thomson, had viewed them abroad. By 1880, nearly 30 percent of U.S. track mileage consisted of steel rails; ten years later that figure increased to 80 percent. (Andrew Carnegie, who as a young man worked for the Pennsylvania Railroad and was a disciple of Thomson, soon became a leader in American steel production; Carnegie honored his mentor by calling his great mill at Pittsburgh the J. Edgar Thomson works.)

What was behind the decision of railroad leaders to switch to steel? Two technical factors were at the forefront. First, steel rails were much more durable than iron rails and thus had to be replaced less frequently. Second, steel rails could support much heavier loads. The latter factor meant that heavier, more powerful locomotives could be used to pull longer trains made up of larger-capacity cars at higher rates of speed.

Signals, Couplers and Brakes.   Lesser but related technological changes went along with steel's important impetus to increased railroad efficiency. Among them were block or interval-distance signaling equipment to coordinate traffic movement with greater safety, automatic coupling devices to facilitate the making up and breaking down of long trains, and air brakes that allowed such trains to run at greater speeds with safety. It has been estimated that if the railroads in 1870, which were mostly without these technological improvements, had been asked to carry the actual traffic of 1910, the incremental cost would have been approximately $1.3 billion greater than the actual cost in 1910. Freight and passenger charges, therefore, would have been correspondingly greater. It is doubtful that these savings would have been as large or as rapid without the intense competitive pressures of late nineteenth-century railroading.

Cooperation: Standardizing Equipment and Time

Cooperation among railroads also aided in the advance of productivity. As noted earlier, competition may in some cases promote a high rate of technological progress. But it may also have negative aspects, such as was seen in railroading when competitive bluffs led to the costly and wasteful construction of parallel lines that threatened the financial stability of some railroads. Similarly, cooperation among railroads had negative effects when its intent was to stifle competition through such devices as pools and cartels designed to raise prices to consumers of transportation services. But cooperation, like competition, also had its positive effects. A steady flow of traffic was important to the operating and financial health of such heavily capital-intensive enterprises. Yet, at the start of the great postbellum surge of railroad growth, there were major barriers to the smooth flow of traffic. Most railroads were small, regional operations, creating a problem of transshipment for the interregional movement of traffic. Either because track gauges and other equipment had not been standardized or because the operating problems of

sharing equipment and revenues had not been worked out, freight and passengers often had to be transferred from one line's equipment and track to another's when moving over long distances. Realizing that this raised costs and otherwise impeded the goal of maximum traffic flow, the railroads began to cooperate in order to standardize equipment and gauges as well as to work out business arrangements for sharing equipment and revenue equitably. By the late 1880s and early 1890s, these various problems had been solved through railroad cooperation.

Another aspect of late nineteenth-century railroad cooperation was also important. In a large country like the United States, the coordination of interterritorial railroad traffic movements ran into a real obstacle: timing. Before the advent of such movements, scattered communities across the American landscape maintained their own local methods of reckoning time. This posed a problem for making up railroad schedules and for ensuring that trains operating under different methods of time reckoning did not bump into one another. In the 1880s, the solution was found in standard time with its twenty-four zones of 15 degrees longitude, starting from the Greenwich Observatory in London, England. American railroad leaders, almost of necessity, were among the prime movers for this worldwide system of time reckoning.

Changes in Managerial Structures

Both the competitive and cooperative aspects of railroad decision making in the late nineteenth century were carried out by a new breed of managers. American railroads, as noted earlier in the chapter, were the progenitors of the modern large-scale, multidivisional enterprise. By 1890, when the Pennsylvania Railroad alone employed 110,000 workers, the giant railroad systems of the United States were the largest business enterprises in the world. While large-scale operations led to efficiency, they also created tremendous problems of administrative coordination. To cope with these new problems, the railroads had to develop complex management structures and then staff them with professional managers. Under a single organization, functions such as finance, operations, and traffic were recognized as separate specialties. In many railroad corporations separate accounting, treasury, legal, purchasing, and freight (similar to marketing) departments emerged. The railroads' large-scale, capital-intensive technology and their massive volume of output meant that professional managers within the enterprise assumed more and more of the coordinating functions that external markets had performed in the earlier era of small-scale enterprise. Business historian Alfred D. Chandler, Jr., aptly described the transition: "The visible hand" of administrative coordination by managers was replacing (or supplementing) Adam Smith's "invisible hand" of market coordination by prices.[1] It should come as no surprise that business schools and degree programs for managers first appeared in the 1880s.

The Social Savings of Railroads

The development of steam-powered railway transportation was a prominent feature of American economic life in the last half of the nineteenth century. The achievements, antics, and failures of railway promoters were watched closely by Americans and others in the world because railroad developments affected them in many ways. European farmers were no less affected than their counterparts in America, for example, and the same was true of bond and stock investors here and abroad. The "romance of the rails" was a captivating event, as generations of children and their parents rode real trains and played with toy model trains. In light of this, it is not surprising that many observers seriously espoused the notion that the railroad was indispensable to the growth of the American economy. If such a notion is taken to mean that the railroad had a profound impact on the course of American economic life as it actually unfolded in the railroad age, few would find it exceptionable. But if it is taken to mean that the American economy without railroads would have grown at a much slower rate and would have attained levels of total and per capita income substantially lower than the ones that actually prevailed with railroads, there are some grounds for doubt. The discipline of economics reveals that among the more powerful and controlling influences on the demand for and supply of any good or service is the availability of substitutes. And economic history usually reveals that the range of available substitutes is wide indeed.

Defining and Measuring Social Saving

Economists define the *social savings* of an innovation as the difference between the actual cost of performing the work done by the innovation and the higher cost of doing the job that would have been entailed with available alternative technologies. In the case of nineteenth-century railroads, the alternative would have been a combination of water and wagon transportation. Calculations of the social savings of American railroads in 1859 and 1890 indicate that the savings were on the order of 5 percent of GNP for both years.[2] In other words, had the railroad not existed, about 5 percent of the resources that the American economy had in fact been able to devote to other productive purposes would have had to be diverted to the transportation sector in order to carry railroad traffic by nonrail means. The 1890 estimate, however, is low because it ignores passenger services and, it is argued, fails to take into account dynamic impacts on the rest of the economy of a greatly enlarged railroad sector. Nevertheless, whether the social savings in 1890 was 5 percent or 10 percent of GNP, the implication of such calculations is that American economic growth would not have suffered greatly had the railroads not been present.

This finding of *cliometrics*—that is, analytic and quantitative history—is significant. No innovation did more to shape the contours of the modern American economy than the nineteenth-century railroad. Its impacts on the location of economic activities, on the mobility of goods and persons, on business organization, on capital markets, and on political and social institutions were pervasive. Yet a modern economy is such a complex organization of resources and decision making that no single innovation or industry is critical to economic progress.

Substitutes for Rail Transportation

The basic reason the railroad does not appear as the indispensable ingredient of nineteenth-century growth that many considered it to be is that other possibilities in transportation existed. This was not the case everywhere in the world, but it was in the United States. Great improvements in river and canal transportation antedated the railroad age and did much to reduce transport costs to levels where water transport was nearly competitive with rail transport. Moreover, had the railroad not come along when it did, water transportation undoubtedly would have been improved and extended. Those who argued that the railroads were indispensable to economic growth probably meant that cheap transportation (with which they associated the railroad for good historical reasons) was indispensable. There were in the United States other means of cheap transportation; they were not quite as efficient as the railroad but they were also not vastly inferior to it. Indeed, to this day on many routes and for many commodities, water trans-

portation remains competitive with railway and other land-based modes of transport.

Railroads and the Political Economy of Regulation

Discriminatory Freight Rates

Although late nineteenth-century railroads carried increasing amounts of traffic at falling charges to consumers of their services, many consumers and railroad leaders were unhappy with the existing situation. The basic problem stemmed from variations in the degree of competition faced by the railroads. On the long hauls between major cities in different regions, competition for traffic was intense; on short hauls between cities and their surrounding countrysides, competition was virtually nonexistent. The strategy of railroad-pricing decisions therefore called for low freight rates on the long hauls and high rates on the short hauls. But this strategy did not sit well with farmers and small-town merchants who had to pay the high short-haul rates. They complained of discrimination in ever-more voluble tones, particularly when they discovered that discrimination was not only by location but also by size of user: certain large users of rail services (notably Rockefeller's Standard Oil Company) were favored with low rates through hidden rebates. Railroad leaders resented the charges made against them—that they charged the small shipper whatever the traffic would bear but gave bargain rates to the big intercity shippers. Although the railroad leaders did not admit so in public, they wanted to charge all shippers what the traffic would bear. To that end, they continually attempted through pools, cartels, and other forms of gentlemen's agreements to maintain rates at monopolistically high levels. But on the long hauls, where a number of separately managed routes, both rail and nonrail, were available, the railroads found that such agreements were exceedingly difficult to maintain.

State Regulation and the Munn Decision

By the early 1870s, in reaction to charges of railroad rate discrimination, several midwestern states passed Granger laws, named after the farmer's organizations that had promoted the legislation. The laws created state commissions empowered to regulate the rates and charges of railroads and other agents with whom the farmers dealt in their purchasing and marketing. Enterprises so regulated protested to the courts that some features of the regulations amounted to illegal confiscation of their property. In 1877, however, the Supreme Court in *Munn v. Illinois,* a case dealing with a grain elevator but extended to railroad cases, held that the states had a right to regulate private enterprises vital to the public interest. This right, strictly speaking, applied only to intrastate shipments because the Constitution reserved to Congress the right to regulate commerce between the states. When the Illinois regulators transgressed this boundary of federalism by attempting to set rates on interstate shipments, the Wabash Railway protested and was sustained by the Supreme Court in an 1886 decision.

Federal Regulation: The ICC

The *Wabash* case helped pave the way for passage by Congress of the Interstate Commerce Act of 1887, which marked the beginning of federal regulation by commission. The newly created Interstate Commerce Commission (ICC) was to see that railroad rates were reasonable and just and to prohibit personal and locational rate discrimination as well as agreements for the pooling of traffic and revenues. Railroads themselves were by no means opposed to all features of the regulatory act. They had long sought ways to bring more order to

their competitive struggles. And, in fact, in its *Second Annual Report,* the ICC went on record as opposing unreasonably low rates as being unfair to investors and a threat to good service. Hence, it is not surprising that federal regulation allowed the railroads to raise their rates on the previously competitive long-haul routes while mollifying the public through less discriminatory rate structures and relative declines in short-haul rates.

Nonetheless, when an individual railroad thought that regulatory decisions went against its particular interests, it instituted actions in the courts. And the railroads were often successful in overturning the authority of the ICC. In the Maximum Freight Rates decision of 1897, for example, the Supreme Court ruled that the ICC had the power to declare existing rates reasonable or unreasonable but not to prescribe future rates; that power remained with the railroads. In the same year, in *Interstate Commerce Commission v. Alabama Midland Railway Company,* the Court, citing some ambiguous language in the 1887 Interstate Commerce Act, overturned the ICC's power to prevent short-haul rates from exceeding long-haul rates on the same railroad. Federal regulation, then, was far from vigorous in solving the problems perceived, from different vantage points, by the railroads and the public.

Since government regulation had initially proved to be a weak method for solving their competitive problems, the railroads continued their earlier efforts to envelop competition by means of giant, consolidated systems. The movement for more regulation was, however, far from dead. When interests of the railroads and of the public coincided, stronger regulatory laws were forthcoming. Thus, the Elkins Act of 1903 was designed to end the practice of rebates to large shippers; the public resented rebates as discrimination in favor of large corporations, whereas the railroads resented the surreptitious competition that rebates fostered. But it required strong presidential and congressional leadership to restore to the ICC the regulatory powers it thought it had before the Supreme Court decisions of the 1890s proved otherwise. With the support of President Theodore Roosevelt, Congress in 1906 passed the Hepburn Act, which gave the ICC the power to prescribe maximum railroad rates. Four years later, the Mann-Elkins Act undid the Alabama Midland decision of 1897 by granting the ICC clear authority over long- and short-haul rate differences. The power of the ICC to regulate railroad rates was thus firmly established. By that time, however, the condition of intense competition on some routes, coupled with monopoly on others (monopoly had provided the initial impetus to regulation), had been altered by the railroads themselves through consolidations. The American people were nonetheless satisfied that the government, through the ICC, was looking after the public interest. In time, as new modes of transportation were developed, the railroads would find that the ICC, by using its regulatory powers to restrict competition in transportation, would look after their interests as well.

Regulation in Historical Perspective

Even a cursory glance at the origins of regulation through supposedly independent government commissions is sufficient to suggest that decisions to regulate were the outcome of complex crosscurrents of economic, social, and political forces. The decisions were not always made to protect consumers from the ill effects of monopoly, as some traditional views of regulation assume. Problems of competition, as perceived by railroad leaders, stood along with problems of monopoly, as perceived by consumers, in the early drive for government regulation. These findings, documented extensively by historical scholarship, are important to a fair understanding of the past. But they also lend perspective to our own era when dis-

affection with the effects of vastly expanded government regulation became widespread. Within a pluralistic American political system, regulation could protect consumers from monopoly. But because business interests were far more concentrated than the diffuse interests of consumers, regulation often did a better job of satisfying the former than the latter. The movements for deregulation in the 1970s and 1980s were based on analyses of regulatory history.

Advances in Communication

Railroads and Postal Service

Modern economies require a huge volume and rapid flow of information for efficient decision making. Advanced technologies of large-scale production in concentrated areas, for example, would be less feasible without a continued flow of up-to-date information on resource prices and market demands in distant places. Seen in this light, the railroad represented enormous advances in rapid communication and the spread of information. It moved both people and informational goods (such as newspapers) at faster speeds than previously had been possible, and through all kinds of weather. The railroad also played a large role in the formation of the modern postal system. In 1847, railroads accounted for some 11 percent of the miles that mail was transported by the federal postal service. Just ten years later, the figure had risen to 33 percent. The efficiency of railroads in carrying mail was reflected in price as well as in volume and speed. In 1850, it cost five cents to send an ounce of mail up to three hundred miles and ten cents beyond that distance. Five years later, the standard rate was three cents per ounce for any distance. The rising efficiency of service and the rising volume of mail transported by rail led to the adoption of new methods for making the posting of a letter more convenient, while at the same time saving on postal labor. The printed postage stamp thus made its first appearance and passed into general use at the time when railroads were revolutionizing mail service. In earlier days, people took their letters to the post office during its hours of operation and paid a clerk the postage charges.

Telegraphy: The Western Union Company

Even though the gains of railways in the speedy movement of people, goods, and mail were great, they did not suffice for all purposes. Railway managers for example, could hardly coordinate the simultaneous movement of a number of trains over their railroads with messages sent by train. The trains might have crashed before the messages designed to prevent such crashes could be delivered. Here the electromagnetic telegraph furnished a solution by providing nearly instantaneous communication between widely separated points. Its first practical demonstration came in the mid-1840s when, with the aid of a federal subsidy, the inventor Samuel F. B. Morse and his associates built a line between Washington and Baltimore. In 1851, the Erie Railroad introduced the telegraph to control train movements, thus commencing a long and fruitful relationship between the two technologies. The railroad supplied an already existing right-of-way for telegraph wires, and the telegraph supplied the quick communications needed to manage efficiently a complex and far-flung enterprise.

With telegraphic technology the advantages of administrative coordination in a single large enterprise over the coordination of many competing firms through markets were demonstrated. By 1866, the Western Union Company had absorbed its rivals, becoming in effect the telegraphic system of the United States. Its near monopoly of telegraphic communication, however, produced no major outcry on the

part of the public, in part because the mails offered a viable alternative in many cases and in part because the threat of potential competition in telegraphy was real. When Jay Gould, the Mephistopheles of Wall Street, who had done so much to convince other railroad leaders of the advantage of building large systems, was putting together his own rail system during the 1870s, he initiated a threat to Western Union by creating a telegraph system to go along with his rail empire. Whether Gould actually wanted his own telegraph company or planned from the beginning to sell out at a profit to a worried Western Union is unclear, but he did take the latter action in 1878. It was a rewarding tactic for the clever and well-heeled financier, an early "greenmailer," and he soon decided to repeat it by forming a second telegraphy company. Word of Gould's new project was sufficient to depress the price of Western Union's stock to the point where even Gould thought it a good buy. By his influence in the decision-making councils of Western Union, secured by his purchase of the firm's stock, Gould encountered few problems in selling his second independent company to the giant of telegraphy.

The Telephone

Although the railroad and telegraph brought about significant improvements in the flow of information required for better decision making in a growing and increasingly complex economic organization, the problem of instantaneous voice communication between individuals separated by various distances remained. It was, in principle, solved when Alexander Graham Bell in 1876 invented and patented a working prototype of the telephone, an instrument that transmitted the sound of a human voice through vibrations produced by an electric current passing through a wire. The development of American telephony over the ensuing four decades

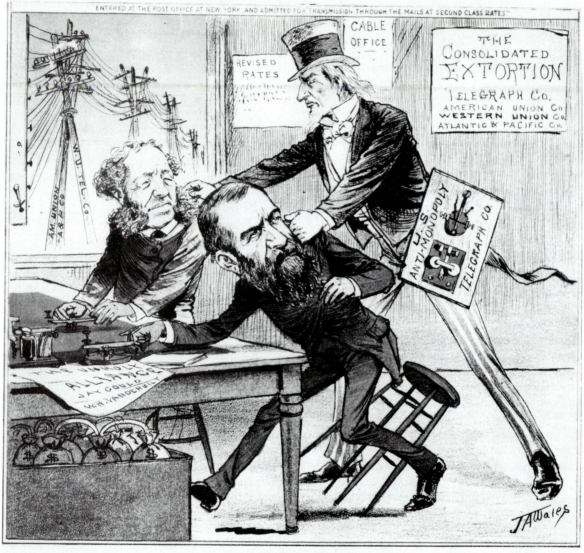

THE BEST REMEDY.

Breaking the Gould–Vanderbilt Telegraph Monopoly.   This 1881 cartoon from the magazine *Puck* shows Uncle Sam getting tough with financiers Jay Gould and William H. Vanderbilt (Commodore Cornelius Vanderbilt's son and heir), who were attempting to merge competing telegraph companies. In less than a decade, the Sherman Antitrust Act (1890) would further restrict business combinations. (The Bettmann Archive)

Theodore Vail of AT&T. Vail, a leading figure in the early decades of the American Telephone and Telegraph Company, is seen here demonstrating one of the keys to that corporation's success in dominating U.S. telephony: its long-distance telephone network. Seated at his desk in New York City, Vail is talking to Honolulu, 4,900 miles away, in 1915. The AT&T strategy of private monopoly subject to government regulation was put in place and matured under Vail. (Courtesy of the AT&T Archives)

furnishes an interesting case study of decision making under both monopoly and competition. It also provides further insight into the mix of motives underlying the historical emergence and early behavior of modern regulatory institutions.

Era of Patent Monopoly, 1876–1893. Within a decade of Bell's initial patent, the organizational structure of the Bell System—the dominant enterprise in American telephony until it was dismembered by the courts a century later—had emerged. Alexander Graham Bell assigned his patents to a company organized by his backers; after several name changes, it became in 1880 the American Bell Telephone Company. In 1882, the Western Electric Company was acquired to manufacture and supply equipment for the system; then, in 1885, the American Telephone and Telegraph Company was organized as a subsidiary to provide long lines, or long-distance phone service. During these years, a number of subsidiary regional companies were formed to lease Bell equipment to local subscribers and to operate local service. Theodore N. Vail, a man experienced in telegraph operations, was brought in as the Bell Company's general manager in 1878; it was his policy to maintain Bell control of the telephone business through large-scale expansion. Vail vacated his position when the company's board of directors, cognizant of their monopoly, opted instead for a policy of limited expansion and a high rate of profit. As we will see later in the chapter, Vail was to return—vindicated—at a later date.

Seventeen years (1876 to 1893) of telephone development under the Bell patent monopoly ended with 266,000 Bell phones in service in the United States. The monopolistic prices charged by Bell had restricted development mainly to the business centers of large urban areas. Many communities on the fringes of these central business areas, as well as smaller towns and rural areas, were largely without telephone service. After 1893, when the first Bell patents expired, such places became prime targets for invasion by independent telephone companies that were organized to compete with Bell. The emergence of independent telephone companies after 1893 is an interesting phenomenon in light of the common view that the business of telephony is, from the nature of its technology, a natural monopoly (i.e., a business in which one producer in principle can supply a market more efficiently than a group of competitive producers). Telephone service may very well be a natural monopoly, at least on the local level. But the emergence of competition in American telephony after 1893 demonstrates a further and perhaps more subtle point: The right to provide telephone service can be opened up to competitive bidding even if the provision of service is best left to one supplier. The independent telephone movement caught on after 1893, when the new companies undercut Bell's monopoly rates and secured franchises to provide service in areas that Bell had ignored.

Competitive Struggles.   The effects of competition in telephony were striking. Between 1893 and 1907, when the independent movement reached its peak in relative terms, the number of phones in the United States increased from 266,000 to 6.1 million. Of these, 3 million were independent and 3.1 million were Bell phones; Bell's market share had fallen from 100 percent to 51 percent. Although its market share had been cut nearly in half, Bell reacted vigorously to the new competition by cutting its

charges to subscribers and by adding more than ten times as many phones in 1893 to 1907 as it had put into service in the era of its monopoly from 1876 to 1893. But the old monopoly, called American Telephone and Telegraph Company (AT&T) after 1900, was not enthusiastic about competition, which had cut its rate of return on investment from over 40 percent under the patent monopoly to only 8 percent over the years 1900 to 1906. AT&T began to propagandize against competition as well as particular competitors. Bell also attempted to weaken its competitors by refusing to sell them equipment or to allow them to connect into Bell's established long-distance network. The former tactic had little effect because several independent telephone-equipment manufacturers filled the void, but Bell's refusal to interconnect with the independents was a more powerful weapon in the competitive struggle.

After 1907, Bell System policies were altered and the company appeared to become more conciliatory toward independent competition. The impetus for this change came from bankers who had observed AT&T investing greater amounts of capital in the effort to keep pace with its competitors while at the same time suffering a falling rate of return on its investments. A New York banking group headed by George F. Baker and J. P. Morgan took control of the Bell System in 1907 and brought Theodore Vail back as president. Vail changed the emphasis of the Bell System's struggle against competition from a private concern for its own financial interests to a "public" concern over the wastefulness and duplication of competition. In terms of tactics, with the independents stymied by Bell's refusal to interconnect, Bell under Vail began to offer them a solution to their problem by acquiring them. It even reversed the ban on equipment sales for two reasons: The independents had grown to such a size that they constituted an attractive equipment market, and Bell's growth through acquisition would be easier if the independents were already using Bell equipment. Vail's policies were effective in turning around the Bell System's trend of market share. By absorption and expansion, Bell added some 2 million phones between 1907 and 1912, whereas the independents collectively grew by only 0.6 million phones.

Regulation Replaces Competition. The cornerstone of Bell's post-1907 corporate policy to reverse its relative decline involved an about-face with respect to regulation. During its thirty years of operation under both patent monopoly and relatively free competition, the Bell System generally had opposed government regulation. In 1907, under Vail, the Bell System became more accommodating. Vail and the bankers, observing the stabilizing effects of the ICC on railroad markets and price structures, concluded that telephony might benefit from similar arrangements. One of the first practical results of Bell's policy shift came in 1910, when the Mann-Elkins Act (noted earlier in connection with railroad regulation) bestowed on the ICC the authority to regulate telephone and telegraph companies. Both the Bell System and the independent telephone industry approved of this extension of federal regulatory power; they were less enamored of the competitive struggle. From then on the Bell System began to invest considerable resources in shaping the new regulatory climate at both the federal and state levels. With the decline of competition and the growth of regulation, Bell's market share increased for several decades and then stabilized at about five-sixths of all U.S. phones. For many years AT&T, in terms of measures such as tangible assets and profits, was the largest private corporation in the world. During the 1970s, however, development of competitive microwave technologies undermined AT&T's case for a natural monopoly of long-distance telephone service. In the 1980s, the company was broken up into independent regional operating companies, with a smaller AT&T emerging as a competitive producer of long-distance service and telephone equipment.

Summary

The railroad, the telegraph, and the telephone were the transportation and communication links that, by the beginning of the twentieth century, bound the distant regions of the United States into a unified economy of unprecedented dimensions in world history. These nineteenth-century innovations had many impacts, but their greatest achievement was the operational meaning they brought to the national economy. The size of the free-trade area within the United States became a source of growth and development; it functioned to stimulate the development of new resources, the implementation of large-scale technologies of production, and continual increases in specialization and division of labor. Although other similar-sized regions of the world possessed resources and technical knowledge equal to that of the United States, none had the opportunity to exploit a marketplace of comparable size. From the time of the signing of the Constitution, the American political and economic environment favored the development of a huge national economy; a century later, technological advances in transportation and communication made that possible.

Endnotes

1. Alfred D. Chandler, Jr., *The Visible Hand: The Managerial Revolution in American Business* (Cambridge, Mass.: Harvard University Press, 1977), Part II.
2. For the 1859 calculation, see Albert Fishlow, *American Railroads and the Transformation of the Antebellum Economy*; for the 1890 calculation, see Robert Fogel, *Railroads, and American Economic Growth*. Full citations are in Suggested Readings.

Suggested Readings

For concise historical surveys of transportation and other economic developments in the 1860 to 1914 period, see Edward C. Kirkland, *Industry Comes of Age: Business, Labor, and Public Policy, 1860–1897* (New York: Holt, 1961); and Harold U. Faulkner, *The Decline of Laissez-Faire, 1897–1917* (New York: Holt, 1951)—both of which are especially helpful on the emergence of railroad regulation. A more analytical economic survey is given in chapter 13 of Lance Davis et al., "Internal Transportation," in *American Economic Growth: An Economist's History of the United States* (New York: Harper & Row, 1971) —in particular, it summarizes the estimates of railroad social savings in 1859 and 1890. For the details of social savings calculations and penetrating analyses of economic issues in railroad development, see Albert Fishlow, *American Railroads and the Transformation of the Antebellum Economy* (Cambridge, Mass.: Harvard University Press, 1965); and Robert W. Fogel, *Railroads and American Growth* (Baltimore: Johns Hopkins University Press, 1964). Passenger social savings are the subject of J. Hayden Boyd and Gary M. Walton, "The Social Savings from Nineteenth-Century Rail Passenger Services," *Explorations in Economic History*, 9 (Spring 1971). The detailed and sometimes controversial debate that arose over interpreting the social-savings findings is dealt with at considerable length in Robert W. Fogel, "Notes on the Social Savings Controversy," *Journal of Economic History*, 39 (March 1979). For a good discussion of the movement from local time to standard time, see Michael O'Malley, *Keeping Watch: A History of American Time* (New York: Viking, 1990).

The prize-winning book of Alfred D. Chandler, Jr., *The Visible Hand: The Managerial Revolution in American Business* (Cambridge, Mass.: Harvard University Press, 1977), analyzes the pioneering contributions of railroads to modern economic organization. Chandler deals to some extent with individual railroad leaders; for a more personal view, Matthew Josephson, *The Robber Barons: The Great American Capitalists, 1661–1901* (New York: Harcourt, 1962), is still fascinating reading. For aspects of railroad finance, see Mira Wilkins, *The History of Foreign Investment in the United States to 1914* (Cambridge, Mass.: Harvard University Press, 1989); Dorothy R. Adler, *British Investment in American Railways, 1834–1898* (Charlottesville: University Press of Virginia, 1970); Stanley L. Engerman, "Some Economic Issues Relating to Railroad Subsidies and the Evaluation of Land Grants," *Journal of Economic History*, 33 (June 1972); and Robert W. Fogel, *The Union Pacific Railroad: A Case in Premature Enterprise* (Baltimore: Johns Hopkins University Press, 1960). The most useful study of the growth of railroad productivity is Albert Fishlow, "Productivity and Technological Change in the Railroad Sector, 1840–1910," in National Bureau of Economic Research, *Output, Employment, and Productivity in the United States After 1800: Studies in Income and Wealth,* vol. 30 (New York: National Bureau of Economic Research, 1966).

Challenging analyses of the early regulatory movement include Gabriel Kolko, *Railroads and Regulation, 1877–1916* (Princeton: Princeton University Press, 1965); Paul MacAvoy, *The Economic Effects of Regulation* (Cambridge, Mass.: MIT Press, 1965); and two books by Albro Martin, *Enterprise Denied: Origins of the Decline of American Railroads, 1897–1917* (New York: Columbia University Press, 1971), a vigorous critique of Kolko's book, and *Railroads Triumphant: The Growth, Rejection, and Rebirth of a Vital American Force* (New York: Oxford University Press, 1992), a full account of railroad-government interactions.

Alfred Chandler's *The Visible Hand*, cited earlier, gives some attention to the communications industries. On early telephony, see the following four volumes published by Johns Hopkins University Press in its series on telephone history: Robert Garnet, *The Telephone Enterprise: The Evolution of the Bell System's Horizontal Structure, 1876–1909* (1985); George David Smith, *The Anatomy of a Business Strategy: Bell, Western Electric, and the Origins of the American Telephone Industry* (1985); Neil H. Wasserman, *From Invention to Innovation: Long-Distance Telephone Transmission at the Turn of the Century* (1985); and Kenneth Lipartito, *The Bell System and Regional Business: The Telephone in the South, 1877–1920* (1989). See also Richard Gabel, "The Early Competitive Era in Telephone Communication, 1893–1910," *Law and Contemporary Problems* (Spring 1969); and J. Warren Stehman, *The Financial History of the American Telephone and Telegraph Company* (New York: Augustus M. Kelley, 1967). The breakup of AT&T in the 1980s is the subject of Peter Temin with Louis Galambos, *The Fall of the Bell System* (Cambridge: Cambridge University Press, 1987).

Chapter 15

The Financial System Under Stress

THE CIVIL WAR, LIKE ALL MAJOR WARS IN THE nation's history, placed great strains on the American financial system. The war created a new financial situation, and from that time forward decision making at the federal level came to predominate. In the period of creative political economy under the Federalist management of Alexander Hamilton in the 1790s, the basic outlines of American arrangements in money, banking, and government finance emerged. Later antebellum decades were marked by backing and filling—in short, marginal adjustments—at the federal level. The more important financial developments of the era emerged from considerable experimentation with new institutional forms and regulatory arrangements, primarily in banking, among private and state governmental decision makers. As a result of these experiments, when the Civil War made it necessary for national leaders to make major financial decisions, there was a wealth of financial experience—both good and bad—from which they could draw. The choices they made affected many generations of Americans. Indeed, most of the financial developments of historical significance during the next half-century were rooted in the decisions of 1861 to 1865.

Legacies of Civil War Finance

The major financial problem faced by governments in wartime is how to divert economic resources from peacetime uses to war efforts. In peacetime, economic resources—labor, capital, and land—are used to produce the consumer and capital goods and services, including governmental goods and services, that satisfy people's present and future wants. In wartime, when the survival of a society is often threatened, ways must be found to reduce the satisfaction of normal private and collective wants in order to win the war.

Three financial methods that a government can use to achieve the necessary diversion of resources to war objectives are *taxation, borrowing,* and *money creation*. Each in its own way removes purchasing power from individuals and private organizations and places it in the hands of the government. In most large-scale wars of modern history, including the American Civil War, policymakers used a combination of these three methods.

Taxation

Taxation is the least complicated and most direct method for a government to finance a war. Taxes embody the idea of compulsory payments to the government, which imposes the taxes and enforces their collection. There has always been a debate between different economic groups over whether raising revenue by taxation, by borrowing, or by creating money is the best alternative. When the Civil War began, there was reluctance by a few federal officials to rely on tax finance. But patriotism made the American people accept more taxation every year. As a result, by 1865, taxes had paid for about one-fifth of the federal government's total wartime expenditures. This precedent made it possible for taxes to cover about two-fifths of the government's expenditures during World War I and three-fifths during World War II.

Civil War Taxes   Although the federal government's tax effort during the Civil War was relatively small in comparison with those during the world wars, it was much more extensive than that of earlier wars. During the War of Independence, for example, the power of the national government to enact formal taxes was essentially nonexistent. During the War of 1812, the government had the ability to raise taxation but the will to do so developed only late in the war. During the Civil War, however, there was not a lack of ability on the part of federal decision makers to collect taxes. Indeed, virtually every kind of tax that had ever been put into effect by any level of government in the United States was adopted by Congress at this time, and some new ones were added to the list. In the former category, tariffs were increased and direct taxes on real property, excise taxes, license taxes, and stamp duties based on earlier federal precedents were revived and extended. All manufactured articles were taxed at either specific or ad valorem rates, and gross receipts taxes were placed on the sale of a variety of services (such as transportation and advertising). In the new-tax category were added income and inheritance taxes. The ratio of tax revenues to total federal expenditures increased from 10 percent in 1862 to 25 percent in 1865.

Postwar Tax Reductions   With the end of the Civil War in 1865, federal expenditures fell sharply. The first of many consecutive years of federal budget surpluses appeared in fiscal year (FY) 1866, creating a favorable climate for tax reduction. But decisions had to be made regarding which taxes to reduce or eliminate. The choice was often cast in terms of tariffs and internal taxes, and when cast in such terms, the choice seemed obvious. Tariffs on imports had been a mainstay of federal finance from the beginning of the government under the Constitution. Unlike internal taxes, customs duties (which had increased markedly during the war) had a large, organized, and influential body of supporters among producers, who were protected in varying degrees from foreign competition by taxes on imports of their products. Internal taxes, in contrast, had no such constituency; instead, they were largely viewed as temporary nuisances or as tending to harm economic development. Farm and labor groups supported the income tax, but manufacturing and financial pressure groups successfully fought it until the Constitution was amended in 1913.

Thus, in the late 1860s and early 1870s, nearly all of the internal taxes imposed during the Civil War were reduced and then eliminated. Of the main revenue-producing taxes, manufacturers' excises and gross receipts taxes were repealed in 1867 and 1868, respectively, and income taxes in 1872. After the latter date, the only high-yielding internal taxes retained were those on liquor and tobacco products, two items of consumption almost unique in their capacity to generate both a steady tax revenue and a popular feeling that they deserve to be taxed.

High Tariffs and Budget Surpluses   In terms of taxation, the significant aspect of wartime financial decisions for later economic developments was a return—one that persisted for decades—to high tariffs on imports as the mainstay of federal finance. Average tariff rates, measured by the ratio of customs duties to the value of taxed imports, had fallen from over 50 percent in the late 1820s to approximately 20 percent in 1860. During the Civil War, the average tariff rate rose to between 40 percent and 50 percent and remained at such levels until 1913. To a great extent, the late nineteenth-century tariffs taxed consumer goods, as did the federal government's two important domestic taxes—those on liquor and tobacco. When the nation's economy expanded at high rates in the postwar decades, the consumption of imports, liquor, and tobacco—and consequently federal revenues—all increased. But federal spending did not increase to the same extent. Post–Civil War administrations were therefore faced with a new financial problem: what to do about the government's budget surpluses. The use, during the Civil War, of another method of diverting resources from private hands to the government—borrowing—furnished a solution to that problem.

Borrowing

The federal government's reluctance to tax during the Civil War meant that borrowing became the primary method of government finance. Borrowing took on two forms. In the first, traditional form, the government swapped its promises to pay given sums of money—principal and interest—at specified times in the future for current purchasing power (i.e., *interest-bearing debt*). In the second form of borrowing, the government issued a *noninterest-bearing debt,* which usually did not have a specific redemption date but an implicit promise or understanding that the paper would be redeemed at some time. This form of debt was essentially the printing of fiat paper money by the government.

During the war years the issue of interest-bearing debt was unprecedented. This form of federal debt rose from $90 million in 1861 to $2322 million in 1866. In current dollar terms (that is, dollars unadjusted for inflation), the government borrowed in a few years a sum roughly twice as large as what had been expended by investors on the construction of antebellum railroads in three decades. Under the stimulus of such massive government borrowing, both financial technologies and financial institutions underwent widespread changes that helped to modernize the American capital market.

Jay Cooke and the Mass Marketing of Federal Securities. In the area of financial technology, the huge volume of federal securities marketed during the Civil War required a vastly different system of distribution. Before the war, most federal and state securities as well as some private securities were sold through a loan-contracting process in which the issuer advertised the amount and terms of a loan and invited bids from interested investors. The highest bids were accepted, and the winning contractors disposed of the securities through private channels of distribution. The loan-contracting system worked fairly well for small and infrequent issues, but the Civil War loans were of a much larger magnitude.

Jay Cooke, 1821–1905. In marketing hundreds of millions of dollars worth of federal government bonds during the Civil War, Jay Cooke & Company, a Philadelphia private banking house founded in 1861, pioneered modern techniques of mass security distribution. After the war, Cooke's firm specialized in marketing railroad securities; it failed during the financial panic of 1873, when it could not market securities it had underwritten. (Historical Pictures/Stock Montage)

After the older methods were tried and found ineffective, the Treasury Department turned over its bond-selling business to the agency of Jay Cooke, a private banker in Philadelphia. Cooke devised new methods of security distribution with great success. From October 1862 to January 1864, Cooke's organization sold $362 million of a $510 million issue of the so-called "five-twenties" (6 percent bonds callable after five years and maturing in twenty years) at par, and other sales were stimulated by his methods. In January 1865, Cooke was again called on by the Treasury to act as general agent in its bond sales; his organization succeeded over several months in selling most of an $830 million issue of so-called "seven-thirties" (7.3 percent notes maturing in three years). By then Cooke's name had become a household word and he was admired as one of the great architects of the Union victory.

Although Cooke's methods were relatively simple, their implementation depended crucially on a large volume of sales, which explains why they had not appeared earlier in the United States. For a payment of only a fraction of 1 percent of the proceeds of the loans, Cooke was able to employ an army of agents and subagents who canvassed the country selling bonds in denominations as low as $50 to people in all walks of life (including federal troops) and at all levels of income and wealth. The agents numbered about 2500 in the "five-twenty" campaign and four thousand to five thousand in the sale of the "seven-thirties." They included most of the country's banks and bankers, who not only retailed the bonds but also bought them for their own accounts and financed other investors' purchases by lending them the money to buy federal bonds.

After the extensive agency system, the next distributional innovation of importance in the success of Cooke's bond campaigns was advertising. Newspapers throughout the nation published Cooke's ads as well as articles written by Cooke and his aides explaining the features of the federal loans and describing the great successes already achieved in their distribution. These, together with numerous handbills circulated by the agents, appealed to the patriotism and economic self-interest of small investors. Large investors were informed that the bonds constituted a first mortgage on all the wealth and income of the country.

The National Banking System.   Cooke's innovations in security distribution were also used to promote another important change in financial technology and institutions resulting from

the war—the National Banking System, established in 1863. The banking bills before Congress in 1862 and 1863 required the proposed national banks to become heavy buyers of federal bonds. Cooke realized that the existence of such banks would aid his bond-selling campaign. But opposition to federally chartered banks was strong, especially on the part of the state banks. Cooke, therefore, decided to urge his agents and the newspapers in which he advertised to tout the advantages of the proposed system over the old state banks. He saw to it, moreover, that members of Congress received word of public opinion thus properly informed. After the bill to charter national banks became law, Cooke helped organize several of the new banks, including the first to receive a charter. He also wrote a pamphlet, distributed in part through his agents, telling others how to form national banks.

Government Finance and Capital Market Integration.   Methods of large-scale security distribution and a system of national banks holding significant amounts of the federal debt were the enduring consequences of the government's debt financing during the Civil War. Numerous individuals and enterprises were introduced to investments in paper wealth. Through the National Banking System, the nation's banks were drawn into a close relationship with federal finances. A single, national capital market began to emerge out of the heterogeneous and loosely related markets of earlier decades. At the center of this capital market was the market for government securities. Here the financial mechanisms created in the war years were kept active after the war, as the government first funded a variety of its short-term obligations into long-term bonds and then, as bond yields fell, refunded large portions of the debt into bonds carrying lower interest rates. While these operations were being carried out during the late 1860s to the early 1870s, as well as in subsequent years, the government helped to spread the new techniques of high finance to other sectors of the capital market through a policy of *debt retirement*. This "policy" of debt retirement was less a conscious policy decision than a course of action thrust on postbellum administrations by growing tax revenues and relatively stable expenditures. The annual budget surpluses generated by tax and expenditure policies were disposed of by retiring outstanding government bonds. In the process, many of the investors who sold their bonds to the government for cash then sought new investment outlets. Through the increasingly organized and efficient capital markets, the nation's growth sectors—transportation, manufacturing, and state and local public works—provided more than an ample supply of new securities to replace the retired government bonds. The money, bond, and stock markets of the nation's financial center in New York City's Wall Street were thus linked with thousands of Main Streets throughout the country.

Money Creation

Inadequate tax finance and problems connected with borrowing early in the Civil War forced the Lincoln administration to turn to still another method of commandeering resources away from private hands: printing and spending paper money. In July 1861, Congress, as a part of a $250 million loan package, had authorized the issue of up to $50 million of noninterest-bearing notes redeemable on demand in specie. These so-called "demand notes" were made acceptable for payments to the government and for some payments by the government (such as government employees' salaries). But with the redeemability feature, they were still a debt instrument.

The Greenbacks and Civil War Inflation. When, at the end of 1861, the banks of the country as well as the government were forced to suspend specie redemption of paper liabilities, the financial emergency that paralleled the military crisis created a situation of desperation for government finance. The result was the Legal Tender Act of February 1862. The new law authorized the Treasury to print and spend $150 million of U.S. notes, called *greenbacks;* they were not specifically redeemable at any future date or in any monetary metal. Greenbacks were declared by law to be full legal tender for almost all public and private debts; they thus were the first fiat paper money issue of the U.S. government. The two exceptions to full legal tender were that greenbacks would not be accepted by the government in payment of customs duties and could not be used by the government to pay interest on the federal debt. Specie payments continued to be required in these transactions throughout the seventeen-year period 1862 to 1878 when the United States was off a specie standard.

The first issue of greenbacks in the spring of 1862 did little to alleviate the Treasury's financial problems. War expenditures were draining off funds as fast as they came in, prompting renewed trips to the printing press. In mid-1862 and again in early 1863, additional $150 million issues of greenbacks were authorized, making the total authorization $450 million.

The result of such a massive infusion of fiat paper money, together with other government debt issues and bank-created money, was a rapid rise in prices. Demand for economic resources exceeded supply at given price levels, and price inflation was the mechanism through which markets were cleared. The extent of the Civil War inflation was evident in a number of areas. Wholesale prices, for example, at their peak in January 1865, were about 2.3 times their level at the outbreak of the war in April 1861, representing an inflation rate of 25 percent per year. Estimates of the cost of living indicate that an approximate doubling of consumer prices took place during the war. Another measure of inflation—the premium on gold—was also dramatic. When, as before

The Greenback, or United States Note.   From February 1862 to March 1863, the federal government authorized and issued $450 million of greenbacks to aid in financing its Civil War expenditures. These legal tender notes were a fiat currency; they could not be exchanged for gold or silver dollars. The greenbacks fueled an inflation that doubled prices between 1862 and 1864. The one-dollar greenback shown here features a portrait of Salmon P. Chase, who as wartime Secretary of the Treasury issued them. In 1864, Chase succeeded Roger Taney as Chief Justice of the United States; on the Supreme Court he contended that the greenbacks were unconstitutional. (The Bettmann Archive)

the war, paper dollars were convertible into gold dollars, there was no premium. Before the first greenbacks were issued in 1862, but after the banks and government had suspended convertibility of paper liabilities into gold at fixed rates, it took $1.02 in paper to buy a gold dollar. In mid-1864, at the peak of the paper dollar's depreciation, it took $2.62 in paper to buy a gold dollar. But by mid-1865, when the war was over, a gold dollar could be purchased for $1.43 in paper. As we will see later in the chapter, one major objective of postwar financial policy was eliminating the discrepancy in value between the gold dollar and the greenback dollar.

The financing of the Civil War by the federal government thus brought about tremendous changes in the American financial system. At the war's end, serious problems remained and effective decisions were needed to resolve them. Increases in old taxes and the imposition

of many new taxes had resulted in a tax contribution of about one-fifth of the government's total war expenditures, yet these taxes were more than adequate to finance the reduced levels of federal expenditures after the war. Although postwar governments eliminated internal taxes (with the exception of the excises on liquor and tobacco products), they maintained for decades the large increases in customs duties enacted during the war. Even with the tax reductions, however, the federal budget was in surplus for over a quarter-century after 1865. Still, a huge war debt had been incurred, so the surpluses were used to reduce that debt by transferring money from taxpayers to bondholders. A new system of national banks had been created to aid war finance, but in 1865 it was not clear whether that new system would play a major role in future American finance. As a result of the various monetary schemes adopted during the war (most notably, the fiat greenback issues), the nation's money supply was greatly enlarged, price levels were doubled, and the paper dollars that most Americans used were worth substantially less than the interconvertible gold, silver, and paper dollars of antebellum decades. The agenda of postwar decision makers in resolving monetary and banking problems would be a large one indeed.

Money and Prices

The story of money and prices in the United States during the half-century following the Civil War is particularly interesting to students of economic history. If one considers the period as a whole, the story represents a continuation of broad trends established earlier. As noted in Chapter 7, during the four decades prior to the Civil War, the nation's money supply grew at a rate of about 5 percent per year, whereas the overall trend of prices was stable or mildly downward. From 1867 to 1914, the *money stock*—defined as coin and paper currency plus commercial bank deposits owned by the public—grew at a rate of about 5.3 percent per year, whereas wholesale prices declined at a rate of 1.3 percent per year. As before the Civil War, there were notable fluctuations in monetary growth and price movements during the postbellum decades. Indeed, most of the attention of both contemporaries and later analysts was devoted to aspects of the shorter-term fluctuations. Before turning to these short-term changes, we need first to look at the long-term trends in order to understand more fully the immediate financial problems.

Growth of the Money Supply

In the United States and elsewhere in the Western world, the monetary and price history of the nineteenth century was markedly differ-

ent from that of earlier centuries as well as the twentieth century. The main difference was the divergent behavior of long-term monetary and price trends. In the nineteenth century, considerable innovations in monetary arrangements, including both the explicit addition of governmental fiat elements to the older metallic bases of monetary systems and a persistent spread of banking institutions that added increasing amounts of bank money to metallic and fiat paper currencies, led to substantial growth of money supplies. The evidence indicates, for example, that the money supply trended upward at an annual rate of over 5.5 percent from 1820 to 1914. Another way of viewing this monetary expansion is to note that the U.S. money supply in 1914 was 190 times its level in 1820, whereas the U.S. population increased only 10.3 times in the same period. Thus, money per capita was $163 in 1914 but only about $9 in 1820. Yet in spite of such high absolute and relative rates of monetary expansion, which both before and after the nineteenth century have usually been associated with rising price levels, the long-term trend of nineteenth-century prices was mildly downward.

Expanding Market Activity and the Demand for Money

Why in this one century did units of money, such as the U.S. dollar and the British pound sterling, become more valuable in terms of their ability to purchase goods despite enormous increases in their supply? One answer is that the demand for money in the nineteenth century increased even more rapidly than the supply of money. But why did this occur? No doubt increases in population and the growth of per capita production through technological improvements, capital accumulation, and the augmentation of all kinds of economic resources account for much of the growth of monetary demand. Neither population nor total economic output, however, grew anywhere near as fast as the supply of money, and so they cannot by themselves account for the excess demand for money that was eliminated by falling price levels for goods. A complete accounting would therefore have to include other factors, the most important being the increase in market-oriented economic activity relative to nonmarket activity over the course of the century.

The effect of an increase in market activity on the demand for money is easily illustrated. Consider the typical American family of the early 1900s versus the typical farm family of the early 1800s. The farm family produced most of what it consumed at home and traded for the rest of its needs with neighbors in the local community. It accumulated wealth mostly in the form of real assets (such as land, buildings, and livestock), while economic security was provided by intergenerational transfers within the family unit. A century later, the typical family—as likely to be urban as rural—specialized in production and sold its resources (e.g., labor) and products in markets for cash, using the proceeds to purchase consumer goods and capital assets. A family's wealth accumulation was as much a matter of purchasing financial assets—money, savings accounts, life insurance policies, even stocks and bonds—as of buying real assets—farms and houses. In part, the motivation for new forms of asset accumulation came from the erosion of older intrafamily forms of lifetime economic security by growing specialization, increased geographic and occupational mobility, and a wider range of economic opportunities. Market exchanges penetrated virtually all areas of economic activity, where a century earlier they had been far less pervasive. Hence, there resulted an increased demand for the medium of exchange—money—that was much greater than the increase of economic activity.

The Gold Standard Constraint

Although the demand for money was growing, the supply of money did not keep up with the demand in the sense that long-term stable price levels were not maintained. The growth of the nineteenth-century money supply was hindered by widespread beliefs that "true" money was made of a precious metal (usually gold) and a "true" monetary unit (such as the dollar) had to represent a fixed quantity of that precious metal. Although many people sought to create and put into use vast quantities of other types of money, the so-called "gold standard" was embodied in laws and institutions and thus remained. It manifested itself in economic policies, deflationary trends that provoked protest movements, and financial upheavals that eventually led to reform of the monetary system in the twentieth century.

The Economics of Resumption

At the end of 1861, American banks and the federal government had to suspend convertibility of their paper monetary liabilities into specie because they did not possess enough metallic money to meet the demands of holders. Paper money issued by the government, such as the legal tender greenbacks or U.S. notes, replaced gold as the monetary base of the nation. For seventeen years starting in 1862, when holders of bank money desired to convert it into "lawful money," they received—much as we do today—paper obligations of the government rather than specie. Under the pressures of war finance, the monetary base of paper and the money supply were greatly enlarged. As a result, the general price level and the price of gold dollars (or equivalent bullion) in terms of paper dollars had roughly doubled during the war.

Deflation With and Without Monetary Contraction

Virtually all of the nation's leading economic and political decision makers in 1865 were in agreement that the monetary and financial consequences of the war, though necessary then for preserving the Union, were abnormal and that measures had to be taken to return the nation to prewar conditions; that is, paper monetary liabilities had to be convertible into specie, dollar for dollar. At the time, the gold dollar sold at a premium of approximately 50 percent over the paper dollar. Secretary of the Treasury Hugh McCulloch thus proposed in 1865 to eliminate the premium on gold by retiring the greenbacks with budget surpluses

and funding short-term "near" monies that the government had issued during the war into long-term bonds. In 1866, Congress authorized McCulloch to implement this policy of monetary contraction. Its economic basis was to reduce the supply of paper money and thus raise its value in terms of both goods and gold. Since paper money was the monetary standard, this meant that the market prices of goods and of gold in terms of paper dollars would have to fall.

And fall prices did. This can be seen in Figure 15–1, which charts the course of wholesale prices in the United States from 1860 to 1914. The fall of prices from the wartime peak in 1864 to 1868 can be attributed largely to policies

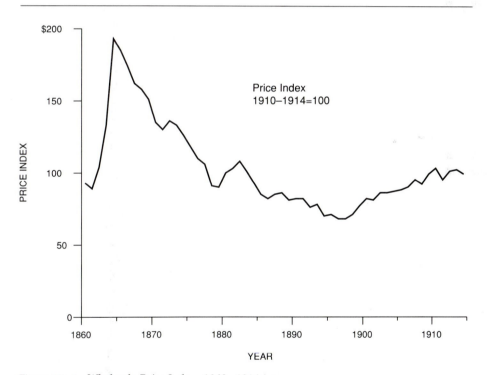

Figure 15–1 *Wholesale Price Index, 1860–1914*
Source: Adapted from George F. Warren and Frank A. Pearson, *Prices* (New York: Wiley, 1933), pp. 11–12.

associated with monetary contraction. However, the decision to give paper dollars more value was not popular among businesspeople and farmers, many of whom had contracted debts at inflated prices and discovered later that the prices of the products they sold—the proceeds of which they used to repay debts—were falling. In 1868, Congress therefore repealed the policy of contracting the outstanding supply of greenbacks. As Figure 15–1 indicates, however, ending the contraction of the paper currency did not end the price decline; instead, it continued almost without interruption until 1879, when prices were at pre-Civil War levels. The prices of gold and of the gold dollar also declined. When on January 2, 1879, in accordance with the Resumption Act passed by Congress in 1875, the U.S. government and the banks of the country once again offered to exchange gold dollars for their paper dollar liabilities, there were few takers. Paper dollars were equal in value to gold dollars and more convenient to use for most monetary purposes.

Deflation with High Real Growth

The resumption of paper dollar–gold dollar convertibility was accomplished, in the decade after policies of explicit paper money contraction were abandoned in 1868, essentially by a very limited expansion of the nation's money supply coupled with a large expansion in the output of goods and services. Figure 15–2 plots the behavior of both the money supply and the monetary base (specie and paper money liabilities of the federal government) from 1867 to 1914. The monetary base exhibited no growth between 1867 and 1879, while the money supply grew very slowly at a rate of just over 1 percent per year—the result of small increases in the ratios of bank deposits to bank reserves and of the public's holdings of bank money to its holdings of coin and paper currency. At the same time, prices declined

rapidly; the wholesale price index, for example, fell at a rate of about 5 percent per year from the end of the Civil War to 1879. Slight increases in the money supply and rapidly falling prices suggest that the income velocity of money (that is, its rate of turnover per year) fell, that the real output of the economy expanded, or that some combination of the two took place. Although the evidence available on total output of the economy for the postwar deflationary period is sketchy, it warrants the conclusion that most of the price decline resulted from an expansion of production.

Thus, the 1879 resumption of gold dollar–paper dollar interconvertibility resulted from replacing the initial postwar policy of explicit and absolute monetary contraction with a new policy of implicit and relative contraction (relative in the sense that monetary growth was kept well below the rate of economic growth). The price the nation paid for this heavy dose of deflation, in terms of perceived business depression, social unrest, and fundamental divisions among groups of Americans about proper monetary arrangements, was considerable. Nonetheless, rather than preventing a high rate of real economic growth, deflation was in large measure the result of a considerable expansion of production.

Deflation and the Gold Standard Orthodoxy

In general, a stable price level or value of money is considered desirable. Much of the utility of money as a social contrivance arises from the economy as well as convenience of information about relative values of goods, services, and productive resources when these values are expressed in terms of a single monetary unit. A changing value of the monetary unit introduces added uncertainty into economic decision making and tends to distort relative values from what they would be under stable price levels. These considerations suggest that it is not at all obvious why a course of

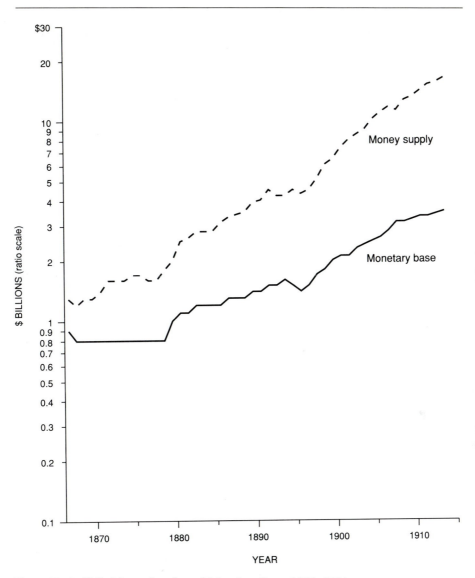

Figure 15–2 *U.S. Money Supply and Monetary Base, 1867–1914*
Source: Adapted from Milton Friedman and Anna J. Schwartz, *A Monetary History of the United States, 1867–1960* (Princeton: Princeton University Press, 1963), pp. 704–708, 799–801.

fairly drastic price deflation was deliberately chosen after the Civil War. The guiding idea of the time was that the gold dollar remained the true standard of value and that the market premium of gold over paper dollars represented a temporary aberration that had to be eliminated. Such a view was reinforced by the use in the greenback era of gold dollars for payment of customs duties and interest on the federal debt. The dominant gold-standard view came under increasing attack as price deflation continued, but it managed to hold its ground and remain financial orthodoxy not only in the United States but in much of the rest of the industrial world as well.

An alternative policy that would have avoided the need for deflation and preserved much of the gold-standard orthodoxy was for the United States to devalue the gold dollar in 1865. Law, it should be noted, defined the gold dollar as 23.22 grains of gold. In 1865, that weight of gold could be purchased on the market for about $1.50 in paper money. Had the law then been changed to redefine the gold dollar as 14.81 grains—two-thirds of its former weight—a paper dollar would have been equivalent to a gold dollar. Such a decision, which would have avoided the rapid deflation of 1865 to 1879, seemed so arbitrary to contemporaries that it was not given any consideration. It would not, however, have been unprecedented. In 1834, Congress reduced the weight of the gold dollar from 24.75 to 23.2 grains in order to encourage the minting and circulation of gold coins. That devaluation achieved its objective. Three decades later, the thinking of monetary policymakers was less flexible, resulting in a long period of deflation and monetary agitation.

Greenbackism and the Free-Silver Movement

Beginning in the late 1860s, currency contraction and deflation were polarizing the monetary thinking of various economic groups in the United States. Foreign traders, eastern bankers, and some manufacturers favored contraction as a means of achieving early resumption of gold–paper interconvertibility at the prewar parity. But farmers, labor groups, western businesspeople and bankers, and

Silver Versus Gold in the 1890s. This pro-silver populist cartoon shows a mechanic and a farmer, their existence already threatened by low wages and prices, coupled with heavy debts, taxes, and transportation charges, about to succumb from the added burden of a permanent gold standard. A big-business monopolist, with Republican presidential candidate William McKinley in his pocket, prepares to apply the coup de grace of gold. McKinley won the 1896 election, and the United States formally adopted the gold standard in 1900. In between, gold production began to rise, and the price deflation of the late nineteenth century came to an end. (Brown Brothers)

other manufacturers sought to reverse policies of contraction in order to stem the depression of prices and their increased debt burdens. The result was an uneasy compromise: The federal government did little to expand or contract the currency, economic growth increased the demand for money, and prices continued to fall.

The Greenback Party

Resistance to continued deflation strengthened in the depression following the financial panic of 1873. In 1874, both houses of Congress passed the Inflation Bill to expand the issue of greenbacks, but President Ulysses Grant, an advocate of resumption, vetoed it and deflation continued. In 1875, various opponents of deflation organized the Greenback party to advance their major goal of currency expansion. Although the party's presidential candidate, the industrialist-inventor Peter Cooper, got less than 1 percent of the vote in 1876, in the 1878 congressional elections it garnered 10 percent of the vote and won fourteen congressional seats. Resumption was accomplished before this Congress took office, however, and by 1880 the Greenback party was no longer a significant political force. By then it was calling for unlimited coinage of silver, a position that remained alive even after the Greenback party had disappeared.

Silver Politics

The "Crime of 1873."   Although at the start of the Civil War the United States in a legal sense was still on a bimetallic monetary standard, full-weight silver coins (371.25 grains to the dollar) had not been in circulation since the 1830s. The reason was that 371.25 grains of silver were worth more than a dollar in the market, so it did not pay for silver owners to take their metal to the U.S. mint for coinage. In the 1850s, a shortage of small coins led to the establishment of a subsidiary silver coinage; that is, coins containing less silver than their face value. But the standard silver dollar remained, in theory if not in practice, a recognized coin. Then, in 1873, Congress brought theory into line with practice in an amendment to the coinage laws that discontinued the coinage of standard silver dollars. Soon thereafter, new mines were opened and the supply of sil-

ver began to increase. At the same time, worldwide demand for silver fell because several European countries abandoned their silver or bimetallic monetary standards in favor of a monometallic gold standard. The price of silver fell to the point where, by 1875, American silver producers would have found it profitable to bring their metal to the mint for coinage had not the 1873 amendment foreclosed that possibility. Reactions were predictable. Silver producers branded the discontinuance of silver-dollar coinage the "Crime of 1873," and they were joined by opponents of deflation (such as Greenbackers) in calling for monetary expansion through a return to free coinage of standard silver dollars, or, as it was often termed, "free silver."

Limited Victories of the Silver Forces.   The free-silver movement won two partial but significant legislative victories in the two decades (1876 to 1896) when it flourished. The first was the Bland-Allison Act of 1878. Originally a free-coinage measure when it passed the House in 1877, the bill was amended in the Senate to limit the amount of silver the federal government would purchase. President Rutherford Hayes vetoed the bill but was overriden by Congress. Under the act's provisions, $2 million to $4 million worth of silver was to be purchased at market prices each month and coined into silver dollars. Despite the legal tender status of these silver dollars, the Treasury often had difficulty keeping them in circulation, in part because of the tendency of gold monometallists and others to pay taxes in silver or silver certificates rather than in gold obligations.

The other legislative triumph of the free-silver forces came in 1890. In return for supporting the protectionist McKinley Tariff Bill that year, the silverites gained sufficient protectionist support to secure passage of the Sherman Silver Purchase Act. The act provided that the Treasury purchase 4.5 million ounces of silver per month at the market price.

This represented an increase in silver purchases as compared with actual amounts purchased under the Bland-Allison Act, which the Sherman Act repealed. Silver was purchased with a new paper currency issue, the Treasury notes of 1890. The notes were made full legal tender and were redeemable in either gold or silver, though in practice the Treasury redeemed them in gold.

Undermining the Gold Standard.

The two major legislative victories of silver adherents were largely in vain. Additions of silver to the U.S. money supply created monetary confusion both within America and abroad, and far from preventing price deflation, they actually contributed to it by halting the growth of (or causing actual declines in) U.S. gold reserves. Within the United States, problems such as those of the Treasury in keeping silver and silver certificates in circulation were not, as the silver forces alleged, part of a plot to prevent monetary expansion but rather a reaction to the relative values of gold and silver. No matter how much Americans may have desired monetary expansion, as long as they knew that the silver in a silver dollar was worth less than a dollar on the market, while a gold dollar was worth a dollar, uncertainty about the monetary standard would lead them to prefer to hold monetary assets in gold or gold equivalents and to make payments in silver. Foreigners were in a similar situation. They were reluctant in the period of silver agitation to invest in the United States because the gold or gold equivalents they would give up to acquire dollar assets might have to be repatriated in silver with consequent capital losses. If foreigners already held dollar assets, they would be tempted to sell them for gold whenever the silver threat to the gold standard grew in the United States. Thus, the incentives of both Americans and foreigners were such, given the silver situation in the United States, as to promote decisions to exchange silver and paper money for gold.

Those decisions tended to reduce the Treasury's gold stock and thus threaten the ability of the government to maintain dollar–gold interconvertibility.

Silver Vanquished; Gold Triumphant.

These monetary problems, present since 1878, came to a head in 1893, when the Treasury's gold reserve fell below $100 million for the first time since resumption in 1879. In May of 1893, financial panic broke out as both Americans and foreigners, fearing that gold payments could not or would not be maintained by the government, liquidated assets in an attempt to get gold or currency still convertible into gold. Bank credit and prices fell rapidly, while unemployment and interest rates rose. President Grover Cleveland summoned a special session of Congress to repeal the Silver Purchase Act, which it did in the fall of 1893.

Silver purchases ceased in 1893, but the political movement for free silver continued with even greater fervor as a result of the legislative setback and the continuance of the business depression that followed the financial panic. Both created great political and economic problems for the federal government. The silver agitation and doubts about the strength of the U.S. economy prompted foreigners to withdraw gold in greater amounts. And the depression reduced government revenues by reducing imports and customs collections. Committed to the maintenance of gold payments, for political as well as economic reasons, the government had little choice but to borrow gold, often on unfavorable terms.[1] Between 1894 and 1896, the Treasury sold some $262 million of new bonds to cover its deficits and replenish its gold reserves. This amounted to an increase of 45 percent in the interest-bearing federal debt in less than three years, an uncommon experience for the United States in times of peace. Both the monetary crisis and the silver agitation ended in 1896, when the great spokesman for free silver, William Jen-

Table 15–1   *Number and Deposits of Commerical Banks in the United States, 1860–1910*

Year	Number of National Banks	Number of State Banks	Number of Private Banks	Total Number of Banks	Total Deposits ($ billions)
1860	0	1,579	1,108	2,687	$ 0.541
1870	1,612	261	1,903	3,776	0.925
1880	2,076	1,051	2,318	5,445	1.431
1890	3,484	2,830	4,365	10,679	3.126
1900	3,731	8,696		12,427	5.432
1910	7,138	17,376		24,514	12.286

SOURCE: Richard Sylla, *The American Capital Market, 1846–1914* (New York: Arno Press, 1975), p. 26.

nings Bryan, was defeated for the presidency by William McKinley, a conservative, sound-money advocate. In 1900, the United States officially adopted the gold standard that, with great difficulties, it had more or less maintained during the two previous decades.

Banking Problems

By 1860, commercial banking had become an important business in the United States. Well over two thousand banks were in operation at this time (see Table 15–1). The majority were banking corporations chartered by state governments, but there were also significant numbers of unincorporated proprietorship and partnership banks. The latter type—the private banks—generally were smaller and less noteworthy than the chartered banks. They also avoided the political problems of chartering and government regulation that impinged upon the chartered banks. The liabilities—deposits and notes—of chartered and private banks made up the larger part of the American money supply, with gold and small amounts of silver coins making up the rest.

During the half-century from 1860 to 1910, commercial banking continued to be a growth

sector of the economy. As Table 15–1 indicates, the number of banks grew ninefold and deposit liabilities increased twenty-three times. The implied rates of expansion far exceeded those of either population or national product during the same period. Despite its robust growth and definite contributions to economic expansion, the American banking system was plagued by serious problems. In particular, there were problems associated with organizing the many component parts of the banking system as well as with the system's tendency to become unglued in periodic financial panics that spread out from the financial sector to weaken the whole economy. Policy decisions gave rise to these problems, and new policy decisions would attempt to overcome them.

Promises and Pitfalls of National Banking

The Civil War contributed to banking problems through one of its major legislative consequences—the federal laws of 1863 and 1864 that established the National Banking System. The intent of these laws was twofold. One objective, a pressing one in 1863 to 1864, was to create a captive market for federal wartime loans by requiring the new national banks to purchase federal bonds. The other major objective, one that antedated the Civil War, was to furnish the nation with a uniform paper currency to replace the variegated note issues of some 1,600 state-chartered banks. National bank notes were to be uniform in design and backed by federal bonds, which the banks would buy and deposit with a newly created Treasury Department office — the Comptroller of the Currency — in return for the notes. Then, should a national bank fail, the bonds could be liquidated and the noteholders compensated without loss.

It was a good idea, with precedents in earlier state banking laws, but its execution was poor. Federal officials had contemplated that all of the nation's note-issuing banks would give up their state charters and join the national system, but many were reluctant. The problem was that the new legislation contained provisions that were more restrictive than those under which existing state-chartered banks had been operating. Among these provisions were bond purchase requirements, especially a limitation on the amount of notes that any one national bank could issue to 90 percent of the par or market value of the bonds deposited with the Comptroller, whichever was less, and a ceiling on the total national bank note issue for the whole country. Still other provisions of the law set minimum capital requirements for national banks that were too high to make national banking feasible and competitive in smaller towns and cities and prohibited loans extended on the basis of real estate collateral (a drawback to national banking in a still largely agricultural nation, with land as the major asset possessed by many people). Faced with these potential restrictions on their business, many existing banks chose to keep their state charters rather than join the new national system.

The Dual Banking System

The recalcitrance of bankers in pursuing their private interests did not sit well in Washington.

Political muscle was flexed. In March 1865, Congress enacted a 10 percent tax, effective in 1866, on any state bank note paid out by any bank. This effectively killed the note-issuing business of most state banks by destroying its profitability. Many banks took out national charters, but some two hundred to three hundred, primarily in cities where depositing banking had eclipsed note issue in importance, remained state banks. And, of course, private banks, which usually did not issue notes, remained and even flourished, unhampered by either federal or state regulation.

Thus was created the so-called *dual banking system* that continues to the present day. From 1864 on, most American banks have operated under either federal or state charter, with different rules and regulations. By the early part of the twentieth century, most private banks had been absorbed into one or the other of the two chartering arrangements. The Civil War objective of making all banks national banks was not achieved. There were important economic effects related to this policy failure in the late nineteenth century. The national banks operating under restrictive laws and regulatory provisions were ill suited to the small towns and agricultural regions of the country. As a result, national banks were heavily concentrated in the northeastern part of the nation. State banking was nearly destroyed by the note-issue tax. It recovered rather slowly as deposit banking habits spread and the states gradually liberalized their laws to make state charters more attractive to would-be bankers. Restrictive provisions on national banking were also gradually relaxed, most notably in 1900, when minimum capital requirements were cut in half. Nonetheless, for some two to three decades after the Civil War, there were inadequate banking facilities throughout much of the country. It is no surprise, then, that the greenback and free-silver movements flourished, that bankers were unpopular, and that widely varying interest rates across regions were deplored. Decisions regarding the organization and expansion of the banking system were the fundamental problems, but as so often happens in political economy, symptoms came to be confused with causes.

Banking Panics

Another major problem that plagued American banking before 1914 was the susceptibility of the banking system to financial panic. Fractional reserve banking of the kind practiced then and now is based on the notion that not every depositor will attempt to convert his or her deposit into base money—be it gold or government-backed paper currency—at the same time. This allows banks to lend out most of their resources while keeping a fractional reserve of base money just in case daily withdrawals exceed daily deposits. Usually, this arrangement presented no problems. The public found it convenient to make payments in bank money by writing checks against deposits and to take out loans in the form of bank deposit credits. Since bank deposits were normally convertible into base money, the public showed no marked tendency to make such conversions, except for day-to-day transactions where cash—coins and paper money—was more convenient than checks.

Cyclical and Seasonal Credit Demands. Two cycles of economic activity served to complicate the usual relationship between bank and customer: the *business cycle*, the ebb-and-flow sequence of economic activity that typically occurred over a period of three to four years; and *seasonal variation* in the demand for cash and bank credit, which was related to agriculture. In the spring of the year and again in the late summer and autumn, seasonal demand would increase in the agricultural regions of the country as farmers first borrowed to plant their crops and later as merchants borrowed to finance marketing or crop moving. When seasonal demand

arose, country banks would draw on the deposits they had made in city banks during times of low seasonal demand for loans in rural areas. The National Banking System encouraged this practice of interbank lending through its reserve system. All national banks were required to hold reserves against their deposit liabilities, but for most national banks half or more of legally required reserves could take the form of deposit balances in city banks. Since the city banks paid interest on these bankers' balances, they were an attractive and liquid investment for banks with excess funds. New York City, then as now the nation's financial capital, was the magnet toward which great amounts of these funds were drawn. The large national banks of New York were able to pay interest on bankers' balances from all over the United States because they in turn could relend the funds to their customers, most notably to individuals and firms that dealt in New York's bond and stock markets.

Peaks of business cycle activity were usually accompanied by heavy commercial loan demand and extensive speculation in the securities markets. When they coincided with peaks in seasonal credit demands from the countryside, the banks of New York and other large cities sometimes found themselves in a bind: they could meet the country withdrawals of cash and deposits only by contracting their own lending, which caused problems for their borrowing customers. At its worst, the shortage of loanable funds led to business failures and securities market liquidation. With the people and enterprises to whom the banks had lent in trouble, depositors in the banks thus become fearful that their own funds were in danger and rushed to the banks to convert their deposits into base money. The result was financial panic. Demands to convert deposits to cash caused further credit contraction, increased business failures, and resulted in securities market declines. Sometimes the banks were forced to suspend conversion of deposits into cash. Panics ended quickly, but the damage inflicted caused business to be depressed for longer periods. This was the case after the panics of 1873, 1884, 1893, and 1907.

Currency Inelasticity and a Central Bank. How to prevent financial panics became, toward the end of the century, a major concern of financial decision makers. The problem they faced was commonly described as one of inelasticity of the money supply. By this some analysts meant that the money supply did not conform to "the needs of trade." For example, at business cycle peaks, credit demand was strong, but the money supply, based on relatively stable stocks of gold and government-backed paper currency, could not expand sufficiently to accommodate all borrowers or prevent rising interest rates. In depressions, however, conditions were said to be such that more money existed than was needed. This interpretation of the inelasticity problem was very popular, but its foundation in economic reasoning is weak. To impart elasticity by creating more and more money when business was booming and both interest rates and prices were rising would have been to run the risk of protracted inflation. And to contract the money supply during depressions would have hindered economic recovery by promoting price declines and preventing interest rates from falling to the point where increased borrowing for investment purposes would have been encouraged. Making the money supply elastic in these senses would have accentuated economic fluctuations and thus would not have been a wise policy decision.

More perceptive analysts realized that the basic problem during financial panics was that the supply of currency—coin and paper money—was inelastic. Panics occurred when a large number of depositors doubted that their banks deposits could be converted into currency; in testing their doubts by lining up at banks to withdraw their deposits, the depositors acted to confirm them. What was needed was some way to expand the volume of currency during incipient panic situations so as to allay rather than confirm the doubts of deposit holders. After the panic of 1907, the federal government acted to deal with the fundamental problem of monetary inelasticity in a systematic way. The first result was the Aldrich-Vreeland Act of 1908, which provided both a temporary solution and an impetus to long-term reform. The temporary solution came in the form of an authorization to groups of banks threatened by depositor panic to issue an emergency currency backed by pledges of certain types of bank assets, with a progressively rising tax on such emergency issues in order to ensure that they would be retired after the emergency had disappeared. The Aldrich-Vreeland Act's impetus to reform came with its provision for a National Monetary Commission composed of senators and representatives authorized to make extensive studies of monetary and banking systems and recommend appropriate reforms of American arrangements. The work of the National Monetary Commission during the next few years led to passage of the Federal Reserve Act in 1913 and establishment of the Federal Reserve System, the central bank of the United States, in 1914. These developments created a momentous change in American institutions.

The Financial Sector and Capital Formation

Role of Financial Intermediaries

A major function of the financial sector in any modern economy is to transfer in an efficient manner the surplus funds of savers into the hands of investors. This is one of the ways—and one that increases in relative terms with higher levels of economic development—that capital formation is financed. Primitive economies do not have much need for a financial sector. To the extent that capital formation occurs in them, it is usually through *self-finance* (e.g., as when a farmer decides to sacrifice leisure and current consumption in order to clear farmland of trees and perhaps make split-rail fences for the fields from the fallen timbers). A more advanced economy features *direct finance*, which is the activity of savers directly lending their funds to investors or buying equity shares in enterprises. The division of labor in finance can be, and customarily is, carried even further, giving rise to *indirect finance*. Savers, instead of lending to enterprises or directly investing in them, place their surplus funds in financial intermediaries, such as banks, investment companies, life insurance companies, and pension funds. The intermediaries attract funds by selling savers products, such as bank deposits, investment diversification, life insurance, or retirement incomes. And the intermediaries, with their economies of scale and advantages of specialization and diversification, in turn invest the pooled resources of savers in the debt and equity instruments offered by productive enterprises whose demand for funds exceeds what they themselves can generate from current income.

As the American economy grew in size and complexity during the late nineteenth century, the number of financial intermediaries increased at a rapid rate and they became ubiquitous features of the economic institutional landscape. In what ways did they affect the performance of the economy? Insofar as they offered savers more attractive products and increased investment yields, the intermediaries acted to raise the attractiveness of saving and investment. And insofar as their larger scale enabled them to gather more information on potential investments and reduce investment risks through diversification, the intermediaries acted to reduce barriers to capital mobility and promote efficient use of savings. In these ways, the intermediaries tended to raise savings and investment rates and to equalize the interregional and interindustry costs of funds to users of financial capital.

There is evidence that intermediaries had both of these effects. Studies of commercial bank-lending rates, for example, show that interest rates to bank borrowers were very different in different regions of the United States during the 1860s and the 1870s, but that by the first decade of the twentieth century, many of the interregional differences had been eliminated. The rapid growth in numbers and competitiveness of bank and nonbank intermediaries during the period played a large role in this fashioning of a more unified national capital market.

The other expected effect of financial intermediation—an increase in the volume of saving and investment—is also evident in the historical record of the post–Civil War decades. An increase in relative levels of saving and investment during these decades is in fact one of the more striking characteristics of that period documented by economic-historical research. Figure 15–3 presents data on the share of aggregate capital formation in total economic product and on one of its key components—the tools, machinery, and equipment represented by manufactured producer-durables. What is striking about the capital formation rates exhibited in the figure is not their rising trend over the decades—that is not an unusual characteristic of developing economies—but rather the magnitude of the overall rise, especially the jump between the pre– and post–Civil War eras. Rates of capital formation, which were rising during the prewar decades, doubled between the 1840s and the 1870s and between the 1850s and the 1890s. Increases in the producer-durable goods component of capital formation were even greater.

Although financial intermediaries undoubtedly contributed to rising rates of capital formation by making savings and investment more attractive, it is unlikely that their development alone explains all or most of the increase. The intermediaries continued to develop in the twentieth century, but rates of capital formation did not maintain the upward

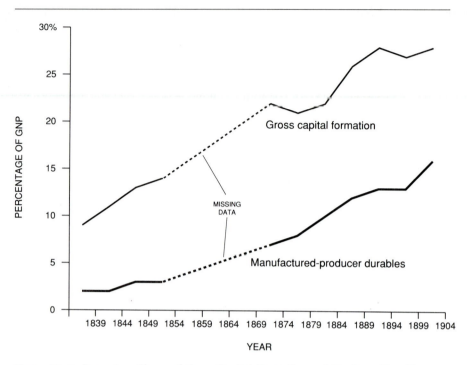

Figure 15–3 *Percentage Shares of Gross Capital Formation and Producer-Durable Capital Formation, 1834–1843 through 1899–1908*

SOURCE: Adapted from Robert E. Gallman, "Gross National Product in the United States, 1834–1909," in National Bureau of Economic Research, *Output, Employment, and Productivity in the United States After 1800: Studies in Income and Wealth,* vol. 30 (New York: Columbia University Press, 1966), pp. 11, 26, 34. Data are not available for 1859–1868.

ward momentum of the late nineteenth century. Other and more specifically historical forces of the period must have aided the rising rate of capital formation, which in its magnitude was most unusual for an economy where decision making by individuals and individual enterprises determined savings and investment behavior.

Federal Budget Surpluses and Debt Retirement

Financial policies of federal decision makers, though perhaps not intended to stimulate cap-

ital formation, may have had that result. One such policy, covered earlier in the chapter, concerned the public debt. As can be seen in Figure 15–4, the federal interest-bearing debt rose to unprecedented levels during the Civil War years. Then, for more than a quarter-century after the war, the federal government took in more money in tax revenues than it spent and used the surpluses to redeem government bonds for cash. (The only significant exception to this pattern came in the late 1870s, when the Treasury floated bonds to purchase gold and resume specie payments.) When the Treasury redeemed bonds, it transformed budget sur-

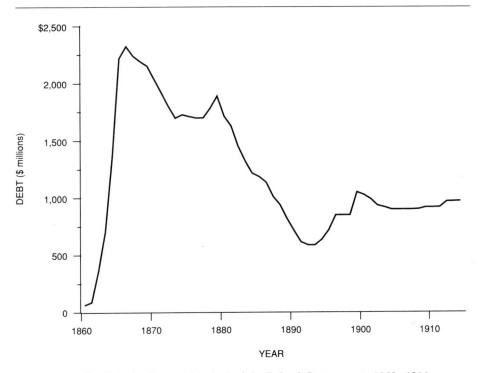

Figure 15–4 *Public Debt (interest-bearing) of the Federal Government, 1860–1914*
SOURCE: Adapted from data in U.S. Bureau of the Census, *Historical Statistics of the United States,* part 2 (Washington, D.C.: GPO, 1975), p. 1118.

pluses into funds available to private investors; this, in turn, increased capital funds and depressed market interest rates and other capital costs. The actual impact of debt retirement on private capital formation was much greater than the nominal amount of debt retired. When the debt was growing during the Civil War, the federal government borrowed inflated greenback dollars, but when it paid interest on its debts and redeemed them with surplus cash after the war, it did so in dollars that had increased in value as a result of falling price levels. Thus, the purchasing power that the Treasury returned to private investors was much greater than what those investors had given up when they bought government bonds during wartime.

A fuller understanding of why the federal debt policies likely increased capital formation can be gained by considering the two main sources of surplus federal revenues. One source was customs duties on imported goods; the duties raised the costs of consumer-goods imports more than the costs of capital-goods imports. The other main source was excise taxes on two popular consumer goods—tobacco products and alcoholic beverages. Thus, the net effect of post–Civil War federal debt, tariff, and tax policies was to transfer purchasing power from consumers to investors. The policies almost certainly promoted higher rates of capital formation and economic growth after the Civil War.

Summary

Civil War finance brought about innovations in taxation, borrowing, paper money, and banking. The financial policy decisions made between 1861 and 1865 helped to solve some of the federal government's pressing problems, but they also sowed the seeds of later financial difficulties and discontents. Disagreements over tariff, tax, and debt questions, over the organization and operation of the banking system, and over the foundation or base of the money supply became staples of the American political economy in the late nineteenth century. Widespread perceptions of the inadequacies of existing financial arrangements led to experimentation with other approaches, but these, too, as in the case of the silver policies, appeared to cause at least as many problems as they had been designed to solve.

Yet the American financial system matured considerably in the decades after 1860. Banks and other financial intermediaries ultimately spread throughout the nation and promoted economic efficiency in the mobilization and distribution of capital. The federal government's tax and debt policies, perhaps inadvertently but nonetheless effectively, stimulated high and ever-rising levels of capital formation. During these decades, the U.S. economy exhibited the highest rates of growth and of tangible capital formation in the two centuries of its history.

Endnote

1. Milton Friedman and Anna J. Schwartz, in *A Monetary History of the United States, 1861–1960* (Princeton: Princeton University Press, 1963), p. 111, assert that abandonment of the gold standard was not "economically undesirable" but rather "politically unacceptable."

Suggested Readings

For more information on the impacts of the Civil War on the American economy, see David T. Gilchrist and W. David Lewis, eds., *Economic Change in the Civil War Era* (Greenville, Del.: Eleutherian Mills Hagley Foundation, 1965); and Stanley L. Engerman, "The Economic Impact of the Civil War," *Explorations in Entrepreneurial History*, 3 (Spring–Summer 1966). Wartime financing problems at the federal level are treated in Bray Hammond, *Sovereignty and an Empty Purse* (Princeton: Princeton University Press, 1970). For a detailed discussion of taxation issues before, during, and after the Civil War, see Sidney Ratner, *Taxation and Democracy in America*, rev. ed. (New York: W. W. Norton, 1967). Ratner's *The Tariff in American History* (New York: Van Nostrand, 1972) is an incisive introduction to the tariff history of the period. On debt policy, see Henrietta M. Larson, *Jay Cooke, Private Banker* (Cambridge, Mass.: Harvard University Press, 1936); and Robert T. Patterson, *Federal Debt-Management Policies, 1865–1897* (Durham, N.C.: Duke University Press, 1954).

For the general financial history of this and other eras of American history, a helpful work is Paul Studenski and Herman Krooss, *Financial History of the United States*, 2d ed. (New York: McGraw-Hill, 1963). The classic work on the monetary history of this and subsequent periods is Milton Friedman and Anna J. Schwartz, *A Monetary History of the United States, 1867–1960* (Princeton: Princeton University Press, 1963). An excellent economic analysis of issues involved in the resumption of specie payments after the Civil War is James K. Kindahl, "Economic Factors in Specie Resumption: The United States, 1865–79," *Journal of Political Economy*, 59 (Feb. 1961).

Banking problems and the evolution of the banking system in these (and earlier) years is the subject of Fritz Redlich's encyclopedic study, *The Molding of American Banking* (New York: Johnson Reprint Corporation, 1968). For more economic analysis of these subjects, see Richard Sylla, *The American Capital Market, 1846–1914* (New York: Arno Press, 1975), which also analyzes the impact of federal debt management on the economy; John A. James, *Money and Capital Markets in Postbellum America* (Princeton: Princeton University Press, 1978); and Eugene N. White, *The Regulation and Reform of the American Banking System, 1900–1929* (Princeton: Princeton University Press, 1983). Richard H. Timberlake, *The Origins of Central Banking in the United States* (Cambridge, Mass.: Harvard University Press, 1978), treats a wide range of monetary, banking, and financial issues in addition to central banking.

The emergence of an efficient national capital market is a major theme of Sylla, *Capital Market*, and James, *Money*, both cited earlier. They were inspired by the pathbreaking study of Lance Davis, "The Investment Market, 1870–1914: The Evolution of a National Market," *Journal of Economic History*, 15 (Sept. 1965), which is worth consulting both for its analysis and its extensive data on interregional interest rates, 1870–1914. Pre– and post–Civil War capital markets are compared and contrasted in Howard Bodenhorn and Hugh Rockoff, "Regional Interest Rates in Antebellum America," in Claudia Goldin and Hugh Rockoff, eds., *Strategic Factors in Nineteenth Century American Economic History* (Chicago: University of Chicago Press, 1992). For detailed information on

the characteristics and performance of various U.S. financial markets, see Sidney Homer and Richard Sylla, *A History of Interest Rates*, 3d ed. (New Brunswick, N.J.: Rutgers University Press, 1991); Kenneth Snowden, "American Stock Market Development and Performance, 1871–1929," *Explorations in Economic History*, 24 (Oct. 1987); Kenneth Snowden, "Historical Returns and Security Market Development, 1872–1925," *Explorations in Economic History*, 27 (Oct. 1990); Kenneth Snowden, "Mortgage Rates and American Capital Market Development in the Late Nineteenth Century," *Journal of Economic History*, 47 (Sept. 1987); Thomas Navin and Marion Sears, "The Rise of a Market for Industrial Securities, 1887–1902," *Business History Review*, 24 (June 1955); and Jonathan B. Baskin, "The Development of Corporate Financial Markets in Britain and the United States, 1600–1914: Overcoming Asymmetric Information," *Business History Review*, 62 (Summer 1988). The investment banking industry is the subject of Vincent Carosso, *Investment Banking in America: A History* (Cambridge, Mass.: Harvard University Press, 1970). Carosso also has a detailed study of its leading firm in *The Morgans: Private International Bankers: 1854–1913* (Cambridge, Mass.: Harvard University Press, 1987); another good study of the same firm is Ron Chernow, *The House of Morgan: An American Banking Dynasty and the Rise of Modern Finance* (New York: Atlantic Monthly, 1990).

The essential findings on economic growth and capital formation trends are set forth by Robert E. Gallman, "Gross National Product in the United States, 1834–1909," in National Bureau of Economic Research, *Output, Employment, and Productivity in the United States After 1800: Studies in Income and Wealth*, vol. 30 (New York: Columbia University Press, 1966). Finally, for a provocative, highly technical economic analysis of financial and other economic issues of the post–Civil War era, see Jeffrey C. Williamson, *Late Nineteenth-Century American Development* (Cambridge: Cambridge University Press, 1975).

Chapter 16

National and World Markets for Mass Production

THE YEARS BETWEEN 1860 AND 1914 WITNESSED major changes in the nation's marketing system, changes that were comparable in importance to those taking place in the methods of production. Crucial developments occurred in the marketing of agricultural commodities. However, the most distinctive marketing development of this period was the emergence of a system of *mass distribution.* Through it the greatly enlarged volume of manufactured goods made possible by mass production was distributed more effectively. Mass retailers—department stores, chain stores, and mail-order houses—were able to reach a growing number of consumers who possessed increasing amounts of disposable income. In addition, as noted in Chapter 12, large manufacturing corporations created their own distribution and purchasing organizations to reach markets and obtain materials and components more efficiently. A closely related development was the emergence of modern advertising—a vastly larger volume of advertising designed increasingly to persuade as well as to inform consumers. All of these changes led, in turn, to questions about the cost of distribution and the purposes of advertising.

In foreign trade, two significant changes reflected the maturing of the American economy. The first, a shift from an unfavorable to a favorable balance of trade, occurred in the mid-1870s. The second important change had to do with the composition of exports. In the quarter-century before World War I, exports of American manufactured goods increased dramatically relative to the exports of agricultural commodities that had long been the staples of American trade with other parts of the world.

Important changes also took place in the nation's commercial policies toward the rest of the world. The level of tariff protection increased markedly, as compared to the pre–Civil War years. As a result, tariff policies became among the most heated issues debated by national decision makers in the 1860 to 1914 period. Even though Congress focused on high tariffs as a tool to discourage imports of foreign manufacturing goods, some members of the executive branch were working to promote the export of American manufactured goods. Finally, the emergence of the United States as a participant in world balance-of-power politics led to territorial acquisitions and a policy of "dollar diplomacy"—that is, the use of economic means to support diplomatic and strategic objectives.

Marketing of Agricultural Commodities

Specialization in the collection and distribution of agricultural products occurred as early as the 1850s and 1860s. The marketing of both grain and cotton was dramatically changed by the expansion of the railroad and telegraph as well as the growth of related enterprises, such as grain elevators, cotton presses, warehouses, and the important new institution of the organized commodity exchange. These exchanges, based on telegraphic communication, made it possible for cotton, grain, and other commodities to be bought and sold while in transit or even before they had been harvested. The merchants who took the lead in standardizing and systematizing the marketing procedures of the commodity exchanges not only reduced their transportation costs but also changed drastically the methods of financing agricultural commodities in the United States.

The first such reforms emerged in the marketing and financing of the grain trade and led to the establishment of the Chicago Board of Trade in 1848. Similar institutions were soon founded in St. Louis, Buffalo, New York, Philadelphia, and other cities. In the post–Civil War period, dealers and brokers on the commodity exchanges distributed and marketed crops like wheat, barley, corn, oats, and rye.

Similarly, once southern railroad and telegraph networks had been rebuilt after the Civil War, the marketing of cotton also changed. Instead of depending on the services of cotton factors—the dominant agents of the antebellum cotton economy—cotton dealers were able to buy directly from planters, small farmers, and general storekeepers. Cotton exchanges were created in New York in 1870 and in New Orleans in 1871.

The administrative networks created by the commodity dealers often were global enterprises, but they did not necessitate more than a small investment in capital facilities and needed only a few managers. The organizations lowered the cost of credit for crop movements and enabled a closer integration of supply and demand through improved information processing and scheduling. As a result, both farmers and buyers of agricultural products had better information on which to base their decisions of sale or purchase. In the 1860 to 1914 period, agricultural exports were extremely important to American economic growth; the development of large commodity dealers and commodity exchanges increased the efficiency of marketing agricultural commodities.

Mass Consumption and Mass Distribution

Mass production involved the application of new technology along a broad front and made available to more consumers a greater volume and wider range of goods than ever before (see Chapter 12). In food processing, refrigeration (particularly the introduction of the refrigerated car) revolutionized meat packing, as did roller grinding for flour milling. Mechanization of processes and advances of scientific knowledge led to the expansion of the canning of food, the bottling of soft and hard drinks, the preparation of dairy products, and the refining of sugar. Even in textiles, America's first factory industry, a large rise in output of cloth accompanied the introduction of new types of spinning and weaving equipment. The knit-goods industry, particularly the production of hosiery and underwear, developed rapidly with the invention of machinery to manufacture seamless and then full-fashioned goods.

The application of new technology in many lines made available goods that were better in quality than homemade articles and lower in price than the products of artisans; sometimes the new technology even produced goods that had not existed before. Adaptation of the sewing machine and the development of cloth-cutting machines and other special equipment accelerated the expansion of the ready-made clothing industry; by 1900, so-called "store clothes" accounted for as much as nine-tenths of the supply of men's clothing for the nation, providing a wide range of quality for different segments of the market. Adaptation of the sewing machine to leather reduced dramatically the price of boots and shoes. For use in the home, carpets made on power looms replaced handmade rugs, and furniture from Grand Rapids and other locations, however unimaginative in style, appeared superior to home-built items and seemed the best possibility for consumers unable to pay for the fine products of skilled artisans. Two new industries provided significant improvements in lighting. The principal product of the petroleum industry before 1900 was kerosene for the oil lamp, which became of particular importance to rural families. Electricity replaced manufactured gas for illumination in urban areas by the end of the nineteenth century, though gas had represented an important advance in lighting in the earlier part of the century. In addition, new ways of making stoves, ice boxes, and plumbing fixtures reduced their prices, making possible more comfortable living for larger numbers of people. Invention of the linotype, coupled with the discovery of processes to make cheap paper, brought im-

Coca-Cola Advertisement Circa 1905. This advertisement is an example of how sellers devised reasons why consumers should buy their wares. (Courtesy of the Coca-Cola Company)

portant changes to printing and publishing—more books, magazines, and newspapers at lower costs. The phonograph, amateur photography, and the movies gave new dimensions to Americans' leisure time. The telephone had its principal effects in business during this period. But the possibility of improved personal transportation was eagerly embraced by consumers—first with the bicycle in the late nineteenth century and then with the automobile after the turn of the century. Rubber, which became an adjunct of the automobile industry, was already experiencing sig-

nificant growth before 1900, with increasing production of rubber footwear and bicycle tires.

The strong demand for all of these new consumer goods ultimately rested on population growth and rising income levels. The population of the United States doubled between 1860 and 1890, and then grew another 68 percent in the ensuing three decades. From the 1870s to 1900, real gross national product per capita almost doubled; it rose another 30 percent by 1920.

The middle-income group was particularly important in expanding consumption along lines suggested some years ago by Elizabeth W. Gilboy: "The introduction of new commodities leads people possessed of an economic surplus to try this and that, and finally to include many new articles in their customary standard of life."[1] The small number of wealthy people could be supplied with expensive handicrafts, while the many poor had little to spend beyond the bare necessities of life. Thus, it was members of the middle class who used their purchasing power to incorporate more and more factory-made goods into their consumption patterns.

New channels of distribution were required to sell large flows of goods to expanding markets. The older system of marketing was not suited to handling the sharp increase in the volume of goods being generated by mass production. The railroad and telegraph, as discussed in Chapter 14, created for the first time a truly national market in the United States. By making possible the movement of goods and messages with unprecedented speed, volume, and regularity, the new transportation and communication innovations formed the basis for the emergence of a modern system of mass distribution.

The Creation of a Nationwide Marketing System

By the middle decades of the nineteenth century, the United States from the Atlantic Coast to the Great Plains had become an integrated

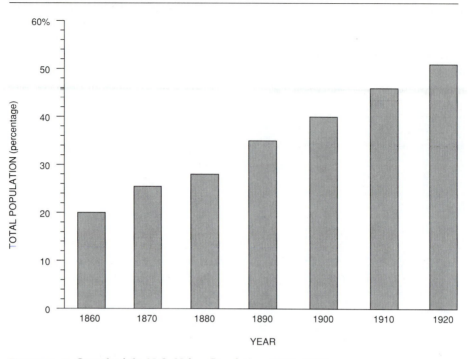

Figure 16–1   *Growth of the U.S. Urban Population, 1860–1920*
SOURCE: Based on data in U.S. Bureau of the Census, *Historical Statistics of the United States, Colonial Times to 1970* (Washington, D.C.: GPO, 1975), pp. 11–12.

market area for many of the products of agriculture and industry. After mid-century, continued population growth and the extension and improvement of transportation and communication technologies continued to expand the size of the nation's market area. Growing concentrations of population in urban areas provided an additional stimulus to trade by reducing costs of wholesale and retail trade. As the percentage of the American population engaged in farming declined, the urban population (that is, people living in places with 2500 or more inhabitants) increased from 20 percent of the total population in 1860 to 51 percent in 1920 (see Figure 16–1). In 1860, only nine cities had more than 100,000 inhabitants; by 1920, however, sixty-eight urban places could claim

this distinction (see Table 16–1). At the time of World War I, the populations of the cities of New York, Chicago, and Philadelphia each surpassed the 1.5 million mark.

Transportation improvements and urban growth led an increasing proportion of the American labor force to become engaged in the distribution of goods as contrasted with their production. The resulting increase in economic specialization led to a greater dependence by individuals, households, and businesses on goods and services sold through markets. The effect of these forces of specialization on the demand for marketing activities is evident in the doubling of the proportion of American workers engaged in trade and transportation from 10 percent in 1860 to 20 percent in 1920.

Table 16–1 *Growth of Large Cities in the U.S., 1860–1920*

| | Cities Over 100,000 Population | | |
Year	Number	Population [in million]	Percentage of Total U.S. Population
1860	9	2.6	8.4%
1870	14	4.1	10.4%
1880	20	6.2	12.4%
1890	28	9.7	15.4%
1900	38	14.2	18.7%
1910	49	20.3	22.1%
1920	68	27.4	25.9%

SOURCE: U.S. Bureau of the Census, *Historical Statistics of the United States, Colonial Times to 1970* (Washington, D.C.: GPO, 1975), pp. 8, 11–12.

Specialization and Integration in Distribution

In the years between 1840 and 1890, a new specialized marketing system developed that met the demands of both the intermediate and the ultimate consumers of goods. The general merchant in the pre-1840 period had combined the functions of the importer, wholesaler, and retailer. But the rising volume of trade brought firms that specialized in one or several functions of the earlier general merchant. Domestic wholesalers became distinct from importers, and dry-goods wholesalers came to specialize in one or several types of goods such as millinery, sheetings, or dress goods. As a result, commission houses and jobbers developed on a wide scale. By 1861 independent wholesalers were in control of the distribution of more than 95 percent of all manufactured products sold in the United States. (An exception was the railroad supply industry, where railroads developed their own contacts with the manufacturers.)

The Independent Wholesaler

The first mass marketer to appear on the scene was the independent wholesaler of traditional goods, including dry goods, hardware, groceries, boots and shoes, and many other lines. Operating out of major commercial centers in the Northeast and Midwest, the wholesaler created an organization to purchase a line of goods from manufacturers as well as a staff of traveling salespeople to sell the goods to country stores in rural communities and specialized retailers in cities and towns across the country. To show the complexity of the jobber's role, a hardware wholesaler typically handled six thousand different items purchased from over one thousand firms and shipped to an even larger number of retailers. The wholesale jobber became the dominant figure in the nation's distribution system during the 1850s and 1860s. By 1861, independent wholesalers were in control of the distribution of more than 95 percent of all manufactured products sold in the United States.

By the early 1880s, however, the position of the independent wholesaler was being challenged by the manufacturing corporation as well as the mass retailer. As noted in Chapter 12, large manufacturing corporations were integrating their operations forward into wholesaling. At the same time, the mass retailers that were emerging were purchasing the goods they sold to consumers directly from manufacturers. Still, the wholesale jobber remained an important link between manufacturer and retailer in a number of lines, such as hardware, groceries, and drugs.

Mass Retailers and a Revolution in Shopping

The Department Store

The first mass retailer to alter so dramatically the structure of the distribution system and consumers' habits of shopping was the department store. The essence of the department store was its unprecedented size and wide variety of goods, in contrast to the small specialized retailers that had long dominated urban retailing. Department stores began to appear

Main Floor of Macy's Department Store, 1882.   In this woodcut prepared for an advertisement, note the neat displays of goods, the well-dressed, middle-class women who comprised the principal clientele of department stores, and the female sales clerks waiting on customers. (Courtesy of Macy Archives)

in the nation's largest cities during the mid-nineteenth century and grew rapidly in the ensuing decades as new urban transportation technologies made it possible for large numbers of people to travel to central business districts. Some of the first such stores, like Marshall Field in Chicago, began as adjuncts to successful wholesale firms. Others, including John Wanamaker in Philadelphia and R. H. Macy in New York, started as small-scale retailers of clothing or dry goods. Whatever the origins, the goals of entrepreneurs in this new field were high volume of sales and high turnover of stock by selling at low prices and low margins. When individual department stores

attained levels of sales as high as those of wholesale firms, they could buy directly from manufacturers for cash. Although they could not eliminate the cost of the wholesaling function, they could reduce it by bypassing the independent wholesaler.

Yet the innovation of the department store involved much more than large size and low prices. Because department stores almost from the beginning employed hundreds of sales clerks to process thousands of transactions, they introduced the one-price system that replaced the old custom of haggling over the price of each sale. They also offered free entry to browsers, with the hope that this would encourage impulse buying. Because department stores emphasized the importance of turning over stock, they marked down prices on slow-moving goods. Above all, department stores sought to make shopping a pleasure, not just a task, particularly for the urban middle-class and upper-middle-class women with discretionary income who constituted the core of their clientele. To this end, the large stores housed their goods in "palaces of consumption," structures with impressive exteriors and elegant interiors. Department stores were among the first important users of elevators and electrical illumination. To make shopping pleasant and interesting, they offered a variety of services to customers, including restaurants (in a period when there were few public eating facilities for women dining alone), lounges and reading rooms, delivery services, and refunds in the case of dissatisfaction with the goods purchased. R. H. Macy of New York, in an 1895 advertisement, neatly summarized the appeal of the department store to middle-class urban consumers: "Ride our bicycles, read our books, cook in our saucepans, dine off our china, wear our silks, get under our blankets, smoke our cigars, drink our wines. Shop at Macy's and life will cost you less and yield you more than you dreamed possible."[2]

The Mail-Order Firm

What the department store brought to middle-class urban consumers, the mail-order house made possible for middle-class families in rural areas—a wide variety of goods at low prices. During the late 1860s and early 1870s, a number of concerns engaged in selling by mail specialized items like books, novelties, and pictures. The first general merchandise mail-order concern was established in Chicago in 1872 by A. Montgomery Ward. Backed by the Grange, a powerful agricultural organization, Ward developed direct mail-order transactions with farmers and small-town people through-

out the United States, thereby enabling them to bypass the monopolistic local storekeeper. From the beginning, his policy was to offer goods at the lowest possible price through cash sales, backed by a warranty for all items and the right of return if the customer was not satisfied. The key to Ward's success was the catalog—the "wish book" for farm families—which by 1887 contained 540 pages offering over 24,000 items. Ward's chief competitor was Sears, Roebuck and Company; founded in 1887 to sell watches by mail, the firm soon began to add other lines. By the end of the century, both Ward and Sears were selling nearly all of the goods offered by country storekeepers. Like their urban counterparts, the department stores, the mail-order houses emphasized lower margins and prices by increasing stock turnover and buying directly from manufacturers. They achieved speed in handling orders with the use of mechanical devices and a tightly controlled schedule system. At Sears, as many as 100,000 orders could be processed in a day, "as many transactions as most traditional merchants in pre-railroad days handled in a lifetime."[3]

The expansion of the mail-order business was further aided by the establishment of rural free delivery in 1896 and parcel-post service in 1912. However, because the rural market was declining by the second decade of the twentieth century, mail-order houses responded in the 1920s by opening retail stores in cities.

The Chain Store

The chain store was another type of mass retailer to attain economies of scale through volume buying and selling. The term *chain store* meant that several retail establishments were combined to operate under one ownership and management. Generally, early chain stores avoided direct competition with the other forms of mass retailing by locating their establishments in small towns or on the outskirts of

Table 16–2 *Chain Stores in the United States, 1885–1915*

Year	All Chains	Number of Chains			
		Grocery	Drugs	Shoes	Ready-to-Wear Clothing
1885	4	2	0	0	0
1890	10	6	1	0	0
1895	21	11	1	1	1
1900	58	21	7	3	5
1905	154	44	19	9	21
1910	257	62	36	13	34
1915	505	112	81	38	73

SOURCE: Data from U.S. Bureau of the Census, *Historical Statistics of the United States,* series 220 (Washington, D.C.: GPO, 1975), p. 847.

metropolitan areas and by specializing on lines where their rivals had not yet become strongly entrenched. Since each chain store remained relatively small and did not offer much in the way of customer services, the cost of sales and overhead were held to a minimum. Like the other mass retailers, chain stores bought directly from the producers of the goods they sold.

The first modern retail chain-store system, the Great Atlantic and Pacific Tea Company, was founded in 1859. Its success in the grocery field encouraged many imitators. F. W. Woolworth's five-and-dime chain was the most successful of the variety stores that began in this period. Starting with six stores selling an assortment of low-priced goods in small towns in southeastern Pennsylvania in the early 1880s, Woolworth was operating over three hundred units by 1909. During the lifetime of its founder, Woolworth's chain offered only items priced at or under ten cents; indeed, at one point Woolworth searched for a manufacturer that could produce a watch to be sold for ten cents. The success of Woolworth stimulated the entry of a number of other firms into the variety field. In addition, by 1900, chains were beginning to appear in fields as varied as drugs, shoes, jewelry, furniture, and cigars (See Table 16–2).

Advertising and the Consumer

During the period from 1860 to 1914, advertising became an integral part of the marketing process in an increasingly consumer-oriented society. Not only was there a tremendous surge of growth in the amount of advertising; even more important, there were also changes in the kind of appeal used by advertisers. Before the Civil War, advertising in newspapers by merchants consisted primarily of information about the arrival of goods and their prices. It was a very important part of the newspaper; indeed, advertising usually appeared on the front page. But early businesspeople held little perception of the possibility of using advertising to persuade readers to use a particular product. They generally relied on word-of-mouth recommendations made by satisfied customers.

Several factors combined in the decades after 1860 to encourage the development of a new style of advertising designed to reach large numbers of people. As stressed earlier in the chapter, the railroad and telegraph created opportunities for more manufacturers to sell their products in a national market. In a number of the new mass-production industries, the high volume of production encouraged manufacturers to use advertising as a way to differentiate their products from those of rivals. (In many cases, the differences between the products advertised were slight and existed mainly in packaging and other minor characteristics.) For the new mass retailers, especially the department stores, there was the need to communicate information to the growing populations of large urban communities.

At the same time that demand for advertising was growing, technological changes in the publishing industry were lowering the cost of advertising space in the print media and broadening the audience that could be reached. New methods of printing and cheaper newsprint significantly reduced the cost of producing newspapers and magazines. Newspaper publishers in major cities across the country were attracting the attention of new readers with pictures, bold headlines, large type, and sensationalism—what was called *yellow journalism*. As a reflection of these developments, the number of daily newspapers in the United States increased from 574 in 1870 to over 2,000 in 1920; circulation rose by almost ten times. Thus, the mass media significantly improved the ability of mass distributors to reach the mass of consumers.

Magazines were also important for advertisers. In addition to the well-established monthlies like *Harper's* and the *Atlantic,* publishers launched several women's magazines in the late nineteenth century. These were aimed at the middle-class woman who made many of the decisions for her family about the purchase of consumer goods. In just fifteen years, from 1890 to 1905, monthly magazine circulations rose from eighteen million to sixty-four million. One magazine alone, the *Ladies' Home Journal,* reached a circulation of nearly one million by the turn of the century. Helping to stimulate this growth was a hefty U.S. postal subsidy provided to publishers of "informative periodicals"; from 1885 to 1917, the second-class rate was one cent per pound, while the Post Office spent about 5.5 cents for each

pound of such mail that it handled. Although advertising had always been a source of revenue to publishers, it had now become far more important than newsstand sales or subscriptions for both newspapers and magazines. (In 1919, advertising accounted for 66 percent of the total receipts of American newspapers and for 65 percent of that of periodicals.) Subscribers were no longer just readers; they were now perceived as consumers to whom merchandisers could appeal. In addition to the print media, advertisers exploited the possibilities for advertising in trolleys, subways, suburban trains, roadside billboards, and illuminated electric signs in major cities.

Department stores were among the early heavy users of advertising, and they increased over the years not only the amount that they spent on advertising but also the ratio of advertising expenses to sales. R. H. Macy, for example, typically placed five- or six-column advertisements in the Sunday editions of several New York newspapers, sometimes on the front page, and at least one single-column advertisement daily.

Through advertising in magazines with national circulation, manufacturers hoped that pressure from consumers would induce retailers and wholesalers to handle their products. The pioneers in employing this tactic were the manufacturers of patent medicines, like Lydia Pinkham, who directed a multitude of vivid but often exaggerated appeals to consumers. However, by 1900, the leading national advertisers were manufacturers of packaged goods—such as cigarettes, soap, and foods—as well as producers of consumer durable goods—such as bicycles and sewing machines, joined very soon by automobiles (see Table 16–3).

With the growth of advertising, the advertising agency emerged as the principal specialized business unit carrying out this part of the marketing process. In the immediate post–Civil War years, advertising agents were little more than "retailers" of space that they had

Table 16–3 *Largest Advertisers in National Magazines, 1914*

Rank	Corporation	Type of Product
1	Procter & Gamble	Household products
2	Quaker Oats	Breakfast cereals
3	American Tobacco	Cigarettes
4	Victor Talking Machine	Phonographs, records
5	Postum Cereal	Breakfast cereals
6	Willys-Overland	Automobiles
7	Goodyear Tire & Rubber	Tires
8	Cudahy Packing	Meat
9	Eastman Kodak	Cameras, film
10	Colgate	Household products
11	Joseph Campbell Company	Canned foods
12	Kellogg Toasted Corn Flakes	Breakfast cereals

SOURCE: Adapted from Daniel Pope, *The Making of Modern Advertising* (New York: Basic Books, 1983), pp. 43–45.

bought at "wholesale" from publishers. Like any merchant with an inventory, their principal concern was to sell that space, whether or not it best fit the needs of specific advertisers. A major step forward was the *open-contract system* (also called the net-cost-plus-commission plan), which spread through the advertising business after its introduction in the 1870s. The advertising agency now received from the advertiser a fixed percentage—usually 15 percent—of the cost of the space, which was purchased specifically for that advertiser. The open-contract arrangement helped to establish the principle that the sole responsibility of the advertising agency was to work on behalf of the advertiser.

As the use of advertising expanded, the intensity of competition among agencies increased. At the same time, advertisers perceived a need to find new ways to convince potential customers to buy their products. These developments, in turn, encouraged the adoption of a new approach to copywriting: An advertisement should be more than a mere claim of superiority of the product or its seller. Increasingly, copywriters, assisted by psychologists and artists on the staffs of their agencies,

sought to write copy that would persuade the consumer to buy the product. The purpose of each advertisement became to link the benefits that the product offered to the needs of the consumer. As one noted agency head proclaimed, the meaningful advertisement had to give the reader a "reason why" he or she should buy the item advertised. Eastman Kodak advertising succinctly put its case like this: "You press the button. We do the rest." Copywriters were learning to apply psychology in order to develop emotional appeals by emphasizing status symbols and fear of social embarrassment. One noted psychologist, Walter Dill Scott, set forth what he thought would become the basic law of the subject when he posed these questions in 1903: "How many advertisers describe a piano so vividly that the reader can hear it? How many food products are so described that the reader can taste the food? How many advertisers describe an undergarment so that the reader can feel the pleasant contact with the body?"[4]

Nineteenth-century publishers and advertisers generally showed little concern about the issue of truth in advertising. However, by the early 1900s, more and more businesspeople in publishing and merchandising were beginning to realize that advertisements offensive to their readers' standards of accuracy created consumer incredulity. Scrupulous and intelligent firms like Wanamaker's and Macy's were among the pioneers in eliminating dishonesty from advertising copy. Groups concerned about enforcing truth in advertising formed vigilance committees and lobbied for truth-in-advertising statutes. The movement concentrated on eliminating factual misstatements to protect reputable advertisers. It did not go into deeper ethical questions concerning the value of "conspicuous consumption" or the issue of "ostentatious display" raised by critics of business like Thorstein Veblen.

Despite its critics, early advertising served to encourage economic growth and helped consumers by bringing information about products to the largest possible audience of potential buyers. In an age that stressed the virtues of frugality, saving against spending, and puritanism in consumption, advertising was the only American social institution that emphasized instead the virtues of increasing one's standard of living and enjoying consumer products. Where to draw the line between abstinence and indulgence required wisdom and knowledge on the part of the consumer; increased consumer education, consumer research, and the setting of standards of purity and quality helped to create those qualities.

The Cost of Distribution

The revolution in mass distribution during the 1860 to 1914 period brought numerous advantages to the general public, but many Americans thought that wholesale- and retail-distribution costs were excessive. The price spread between what the producer received for goods and what the consumer had to pay for goods seemed too high, presumably because of unnecessary waste or distributive profits or both. The best statistical study on distribution costs in the United States during

the post–Civil War period showed a small but steady rise in the cost of wholesale and retail charges to the consumer (when measured as a percentage of the retail value of all commodities sold on the retail market) from about 33 percent of retail value in 1869 to about 37 percent in 1909. These figures omitted the cost of national advertising by manufacturers of consumer goods and the merchandising activities of producers or distributors of unfinished goods. Including these costs would raise the figures for distribution costs between 1869 and 1909 by at least 10 percent and perhaps as much as 17 percent. Such a revision would mean that distribution costs ranged from about 48 percent of retail prices in 1869 to over 50 percent in 1909.

Did distribution cost too much? Some contended, on the one hand, that the evolving distribution process resulted in unnecessary duplication of sales efforts, a multiplicity of sales outlets, excessive customer services, too many brands of essentially similar products, and wasteful advertising. On the other hand, the distribution process gave consumers greater varieties of goods and retail outlets, greater convenience of shopping, more personal services in the stores, other services like home delivery and the privilege of returning goods, and more information to aid in purchasing decisions. The critics of distribution costs likely did not consider whether, if American consumers had preferred lower prices at the cost of forgoing these conveniences and services, entrepreneurs would not have taken advantage of that preference. Beyond these considerations, the most significant point is that the new system of distribution was capable of rapidly moving the high volume of goods necessary to support a high level of mass consumption.

The United States in a Growing World Economy

From 1860 to 1914, as we have seen, the United States was building up a great nationwide distribution network that allowed the free movement of goods and services over an area as large as Europe. But during this same period, the United States, in its commerce with other countries, frequently erected barriers to free international trade by imposing tariffs on imports. Nevertheless, so rapid was the development of the American economy that even highly protective policy decisions did not prevent the United States from becoming an increasingly important participant in world commerce.

The rise of the United States in the world economy was not the result of slowed growth in world trade. Quite the contrary, the advantages of an international division of labor were so great that during the nineteenth century the network of international trade grew in size and activity to levels never before reached. The ratio of world trade (exports and imports combined) to world production is estimated to have risen from about 3 percent in 1801 to 16 percent in 1860 and to 33 percent in 1914. In 1867/68, the total value of world trade came to about $10.5 billion; by 1913, it had increased to about $40.6 billion, implying a rate of growth of over 30 percent per decade. The share of combined American exports and imports in these world values was roughly 6 percent in 1867/68 and 11 percent in 1913.

As world trade grew relative to world production, most of the major industrial countries of Western Europe and Japan also experienced an increase in their foreign trade-production ratios. The United States, however, did not. The American ratio was about 15 percent in the early 1870s and only 11 percent in 1913. The size and diversity of the United States in terms of its natural and human resources were so great that the possibilities for internal specialization and exchange were much more extensive than they were for other nations.

It may seem like a paradox that the United States was becoming relatively more important in the world economy at the same time that the world economy was becoming relatively less important to the United States. However, it is

important to note that economic growth was more rapid in the United States than elsewhere at this time. In the setting of world trade and production from the time of the American Civil War to World War I, the United States developed into the most powerful industrial nation while also maintaining and even increasing its importance as a major supplier of foodstuffs and raw materials to Western Europe and other parts of the world. American industrial growth was the key factor in its rise to economic preeminence. In 1870, the U.S. share of world manufacturing output was 23.3 percent, second to that of Great Britain. But by 1913, the U.S. share rose to 35.8 percent and greatly outdistanced the shares of Britain, Germany, and France, its major rivals in manufacturing.

Trends in Foreign Trade and Payments

Between 1860 and 1914, dramatic increases in the value of U.S. merchandise exports and imports occurred, as shown in Figure 16–2. Exports rose from about $340 million to a figure six times as large, $2.4 billion; imports grew from $360 million to $1.9 billion, a fourfold increase. From 1860 to 1873, with the one exception of 1862, American imports exceeded exports. Then, in 1874 a major change in American foreign trade occurred: From then until 1914 (with the exceptions of 1875, 1888, and 1893), American exports exceeded American imports in value. However, as spectacular as these increases in exports and imports were, they represented a relatively small and declining percentage of the gross national product. Exports, for instance, reached a high of 9 percent of the GNP in 1879 but then slowly sank to 6 percent in 1914; during the same period, imports reached a peak of 7.1 percent in 1869 and gradually declined to 5.3 percent in 1914.

The maturing of the American economy was evident in the dramatic changes that occurred in the composition of American trade between the 1870s and the 1910s. In the 1870s, over four-fifths of American exports consisted of

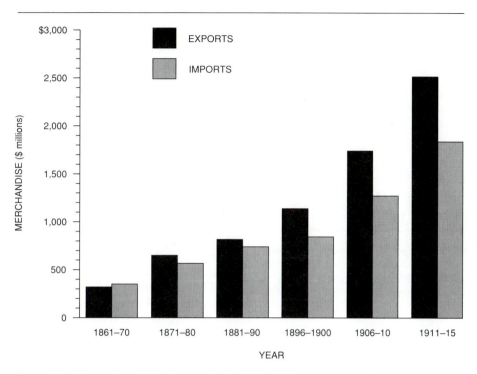

Figure 16–2 *Expansion of U.S. Foreign Trade, 1861–1915*
SOURCE: Data adapted from U.S. Bureau of the Census, *Statistical Abstract of the United States* (Washington, D.C.: GPO, 1957), pp. 888–89.

raw materials and foodstuffs, whereas less than one-fifth was nonfood manufactures. By the 1910s, the share of nonfood manufactures rose to about one-half. On the import side, the changes were not quite so marked; however, the share of imported manufactures declined somewhat while that of raw materials increased quite rapidly. In short, between the Civil War and World War I, the nature of the United States' comparative advantage in the world economy shifted away from agriculture and toward manufacturing.

The export of American manufactured goods to Europe and other parts of the world from 1890 to 1914 was considered so great that some writers described it as an American "commercial invasion" of Europe. The most important manu-

factured exports in terms of value were iron and steel manufactures, refined petroleum, copper, cotton goods, leather and leather products, and agricultural implements. Among the specific articles listed under the heading of iron and steel manufactures were electrical machinery, sewing machines, typewriters, locomotives, cash registers, and shoe-making machinery (see Table 16–4). These manufactured exports reflected the industrialization of the American economy as well as the increasing ability of various American manufacturers to compete in foreign markets with leading European industrial powers like Great Britain and Germany. At the same time, imports of crude materials other than foodstuffs became relatively more important to the American economy, reflecting the growing economic

Table 16–4 *Exports of the U.S., 1872–1913* (*in $ millions, current prices*)

Category	1872	1900	1913
Raw materials	$250	$ 542	$1,031
Food, drink, tobacco[a]	187	568	513
Metals manufactures	5	139	348
Machinery	7	72	186
Transportation	3	15	64
Chemicals	11	35	69
Textiles	4	27	76
Others	13	55	149
Total	$480	$1,453	$2,436

[a]Includes both processed and unprocessed food exports.
SOURCE: Adapted from William H. Becker, *The Dynamics of Business-Government Relations: Industry and Exports, 1893–1921* (Chicago: University of Chicago Press, 1982), p. 10.

relations between the United States and various supply-source areas in Asia, Oceania, the Middle East, Canada, and Latin America.

From 1860 to 1914, Europe was America's greatest market and chief source of imports. In 1870, that continent, including the United Kingdom as a leading customer, took 80 percent of American exports; gradually, the figure fell but in 1914 it was still 64 percent. As for imports, 55 percent came from Europe in 1870; by 1914, its share dropped to 46 percent. As American trade with Europe declined, Asia—especially Japan, the Philippines, and Indonesia—grew in importance as a supplier of products for the American market and as an absorber of American exports. Next to Asia in economic importance were America's commercial relations with Canada and Latin America. U.S. trade with Africa and Oceania increased rapidly in the pre-1914 era, but the amounts involved were still small.

Changes in the United States' balance of payments with the rest of the world during the late nineteenth century also reflected the maturing of the American economy (see Table 16–5). In earlier decades, imports of goods and

services typically exceeded exports, and the United States financed its deficit on current account by means of loans from foreigners eager to earn the high returns on capital invested in America. Payments deficits on current account thus were balanced by surpluses, or net credits, on capital account. During the 1870s, the balance of commodity trade shifted from deficit to surplus. However, for some decades the whole current account remained in deficit because trade surpluses were more than offset by payments to foreigners in the forms of interest and dividends, tourist expenditures overseas, transportation charges, and remittances from immigrants (who sent some of what they earned in the United States to relatives and friends in their native lands).

The continuing deficits on current account from the 1870s to 1890s were offset, as they had been earlier, by credits arising from the flow of foreign capital to the United States as well as from small exports of specie. In these decades, the capital coming to America from overseas—mostly from Europe—went into the development of American railroads and cattle, land, and mining enterprises. During the 1890s, however, there were signs that the centuries-old pattern of Americans importing capital was beginning to change. The current account of the balance of payments followed one of its components, the commodity trade account, into surplus, and America's net current earnings from international commerce were used to finance investments in other countries. The United States had thus transformed itself from a capital-poor to a capital-rich economy (see Table 16–6).

The Protective Tariff

The increase in U.S. exports from 1860 to 1914 was higher than that of imports by a ratio of three to two. A major reason for the disparity was the use of the protective tariff by the Republican party to "protect" various American

Table 16–5 *U.S. International Balance of Payments, 1869–1913, 5 Year Totals (in $ millions)*

Period[a]	Merchandise (net)	Services: Income on Investments (net)	Other Services	Net Unilateral Transfers	Current Account Balance	U.S. Capital[c]	Foreign Capital[b]	Capital Account Balance	Net Change in Monetary Gold Stock[c]	Errors and Omissions
1869–73	$ −553	$ −418	$ +170	$ +16	$ −785	$ 0	$ 0	$ +786	$ 0	$ +1
1874–78	+488	−459	+151	−60	+120	0	0	−48	−71	−1
1879–83	+820	−418	−16	−52	+334	0	0	−10	−324	0
1884–88	+278	−474	−311	−137	−644	0	0	+794	−150	0
1889–93	+290	−659	−176	−237	−782	0	0	+719	+63	0
1894–98	+1,316	−621	−114	−243	+338	0	0	−191	−148	1
1899–1903	+2,612	−463	−179	−487	+1,483	0	0	−848	−424	−211
1904–08	+2,500	−339	−565	−786	+810	−454	+454	0	−465	−345
1909–13	+2,265	−351	−937	−1,034	−57	−699	+1,171	+472	−249	−166

[a]Fiscal years through 1900; thereafter, calendar years.

[b]An outflow of funds is shown as negative.

[c]An increase is shown as negative.

NOTE: From 1869 to 1898, the capital account balance functions in the same way as the errors and omissions item does from 1899 to 1913. From 1881 to 1899, the figures for net change in the monetary gold stock are also included in the totals for the capital account balance.

SOURCE: Adapted from data in U.S. Bureau of the Census, *Statistical History of the United States from Colonial Times to the Present* (New York: Basic Books, 1976), pp. 864–68; and Harold G. Vatter, *The Drive to Industrial Maturity* (Westport, Conn.: Greenwood Press, 1975), p. 310.

Table 16–6 *Estimates of U.S. Direct Foreign Investments, 1914*

Industry	Europe	Canada	Latin America	Asia	Other
Manufacturing	$200	$221	$ 37	$ 10	$10
Sales	85	27	34	15	9
Petroleum	138	25	133	40	7
Mining	5	159	549	3	4
Agriculture	0	101	243	12	0
Utilities	11	8	98	16	0
Railroads	0	69	176	10	0
Total	$439	$610	$1,270	$106	$30

SOURCE: Adapted from Mira Wilkins, *The Maturing of Multinational Enterprise: American Business Abroad from 1914 to 1970* (Cambridge: Harvard University Press, 1974), p. 31.

industries by excluding or limiting the flow of competing products from abroad, particularly those from the United Kingdom and Germany. Because changes in tariff rates could either increase or decrease competition from foreign producers, they had important short-term effects on the profits of particular industries and the economic welfare of all connected with those industries. Policy decisions on the tariff thus became the focus of intense lobbying and pressure politics as various producing groups tried to use governmental powers and processes to further their private economic interests. Considerations of consumer welfare were not very important in the policy debates and decisions. Because there were many more consumers than producers and because the interest of any individual consumer in a decision usually was not great, it was difficult to organize effective consumer opposition to highly protective duties. Tariff policies, therefore, affected economic welfare by redistributing income from consumers to producers as well as among various groups of producers. Whether the protective tariff had much effect on the nation's economic growth is less certain.

During the three decades before the Civil War, the average ad valorem duties on imports moved downward from 49 percent to 20 per-

cent and reversed in large measure the protectionist trend that had developed between 1816 and 1832. But the secession of eleven southern states enabled organized northern industrial groups, with their free-soil farming allies in the Republican party, to gain control of Congress. They then enacted high protective tariff legislation, partly to get revenue for waging the Civil War and partly to aid American manufacturers in meeting foreign competition while burdened by heavy internal taxes during the war. Three minor tariff acts were passed between March 2 and December 24 in 1861. As the war progressed and the need for revenue increased, Congress was induced by different pressure groups, led by iron, cotton, and woolen manufacturers, to enact two major tariff statutes—in July 1862 and in June 1864. The average ad valorem rates on dutiable commodities were increased from 37.3 percent under the 1862 act to 49 percent in 1864.

At the end of the Civil War, federal revenues exceeded the needs of the national government. By 1872, most of the internal taxes, including the income tax, had been abolished in response to strong pressures for relief from the heavy Civil War taxes. But no similar drastic action was taken toward the reduction of import duties. The 1864 Morrill Tariff Act, although an emergency war measure, remained virtually unchanged for over twenty years. Although most Democrats and some Republicans favored a tariff for revenue, the latter group controlled Congress for most of the period between 1865 and 1912 and was able to retain or increase most Civil War tariff duties.

After 1880, the large Treasury surpluses created public pressure for reduction of high protective tariff duties, but no effective decrease was achieved for decades. In 1890, the Republicans achieved a drastic extension of high protection through the McKinley Tariff Act. Average customs rates on dutiable items came to 49 percent. One concession to consumers was the putting of raw sugar on the free list, but a bounty was given for the production of sugar within the United States.

Four years later, in 1894, the Democrats made a gallant effort to reduce the protective duties on manufactured goods through the Wilson-Gorman Tariff Act. But protectionist Republicans and Democrats in the Senate prevented tariff reform, and the act had only a slightly moderated protective intent. The average ad valorem rate on dutiable goods was 41 percent. A duty was again imposed on raw sugar; this benefited the sugar growers of Louisiana but harmed Cuban sugar interests.

The 1896 election was waged primarily on the free-silver issue, though the victorious Republicans acted as if they had received a mandate for a high protective tariff. The next year they pushed through Congress the Dingley Tariff Act, which created the second highest average rate on dutiable goods in American history—52 percent. During the twelve years that the Dingley Tariff Act was enforced, a strong public opinion developed in favor of downward revision of the tariff. However, the Payne-Aldrich Tariff Act of 1909 preserved the extremely high rate as well as the hostile attitude toward foreign trade of the earlier 1890 and 1897 tariff measures. Nevertheless, the average ad valorem duty on dutiable goods went

downward to about 42 percent. For the first time in decades, the extreme champions of protection were on the defensive.

In the election of 1912, President Woodrow Wilson came to power on a reform program directed against high protective tariffs and monopolistic big business. The next year he succeeded in getting Congress to pass the Underwood-Simmons Tariff Act, in defiance of powerful lobbying by industrial interests. The new law greatly expanded the "free list" of articles excepted from tariff duties, yet moderate protection was given to "legitimate" domestic industries. Hence, the average ad valorem rate on dutiable goods fell only to 36 percent during the first year the new tariff was in effect. With the return to moderate protection went a provision for an income tax, which had been made possible by enactment of the Sixteenth Amendment to the Constitution. As a result, the burden of taxation was shifted from low-income groups to high-income classes and the cost of living for consumers was reduced.

Discussions of the protective tariff have usually stressed the nominal rates imposed on specific commodities and have given the average ad valorem rate as a measure of the protection given to domestic industries. However, careful study of the data indicates that the effective rates of protection were often much higher than the nominal rates. This occurred, for example, when finished goods like woolen and cotton textiles and steel rails were made from raw materials and components taxed at lower rates. In the case of cotton textiles, if the value of cotton produced domestically or imported free of duty made up half the value of the final product, then the effective tariff duty on cloth was twice the nominal duty, say 20 percent rather than 10 percent. The implication of these new analyses for tariff history is that the profits made by industrialists and the costs imposed on consumers were much greater than early opponents of the protective tariff realized.

Although tariffs redistributed income from consumers to producers as well as between various groups of producers that were protected to different degrees, economists disagree about the effects of tariffs on the nation's economic growth. The judgment of most economists is that tariffs are barriers to trade that hinder economic growth by interfering with international specialization and the exploitation of comparative advantages. In the United States, however, rates of economic growth during the period of high tariffs from the Civil War to World War I were as high as at any other time in the nation's history. Protectionist economists argue that the potentially adverse effects of tariffs on economic growth may have been offset in part by the absence of restrictions on the flow of labor and capital to the United States from abroad and by the increased capital investment in, and efficiency of, some, if not all, of the protected industries.

Another consideration that economists invoke relates to government finance. Tariff duties furnished a large part of federal revenue. To have maintained the same revenue in the absence of protection would have required other forms of taxation, with other effects on economic efficiency and growth. To have reduced revenues through lower customs duties would have meant reduced budget surpluses or increased federal deficits. These, too, would have necessitated other policy changes affecting growth and welfare. Reduced budget surpluses, for example, would have meant less federal debt retirement in the late nineteenth century. As noted in Chapter 15, debt retirement may have stimulated capital formation and economic growth. Considerations such as the foregoing illustrate the problems that arise in attempting to reach sound conclusions about the effects of tariffs on growth and welfare.

Promoting American Business Abroad

As part of an enhanced interest among the nation's political leaders in world affairs, the U.S. government between the 1890s and World War I significantly expanded its efforts to promote the growth of American export trade. It was assumed that a major obstacle for business was lack of knowledge about the foreign field. Thus, accurate commercial information was thought to be the key to linking U.S. producers with potential customers abroad. This approach was perceived as politically more feasible than other proposals considered at the time, such as subsidizing the merchant marine or extending tariff reciprocity.

Major improvements were made in the operation of the consular service, operated by the Department of State. Consuls, traditionally appointed under the political spoils system, were brought under modified civil service regulations and given better staff support in their offices around the world. Their mission was clear: to promote American export trade by making regular reports on foreign tariffs and customs regulations, transportation, currency, local buying habits, and other items of interest to U.S. exporters. The State Department also operated a Bureau of Statistics, which issued many publications and answered inquiries from business firms and trade associations.

When the Department of Commerce and Labor was established in 1903, it too was assigned responsibility for promoting the nation's export trade. The Bureau of Manufactures (later called the Bureau of Foreign and Domestic Commerce) within the Department of Commerce and Labor employed special agents who traveled widely to study foreign markets. The bureau compiled lists of reputable foreign merchants willing to handle American merchandise in their countries; it also published daily editions of consular reports and confidential bulletins on subjects of interest to U.S. manufacturers.

Somewhat paradoxically, however, the expansion of government activities in promoting foreign trade had little to do with the surge of American exports in the quarter-century prior to World War I, as the research of William

Table 16–7 *Manufacturing Operations Established by U.S. Manufacturing Corporations in Great Britain and Germany, 1900–1917*

Industry	Number of Operations		
	Great Britain 1900–1917	Germany 1900–1913	Total in Both Countries
Machinery	8	8	16
Electrical machinery	4	0	4
Transportation equipment	4	0	4
Stone, clay, glass	1	2	3
Food	2	0	2
Petroleum	0	2	2
Fabricated metals	1	1	2
Instruments	1	1	2
Industrial chemicals	1	0	1
Total	22	14	36

SOURCE: Adapted from Alfred D. Chandler, Jr., *Scale and Scope: The Dynamics of Industrial Capitalism* (Cambridge: Harvard University Press, 1990), pp. 158–59.

Becker clearly shows.[5] During this period, machinery, metal products, processed foods, and oil consistently dominated exports, accounting by the time of World War I for over 80 percent of total American exports of manufactured goods. These were the products made by the pioneers of mass production and mass distribution, who began early to expand their markets across international boundaries. With superior technology and skillful marketing, these giant corporations found success in selling their wares in western European nations with income structures and demand patterns similar to those of the United States, as well as to nearby Canada and Mexico. They neither needed nor sought government help to expand their exports. They had their own foreign sales organizations to gather information and distribute goods. When foreign governments imposed tariffs and other restrictions to protect their own business interests, American corporations did not seek the support of their government. Rather, they developed private strategies to deal with their problems. These firms became the first American multinational corporations when they established foreign manufacturing plants in order to jump the tariff walls imposed by foreign governments on their U.S.-produced goods (see Tables 16–6 and 16–7).

Certain firms, however, did look to government for help in expanding their exports. These included small- and medium-sized manufacturers of undifferentiated products like hats, clothing, textiles, pottery, and leather goods—industrialists who held no particular technical or marketing advantages over foreign competitors. Their interest in foreign trade peaked during years of depression, such as the 1890s, when they perceived exporting as a solution to the problem of excess capacity that developed when domestic demand turned down. Their trade associations, the National Association of Manufacturers, and other organizations applied pressure on the government to help them sell abroad. Then, with the return of prosperity in the United States, their interest in export markets waned.

According to research conducted by Becker and by Herman Werking,[6] it was government bureaucrats who supplied much of the initiative that built the foreign service apparatus dedicated to the promotion of American exports. The principal agents of this bureaucratic expansion were in middle-echelon positions in the Departments of State and Commerce. Cosmopolitan in their outlook, they believed that America was destined to play a larger role in world balance of power politics based on its economic strength. The bureaucrats also realized that promotion of foreign trade would be useful to them as careerists, in that they would gain the political support of a business constituency in their dealings with Congress for increased responsibilities and appropriations. In any event, the interest of these government officials in promoting American exports during these years was clearly more consistent than was the attention paid to foreign trade by the small manufacturers most in need of government assistance.

Territorial and Economic Expansion Overseas

The Spanish-American War (1898) marked the emergence of the United States as a player in the world balance of power politics. Throughout most of the nineteenth century, the country concentrated its efforts on settling and developing a continent; however, the 1867 purchase of Alaska from Russia for $7.2 million was too good a bargain to pass up. The doctrine of two spheres, originally established by the Monroe Doctrine of 1823, continued to prevail, but concern about European activity in the Western Hemisphere lessened with distance from the United States. After the Civil War, little attention was given to the nation's military establishment, except for the role of the army in waging war against the native population in the West. Only in the 1890s, when it was apparent that new developments in naval technology had effectively shrunk the distance between America and potential rivals in Europe and Asia, did political-strategic decision makers begin to articulate the need for a

"two-ocean" fleet to defend both coasts. They were aware of the growing naval power of Japan in the Far East and the militant foreign policy and naval buildup of Germany in Europe.

As a direct result of the war, the United States annexed the former Spanish colonies of Puerto Rico, the Philippine Islands, and Guam. Cuba, whose struggle for independence from Spain had led to the war, became in effect a self-governing protectorate of the United States. The Cubans were required to write into their constitution provisions authorizing U.S. intervention to maintain law and order as well as the leasing of land for a U.S. naval base. As a by-product of hostilities, previously independent Hawaii was annexed, partly for strategic reasons (naval bases on the route to Asia) and partly for economic reasons. (Hawaii had fallen under the control of American sugar planters in 1893, so annexation made Hawaiian sugar a domestic American product with duty-free entry to the mainland.)

The Spanish-American War not only gave the United States colonies in the Caribbean and in Asia; it also demonstrated the need for a canal across Central America to move the nation's growing two-ocean navy from one coast to the other. After tacitly helping Panama to achieve its independence from Colombia, the Theodore Roosevelt administration concluded an agreement with the new republic in 1904, granting the United States in perpetuity the use and control of a canal zone across the Isthmus. Construction of the canal, begun earlier by a French company, was completed in 1914.

With the canal a basic element in U.S. defense strategy, President Theodore Roosevelt and other political leaders were determined to acquire effective control over surrounding territory in Central America, northern South America, and the islands of the Caribbean so as to ensure that no hostile foreign power could threaten the canal. The small nations in

Construction of the Panama Canal.   The canal, opened to traffic in 1914, had an important impact not only on commercial shipping patterns but also on U.S. strategic defense planning. (Brown Brothers)

this area were economically underdeveloped, dependent on outside capital (sometimes even to finance their governmental operations), and politically unstable, with revolutionary regimes often repudiating government debt and confiscating property owned by foreigners. American political-strategic-military decision makers were concerned that repudiation of debts owed to European investors would lead to intervention by their governments and possibly the establishment of naval bases in the region. Thus, Roosevelt proclaimed his own corollary to the Monroe Doctrine, by which the United States, as the "policeman" of the Western Hemisphere, would intervene in Latin American countries to collect debts owed to

European investors. To reduce further the possibility that European investment would lead to foreign intervention in the affairs of Caribbean nations, the Taft administration pursued a policy of "Dollar Diplomacy." Potential U.S. investors received informal assurance that armed force would be used swiftly in the event of repudiation of bonds or confiscation of property by governments in the region. In other words, economic means would be employed to achieve strategic goals. During the first two decades of the twentieth century, American military interventions, followed by the establishment of quasi-protectorates, occurred in Cuba in 1906 to 1909, in the Dominican Republic in 1905 and 1916, in Nicaragua in

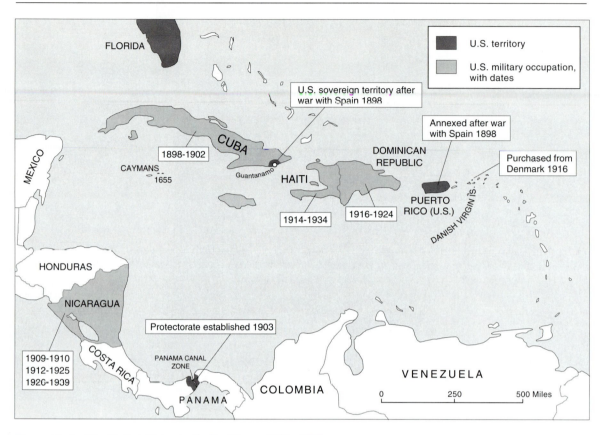

Figure 16–3. *The United States in the Caribbean, 1898–1939*
Source: Adapted from Martin Gilbert, *American History Atlas* (New York: Macmillan, 1968), p. 67.

1912, and in Haiti in 1915. In Nicaragua, for example, the U.S. government gained the right to build a canal and a naval base, while American bankers won control over Nicaragua's finances, banking, and railways. As a result of U.S. actions from 1898 on, including the purchase of the Virgin Islands in 1917, the Caribbean had become an "American lake" (see Figure 16–3). U.S. intervention to maintain stability and order in the affairs of sovereign nations achieved the short-term goal of protecting the sea lanes of the Caribbean from potentially hostile European powers, particularly Germany. However, that success was gained at a high price in terms of the hostile attitudes of virtually all Latin Americans toward the "Yankee colossus" to the north. U.S. military intervention for this purpose was thus abandoned in the 1930s.

American interests were also involved in Mexico, where a series of revolutions occurred between 1910 and 1920. American business held large investments in Mexican mines, oil fields, railroads, and rubber plantations. Despite pressure from U.S. business, President Wilson refused to follow the lead of the European powers in recognizing the conservative government established by force under General Huerta. Instead, the Wilson administration worked to force Huerta out of office by ordering U.S. naval forces to prevent European shipments of war materials to the Huerta regime, by allowing munitions from the United States to reach Huerta's opponents, and by promising to encourage American bankers to make loans to a new Mexican government. The two countries came close to war in 1914, when American forces bombarded Vera Cruz and occupied the city. Finally, in 1917, Wilson recognized the leader of the popular party, Venustiano Carranza, as Mexican president. Yet American support for the new government did not prevent the Mexican constitution of 1917 from vesting all subsoil rights in the Mexican people, thereby furnishing the legal basis for Mexico's expropriation of foreign oil holdings in 1938.

In China, the United States also attempted to gain influence but with less success than in Latin America. After the defeat of China by Japan in 1895, England, France, Germany, and Russia had obtained naval bases, ports, and spheres of influence from the weak Chinese government. American business feared that China would be closed to American trade, and missionaries argued that they needed government protection to operate in the Far East. Thus, in 1899 and 1900, the United States asked the European powers to accept an "open-door" policy in China; it was intended to grant free trading opportunities to all nations. When all the powers involved except Russia agreed, Secretary of State John Hay announced that the policy was in operation. During the Taft administration (1909–1913), the State Department tried to get American bankers to join European financiers in making investments in Chinese railroads. But the outbreak of revolution in China in 1911 threatened the success of this enterprise; in addition, American bankers, perceiving greater opportunity elsewhere, were reluctant to commit their funds to such projects. In 1913, President Wilson withdrew American support from the venture, fearing that it impinged on China's sovereignty and might invite foreign intervention.

Summary

In the new national market created by the railroad and telegraph, a system of mass distribution emerged to handle the vastly larger flow of goods made possible by mass production. From the 1850s to the early 1880s, wholesalers dominated the American distribution system. They performed many valuable services as middlemen between domestic and foreign manufacturers on the one hand, and between general country stores and urban retailers on the other. However, the position of wholesalers was undermined with the development of other forms of marketing. Giant manufacturing corporations assumed for their product lines the marketing functions formerly performed by wholesalers. Growing urban and rural populations, along with rising levels of income, led to the development of mass retailers—department stores, chain stores, and mail-order houses—that typically purchased their stocks of goods directly from manufacturers. The new mass marketers gave consumers access to a greater variety of goods than ever before, often at lower prices and with greater convenience. Advertising grew in volume and changed in purpose as sellers sought ways to reach the mass market and encourage a high level of consumption.

As the United States rose to industrial preeminence, the nation's long-established patterns of economic relations with the rest of the world were altered. The balance of foreign trade became favorable, with merchandise exports exceeding imports, and by the early twentieth century the United States became a net exporter of capital. Although traditional exports of agricultural commodities continued to increase, exports of American manufactures grew much more rapidly. The United States was developing at home the largest free trade area in world history, but its stance toward the rest of the world during and after the Civil War became highly protectionist. Well-organized manufacturing interests secured economic gains at the expense of consumers and foreign producers through steep tariffs on imported goods.

Decisions to erect barriers to the flow of foreign products into the United States did not reflect a policy of isolation. Rather, like other industrial powers, the United States became caught up in the scramble for overseas territories and spheres of influence. The purchase of Alaska, the annexation of Hawaii, and the acquisition of territories resulting from the brief war with Spain were motivated more by strategic and political than by economic considerations. In the early years of the twentieth century, the nation's political decision makers fashioned a policy of Dollar Diplomacy in the Caribbean and the Far East, by which they sought to use economic means to advance what they perceived to be the strategic goals of the United States as a participant in the world balance of power politics. While military intervention in sovereign nations in the Caribbean may have prevented potentially hostile European powers from establishing bases in that region, such actions caused considerable hostility toward the United States throughout Latin America.

Endnotes

1. Elizabeth W. Gilboy, "Demand as a Factor in the Industrial Revolution," in *Facts and Factors in Economic History: Articles by Former Students of Edwin Francis Gay* (Cambridge: Harvard University Press, 1932), p. 626.

2. Quoted in Ralph M. Hower, *History of Macy's of New York, 1858–1919: Chapters in the Evolution of the Department Store* (Cambridge: Harvard University Press, 1943), p. 273.

3. Alfred D. Chandler, Jr., *Visible Hand: The Managerial Revolution in American Business* (Cambridge: Harvard University Press, 1977), p. 232.

4. Walter Dill Scott, "The Psychology of Advertising" (1903), quoted in David M. Potter, *People of Plenty: Economic Abundance and the American Character* (Chicago: University of Chicago Press, 1954), pp. 171–72.

5. William H. Becker, *The Dynamics of Business-Government Relations: Industry and Exports, 1893–1921* (Chicago: University of Chicago Press, 1982).

6. Richard H. Werking, *The Master Architects: Building the United States Foreign Service, 1890–1913* (Lexington: University Press of Kentucky, 1977).

Suggested Readings

Alfred D. Chandler, Jr., *The Visible Hand: The Managerial Revolution in American Business* (Cambridge: Harvard University Press, 1977) places the marketing changes in the context of his account of the rise of large-scale enterprise. Thomas C. Cochran, *200 Years of American*

Business (New York: Basic Books, 1977) relates developments in marketing to those taking place in other business sectors. Harold Barger, *Distribution's Place in the American Economy Since 1869* (Princeton: Princeton University Press, 1950) furnishes an able statistical summary of trends in the domestic marketing system. Changes in the marketing of agricultural commodities are discussed in Henrietta M. Larson, *The Wheat Market and the Farmer in Minnesota, 1858–1900* (New York: Columbia University Press, 1926); Morton Rothstein, "America in the Rivalry for the British Wheat Market, 1860–1914," *Mississippi Valley Historical Review*, 47 (1960); and Harold D. Woodman, *King Cotton and His Retainers: Financing and Marketing the Cotton Crop of the South, 1800–1925* (Lexington: University Press of Kentucky, 1968).

Daniel J. Boorstin, *The Americans: The Democratic Experience* (New York: Random House, 1973) discusses some of the social aspects of mass consumption; while Daniel Horowitz, *The Morality of Spending: Attitudes Toward the Consumer Society in America, 1875–1940* (Baltimore: Johns Hopkins University Press, 1985) analyzes changing attitudes about consumer spending. Glenn Porter and Harold G. Livesay, *Merchants and Manufacturers: Studies in the Changing Structure of Nineteenth Century Marketing* (Baltimore: Johns Hopkins University Press, 1971) analyzes the place of the wholesaler in the distribution system; Lewis Atherton, *Main Street on the Middle Border* (Bloomington: Indiana University Press, 1954) discusses the role of country stores.

The most useful scholarly histories of mass marketing firms that emerged during this period are Ralph M. Hower, *History of Macy's of New York, 1858–1919: Chapters in the Evolution of the Department Store* (Cambridge: Harvard University Press, 1943); Robert Twyman, *History of Marshall Field Co.* (Philadelphia: University of Pennsylvania Press, 1954); and Boris Emmet and John D. Jeuck, *Catalogues and Counters: A History of Sears, Roebuck and Company* (Chicago: University of Chicago Press, 1950). Daniel A. Pope, *The Making of Modern Advertising* (New York: Basic Books, 1983) is a valuable, comprehensive account. Ralph M. Hower, *The History of an Advertising Agency: N. W. Ayer & Son at Work, 1869–1949* (Cambridge: Harvard University Press, 1949) is the best history of an individual firm in this field. Merle Curti, "The Changing Concept of 'Human Nature' in the Literature of American Advertising," *Business History Review*, 41 (1967) and Richard Kielbowicz, "Postal Subsidies for the Press and the Business of Mass Culture, 1880–1920," *Business History Review*, 64 (1990) provide details on two important developments having implications for the growth of advertising during this period. Richard S. Tedlow, *New and Improved: The Story of Mass Marketing in America* (New York: Basic Books, 1990) offers some useful insights into the subject.

The importance of foreign commerce is brought out in Robert E. Lipsey, *Price and Quantity Trends in the Foreign Trade of the United States* (Princeton: Princeton University Press, 1963); that of the protective tariff in Sidney Ratner, *The Tariff in American History* (New York: D. Van Nostrand, 1972).

The study of the relationship between business-economic interests and political-diplomatic-strategic considerations in American territorial and commercial expansion during this period has elicited sharply conflicting interpretations. William H. Becker, *The Dynamics of Business-Government Relations: Industry and Exports, 1893–1921* (Chicago: University of Chicago Press, 1982); Richard H. Werking, *The Master Architects: Building the United States Foreign Service, 1890–1913* (Lexington: University Press of Kentucky, 1977); and William H. Becker and Samuel F. Wells, Jr., eds., *Economics and World Power: An Assessment of American Diplomacy Since 1789* (New York: Columbia University Press, 1984), especially the essays by David M. Pletcher and by Becker, offer a serious challenge to the interpretation made by Walter LaFeber, *The New Empire: American Expansion, 1860–1898* (Ithaca: Cornell University Press, 1963) and other critics of American foreign economic policy. See also Robert Zevin, "An Interpretation of American Imperialism," *Journal of Economic History,* 32 (1972); James A. Field, Jr., et al., "American Imperialism." *American Historical Review.* 83 (1978); Paul S. Hobo, "Economics, Emotion, and Expansion," in H. Wayne Morgan, ed., *The Gilded Age,* rev. ed. (Syracuse: Syracuse University Press, 1970); John A. S. Grenville and George B. Young, *Politics, Strategy, and American Diplomacy, 1893–1917* (New Haven: Yale University Press, 1966). Marilyn B. Young, *The Rhetoric of Empire: American China Policy, 1895–1901* (Cambridge: Harvard University Press, 1968); Clarence B. Davis, "Financing Imperialism: British and American Bankers as Vectors of Imperial Expansion in China, 1908–1920," *Business History Review,* 56 (1982); Lester D. Langley, *The Banana Wars: An Inner History of American Empire, 1900–1934* (Lexington: University Press of Kentucky, 1983); and William Schell, Jr., "American Investment in Tropical Mexico: Rubber Plantations, Fraud, and Dollar Diplomacy, 1897–1913," *Business History Review,* 64 (1990) focus on American business activity in particular areas. Cleona Lewis, *America's Stake in International Investments* (Washington, D.C.: Brookings Institution, 1938) is still useful. Mira Wilkins, *The Emergence of Multinational Enterprise: American Business Abroad from the Colonial Era to 1914* (Cambridge: Harvard University Press, 1970) is the basic work on the subject of American corporate investment outside the United States. Mira Wilkins, ed., *The Growth of Multinationals* (Brookfield, VT: Edward Elgar Publishing Co., 1991) includes important journal articles on this subject. David K. Fieldhouse, *Economics and Empire, 1830–1914* (Ithaca: Cornell University Press, 1973); William Ashworth, *A Short History of the International Economy Since 1850,* 3rd edition, (London: Longman, 1975); and W. Arthur Lewis, *Growth and Fluctuations, 1871–1914* (London: Allen & Unwin, 1978) furnish penetrating analyses and balanced perspectives on the world scene.

Part IV

Prosperity, Depression, and World Wars

1914–1945

THE CHIEF EPISODES OF AMERICAN ECONOMIC history during the period from 1914 to 1945 included a world war, a decade of high prosperity followed by one of severe depression, and another world war. Over these three decades, the U.S. economy made great advances. Real gross national product per capita doubled between 1914 and 1945, while national wealth in constant dollars advanced by 64 percent. Behind these gains was significant growth in productivity, as a more than doubling of gross domestic product per unit of total factor input reflected capital investment in machinery and equipment as well as the education and skill of the American labor force.

Major advances in science and technology continued to promote increases in the variety of available goods. New industries emerged, such as synthetic fibers and aircraft, and new power sources, such as electricity, and new forms of transport, such as the automobile, changed the American way of life. A high level of consumption was becoming a reality for greater numbers of people as the consumer durable goods revolution of the 1920s created major changes in the spending and saving behaviors of American households. It was this "taste of the good life" experienced during the prosperity of the 1920s that made the Great Depression of the 1930s so bitter for many Americans.

War and depression led to greatly expanded government decision making in the economic affairs of the nation. During World War I, for the first time in American history, extensive government controls were implemented to mobilize the economic resources necessary for military victory. Government agencies were created to control production and prices and to allocate material and human resources. Although these agencies were quickly dismantled after victory was achieved, an even-greater web of government controls was utilized during World War II to mobilize economic resources for this larger military effort.

The near collapse of the U.S. economy in the Great Depression of the 1930s created overwhelming pressures for government to play a more important economic role than ever before. Out of the economic and political circumstances of these years emerged new concepts of using fiscal policy—or of the relationship between government spending and revenues—as stabilizing tools. Particularly important was the development of the concept that government deficits could provide the purchasing power needed to promote economic recovery. The Federal Reserve System, established in 1913 and greatly strengthened in the 1930s, possessed a set of monetary tools with which it sought to influence the general level of economic activity. There existed a widespread belief that business practices had contributed significantly to the economic hard times of the 1930s. In addition, small business worried about the competition and power of giant corporations, and farmers were concerned about their economic survival and welfare. Industrial workers complained about job insecurity, low wages, and other grievances against employers. All of these groups turned to the government to provide remedies for their problems. As a result, more areas of business were brought under government regulation during the 1930s than at any earlier time in American history. The economic plight of large numbers of people in the Depression also led to the adoption of welfare programs, which later resulted in a dramatic increase in government-transfer payments.

Industrialization and the revolution in internal transportation are today viewed as the most outstanding economic features of nineteenth-century America. Historians of the twenty-first century may well look back at the enlarged role of government and the accelerated trend toward a consumer society as the most significant economic features of twentieth-century American history.

Between 1914 and 1945, the United States increased its position as the foremost industrial power of the world. Superiority in manufacturing production during World War I enabled the nation to serve as the arsenal for the Allied combatants in Europe and then to mount a major military effort of its own. America, which had always been a debtor to Europe, suddenly became a great creditor nation, with New York replacing London as the world's leading financial center. Then, in World War II, American industrial might was again decisive in the military defeat of the Axis powers. The wartime damage to most of the other major industrial powers, combined with the strength of the American economy, created a unique set of circumstances that enabled the United States to become the world's dominant economic power.

Chapter 17

The Economic Impact of World War I

SINCE THE TURN OF THE CENTURY, THE UNITED States had been an active participant in world balance of power politics, a role made possible by its economic strength. Soon after war broke out in Europe in 1914, the United States began to play a decisive role as "arsenal and granary" for one set of belligerents. American entry into the war in 1917 provided the military strength to break the deadlock in favor of Britain and France and against Germany. The wartime events had the results of increasing the economic strength of the United States while undermining that of the European powers, the victors as well as the losers. By the end of the war, the United States had made the transition from a net debtor to a net creditor nation, and New York had displaced London as the world's financial center. Thus, World War I (1914–1918) marked the transfer of world economic leadership from Europe to America.

Industrialization and the development of new military technology made the engagement of economic resources in World War I much greater than in any previous conflict. As a result of the need to mobilize economic and human resources for the war effort, the U.S. government assumed a significant role in economic management.

The Road to World War I

When war broke out in Europe in August 1914, President Woodrow Wilson proclaimed the neutrality of the United States, advising Americans to be "impartial in thought as well as in action." Most of the president's fellow Americans believed at the time that a war between the *Allies*—Britain, France, and Russia—and the *Central Powers*—led by Germany and Austria-Hungary—carried on three thousand miles or more away was not their concern. However, because the United States had been

a player in world balance of power politics since the turn of the century, it was impossible for the nation to maintain impartiality with respect to the ongoing conflict among the leading European nations (particularly as its own economic prosperity became closely intertwined with the military fortunes of one set of belligerents).

In a serious recession from 1913 to 1914, the United States welcomed purchases of war goods, food, and other materials by both sides in the European war. However, an effective British naval blockade of the Central Powers meant that most of the wartime trade went to the Allied countries. In 1915, the belligerents started to sell bonds to private investors in the United States to finance continued purchases of military material. By the time of U.S. entry into the war in April 1917, American investors had purchased $2.3 billion worth of bonds from the governments of the Allied countries, compared with only $27 million of German and Austrian bonds. U.S. exports to the Allied powers rose from around $800 million in 1914 to around $3 billion in 1916, whereas exports to Germany and Austria-Hungary declined from around $169 million to only slightly more than $1 million during these years. Allied orders for steel, gunpowder, small arms, food, and a host of other items fueled an economic boom that benefited the entire country. (see Table 17–1). It was recognized that eventual repayment of the loans would be dependent on an Allied victory.

Economic considerations thus played an important role in shaping American attitudes toward the European belligerents. These considerations reinforced the cultural and linguistic ties between Americans and the British. In addition, leading political, diplomatic, and military strategists were convinced that a German victory, by upsetting the existing world balance of power, would be detrimental to long-term American interests.

Violation of America's neutral rights proved to be the factor that precipitated the entry of

Table 17–1 *Exports from the United States, 1914–1920*

Year	Exports of U.S. Merchandise [$000,000]	Exports as Percentage of GNP
1914	$2,330	6.1%
1915	2,716	6.6
1916	5,423	11.5
1917	6,170	10.5
1918	6,048	9.3
1919	7,750	10.0
1920	8,080	9.3

SOURCE: Data from U.S. Bureau of the Census, *Historical Statistics of the United States* (Washington: 1975), pp. 884, 887.

the United States into the war. In early 1917, the German high command, in a desperate attempt to cut off American supplies to the Allies, decided to employ the only effective naval technology that it possessed—the submarine. While British violation of U.S. neutral rights caused resentment, German submarines that attacked armed merchant ships led to the loss of American lives. In response to President Wilson's call, Congress declared war on Germany in early April 1917.

Mobilization of Manpower

Once the United States had become a belligerent, policymakers were determined to expand the nation's role as arsenal and granary for the Allied powers. Furthermore, to assure a German defeat, an American Expeditionary Force would be deployed to the western front to reinforce the position of British and French troops nearly worn out after three years of trench warfare.

Less than a year prior to entry into the war, the United States military forces consisted of only 179,000 troops on active duty. Even

though the U.S. Army lacked plans for organizing and equipping a large military operation as late as six weeks prior to the declaration of war, the government rapidly built up a force that eventually involved more than 4.7 million men under arms (compared with 2.2 million Union forces in the Civil War and 307,000 troops in the Spanish-American War). To mobilize a force of this size in such a short time, the Selective Service Act (1917) provided legal authority to conduct a draft of the country's young men. To overcome potential opposition to a draft, initially characterized by some congressional opponents as a "Prussianization" of American life, President Wilson defined conscription as "selection from a nation that has volunteered in mass" and assigned responsibility for administering the draft to boards of local citizens.[1]

The Selective Service Act enabled the government to recruit for hazardous duty a large force of young men at something less than a market rate, though for many of those who had lived in urban or rural slums military service may have represented an improvement in living standards. Between 1917 and 1918, some 2.8 million American men between the ages of twenty-one and thirty were drafted, constituting about 70 percent of those who served in the army. Local civilian draft boards, with responsibility for administering the law, were authorized to grant deferments to men employed in essential war industries. Eventually, the armed services accounted for about 16 percent of the nation's male labor force.

Housing, feeding, clothing, and equipping the American armed forces involved substantial organizational efforts and expenditures. According to economic historian George Soule, the care and sustenance of military personnel, not counting pay, accounted for at least one-quarter of the total cost of World War I, with the government spending $6.2 billion on such supplies, over $2 billion more than it expended on munitions. Expenditures on the

Draftees Checking in at Fort Slocum, New York, 1917.   An estimated five million men between the ages of 21 and 35 were subject to military conscription in World War I. (UPI/The Bettmann Archive)

construction of military camps alone stood at $800 million.[2]

Eventually, about two million men served in the American Expeditionary Force in France, under the leadership of General John J. Pershing. They provided the fresh strength needed to repel a major German offensive launched in the spring of 1918. The human costs of the war to America included 116,500 dead and 204,000 wounded.

Mobilization of Economic Resources

More than ever before in U.S. history, World War I required the mobilization of all of the nation's economic resources to achieve victory on the battlefield. To coordinate the country's economic efforts for military purposes, the government assumed unprecedented control over key areas of economic decision making that had traditionally been in the sphere of private business. Even before the United States

became a belligerent, Congress passed legislation that gave sweeping powers to the president in time of war—the power to procure munitions at prices determined by the government and to take possession of any system of transportation deemed necessary for the movement of troops or military materials.

Although the Council of National Defense, composed of cabinet officers and an advisory committee of business leaders, had been in existence since 1916, neither government nor industry had made effective preparations for conversion to full-scale war production. An economy already operating at a high level of capacity had to find the means to expand the shipment of materials to the Allied powers as well as supply a large overseas military effort. Confusion was compounded as the armed forces and private suppliers of war goods bid against each other for scarce labor and materials. In the winter of 1917/18, there existed the possibility of a total breakdown of the war economy. There was widespread acceptance of the principle that government would have to exercise responsibility for coordinating the mobilization of economic resources for the war effort. The problem was how to develop an administrative and political structure through which that goal could be achieved.

In the spring of 1918, the War Industries Board (WIB), with financier Bernard Baruch as chairman, emerged as the agency with final authority to coordinate war industry. President Wilson conferred upon the WIB sweeping power to create new facilities for war production, convert existing facilities to new uses, determine priorities of production and delivery of articles in short supply, and make purchases for the Allies. As Baruch later explained, the most important power held by the WIB was that of determining priority, which he regarded as a complex responsibility:

> Should locomotives go to [General] Pershing to carry his army to the front or should they go to Chile to haul nitrates needed to make ammunition for Pershing's troops? Should precedence be given to destroyers needed to fight the U-boats or to merchant ships whose numbers were being decimated by the German subs? Should nitrates be allocated to munitions or to fertilizers?[3]

Since priorities provided guidance to manufacturers in the filling of orders, businesspeople generally viewed the system with favor. To discourage sharp increases in the prices of scarce commodities, a Price Fixing Committee of the WIB negotiated with individual manufacturers to conclude voluntary agreements. If appeals to patriotism failed to bring voluntary cooperation on the part of a business firm, Baruch could threaten to use the government's power to commandeer plants, deny transportation services, or curtail the output of an industry.

Of equal importance to the WIB's role in economic mobilization for war was the U.S. Food Administration, created in 1917 and headed by future President Herbert Hoover. This govern-ment agency had virtually complete control over the industries producing and distributing food. The combined foreign and domestic demand for American food products had put great pressure on U.S. agricultural production, reflected in an increase of 135 percent in the average price of farm products between 1913 and mid-1917. To conserve scarce food supplies, the Food Administration exhorted consumers to observe "wheatless" and "meatless" meals. The licensing power over firms engaged in the distribution of foodstuffs enabled the Food Administration to exercise control over prices at the retail level through agreements with middlemen to limit markups. Local newspapers published fair-price lists, which consumers could check against prices actually charged in food establishments. The centralization of Allied purchasing in the Food Administration also helped to keep prices under control. To increase production, the agency guaranteed a minimum price on wheat and stabilized prices on other products at levels that gave farmers a substantial profit. The government-owned U.S. Grain Corporation effectively fixed the price of wheat by largely eliminating competitive buying at country grain elevators and then making allotments of the available grain to flour-milling companies according to the amount each used in previous years. A Sugar Equalization Board played a similar role in the sugar market by purchasing raw sugar from different producing regions, within and outside the United States, at the price appropriate for each region. In order to increase the production of hogs to meet the needs of the United States and its allies, the Food Administration fixed the price of hogs at a high level in relation to the price of corn to encourage farmers to concentrate on the raising of hogs.

War time government controls also extended to fuels, with the creation of the U.S. Fuel Administration in 1917. Due to strong demands for fuel from railroads, shipping, and industry, the price of coal, the nation's principal energy source at the time, had risen spectacularly from between $1.25 and $1.50 in mid-1916 to between $7 and $8 a year later. However, because of the method used to apply price controls, the Fuel Administration brought on a severe shortage of coal in the winter of 1917/18. Only by imposing a "fuel holiday" on much of industry and "heatless Mondays" on both businesses and households was enough coal diverted to fuel the ships carrying munitions and other military supplies to the European theater of operations. During the remainder of the war, the Fuel Administration used a system of priorities to allocate fuels to various types of users.

In addition, the government became involved with the operation of the nation's transportation system. The numerous railroad companies were unable to coordinate their work in meeting the increased transportation demands arising from the war effort, particularly since a large part of the growing volume of traffic involved the shipping of goods from the Midwest (where much of the country's metallurgical industry was located) to the East Coast for shipment to Europe. By late 1916, there was a serious shortage of freight cars, primarily because so many of them were being used as storage facilities. In December 1917, President Wilson created the U.S. Railroad Administration to take control of the operation of the railroads. While this governmental innovation proved successful in meeting the nation's wartime transportation needs, railroad corporations suffered financial losses owing to increased wages and prices not covered by corresponding increases in rates and fares.

Ocean transport also posed problems that required government intervention. As America expanded its exports of war goods and other materials to Europe during the period of official neutrality, a serious shortage of shipping developed. The U.S. Shipping Board, created in 1916, was empowered to construct

ocean vessels through its subsidiary, the Emergency Fleet Corporation. This government-owned corporation embarked on an ambitious program with the goal of building "a bridge of ships" across the Atlantic. Notable was the application of mass-production techniques to the construction of ships at government shipyards in several locations. During 1917 and 1918, American yards launched almost 3.5 million tons of ships. At the same time, the Shipping Board assumed effective control of the entire existing American merchant marine, with the ships being operated by their owners under charter to the U.S. government. The wartime experience reversed a long-term decline of the American merchant marine. (Between 1860 and 1910, U.S. tonnage registered for foreign trade had decreased by two-thirds. During those same years, the value of foreign commerce quadrupled, but the share carried in American bottoms dropped precipitously from 66 percent to 8 percent.) By 1921, the ambitious shipbuilding program had resulted in the United States displacing Great Britain from first place among the world's merchant fleets.

There was an international dimension to the mobilization of resources for war. The Trading-with-the-Enemy Act (1917) authorized the creation of the War Trade Board, which had the power to license exports and imports and to investigate all those engaged in foreign trade. Under this law, enemy property in the United States, including industrial plants, could be seized by the government. The Inter-Allied Purchasing Commission helped to coordinate the demands for munitions and other materials made by the various Allied powers.

Financing the War Effort

After the U.S. entry into World War I, federal government expenditures soared. At the peak of military spending in 1918, nearly one-

Table 17-2 *Federal Individual Income-Tax Exemptions and First and Top Bracket Rates, 1913–1920*

Year	Personal Exemptions[a]	First Bracket		Top Bracket	
		Tax Rate	Income	Tax Rate	Income Over
1913	$4,000	1%	$20,000	7%	$ 500,000
1916	$4,000	2%	$20,000	15%	$2,000,000
1917	$2,400	2%	$ 2,000	67%	$2,000,000
1918	$2,400	6%	$ 4,000	77%	$1,000,000
1919	$2,400	4%	$ 4,000	73%	$1,000,000

[a]Married with two dependents.

SOURCE: Data from U.S. Bureau of the Census, *Historical Statistics of the United States: Colonial Times to 1970* (Washington, D.C.: GPO 1975), p. 1095.

quarter of the national income was allocated to the war effort. Thus, it was fortunate that the government had a recently enacted form of taxation that it could use to pay for a significant part of the cost of the war.

Taxation

The fundamental change in taxation that began during the era of World War I may be described compactly as a shift away from *indirect taxation* and toward *direct taxation*. Until this time, the federal tax structure was little changed from the system established during the first administration of President George Washington. In 1913, customs duties on imports supplied 47 percent of federal tax revenues, while 46 percent came from internal excise taxes (chiefly on alcoholic beverages and tobacco products). All taxes are, of course, ultimately paid by people, not by alcohol, tobacco, or imports. But when these latter products are taxed, people pay the taxes indirectly. When taxes are levied on incomes, wealth, or payrolls, people are taxed directly.

Direct taxation in the United States received a major boost with the adoption of the Sixteenth Amendment to the Constitution in 1913. It explicitly granted Congress the power to levy income taxes without apportionment among the states according to population. Article 1, section 9, of the Constitution had stated that "no capitation or other direct tax shall be laid, unless in proportion to the census. . . ." Before 1895, federal income taxes were considered constitutional; but from 1895 to 1913, a conservative Supreme Court made these taxes unconstitutional. The mild 1 percent tax on the net income above $5,000 of every corporation organized for profit, enacted in 1909, illustrates the problems faced in income taxation before 1913. This tax had been devised by conservatives to stave off growing pressure for taxation on individual incomes, but, since in law the corporation is a legal person, opponents of the 1909 tax claimed that it violated the Constitution. The Supreme Court sustained the corporation tax but only by declaring it an excise rather than a direct tax.

An individual income tax with progressive rates of up to 7 percent was enacted in 1913 to go along with the corporation income tax. The advantages and flexibility of these relatively new forms of taxation were quickly demonstrated during World War I. As indicated in Table 17–2, tax rates were raised to unprecedented heights—as high as 77 percent in the case of individual incomes over $1 million. Individual income taxes paid by the American public rose from $41 million in 1914 (the first full year for which the tax was in effect) to over $1 billion in 1918. Corporate income-tax rates

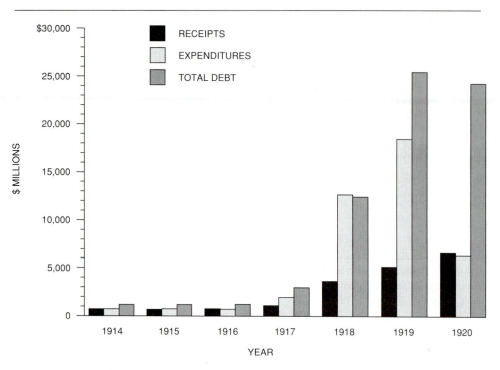

Figure 17–1 *Federal Government Finances, 1914–1920*
Source: Data from U.S. Bureau of the Census, *Historical Statistics of the United States: Colonial Times to 1970* (Washington, D.C.: GPO, 1975), p. 1104.

were also raised, so that corporations paid $643 million in that year. These two forms of taxes brought in well over one half of all federal tax revenue to support the American war effort. In addition, an excess profits tax was imposed on corporate earnings deemed to be beyond a reasonable return on capital invested; this yielded $2.5 billion in 1918. The proceeds from excise taxes levied on a variety of items (including beverages, tobacco, furs, and other "luxury" goods) also contributed funds to finance the war effort.

Borrowing and Credit Expansion

As great as were the increases in taxes levied on the American people, the government still had to rely on borrowing to pay about two-thirds of the cost of World War I. As a result, the federal government debt rose from about $1.2 billion in 1916 to over $25 billion in 1919; per capita debt advanced from less than $12 in 1915 to $242 in 1919 (see Figure 17–1). With great ballyhoo, the government urged citizens to show their patriotism by purchasing Liberty bonds, which paid interest of 3.5 percent to 4.75 percent (compared to a 2 percent interest rate on most of the federal debt in 1916). Low-income groups purchased war savings stamps for as little as 25 cents, which were then accumulated and exchanged for war certificates with a maturity value of $5. Overall, individuals with incomes under $2000 purchased nearly one-third of all the war bonds issued.

A Liberty Loan Campaign.   Government bond drives made a strong appeal to patriotism in urging citizens to support the war effort. This campaign, the third of four such drives during the war and one afterwards, raised $4.2 billion in May 1918. (The Bettmann Archive)

In previous major conflicts, the government had paid for a substantial part of the cost of war by printing money. In World War I, however, the government did not print money; rather, the newly organized Federal Reserve System, or the Fed, performed a similar function in a more sophisticated manner. (The Fed's origin and early operation are discussed later in the chapter.) Federal Reserve Banks purchased bonds by creating, in the form of deposits and Federal Reserve notes, money

(i.e., claims on goods and services) that had not existed before. This new money, when deposited by suppliers of goods to the government, increased the amount of money in circulation and expanded the ability of the banking system to extend credit, creating still more money. Further, commercial banks were encouraged to lend funds to customers who wanted to buy government bonds. The Federal Reserve banks readily discounted the customers' promissory notes, thereby putting still more deposits into the banking system.

From 1914 to 1920, U.S. wholesale prices rose at an annual rate of 15 percent, representing a doubling of the price level. The inflation was supported by Federal Reserve management of the U.S. money stock; it increased at an annual rate of 13 percent during these years. Before the United States entered actively into the hostilities in 1917, the primary impetus to monetary expansion came from gold flows into the United States, mostly from Europe, to finance purchases of war materiel. The Federal Reserve System, as the country's central bank, in effect created dollars to purchase the gold, which added to the nation's monetary base. Once the United States entered the war, huge deficits in the federal government's budget were financed by Fed-created dollars that underwrote the government's bond sales to the public, to the banking system, and to the Fed itself. The Fed's decisions in this war period undoubtedly caused monetary expansion and price inflation. But the Fed did not really have much latitude in its decision making during this national emergency. The goal of moderate monetary expansion consistent with price stability was compounded by abnormal gold inflows and ultimately sacrificed in favor of the more-pressing and immediate goal of financing a successful war effort. However, to the extent that this method of paying for a part of the cost of the war inflated the price level, it constituted an indirect tax.

Table 17–3   *Real Gross National Product, 1914–20.*
Total and Per Capita (in 1958 prices)

Year	Total GNP (in $ billions)	GNP per Capita (in dollars)
1914	$125.6	$1,267
1915	124.5	1,238
1916	134.3	1,317
1917	135.2	1,310
1918	151.8	1,471
1919	146.4	1,401

SOURCE: Data from U.S. Bureau of the Census, *Historical Statistics of the United States: Colonial Times to 1970* (Washington, D.C.: GPO, 1975), p. 224.

American Industry During the War Years

During World War I, the demand for American industrial products increased as never before. Real gross national product advanced by almost 21 percent between 1914 and 1918; real gross national product per capita rose by slightly over 16 percent (see Table 17–3). The physical volume of all manufacturing industries increased by 17 percent between 1914 and 1919. Value added by manufacture recorded a gain of approximately 25 percent in real terms.

The metallurgical and engineering industries were major suppliers of a wide range of military products for the Allied powers and later for the U.S. armed forces. To protect their trenches in the war zone, Britain and France turned early to American iron and steel manufacturers for barbed wire, a product that the United States had long supplied to the entire world. The demand broadened to include shell steel and shrapnel, locomotives, motor vehicles, tractors, gun carriages, and aircraft. As a result, the output of aluminum and steel at least doubled during the war years. The chemical industries significantly expanded their facilities to supply explosives and synthetic dyestuffs, the latter to make up for the loss of imports from Germany. Meat packers, can-ners, flour millers, and other food processors sought to fill huge orders as America became the granary as well as the armory of the Allied powers. The textile industries produced cloth used by apparel manufacturers to make uniforms, tents, and bandages. The tobacco industry increased its output of cigarettes, for both soldiers and civilians, by 2.6 times between 1914 and 1918.

Much of the large investment in plant and equipment that had been made for military purposes could be converted to production for peacetime. Thus, the nation came out of the war with a significant increase in manufacturing capacity. In qualitative ways as well, the wartime experience of American industry was more than transitory. To meet the need for huge outputs of steel, manufacturers rapidly extended the use of electricity for making steel and for heat-treating steel products. The demand for ordnance promoted the production of alloy steels, which met the exacting requirements of the automobile industry as well. When car production for the civilian market had to be curtailed to conserve steel and other materials for war goods, automobile manufacturers turned to the production of tractors, aircraft engines, and refrigerators—products they continued to produce after the war. The chemical industry was stimulated by the cessation of German imports of coal-tar products—dyes and industrial solvents—to undertake the manufacture of these products in the United States. Government seizure of enemy-held patents for synthetic dyes and other chemical products enabled American corporations to make great strides in an industry long dominated by German corporations.

The wartime experience made a broad range of industrialists aware of the economic benefits to be gained by reducing the number of styles and sizes of their products. For example, manufacturers reduced the different colors of typewriter ribbons from 150 that had existed in 1914 to just 4; 150 auto tire sizes were reduced to 3,232 varieties of buggy wheels to 4, and 326 models of plows to 76. To meet the problems resulting from a wartime labor shortage, personnel management came to be recognized as an increasingly important function in industrial enterprises. The excess-profits tax levied during the war, by encouraging corporations to inflate costs, led to a significant increase in the use of advertising by business whenever it could be rationalized as promoting good will.

Agriculture During the War Years

The combined foreign and domestic demand for American food products put great pressure on the United States for increased farm production during the war years. Yet agricultural production grew by only 10 percent between 1913 and 1919. The failure of agriculture to expand beyond this peak figure stemmed from several factors present at the outbreak of the war: there was little slack in farm resources; important innovations in farm technology were not yet available; massive additions to the land stock through an expansion of the frontier was no longer feasible. Yet the 10 percent increase in production was sufficient to save Great Britain, France, and Italy from critical food shortages. The United States ensured an adequate flow of food exports (especially wheat, hogs, and sugar) to its allies by a partial embargo on food shipped to neutral countries and by inducing the American public to cut out the 15 percent to 20 percent of its food consumption in excess of what was necessary to maintain public health. By 1919, farm-commodity exports amounted to nearly 20 percent of the total American farm production.

During World War I, the great majority of American farmers made important gains in real income. Their numbers did not increase, but the prices paid for their products did, and their total output was sustained. Prices re-

ceived by farmers for their products more than doubled between 1913 and 1918. The purchasing power of the realized income (i.e., the net income available for spending after paying income taxes) of all those obtaining income from agriculture was 25 percent higher in 1918 than in 1915, with the major part of the gain going to farm owners rather than farm workers.

The total net income of farmers, measured in current dollars, more than doubled between 1914 and 1918, rising from $4 billion to $10 billion. In that same period, the value of farm property (including farmland, buildings, machinery, and livestock) rose from $47.4 billion to $61.5 billion. These increases in income and capital value induced many farmers to invest their savings in more farmland, often supplementing their own capital with mortgage loans. At the time this seemed like a sound investment, but the future proved it to be unwise speculation (as we will see later in the chapter).

The Labor Force in Wartime

While the expansion of industrial activity after 1914 increased the demand for labor, an important source of supply of labor for the American economy was being sharply curtailed. Immigration into the United States, mostly from Europe, had been running at about one million per year in the decade prior to the outbreak of World War I. After the start of hostilities, the men that had long been regarded by European nations as surplus became valuable as "cannon fodder" for the mass armies being fielded by the belligerents. As a result, immigration into the United States dropped sharply—to a low of about 111,000 by 1918. In addition, the military buildup in the United States drained the nation's labor supply. Thus, the country's rate of unemployment declined from 8.5 percent in 1915 to just 1.4 percent in 1918 and 1919 (see

Table 17–4 *Unemployment, 1914–20*

Year	Number of Unemployed (in thousands)	Percent of Civilian Labor Force
1914	3,120	7.9%
1915	3,377	8.5
1916	2,043	5.1
1917	1,848	4.6
1918	536	1.4
1919	546	1.4
1920	2,132	5.2

SOURCE: Data from U.S. Bureau of the Census, *Historical Statistics of the United States: Colonial Times to 1970* (Washington, D.C.: GPO, 1975), p. 135.

Table 17–5 *Average Annual Earnings of Employees, 1914–1920*

Year	When Employed	
	Money Earnings	Real Earnings (in 1914 dollars)
1914	$ 639	$639
1915	635	628
1916	705	648
1917	807	632
1918	994	663
1919	1,142	662
1920	1,342	672

SOURCE: Data from U.S. Bureau of the Census, *Historical Statistics of the United States: Colonial Times to 1970* (Washington, D.C.: GPO, 1975), p. 164.

Table 17–4). The result was rapid labor turnover and upward pressure on wages, especially in industries producing for the war effort. Real earnings in manufacturing grew by 3.26 percent per year between 1914 and 1919, compared to a rate of 1.4 percent between 1900 and 1914 (see Table 17–5). In addition, by 1919, nearly one-half of the nation's manufacturing wage earners had achieved an eight-hour day, in comparison with only one-twelfth a decade earlier.

The labor shortage encouraged industrial employers to look to new sources of labor supply. As indicated in Chapter 13, the great majority of the African-American labor force was employed in agriculture and resided in the southern states. They had many reasons for leaving the South, including low levels of income derived from cotton production under the sharecropping system, economic dislocation resulting from damage to the cotton crop from the continuing spread of the boll weevil infestation, lack of basic political rights and educational opportunities for their children, and threats of physical violence (in the forms of lynchings and beatings). These situations constituted a strong push to migration. The pull came when northern businesspeople began in 1916 to use agents to recruit blacks residing in

rural areas of the South, sometimes offering free transportation to northern industrial centers. Southern landowners, dependent on a low-paid black labor force to work their land and perform a variety of routine tasks, resorted to coercion as well as persuasion to halt the exodus, but to no avail. An infrastructure quickly developed to organize the beginning of what came to be called the *Great Migration* of blacks from the rural South to the urban North. In the years from 1916 to 1919 alone, about 500,000 black southerners moved north, with nearly one million following them in the 1920s.

As a result of migration, the number of African-American wage-earners in industry increased significantly. By 1920, 31 percent of the black labor force in the United States was employed in manufacturing, trade, or transportation, up from only 13 percent two decades earlier. Without industrial experience or educational background, however, most black male migrants found jobs as unskilled laborers in industries like meat packing and steel making. Others moved into unskilled nonindustrial work as porters, waiters, and janitors. Many of the female black migrants took jobs in house-

Women Workers, 1918. Because of wartime labor shortages, women made important contributions to the war effort by undertaking many kinds of work previously performed by men, including work in a munitions factory in Detroit, pictured here. (UPI/The Bettmann Archive)

hold service. Those African-Americans who moved to the urban North did not escape the effects of racism. They continued to suffer from various forms of discrimination, including inadequate training and the refusal of most established trade unions to admit them to membership.

The wartime labor shortage also provided new employment opportunities for women. Some women were hired for what had previously been regarded as "men's jobs" as production workers in basic industries like chemicals, automobiles, and iron and steel as well as in a range of occupations as varied as bank teller and streetcar conductor. However, with the demobilization of the armed forces at the end of the war, many of the gains made by women in entering the realm of "men's work" evaporated. Still, the continued growth of the office and of merchandising generated increasing employment opportunities for women in

what had been defined before the war as "female occupations" such as filing clerks, bookkeepers, telephone operators, and sales clerks. According to the Census of 1920, more women were employed in white-collar work than in manufacturing, domestic service, or agriculture (see Table 17–6).

Growth of Labor Unions

During World War I, the strong demand for workers coinciding with the labor shortage and the conciliatory attitudes of employers and the national government led to unprecedented growth in union membership—from 2.7 million in 1916 to 5 million in 1920 (see Table 17–7). The support of the American Federation of Labor (AFL) for the war effort was rewarded by the appointment of AFL officers to most of the war boards organized by the government. Special labor-adjustment boards were set up for the shipbuilding, railroad, and maritime industries. For other war industries a National War Labor Board was established to mediate disputes; it encouraged employers to recognize workers' right to organize and engage in union activities.

However, after the Armistice in November 1918, the government, employers, and the public became hostile toward the American labor movement, based in part on the fear generated by the Bolshevik Revolution in Russia. This affected public attitudes toward the numerous strikes that broke out in 1919, involving more than four million wage earners. The important strike against the U.S. Steel Corporation, organized by the AFL in 1919, failed when the company refused to negotiate and broke the strike by using scare propaganda and black strikebreakers.

New Developments in Finance

As discussed in Chapter 15, the banking system tended to produce, or contribute to, the

Table 17–6 *Women in the Labor Force, 1910 and 1920*

	1910	1920
Women as proportion of total labor force	19.8%	20.4%
Women as proportion of white collar labor force	23.8%	32.4%

SOURCE: Data from U.S. Bureau of the Census, *Historical Statistics of the United States: Colonial Times to 1970* (Washington: D.C., GPO, 1975), pp. 139–40.

Table 17–7 *Labor Union Membership, 1914–1920*

Year	Number of Union Members (thousands)		
	Total All Unions	American Federation of Labor	Other Unions
1914	2,687	2,061	626
1915	2,583	1,968	614
1916	2,773	2,124	649
1917	3,061	2,457	605
1918	3,467	2,825	642
1919	4,125	3,339	786
1920	5,048	4,093	955

SOURCE: Data from U.S. Bureau of the Census, *Historical Statistics of the United States: Colonial Times to 1970* (Washington, D.C.: GPO, 1975) p. 177.

financial panics that periodically undermined the stability of the U.S. economy. A giant step in the direction of solving that recurring problem came with the establishment of the Federal Reserve System in 1914. With the creation of the Fed (as it is often called), the United States somewhat belatedly followed the example of other leading nations in establishing a central bank—one that would act as a bankers' bank, as the government's bank and fiscal agent, and as a means of promoting economic stability through centralized control of the nation's supplies of money and credit.

The Structure of the Federal Reserve System

Americans have always had a pronounced—many would say healthy—fear of the concentration of economic and political power; those

who created the Fed in 1913/14 were no exceptions. Through extensive studies under the National Monetary Commission of 1908 to 1912, they had familiarized themselves with the structure and operations of banking systems in other countries. But rather than establishing a single central bank on the pattern of the Bank of England and other European central banks, they divided the United States into twelve districts with a Federal Reserve Bank in each (see Figure 17–2). All national banks were required to become members of the Federal Reserve System by purchasing capital stock in the Reserve Banks of their respective districts and by holding their reserves as deposits in the Reserve Banks. State banks were given the option of becoming members on the same terms. Ownership of the Fed, however, was divorced from control; the member banks who owned the capital stock of the system were granted 6 percent dividends, but control lay elsewhere. At the head of the system was the Federal Reserve Board in Washington, D.C., consisting of seven members: the secretary of the treasury and the comptroller of the currency (both ex officio) as well as five others appointed by the president. Each of the twelve district Reserve Banks had nine directors, three appointed by the Board and six—of whom only three could be bankers—elected by the member banks of the district.

Thus, checks and balances were in the structure of the Fed as well as in its vaults and ledgers. It was a typically American institution, rather like the national and state governments

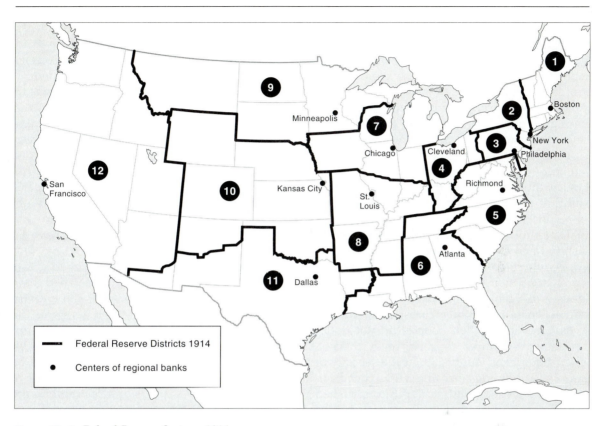

Figure 17–2   *Federal Reserve System, 1914*

under the Articles of Confederation, and with time it, too, evolved toward more centralized control. For nearly two decades after 1914, the individual Reserve Banks exercised considerable autonomy. Their boards elected governors to serve as operating heads. The governors, individually and as a group, exercised considerable policy power within the Federal Reserve System. This was especially true of the New York Reserve Bank, located at the center of American finance, and of its governor, Benjamin Strong. From the inception of the New York Reserve Bank in 1914 until his death in 1928, Strong was the dominant figure in the Fed. The Federal Reserve Board in Washington attempted to coordinate system policies and actions, but considerable Reserve Bank autonomy characterized the early years of the Fed.

Functions and Tools of the Fed

Central banks everywhere perform a number of routine service functions for individual banks and the government; their more important functions lie in the ability to control the supply of money and credit throughout the economy. These control functions are directed toward economic stabilization.

The impetus for establishing the Fed came from the periodic financial panics in the decades prior to 1914. At that time, the banks of the nation held their reserves of base money—coin and government-backed paper currency—as cash in their own vaults or in the form of deposits at other banks. There was no central pool of reserves, though the large national banks of New York City came close to functioning as one. Reserves were necessary because the banks had a contract with their depositors to pay them base money on demand—in short, to cash their checks. The flaw in the system that produced the panics was that the total supply of base-money reserves in the nation was much less than the total amount of deposits that holders might wish to cash. Usually, the flaw was not apparent. People preferred the convenience of holding most of their money in the form of bank deposits subject to withdrawal by check rather than in coins and paper currency in normal times (i.e., times when people did not doubt the ability of banks to cash their checks). When Americans' doubts about the security of their bank holdings became widespread, financial panics occurred as depositors rushed to the banks to cash checks. There simply was not enough cash for the banks to cash all the checks and pay off the depositors at one time.

In order to prevent financial panics, a method of expanding the supply of reserves of base money during incipient panic situations was needed to allay the fears of depositors. The Fed embodied several such methods. For example, member banks of the Federal Reserve System were required to hold a percentage of their deposits in a reserve account at the Fed. The required reserves were not so much a pool of funds from which the member banks might draw when cash was needed as a method of controlling the nation's total supply of money and bank credit. By becoming members of the Federal Reserve System, however, individual banks gained the privilege of borrowing from the Fed, using some of their own assets as collateral for the loans. In this way, bank loans

could be rediscounted or converted into cash at the Fed, which charged the banks an interest or discount rate that it could vary down or up depending on whether it wanted to encourage or discourage the borrowing of the member banks. Under this method, then, there was no reason for a general financial panic to occur. A solvent but illiquid bank—one basically sound but short of cash reserves—could convert some of its illiquid assets into cash by rediscounting them at the Fed, the bankers' bank. Knowing this, the depositors of any properly managed bank would have no reason to doubt that their deposits would be converted into cash on demand, and so they would have no reason to demand cash en masse.

The Fed, in short, had the power to create additional bank reserves when it deemed them necessary. The monetary base of the country no longer consisted simply of the sum of the coins, bullion, and paper currency that happened to be in the bank vaults at any given moment. Instead, the monetary base could be expanded or contracted by the Fed almost at will—"almost" because some restraints were placed on the Fed's power to create reserves. One was a qualitative restraint: Only certain types of the assets of member banks were eligible for rediscount at the Fed. Another was a quantitative restriction: Just as member banks were required to hold reserves equal to some percentage of their deposit liabilities, so too the Fed was required to hold gold reserves equal to a percentage of its liabilities of Federal Reserve notes (a new form of paper currency in the United States in 1914) and similar fractional gold reserves against its own deposit liabilities that were the reserves of member banks. Although this seemed to base the revamped monetary and banking systems on a foundation of gold, in reality the flexibility of the Fed's powers marked another step away from a metallic-based system.

The rediscounting mechanism was initially regarded as the main method by which the Fed would control supplies of money and credit in the United States and eliminate the threat of financial panic. But controlling bank reserves through the rediscounting mechanism relied on the willingness and ability of member banks to take an active role; if the banks had adequate reserves from their own point of view, they might refuse to borrow from the Fed even if the Fed thought more reserves and money were needed to achieve some broader economic objectives. The Fed would learn by the 1920s that it could directly control the quantity of bank reserves in existence by purchases and sales of open-market securities, usually U.S. government securities. Open-market purchases of securities by the Fed added to bank reserves as the private sellers deposited the Fed's checks in their own commercial banks. Similarly, the Fed's open-market sales destroyed bank reserves as the purchasers drew down their commercial bank balances to pay the Fed. Control of total bank reserves through open-market operations, though it appears to have been discovered as a by-product of other Federal Reserve Board activities, quickly became the chief method of implementing Fed policy.

The original objective of the Federal Reserve System, as stated in the 1913 legislation that created it, was "to furnish an elastic currency." Some interpreted this to mean a currency that would expand when the economy was expanding and decline when the economy was contracting. Today, this position of calling for the money supply to expand and contract according to the alleged "needs of trade" is discredited because it would serve to increase rather than reduce economic instability. Another interpretation of "elastic currency" made more sense. Financial panics occurred because one component of the money supply—the public's holdings of bank deposits—could not be exchanged on a large scale for the base money of currency and coins that had been created by the government. Through its pow-

ers of rediscounting member bank assets and purchasing open-market securities, the Fed could make the supply of base money elastic, thereby eliminating the major cause of panics. In the situations leading up to the panics, prices were usually rising and unemployment was low, while during and after the panics prices fell and unemployment soared. Hence, the power of the Fed to prevent panics implied a power to make both the general level of prices and the level of unemployment more stable than they otherwise would have been. In time, the stabilizing powers of the Fed were increasingly understood. It is widely recognized today that the Fed has a responsibility to promote price stability and full employment.

As noted earlier in the discussion of the financing of the war, the government's Wholesale Price Index roughly doubled between 1915 and 1920. As was the case with pre-1914 periods of sharp price inflation in the United States, this inflationary burst was associated with the effort on the part of the federal government to divert economic resources on a large scale from peacetime civilian uses to war-related activities. Although the Fed began its work with the responsibility of furnishing an elastic currency to prevent financial panics, and in time assumed responsibilities in the areas of price stability and employment, it should be recognized that a war caused the Fed to sacrifice its normal economic objectives in order to solve what seemed to be more pressing problems.

Greatly enlarged government spending to achieve military victory, accompanied by accommodating money creation by the Fed, had beneficial effects on the rate of unemployment. High when the war period began, unemployment was rapidly reduced by government spending and monetary expansion. However, for the same reasons that it would be wrong to be unduly critical of federal budgetary and monetary policies in causing inflation during a war era, so it would be wrong to give them major credit for promoting full employment in these years. The policies were motivated more by major overseas political events impinging directly on the national security of the United States than by the conscious efforts of Fed decision makers to promote national economic goals.

However, the Fed had a large role in the instability that plagued the American economy after the end of the war. During 1919, the Fed took no effective action to stem the continuing inflation; instead, perhaps to aid Treasury financial goals by maintaining low yields and high prices on government securities, the Fed maintained its discount rate at below-market levels and thus encouraged the nation's banks to make more loans based on Fed-created dollars. Inflation accelerated. Sensing this, rather belatedly, the Fed moved abruptly against inflation. The rediscount rate—then the Fed's major policy weapon—had been held at 4 percent in New York from April 1918 to November 1919. Between then and June 1920, it was raised in a series of abrupt steps to 7 percent, where it remained for nearly a year. Although there were signs that the economy was already weakening as the Fed took these actions, their effect was to turn a decline into a rout. The money supply exhibited one of its rare declines on a year-to-year basis, falling some 9 percent between 1920 and 1921. Unemployment soared from 4 percent to nearly 12 percent in the same period, and wholesale prices in 1921 on average were nearly 40 percent below their 1920 levels. The price collapse of 1920 to 1921 was perhaps the sharpest in U.S. history.

The New U.S. Position in the World Economy

From the nation's very beginnings, America had been Europe's debtor. As noted in Chapter 16, in the decades prior to World War I, American investments overseas grew faster than foreign investments in the United States, making it likely that the country would eventually become a net creditor nation. The events of the war years accelerated that trend already under way. As a net debtor nation in 1914, U.S. assets abroad came to $3.5 billion, whereas some $7.2 billion represented European investments in this country. The great wartime demand by the Allied powers of Europe for American goods and services was financed in part by the liquidation of foreign-owned American securities (British and French citizens disposed of about 70 percent of their holdings of American stocks and bonds); in part by the shipping of gold to the United States; and in largest part by loans from the U.S. government to the governments of the Allied powers after American entry into the war. Furthermore, during the war years, American corporations continued to expand their foreign investments, primarily in the production and processing of minerals and agricultural commodities in Central and South America. As a net creditor nation in 1919, the United States' foreign private investments stood at $7 billion, whereas foreigners held $3.3 billion of investments in the United States. In addition, foreign governments, primarily those of the Allied powers in Europe, owed the U.S. government about $9.6 billion. In just five years, then, the United States had changed from a debtor nation that owed foreigners $3.7 billion to a creditor nation owed $12.6 billion by foreigners.

America's new position as the world's leading economic power and largest creditor nation had significant implications. However, not all of the implications were carefully considered at the time because the change in economic status had appeared to come so suddenly. Foreigners as debtors would have to find dollars to pay dividends and interest, but this they could do only if they could sell more goods and services to Americans than they bought from them. However, the long experience of the United States as a debtor nation meant it was ill prepared to adjust to the new economic reality. Industrial and agricultural interests continued to seek tariff protection in order to keep foreign goods out of the domestic market.

For over half a century, Britain had stood at the center of an international system of exchange as the world's leading economic power. But World War I disturbed the financial institutions in London that had contributed so importantly to the smooth functioning of the multilateral system of international trade developed over the course of the nineteenth cen-

tury. However, even though world economic leadership had now passed to the United States, the nation was slow to recognize the need for it to assume greater responsibility. A restoration of the kind of international economic stability that prevailed prior to 1914 could be achieved only if America adapted its institutions and policies to reflect its new responsibilities. The United States was not the only country to put domestic economic and political considerations above the smooth operation of the international economy, but the consequences of the new world leader's actions had far greater impact, as we will see in Chapter 18.

Summary

As the leading neutral country after war broke out in Europe in 1914, America prospered as a producer of munitions and other military goods as well as foodstuffs for one set of belligerents. After U.S. entry into World War I, government control of much of the economy was needed to mobilize resources to support the military effort; this was the nation's first attempt at using economic management for a national purpose. Although the WIB and other government agencies were dismantled soon after hostilities ended, the experience of government direction of the economy set a precedent. Economic and political decision makers later turned to that precedent to deal with another crisis—the Great Depression of the 1930s.

World War I was financed in part by a significant increase in the level of taxation, most notably through the newly enacted income tax; in part by drawing on the savings of individuals through the sale of bonds to the public; and in part by the creation of money through the operation of the banking system. This last method of war finance promoted inflation and thereby constituted a hidden tax.

The events of the war years strengthened many sectors of American industry and contributed to the prosperity of the nation's agriculture. The war gave the Federal Reserve System its first opportunity to test the tools it had been given to perform its role as the nation's central bank. However, the Fed gave priority to facilitating government finance in a time of national emergency over its responsibilities to prevent inflation.

Although wartime labor shortages encouraged the entry of women into new kinds of occupations, most of the gains were only temporary. More far-reaching in economic and social influence was the stimulus that labor shortages gave to the beginning of the Great Migration of a large portion of the nation's African-American population from the rural South to the urban North.

World War I served to strengthen America and weaken Europe. In the process of becoming the world's leading economic power, the United States made the transition from a net debtor nation to a net creditor nation. However, Americans were slow to recognize that different economic policies were needed for the nation's new position in the world economy.

Endnotes

1. Quoted in Robert Higgs, *Crisis and Leviathan: Critical Episodes in the Growth of American Government* (New York: Oxford University Press, 1987), p. 132.
2. George Soule, *Prosperity Decade: From War to Depression, 1917–1929* (New York: Rinehart, 1947), pp. 37–38.

3. Bernard Baruch, *Baruch: The Public Years* (New York: Holt, Rinehart & Winston, 1960), quoted in Higgs, *Crisis and Leviathan*, p. 129.

Suggested Readings

For a well-organized survey of the economic experience of the World War I period, see George Soule, *Prosperity Decade: From War to Depression, 1917–1929* (New York: Rinehart, 1947). John Maurice Clark, *The Costs of the War to the American People* (New Haven: Yale University Press, 1931), and Simon Kuznets, *National Product in Wartime* (New York: National Bureau of Economic Research, 1945), are important statistical analyses. Arthur Link, *Wilson: The Struggle for Neutrality, 1914–1915* (Princeton: Princeton University Press, 1960), and Link's *Wilson: Campaign for Progressivism and Peace* (Princeton: Princeton University Press, 1965), deal with the diplomatic and political aspects of the road to war. Other general works on the war period include Arthur A. Stein, *The Nation at War* (Baltimore: Johns Hopkins University Press, 1980); David M. Kennedy, *Over Here: The First World War and American Society* (New York: Oxford University Press, 1980); and Gerd Hardack, *The First World War, 1914–1918* (Berkeley: University of California Press, 1977).

Milton Friedman and Anna Jacobson Schwartz, *A Monetary History of the United States, 1867–1960* (Princeton: Princeton University Press, 1963), analyzes the financial experience of the war years in a larger perspective; while Charles Gilbert, *American Financing of World War I* (Westport, Conn.: Greenwood Press, 1970), contains a detailed description of the subject. For differing views about the founding of the Federal Reserve System, see Richard H. Timberlake, Jr., *The Origins of Central Banking in the United States* (Cambridge: Harvard University Press, 1978); James Livingston, *Origins of the Federal Reserve: Money, Class and Corporate Capital, 1890–1913* (Ithaca: Cornell University Press, 1986); and Eugene N. White, *The Regulation and Reform of the American Banking System, 1900–1929* (Princeton: Princeton Unversity Press, 1983).Sidney Ratner, *Taxation and Democracy in America* (New York: Wiley, 1967), and Paul Studenski and Herman Krooss, *Financial History of the United States* (New York: McGraw-Hill, 1963), are also worth consulting.

The most important study of the roles of business and government in mobilizing industry for the World War I effort is Robert D. Cuff, *The War Industries Board: Business-Government Relations During World War I* (Baltimore: Johns Hopkins University Press, 1973). Other works that deal with this topic include Hugh Rockoff, *Drastic Measures: A History of Wage and Price Controls in the United States* (New York: Cambridge University Press, 1984); Robert Higgs, *Crisis and Leviathan: Critical Episodes in the Growth of American Government* (New York: Oxford University

Press, 1987); Carroll W. Pursell, Jr., ed., *The Military-Industrial Complex* (New York: Harper & Row, 1972); Paul A. C. Koistinen, "The 'Military-Industrial Complex' in Historical Perspective: World War I," *Business History Review*, 41 (1967); and Melvin Urofsky, *Big Steel and the Wilson Administration: A Study in Business-Government Relations* (Columbus: Ohio State University Press, 1969). Individual areas of government regulation are discussed in Tom G. Hall, "Wilson and the Food Crisis: Agricultural Price Control During World War I," *Agricultural History*, 47 (1973); and K. Austin Kerr, *American Railroad Politics, 1914–1920* (Pittsburgh: Pittsburgh University Press, 1968). Victor S. Clark, *History of Manufactures in the United States, 1893–1928*, vol. 3 (New York: Peter Smith, 1949; reprinted) surveys the course of development in the nation's leading industries. Paul A. Samuelson and Everett E. Hagen, *After the War—1918–1920* (Washington, D.C.: National Resources Planning Board, 1943), deals with events in the postwar years.

Among the general histories of organized labor containing discussion of the wartime experience are Melvyn Dubofsky, *Industrialism and the American Worker, 1865–1920* (New York: Harlan Davidson 1975); and Philip Taft, *The A. F. of L. in the Time of Gompers* (New York: Harper & Row, 1957). For a discussion of one aspect of working conditions during the war years, see Robert Whaples, "Winning the Eight-Hour Day, 1909–1919," *Journal of Economic History*, 50 (1990). David Brody, *Labor in Crisis: The Steel Strike of 1919* (Philadelphia: Lippincott, 1965), is the most useful analysis of that important event. James R. Grossman, *Land of Hope: Chicago, Black Southerners, and the Great Migration* (Chicago: University of Chicago Press, 1989), is an excellent case study of the beginnings of the mass migration of African-Americans from the rural South to the urban North. Maurine Weiner Greenwald, *Women, War, and Work: The Impact of World War I on Women Workers* (Westport, Conn.: Greenwood Press, 1980), is a good survey of the role of women in the war.

William H. Becker and Samuel F. Wells, Jr., eds., *Economics and World Power: An Assessment of American Diplomacy Since 1789* (New York: Columbia University Press, 1984), contains a useful summary statement of U.S. foreign economic policy in the war and immediate postwar years. Mira Wilkins, *The Maturing of Multinational Enterprise: American Business Abroad from 1914 to 1970* (Cambridge: Harvard University Press, 1974), includes a discussion of direct foreign investment by U.S. corporations in this period. William Ashworth, *A Short History of the International Economy Since 1850* (London: Longman, 1975), places American economic developments in the perspective of the world economy.

Chapter 18

The 1920s: A Taste of Affluence

THE 1920S BROUGHT TREMENDOUS ECONOMIC EXpansion and prosperity to the United States like never before in the nation's history. New consumption patterns, especially the purchase and use of major consumer durable goods like automobiles and household appliances, rested on advances in mass production and mass distribution. These advances made it possible for large numbers of Americans—including a significant portion of the nation's blue-collar workers—to achieve many conveniences of living previously enjoyed only by the wealthy. It seemed to many Americans that the nation had entered a "new era" of permanent prosperity.

However, even prosperity had its problems. By no means did all members of American society partake of the fruits of prosperity, as whole sectors of the economy experienced difficult times. In addition, the experience of the 1920s did not prepare even those who did prosper for the tragic economic fate of the 1930s—the Great Depression (as we will see in Chapter 19). Thus, despite the widespread assumption that a new era of permanent abundance had arrived in the 1920s, hard times had not been abolished.

The Contours of Economic Change in the New Era

Statistics show some of the dimensions of economic advance in the United States during the "new era." Between 1921 and 1929, real gross national product grew by 59 percent and real gross national product per capita by 42 percent (see Table 18–1). In addition, personal income advanced by 38.3 percent (see Table 18–2). Productivity showed impressive gains as well, with output per worker hour increasing by 26.6 percent and output per unit of total factor input by 21.8 percent between 1919 and 1929. These productivity gains were a major force

Table 18–1 *Real Gross National Product, Total and per capita, 1920–1929 (in 1958 prices)*

Year	Total GNP (in $ billions)	GNP per Capita (in dollars)
1920	$140.0	$1,315
1921	127.8	1,177
1922	148.0	1,345
1923	165.9	1,482
1924	165.5	1,450
1925	179.4	1,549
1926	190.0	1,619
1927	189.8	1,594
1928	190.9	1,584
1929	203.6	1,671

SOURCE: Data from U.S. Bureau of the Census, *Historical Statistics of the United States: Colonial Times to 1970* (Washington, D.C.: GPO 1975), p. 224.

Table 18–2 *Personal Income, 1920–1929*

Year	Personal Income (in $ billions)
1920	$73.4
1921	62.1
1922	62.0
1923	71.5
1924	73.2
1925	75.0
1926	79.5
1927	79.6
1928	79.8
1929	85.9

SOURCE: Data from U.S. Bureau of the Census, *Historical Statistics of the United States: Colonial Times to 1970* (Washington, D.C.: GPO, 1975), p. 224.

behind the rise of 91.7 percent in the index of manufacturing production (see Table 18–3). These years, often referred to as "the high tide of the Reserve System," were marked by moderate monetary expansion and a stable price level.

Table 18–3 *Index of Manufacturing Production (Federal Reserve Board), 1920–1929*

Year	Index (1967 = 100)
1920	15
1921	12
1922	15
1923	18
1924	17
1925	19
1926	20
1927	20
1928	21
1929	23

SOURCE: Data from Bureau of the Census, *Historical Statistics of the United States: Colonial Times to 1970* Washington, D.C.: GPO, 1975), p. 667.

Advertisement for the Ford Runabout. In the early 1920s, Ford was in almost complete possession of the low-price field. Most Ford purchasers were first-time car buyers. The pioneer in making cars for the masses would face increasing competition from General Motors during the decade. (Brown Brothers)

Growth Industries

The Automobilization of America

At the center of much of the growth of the 1920s was the automobile industry, important in terms of its own rise to prominence as America's leading industry in value of product as well as in its impact on a wide range of other economic activities. The automobile, initially considered a luxury for the rich, became a convenient, low-cost form of personal transportation for large numbers of Americans. More than any other individual, Henry Ford was responsible for making the automobile available to the average American—first by his design of the Model T in 1909 as a practical and reliable car and then by a significant reduction of manufacturing costs through his application of mass-production techniques. The moving assembly line, introduced in 1913 and 1914, was a major element of what was sometimes called the "Ford system" of production. Continuing improvements in productivity were made in the 1920s, as the labor hours per unit of prod-

uct fell an average of 7.4 percent a year between 1919 and 1929 (see Figure 18–1).

The trend to the closed car as well as innovations like the self-starter and pneumatic tires further enhanced the appeal of the automobile. Alfred P. Sloan and General Motors organized a line of cars ranging from the top-of-the-line Cadillac to the Chevrolet, a low-priced car that offered somewhat more luxury than the Ford. As one would expect of an oligopoly, automobile manufacturers no longer responded to an insufficiency of demand with a reduction of prices; rather, they curbed their

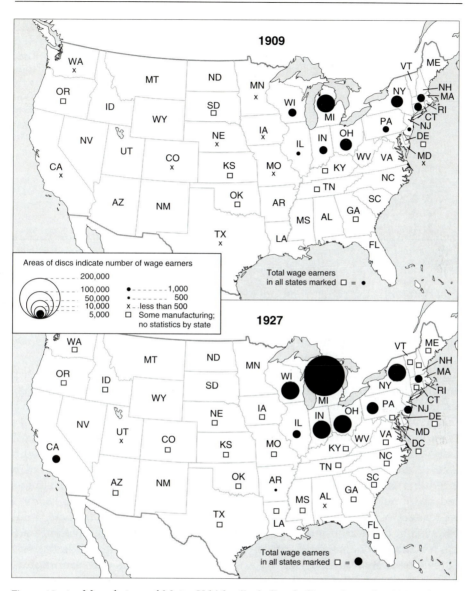

Figure 18-1. *Manufacture of Motor Vehicles (including bodies and parts), 1909 and 1927.*

Source: Charles O. Paullin, *Atlas of the Historical Geography of the United States* (Washington D.C.: Carnegie Institution, 1932).

Table 18–4 *Automobilization of America, 1920–29*

Year	Automobile Registrations (million)	Passenger Car Sales (million)	Travel by Motor Vehicle (billion miles)	Motor Fuel Usage (billion gallons)	Roads, Surfaced (thousand miles)
1920	8.1	1.9	—	3.1	369
1921	9.2	1.5	55.0	4.1	387
1922	10.7	2.3	67.7	5.0	412
1923	13.3	3.6	85.0	6.3	439
1924	15.4	3.2	104.8	7.8	472
1925	17.5	3.7	122.3	9.1	521
1926	19.3	3.7	140.7	10.6	550
1927	20.2	2.9	158.5	11.9	589
1928	21.4	3.8	172.9	13.1	626
1929	23.1	4.5	197.7	15.1	662

SOURCE. U.S. Bureau of the Census, *Historical Statistics of the United States: Colonial Times to 1970* (Washington, D.C.: 1975), pp. 710, 716, 718.

output. Product differentiation rather than price thus became the key competitive weapon.

Table 18–4 shows how the automobile took off in the 1920s. Annual sales of passenger cars more than doubled between 1920 and 1929, and automobile registrations almost tripled. By the end of the decade, nearly 60 percent of all American families owned automobiles.

Automobilization also led to far-reaching changes in other industries. The petroleum industry, as it moved from the age of illumination to the age of energy, was stimulated to develop new refining techniques and additives that produced gasoline to power cars more smoothly; the leaders of the industry also organized a new system of distribution of petroleum products for automobile users. Burgeoning sales of steel for motor vehicles led to a significant shift in the product mix of the steel industry away from rails and other heavy products to sheet and strip steel. As a result of the increased use of closed cars, the automobile industry became the largest consumer of glass, encouraging the latter industry to develop new products like safety glass. More motor vehicles on the road required more tires, so rubber manufacturers sought ways to manu-

facture more durable tires. The automobile, as a piece of mechanical equipment, needed service and repair facilities, which stimulated the emergence of a whole new sector of economic activity. The automobile also provided a boost to the insurance industry, which provided financial protection for a costly investment.

A new attention to road building by government at all levels was both a result and a cause of the increased use of automobiles. During the 1920s, the mileage of surfaced highways in the country grew by 79 percent, from 369,000 in 1920 to 662,000 in 1929, as the value of new construction of highways, roads, and streets put in place doubled, from $656 million to $1.3 billion. While the Federal Aid Road Act of 1916 provided for federal funds to assist state and local governments with grants and in the planning of a national highway network, the actual construction and maintenance of roads were left to the states and localities. Even though federal government spending on the federal-aid highway system did not exceed $100 million in any year during this period, there were nearly 190,000 miles of highways designated as U.S. routes by 1929. As a result of the growing numbers of cars on the expanding network of roads in the nation, usage of motor fuel more than quadrupled and miles of travel increased by 3.6 times during the decade.

The greater flexibility of the private automobile, as compared to commuter rail lines and streetcar systems, facilitated the movement of more people and economic activities to the suburbs of the nation's large cities. This, in turn, stimulated a significant amount of investment in residential, commercial, and industrial construction. The flexibility of the automobile also brought new possibilities for tourism and travel, encouraging the creation of roadside facilities for the accommodation of travelers (tourist cabins, e.g., were the forerunner of the motel business).

The Electrification of America

Although most electricity was generated by water or steam power, the convenience and ease of transmission of electricity to factories and homes were so great as in many ways to make the twentieth century the age of electricity. Electrification began in the 1890s, but it had its first great development only after the steam turbine had been made sufficiently efficient for the establishment of thermal power stations and highly centralized electric-power generation. The use of electric power rose from just 6 billion kilowatt hours in 1902 to 57.1 billion hours in 1920 and to 117 billion hours in 1929.

In manufacturing, the proportion of power supplied by electric motors rose from only 5 percent in 1899 to 55 percent in 1919 and to about 70 percent in 1919. Expanded use of electricity as a source of power made its mark on industry in several ways. It strengthened the trend toward mass-production technology in large energy-using industries, particularly those producing aluminum, magnesium, other nonferrous metals, steel, paper, and various chemical products. The widespread availability of electric power at low cost enabled manufacturers to change the location and design of their plants because they no longer had to con-

sider the availability of coal as a crucial determinant of location. Moreover, small enterprises were able to compete with larger firms by taking advantage of the efficient, small-scale use of electric power and of truck deliveries for small shipments of goods. While the largest corporations were utilizing mass-production economies to center their resources on a few standardized models, small specialty shops had greater opportunities for producing the variety their customers wanted at a somewhat higher price.

The use of electricity in urban residences also grew rapidly during the 1920s. At the beginning of the decade, slightly less than one-half of all urban-dwelling units had electric service; by 1930, the proportion was 85 percent. More households were consuming more electricity, with the average kilowatt hours per customer growing from 339 in 1920 to 502 in 1929, encouraged in part by a decline in the average price per kilowatt hour from 7.45 cents to 6.33 cents. Electricity supplied not only improved lighting for the home; it also provided the power for a variety of new kinds of household appliances purchased by middle-class urban families in increasing numbers during the 1920s—washing machines, vacuum cleaners, refrigerators, fans, toasters, and irons, all of which made life more convenient. (Consumer spending on all types of household appliances more than doubled from the decade before World War I to the decade after.) As leading home economists noted at the time, these new devices would help to integrate the individual household with the technological world of which it was a part.

By the end of the 1920s, the generation of electric power had become a major industry, with the United States producing more of this kind of energy than the rest of the world combined. This required a large investment of capital, with the value of power-generating facilities estimated at $10 billion. As Thomas Cochran notes, during the three decades from 1900 to

1930, "an investment numerically as large as that in railroads in the nineteenth century was made in urban power and light stations."[1]

Chemicals: Pioneering in Science-Based Industry

Although chemistry and chemical processes in American industry had undergone considerable development in the late nineteenth and early twentieth centuries, the military demands of World War I more than doubled the earlier U.S. output of chemical products. In the 1920s, as American firms turned to the peacetime manufacture of carbon, nitrogen compounds, sodium, and other basic chemicals, the United States became the world's leader in chemicals, supplanting Germany, which had occupied that position prior to 1914. The manufacture of synthetic dyes utilized German patents that had been seized by the government during the war and then distributed to American manufacturers. Production of rayon, which had come on the market just before World War I, more than tripled during the 1920s, as the characteristics of this synthetic fiber improved and its price declined.

The most important growth factor for chemicals was the industry's leadership in organized research and development. As discussed in Chapter 12, nineteenth-century innovations in industry had sprung in large part from predominantly empirical inventive activity and owed little to abstract scientific principles or organized knowledge. Twentieth-century technology, however, saw a shift in inventive activity away from the empirically based and toward the newer science-based industries. Instead of the crude empiricism and trial-and-error methods of previous generations, the new technology was based on the mastery of systematic, complex bodies of knowledge. But innovation in industrial technology was not just generating new ideas; it was also creating new products and processes. Thus, the application of

scientific knowledge could take place most effectively within the industrial firm.

Chemical producers like DuPont were among the first large corporations to establish research and development laboratories at the turn of the century. Throughout the 1920s, the chemical industry ranked first in research intensity among American manufacturing industries, accounting for about 30 percent of all scientists and engineers employed by U.S. manufacturers. Based on in-house research, chemical manufacturers in the 1920s and 1930s applied discoveries in molecular chemistry to the development of a variety of organic polymers, including plastics, synthetic fibers, and packaging materials. Those same corporations exploited the achievement of chemists in the transformation of materials through changes in atomic or molecular structure to obtain the refinement of fuels like petroleum, natural gases, and coal, and of basic raw materials needed for the production of cement, rubber, and glass.

The research of chemists in industrial laboratories resulted in the development of a range of new products—from insecticides and linseed-based cattle feed by paint manufacturers to milk-based chemicals for use in paint and other coatings by food processors. In the diffusion of industrial technology to a wide range of other industries, as David C. Mowery and Nathan Rosenberg suggest, the chemical industries during the interwar years played a role similar to that of the machine-tool industry in the nineteenth century.[2]

Other Growth Sectors

Telephone Service.   In the area of mass communications, the use of telephones continued to expand along the lines developed by Theodore Vail and the American Telephone and Telegraph Company (AT&T) before 1914 (see Chapter 14). Indeed, the telephone was well on its way to becoming a necessity of modern life for social as well as business communication, as the percentage of American households with telephone service grew from 35 percent in 1920 to 42 percent in 1929. While the majority of calls were local, the use of long-distance service was growing, encouraged by a substantial decrease in toll rates (e.g., the cost of a call between New York and San Francisco, a service introduced in 1915, dropped from $16.50 in 1919 to $9 in 1929). Furthermore, as the result of the continuing acquisition of local companies by AT&T, most households across the country were connected to a national communication system by the end of the 1920s.

Motion Pictures. The motion picture industry, an important dispenser of mass entertainment soon after its origin at the turn of the century, grew rapidly in the decade of the 1920s. The net per capita output of the motion picture industry—reflecting the cost of films at the point of production—more than doubled between 1921 and 1929. Average weekly attendance also more than doubled from 1926 to 1930, stimulated by the introduction of sound in 1926 and color in 1929. The structures in which movies were shown had become veritable palaces. As a noted sociologist commented in 1933, the role of the motion picture "in the leisure time of the masses can hardly be exaggerated. Moderate in cost and almost universal in its appeal, it provides an easily accessible form of recreation especially adapted for a temporary escape from the routine of daily life."[3]

Radio Broadcasting. The growth of radio was even more dramatic. The nation's first radio broadcasting station inaugurated service in Pittsburgh in the fall of 1920, just in time to broadcast the presidential election results to listeners in that area. By 1929, with more than six hundred stations in operation across the country, radio broadcasting had assumed its mature form as a medium of mass entertainment. Advertising began to support programming in 1925, and networks were organized the following year to send out programs of national scope that appeared at scheduled times, with the more successful programs gaining large public followings.

The earliest receiving sets were complicated mechanisms requiring the use of external batteries and headphones, with most sets being assembled by users from kits of components. As the technology of radio advanced, manufacturers began to mass produce for a growing mass market radio sets giving improved performance, often housing them in elaborate cabinets. Sales grew steadily from 1.5 million radios in 1924 to 4.4 million in 1929, at which time nearly 40 percent of all American households were equipped with a radio set.

Nondurable Goods. Manufacturers producing a variety of nondurable goods for mass markets also participated in the prosperity of the 1920s. Consumers increased their purchases of branded, packaged goods like breakfast cereals and soups as well as ice cream and carbonated beverages, partly making up for the legal absence of alcoholic beverages as the result of Prohibition. While the tobacco industry sold fewer cigars, its sales of cigarettes soared during the decade, partly as the result of aggressive advertising designed to encourage women to take up smoking. (Women consumed an estimated 12 percent of all cigarettes sold in 1929.) A new emphasis on style and fashion for women heightened the demand for dresses and cosmetics. Pharmaceutical research led to the development of vitamins and hormones that could be mass-produced and mass-marketed. Goods as varied as toys and games and fountain pens and mechanical pencils also found mass markets.

Mass Marketers and Mass Consumption

The rapid growth of mass distribution in the 1920s reflected an adjustment to major changes in the number, distribution, and purchasing habits of Americans as well as in the availability of vastly increased quantities and varieties of goods. Equally important was the continuing migration from rural to urban areas, which greatly increased the demand for finished goods. In 1920, for the first time in American history, the urban population exceeded the rural population. By 1930, the rural population constituted less than 44 percent of the national total. The continuing growth of large cities and their suburbs contributed to the concentration and expansion of large-scale wholesale and retail trade. By 1930, cities with populations of over 500,000 accounted for 17 percent of the nation's total, up from 10.7 percent at the turn of the century.

Prior to 1919, wholesalers and manufacturers played leading roles in directing the production and marketing of consumer goods in the United States. But after World War I, retailers came to assume an increasingly important place in this activity. Large-scale retailers not only began to introduce their own brands of merchandise but also sought actively to create consumer loyalty to themselves as against the manufacturers. The manufacturers, however, managed to retain a special place in the market through advertising and other means.

During the 1920s, department stores were able to maintain their position in the retail distribution structure. However, chain stores became the fastest-growing channel of retail distribution, expanding more rapidly than either new department stores or mail-order houses. Between 1918 and 1929, the number of chain-store units increased more than fivefold. Chain stores also improved their position in the drug, grocery, and other trades previously dominated by the wholesaler and small retailer.

Mail-order houses, such as Sears, Roebuck and Montgomery Ward, found their rural markets declining in the 1920s and built chains of retail department stores to gain sales in urban and suburban markets.

In the 1920s, American consumers significantly changed their buying habits as they acquired a liking for new products. Recent research conducted by economist Martha Olney establishes that a "consumer durable goods revolution" occurred during the decade, as a large number of households made significant changes in their spending and saving habits. Households increased their allocation of disposable income to the purchase of major durable goods like automobiles and appliances. In part, this was because they spent a lesser proportion on minor durable goods, like china and books, and on perishables. More important, to increase their purchases of durable goods, households decreased the portion of their incomes going to savings by nearly one-third. Sales finance companies emerged as major suppliers of the consumer installment credit needed by most households to purchase "big-ticket" items. Reducing the amount of required down payment and lengthening the term of payment were even more important than rising income levels in broadening the market for consumer-durable goods. Advertising was also an important element in propelling the "consumer durable goods revolution," not only in informing consumers about the attributes of particular products but also in fostering the style consciousness that increasingly affected decisions about the purchase of many kinds of goods.[4]

The iconoclast economist Thorstein Veblen had earlier satirized the "conspicuous consumption" of the idle rich. To many members of the middle and working classes, however, the new mass-produced and mass-marketed functional equivalents of the luxuries of the wealthy did not appear to be socially objectionable since they were not restricted to a favored few.

6^{25}
is all you need pay down to secure a Hoover complete with household cleaning attachments. Now, anyone can afford a Hoover. Have yours delivered today!

It beats **rugs** gently; sweeps as no broom can; and thoroughly air-cleans — *electrically!* Its handy new air-cleaning tools dust, *dustlessly.* It keeps your home immaculate; saves time, strength, health; makes rugs wear years *longer.* Certainly, it's a Hoover! Delivered to any home upon payment of only $6.25 down! Your Authorized Hoover Dealer will explain our easy purchase plan.

THE HOOVER COMPANY, NORTH CANTON, OHIO
The oldest and largest maker of electric cleaners
The Hoover is also made in Canada, at Hamilton, Ontario

The HOOVER
It BEATS ... as it Sweeps   as it Cleans

[1924]

Advertisement for Hoover Vacuum Cleaners, 1924. Credit played a crucial role in expanding sales of consumer durable goods like the vacuum cleaner pictured here. (Historical Pictures/Stock Montage)

Depressed Industries

The developments surveyed thus far in the automobile, electrical, chemical, and other growth industries represented the intricate interplay of factors that produced the phenomenal upswing of American manufacturing during the 1920s. A major economic fact of life in this period of change was the extent to which scientific discoveries, inventions and innovations, and new manufacturing methods created in one industry led to successive repercussions in other industries.

Yet the impact of new products, new methods of production, and new modes of organization on participants in older, established industries was rarely as dramatic as implied by economist Joseph Schumpeter's phrase, "the gale of creative destruction." For example, the automobile appealed to many urban dwellers who had never owned a horse-drawn vehicle. Very often, existing enterprises and their workers could easily move into closely related fields, such as those who transferred their facilities and skills from making lamps for horse-drawn carriages to producing automobile headlights or from hand-wound Victrolas to electric phonographs. In other cases, a segment of an industry fared better than the industry as a whole, as in the case of the piano when increasing numbers of households turned to the radio for home entertainment; production of pianos dropped by 67 percent during the decade, but the sale of grand pianos increased threefold as concert attendance rose dramatically.

However, major problems arose in several large and old industries that faced stagnating markets and intensifying competition. Firms in these industries usually implemented a strategy that relied on minor innovations, improvements in existing technology, and some rationalization of operations, the latter usually resulting in a shrinkage of the work force.

Three of the largest depressed industries of the 1920s were railroads, coal mining, and textile manufacturing, none of which succeeded in making adequate adjustments to new economic conditions.

The Railroads

In the 1920s, the railroads suffered their first serious competition from other carriers—motor trucks and passenger cars as well as intercoastal steamships operating through the Panama Canal. As trucks were replacing horse-drawn vehicles in the movement of local freight, they were also beginning to take the business of short hauls of less-than-carload lots away from the railroads. In addition, cars were making inroads on branch-line passenger traffic.

Railroad corporations faced a series of problems in meeting the new challenge of competition. Unlike other business enterprises, tight government regulation limited the flexibility of railroad management. Almost any decision made by managers had to be approved by the Interstate Commerce Commission (ICC), including whether to raise or reduce rates, to build new lines, to abandon old lines, or to issue securities in order to acquire new equipment. The Transportation Act of 1920, which returned the railroads to private ownership after government operation during World War I, authorized the ICC to formulate a plan for consolidating all of the nation's railroads into a limited number of large and financially strong systems. But this effort to improve efficiency through eliminating duplication of service was never realized. Furthermore, powerful railroad unions hindered efforts to install labor-saving equipment and improved work practices. Yet even if these "external" problems had not existed, a structure of bureaucratic management that had evolved in the railroad business appeared to dull the initiative of executives in introducing innovations.

In spite of the various obstacles to change, some significant technical improvements were made in railroad operations during the 1920s, including more efficient steam engines, longer trains, and a reduction in the hauling of empty cars. But the changes turned out to be too little too late. While annual ton-miles of freight hauled by the nation's railroads increased from 413.7 million in 1920 to 450.2 million in 1929, annual passenger miles decreased from 47.4 million to 31.2 million between those years. Total operating revenues remained stagnant over the decade. With the economic decline after 1929, the railroad rapidly lost ground to more vigorous automotive competitors. Indeed, for the first time in American history, the miles of railroad track decreased in 1931.

Bituminous Coal Mining

Bituminous coal was still the chief source of industrial energy and was widely used for residential heating in the 1920s. Yet chronic overproduction put great pressure on prices, profits, and wages in coal mining. This was in part the result of a significant expansion of the industry to meet the fuel needs of World War I. In addition, an industry that already had excess capacity faced growing competition from oil and natural gas as energy sources for industry and utilities, as well as water power for the latter. As a result, the ratio of coal to total energy consumption steadily declined, from nearly 90 percent at the turn of the century to 84 percent on the eve of World War I to just 60 percent in 1929. An equally serious problem for coal was the significant increase in the efficiency of energy use by its users, the result of many small advances made in manufacturing industries like iron and steel, in power generation, and in railroading. For example, the amount of coal needed to generate one kilowatt hour of electricity declined from 3.20 pounds in 1919 to 1.84 pounds in 1927.

In the face of these adverse trends affecting the consumption of coal, production declined only slightly during the 1920s; in fact, it stood in 1929 at a level that exceeded by about 35 percent the average annual production in the decade prior to 1914. It is not surprising that the market adjusted with a sharp drop in the price paid for bituminous coal, from an average of $3.75 per short ton in 1921 to $1.78 in 1929. Some coal mine owners attempted to deal with the problem of low profits through mechanization of the cutting and loading operations, resulting in an increase in the productivity of the industry as a whole. But only a reduction of capacity could have solved the basic problem of chronic overproduction. In an industry characterized by a large number of firms, individual owners were not willing to accept the financial losses that would result from voluntary withdrawal when others would receive the benefits. Instead, coal miners bore much of the burden of competitive conditions in the industry, suffering from some of the worst working and living conditions of any group of workers in the United States.

The Textile Industries

Trends in the textile industries were also running against the generally rising economic tide of the 1920s. People still bought clothing and other goods made from textile products, but they were allocating a smaller portion of their growing incomes to this category of consumption. However, changes in living habits associated with the closed automobile and more extensive use of central heating encouraged a shift to lighter-weight fabrics for both men's and women's clothing, creating particularly difficult problems of adjustment for the woolen industry. Rayon was beginning to be used in the manufacture of some types of clothing, again more damaging to wool than to cotton. New styles of women's clothing, especially shorter skirts, required fewer yards of cloth per garment. Some of these losses were offset by the development of new industrial applications like cotton cords for automobile tires. However, the net result of these influences was a rise in the physical output of the textile industries as a whole in the 1920s, but at a slower rate than earlier. At the same time, because of falling prices, the value of products steadily declined. The basic problem for textiles, as for bituminous coal, was excess capacity in a highly competitive industry composed of many firms producing a standardized, unbranded commodity-like product for a market that was growing only slowly.

Members of the textile industries sought to improve performance through both collective and individual action. Trade associations conducted market studies and encouraged the dissemination of improved merchandising methods. Some firms sought to shift product lines to meet the changing needs of apparel manufacturers more effectively. Improved machinery and production methods brought productivity gains to the industry, though these gains were lower than the average for manufacturing as a whole. To take advantage of lower labor costs, more of the cotton textile industry migrated to the South, where hourly earnings were 25 percent to 60 percent lower than in the New England and other northeastern states. By 1930, the South accounted for over 60 percent of total U.S. employment in cotton textiles.

The Government of the Business System

As pointed out in Chapter 12, the growth of the large corporation in the late nineteenth century caused widespread alarm about an increasing concentration of economic power in the hands of big business. This, in turn, led to the passage of antitrust legislation—the

Sherman Act in 1890 and the Clayton Act and the Federal Trade Commission Act in 1914. However, the enforcement of the antitrust laws depended on interpretation by the courts. Thus, in 1920, the Supreme Court, following the "rule of reason" set forth in 1911, declared that the large size and potential monopoly power held by the United States Steel Corporation were not legally relevant because "the law did not make mere size an offense or the existence of unexerted power an offense." This interpretation of what constituted a violation of the antitrust laws remained the law of the land for the next two decades.

After the first great merger movement of 1895 to 1903, mergers were made at a relatively slow rate during the next two decades. However, a second wave of mergers developed between 1925 and 1931 as entrepreneurs made decisions resulting in 5846 mergers, with a peak of 1245 mergers in 1929 alone. The major effect of the mergers was that the share of total manufacturing assets held by the one hundred largest industrial firms rose from 35.6 percent in 1925 to 43.9 percent in 1931.

The merger movement of 1925 to 1931 accelerated the trend toward oligopoly (in which a few firms dominate a market) already under way prior to 1914. This was due in large part to the fact that the new mergers were undertaken, not by the largest firms in an industry, but by those in the second rank. Such activity took place in cement, cans, petroleum, automobiles, agricultural implements, glass, and steel. In the steel industry, for example, the chief firms participating in mergers were those known as "Little Steel"—Bethlehem and Republic—not "Big Steel"—U.S. Steel. In the food industry, considerable merger activity took place, with National Dairy, Borden, General Foods, and General Mills as the leaders. On the whole, such mergers led to local oligopoly in the primary products—for example, fluid milk and bread—and to national oligopoly in lesser products—such as cheese.

Reinforcing the trend toward bigness in business was the decision by large manufacturing corporations to diversify by expanding into new products for new markets. This became an explicit strategy of growth, as top managers searched for new products and new markets. The aim was to promote the long-term health of an enterprise by more profitably using its managers, facilities, and specific technological resources. In the 1920s, for example, chemical companies like DuPont and electrical manufacturers like General Electric expanded by developing new product lines.

Managerial Enterprise

By the 1920s, most of the nation's large industrial corporations had come to be characterized by separation of ownership and management, long regarded as the functions of private property (the "splitting of the atom of property," as Berle and Means phrased it in their notable book, *The Modern Corporation and Private Property* (1934). The original founders had by now passed from the scene, and their heirs were often more interested in spending money than in making it. As a result, the ownership of many large corporations had become widely dispersed among a multitude of small shareholders who lacked the ability to participate effectively in the management of the property they legally owned. At the same time, the influence of financiers, related to their control of access to capital, was declining, as managers of industrial, utility, and transportation corporations increasingly used retained earnings as a source of funds to finance expansion.

By the 1920s, greater size and more extensive diversification created the need for a new structure of decision making within the large corporation. The management hierarchy created earlier to govern the corporation that manufactured one line of products for one market found difficulty in making decisions about the manufacture and distribution of several sets of products sold in different markets. The organizational innovation of the 1920s was the *multidivisional, decentralized corporate structure.* Autonomous *operating divisions* were headed by managers responsible for coordinating the production and distribution of one major product line for one major market. Top executives in a *general office,* with no operating responsibilities, concentrated on appraising the results of divisional management as well as determining strategy for the corporation through control of allocation of resources. Large size and a broad range of corporate activity also stimulated the widespread adoption of new accounting, budgeting, and forecasting methods. The decentralized, multidivisional structure thus became widely diffused as a system of management in large, diversified industrial corporations.

Separation of ownership and management encouraged a new perception of the role of corporate managers. No longer did decision makers in large corporations see themselves as merely profit seekers; rather, they increasingly perceived themselves as professionals like lawyers and physicians. A basic element of professionalism was professional education, which was offered by a growing number of universities and colleges in the 1920s. Although individual businesspeople had long made donations to charitable causes, the large corporation, as a part of providing service to society beyond efficiently making good products, became a dispenser of philanthropy through participation in community chests and other organizations. With widespread public approval of businesspeople as professionals serving society, corporate executives took on a wider role as community decision makers through membership on the boards of trustees of universities and other institutions.

Small Business and the Trade Association Movement

In oligopolist industries inhabited by large firms, price became less of a competitive wea-

pon as sellers came to employ such tactics as product differentiation through advertising and other marketing techniques. However, in many industries populated by small- and medium-sized firms, a pattern of less restrained competition stimulated participants to seek greater price stability and control of their markets through some form of cooperative action. Arthur J. Eddy, author of an influential book published in 1912, described what he called "the new competition" in this way: "The basis of the old competition is secrecy, the strength of the new is knowledge. The essence of the old is deceit, the spirit of the new is truth."[5]

During World War I the government encouraged trade association activity as a way for individual firms to coordinate their efforts in the production of war goods. About a thousand national trade associations were in operation by the end of the war. In the 1920s, government officials like Secretary of Commerce Herbert Hoover further encouraged cooperation between business and government, a movement that historians later termed the "associative state." An important key to controlling unbridled competition was the open-price policy, by which each member firm posted its price with an industrywide trade association, which, in turn, circulated the information among its members. While collusive action to control competition had long been illegal under the antitrust laws, the Supreme Court in 1925 held to be legal the exchange of information that was not used as a means of controlling prices (*Maple Floor Manufacturers Association v. U.S.*). In spite of the widespread use of the open-price policy, price stability remained more of a goal than an achievement, even in the generally prosperous 1920s; eventually, it broke down completely with the severe economic downturn after 1929. More successful, however, was the work of trade associations in lobbying and public relations on behalf of small- and medium-sized firms that could not afford to support these functions individually.

Changes in the Labor Force

As the population of the United States grew by 15.7 percent between 1920 and 1930, the labor force (those gainfully employed) increased by 17 percent. The rate of population growth in the 1920s was slightly higher than the 15.4 percent experienced between 1910 and 1920 but lower than that of earlier decades. Thus, the labor participation rate inched up, reflecting the long-term tendency of the U.S. work force to grow slightly more rapidly than the population.

The most striking development affecting the growth of population and labor force was the sharp curtailment of immigration. Traditionally, employers had supported unrestricted immigration because it provided them with what seemed like an unlimited flow of low-cost labor. Among most segments of the American public, there was a widespread assumption that immigration represented opportunities for those suffering from political repression or economic deprivation in Europe. However, in the aftermath of World War I, many employers came to believe that immigrants played a major role in labor unrest and other "un-American" activities. In addition, many leaders of the trade union movement viewed immigrants as competitors in the labor market. Congress passed legislation in 1921 and 1924, creating quotas for national groups based on the origins of the U.S. population. The effect of the legislation was to discriminate against potential immigrants from southern and eastern Europe, since a large majority of the immigrants to the New World had come from northern and western Europe. From an average of about one million persons per annum before World War I, immigration from Europe slowed to under 160,000 each year between 1925 and 1929. One significant result of immigration restriction was to encourage the continued migration of African-Americans from the rural South to the urban North to fill the unskilled jobs that European immigrants might otherwise have taken.

Most of the growth in the American population and labor force for the decade came from natural increase—that is, an excess of births over deaths. The birthrate continued to decline, reflecting decisions in favor of smaller families characteristic of urban societies. The major factor in the natural increase of population was the sharp drop in the death rate, resulting from improved living standards as well as medical advances. The decline in infant mortality was particularly striking.

Significant changes were taking place in the composition of the labor force in the 1920s. The proportion of workers engaged in agriculture had long been declining; the absolute numbers were now also declining. Manufacturing saw a small decrease in relative importance, although the number of workers increased. The largest increase in the labor force occurred in the service sector.

In terms of major occupational groupings, white-collar workers increased in numbers almost twice as fast as did manual and service workers (see Table 18–5). Moreover, many types of service work required high-level skill and training, involved personal contact with the consumer or business user of the product or service, and allowed a wider gamut of satisfying work activity. Many white-collar occupations also required a higher level of educational attainment than did manual work. Thus, it is not surprising that the U.S. work force was becoming a more educated one. The number of high school graduates more than doubled between 1920 and 1930; in the latter year, 28.8 percent of the age-seventeen group completed secondary education compared to just 16.3 percent a decade earlier. Higher education also experienced a significant expansion, with the number of bachelor's degrees growing by more than 150 percent during the decade; fifty-seven men and women in every thousand of the age-twenty-three group graduated from

Table 18–5 *Major Occupational Groups, Civilian Labor Force, 1920 and 1930*

Occupation	Thousands of Persons, Age 14 and Older		Percent Change (1920–1930)
	1920	1930	
White-collar	10,529	14,320	+36.0%
Manual/service	20,287	24,044	+18.5%
Farm	11,390	10,321	−9.4%

SOURCE: Data from U.S. Bureau of the Census, *Historical Statistics of the United States: Colonial Times to 1970* (Washington, D.C.: GPO, 1975) pp. 139–40.

Table 18–6 *Women in the Labor Force, 1920 and 1930*

	1920	1930
Female labor force participation rate		
All women	23.7%	24.8%
Married women	9.0	11.7
Single women	46.4	50.5
White women	21.6	23.7
Nonwhite women	43.1	43.3
Women as proportion of total labor force	20.5%	22.1%
Proportion of women in labor force employed in white-collar occupations	38.8	44.2
Women as proportion of white collar labor force	31.8	33.2

SOURCE: Data from Claudia Goldin, *Understanding the Gender Gap: An Economic History of American Women* (New York: Oxford University Press, 1990), p. 17; and U.S. Bureau of the Census, *Historical Statistics of the United States: Colonial Times to 1970* [Washington, D.C.: GPO, 1975], pp. 139–40.

college in 1930, up from only twenty-six graduates per thousand in 1920.

The labor participation rate for women increased from 23.7 percent to 24.8 percent between 1920 and 1930. By the latter date, women accounted for 22.1 percent of the labor force, up from 20.5 percent a decade earlier. Gains in female employment, as in earlier decades, were greatest in white-collar work, where women's proportion of that segment of the labor force grew from 31.8 percent in 1920 to 33.2 percent in 1930 (see Table 18–6).

Finally, although a constitutional amendment designed to give Congress the power to regulate the work of children failed, effective child-labor and compulsory school-attendance laws in most northern states resulted in a continuing decline in the full-time employment of children under age sixteen.

A Rise in Real Wages

Despite the hard times of 1920 to 1921, labor was able to preserve the economic gains made during World War I and then to record new advances. From 1920 to 1929, the average real annual earnings of employed nonfarm workers in the United States rose by 24 percent (see Table 18–7). The $834 (in 1914 dollars) that the average worker received in 1929, for example,

Table 18–7   *Average Annual Earnings of Employees, 1920–1929*

| | When Employed | |
Year	Money Earnings	Real Earnings (in 1914 dollars)
1920	$1,342	$672
1921	1,227	689
1922	1,190	718
1923	1,278	753
1924	1,293	759
1925	1,317	753
1926	1,346	764
1927	1,380	799
1928	1,384	810
1929	1,425	834

SOURCE: Data from U.S. Bureau of the Census, *Historical Statistics of the United States: Colonial Times to 1970* (Washington, D.C.: GPO, 1975), p. 164.

Table 18–8   *Average Weekly Hours of Production Workers in Manufacturing, 1914 and 1920–1929*

Year	Average Weekly Hours
1914	49.4
1920	47.4
1921	43.1
1922	44.2
1923	45.6
1924	43.7
1925	44.5
1926	45.0
1927	45.0
1928	44.4
1929	44.2

SOURCE: Data from U.S. Bureau of the Census, *Historical Statistics of the United States: Colonial Times to 1970* (Washington, D.C.: GPO 1975), p. 170.

was nearly one-third above that achieved in the best prewar year—$640 in 1913. Meanwhile, as shown in Table 18–8, the average weekly hours of production workers in manufacturing declined from 49.4 hours in 1914 to 47.4 hours in 1920 and to 44.2 hours in 1929, providing added leisure time for more members of the nation's work force. Another favorable factor for the average worker was the low rate of unemployment experienced between 1923 and 1929 (see Table 18–9).

However, it should be emphasized that the experience of individual workers varied widely from the averages indicated in Tables 18–7 and 18–8. A major difference continued to exist between the average earnings of men and women. The ratio of female to male weekly earnings in twenty-one manufacturing industries through most of the 1920s was 60 percent or lower, reflecting in large part the occupational segregation of women in the labor force—that is, the concentration of large numbers of women in low-paying occupations. There was also a significant skill differential in weekly earnings—about one-third for skilled men over unskilled men in major manufactur-

Table 18–9   *Unemployment in the United States, 1920–1929*

Year	Number of Unemployed (in thousands)	Percentage of Civilian Labor Force
1920	2,132	5.2%
1921	4,918	11.7
1922	2,859	6.7
1923	1,049	2.4
1924	2,190	5.0
1925	1,453	3.2
1926	801	1.8
1927	1,519	3.3
1928	1,982	4.2
1929	1,550	3.2

SOURCE: Data from U.S. Bureau of the Census, *Historical Statistics of the United States: Colonial Times to 1970* (Washington, D.C.: GPO, 1975), p. 135.

ing industries. Steady jobs paying good wages were generally more plentiful in growth industries like automobiles than in depressed industries like textiles and coal mining.

Table 18–10 *Labor Union Membership, 1920–1929*

	Number of Union Members (in thousands)		
Year	Total All Unions	American Federation of Labor	Other Unions
1920	5,048	4,093	955
1921	4,782	3,967	815
1922	4,027	3,273	754
1923	3,622	2,919	703
1924	3,536	2,853	683
1925	3,520	2,831	689
1926	3,503	2,715	788
1927	3,546	2,759	787
1928	3,480	2,809	671
1929	3,461	2,770	691

SOURCE: Data from U.S. Bureau of the Census, *Historical Statistics of the United States: Colonial Times to 1970* (Washington, D.C.: GPO, 1975), p. 177.

The Decline of Unionism

Throughout American history, labor unions usually expanded their membership during periods of prosperity. But the experience of the 1920s was an exception to this generalization. Between 1920 and 1929, membership in American trade unions declined by nearly one-third. In just ten years, organized labor lost over 1.5 million members (see Table 18–10).

A major part of the membership problem was internal to the union movement itself. William Green, who succeeded Samuel Gompers as president of the American Federation of Labor in 1924, displayed little daring or imagination about devising new ways to organize the unorganized segments of the work force. More fundamentally, the structure of the AFL was oriented toward craft unionism—that is, organizing workers by skill—which was not suited to promoting unionism among the semiskilled and unskilled workers in the mass-production industries, then the fastest-growing manufacturing sector. The position of organized labor is aptly summarized by a noted scholar in this way: "While the country as a whole was completing its transition from the horse-and-buggy era to the automobile age, the labor movement as a whole . . . remained in the horse-and-buggy stage."[6]

Yet even a better-organized union movement would have encountered difficulty in dealing with the external problems of the politico-economic environment. Government continued to take the side of management in labor disputes, with the courts upholding the use of injunctions and the legality of yellow-dog contracts. At the same time, corporations expanded the system of welfare capitalism, started prior to the war, to ensure that management retained full authority over the terms of employment. Based on a paternalistic concept of responsibility by business for the well-being of employees, welfare capitalism included safety programs, group insurance, stock-purchase opportunities, pension plans, encouragement of home ownership, and employee-representation plans (or what later came to be called company unions).

More than any other factor in accounting for the poor performance of unions during the 1920s was the prosperity of the era. It functioned to undermine the sense of working-class consciousness. As a former Socialist explained in 1929, workers in America "have enjoyed a constantly widening circle of increasing physical comfort and even of luxury . . . which the workers of fifty years ago regarded as unattainable."[7] Even if a "de-skilling" of labor had taken place in much of mass-production industry, large numbers of workers had come to share with members of the middle class satisfactions as consumers of the great variety of new goods turned out by the American productive system. Disillusionment would set in with the onset of the Great Depression after 1929 (see Chapter 19).

Problems in the Agricultural Sector

Within eighteen months after the end of World War I, American farm prices suffered a severe reduction. Between 1919 and 1921, the prices received by farmers declined by almost 40 percent. The economic distress of farmers, especially those farming the spring wheat region and the Corn Belt, was intensified by the legacy of the wartime speculative rise in the prices of farmland and the heavy increase in farm-mortgage debt, which led to many foreclosures of farm property during the mid-1920s. The rest of the American economy soon recovered from the downturn in the business cycle and, by 1921, the prosperity of the 1920s seemed firmly established. Yet agriculture did not share proportionately in this upward trend.

A number of factors combined to keep American agriculture depressed. One was that agriculture in the war-devastated areas of Europe and elsewhere recovered rapidly from the effects of the war and expanded through progress in technology. Another was that, since the United States insisted on the repayment of war loans and enacted high protective tariffs, foreign countries had reduced means for buying American food exports and were forced to cut their imports. Hence, many European nations encouraged an increase of farm production at home and made foreign purchases from those countries that accepted industrial goods in payment.

Nevertheless, since domestic consumption rose enough to counterbalance the decline in foreign demand, income in agriculture recovered by the mid-1920s and stayed on something of a plateau from 1925 until 1929. Technological advances, however, continued to increase farm output considerably. The use of tractors, trucks, and automobiles grew rapidly, and the all-purpose tractor prompted a movement toward large-scale farming. Although the productivity of agriculture in this period rose less rapidly than that of industry, the number of persons supplied by one farm worker rose from about eight in the 1917 to 1920 period to almost ten in 1930. But the domestic demand was too inelastic to absorb a constantly increasing supply. Not only did the population increase less rapidly than before the war, but, even more important, most American consumers decided to use their higher incomes to buy the new products of industry (such as automobiles and refrigerators) rather than more food. This imbalance kept farm prices and incomes from rising to levels considered adequate by farmers.

However, some types of farming, taking advantage of the changing eating habits of middle-class urban dwellers, experienced much the same kind of success as the expanding manufacturing industries of the decade. The growing numbers of Americans in white-collar sedentary occupations consumed less heavy food like bread and more dairy products (e.g., fluid milk, cheese, and ice cream), poultry and eggs, and vegetables and fruits. Unfortunately, the number of farmers in these specialties was much smaller than that in the old staple commodities.

Government Decisions and Controls

Adverse conditions in many segments of agriculture initiated a trend toward increasing centralization of decision making. Farmers formed a new organization, the American Farm Bureau Federation, which joined with the older National Grange and the Farmers' Union to create a bipartisan farm bloc in Congress that worked for agrarian legislation. Congress responded in 1921 by reviving the War Finance Corporation as a lending agency to finance the export of farm surpluses, and by passing a Futures Trading Act that curbed speculation in grain prices. In 1922, a Co-operative Act exempted agricultural cooperatives from the antitrust laws, and the next year an Intermediate Credits Act established a system of twelve intermediate credit banks. These aided farmers in the more orderly marketing of their products and enabled them to borrow against crops in storage in order to hold them for hoped-for higher prices on the market.

The slogan "Equality for Agriculture" inspired the farm bloc to get through Congress the McNary-Haugen bill, which provided for a two-price plan highly favorable to farmers. But President Calvin Coolidge vetoed the measure in both 1927 and 1928. The farm bloc succeeded, however, in its push for enactment of the Agricultural Marketing Act of 1929, which created the Federal Farm Board to promote cooperative marketing agencies for farm commodities. The board was equipped with a revolving fund of $500 million so as to enable producers to achieve a high degree of price control. The experiment failed because of lack of measures for production control and the adverse effects of the Great Depression on consumer demand for food products.

In addition to these appeals for government intervention, American farmers in the late 1920s established large national cooperatives in the hopes of expanding consumer demand through quality control and of raising farm prices through market management. But these attempts at self-help proved unsuccessful because there was no effective control of production. Hence, most American farmers came to look to the government for mechanisms that would overcome the deficiencies of voluntary organizations.

The United States in the World Economy

As a result of the U.S. experience in World War I, America became the world's leading economic power. While Europe had been weakened by the war, the United States continued to gather strength in the 1920s. In the aftermath of the emergence of the United States as a net creditor nation, New York gradually built up the institutional structure that enabled it to replace London as the world's financial center.

Underpinning America's economic power was its industrial strength; the nation's share of the world's manufacturing output increased from 36 percent on the eve of the war to 42 percent in the late 1920s.

In the decade following World War I, American policymakers extolled the virtues of the open-door policy, applied earlier to the Far East and now to the entire world—the right of Americans to trade and invest on equal terms with all nations. The open-door approach, its advocates believed, would not only advance American material interests but also contribute to a stable world order and international prosperity. However, it should be emphasized that the steady growth of U.S. foreign trade and overseas investment during the 1920s owed far more to decisions made by private business than to the efforts of government officials to promote American interests abroad. The United States became the world's leading exporter and chief investor and the second most important importer.

Foreign Trade

American exports grew by over one-third from 1922, by which time the war boom and postwar recession had run their course, to 1929 (see Table 18–11). Most spectacular was the growth of exports of finished manufactured goods, which almost doubled during these years; this category, which constituted less than one-third of exports before the war, made up almost one-half in 1929. Automobiles, an industry in which the United States could then claim superiority in design and production methods, accounted for almost 10 percent of all exports. In the late 1920s, for example, Ford and General Motors manufactured in their American plants nearly all the cars sold in Japan; automobiles were shipped knocked down and assembled in U.S.-owned facilities.

Other mass-manufactured products that had led the way into foreign markets in the prewar

Table 18–11　*Foreign Trade of the United States, 1920–1929*

Year	Merchandise Surplus (in $ millions)	Percent of GNP	
		Exports	Imports
1920	$2,950	9.3%	5.9%
1921	1,976	6.1	3.4
1922	719	5.2	4.2
1923	375	4.8	4.4
1924	981	5.2	4.1
1925	683	5.4	4.6
1926	378	4.9	4.5
1927	681	5.1	4.3
1928	1,037	5.2	4.2
1929	842	5.0	4.2

SOURCE: Data from U.S. Bureau of the Census, *Historical Statistics of the United States: Colonial Times to 1970* (Washington, D.C.: GPO, 1975), pp. 884, 887.

years—such as cash registers, typewriters, sewing machines, and agricultural machinery—also found growing sales abroad. Europe continued to be the most important foreign market for U.S. exports, though its share of the total declined from almost two-thirds before the war to under one-half in 1929. Canada, Latin America, Asia, Africa, and Oceana all took growing proportions of American exports in the 1920s.

Imports grew by 41 percent, an even faster rate of growth than exports, though the United States recorded a surplus in its trade balance each year. Especially important components were supplies of raw materials like wood pulp, newsprint, silk, rubber, and petroleum, necessary inputs for the nation's industrial economy. Indeed, as Secretary of Commerce Hoover explained in 1927: "Upon these highly essential imports is dependent not only much of our comfort but even the very existence of the major part of our industrial life."[8] However, imports of manufactured goods grew by 50 percent in spite of the enactment in 1922 of the Fordney-McCumber Tariff, which increased rates on this category

of imports by up to 25 percent. Europe was the leading source of imports, but its share of the total declined from over one-half in 1910 to under one-third in 1929. By the latter date, Asia was exporting to the United States almost as much as was Europe.

Foreign Investment

Direct investment by American corporations abroad nearly doubled during the 1920s, building on the base established earlier. *Market-oriented investments* were made by American multinational corporations in foreign manufacturing facilities to sell goods in foreign markets, primarily in Western Europe, Canada, and Australia. The leading market-oriented investors were corporations making automobiles, electrical equipment, certain kinds of machinery and metal products (e.g., office equipment, sewing machines, and radiators), aluminum, petroleum products, and trademarked packaged foods and beverages. The research of Mira Wilkins has defined certain characteristics of the market-oriented multinational corporation as follows: They were likely to be large firms in relatively new industries making distinctive products; they possessed superior technology; and they used advanced marketing methods. Generally, these corporations were already major exporters, but they perceived new opportunities by investing in manufacturing facilities abroad (e.g., they sought to jump the tariff wall, achieve lower production costs, and meet the special needs of foreign consumers). Some corporations built branch plants abroad, as did Ford in England; others acquired existing companies whose production facilities and marketing organizations they then "Americanized," as did General Motors in England and Germany.[9]

In contrast to market-oriented investment by American multinational corporations, *supply-oriented investment* was made primarily in lesser-developed countries to secure supplies of raw materials for export to the United States or other industrial nations. American corporations made substantial investments in Latin America and Canada for the mining of a wide range of minerals, including nitrates, copper, tin, and nickel. In agriculture, U.S. corporations operated facilities to produce commodities as varied as tropical fruit in Central America, sugar in Cuba, and rubber in the Far East and Africa. Concern about dwindling reserves of oil within the United States stimulated a worldwide search for new sources of petroleum. The major move in this area during the 1920s was the application of U.S. capital to develop vast new oil fields in Venezuela. By the end of the decade, American corporations had gained a foothold in the oil fields of the Middle East.

During the 1920s, American business successfully challenged European business in areas where the latter had long dominated. Indeed, in 1922, the value of U.S. investment in Canada for the first time exceeded that of British holdings there, despite Canada's political ties to Britain. In 1929, the United States for the first time surpassed Britain in the value of investment in Latin America. Even in Western Europe, American business had mounted a second "invasion" in the 1920s, matching that made at the turn of the century.

It should be emphasized, however, that foreign economic interests, though important, did not gain proportionately greater significance in the perspective of the whole American economy. The 1929 book value of U.S. direct foreign investment overseas was equivalent to 7 percent of that year's gross national product (GNP)—the same percentage as in 1914. Likewise, the nation's exports and imports in the late 1920s accounted for about the same proportion of GNP as in the years just before World War I.

The Legacy of War Debts and Reparations

The treaty ending World War I required that Germany pay to the victors the huge costs of the war. While the United States demanded no reparations for itself, it nevertheless became involved in the problems surrounding these payments. The British government announced that it would collect from Germany only such amounts as would equal Britain's payments on its war debt to the United States, so in effect the German reparations payments would go ultimately to the latter country.

Regular payments of both German reparations to the Allies and Allied war debts to the United States began in the mid-1920s. In theory, Germany was transferring to Great Britain and France the proceeds of an export surplus, which, in turn, was being transferred to the United States. In actuality, though, American investors had extended large loans to Germany, which it used to make the reparations payments to the Allies, who then sent this American money back to the United States. As economic historian George Soule comments: "This curious result was hardly the consequence of a plot or of a conscious design on anybody's part. Rather, it was an example of the way in which the conventions of finance may for a time conceal fundamental anomalies in international transactions."[10]

The episode served to illustrate a larger problem, one stemming from America's failure to adjust to its new role as a net creditor nation. Political decision makers were determined on a policy of high protective tariffs to protect the domestic market from foreign competition, thereby maintaining a favorable balance of trade. Hence, the proceeds of foreign loans could provide the dollars needed by foreigners to pay for American goods as well as to repay war debts.

American investment bankers quickly responded to the opportunity, floating loans to foreign business corporations as well as to national, provincial, and municipal governments. During the decade as a whole, Europe supplied 41 percent of the foreign securities sold in the United States, followed by Canada with 25 percent, Latin America with 22 percent, and the rest of the world, principally Asia, with 12 percent. Investors in the United States, tempted by high interest rates, were willing purchasers of foreign securities, which accounted for between 10 percent and 18 percent of all new capital issues sold in the United States from 1920 to 1928. Large underwriting profits stimulated investment-banking firms to search for borrowers. Often the real needs of borrowers were less important than the pressure from lenders. For example, a Bavarian hamlet in need of $125,000 was persuaded by American bankers to issue $3 million in bonds.

For much of the decade, a large outflow of American capital made possible an efficient functioning of the international economy, in spite of the determination of the world's largest creditor nation to maintain a favorable balance of trade. The peril of the situation, however, appeared by the middle of 1928, when American foreign lending began to decline sharply, in large part because of the perceived opportunity for even greater profits in stock-market speculation. When the outflow of capital was further curtailed after the onset of depression in 1929, foreigners would no longer have dollars to pay their debts or to buy American goods.

That Bull on Wall Street

Like most periods of high prosperity, the decade of the 1920s was not without a large measure of speculative froth. A boom and bust of speculation in inventories of manufactured goods and raw materials opened the 1920s. In the middle of the decade, speculative interest focused on Florida land. Before this boom collapsed, thousands of small investors had squandered their savings on the purchase of unimproved tracts, some of them under water, in the hope that a "greater fool" would pay more than they had. But the greatest excitement revolved around the bull market of stocks that climaxed in 1929.

From 1924, when the bull market began its long upward drive, to 1929, the Standard and Poor index of common stocks almost tripled. Glamour stocks representing the exciting new growth industries of the era, like Radio Corporation of America, recorded even more spectacular gains. The break in the stock market in the fall of 1929 came in the form of several weeks of alternating panic followed by anemic recovery of stock prices. After the first sharp decline in late October, the efforts of Wall Street leaders to shore up the market, supported by New York banks, were only temporarily successful. By mid-November, the *New York Times* average of stock prices stood at about one-half of the high recorded just two months earlier. After what turned out to be a false recovery in early 1930, the market resumed its downward course. By the low point in 1932, more than 85 percent of the 1929 peak stock values had been wiped out.

Legend has it that the promise of quick profits to be made in buying and selling stocks lured bootblacks, taxi drivers, and every other kind of person into what was widely viewed as a gambling spree. In actuality, the number of stockholders was never more than nine million, out of about thirty million households in America, and the typical investor was likely to be a businessperson or professional investing in what was perceived to be the economic future of the country. The optimism of the day was by itself enough to encourage widespread interest in the stock market. Salespeople from brokerage houses further stimulated excitement with telephone solicitations and even house-to-house canvasses of upper-middle-class neighborhoods. Securities firms issued market letters with advice on the best prospects, and "experts," like a university professor in Chicago, provided tips on regularly scheduled radio broadcasts. Persons seeking professional management of their funds could purchase shares of investment trusts, financial institutions that bought common stocks or other securities; for the professional management, investors paid a large premium over the net asset value of the securities owned by the investment trust.

While the prices that investors paid for shares of stock in the late stages of the bull market were high in terms of the fundamentals—dividend yields and price-earnings ratios—expectations of future expansion of the economy and increasing profits of leading growth corporations seemed to justify the high valuations. Recent research suggests that stock prices in the late 1920s were on average at least 30 percent higher than the fundamentals would have warranted.[11] But only hindsight would reveal that investors were discounting not only the future but in some cases the hereafter as well.

The true speculative excesses of Wall Street in the 1920s derived largely from the leverage that many of the players employed to multiply their gains. Indeed, much of the rise in stock prices was fueled by the great increase in credit made available in the form of brokers' loans. Traders could buy stocks on margin, putting up only 10 percent or 20 percent of the purchase price and using the securities as collateral for the loan. The loans were callable if there was danger that the price of the collateral stock would drop below the amount of the loan. A tremendous volume of funds flowed into this call-loan market, not only from commercial banks but even more from domestic and foreign corporations and individuals attracted by high interest rates for loans that were presumed to be highly liquid and secure. When the market turned down and their loans were called, margin buyers saw the entire value of their equity wiped out. In contrast, those who had paid cash for solid blue-chip stocks, even at inflated prices, had the satisfaction of seeing valuations return to the peak levels of 1929 a quarter-century later.

The founders of the Federal Reserve System had hoped that a central bank would be able, through use of its monetary tools, to curtail the kind of speculative excess that led to financial panic in 1929. Yet it is evident that the Federal Reserve played a role in bringing on the Wall Street collapse. In 1927, the Fed, worried about signs of emerging weakness in the economies of the United States and Europe, adopted a policy of monetary ease by lowering discount rates and engaging in open-market purchases. These measures, which came at a time when the volume of credit created for speculation in stocks was rising, served to stimulate even more of that speculation. By 1928, the economy had recovered from its pause so that the continuing securities speculation on credit became a major concern of the Fed. Discount rates were raised (in New York) to 5 percent in July 1928, their highest level since 1921. The speculation continued into 1929, even though the economy again showed signs of weakness. Concentrating on the speculation, the Fed again raised its discount rate to 6 percent in August 1929. But speculators were not discouraged by a rise in interest rates if they believed that they could use borrowed money to make a killing in the stock market.

The End of the New Era

The stock market crash of October 1929 is widely associated with the onset of the Great Depression. While the direct effects of the crash on the economy's subsequent performance are often exaggerated, its indirect effects through the negative impact it had on the confidence of businesspeople, consumers, and investors were of some importance.

Despite widespread optimism in 1929, there were underlying problems, not all of which were entirely apparent to contemporary observers. A great surge of residential construction,

Wall Street, 29 October 1929.   Crowds usually gathered on Wall Street during a financial panic. On this "Black Tuesday," a crowd assembled on the steps of Federal Hall, across the street from the New York Stock Exchange, as if watching a fire or other disaster. For stockholders, especially those who had bought on margin, this was a disaster—the greatest fall in stock prices up to that time. (Brown Brothers)

resting in part on the move to the suburbs, peaked in 1925 and 1926 and then began to decline as the market for new housing became satiated at existing price and income levels. At the same time, other forms of capital formation were slowing, as there appeared to be fewer major capital-absorbing changes in technology that would generate attractive investment opportunities. The boom in consumer durable goods threatened to run out of steam; outstanding consumer installment debt rose to 9.34 percent of household income in 1929 (compared to less than 6 percent in the decade prior to World War I). Passenger-car registrations showed a declining rate of annual increase, from 24 percent in 1923 to between 5 percent and 10 percent in the late years of the decade. Clearly, the automobile industry was

maturing as it became increasingly dependent on replacement sales as opposed to first-time car buyers. Electrification was nearing its limits, too; most of the nation's urban households had been tied into the electrical distribution system, and power companies were reluctant to invest in rural areas with low population density. The proportion of funds raised through new financing that resulted in additions to physical equipment declined from 76 percent in 1924 to only 35 percent in 1929, with a growing amount of the dollars of investors (that is, savers) going into speculation in commercial real estate and stocks. It appeared that American productive investment had come to rest at a level that was insufficient for the continued expansion of the economy.

While opportunities for useful, labor-employing capital apparently were growing scarce, saving, or the accumulation of funds to invest, was growing. This, in turn, was related to the pattern of income distribution. Research conducted by Charles Holt shows that most of the gains in income during the 1920s went to the top income receivers. From 1923 to 1929, average real disposable income per capita of the top 1 percent of nonfarm income receivers rose by 63 percent, compared to an average increase of 9 percent for all nonfarm income receivers.[12] In other words, the share of total income going to the top 1 percent of income receivers rose from 13.1 percent in 1923 to 18.9 percent in 1929 and that of the top 5 percent from 27.1 percent to 33.5 percent.

Summary

There appeared to be much reason for the widespread belief in the 1920s that America had attained a state of permanent prosperity, a view articulated not only by business and political leaders but by respected academics as well, including Irving Fisher and Wesley C. Mitchell, two noted economists. Increased levels of production, sustained high employment, and a stable price level all contributed to the ability of larger numbers of people than ever before to participate in the fruits of technological and economic progress. Indeed, it seemed to some observers, like presidential nominee Herbert Hoover in 1928, that the nation was on the verge of a final triumph over poverty.

It is true that some industries, regions, and groups lagged badly, but "uneven development" was not a unique characteristic of the 1920s. Rarely had all sectors of the economy and all segments of society marched together in lockstep, participating equally in national economic prosperity. There were failures, most notably in dealing with the problems of depressed industries (including agriculture) and in formulating a meaningful foreign economic policy that reflected America's new position in the world. The 1920s led to the Great Depression of the 1930s, but the decade also foreshadowed in many ways the economic experience of the quarter-century after World War II, when high employment and mass consumption spread their net more widely and evenly throughout America.

Endnotes

1. Thomas C. Cochran, *American Business in the Twentieth Century* (Cambridge: Harvard University Press, 1972), p. 21.
2. David C. Mowery and Nathan Rosenberg, *Technology and the Pursuit of Economic Growth* (New York: Cambridge University Press, 1989), p. 77.
3. J. F. Steiner, "Recreation and Leisure Time Activities," in President's Research Committee on Social Trends, *Recent Social Trends in the United States* (New York: McGraw-Hill, 1933), p. 941.
4. Martha L. Olney, *Buy Now, Pay Later: Advertising, Credit, and Consumer Durables in the 1920s* (Chapel Hill: University of North Carolina Press, 1991), passim.
5. Quoted in Cochran, *American Business* p. 69.

6. Carroll R. Daugherty, "Labor [1919–1950]," in Harold F. Williamson, ed., *The Growth of the American Economy,* 2nd ed. (Englewood Cliffs, N.J.: Prentice-Hall, 1951), pp. 847–48.

7. Quoted in David Brody, *Workers in Industrial America* (New York: Oxford University Press, 1980), p. 62.

8. Quoted in Melvyn P. Leffler, "Expansionist Impulses and Domestic Constraints, 1921–1932," in William H. Becker and Samuel F. Wells, Jr., eds., *Economics and World Power: An Assessment of American Diplomacy Since 1789* (New York: Columbia University Press, 1984), p. 247.

9. Mira Wilkins, *The Maturing of Multinational Enterprise: American Business Abroad from 1914 to 1970* (Cambridge: Harvard University Press, 1974), pp. 89–91 and passim.

10. George Soule, *Prosperity Decade, From War to Depression: 1917–1929* (New York: Rinehart, 1947), p. 264.

11. J. Bradford De Long and Andrei Shleifer, "The Stock Market Bubble of 1929: Evidence from Closed-end Mutual Funds," *Journal of Economic History,* 51 (1991), p. 697.

12. Charles Holt, "Who Benefited from the Prosperity of the Twenties?" *Explorations in Economic History,* 14 (1977), p. 283.

Suggested Readings

George Soule, *Prosperity Decade: From War to Depression: 1917–1929* (New York: Rinehart, 1947) is still the most comprehensive account of the economic history of the 1920s. Able surveys of the general history of the decade are contained in William E. Leuchtenberg, *The Perils of Prosperity, 1914–1933* (Chicago: University of Chicago Press, 1955) and Ellis W. Hawley, *The Great War and the Search for a Modern Order* (New York: St. Martin's Press, 1979). Two works by Thomas C. Cochran, *American Business in the Twentieth Century* (Cambridge: Harvard University Press, 1972) and *200 Years of American Business* (New York: Basic Books, 1977) are excellent general studies containing information on this period. For specialized and still useful reports written at the end of the decade, see the essays in President's Committee on Economic Trends, *Recent Economic Changes in the United States* (New York: McGraw-Hill, 1929) and President's Research Committee on Social Trends, *Recent Social Trends in the United States* (New York: McGraw-Hill, 1933).

Developments in individual industries or major corporations are discussed in the following: John B. Rae, *The American Automobile Industry* (Boston: Twayne Publishers, 1984); John B. Rae, *The Road and the Car in American Life* (Cambridge: MIT Press, 1971); James Flink, *The Car Culture* (Cambridge: MIT Press, 1975); Allan Nevins and Frank Hill, *Ford: Expansion and Challenge, 1915–1933* (New York: Scribner's, 1957); Michael J. French, *The U.S. Tire Industry* (Boston: G. K. Hall, 1990); Graham D. Taylor and Patricia E. Sudnik, *DuPont and the International Chemical Industry* (Boston: Twayne Publishers, 1984); Harold F. Williamson et al., *The American Petroleum Industry: The Age of Energy, 1899–1959* (Evanston: Northwestern University Press, 1963); George David Smith, *From Monopoly to Competition: The Transformations of Alcoa, 1888–1986* (New York: Cambridge University Press, 1988); Albro Martin, *Railroads Triumphant: The Growth, Rejection, and Rebirth of a Vital American Force* (New York: Oxford University Press, 1992); Ari Hoogenboom and Olive Hoogenboom, *A History of the ICC: From Panacea to Palliative* (New York: W. W. Norton, 1976); Donald M. Itzkoff, *Off the Track: The Decline of the Intercity Passenger Train in the United States* (Westport, Conn.: Greenwood Press,

1985); Maury Klein, *Union Pacific: The Rebirth, 1894–1969* (New York: Doubleday, 1989); John B. Rae, *Climb to Greatness: The American Aircraft Industry, 1920–1960* (Cambridge: MIT Press, 1968); and Warren James Belasco, *Americans on the Road: From Autocamp to Motel, 1910–1945* (Cambridge: MIT Press, 1979). David C. Mowery and Nathan Rosenberg, *Technology and the Pursuit of Economic Growth* (New York: Cambridge University Press, 1989) analyzes the role of research and development in economic growth; specific developments in this area are studied in David A. Hounshell and John Kenly Smith, Jr., *Science and Corporate Strategy: DuPont R & D, 1902–1980* (New York: Cambridge University Press, 1988), and Margaret B. W. Graham and Bettye H. Pruitt, *R & D for Industry: A Century of Technical Innovation at Alcoa* (New York: Cambridge University Press, 1990).

Mass marketing is covered in the following works: Daniel Horowitz, *The Morality of Spending: Attitudes Toward the Consumer Society in America, 1875–1940* (Baltimore: Johns Hopkins University Press, 1985); Daniel Pope, *The Making of Modern Advertising* (New York: Basic Books, 1983); Roland Marchand, *Advertising the American Dream: Making Way for Modernity, 1920–1940* (Berkeley: University of California Press, 1985); and Richard S. Tedlow, *New and Improved: the Story of Mass Marketing in America* (New York: Basic Books, 1990). Martha L. Olney, *Buy Now, Pay Later: Advertising, Credit, and Consumer Durables in the 1920s* (Chapel Hill: University of North Carolina Press, 1991) analyzes the "consumer durable goods revolution" that took place in the decade; but for another view, see Harold G. Vatter, "Has There Been a Twentieth-Century Consumer Durables Revolution?" *Journal of Economic History,* 27 (1967). Harold Barger, *Distribution's Place in the American Economy Since 1869* (Princeton: Princeton University Press, 1955) puts developments into long-run historical perspective.

Ralph L. Nelson, *Merger Movements in American Industry 1895–1956* (Princeton: Princeton University Press, 1959) is a valuable analysis of trends. For changes in the organization of decision making in large corporations, the following works by Alfred D. Chandler, Jr. are essential: *Strategy and Structure: Chapters in the History of the Industrial Enterprise* (Cambridge: M.I.T. Press, 1962), *The Visible Hand: The Managerial Revolution in American Business* (Cambridge: Harvard University Press, 1977), and *Scale and Scope: The Dynamics of Industrial Capitalism* (Cambridge: Harvard University Press, 1990). Mansel G. Blackford, *A History of Small Business in America* (New York: Twayne Publishers, 1991) surveys developments in that sector of the business system. Louis Galambos, *Competition and Cooperation: The Emergence of a National Trade Association* (Baltimore: Johns Hopkins University Press, 1966) is a solid case study of one industry. Ellis W. Hawley, "Herbert Hoover, the Commerce Secretariat, and the Vision of an 'Associative State,' " *Journal of American History,* 61 (1974) focuses on government-business relations. Morrell Heald, *The Social Responsibilities of Business: Company and Community, 1900–1960* (Cleveland: Press of Case Western Reserve University, 1970) provides an account of organized corporate philanthropy, while Richard S. Tedlow, *Keeping the Corporate Image: Public Relations and Business, 1900–1950* (Greenwich, Conn.: JAI Press, 1979) surveys the evolution of public relations as a business function.

Useful works on labor during the 1920s include Irving Bernstein, *The Lean Years* (New York: Houghton Mifflin, 1960); David Brody, *Workers in Industrial America: Essays on the Twentieth Century* (New York: Oxford University Press, 1980); Daniel Nelson, "The Company Union Movement, 1900–1937: A Reexamination," *Business History Review,* 46 (1982); Philip Taft, *The A.F. of L. in the Time of Gompers* (New York: Harper & Row, 1957); and Philip Taft, *The A.F. of L. from the Death of Gompers to Taft-Hartley* (New York: Harper & Row, 1959). James R. Green, *The World of the Worker* (New York: Hill & Wang, 1980), and Robert H. Zieger, *American*

Workers, American Unions, 1920–1985 (Baltimore: Johns Hopkins University Press, 1986) are recent assessments of the history of American labor. On agriculture, two useful surveys of long-run development in the sector are Murray R. Benedict, *Farm Policies of the United States, 1790–1950* (New York: Twentieth Century Fund, 1953) and John T. Schlebecker, *Whereby We Thrive: A History of American Farming, 1607–1972* (Ames: Iowa State University Press, 1975). Harold Barger and H. H. Landsbert, *American Agriculture, 1899–1939: A Study of Output, Employment, and Productivity* (New York: National Bureau of Economic Research, 1942) is an important statistical analysis. John L. Shover, *First Majority, Last Minority: The Transformation of Rural Life in America* (DeKalb, Ill.: Northern Illinois University Press, 1976) discusses changes in farming in twentieth-century America, while Robert C. Williams, *Fordson, Farmall, and Poppin' Johnny: A History of the Farm Tractor and Its Impact on America* (Urbana: University of Illinois Press, 1987) deals with the effects of mechanization.

Melvyn P. Leffler, "Expansionist Impulses and Domestic Constraints, 1921–1932," in William H. Becker and Samuel F. Wells, Jr., eds., *Economics and World Power: An Assessment of American Diplomacy Since 1789* (New York: Columbia University Press, 1984) surveys the evolution of foreign economic policy during the decade. Joan Hoff Wilson, *American Business and Foreign Policy, 1920–1933* (Lexington: University Press of Kentucky, 1971) is also useful. Mira Wilkins, *The Maturing of Multinational Enterprise: American Business Abroad from 1914 to 1970* (Cambridge: Harvard University Press, 1974) is the authority on corporate foreign investment. Sidney Ratner, *The Tariff in American History* (New York: Van Nostrand, 1972) surveys well that subject. William Ashworth, *A Short History of the International Economy since 1850* (London: Longman, 1975) puts American developments into global perspective.

The rise and fall of the stock market are the subject of two well-written books: J. K. Galbraith, *The Great Crash* (Boston: Houghton Mifflin, 1954) and Robert Sobel, *The Great Bull Market: Wall Street in the 1920s* (New York: W. W. Norton, 1968). Vincent Carosso, *Investment Banking in America: A History* (Cambridge: Harvard University Press, 1970) includes a discussion of practices in the industry during the 1920s. For an analysis of special aspects of stock-market performance during the boom, see J. Bradford De Long and Andrei Shleifer, "The Stock Market Bubble of 1929: Evidence from Closed-end Mutual Funds," *Journal of Economic History*, 51 (1991) and Alexander J. Field, "A New Interpretation of the Onset of the Great Depression," *Journal of Economic History*, 44 (1984). Valuable analyses of the distribution of income and wealth are contained in Jeffrey Williamson and Peter Lindert, *American Inequality: A Macroeconomic History* (New York: Academic Press, 1981), and Charles Holt, "Who Benefited from the Prosperity of the 1920s?" *Explorations in Economic History*, 14 (1977).

Chapter 19

The Great Depression and the Expanding Role of Government

THE SEVERITY OF THE SHIFT FROM THE HIGH PROSperity of the 1920s to the deep depression of the 1930s was unprecedented in American history. The economic downturn was an extremely steep one, and the economy continued to perform at a low level for a decade. Business and political decision makers, lacking a full understanding of the reasons for the decline, offered a variety of prescriptions to cure the nation's economic ills. There is still no consensus among historians as to the causes of the Great Depression. However, the results of it are clear. With the goals of creating greater stability for the economy and more security for members of society, the scope of federal government control of economic activity became much larger and more complex than ever before. Government became a permanent and powerful participant in economic decision making across a wide range of activities.

Table 19–1 *Real Gross National Product, 1929–1941, Total and Per Capita (in 1958 prices)*

Year	Total GNP (in $ billions)	GNP per Capita (in dollars)
1929	$203.6	$1,671
1930	183.5	1,490
1931	169.3	1,364
1932	144.2	1,154
1933	141.5	1,126
1934	154.3	1,220
1935	169.5	1,331
1936	193.0	1,506
1937	203.2	1,576
1938	192.9	1,484
1939	209.4	1,598
1940	227.2	1,720
1941	263.7	1,977

SOURCE: Data from U.S. Bureau of the Census, *Historical Statistics of the United States: Colonial Times to 1970* (Washington, D.C.: GPO, 1975), p. 224.

A Downward Spiral of Economic Activity

In just three years—from 1929 to 1932—a whole decade of economic growth was wiped out, as real gross national product dropped by almost one-third, back to the level of the early 1920s (see Table 19–1). Personal income declined by 45 percent, while industrial production was cut almost in half (see Tables 19–2 and 19–3). Private building construction, the largest form of capital investment, declined by 1932 to just one-sixth of the 1929 level. State and local government construction also dropped sharply. Overall, real gross investment declined by a sickening 98 percent between 1929 and 1932. Unemployment increased rapidly. By 1932, about one-fourth of the U.S. labor force was totally unemployed (see Table 19–4). Since many employers encouraged workers to share jobs, the labor hours worked in 1932 were 40 percent below those in 1929. Business failures rose by 39 per-

Table 19–2 *Personal Income, 1929–1941 (in current prices)*

Year	Personal Income (in $ billions)
1929	$85.9
1930	77.0
1931	65.9
1932	50.2
1933	47.0
1934	54.0
1935	60.4
1936	68.6
1937	74.1
1938	68.3
1939	72.8
1940	78.3
1941	96.0

SOURCE: Data from U.S. Bureau of the Census, *Historical Statistics of the United States: Colonial Times to 1970* (Washington, D.C.: GPO, 1975), p. 224.

Table 19–3 *Index of Manufacturing Production (Federal Reserve Board), 1929–1941*

Year	Index 1967 = 100
1929	23
1930	19
1931	15
1932	12
1933	14
1934	15
1935	18
1936	22
1937	23
1938	18
1939	22
1940	25
1941	32

SOURCE: Data from U.S. Bureau of the Census, *Historical Statistics of the United States: Colonial Times to 1970* (Washington, D.C.: GPO, 1975), p. 667.

Table 19–4 *Unemployment in the United States, 1929–1941*

Year	Number of Unemployed (in thousands)	Percent of Civilian Labor Force
1929	1,550	3.2%
1930	4,340	8.7
1931	8,020	15.9
1932	12,060	23.6
1933	12,830	24.9
1934	11,340	21.7
1935	10,610	20.1
1936	9,030	16.9
1937	7,700	14.3
1938	10,390	19.0
1939	9,480	17.2
1940	8,120	14.6
1941	5,560	9.9

SOURCE: Data from U.S. Bureau of the Census, *Historical Statistics of the United States: Colonial Times to 1970* (Washington, D.C.: GPO, 1975), p. 135.

cent between 1929 and 1932, with many of the surviving firms just barely hanging on. The impact of unemployment was especially devastating on communities that were dependent for most of their jobs on one company that failed.

Consumption declined drastically, as even those who held on to their jobs feared layoffs. Households could defer the purchase of consumer durable goods such as automobiles and appliances, which had become such an important part of the consumption pattern in the 1920s. In addition, to avoid repossession of durable goods purchased earlier on installment credit, households often cut back on their consumption of nondurable goods.

Crisis in the Financial System

Contributing mightily to the economic catastrophe was the collapse of the nation's financial structure. The Federal Reserve System had contributed to the crash of the stock market. It also played a large role in making the Depression as severe as it was.

After the crash on Wall Street, there followed a year or so of contraction of both money and prices. While matters were not yet out of hand, the Fed did next to nothing to reverse these developments. The monetary base was allowed to decline somewhat in 1930. The Fed's inactivity in this period seems to have followed from its interpreting declining market interest rates as a sign of monetary ease, even though the supply of money was falling. During the first year of the Depression, economic and psychological factors reduced the demand for money; rather than let the supply of money decline in response to these factors (in line with the perverse notion of elastic currency), the Fed should have maintained or increased the money supply and eased credit costs in the process. Such a policy decision might have mitigated or even reversed the initial economic decline.

Instead, the money and banking situation turned from bad to worse. In the fall of 1930 began the first of three great waves of bank failures that culminated in the proclamation of the nationwide bank "holiday" by President Franklin Delano Roosevelt in March 1933, when all U.S. banks were ordered closed for about a week. Although bank failures had been frequent during the 1920s, there were major differences between these failures and the failures of 1930 to 1933. Many more banks failed per year during the latter period and, more important, unlike the failures of the 1920s, the 1930s failures were accompanied by sizable declines in the money supply. The number of bank suspensions during the early 1930s was as follows: 1930 — 1,350; 1931 — 2,293; 1932 — 1,453; and 1933 — 4,000. Not all suspending banks failed, but the majority never reopened.

The bank failures of the early 1930s played a major role in causing the Depression to become "Great" because they caused much of the severe monetary contraction. These failures had this effect primarily because of their impact on the behavior of the nation's banks and the American public. Witnessing other banks failing, remaining banks became very cautious in their lending policies and attempted to hold more reserves per dollar of their deposit liabilities. The ratio of deposits to reserves at commercial banks fell from over thirteen in 1929 to less than eight in 1933. Even more severe were the effects of bank failures on the nonbank public. Americans held more than $11 of commercial bank deposits per dollar of coins and paper currency in 1929; by 1933, reflecting the growing distrust of banks, this proportion had fallen to about $5.

The nation's money supply, as measured by M_1, declined by over one-quarter between 1929 and 1933. The sharp drop in the price level that accompanied this contraction increased the real burden of debt and may have encouraged households and businesses to de-

fer purchases in the belief that prices would continue to fall even further.

The Fed might have prevented, or at least counteracted, these contractive effects of bank and public behavior on the money supply through sufficient increases in the monetary base of currency and bank reserves, but it did not. In short, the Fed did not do in the 1930s what it had been designed to do in 1913, namely, to prevent banking panics and failures by making the monetary base elastic in times of incipient banking panic. Why the Fed failed to discharge this duty is far from clear. Some scholars argue that the Fed's attention was focused on international considerations such as the U.S. gold position; this might explain why the Fed acted to tighten credit conditions in late 1931, in the midst of the Depression, when gold began to leave the United States due to European fears about maintenance of the international gold standard. If so, the Fed's priorities were misdirected. Others argue that the Fed did not move to stem bank failures because it thought they were attributable to bank mismanagement (as, for example, in the form of questionable loans both at home and abroad during the economic euphoria of the 1920s). To a certain extent, some banks may have been mismanaged. But during the deflation of the early 1930s, even the soundest bank loans could become questionable since lenders and borrowers could not have fully anticipated the drop in prices, production, and demand that occurred. Thus, it must be concluded that the Fed was negligent in allowing the Depression to become as severe as it did.

Anti-Depression Policies of the Hoover Administration

President Herbert Hoover did more than any previous chief executive to alleviate Depression conditions, but neither the prevailing economic beliefs nor his own personal outlook al-

Hunger Marchers in Washington, D.C., January 1932.   So desperate were conditions in early 1932 that 10,000 unemployed men demonstrated at the national Capitol. (Springer/The Bettmann Archive)

lowed him to take sufficient action to turn the situation around. Hoover believed strongly in voluntary cooperation. He urged business to maintain current levels of wages and employment, though few firms could do so for long in view of the continuing decline. Hoover advocated an increase of federal expenditures on public works, but not of such a magnitude as to offset the sharp decline in construction spending by state and local governments and private business. In 1931, Congress raised tariffs significantly in the Hawley-Smoot Act in a misguided effort to "protect" American producers. This action brought reprisals from foreign nations and thereby contributed to a decline in U.S. exports.

A major turning point in government policy was the creation of the Reconstruction Finance Corporation (RFC) in 1932. Never before had the federal government assumed any responsibility for relieving the conditions caused by an economic depression. Fearing that the top layer of the business community might be swept away, taking the rest of the system with it, Congress authorized the RFC—a government agency with $500 million of public funds—to make loans to large corporations such as banks, insurance companies, and railroads. Later in the same year, Congress gave the RFC power to lend funds to state governments for the relief of the unemployed—another important first in American history.

After three years of deficits unwillingly incurred because of the sharp drop in the revenue base, President Hoover and most other political leaders (of both major parties) concluded that a balanced budget was necessary to restore business confidence, regarded as the key to economic recovery. To achieve this goal, the Republican administration and Democratic Congress agreed on a significant rise in personal and corporate income taxes, which had the effect of draining money out of the economy even though revenues still proved to be insufficient to balance expenditures.

Roosevelt's New Deal

Despite the economic plight of the country in 1932, the battle for the presidency was essentially an election without issues. The Democratic party's nominee, Governor Franklin D. Roosevelt of New York, lacked major plans for curing the nation's economic ills, and he attacked incumbent Republican Hoover for not balancing the budget. The Democrats won in a landslide, following an old American tradition of pinning the blame for economic hard times on the incumbent party. Once in office, the Roosevelt administration proposed a *New Deal* entailing action along a broad front to start a stalled economy and to provide a greater measure of security and protection for the population. To a people in despair, the new president proclaimed in March 1933: "The only thing we have to fear is fear itself."

Relief Programs

Relief of the unemployed was the most pressing problem confronting the new administration in March 1933. With a quarter of the labor force out of work, state and local governments and private charities (the traditional dispensers of relief) were running out of resources. A newly established Federal Emergency Relief Administration, headed by former social worker Harry Hopkins, was authorized to make grants—not loans—to the states for distribution to the needy.

With continuing large-scale unemployment, Hopkins organized in 1935 a large-scale jobs program—the Works Progress Administration (WPA)—which employed at its peak more than three million persons and over six years a total of over eight million different individuals (one-fifth of all the workers in the country). While Hopkins created imaginative programs to make work for scholars, artists, and actors, the largest part of the $11.4 billion spent on WPA projects between 1935 and 1941 provided work on roads and parks for the unskilled with little schooling, a group that comprised a disproportionate share of the long-term unemployed in the 1930s. Although WPA jobs generally paid less than work in the private sector, they provided a measure of stability and security of employment for participants.

During these years, the Public Works Administration, directed by Secretary of the Interior Harold Ickes, created jobs on larger projects like schools, bridges, hospitals, and post offices. A still different approach to job creation was the establishment of the Tennessee Valley Authority in 1935. It was a comprehensive program of regional development in one of the poorest sections of the country, with a special focus on the generation of electric power, flood control, and navigation (see Figure 19–1). Other programs cared for the special needs of young people. The Civilian Conservation Corps employed as many as 500,000 young men on reforestation, soil erosion, flood control, and similar projects under the direction of army officers. The National Youth Administration provided funds for part-time jobs that enabled young people to stay in college or high school, accomplishing the twin goals of increasing the nation's stock of human capital and encouraging the participants to delay their entry into the labor market.

With the downturn of economic activity, the business failure rate rose dramatically, contributing further to the growing rolls of the unemployed. To stem the tide, the RFC, established

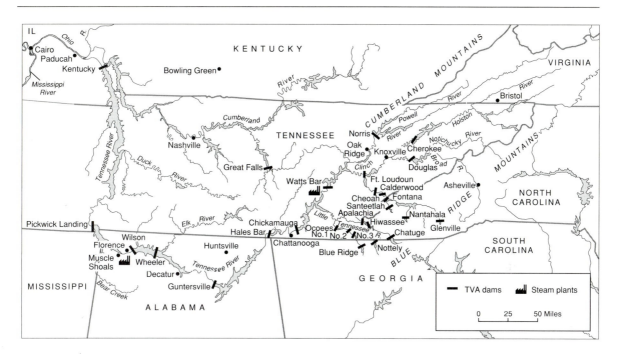

Figure 19–1 *The Tennessee Valley Authority, 1933–1945*
SOURCE: Adapted from *American Heritage Pictorial Atlas of the United States* (New York: American Heritage Publishing Co., 1966).

in 1932 primarily to salvage large corporations, was authorized to make loans to small businesses, including both new entrants and established firms. Another category of the population needing relief comprised homeowners threatened by mortgage foreclosures. To deal with the problem, Congress created the Home Owners Loan Corporation with government capital to refinance nonfarm home mortgage debts.

An Effort to Stimulate Industrial Recovery

While relief was being dispensed to the needy, the New Deal was also seeking ways to counteract the deflationary forces that had caused the collapse of profitability and private investment as well as purchasing power and effective demand. With orthodox policies discredited by the economic events that had taken place between 1929 and 1933, what characterized the Roosevelt administration was its willingness to proceed by trial and error to find ways to promote recovery, even if that meant adopting sometimes contradictory policies.

To the president and his advisers, a reflation of the price level was a principal objective of an expansionist recovery policy. Believing that a devaluation of the dollar in terms of gold would result in a general rise in the internal price level, Roosevelt set the value of the dollar at 59 percent of its former worth. Although this action, without theoretical underpinning, was condemned by conservatives as economic destruction, it was a sign that the New Deal was determined to pursue unorthodox policies to achieve a rise in prices and thus a rise in the level of economic activity.

The National Recovery Administration

The cornerstone of the early New Deal's recovery effort was the National Industrial Recovery Act of 1933, to be administered by the National Recovery Administration (NRA), a government agency with broad powers to regulate the whole American business system. Viewing the Depression as an emergency like war, business and political leaders as well as academics looked back to the precedent of World War I. If a partnership of government and organized business, with the cooperation of organized labor, could plan industrial production for a massive war effort, such a partnership could surely plan a swift revival of industrial production from the depths of Depression. The antitrust laws were suspended so that business firms in each industry, usually working through a trade association, could agree on a code of "fair competition." The codes, when approved by the NRA, typically set minimum prices and/or production quotas, minimum wage rates, and maximum hours of labor. (Labor's right to collective bargaining, guaranteed under section 7A of the law, is discussed later in the chapter.) It was assumed that a reasonable profit to industry would encourage a resumption of business investment, while an increased wage for workers would expand the purchasing power necessary to absorb the products of industry. Businesses that assented to codes could display the emblem of the "Blue Eagle," which assured the public that such firms were patriotic fighters in the war against the Depression. The enemy's major supporter was the "chiseller" who cut prices.

Most decision makers professed to see the logic of this plan to raise prices and wages as a means of reversing the spiral of deflation.

However, disillusionment quickly set in. Small businesses complained that the codes favored the larger firms in an industry, while workers maintained that code authorities often did not live up to the labor provisions. Conflicts among government officials prevented agreement on a master plan of recovery through which the many codes of individual industries could be coordinated. When the Supreme Court declared the National Industrial Recovery Act unconstitutional in May 1935, less than two years after it began operations, most business owners and executives as well as government administrators were not displeased to see the experiment terminated.

However, the NRA had supplied a certain amount of psychological stimulus in helping to get the country past the sense of impending doom that had been prevalent in 1933. Gross national product and industrial production advanced by 28 percent between 1933 and 1935, though these gains could be attributed more to the purchasing power generated by government spending on New Deal relief and public works programs than to the NRA codes. The basic problem was the contradiction built into the program. What was needed to stimulate economic recovery was an expansion of production, not the imposition of cartel-like restrictions to reduce output. It was unlikely that new investment would be made in any industry in which production was restricted by law, however high prices might rise.

In the Aftermath of the NRA

The demise of the NRA did not mean the abandonment of efforts by business to use the power of government to develop a program of market controls. However, instead of attempting to achieve a major reorganization of the whole business system, attention now shifted to the special problems of individual industries or sectors of the economy to justify a departure from competitive standards.

The NRA codes brought some relief to industries that had been depressed even in the generally prosperous decade of the 1920s. With the end of the NRA, leaders of some of these industries tried to secure special legislation to deal with the problems stemming from overcapacity and intense competition for a declining market. For bituminous coal, the Guffey-Vinson Act (1937) created a commission to set minimum prices and marketing rules. However, disagreement among coal producers as well as protests by coal users limited the progress that was made toward stability in that industry. Firms in the cotton textile industry, particularly those in New England, proposed a variety of measures to stabilize prices, including the formation of pooling agreements, the establishment of individual quotas, schemes to finance the scrapping of what was regarded as surplus equipment, the limitation of imports, and export subsidies. The United Textile Workers advocated the development of labor standards for the industry as well as controls to prevent overproduction. Mill owners were solidly opposed to public supervision of their labor practices. Neither they nor their union possessed sufficient political clout to secure favorable legislation. Conditions in the 1930s only served to accelerate the shift of the cotton textile industry away from New England and toward the South.

A greater measure of success in achieving stabilization was attained by the petroleum industry. The nature of oil property ownership encouraged each producer in a field to draw as much oil as possible, resulting not only in waste but overproduction as well. Declining demand for petroleum products after 1929, combined with the discovery of vast new fields of oil, put great pressure on prices, stimulating leaders of the petroleum industry to seek government regulation of production. To support its quest for political machinery in order to achieve private goals, the petroleum industry appealed to the American tradition of conservation of natural resources. State prorationing laws limited the total amount of oil produced

to what could be sold at a profitable price and allocated production among oil fields. The U.S. Bureau of Mines, working in cooperation with the American Petroleum Institute, provided the statistics for determining market demand. The Interstate Oil Compact of 1935 enabled agencies of the oil-producing states to work together, and the Connally Act of the same year prohibited the shipment in interstate commerce of oil produced in violation of state laws. This system, based on the cooperation of federal and state governments with private business, remained a basic element in the decision-making structure of the petroleum industry for many decades.

Small enterprises in retail trade constituted another segment of the American business system that appealed to American tradition—not only to preserve a way of life but also to support the use of government power to preserve its competitive position. The Robinson-Patman Act (1936), by prohibiting a seller from discriminating as to price among various customers who bought for resale, was designed to ensure that small retailers could purchase their stocks of goods as cheaply as the large chain stores. So-called fair-trade laws were passed by many states, enabling manufacturers of branded goods to fix the retail prices of their products through agreements with retailers. (A contract stipulating the price made with just one retailer in a state was made binding on all other sellers in that state.) With the Miller-Tydings Act (1937), Congress exempted such agreements from the federal antitrust laws. Independent retailers benefited, as did large manufacturers, who gained countervailing power in dealing with chain stores and other large retailers.

New Deal Farm Programs

Despite the private and public efforts made in the 1920s to deal with the problems of the

Dr. New Deal. The New Deal proposed a variety of remedies to cure the ills of the Great Depression. A willingness to experiment characterized the approach of the Roosevelt Administration in seeking solutions for economic problems. (Historical Pictures/Stock Montage)

The Hope of Us All. This drawing conveys the critical shift in the 1930s by a majority of Americans from "free enterprise" to a mixed economy of government planning and private enterprise. (Historical Pictures/Stock Montage)

agricultural sector, the plight of the farmer worsened with the downward spiral of economic activity after 1929. Between 1929 and 1932, the realized gross income of farm operators fell 54 percent. Because the cost of production did not decrease proportionately, the net income of farmers fell nearly 70 percent. The situation was caused in large part by a sharp decline in domestic and foreign demand for farm products, while total farm output held steady and then in 1931 and 1932 increased slightly above the 1929 level. Moreover, the farm problem was intensified by changes in the farm population; declining by almost 1.4 million between 1920 and 1929, the number of farmers grew by more than 1 million between 1929 and 1933. Paradoxically, instead of people leaving agriculture as farm prices declined, they stayed, and other people migrated from the city back to the farm, impelled by the scarcity of employment opportunities in urban occupations.

With such great distress in agriculture, Franklin D. Roosevelt and the Democrats won the support of a large majority of farmers in the 1932 election. The New Dealers then launched a bold, innovative program for recovery in agriculture. Given the apparent failure of the farmers' previous reliance on the competitive market system and commodity cooperatives, federal decision makers chose to replace highly competitive commodity markets with a cartel form of organization in agriculture. In the same way that the National Industrial Recovery Act sought to promote the recovery of industry by raising prices, reductions in production and price fixing were perceived as the preferred means of bringing higher income to farmers. The approach, focusing on farm prices as the main objective of farm policy, reflected pressures from an agricultural hierarchy dominated by prosperous farmers—the American Farm

Bureau—and various agricultural economists concerned more with the efficiency of large-scale farming than with the welfare of small farmers, tenant farmers, and farm workers.

The first major New Deal farm legislation was the Agricultural Adjustment Act (AAA) of 12 May 1933. The measure aimed at a drastic reduction in the production of certain basic farm commodities, especially corn, wheat, cotton, tobacco, and hogs. Cash payments to producers participating in the program were funded by new taxes imposed on the sale of these products to processors. The Commodity Credit Corporation (CCC) was established to keep products temporarily off the market when necessary. The program ended, however, in January 1936, when the Supreme Court ruled that the act was unconstitutional.

To replace the AAA, Congress took swift action by passing the Soil Conservation and Domestic Allotment Act (1936). The new law attempted to reduce the production of future surplus crops through payments to farmers from federal funds for improved land use and conservation practices. Whereas the 1933 AAA had tried to restore prices to the level prevailing during "agriculture's golden age" (1909 to 1914), the 1936 legislation had as its goal *income parity*—the ratio of purchasing power of the net income per person on farms to that of the income per person not on farms that had prevailed during the period from August 1909 to July 1914.

The decline in farm prices that followed large crops in 1937 soon brought pressure for a new farm program. The Agricultural Adjustment Act of 1938 authorized comprehensive supply-adjustment programs for each of the major crops. Provisions were made for (1) mandatory price-support loans at 52 percent to 75 percent of parity on corn, wheat, and cotton; (2) necessary marketing quotas that were geared to acreage allotments on tobacco, corn, wheat, cotton, and rice; and (3) permissive supports for other commodities.

Although subsequently amended in various ways, the 1938 act established the basic framework for all the major farm programs since that time. The Commodity Credit Corporation continued under the act as the principal price-supporting agency of the government. When it could not support prices through loans or purchase agreements, the agency bought farm commodities outright and disposed of them in ways that would not disrupt the farm price levels. Between 1937 and 1941, the CCC accumulated 10 million bales of cotton, 419 million bushels of wheat, and 403 million bushels of corn.

Economic and Social Effects

To evaluate the New Deal's agricultural programs in a balanced way is difficult. A statistical analysis shows that both farm income and farm prices rose markedly from the low levels of 1932. By 1937, the net income of persons on farms from farming (including the wages paid to farm workers living on farms) had increased more than two-and-one-half times.

In the 1937 to 1938 recession, net farm income fell from the 1937 level, but it was still twice as high as the 1932 low. A substantial part of the improvement in farm net income came from the general rise of national income, which in turn increased the demands for farm products. Another favorable influence on prices came from the recurrent and severe droughts of the mid-1930s, which had the effect of reducing the production of some farm commodities. In addition, farmers benefited from subsidy payments granted to them for their reductions in acreage of certain major crops through what were called CCC nonrecourse loans to farmers, representing the difference between the current market prices and the parity prices set by the government.

The acreage-reduction program of the 1933 AAA, however, did not lead in general to a reduction in the production of the major farm products. Moreover, the 1933 price supports

Destitute Southern Sharecropper Family, 1930s.   Photographers working for federal government agencies in the 1930s helped to bring to national attention the eviscerating poverty that the southern sharecropping system imposed upon its participants, both black and white. (The Bettmann Archive)

encouraged farmers to devote their resources to certain products, irrespective of current demand and varying rates of technological improvements in different areas of agriculture. The AAA of 1938 improved on the 1933 statute by introducing the principle of the ever-normal granary. The application of this principle by the CCC led to the accumulation of large stocks of wheat, corn, cotton, and tobacco, which later were sold at a profit when the United States became involved in World War II. If it had not been for the war, the CCC's action would have been criticized for establishing minimum prices that falsely inflated farmers' price expectations.

The New Deal contributed much to agriculture in terms of improved efficiency. The use of machines was encouraged. Measures were de-veloped for reducing soil erosion. Farmers were taught methods of contour plowing and dry farming. Programs were set up for conservation and land rehabilitation.

However, New Deal price supports and production controls encouraged American agriculture to overproduce as well as overvalue farm resources. Owing to a rise in land values based on the expectation of profits due to government programs, the use of land for farming increased during the period, though farm employment decreased by 1.5 million. At the same time, farmers increased their investment in most types of durables and expendables. The controls that might be considered justifiable temporary measures produced situations that were economically questionable in the long run.

The New Deal in agriculture was least successful from the human point of view. The 1933 AAA did not benefit tenant farmers, especially Southern share-croppers, most of whom were African-Americans and many of whom were evicted by their landlords. Instead, the major benefits of the act went to wealthy farmers because the subsidies were based on the size of the farm (the larger the farm, the higher the subsidy). The New Deal led to a heavy labor outflow from agriculture into manufacturing and the service industries and into the cities. Many who could not find employment swelled the ranks of those on relief. Although farm wage rates increased, they did not rise as much as nonfarm wage rates.

Pressure politics, as exerted by the farm bloc, probably had more to do with directing the course of agricultural policy in the 1930s than did economics. A major source of difficulty for the agricultural sector was the slow expansion of industrial production in the 1930s, just one-half of the rate of growth in the 1920s. The limited expansion of domestic markets for agricultural commodities, along with the deterioration of foreign markets, appeared to many decision makers as the primary causes of the farm problem that New Deal planners found so formidable until the needs of World War II provided a solution.

The Impact of the Depression on the Transportation Sector

Competing Modes of Transportation

The Great Depression exacerbated the problems of the railroads, long the most important single element in the nation's transportation system. With the declining level of economic activity in the 1930s, rail revenues declined drastically. Loans from the Reconstruction Finance Corporation did not prevent the operators of one-third of the nation's railroad mileage from going into bankruptcy and receivership by 1937. Most of the receiverships were eliminated through the financial reorganization of the railroads in the late 1930s.

As the economy improved, the railroads had to face increasing competition from trucks, buses, airplanes, water carriers, and pipelines. Thus, the railroads began to shrink in the 1930s, in absolute as well as relative terms. First, mainline track in operation declined from an all-time peak of 260,570 miles in 1929 to 245,740 miles in 1940. Freight ton-miles dropped during these years as well—from 450.2 million to 375.4 million. Passenger miles decreased from 31.2 million to 23.8 million.

Although motor freighting suffered some setbacks in the extremely depressed years of the early 1930s, the trucking industry resumed the steady growth that it had experienced in the 1920s. Indeed, the low capital requirements for buying a second-hand truck attracted many unemployed Americans into the industry.

The number of registered trucks in the United States increased from 3.5 million in 1929 to 4.9 million in 1940. By the latter year, motor trucks were hauling 9.5 percent of the total domestic intercity freight traffic, compared to 63.7 percent for the railroads. Several factors accounted for the increase. First, there was the economic advantage of trucks against railroads for short hauls and small shipments. Second, motor trucks offered certain services that the railroads could not match, such as relatively flexible schedules and complete door-to-door service. Third, trucking rates could be made lower than railroad rates because the required plant investment was proportionately far less than that of the railroads and because the costs of going over the highways (despite user charges and gasoline taxes) was less than the costs of constructing and maintaining railbeds and rail track. Improved vehicles and better highways enabled trucks increasingly to push into long-haul traffic. Finally, the Interstate Commerce Commission functioned to protect the motor trucking industry from railroad competition.

In competition with the railroads, motor buses shared many of the advantages held by motor trucks. The number of registered buses almost tripled between 1929 and 1940 — from 34,000 to 101,000. The Depression benefited bus operators in that they could offer budget-minded commuters and travelers a lower fare.

In passenger travel, however, the greatest gains were made by the private automobile. After declining slightly in the worst years of the early 1930s, passenger-car registrations resumed their upward course. By 1940, they stood at 19 percent above the level of 1929. Not even the Depression could do more than delay America's embrace of the car culture, as the 128.6 million automobiles sold in the five years between 1936 and 1940 exceeded the 101.4 million sold between 1925 and 1929. Miles of travel by private automobiles in the second half of the 1930s exceeded by almost 75 percent the level of the second half of the 1920s.

Although air transport began with the first controlled flight by the Wright brothers in 1903, it emerged as a commercial enterprise only after World War I. The war stimulated aircraft development and trained some ten thousand men to fly; many of them became the entrepreneurial reserve for the airlines founded in the late 1920s and early 1930s. The first regular commercial passenger air service was established between Florida and Cuba in 1920, the first domestic scheduled passenger service in 1925, and the first domestic freight service in 1925.

A series of government decisions favorable to private enterprise contributed to the takeoff of commercial aviation. In 1925, Congress authorized the Post Office to begin contracting with commercial airlines on the basis of competitive bids, a move that stimulated the development of commercial aviation since the carriers were required to transport passengers as well as mail. Another advance occurred

when the government assumed responsibility for aids to navigation, safety regulations, and the development of the airways. These were achieved through the Air Commerce Act of 1926, which established what is today the Federal Aviation Agency (FAA), now in the Department of Transportation.

Encouraged by a sharp drop in fares as well as the increased speed of travel, revenue passenger miles flown in domestic airline operations increased from just 85 million miles in 1930 to 1052 billion miles in 1940, an astonishing rise of twelve times. Increased air travel by the public was encouraged not only by lower fares but also by marked improvements in comfort, speed, and safety during the course of the decade.

Government Regulation of Transportation

From the beginning of government regulation of railroads, agencies focused on the rates that carriers charged (usually so as to preclude monopoly profits) as well as on the quality and safety of the services they provided. Federal and state railway commissions also controlled entry into the industry, financial practices, and accounting methods.

In 1920, Congress directed the Interstate Commerce Commission (ICC) to set railway rates at a level that would permit the railroads to earn an average return of 5.5 percent; this was regarded as a fair return on the value of their properties. When the objective was not achieved, however, Congress in 1933 directed the ICC to consider the effect of rates on the movement of traffic. In other words, it called for returns that would enable the railroads to attract new capital. Congress thus recognized that in the competition with other modes of transport, the desired level of earnings in rail transport might best be obtained by lowering, rather than raising, rates.

The entry of many small operators into motor trucking in the early 1930s resulted in severe competition and instability of rates, with repercussions not only on the larger trucking firms but also on the railroads. As a result, the large trucking firms, seeking to reduce the intense competition, pressured a majority of the states to institute some form of control over common and contract carriers. Dissatisfaction with the workings of the NRA code for the industry induced Congress in 1935 to pass the Motor Carrier Act. It gave the ICC the powers to (1) control maximum and minimum rates for common carriers and minimum rates for contract carriers and (2) set the conditions for entry into the industry.

The Motor Carrier Act of 1935 and the Transportation Act of 1940 made the ICC the regulator of both the railroads and their competitors—the trucks, buses, and inland water carriers—even though motor transport did not have the monopolistic characteristics of railroads. The ICC allowed both railroads and trucks to share in most of the traffic. Keeping truck and rail rates close to parity meant that the lower-cost carrier was not able to reduce rates to obtain all the traffic for which it had a cost advantage. As a result, each form of transportation carried traffic for which its competitor had a cost advantage. But since trucking, unlike the railroad, could provide flexible door-to-door service, a policy of rate equality encouraged the growth of trucking at the expense of the railroads. Since the railroad rate structure was based on the principle that the higher the value or selling price of a commodity, the higher the rate, trucks tended to take over the high-valued commodities, whereas the low-valued ones continued to be carried by the railroads.

The policy resulted in the continual decline of the railroads after a temporary revival during World War II. It also had important effects on the postwar structure of the motor trucking industry. Adoption by the trucking industry (with the encouragement of the ICC) of a "value of service" rate structure similar to that of the railroads provided an incentive to shippers to avoid the higher rates on high-valued commodities by using their own trucks. Consequently, private trucking experienced an enormous expansion after World War II, not because it was inherently more economical but because of the special transportation pricing system that the common-carrier segment of the trucking industry had adopted.

Other transportation policy was embodied in the Civil Aeronautics Act of 1938. This statute established what was later known as the Civil Aeronautics Board (CAB) with the power to regulate the conditions of routes, fares, and entry and exit in the air-transport industry; it also created a regulatory shelter for established carriers.

One result of the legislation enacted in 1938 and earlier years was a division of activities: government ownership and operation of the airways and private ownership and operation of the commercial airlines, subject to control by the CAB. Another result was the way these acts promoted the economic progress of commercial aviation in several directions along lines discussed earlier in the chapter. There is no doubt that the CAB attempted to build up the air-transport industry by favoring rates and subsidies that enabled most of the companies to survive and prosper. Despite the progress of the commercial airlines, however, economists some decades later criticized both Congress and the CAB for various inadequacies: Congress erred in presuming that the air-transport industry needed the type of control developed for rail carriers in a monopolistic industry, while at the same time stressing the need for competition and the prevention of monopoly. It appeared that the CAB could not decide conclusively for many years whether air transport should be controlled as a monopoly or treated as a competitive industry.

Reform of the Financial Sector

No other sector of the economy seemed to be in greater need of major reform than the nation's financial system; it was nearing total collapse when the New Deal took office. The bank holiday proclaimed by President Roosevelt in March 1933 brought to a halt the panic that threatened to drain banks of their resources and leave communities without the financial facilities needed to transact business. The Emergency Banking Act (1933) then authorized the RFC to provide financial aid to sound commercial banks by purchasing their preferred stock and other securities.

More important in the long term were the basic changes embodied in the Banking Acts of 1933 and 1935. One fundamental development was the establishment of deposit insurance, a long overdue reform still strongly opposed by most bankers. All member banks of the Federal Reserve System were required to join the newly created Federal Deposit Insurance Corporation (FDIC), which insured the deposits of a single depositor up to a maximum of $2500 (subsequently raised many times, up to $100,000 by the 1980s). Thus, the law removed the possibility of the kind of bank runs that had occurred when depositors became fearful about the safety of their deposits. Few of the innovations in governmental economic policy induced by the Great Depression had a more lasting and generally beneficial impact on economic stability than the FDIC.

Changes in the Federal Reserve System

Another lasting change affecting the performance of the commercial banking system was the centralization and extension of the powers of the Federal Reserve System. The Federal Reserve Board became the Board of Governors, and all of its members were appointed by the president. (The two ex officio members—the treasurer and the controller of the currency—were removed from the governing body.) The president chose the chairperson of the Board of Governors but could not remove the chair at will. The appointment of the operating head of a district Reserve Bank, whose title was

changed from governor to president, was subject to the approval of the Board of Governors. From that time on, control of the policies of the Federal Reserve System rested with the Board of Governors in Washington, D.C. Congress gave the board control of the system's main policy tool—*open-market operations,* or the purchase and sale of government securities. The Federal Open Market Committee, which determined policy, consisted of the seven members of the Board of Governors plus five of the twelve district bank presidents, always including the president of the Federal Reserve Bank of New York because of its strategic position in American finance. The Fed also received a new power—the ability to vary reserve requirements within limits established by the law. Changing reserve requirements affected the amount of reserves available to support new bank lending and so could have a pronounced impact on the money supply and credit conditions.

Because changes in reserve requirements had such pervasive impacts on all member banks, they were changed infrequently and then only by small amounts. Rediscounting was important in the early years of the Fed, but because it relied on member banks rather than the Fed to play the active role, rediscounting declined in importance after the 1930s. As a result, open-market operations, chiefly in the market for U.S. government securities, became the primary method of Federal Reserve control over money and credit. Out of the debacles of the 1930s emerged a more fully centralized central banking institution in the United States. It was more responsive to Washington than to New York or other regional centers of economic power, and it possessed a complete set of central banking tools with which it could influence the course of economic events.

Regulation of the Securities Industry

For Wall Street, the catastrophic drop in stock values after 1929 was more than enough to cause embarrassment. However, a congressional probe of securities markets—the Gray-Pecora investigation—disclosed the extent of abuses and excesses committed on Wall Street during the boom and subsequent collapse of the stock market. It turned out that even some of the most respected securities firms had abused the trust of investors.

Sweeping legislation provided the federal government with new powers over this part of the financial sector, conferring wide supervisory authority to a new government agency called the Securities and Exchange Commission (SEC). To be the chief police officer of Wall Street as the first chairman of the SEC, President Roosevelt appointed the wealthy financier Joseph P. Kennedy, perhaps because, as one member of the administration commented, he knew all the tricks of the trade. Federal law now prescribed and strictly defined the standards of disclosure for issuers and underwriters of securities offered to the public. Under the provisions of the Public Utility Holding Company Act of 1935, the SEC was assigned the responsibility of supervising the break-up of the pyramided holding companies that controlled many of the electric-generating companies across the country. Investigations had concluded that many of these holding companies had been formed in the 1920s primarily for promotional and manipulative purposes. The Glass-Steagall Act (also known as the Banking Act of 1933) decreed a separation of commercial and investment banking, the result of disclosures that the participation of commercial banks in the underwriting of securities, through their security affiliates, had contributed to the weaknesses of the financial system.

The Revival of Antitrust

The Great Depression and the measures of the New Deal seemed to do little to alter the overall structure of the business system. There were relatively few mergers in the 1930s as compared with the 1920s. The share of the top 5 percent of corporate income receivers in total corporate income stood at the same level (84 percent) in 1939 as in 1929, while the share of the smallest 75 percent declined only slightly from 3.97 percent to 3.4 percent.

Over these years, though, the approach of the Roosevelt administration toward business regulation did change markedly. The early New Deal believed that a productive partnership of business and government was essential to economic recovery. As noted earlier in the chapter, the National Industrial Recovery Act suspended the operation of the antitrust laws to allow business to form cartels with the goals of reducing competition in order to raise prices. By the late 1930s, many New Dealers were arguing that the monopolistic practices of big business contributed to high prices, which reduced consumer purchasing power, thereby preventing full recovery of the economy.

In 1938, President Roosevelt called for the creation of the Temporary National Economic Committee (TNEC), charged with the task of studying the concentration of economic power and its effect on the decline of competition. The committee held extensive hearings and published the results of its investigations in over forty monographs and eighty volumes of testimony. The final report was somewhat critical of large corporations, but it made no specific recommendations. The mountain of facts accumulated by the TNEC served to demonstrate the complexity of the problem and did not lead to any magic formula by which the nation's economic ills could be cured to the satisfaction of all factions.

More important for the long-term evolution of government-business relations was the revival of vigorous antitrust enforcement, marked by the appointment in 1938 of Thurman Arnold as head of the Antitrust Division in the Department of Justice. Arnold's philosophical emphasis was on using the antitrust laws to supervise the behavior of business in order to protect consumers and increase consumer purchasing power rather than breaking up otherwise efficient large corporations. He compared the role of the Antitrust Division to that of a traffic officer—to publicize the rules of the road and make arrests for their deterrent effect, understanding that the objective of the exercise was to facilitate the movement of traffic.

Arnold launched prosecutions against a myriad of corporations whose practices, the government contended, imposed restrictions that interfered with the working of a freely competitive market. Major victories included the Paramount case, which divorced motion picture production from exhibition, and the Pullman case, which separated the manufacture of sleeping cars from their operation. Most important of all the cases filed by Arnold was that involving the Aluminum Company of America (resolved in 1945). The court held that Alcoa, because it controlled practically all the output of newly refined aluminum (90 percent), violated the antitrust laws. For the first time, the court used market structure rather than overt market behavior as a test of legality.

The Labor Force in the Depression Years

The population of the United States increased by only 7.2 percent from 1930 to 1940—a rate of growth less than one-half that of the previous decade and the lowest by far in American history. The birthrate dropped sharply, as Depression conditions encouraged Americans to defer marriage and have fewer children. The death rate continued its decline from the 1920s, with an especially marked reduction in infant and child mortality. As a result of the continuing high unemployment in the United States, the 1930s marked the only decade in American history that more foreign-born people departed from the country than entered it.

Growth of the labor force in the 1930s— 14.3 percent—was somewhat less than in earlier

Table 19–5 *Major Occupational Groups, Civilian Labor Force, 1930 and 1940*

Occupation	Thousands of Persons, Age 14 and Older		Change, 1930–1940
	1930	1940	
White-collar	14,320	16,082	+12.3%
Manual/service	24,044	26,666	+10.9
Farm	10,321	8,995	−12.8

SOURCE: Data from U.S. Bureau of the Census, *Historical Statistics of the United States: Colonial Times to 1970* (Washington, D.C.: GPO, 1975), pp. 139–140

decades, though most of the trends that had been changing its composition remained in force. Workers in agriculture, despite an escape-to-the-land movement in the early years of the Depression, declined between 1930 and 1940. Gainful workers in manufacturing increased slightly, both absolutely and relatively, while the service sector recorded significant gains.

The number of white-collar employees grew in the 1930s at only about one-third the rate of the 1920s and only slightly higher than that of manual and service workers. (See Table 19–5). Yet the educational level of the labor force continued to improve. High school graduates almost doubled in number between 1930 and 1940, with nearly one-half of the age-seventeen segment of the population receiving a high school diploma by the end of the decade. Numbers of college graduates increased by almost 50 percent during the decade, with 81 per 1000 population of age twenty-three receiving a bachelor's degree in 1940.

Depression conditions slowed but did not reverse the trend toward a higher female labor participation rate (see Table 19–6). A major form of discrimination hindering the economic progress of women was the marriage bar—a practice used by employers to prohibit the hiring of married women and the retention of female employees when they married. The mar-

Table 19–6 *Percentage of Women in the Labor Force, 1930 and 1940*

	1930	1940
Female labor force participation rate		
All women	24.8%	25.8%
Married women	11.7	13.8
Single women	50.5	45.5
White women	23.7	24.5
Nonwhite women	43.3	37.6
Women as proportion of total labor force	22.1%	24.3%
Proportion of women in labor force employed in white-collar occupations	44.2	44.9
Women as proportion of white collar labor force	33.2	35.1

SOURCE: Data from Claudia Goldin, *Understanding the Gender Gap: An Economic History of American Women* (New York: Oxford University Press, 1990), p. 17; and U.S. Bureau of the Census, *Historical Statistics of the United States: Colonial Times to 1970* (Washington, D.C.: GPO, 1975), pp. 139–40.

riage bar had been introduced in teaching and clerical work—occupations with large numbers of women—in the late nineteenth and early twentieth centuries. The perception that jobs had to be rationed in an environment of high unemployment in the 1930s served as a rationale to reinforce the imposition of the marriage bar, making it a strict policy where it had previously been discretionary and extending it into more occupations and employment sectors. School districts, insurance companies, publishing firms, banks, public utilities, and government on the federal, state, and local levels were among the leading practitioners of the marriage bar. According to calculations made by Claudia Goldin, the marriage bar at its height on the eve of World War II was the policy of 87 percent of all school districts in the country and more than 50 percent of all offices.[1] Denial of jobs to married women seemed to have widespread public approval,

reflected in pollster George Gallup's comment that he had never seen people "so solidly united in opposition as on any subject imaginable including sin and hay fever."[2] The New Deal did little to close the gender gap in earnings. Many industries even incorporated the traditional sex differentials into their NRA codes.

A scarcity of jobs stimulated an escalation of racism as well as sexism in the labor market of the 1930s. Estimates indicate that nationally, black unemployment rates substantially exceeded those of whites. For example, a survey of eighty-three cities, made in the winter of 1935 to 1936, revealed that about one-third of all African-American heads of households were unemployed, a rate double that of whites. This was due in part to a concentration of blacks in unskilled occupations and in industries (like construction) that experienced higher than average levels of unemployment. But the racial unemployment gap also resulted from discriminatory employment policies applied to African-Americans, as employers often replaced black workers, even those who were equally qualified, with unemployed whites. The National Urban League reported: "So general is this practice that one is warranted in suspecting that it has been adopted as a method of relieving unemployment of whites without regard to the consequences upon Negroes."[3]

Government policies also seemed to work sometimes to the detriment of members of the black work force. The NRA was called by some African-American leaders the "Negro Removal Act" because the upward pressure on wage rates contained in NRA codes resulted in the introduction of mechanization, which eliminated many of the unskilled jobs held by blacks. (For example, the percentage of jobs in tobacco manufacturing held by black workers declined from 68 percent in 1930 to 55 percent in 1940.)

In southern agriculture, African-Americans bore much of the burden of the massive changes that took place in the 1930s. The process of agricultural change, especially in cotton production, created a large stock of unskilled labor, largely black, with no longer a place in the southern economy. This development prepared the way for a new and expanded stage in the "great migration" of African-Americans from the rural South to the urban North in the 1940s and 1950s.

Unemployment in the Great Depression

Never before in American history had large-scale unemployment persisted for so long as in the 1930s. For ten years, from 1931 to 1940, the unemployment rate remained above 14 percent (see Table 19–4). Then too, the burden of unemployment fell most heavily on unskilled workers instead of being shared fairly evenly among most segments of the blue-collar work force, as in earlier hard times. Finally, many able-bodied individuals, perhaps one-tenth of the labor force, experienced long durations of unemployment—again a new phenomenon.

In spite of a high rate of unemployment, real wages for those who were employed held fairly steady during the economic downturn from 1929 to 1933 and then increased steadily with the growth of the economy after 1933. As shown in Table 19–7, annual money earnings declined by slightly over 25 percent from 1929 to 1933–34, but the sharp drop in the price level during these years meant that real earnings decreased by only 4 percent. Then from 1934 to 1941, real annual earnings for those employed advanced by almost 28 percent.

The combination of steady or rising real wages for those with jobs, and high aggregate unemployment, seems to run contrary to the expectation that employers would take advantage of the existence of a large army of job seekers to reduce wages. However, recent research suggests that it was not necessarily in the interest of business to cut wage rates to reduce costs. With the need to adjust to declin-

Table 19–7 *Average Annual Earnings of Employees, 1929–1941*

| | When Employed | |
Year	Money Earnings	Real Earnings (in 1914 dollars)
1929	$1,425	$ 834
1930	1,388	834
1931	1,298	857
1932	1,141	838
1933	1,045	811
1934	1,066	800
1935	1,115	816
1936	1,146	830
1937	1,259	880
1938	1,221	868
1939	1,266	915
1940	1,315	943
1941	1,492	1,018

SOURCE: Data from U.S. Bureau of the Census, *Historical Statistics of the United States: Colonial Times to 1970* (Washington, D.C.: GPO, 1975), p. 164.

ing sales and product prices, many employers realized that wage reductions across the board would hurt worker morale and lead to loss of their best workers. Instead, they cut costs by laying off their least productive workers, primarily the unskilled. (Some corporations assigned foremen and skilled workers to unskilled work, just to keep them on the payroll for a future rebound of business.) Employees who were retained often worked even harder to prove their worth. However, what employers were doing was to apply a concept developed by a number of large corporations in the 1920s—that the optimal wage was an "efficiency wage." According to this concept, the higher wages that were paid to efficient workers normally improved productivity in the plant and office and thus contributed to increased profits. Personnel departments were assigned the responsibility of developing procedures to identify efficient workers—those with the appropriate skills, learning ability, and willingness to work diligently.

With efficiency still an important factor when the economy began to recover after 1933, corporate personnel departments again carefully screened job applicants to identify the most productive workers. Those who did not meet the test—primarily the unskilled with little formal schooling—came to form a hard core of long-term unemployed. It was toward this segment of the labor force that the New Deal directed its jobs programs like WPA and CCC. However, these programs did little to upgrade the skills of the unskilled, primarily due to union opposition. Evidence indicates that many WPA workers made little effort to search for private-sector jobs, believing that such a quest would prove to be fruitless. As one WPA worker explained: "My advice, Buddy, is better not take too much of a chance. Know a good thing when you got it."[4] The problem of hard-core, long-term unemployment disappeared only when the needs of World War II provided a massive and persistent demand for labor and thus encouraged employers to hire and train the unskilled, resulting in a decline in the unemployment rate from 14.6 percent in 1940 to 1.2 percent in 1944.

The Emergence of Big Labor

The onset of the Great Depression intensified the problems that organized labor had encountered in the 1920s. From 1929 to 1933, the membership of the American Federation of Labor (AFL), the leading union in the United States, declined by almost 15 percent (see Table 19–8). With 2.3 million members in 1933, the AFL represented no larger a percentage of the nonagricultural labor force than it had in the early years of the century. However, the New Deal opened the way for a tremendous surge in unionization by shifting the power balance in industrial relations in favor of organized labor. Equally important was the emergence of a

Table 19–8 *Labor Union Membership, 1929–1941 (in thousands)*

Year	Total	AFL	CIO	Other unions
1929	3,461	2,770		691
1930	3,416	2,745		671
1931	3,379	2,743		636
1932	3,191	2,497		694
1933	3,048	2,318		730
1934	3,713	3,030		683
1935	3,753	3,218		535
1936	4,107	3,516		591
1937	5,780	3,180	1,991	609
1938	6,081	3,547	1,958	575
1939	6,556	3,878	1,838	840
1940	7,282	4,343	2,154	785
1941	8,698	5,179	2,654	865

SOURCE: Data from U.S. Bureau of the Census, *Historical Statistics of the United States: Colonial Times to 1970* (Washington, D.C.: GPO, 1975), p. 177.

new structure of union organization to take advantage of the changed political climate.

A New Legal Environment for Organized Labor

Even before the New Deal came on the scene, some of the legal restrictions on unions were removed. The Norris-LaGuardia Act (1932) forbade the use of injunctions to enforce yellow-dog contracts or to prevent strikes and picketing. Then, in the first days of the Roosevelt administration, Section 7A of the National Industrial Recovery Act required employers bound by codes to recognize unions and to bargain collectively. Unions affiliated with the AFL achieved a few successes. But most large corporations sought to comply with the law by expanding or forming company unions dominated by management. It is not surprising that some union leaders concluded that the NRA was, for them, the "National Run Around."

The National Labor Relations Act of 1935 (also called the Wagner Act) was truly the

"Magna Carta" of organized labor. The law not only proclaimed a guarantee of the right of workers to engage in collective bargaining with employers through a union of their own choice; it also defined what constituted unfair labor practices on the part of management and established effective enforcement machinery. No longer could company unions satisfy the requirements of federal law. The National Labor Relations Board (NLRB), appointed by the president, had the power to issue cease-and-desist orders enforceable through the federal courts. Under the new rules, the NLRB conducted secret elections in which workers determined the bargaining agent of their choice. Union organizers had free access to workers, while employers were hindered in their efforts to wage a campaign against the union. The union winning the election was required to represent all employees in the bargaining unit, but, in turn, all employees in the bargaining unit were compelled to join the union and pay dues. Most industrial states soon passed labor-relations laws modeled on the Wagner Act. Clearly, government was now on the side of organized labor, a nearly one-hundred-and-eighty-degree turn from previous eras.

Organizing Mass-Production Workers

To seize the opportunity afforded by the new politico-legal environment, John L. Lewis, president of the United Mine Workers, urged AFL leaders to launch industrial unions so as to organize all workers in the mass-production industries, where unskilled and semiskilled workers greatly outnumbered skilled workers. Most of the old-line craft unions, however, were reluctant to surrender their craft jurisdictions. Lewis nevertheless took the lead in 1935 in forming the Committee for Industrial Organization (CIO) to promote industrial unionism within the AFL. (The committee became the Congress of Industrial Organizations, separate from the AFL, in 1937.) The CIO proceeded to launch vigorous and well-financed organizing drives in the steel, automobile, rubber, and other mass-production industries. The sit-down strike, in which workers occupied their employer's plant, played a key role in achieving victory in the battle with General Motors—a major breakthrough in organizing the labor force of a leading corporation whose management was strongly dedicated to defeating unionism.

The combination of government support, the industrial union structure, and militant leadership resulted in the vigorous growth of the CIO in spite of a continuing high level of unemployment, which in earlier eras had reduced union membership. The success of the CIO in turn stimulated the AFL to charter its own industrial unions and develop a more vigorous approach to the organization of the unorganized. The greater abundance of job opportunities that resulted from increased government expenditures on defense at the end of the decade was the final ingredient that made mass unionism an integral part of the decision-making structure of large segments of the American economy. By 1941, total union membership stood at a level almost three times higher than that in 1933, with 5.2 million in the AFL and 2.7 million in the CIO. Within less than a decade, the American labor movement had moved from one of the weakest to one of the strongest in the industrialized world.

Establishment of minimum standards in the workplace was another way in which the federal government aided labor. Unlike earlier "protective" state laws that applied only to female workers, the Fair Labor Standards Act of 1938 prescribed minimum wages for men as well as women. The standard workweek was fixed at forty hours; employers who made their employees work longer were required to pay overtime for the hours over forty. Finally, the act effectively abolished child labor for all firms engaged in interstate commerce.

Security in an Industrial Society

An important innovation of the federal government in the 1930s was the development of programs to deal with some of the hazards of living and working in an industrial society. It is not difficult to understand why Americans became more concerned with income security at this time; unemployment was high and the wealth of many citizens had been greatly reduced by the economic disaster. Still, longer-term forces were at work. A century of economic development had changed the United States from an agricultural and commercial society to an industrial, highly mobile, and technologically oriented one with substantially higher incomes. In such a society, old-age security could not so easily be internalized within the family or community as it had been on the family farm. At the same time, improvements in health technologies combined with declining population growth were giving rise to relative increases in the ranks of the elderly. Indeed, most industrial nations some decades earlier had passed legislation giving individuals income security against such risks as old age and unemployment.

The Social Security Act

In 1934, President Roosevelt appointed the Committee on Economic Security, whose staff included the leading economic specialists in this field. In the meantime, political pressures were growing, as the costly Townshend Plan for paying all those over age sixty a monthly pension of $200 was gaining popularity among the elderly and their adult children, who might otherwise have to provide financial support for indigent parents.

Out of the work of the Committee on Economic Security and the deliberations of Congress came the Social Security Act of 1935. It created the Social Security Board as a permanent administrative agency; by mid-1941, this new government bureaucracy employed over twelve thousand people and operated nearly five hundred regional offices. Under the Social Security Act, the federal government assumed different kinds of responsibility for action in several areas of social welfare.

To deal with the problem of unemployment, the act established a program of social insurance. Unemployment compensation was to be administered by state governments, but it was financed by a federal tax on payrolls, with 90 percent of the revenues from this tax to go to states that established programs meeting federal standards. Framers of the law contemplated that the tax would pay those workers who were insured about half of their wages for a period of twelve weeks after a waiting period of four weeks. Under the original provisions, large segments of the labor force were excluded, including agriculture, domestic service, government, and educational institutions, as well as all who worked for small firms.

In the area of old age, the law established a social insurance program. Unlike unemployment compensation, old-age and survivors' insurance was provided directly to beneficiaries by the federal government, with no local or state involvement. Those over age sixty-five would receive an annuity financed by a tax levied in equal amounts on employers and employees. What gave the concept of old-age insurance broad support was its reliance on the "contributory-contractual" principle, which allowed people to perceive of Social Security as equivalent to a private insurance plan that they had purchased, not as a welfare payment. As a form of social insurance, entitlement to benefits was associated with prior employment rather than with need.

Federal funding was also provided on a regular basis for social-assistance programs administered by state governments. These were means-tested programs covering certain categories of the population, for which the federal government would make grants to match the amounts contributed by state governments. From the point of view of later history, the most important of these was the Mothers' Pension program, under which a small amount was given to destitute widows with young children, initiated by many state governments in the earlier part of the century. The program was expanded and renamed Aid for Dependent Children, or ADC. (The benefits paid under ADC and its successor programs would later stand at the center of the "welfare problem" in America from the 1960s into the 1990s.)

Performance of the American Economy

Recovery from the depths of the Great Depression was exceedingly rapid during the four years after 1933. In this recovery, the money supply, wholesale prices, and total output of the economy in real terms all increased at annual rates of between 10 percent and 12 percent. While unemployment was still distressingly high at over 14 percent of the labor force in 1937, the rate of unemployment had fallen by over 10 percent from the 1933 level. Then, in the second half of 1937, the economy plunged into deep recession, with almost all parts of the private economy suffering a decline and unemployment rising to 19 percent. Despite widespread discouragement, recovery quickly resumed, though nearly one-tenth of the labor force was still out of work during 1941.

Monetary Policy

The Federal Reserve Board was essentially passive during the recovery of 1933 to 1937. Increases in the money supply emanated from two other sources. One was the increase in the

U.S. gold stock, resulting in part from devaluation of the dollar in 1934 (which made the then-nationalized gold stock worth more dollars) and in part from gold imports between 1934 and 1937. When the Treasury Department purchased virtually all of the monetary gold held by Americans in 1933 and early 1934, and then purchased gold flowing in from abroad in 1934 to 1936, it did so in effect by printing the money and increasing the monetary base.

The other source of monetary growth was a rise in the proportion of the public's money holdings held in the form of bank deposits. When the public lost confidence—with good reason—in the banking system during 1929 to 1933, its ratio of deposits to currency fell sharply and accentuated the collapse of the money stock. But after the bank holiday of 1933, the ratio began to rise; it went from less than five in that year to more than seven by 1936. An important reason for the public's renewed confidence in bank money was federal insurance of bank deposits, initiated at the beginning of 1934.

The confidence of the nation's bankers, however, did not return so quickly after the debacle. Instead of creating more deposits per dollar of bank reserves held, after 1933 bankers continued to increase the ratio of reserves to deposits. In doing so, they conformed to a pattern characteristic of the aftermath of earlier banking panics. But the rise of bank reserves in relation to deposits continued until 1940, an uncharacteristically long time. In any case, by the mid-1930s, the Federal Reserve Board, noticing the recovery of prices and production, began to worry that the excess reserves of bankers carried a potential threat of runaway inflation. By this time, the Fed had acquired the power to vary the reserve requirements of member banks.

The Fed did not wait long to employ its new powers in attacking the source of its worry. Between August 1936 and May 1937, bank reserve requirements were doubled in three steps. The policy decisions in effect wiped out a large part of the banks' desired excess reserves; in an effort to rebuild them, the banks contracted their lending. As a result, the money supply contracted, prices fell, and unemployment rose—from 14 percent in 1937 to 19 percent in 1938. From that time forward, the Fed was more cautious in changing reserve requirements.

Federal Reserve Board monetary policy had been the primary method of economic stabilization used by government decision makers from 1914 into the early 1930s. The persistence of the Great Depression then caused many to doubt whether monetary policy could by itself give rise to an effective stabilization program. The view was exaggerated, but when it grew out of an examination of what the Fed had actually done, rather than what it might have and probably should have done, the view contained an element of validity. In any event, the Depression era marked the beginning of experimentation with other types of stabilization policies. Concentrated in the fiscal area, the policies consisted of varying governmental expenditures and taxation with a view to promoting stabilization goals. The framework of modern fiscal policies rested, in turn, on the foundation of a greatly enlarged share of government spending and revenues in the American economy.

A Keynesian Approach to Fiscal Policy

Fiscal policy may be defined as governmental decision making about the levels and types of public expenditures and taxes and, as a consequence, the balance of the government budget. Although economists and public officials were long aware that increased public spending had beneficial effects on employment and business conditions when and where the funds were expended, significant use of this insight to attack an economywide problem did not come until the Great Depression of the

1930s. Then it came in response to the magnitude of the disaster and was motivated by the seeming inability of Federal Reserve monetary policy to bring about the recovery of employment and production. It took the form of a host of federal spending programs that were part of President Roosevelt's New Deal program of relief and recovery.

At the same time that the New Deal was searching for fiscal solutions to unprecedented economic problems, a conceptual and theoretical rationale for its fiscal activities came forth from the eminent British economist John Maynard Keynes. Keynes's 1936 book, *The General Theory of Employment, Interest and Money,* demonstrated in theory that an economy could become stuck in an equilibrium of less-than-full employment and that attempts to raise employment through increases in the supply of money could prove ineffective if the new money was in some sense hoarded rather than spent. In the United States, the persistence of high levels of unemployment throughout the 1930s, as well as the tendency of banks to hold large excess reserves rather than engage in more lending, appeared to be explained by Keynes's theories. From a theoretical explanation of the fact of depression, Keynes proceeded to a theory of how it might be alleviated or even ended. The problem, as he saw it, was a level of spending or aggregate demand on the part of consumers, investors, and government that was insufficient to employ all of the economy's resources, and the solution was for government to eliminate the deficiency of demand by its own increased spending. The government budget would have to be deliberately unbalanced—that is, expenditures would have to exceed tax revenues—at least until resources were fully employed.

Keynes's novel ideas had a limited impact on U.S. fiscal policy in the 1930s. The New Deal spending measures before 1938 were based more on pragmatic experimentation than on a new conceptual framework of economic theory. But by the end of World War II, the idea that massive government budget deficits could end a depression and restore full employment appeared to have been demonstrated. The Keynesian framework of thinking was by then widely accepted, and economists and public decision makers were prepared to refine and adapt it to problems of maintaining economic stability.

New Deal Fiscal Practices

Despite large increases in both federal spending and federal budgetary deficits under the New Deal of the 1930s, recovery from the Depression was painfully slow. The strong expansion of 1933 to 1937 came to an end in the severe recession of 1937 to 1938. Hence, in 1939, the unemployment rate was still 17.2 percent of the labor force and the real GNP (adjusted for price level changes) was about the same as it had been a decade earlier despite increases in the population and labor force. Those who favored limited government and balanced budgets while distrusting both Roosevelt and Keynesian ideas pointed to this record in support of their view that deficit spending was ineffective or counterproductive or both. Supporters of the New Deal, however, argued that the deficit-spending policies had substantially improved the economic situation following the trough of the Depression in 1933 (see Figure 19–2).

We know today that both these views are open to correction. The budget deficits of the 1930s, both before and after the New Deal, were largely the result of the Depression rather than a means of recovery from it. The collapse of incomes during the early years of the Depression led to declining tax revenues for all levels of government taken together, and this revenue decline, more than expenditure increases, produced the deficits of those years. In response to the revenue fall-off, taxes at both the federal and state–local levels were ac-

tually increased during the Depression. Later, New Deal deficits tended mainly to offset the demand-reducing effects of this and other tax increases, so that the stimulating effects of government fiscal policies on the economy, while considerable up to 1937, were not as high as they could have been. When the Roosevelt administration sharply cut spending on public works and work relief in the second half of 1937 in an effort to balance the budget (at the same time that the Fed put on the monetary brakes), the economy suffered a severe recession, which was arrested only by a new public works program and increased military expenditures.

A useful way to evaluate the stimulus of fiscal policies, some economists argue, is to determine what they imply about the balance of the government budget at a full-employment level of national income rather than at actual existing levels. Since tax collections depend to a large extent on income, they tend to increase as the economy expands from lower income or output levels with unemployment toward higher levels of production consistent with full employment of resources. It was from this point of view that New Deal fiscal policies were deficient; the actual budget deficits of the 1930s, with unchanged levels of government spending, would have turned into substantially lower deficits or perhaps even surpluses had the economy been at or near full employment. In effect, American governments counteracted with increases in tax rates much but not all of what they were attempting to do with increased spending. This partly explains why recovery from the Great Depression was good from the contemporary point of view up to 1937 and in 1939 to 1940 but not adequate from the viewpoint of many present-day economists.

America and the World Economy

The worldwide economic downturn after 1929 brought to the surface the basic problem cre-

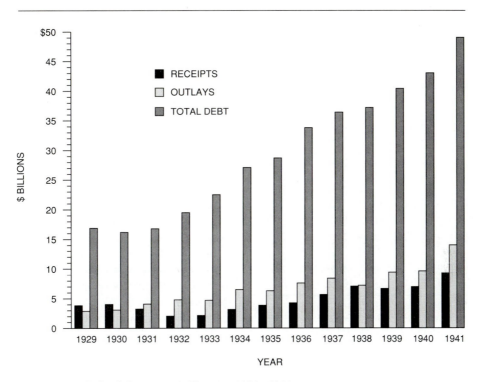

$ BILLIONS

- ■ RECEIPTS
- □ OUTLAYS
- ▨ TOTAL DEBT

YEAR

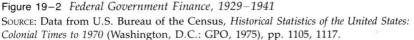

Figure 19–2 *Federal Government Finance, 1929–1941*
SOURCE: Data from U.S. Bureau of the Census, *Historical Statistics of the United States:
Colonial Times to 1970* (Washington, D.C.: GPO, 1975), pp. 1105, 1117.

ated by the inability of the United States to adjust to its emergence as the world's leading creditor nation. In this time of great adversity, there was no leadership to stabilize the international economic system. The leader of the pre-1914 era, Great Britain, was economically too weak, and the United States was unwilling to abandon its traditional policy of protectionism for domestic industry and agriculture and export surpluses. One of the authors of the Hawley-Smoot Act of 1931, which increased substantially the tariffs on American imports, proclaimed that the measure would bring prosperity back to the United States within a few months. Instead, it brought retaliation by other nations in the forms of tariffs, quotas,

debt defaults, and exchange controls, as political leaders everywhere desperately groped for solutions to their own economic problems.

Financial crises in Austria and Germany in 1931 prompted President Hoover to declare a moratorium on all intergovernmental debts from the war, which led by 1933 to the effective end of the tangle of reparations and war debt payments. The international gold standard, long the basis of a multilateral world trading system, crumbled after its abandonment by Great Britain in 1931 and by the United States in 1933. After the breakdown of the World Economic Conference in 1933, which had been organized by the League of Nations to restore monetary stability, the restoration of

Table 19-9 *Foreign Trade of the United States, 1929-1941*

Year	Merchandise Surplus (in $ millions)	Percent of GNP Exports	Percent of GNP Imports
1929	$ 842	5.0%	4.2%
1930	782	4.2	3.4
1931	334	3.2	2.7
1932	288	2.8	2.3
1933	225	3.0	2.6
1934	478	3.3	2.5
1935	235	3.1	2.8
1936	33	3.0	2.9
1937	265	3.7	3.4
1938	1,134	3.6	2.3
1939	859	3.5	2.5
1940	1,396	4.0	2.6
1941	1,802	4.1	2.7

SOURCE: Data from U.S. Bureau of the Census, *Historical Statistics of the United States: Colonial Times to 1970* (Washington, D.C.: GPO, 1975), pp. 884, 887.

Foreign Trade of the United States

Following swiftly on the heels of the stock-market crash was a sharp drop in the foreign trade of the United States (see Table 19-9). Reduced earnings from exports of raw materials led the less-developed countries to cut back on their imports of manufactured goods from developed countries. Protectionist policies that were implemented everywhere, along with the contraction of purchasing power, contributed to the downward spiral of world trade, as the value of international commerce (measured in gold dollars) declined by nearly 60 percent from 1929 to 1932. During these years, American foreign trade suffered an even-sharper contraction, with exports and imports falling by 69 percent.

To assist in the recovery of the depressed export industries, including agriculture, the Roosevelt administration launched a New Deal for foreign trade. While Roosevelt's decision to devalue the dollar was made primarily in the hope of boosting domestic prices, the action also gave a 40 percent bounty to American exports, thereby improving their position in world markets. Another device to open markets was to extend credits to foreign purchasers of American exports, a function of the Export-Import Bank, a government-owned corporation created in 1934.

The New Deal's cornerstone for foreign trade was the Reciprocal Trade Agreements Act of 1934, embodying concepts strongly urged by Secretary of State Cordell Hull. A basic assumption of Hull and other proponents of the measure was that foreign trade was a two-way process—that American exports could increase only if foreign buyers could sell their goods in the United States. This meant, in turn, the abandonment of the nation's high level of protectionism. Hull realized that a unilateral reduction of tariffs by the United States—the simplest way to stimulate international trade—was politically impossible. Thus, the Reciprocal Trade Agreements Act implemented a policy of bilateral bargaining with foreign countries. Under this act, the president could enter into agreements with individual countries to reduce by up to 50 percent tariffs on imports into the United States, in return for corresponding reductions in tariffs on American exports to that country. Incorporating the most-favored-nation principle, any reductions of duties were extended to all other countries, except those that discriminated

international economic cooperation to deal with the problems of the Great Depression was no longer politically possible. Through the decade of the 1930s, the international political situation steadily deteriorated with Japan's aggression in the Far East, Germany's rearmament for war, and Italy's invasion of Abyssinia. From the mid-1930s on, preparation for war and defense increasingly influenced the foreign economic policies of all of the Great Powers of the world.

against American trade. The act also included safeguards for domestic interests, including consultation, administrative hearings, and legal action.

During the five years between 1934 and the outbreak of war in Europe in 1939, the United States negotiated trade agreements with twenty countries. Half of these trade treaties were with Latin American nations, whose tropical or semitropical products were already dependent on the U.S. market. Although these treaties had a minor effect on trade, they formed a part of the Roosevelt administration's Good Neighbor policy toward this area of the world. An agreement with Canada in 1935 brought that country even closer economically to the United States by allowing free entry of forest products and other raw materials in return for reductions of Canadian duties on many U.S. manufactured goods. The outstanding success of the program was the conclusion of a treaty with Great Britain in 1938, a notable achievement on two scores: Britain's industrial exports were generally competitive with the products of American industry, and Britain was the largest potential market for U.S. farm products and other raw materials. Altogether, the trade treaties made reductions in over 1000 of the 3200 rates in the American tariff schedule, with almost one-half of these reductions amounting to 40 percent to 50 percent of the original rates established by Congress.

American foreign trade revived from the low levels reached during the depth of the Depression, with exports nearly doubling between 1932 and 1939 and imports rising by 72 percent. And the U.S. share of the value of world trade increased—from 9.9 percent in 1933 to 11.8 percent in 1937. But the value of the country's foreign trade was still well below pre-Depression levels. Not until after the outbreak of war in Europe did American exports approach the level of 1929, primarily due to increased shipments of military goods to Britain and other countries regarded as potential allies

of the United States. Furthermore, while exports increased more than did imports during the 1930s, the major gains were made in manufactured goods. The revival of American foreign commerce had done little to solve the problem of large agricultural surpluses. Even with a program of export subsidies for wheat and cotton introduced in 1938, the value of American farm exports in 1940 was lower than in any year since 1888.

The Hull program of reciprocal trade agreements did nothing to remedy the basic problem that had contributed so importantly to world economic problems—the incongruity between America's creditor position and large trade surpluses. In the 1920s, American foreign lending had offset this surplus, making it possible for foreigners to pay for purchases of U.S. goods. In the 1930s, foreign lending dried up almost completely. Thus, during the Depression decade, the American export surplus was paid for in gold, with the result that the United States by 1939 held 59 percent of the world's stock of monetary gold. The large American trade surplus and the drain of gold to the United States put pressure on debtor countries not only to transfer their purchases from the United States to other countries but also to develop methods of international trade that did not depend on the use of gold and foreign exchange.

The reciprocal trade agreement program was not without its limitations. Its success in dismantling trade barriers was far from complete. Furthermore, it is clear that the program, to the extent that it was adopted, was perceived by its proponents as in the national interest of the United States rather than a matter of altruism. Yet, Hull's policy of freer world trade clearly demonstrated that the goal of New Deal economic diplomacy was not a retreat to isolationism. As economic historian Charles Kindleberger observes, the Reciprocal Trade Agreements Act, passed "at the faint beginnings of recovery, remains a remarkable and unpredictable step reversing the direction of movement in the world's economy."[5]

Foreign Investment by the United States

The Depression brought to a halt the strong growth of direct investment by American multinational corporations. In 1933, for the first time since before the turn of the century, there was a net *inflow* for direct investment. And the net inflow continued through the rest of the decade. Between 1929 and 1940, the value of U.S. direct foreign investment declined from $7.5 billion to $7 billion, or by 7.3 percent.

The most severely affected overseas operations were those in mining. Governments of countries in Latin America increased taxes and imposed various cost-increasing regulations, such as limiting the number of alien employees, requiring the employment of native persons in managerial and technical positions, and mandating expanded fringe benefits. However, the basic problem for the mining companies was the low level of prices prevailing for copper, lead, zinc, nitrate, tin, and other commodities. U.S. corporations engaged in foreign agriculture faced similar problems.

In manufacturing, some American corporations retreated from overseas, but a greater number increased their foreign investments (although at a much slower pace than in the 1920s). The major incentive to market-oriented investment abroad in the 1930s was to vault the tariff barriers and other forms of protectionism implemented by nations around the world. The increase in U.S. investment was larger in Germany than in any other country, primarily because government regulations limited the outflow of funds, thereby forcing American corporations to reinvest their profits in that country.

In petroleum, the Mexican government in 1938 expropriated most of the foreign oil industry, including the property of leading U.S. corporations. (Despite political pressures applied by the oil companies, the Roosevelt administration declined to intervene on their behalf.) American corporations in 1939, as in 1929, had their principal foreign investments in crude oil production in the Western Hemisphere, notably in Venezuela, but they had expanded their stakes in the Middle East and Dutch East Indies. By the end of the decade, the modern structure of the international petroleum industry had taken shape: domination by the group which came to be called the "Seven Sisters": five American and two European corporations—Jersey Standard, Socony-Vacuum (later called Mobil), Gulf, Standard of California, Texaco, Royal Dutch Shell, and the Anglo-Iranian Oil Company (later called British Petroleum)—each a huge, integrated, multinational enterprise.

Summary

Never before in American history had there been an economic downturn so deep and so long lasting as the Great Depression of the 1930s. Without precedent to guide them, and in an atmosphere of crisis and collapse, the New Dealers used the powers of the federal government to experiment with a broad range of programs to deal with the problems of the Depression.

Emergency relief was dispensed to the unemployed, and jobs programs were created. Through the National Industrial Recovery Act for business and the Agricultural Adjustment Act for agriculture, the early New Dealers sought to promote economic recovery through restricting output and raising prices. Federal regulation was also applied to bring order to the new forms of transportation—motor trucking and aviation. The Federal Reserve System, as the nation's central bank, was given new powers, and its decision making with respect to monetary policy became more oriented to public control. Federal deposit insurance was introduced to prevent the bank runs that had contributed to the near collapse of the commercial banking system. With Wall Street in disgrace, federal regulation of the securities industry was imposed. Government policy, previously on the side of management in labor disputes, now favored unions. The circumstances of the Depression brought to the surface the problems of dealing with the hazards of an industrial society, resulting in social insurance programs for the elderly and unemployed. While the New Deal represented a "go-it-alone" approach toward dealing with the problems created by the Depression, the Reciprocal Trade Agreements program marked the beginning of a move away from America's traditional high tariff policy.

With the growth of reservations about the effectiveness of Federal Reserve monetary policy as an economic stabilizer, attention turned to fiscal policy. Recovery from the Depression, however slow, appeared to many New Dealers to be the result of large increases in federal spending and federal budgetary deficits.

The New Deal, in historical perspective, represented a decisive movement away from reliance on a traditional laissez-faire economy toward a mixed economy, with government involvement in economic stabilization, social security, and labor-management relations. Government now participated in many areas of economic decision making that were previously the exclusive prerogative of private business. Complete recovery from the Depression and full employment of the nation's economic and human resources came with the massive government expenditures of World War II (as we will see in Chapter 20).

Endnotes

1. Claudia Goldin, *Understanding the Gender Gap: An Economic History of American Women* (New York: Oxford University Press, 1990), pp. 162–64.
2. Quoted in Irving Bernstein, *A Caring Society: The New Deal, the Worker, and the Great Depression* (Boston: Houghton Mifflin, 1985), p. 291.
3. Quoted in William A. Sundstrom, "Last Hired, First Fired? Unemployment and Urban Black Workers During the Great Depression," *Journal of Economic History*, 52 (1992), p. 421.
4. Robert A. Margo, "The Microeconomics of Depression Unemployment," *Journal of Economic History*, 51 (1991); and Richard J. Jensen, "The Causes and Cures of Unemployment in the Great Depression," *Journal of Interdisciplinary History*, 19 (1989). The quotation is from Margo, p. 340.
5. Charles P. Kindleberger, *The World in Depression, 1929–1939* (London: Penguin, 1973), p. 237.

Suggested Readings

Few events in American history, except for war, have produced a larger volume of literature than the Great Depression of the 1930s. For excellent surveys of the economic events of the decade, see Broadus Mitchell, *Depression Decade: From New Era Through New Deal, 1929–1941* (New York: Rinehart, 1947) and Lester Chandler, *America's Greatest Depression: 1929–1941* (New York: Harper & Row, 1970). The following works place the American experience in the context of the world economy: Charles P. Kindleberger, *The World in Depression, 1929–1939* (Berkeley: University of California Press, 1973); Peter Temin, *Lessons from the Great Depression* (Cambridge: MIT Press, 1989); and H. W. Arndt, *The Economic Lessons of the Nineteen-Thirties* (Reprinted. London: Frank Cass & Company, 1963).

The policies of the Hoover Administration in dealing with the Depression are covered in Joan Hoff Wilson, *Herbert Hoover, Forgotten Progressive* (Boston: Little, Brown, 1975); the essays in Martin L. Fausold and George T. Mazuzam, eds., *The Hoover Presidency: A Reappraisal* (Albany: State University of New York Press, 1974); Albert U. Romasco, *The Poverty of Abundance: Hoover, the Nation, the Depression* (New York: Oxford University Press, 1965); William J. Barber, *From New Era to New Deal: Herbert Hoover, the Economists, and American Economic Policy, 1921–1933;* and James Olson, *Herbert Hoover and the Reconstruction Finance Corporation* (Ames: Iowa State University Press, 1977).

Good surveys of the politics as well as the economics of New Deal activities include William E. Leuchtenberg, *Franklin D. Roosevelt and the New Deal* (New York: Harper & Row, 1963); Arthur M. Schlesinger, Jr., *The Coming of the New Deal* (Boston: Houghton Mifflin, 1959); Albert U. Romasco, *The Politics of Recovery: Roosevelt's New Deal* (New York: Oxford University Press, 1983); and John A. Garraty, *The Great Depression: An Inquiry into the Causes, Course, and Consequences of the Worldwide Depression of the Nineteen-Thirties* (New York: Harcourt Brace Jovanovich, 1986).

Ellis W. Hawley, *The New Deal and the Problem of Monopoly: A Study in Economic Ambivalence* (Princeton: Princeton University Press, 1966); Sidney Fine, *The Automobile Under the Blue Eagle* (Ann Arbor: University of Michigan Press, 1963); and Robert F. Himmelberg, *The Origins of the National Recovery Administration: Business, Government, and the Trade Association Issue, 1921–1933* (New York: Fordham University Press, 1976) focus on business-government relations, especially the NRA. Michael A. Bernstein, *The Great Depression: Delayed Recovery and Economic Change in America, 1929–1939* (New York: Cambridge University Press, 1987) discusses the differing experiences of individual industries, while Timothy F. Bresnahan and Daniel M. G. Raff, "Intra-Industry Heterogeneity and the Great Depression: The American Motor Vehicles Industry, 1929–1935," *Journal of Economic History,* 51 (1991) analyzes the role of plant closures in adjustment to the Depression. Jesse H. Jones, *Fifty Billion Dollars: My Thirteen Years with RFC* (New York: Macmillan, 1951) is the tale of a participant. David Lynch, *The Concentration of Economic Power* (New York: Columbia University Press, 1946) provides a review of the work of the Temporary National Economic Committee.

Exploring various aspects of fiscal and monetary policy are Milton Friedman and Anna Jacobson Schwartz, *A Monetary History of the United States, 1867–1960* (Princeton: Princeton University Press, 1963); Lester V. Chandler, *American Monetary Policy, 1928–1941* (New York: Harper & Row, 1971); Peter Temin, *Did Monetary Forces Cause the Great Depression?* (New York: Norton, 1976); David C. Wheelock, *The*

Strategy and Consistency of Federal Reserve Monetary Policy, 1924–1933 (New York: Cambridge University Press, 1991); Susan Estabrook Kennedy, *The Banking Crisis of 1933* (Lexington: University Press of Kentucky, 1973); Herbert Stein, *The Fiscal Revolution in America* (Chicago: University of Chicago Press, 1969); Lewis H. Kimmel, *Federal Budget and Fiscal Policy, 1789–1958* (Washington: Brookings Institution, 1959); Robert M. Collins, *The Business Response to Keynes, 1929–1964* (New York: Columbia University Press, 1981); Robert Lekachman, *The Age of Keynes* (New York: Random House, 1966); Kenneth D. Roose, *The Economics of Recession and Revival* (New Haven: Yale University Press, 1954); E. Cary Brown, "Fiscal Policy in the Thirties: A Reappraisal," *American Economic Review,* 46 (1956); Larry Peppers, "Full Employment Surplus Analysis and Structural Change: The 1930's" *Explorations in Economic History,* 10 (1973); Gavin Wright, "The Political Economy of New Deal Spending: An Econometric Analysis," *Review of Economics and Statistics,* 56 (1974); and John Joseph Wallis, "The Birth of the Old Federalism: Financing the New Deal, 1932–1940," *Journal of Economic History,* 44 (1984).

Michael Parrish, *Securities Regulation and the New Deal* (New Haven: Yale University Press, 1970) and Vincent P. Carosso, *Investment Banking in America: A History* (Cambridge: Harvard University Press, 1970) deal with the causes and consequences of the regulation of Wall Street. Aspects of transportation and energy policies are discussed in Albro Martin, *Railroads Triumphant: The Growth, Rejection, and Rebirth of a Vital American Force* (New York: Oxford University Press, 1992); William R. Childs, *Trucking and the Public Interest: The Emergence of Federal Regulation, 1914–1940* (Knoxville: University of Tennessee Press, 1985); John G. Clark, *Energy and the Federal Government: Fossil Fuel Policies, 1900–1946* (Urbana: University of Illinois Press, 1987); and Thomas McCraw, *TVA and the Power Fight,*

1933–1939 (New York: Lippincott, 1971). Mansel Blackford, *A History of Small Business in America* (New York: Twayne Publishers, 1991) covers government policies dealing with this sector of the business system.

Various welfare policies are treated in Edward Berkowitz and Kim McQuaid, *Creating the Welfare State: The Political Economy of Twentieth Century Reform* (New York: Praeger, 1980); W. Andrew Achenbaum, *Social Security: Visions and Revisions* (New York: Cambridge University Press, 1986); James Patterson, *America's Struggle Against Poverty, 1900–1985* (Cambridge: Harvard University Press, 1986); Searle F. Charles, *Minister of Relief: Harry Hopkins and the Depression* (Syracuse: Syracuse University Press, 1963); Roy Lubove, *The Struggle for Social Security* (Cambridge: Harvard University Press, 1968); Michael B. Katz, *In the Shadow of the Poorhouse: A Social History of Welfare in America* (New York: Basic Books, 1986); and Daniel Nelson, *Unemployment Insurance: The American Experience, 1915–1935* (Madison: University of Wisconsin Press, 1969). William Mullins, *The Depression and the Urban West Coast, 1929–1933: Los Angeles, San Francisco, Seattle, and Portland* (Bloomington: Indiana University Press, 1991) is a useful regional study.

Claudia Goldin, *Understanding the Gender Gap: An Economic History of American Women* ((New York: Oxford University Press, 1990) analyzes the impact of the Depression on women in the labor force. William A. Sundstrom, "Last Hired, First Fired? Unemployment and Urban Black Workers During the Great Depression," *Journal of Economic History,* 52 (1992) and Raymond Wolters, *Negroes and the Great Depression: The Problem of Economic Recovery* (Westport, Conn.: Greenwood, 1970) examine the impact of the Depression on African-American workers. On unemployment, see John A. Garraty, *Unemployment in History: Economic Thought and Public Policy* (New York: Harper Row, 1978); Robert A. Margo, "The Microeconomics of Depression Unemployment," *Journal of Economic*

History, 51 (1991); Richard Jensen, "The Causes and Cures of Unemployment in the Great Depression," *Journal of Interdisciplinary History,* 19 (1989); and Michael Darby, "Three and a Half Million U.S. Employees Have Been Mislaid: Or an Explanation of Unemployment, 1934–41," *Journal of Political Economy,* 84 (1976).

Irving Bernstein, *Turbulent Years: A History of the American Worker, 1933–1941* (Boston: Houghton Mifflin, 1970), and the same author's *A Caring Society: The New Deal, the Worker, and the Great Depression* (Boston: Houghton Mifflin, 1985) are good surveys of labor history during the decade. The emergence of industrial unionism is traced in David Brody, *Workers in Industrial America: Essays on the Twentieth Century* (New York: Oxford University Press, 1980) and Walter Galenson, *The CIO Challenge to the AFL* (Cambridge: Harvard University Press, 1960). Harry A. Millis and Emily C. Brown, *From the Wagner Act to Taft-Hartley* (Chicago: University of Chicago Press, 1950), and Christopher Tomlins, *The State and the Unions: Labor Relations, Law, and the Organized Labor Movement in America, 1880–1960* (New York: Cambridge University Press, 1985) deal with the evolving legal framework for organized labor. Important biographical studies of labor leaders of the era include Melvin Dubofsky and Warren Van Tine, *John L. Lewis: A Biography* (New York: Quadrangle, 1979); John Barnard, *Walter Reuther and the Rise of the Auto Workers* (Boston: Little, Brown, 1983); and Matthew Josephson, *Sidney Hillman* (Garden City, N.Y.: Doubleday, 1952).

On changes in agriculture, see John T. Schlebecker, *Whereby We Thrive: A History of American Farming, 1607–1972* (Ames: Iowa State University Press, 1975); John L. Shover, *First Majority, Last Minority: The Transformation of Rural Life in America* (DeKalb, Ill.: Northern Illinois University Press, 1976); and Mark Friedberger, *Farm Families and Change in Twentieth-Century America* (Lexington: University Press of Kentucky,

1988). Gilbert C. Fite, *Cotton Fields No More: Southern Agriculture, 1865–1980* (Lexington: University Press of Kentucky, 1984); Pete Daniel, *Breaking the Land: The Transformation of Cotton, Tobacco, and Rice Cultures since 1880* (Champaign: University of Illinois Press, 1985), and Gavin Wright, *Old South, New South: Revolutions in the Southern Economy Since the Civil War* (New York: Basic Books, 1986), in different ways, deal with the major changes that occurred in southern agriculture in the 1930s. Theodore Saloutos, *The American Farmer and the New Deal* (Ames: Iowa State University Press, 1982) discusses the effects of the New Deal on agriculture, while Robert C. Williams, *Fordson, Farmall, and Poppin' Johnny: A History of the Farm Tractor and Its Impact on America* (Champaign: University of Illinois Press, 1987) and Sally Clarke, "New Deal Regulation and the Revolution in American Farm Productivity: A Case Study of the Diffusion of the Tractor in the Corn Belt, 1920–1940," *Journal of Economic History,* 51 (1991) focus on the adoption of the tractor by American farmers.

On America's role in the international arena, Robert M. Hathaway, "Economic Diplomacy in a Time of Crisis, 1933–1945," in William H. Becker and Samuel F. Wells, Jr., eds., *Economics and World Power: An Assessment of American Diplomacy Since 1789* (New York: Columbia University Press, 1984) provides a succinct statement. A good discussion of the reciprocal trade agreements is presented in Sidney Ratner, *The Tariff in American History* (New York: D. Van Nostrand, 1972). The following works deal with various aspects of foreign economic policy during the 1930s: Lloyd C. Gardner, *Economic Aspects of New Deal Diplomacy* (Madison: University of Wisconsin Press, 1964); Frederick C. Adams, *Economic Diplomacy: The Export-Import Bank and American Foreign Policy, 1934–1939* (Columbia: University of Missouri Press, 1976); Irvine H. Anderson, Jr., *The Standard-Vacuum Oil Company and United States*

East Asian Policy, 1933–1941 (Princeton: Princeton University Press, 1975); and Bryce Wood, *The Making of the Good Neighbor Policy* (New York: Columbia University Press, 1961). Mira Wilkins, *The Maturing of Multinational Enterprise: American Business Abroad from 1914 to 1970* (Cambridge: Harvard University Press, 1974) is the key work on American foreign corporate investment.

Chapter 20

The Planned Economy of World War II

TWO WORLD WARS, THE KOREAN WAR, AND THE Vietnam War have made many in America and elsewhere acutely aware of the tragic loss of life and use of material resources that war entails. Yet the study of past wars can have a positive value. The history of the United States in World War II, especially, shows us a nation combining all its forces to confront the seemingly invincible power of the Axis dictatorships. The American government and people courageously experimented with new political, economic, and military institutions, discarding false starts and devising new strategies. The successful wartime innovations in economic theory and practice provide the basis for understanding how new insights can help in conquering peacetime crises.

The World War II International Background

The American economic and political system was shaken to its depths by Germany's invasion of Poland in September 1939; its conquest of Western Europe from Norway to France between April 9 and June 22, 1940; and its air attacks on Britain from July 1940 to June 1941. These events drastically changed American foreign policy. Isolationism gave way to all-out aid short of war to the countries endangered by German aggression. The U.S. military defense program was initiated in June 1940. The first peacetime conscription in American history occurred in October 1940.

In March 1941, Congress passed the Lend-Lease Act, which granted financial aid to Great Britain and any country whose defense the president deemed vital to that of the United States. Lend-Lease to the Soviet Union was granted in November 1941, five months after Germany's invasion of Soviet Russia. Between 1941 and 1945, the United States furnished about $48 billion of Lend-Lease weapons,

foodstuffs, and services. Three-fifths went to the United Kingdom, one-fifth to Soviet Russia, and the remainder to France, China, and other countries. In return, the United States received more than $7 billion in reverse Lend-Lease for military purchases and expenditures for American troops abroad, of which $5 billion came from Britain.

Tension between Japan and the United States had been building up for some time. The Japanese invasion of Manchuria in 1931, of the rest of China in 1937, and of Indochina in 1940 led in 1941 to America's closing the Panama Canal to Japanese shipping, freezing Japanese assets in the United States, and prohibiting the export of steel and pig iron to Japan. German military victories from 1939 to 1941 inspired the Japanese high command to respond to these American actions. Their attack on the American naval base and ships at Pearl Harbor on December 7, 1941 unleashed America's all-out war effort against Japan, Germany, and Italy.

Strategic Military and Economic Decisions

The factors shaping the American economy in World War II were America's resources, on the one hand, and the primary strategic military decisions of the United States, Great Britain, and Soviet Russia, on the other. The major military decisions that set the goals for the U.S. economy were to (1) wage total war and achieve the complete defeat of the Axis powers; (2) target Germany as the primary enemy and Japan as the secondary one; (3) launch offensives in North Africa, Italy, and France; (4) rely more heavily on strategic air attacks on German industrial and military targets than on British-American combat ground forces until the Normandy invasion of June 1944; and (5) limit the offensives in the Pacific until 1944 but then encourage strong naval and air action

Table 20–1 *World War II Industrial Mobilization, 1939–1947*

Date	GNP (in $ billions, current prices)	GNP (in $ billions, 1958 prices)	Manufacturing Output (in $ billions, current prices)	Armaments (in $ billions, mid-1945 prices)
1939	$ 90.5	$209.4	$ 49.0	—
1940	99.7	227.2	56.0	$ 2.1
1941	124.5	263.7	72.5	8.6
1942	157.9	297.8	93.6	30.5
1943	191.6	337.1	120.4	52.4
1944	210.1	361.3	132.3	57.7
1945[a]	211.9	355.2	128.9	33.2
1946	208.5	312.6	124.9	—
1947	231.3	309.9	139.7	—

[a]The 1945 figures cover eight months of that year.
SOURCES: Data from U.S. Census Bureau, *The Statistical History of the United States* (New York: Basic Books, 1976), p. 224, Series F-1–5; p. 228, Series F-32–46; and R. E. Smith, *The Army and Economic Mobilization* (Washington, D.C.: GPO, 1959), p. 5.

against Japan. The latter reached its climax in two atom bomb attacks on Japan and the surrender of Japan in August 1945. Germany had surrendered four months earlier.

War Production: Problems and Achievements

The military decisions made during World War II had far-reaching implications for economic decisions at all levels, from production goals to rationing of consumer goods. Perhaps the most important economic problem that the Allied architects of victory had to face was the great disparity between the Allied and Axis outputs of combat munitions. In 1939, the United States, Britain, and Canada could account for only one-fourth of the combat output of Germany, Italy, and Japan and only one-sixth of their output and that of the Soviet Union (their economic ally from August 1939 to June 1941). After Soviet Russia and the United States joined Great Britain and Canada

as allies in June and December 1941, respectively, the new Allied coalition increased its weapon strength, by 1944, to a combined supply of combat arms exceeding that of the Axis by three to one.

In the Allied coalition, the war production of American industry was crucial. Adolf Hitler and other Axis leaders had viewed the United States as an inferior, decadent country, militarily unskilled, incapable of the mass production needed for victory in war. How wrong they were the statistics and the course of history soon demonstrated. Between 1939 and 1944, the gross national product (GNP) of the United States, measured in current dollars, rose from $90.5 billion to $210.1 billion (see Table 20–1). The volume of manufactured goods in these same years nearly tripled. Total munitions production from July 1940 through August 1945 amounted to some $183 billion. Meanwhile, the output of raw materials increased by 60 percent.

By 1944, the United States had indeed become "the arsenal of democracy." In combat

The United States Arsenal of Democracy.　World War II brought an all-out mobilization of industry. Ford steel tanks were manufactured on assembly lines in record time. (UPI/The Bettmann Archive)

munitions, it out-produced Germany and Japan almost twofold and in 1944 accounted for about 40 percent of the world's armaments production. This achievement was due in part to America's greater material resources. Another important, though often neglected, factor was the higher American output per labor hour—about twice that of Germany and five times that of Japan.

An analysis of American war production shows that aircraft, ships, and combat and motor vehicles made up nearly three-fifths of the total munitions output. The United States had succeeded in building the world's largest navy, merchant fleet, and air force, as well as one of the world's largest armies. However, these bare statistics do not do justice to what pro-

duced them—the unprecedented integrated economic, political, and social efforts of the American people.

Government Control of the Economy

The precedent for centralized government control of the U.S. economy had been established during World War I and in the New Deal. In 1940 and 1941, President Roosevelt created several defense-control or mobilization agencies, though he rejected the idea of one agency with centralized control over production, prices, and labor. In 1942, he established the War Production Board (WPB), under Donald M. Nelson, with the authority to control the production of all raw materials and finished goods, military and civilian, but with no control over food, housing, and transportation. The WPB's authority over military goods was, however, soon challenged by the powerful ordnance representatives of the army and navy. One major victory of the WPB occurred in October 1942, when with the aid of a presidential adviser, Leon Henderson, the board persuaded the armed forces to reduce their tremendous military production goals to the feasible production capacity level of American industry.

Nevertheless, various defects in the administration of the WPB led President Roosevelt in May 1943 to set up the Office of War Mobilization and Reconversion (OWMR), with former Justice James F. Byrnes as its head. This agency had the authority to make priority decisions binding on all other economic agencies as well as the armed forces. Acting for the President, it served as the supreme umpire over the conflicting claims of different government agencies.

Other control agencies important to the functioning of the economy included the War Manpower Commission, the Office of Price Stabilization, the Petroleum Administration for War, the Solid Fuels Administration, and the Office of Defense Transportation. Among the agencies with conflicting claims in finished goods, materials, and facilities were the National Housing Agency and the Maritime Commission with its responsibility for shipbuilding. Ocean shipping was under the control of the War Shipping Administration; the powerful claims of the army and navy were funnelled through the Army-Navy Munitions Board. In the area of U.S. foreign economic relations, the Lend-Lease Administration and Board of Economic Warfare were important supplementary agencies to the State Department until 1943, when their personnel and functions were consolidated into the Foreign Economic Administration.

The new agencies controlling most of the national economy depended in large part for their executives on recruiting formerly important officials of the New Deal and prominent individuals from private enterprise. Business executives received "a dollar a year" as token government salaries but depended on their corporations for their customary salaries. The lower government positions were filled by recruitment from the more highly educated general population. Between 1940 and 1945, the number of civilian federal employees rose from 1.1 million to almost 3.4 million.

Mobilization of Military Troops and the Civilian Labor Force

Once Congress declared war in December 1941, there was an urgent need for the speedy recruitment of men and women for the armed forces and for the procurement of military equipment. The total number of military personnel in 1939 was 334,000, of whom 190,000 were in the army and 125,000 in the navy. By 1945, the total number rose to 12 million: 8 million in the army and 3.4 million in the navy (see Table 20–2).

Meanwhile, the civilian nonagricultural labor force rose from thirty-six million in 1939 to forty-five million in 1944, an increase of 25 percent. At the same time, the percentage of unemployed civilians experienced a dramatic drop—from 17.2 percent in 1939 to 1.2 percent in 1944. This was due in part to the transfer of about 22 percent of the prewar labor force to the armed forces. Black industrial workers accounted for only 17 percent of all black employees in early 1940, but this ratio rose to almost 30 percent in 1944. Similarly, the number of black women in industrial operations jumped from 6.3 percent of all employed females in April 1940 to 17.3 percent in April 1944.

The additional prime-age labor force of some twenty-one million came mainly from new en-

Table 20–2 *Mobilization, 1939–1947*

Year	Military Personnel (in millions)	Nonagricultural Labor Force (in millions)	Unemployment Percentage
1939	0.3	36.0	17.2%
1940	0.4	37.9	14.6
1941	1.8	41.2	9.9
1942	3.8	44.5	4.7
1943	9.0	45.3	1.9
1944	11.4	45.0	1.2
1945	12.1	44.2	1.9
1946	3.0	46.9	3.9
1947	1.6	49.5	3.9

SOURCE: Data from U.S. Census Bureau, *The Statistical History of the United States* (New York: Basic Books, 1976), p. 126, Series D-1–10; p. 1141, Series Y-904–16.

trants into the national civilian labor and military forces. About half were civilian women. The next largest percentage came from previously unemployed workers.

Agriculture was an important and historically neglected source of new civilian labor. Given the drop of the farm population between 1940 and 1944 to 5.7 million, it is estimated that agriculture contributed over 1.25 million Americans to the nonagricultural labor and military forces.

The number of civilian unemployed workers fell from 9.5 million in 1939 to 1 million in 1945 (or from 17.2 percent to 1.9 percent). This tremendous change from the devastating unemployment of the 1930s demonstrated the wisdom of those who urged the creation of employment during depressions through massive government expenditures.

War Finance

The financing of World War II was modeled in large part on the financing of World War I, though on a much larger scale. Another great influence on American wartime fiscal policy came from the writings of John Maynard Keynes, especially his *General Theory of Employment, Interest, and Money* (1936) and his brilliant 1940 brochure, *How to Pay for the War* (1940).[1] He argued persuasively for achieving high war production through an unbalanced budget and with government expenditures far in excess of taxes, with large government loans from the public to prevent consumers from misusing their funds in excessive purchases. Keynes also urged the creation of an "iron ration" for absolute necessities to protect those with low incomes from variations in cost or consumption as general prices changed. Finally, to prevent an increase in economic inequality, he advocated high, progressive income taxation.

Heavy Taxation

The president and Congress were convinced that enormous war production required great military expenditures and revenue measures. Federal expenditures from July 1, 1940 to June 30, 1946 amounted to $387 billion, 75 percent of which ($293 billion) was for defense and war (see Table 20–3). This sum was more

Table 20–3 *Federal War Finance, 1939–1947 (in $ billions)*

Year	Total Expenditures	Military Expenditures	Receipts	Surplus (+) or Deficit (−)	Gross Federal Deficit	Money Supply M₁	Money Supply M₂	Personal Income Tax Receipts
1939	$ 9.4	$ 1.4	$ 6.6	$ −2.9	$ 48.2	$ 34.15	$ 49.27	$ 1.0
1940	9.6	1.7	6.9	−2.7	50.7	39.65	55.26	0.9
1941	14.0	6.2	9.2	−4.8	57.5	46.52	62.51	1.4
1942	34.5	22.9	15.1	−19.4	79.2	55.36	71.16	3.2
1943	78.9	63.4	25.1	−53.8	142.6	72.24	89.91	6.6
1944	94.0	75.9	47.8	−46.1	204.1	85.34	106.82	18.2
1945	95.2	80.5	50.2	−45.0	260.1	99.23	126.63	19.0
1946	61.7	43.1	43.5	−18.2	271.0	106.46	138.73	18.7
1947	36.9	14.8	43.5	+6.6	257.1	111.79	146.00	19.3

SOURCE: Data from U.S. Census Bureau, *The Statistical History of the United States* (New York: Basic Books, 1976), p. 1105, Series Y-339–42; p. 1114, Y-457–65; p. 224, Series F-6–9; p. 992, Series X-410; and p. 1107, Series Y-358–72.

than ten times the amount spent in World War I and about sixty times that spent in the Civil War.

Throughout World War II, the Roosevelt administration vigorously urged heavy tax increases to pay for the war expenditures and to lessen the inflationary effect on large-scale governmental borrowing. It succeeded in obtaining through taxation about 40 percent of the total federal revenue from June 1940 to December 1945. (The national debt, however, rose from $48.2 billion at the end of 1940 to $271 billion by June 1946.) The 40 percent of total revenue achieved through taxation in World War II was higher than the 33 percent in World War I. It was achieved by congressional enactment of six important revenue measures between June 1940 and May 1944. The acts progressively raised the rates of personal income to a maximum of 94 percent and lowered the exemption to $500 per person, whether married, single, or dependent. As a result, the number of income tax payers rose from 4 million in 1939 to 42.7 million in 1945. The lowering of the tax exemption helped to restrain inflation, as did the congressional imposition of heavy excises on liquor and luxury goods.

To prevent or lessen war profiteering and thereby boost war morale of the low- and middle-income classes, Congress enacted unprecedently high increases in corporate and excess-profits taxes along with important price-control and war-contract renegotiation measures. The rates of estate and gift taxes were greatly increased in 1941 as part of the effort to equalize the financial burden of the war for all economic classes.

A very important event in tax administration was the introduction in 1943 of the pay-as-you-earn individual income tax. It replaced the onerous one-time payment each year in income earned the previous year. Instead, each employer was required to collect for the Internal Revenue Service the income taxes from employees' salaries as they earned their incomes. The new procedure increased the efficiency and equity of federal tax collections.

Borrowing Policy and Operations

Congress, limiting the percentage of total war expenditures from taxation to 40 percent, financed the remaining 60 percent of expenditures through government borrowing. Starting in December 1942, the Treasury Department organized seven bond drives, culminating in a victory drive at the end of 1945, and succeeded in selling a total of $156.9 billion in government bonds. The Treasury made an effort to borrow mainly from nonbank resources in order to minimize the creation of new money. As a result, between June 1939 and June 1946, some 62 percent of Treasury offerings came from nonbank investors, of which individual buyers of government securities comprised 25 percent. Commercial banks bought 29 percent of all Treasury offerings, while the Federal Reserve purchased 10 percent.

To keep the interest rates on government securities as well as the government's cost of the war as low as possible, from April 1942 on the Federal Reserve authorities used their financial powers to limit the yield on short-term Treasury notes to three-eighths of 1 percent and the yield on bonds, certificates, and Treasury notes to 2.5 percent. Nevertheless, payments of interest rose to 3.5 percent of the national income, compared to 2 percent after World War I and 2.6 percent after the Civil War.

The Money Supply, Prices, and Price Controls

The Treasury's need for an increasingly large money supply during World War II was met mainly by the new currency and bank reserves credited by the Federal Reserve. Additional deposits were created by the banking system, over which the Federal Reserve could maintain some control. The money supply (currency plus demand and time deposits in commercial banks) increased from $55.2 billion in 1940 to $126.6 billion in 1945 and to $138.7 billion in 1946 (see Table 20–3).

A runaway inflation was prevented in part by the price control system adopted concurrently with the initiation of the easy money policy of the Federal Reserve. The Office of Price Administration, created in April 1941, instituted effective control of many prices in March 1942. This control was expanded by the general freeze on wages and prices ordered in April 1943 by President Roosevelt. The regulations were vigorously enforced until June 1946. During this period, monetary expansion did not increase measured prices to any substantial extent, though monetary expansion likely contributed to concealed price increases and black-market transactions. As evidence of this point, the money supply grew at an annual rate of 17.25 percent from April 1942 to June 1946, whereas wholesale prices rose at an annual rate of only 3.23 percent. In short, the price controls in effect during the war played a crucial role in safeguarding the welfare of the American consuming public (especially those with low or middle incomes) against a great decline in consumption.

The Wartime Labor Force

Gender and Racial Issues

Before and for some years after Pearl Harbor, there was no labor shortage in the United States. Shortages of skilled and unskilled workers did not become acute until 1943, and then only in a few production areas. The number of unemployed workers fell from 9.4 million in 1939 to 1.04 million in 1945. Another dramatic change was an increase in the total U.S. labor force (including the military) from 55 million in 1940 to 62 million in 1944. In June 1944, the total number employed in industry was 8.3 million higher than the monthly average for 1939; however, in that same period, the total number employed in agriculture was 1.3 million lower (see Table 20–4).

The growing labor force included several million young people—males and females aged sixteen to nineteen. The labor force participation rates for teenagers were 66 percent for males and 38 percent for females. Almost half of the men aged sixty-five and over were

Table 20–4 *The U.S. Labor Force: Gender and Age Participation, 1940–1947*

| | | Percent Distribution | | | | | |
| | | Males | | | Females | | |
Year	Total Labor Force (in millions)	Total	Aged 25–44 Years	Aged 45–64 Years	Total	Aged 25–44 Years	Aged 45–64 Years
1940	55.2	74.8%	—	—	25.2%	—	—
1944	62.2	70.8	30.5%	20.0%	29.2	12.6%	6.5%
1946	55.8	72.2	32.1	22.1	27.8	12.2	6.6
1947	58.9	72.6	33.1	22.2	27.4	12.2	7.0

SOURCE: Data from U.S. Census Bureau, *The Statistical History of the United States* (New York: Basic Books, 1976), p. 132, Series D-29–41.

gainful workers. For that age group, peacetime leisure habits gave way to the demands of war.

The role of women workers during the war cannot be overstressed. More than half of the new entrants in the total U.S. labor force between 1940 and June 1944 were women. During this period, employment of women increased most among those aged fourteen to nineteen and over forty-five. The increase among women aged forty-five to sixty-four was 65 percent; for those sixty-five and over, 97 percent; and for those fourteen to nineteen, over 200 percent. Women distinguished themselves in noncombat units of the armed forces as well as in many traditionally male positions in industry. The posters showing "Rosie the Riveter," a young woman doing factory work, conveyed a truth about sexual equality in many economic areas that the feminist movement would build on in later decades.

Four dramatic wartime changes occurred in the status and occupation of African-Americans. The first was an increase of 600,000 black workers in manufacturing; the second, the enrollment of almost 700,000 blacks in labor unions; the third, the induction of 1.5 million blacks into the armed forces; and the fourth, the migration of almost a million blacks from southern farms and rural communities to northern, southern, and

Women Industrial Workers in World War II.
Pictures of women riveters inspired songs about "Rosie, the Riveter." (Photo Researchers)

western industrial centers. These events demonstrated a decided movement from agriculture to industry and the service occupations.

In 1940, one-fifth of all African-American men were farmers or farm managers; another fifth were farm laborers. By April 1944, only 14 percent of each of these groups was still engaged in farming. Between April 1940 and April 1944, the number of black women industrial operatives grew from 6.3 percent to 17.3 percent of all employed females. In this same period, the percentage of black female domestic workers dropped from 60 percent to 45 percent. The exodus of African-American women from paid farm labor during these years resulted in a drop, from 13 percent to about 5 percent, of all paid farm workers.

Racial Discrimination

Although the United States fought against Nazi Germany's appalling racial policies and practices, many American employers still exhibited bias against African-Americans and other minority groups in their hiring, wage, and promotion procedures. The threat that blacks would march on Washington for equal job opportunity induced President Roosevelt in June 1941 to issue an executive order prohibiting job discrimination in defense industries. That order, demonstrating that black militancy could be effective, was an important influence on the African-American protest movements of the 1950s and 1960s. In the armed forces, segregation of blacks in combat and service units prevailed during the early war years. Later in the war, however, considerable integration developed; it achieved great public attention when black volunteer troops were used in desperate military engagements during the critical Battle of the Bulge in December 1944.

One of the most regrettable acts of American racial bigotry occurred early in 1942 with the forcible uprooting of 110,000 Japanese (including 75,000 U.S. citizens) from their homes, farms, and businesses on the West Coast. They were relocated in internment camps from March 1942 to 1945. The excuse given by the government for its action was that the Japanese-Americans were considered a greater risk to U.S. security than German- or Italian-Americans. Forty-six years later, in 1988, Congress formally apologized to the former internees and appropriated $1.25 billion in compensation to the sixty thousand survivors.

Wages and Wage Controls

The extraordinary war demand for the limited but expanding supply of military and civilian products of the manufacturing industry brought about a correspondingly high demand for factory workers as well as an increase in their bargaining power. Average real weekly earnings in manufacturing rose from $24.96 in 1940 to $45.76 in 1944 (or over 90 percent). Real hourly earnings rose from 72 cents to $1.11 (or over 55 percent). Overtime was a major factor in the increased weekly earnings of workers during this period. The average annual earnings of employees between 1940 and 1947 are shown for several industries in Table 20–5.

The pressures of the war caused the government to impose federal controls on labor relations. The War Labor Board (WLB), with representatives from labor, management, and the public, imposed compulsory arbitration even though the courts ruled that its "directive orders" were only advisory. The WLB attempted to stabilize wage rates after January 1941 by tying wage increases to the rise in the cost of living. When this ruling aroused great discontent among union members, the WLB began approving "fringe benefits" rather generously. It also ruled that women deserved equal pay for equal work—a major victory for the feminist cause during the war.

Numerous labor strikes between 1942 and 1943, especially the United Mine Workers strike, led Congress to pass the Smith-Connally War Disputes Act (1943) over President Roosevelt's veto. The act authorized the president to take over plants closed by labor disputes and make violators subject to fines and imprisonment. Despite the sixty-six presidential seizures made

Black Soldiers in World War II.   Some 1,150,000 blacks were inducted into the U.S. armed forces in World War II. This picture shows a black artillery unit in action in France in 1944. (The Bettmann Archive)

Table 20–5   *Average Annual Earnings of Full-Time Employees, 1940–1947*

Year	Total All Industries	Agriculture, Forestry, Fishing	Manufacturing	Mining	Construction	Services
1940	$1,299	$ 407	$1,432	$1,388	$1,330	$ 953
1944	2,109	1,021	2,517	2,499	2,602	1,538
1946	2,359	1,200	2,517	2,719	2,537	1,863
1947	2,589	1,276	2,793	3,113	2,829	1,996

SOURCE: Data from U.S. Census Bureau, *The Statistical History of the United States* (New York: Basic Books, 1976), p. 164, Series D-722–27; pp. 166–67, Series D-739–64.

under the act, it did not seriously weaken trade unions or stop strikes. Rather, labor union membership rose from 8.9 million in 1940 to 14.8 million in 1945. This gain of about 60 percent was due in large part to the recruiting efforts of the Congress of Industrial Organizations (CIO) and the American Federation of Labor (AFL).

The War's Effect on U.S. Food Outputs and Agriculture

World War II reversed the New Deal emphasis on restricting food output as a means of raising farm income. A tremendous demand for American food developed after the attack on Pearl Harbor, from both the U.S. armed forces and America's allies (Britain, Soviet Russia, and China). By 1943, U.S. food exports represented about 14 percent of the total farm output. The exports relieved the Allies' desperate food shortages and made American agriculture a vital strategic factor in the Allied war effort. As a result, the "Food for Freedom" program of American farmers was a success.

Between 1939 and 1944, total farm output rose 25 percent. Although in the same period the proportion of farm laborers in the nation's work force dropped from about 20 percent to 15 percent, the output per worker increased by more than one-third. In 1939, the average wage of a hired farm worker was less than one-third of the wage of the industrial worker; by 1945, however, the average farm wage had almost tripled.

Almost one-fourth of U.S. total food output during World War II went to the armed forces and to America's Allies through the Lend-Lease program. Nevertheless, civilian food consumption in the United States reached its highest level in American history: Civilian per capita food consumption was 9 percent above the 1935 to 1939 level.

Transportation: Wartime Demand and Supply

During World War II, the railroads successfully met extraordinary military and civilian demands. They were able to handle twice the traffic of World War I, with one-fourth fewer cars, one-third fewer locomotives, and nearly one-third fewer workers than in World War I. Despite increases in wages and in the prices of materials and supplies, railway rates and fares remained the same. The railroads were of special importance to the armed forces in transporting heavy military equipment and military personnel from one end of the country to the other.

Motor transportation furnished a larger volume of passengers and nonmilitary freight transportation than either the railroads or the airways. Yet during the war, because of gasoline and other restrictions, passenger and motor freight transportation suffered some setbacks. Meanwhile, the number of military and special-purchase aircraft produced between 1939 and 1945 came to almost 300,000. However, in the same period, civilian air transportation (passenger and freight) remained relatively insignificant.

Family Income Distribution

During World War II, as in World War I, increased equality in income distribution was made possible by progressive income taxation and by the great gain in employment achieved through government expenditures. Between 1941 and 1945, the lower- and middle-income classes moved modestly to higher levels in the family personal income scale. The average before-tax family income (in current dollars) rose from $2,209 in 1939 to $3,614 in 1944 and to $3,940 in 1946.

Table 20–6 *Aggregate Family Income Distribution, 1935–1946*

Income class	Percent Distribution		
	1935–1936	1944	1946
Lowest fifth	4.1%	4.9%	5.0%
Second fifth	9.2	10.9	11.1
Third fifth	14.1	16.2	16.0
Fourth fifth	20.9	22.2	21.8
Highest fifth	51.7	45.8	46.1
Top 5 percent	26.5	20.7	21.3

SOURCE: Data from U.S. Census Bureau, *The Statistical History of the United States* (New York: Basic Books, 1976), p. 301, Series G-319–36.

The percent changes in income distribution are shown in Table 20–6. Slight gains of 1 percent to 2 percent were made in varying degrees by each of the four income classes below the top fifth. Both the highest 20 percent and the top 5 percent lost more than 5 percent of the aggregate family income. Nevertheless, the income of the highest 20 percent income class was greater than the combined income of the lowest 60 percent. The income of the top 5 percent was higher than the combined income of the lowest 40 percent. However, this degree of inequality was less than that of the 1930s.

Investment in the War Effort: Public and Private

One of the great, but rarely noted, paradoxes of World War II is that the U.S. war effort depended heavily on public investment, despite the general impression that the American economic system has been dominated by private enterprise except in crises like the Great Depression. The facts reveal a far more complex relationship between business and government.

During the war, private domestic investment actually fell by more than a third—from $17.9 billion in 1941 to $5.7 billion in 1943. De-

Table 20–7 *Personal Savings and Private Investment, 1940–1947 (in $ billions)*

Year	Gross Personal Savings	Gross Private Domestic Investment
1940	$ 3.8	$13.1
1941	11.0	17.9
1942	27.6	9.8
1943	33.4	5.7
1944	37.3	7.1
1945	29.2	10.6
1946	15.2	30.6
1947	7.3	34.0

SOURCE: Data from U.S. Census Bureau, *The Statistical History of the United States* (New York: Basic Books, 1976), p. 234, Series F-144–62; p. 263, Series F-552–65.

spite a rise to $10.6 billion in 1945, the persistent decline of private investment from the 1941 figure is especially notable, since personal savings increased dramatically from $11 billion in 1941 to $37.3 billion in 1944 (see Table 20–7).

Nevertheless, between mid-1940 and 1945, American manufacturers spent more on new plants and equipment than they had in the whole prewar decade of the 1930s—a total of $11.4 billion (valued at original cost). Yet this expenditure represented only 16 percent of the 1940 manufacturing capital stock, a moderate increase when compared to the 95 percent rise in real manufacturing output from 1940 to 1945. This remarkable expansion was mainly due to government financing of manufacturing plants and equipment built between July 1, 1940 and December 31, 1945. Some $15.98 billion went to private firms operating government-owned plants; only $1.65 billion went to plants owned and operated by the government.

An analysis of public and private industrial wartime expansion by a brilliant young economist named Robert J. Gordon in 1969 demonstrated that the government, not private industry, financed almost all military needs. For instance, the government financed 93 percent of facilities expansion in the war-oriented explosives, ammunition, ordnance, aircraft, and ships categories. One important government investment came in forty-four synthetic rubber plants, costing $670 million to build during the war. These privately operated, government-owned plants contributed almost 100 percent of the U.S. rubber supply after the Japanese invasion of Malaya in 1942. This extraordinary wartime partnership between government and business was not fully realized until Gordon's research was published in the *American Economic Review.*[2]

Government aid to business expansion in World War II began when the Reconstruction Finance Corporation (RFC) was empowered in 1940 to build plants essential for defense. This it accomplished through its subsidiary, the Defense Plant Corporation (DPC), which invested $7 billion in commercial plants that otherwise may not have been constructed. As a result, by June 30, 1945 when it was dissolved, the Defense Plant Corporation owned more than 10 percent of the country's plant capacity. In addition to making direct plant and land investments, the federal government, through such agencies as the RFC and DPC, guaranteed large loans to business corporations and made substantial advances on war contracts. Public and private enterprise thus intermeshed in ways that neither Adam Smith nor Karl Marx could have anticipated.

War-Related Technology and Industrial Change

Great advances in technology were achieved from the scientific research and industrial developments that were so important to the conduct of the war as well as to the postwar economy. Among the most notable innovations were jet engines, rocket propulsion, gas-turbine engines, synthetic rubber, plastics, and electronics, especially television and radar.

Medical breakthroughs included penicillin, synthetic quinine, atabrine, and sulfa drugs.

The most lethal mass-destructive weapon created by World War II technology was the atom bomb, produced at a cost of $2 billion and in response to Nazi Germany's attempts at creating such a bomb. The two atom bombs delivered in August 1945 at Hiroshima and Nagasaki precipitated Japan's unconditional surrender on September 2, 1945. While these powerful weapons shortened the war and saved at least a million lives, the postwar proliferation of nuclear bombs caused many to regret their invention. The one important global benefit has been the controversial development of peacetime nuclear energy as a substitute for petroleum and coal.

World War II Casualties

Between July 1, 1940, and June 30, 1946, as noted earlier in the chapter, the federal government spent $387 billion, of which 75 percent ($293 billion) went for defense and war. The human costs of World War II, however, included 405,399 deaths in the U.S. armed forces, almost four times the number of losses in World War I and two-thirds of those in the Civil War. The losses in Europe and Asia were even greater. German military casualties totaled 3.25 million; the Japanese lost 2.1 million, and the Chinese even more. About three million Soviets perished in battle and another three million died while in German prison camps. The total loss of life—civilian and military—in World War II is estimated at over forty million (three times the total number in World War I). Of this number, between five million and six million European Jews were exterminated in Nazi concentration camps.

The terrible alternatives to U.S. participation in World War II would have included the destruction of millions of non-Aryans in Europe and of Chinese in Asia, the end of democracy in Western Europe and elsewhere, and a great loss of freedom of thought and human dignity. This is why Bertrand Russell, a lifelong pacifist, believed the war was justified.[3] As the innovative economic theorist Mancur Olson puts it, some values are beyond the measuring rod of money.[4]

The Keynesian and Mixed Economy Lessons of the War

World War II fundamentally altered the climate of U.S. government decision making and demonstrated what an active Keynesian fiscal policy might accomplish. While tax revenues rose through progressive increases in tax rates and the passage of new tax laws, government spending increased much more rapidly, giving rise to unprecedented budget deficits. Meanwhile, the Federal Reserve created enough money to keep at low levels the interest rates on government securities issued to finance the deficits.

At the same time, resources were diverted from civilian consumption and investment to war purposes through a system of rationing and price controls. Far-reaching government controls were developed over the procurement and production of raw materials and finished goods, military and civilian. Agencies like the War Production Board and the Office of Price Administration worked out specific controls that supplemented and corrected the supply-demand factors in what otherwise would have been a free market economy.

The result was that the American economy, influenced in part by the New Deal, emerged as a mixed economy. A *command economy* is one in which the government makes all or most decisions about production and distribution. A *market economy* is one in which private individuals and firms make the major decisions about production and consumption. Finally, a *mixed*

economy (like that of the United States in World War II) combines major elements of the market economy with a carefully circumscribed use of the centralized planning and control of strategic resources and government ownership of property. Despite various flaws and errors in the setting up of these war controls, the successes they achieved were so great that many democratic governments in America and Western Europe after 1945 concluded that certain forms of economic planning could be used to avoid depressions and to promote economic welfare.

Demobilization

The end of World War II, coming first in Europe and then in Asia, led to a rapid decline in government war orders after May 7, 1945 and a drastic drop after August 15. Total government purchases of goods dropped from an annual rate of nearly $100 billion in the first three months of 1945 to about $35 billion in the first quarter of 1946. Within only one year, the government lessened its contribution to aggregate demand by an amount equal to almost 30 percent of total GNP at the start of 1945.

Many economists and public figures feared that a massive fiscal deflation would result in a deep recession. In the summer of 1945, they argued that widespread unemployment would become a serious problem by the winter of 1945 to 1946. Some economists even predicted a postwar depression as severe as the Great Depression and the possibility of a social revolution. Their forecasts, however, proved to be untrue. Total GNP decreased by considerably less than half the drop in government spending between the first quarter of 1945 and that of 1946; by the end of 1946, however, it had nearly regained its wartime peak. Unemployment rose from 1.9 percent in 1945 to less than 4 percent in 1946 to 1947. Consumer spending did not decline after Germany's surrender; rather, it increased with great rapidity after V-J day. From early 1946 on, prices began to rise rapidly as controls were relaxed. The great economic problem in 1946 was a tremendous pent-up demand for peacetime goods and services far in excess of existing supplies. Despite the decline in government spending, aggregate demand was great enough to sustain full employment. By June 1946, a vigorous inflationary boom was well under way.

To explain the brief recession and subsequent boom, an analysis of the behavior of private investment and consumer expenditures is needed. Between the first quarter of 1945 and the first quarter of 1946, private spending—including consumer spending, domestic investment, and foreign investment—rose by about 40 percent. Businesspeople converted war facilities to peacetime production in order to meet the high level of existing or anticipated demand. As government orders declined and war controls were lifted, industry was able to absorb the workers and materials released from war production.

The Postwar Labor Force

Gender and Racial Changes

Manufacturing, the service industries, and transportation in 1946 rose to the challenge of employing nine million former military personnel who had been released from active duty by the armed forces. In 1947, another 1.5 million Americans were available for private employment.

Some of the gains in employment made by women during the war were lost in the immediate postwar years. The number of women workers fell from 19 million in 1945 to 16.7 million in 1946. The decrease was especially prominent among young women, who left the labor force to pursue an education or to marry and start a family. However, the number of married women over age forty-five remained high in the postwar labor force.

Black male workers from 1946 on continued the gains they had made in World War II. Between 1940 and 1980, the greatest improvement in narrowing the wage gap between black and white workers occurred in the 1940s, when a 25 percent expansion in the relative wages of black men was realized. It is likely that black women from 1946 on also retained or increased the gains they had made during the war; however, the available statistics are not adequate for conclusive judgment.

Government and Labor

A momentous change in postwar governmental labor policy came with the Employment Act of 1946. It inaugurated a new era of national government responsibility for using all practical means "to promote maximum employment, product, and purchasing power." The general public interpreted the specific goals of the act to mean full employment and healthy economic growth. To achieve these goals, the legislation set up the Council of Economic Advisors and the Joint Economic Committee of Congress to help the president and Congress formulate policies.

Although the Employment Act was explicit on the importance of maintaining employment, it was silent on wage regulation and price stability. As a result, from 1946 to 1948, the various federal wage and price controls of World War II were allowed to expire. Most economists, however, argue that price and wage controls, while effective in war, are not cost-effective in peacetime.

After the end of World War II hostilities, labor unions sought large wage increases for their members and engaged in a great wave of strikes in 1945 and 1946. The business and public reactions against strikes led Congress in

1947 to pass the Taft-Hartley Labor Management Relations Act over President Harry Truman's veto. It imposed various restrictions on unions and prohibited the closed shop. Despite this setback to organized labor, union membership continued to grow during the 1940s. The Taft-Hartley Act thus served to correct union excesses without undermining the collective bargaining process.

Postwar Finance

Even before Japan's surrender, Congress began easing the capital-reconversion tax burden of American business. In November 1945, Congress repealed the capital-stock tax and the excess-profits tax, the latter effective at the end of 1945. Corporate and personal income tax rates were moderately lowered, and tax exemptions on service pay received during the war were granted to members of the armed forces below the rank of commissioned officer. But Congress postponed for many years the reduction of many wartime excise taxes that were about to expire in 1945.

While the tax-reduction process was under way, federal expenditures continued to be high. Although expenditures dropped after 1946 to 40 percent of the wartime peak, they were still 4.6 times greater than the five-year prewar average. Military expenditures fell from $48.1 billion in 1946 to $11.1 billion in 1948; they then rose from 1950 on as the superpower competition known as the *Cold War* intensified. Veterans' benefits, under the GI Bill of Rights, rose from $4.3 billion in 1946 to $7.3 billion in 1947. Interest payments on the public debt remained relatively stable, owing to low interest rates; they amounted to only about $5 billion a year in the 1946 to 1947 period, or roughly 12.5 percent of total federal expenditures. For further discussion of these matters, see Chapter 21.

International Finance and Trade

During World War II, the governments of the United States and Western Europe began planning for the liberalization of foreign trade and the creation of a stable world economy. Congress passed the Bretton Woods Agreements Act in July 1945, authorizing the United States to join other UN governments (but excluding Soviet Russia) in creating two new financial institutions—the International Monetary Fund (IMF) and the International Bank for Reconstruction and Development (IBRD, or the World Bank). The long-term goal of the IMF was to encourage the relative stability of exchange rates and ultimately the free convertibility of national currencies. The World Bank was geared to the promotion of international investment as a means of fostering recovery and economic development, especially in underdeveloped countries. It sought to guarantee and supplement private international investment throughout the world.

The United States and other UN governments, without the cooperation of the Communist bloc, also attempted to reduce tariff barriers—first through the International Trade Organization (ITO) and then through various bilateral understandings that were combined to form the General Agreement on Tariffs and Trade (GATT, generally referred to as the General Agreement of 1947). This became the basis for a series of important tariff reductions over the coming decades.

Meanwhile, European countries were being drained of their gold and dollar reserves despite such measures of assistance as the U.S. sale of surplus government supplies, UN Relief and Rehabilitation, U.S. Export-Import Bank loans, and the special U.S. loan of $2.1 billion in 1947 to the United Kingdom. Between June 30, 1945, and June 30, 1947, Europe experienced a net loss of over $2 billion in its gold and dollar reserves and was forced to impose drastic foreign-exchange restrictions.

As a result, the U.S. State Department initiated in 1946 an $8 billion transfer of government surplus materials overseas to the devastated areas of Europe and Asia in need of rehabilitation and reconstruction.[5] More important in terms of American economic assistance in European rehabilitation and recovery was the 1948 Marshall Plan. The United States, determined to strengthen Europe against Soviet expansion and aggression, made West Germany part of a federation of democratic nations in the hope of preventing a future war. By mid-1951, the European countries receiving aid from the Marshall Plan had achieved most of the recovery they needed. In return, the countries of Europe agreed to eliminate restrictive trade barriers and to check inflation as a precondition to the most effective use of the Marshall Plan aid.

The Challenges of the Postwar Era

The United States had successfully managed the greatest war in its history. How the nation would meet the challenges of demobilization and reconversion to a peacetime economy without undergoing the crisis of massive unemployment worried economists and the American public alike. But tremendous pent-up consumer demand, unusual private entrepreneurship, and supportive governmental intervention in various areas brought economic recovery in the following decades. This was an achievement of great magnitude, as we will see in Chapter 21.

Summary

After entering the war against the Axis powers, the United States moved from the New Deal's partial recovery during the Depression to a period of full employment and high investment. Economic controls by the federal government regulated an increasingly planned economy.

Major military decisions determined programs and levels of production in manufacturing and other areas of the American economy, influenced mobilization and makeup of the military and civilian labor forces, and necessitated a vast war-finance program. The very high demand for labor and food led to government controls on wages and food prices and to increases in output by factory laborers and farmers. Social and economic changes, especially affecting women and blacks, occurred in the labor force.

In the area of investment in war industries, the federal government came to play a larger role than private investors. The great advances in technology during this period laid the basis for new postwar industries.

During World War II, a movement toward a decrease in inequality of income distribution resulted from progressive income taxation and the great increase in employment because of huge government expenditures. An extremely important change in the structure of the American economy developed from government controls over (1) the procurement and production of war materials and goods, (2) regulation of the money supply, taxation, and spending, and (3) rationing and pricing of civilian goods. The American economy became a *mixed economy*. In contrast to a command economy and a classic free-enterprise system, the mixed economy combined elements of the market economy with a limited use of centralized planning, control of strategic resources, and some government ownership of property.

The end of World War II brought an extensive demobilization of the American war economy. Although some economists feared a severe postwar depression, the period from August 1945 to 1948 was one of vigorous prosperity. The United States became a leader in the liberalization of international trade and in the creation of a stable world economy. The Marshall Plan was perhaps the best example of American generosity and leadership of the free world.

Endnotes

1. John Maynard Keynes, *General Theory of Employment, Interest, and Money* (New York: Harcourt Brace, 1936); and *How to Pay for the War* (New York: Harcourt Brace, 1940).
2. Robert J. Gordon, "$45 Billion of U.S. Private Investment Has Been Mislaid," *American Economic Review,* 59 (June 1969).
3. Bertrand Russell, *The Autobiography of Bertrand Russell, 1914–1944* (Boston: Little, Brown, 1951), p. 287.
4. Mancur Olson, "Toward a Unified View of Economics and the Other Social Sciences," *Perspectives on Positive Political Economy,* eds. James E. Alt and K. A. Shepsle (New York: Cambridge University Press, 1990), pp. 212–30.
5. U.S. Department of State, Office of Foreign Liquidation Commission, *Report to Congress on Foreign Surplus Disposal, January 1947* Publication 2722 (Washington, D.C.: GPO, 1947). The economist in the State Department who originated this $8 billion surplus disposal was the senior author of this text. He also worked out a plan that helped to secure the critically needed supplies from Europe for the U.S. landing craft used in the Normandy invasion.

Suggested Readings

An excellent survey and analysis of the economics of the major powers in World War II is Alan S. Milward, *War, Economy, and Society: 1939–1945* (Berkeley: University of California Press, 1977). A useful introduction to major writings on World War II is Sidney Ratner, "The Economic History of the Second World War," *Journal of Economic History,* 12 (1952). A critical administrative and economic history of the American war effort is Eliot Janeway, *The Struggle for Survival* (New Haven: Yale University Press, 1951). Harold G. Vatter, *The U.S. Economy in World War II* (New York: Columbia University, 1985), has valuable analyses of important topics. Among the most useful studies of governmental war agencies are U.S. Bureau of the Budget, *The United States at War* (Washington, D.C.: GPO, 1946); R. H. Connery, *The Navy and Industrial Mobilization in World War II* (Princeton: Princeton University Press, 1951); R. E. Smith, *The Army and Economic Mobilization* (Washington, D.C.: GPO, 1959); and Herman Miles Somers, *Presidential Agency: OWMR* (Cambridge: Harvard University Press, 1950). An important article on government financing of war manufacturing construction is Robert J. Gordon, "$45 Billion of U.S. Private Investment Has Been Mislaid," *American Economic Review,* 59 (June 1969).

A concise guide to fiscal-monetary policies is Robert A. Gordon, *Economic Instability and Growth* (New York: W. W. Norton, 1977). Authoritative studies of wartime fiscal-monetary history include Milton Friedman and Anna J. Schwartz, *A Monetary History of the United States, 1867–1960* (Princeton: Princeton University Press, 1963); Sidney Ratner, *Taxation and Democracy in America* (New York: Wiley, 1967); Herbert Stein, *The Fiscal Revolution in America* (Chicago: University of Chicago Press, 1969); and Paul Studenski and Herman Krooss, *Financial History of the United States,* 2nd ed. (New York: McGraw-Hill, 1963).

On price-wage controls, the most important studies are John K. Galbraith, *A Theory of Price Control* (Cambridge: Harvard University Press, 1952); and Hugh Rockoff, *Drastic Measures: A History of Wage and Price Controls in the United States* (New York: Cambridge University Press, 1984). On wartime industry, very helpful volumes are Walter Adams (ed.), *The Structure of American Industry,* 4th ed. (New York: Macmillan, 1971); Carroll W. Pursell, Jr. (ed.), *The Military-Industrial Complex* (New York: Harper and Row, 1972); and Nathan Rosenberg, *Technology and American Economic Growth* (New York: Harper & Row, 1972). Indispensable works on industrial capital and productivity are Daniel Creamer et al., *Capital in Manufacturing and Mining* (Princeton: Princeton University Press, 1960); John W. Kendrick, *Productivity Trends in the United States* (New York: National Bureau of Economic Research, 1961); John W. Kendrick, *Postwar Productivity Trends in the United States, 1948–1969* (New York: NBER, 1973); and Edward F. Denison, *Trends in American Economic Growth, 1929–1982* (Washington, D.C.: Brookings Institution, 1985).

Two scholarly analyses of wartime agriculture are Walter Wilcox, *The Farmer in the Second World War* (Ames: Iowa State College Press, 1947); and Bela Gold, *Wartime Planning in Agriculture* (New York: AMS Press, 1968). Valuable studies on wartime social changes include Claudia Golden, *Understanding the Gender Gap: An Economic History of American Women* (New York: Oxford University Press, 1990); Richard

Polenberg, *War and Society: The United States, 1941–1945* (Philadelphia: Lippincott, 1972); and Charles E. Silberman, *Crisis in Black and White* (New York: Random House, 1964).

Strong criticism of the accepted wartime national income statistics are presented in Simon Kuznets, *National Product in Wartime* (Princeton: Princeton University Press, 1945), Robert Higgs, "Wartime Prosperity?" *Journal of Economic History,* 52 (1992), and Mancur Olson, *Beyond the Measuring Rod of Money* (unpublished manuscript, University of Maryland, Economics Department). On income distribution, the standard work of Hugh P. Miller, *Income Distribution in the United States* (Washington, D.C.: GPO, 1966).

On wartime labor, the most useful works are Joel Seidman, *American Labor from Defense to Reconversion* (Chicago: University of Chicago, 1976). Sherrie A. Kossoudi and Laura J. Dresser, "Working Class Rosies: Women Industrial Workers during World War II, " *Journal of Economic History,* 52 (June 1992) and two already cited works: Claudia Golden, *Understanding the Gender Gap* and Harold S. Vatter, *The U.S. Economy in World War II.* The most comprehensive study of the various modes of transport is Harold Barger, *The Transportation Industries, 1889–1946* (New York: National Bureau of Economic Research, 1951). Incisive treatments of wartime and postwar foreign trade and balance-of-payment problems are presented in Robert Gilpin, *The Political Economy of International Relations* (Princeton: Princeton University Press, 1987); Charles Kindleberger, *Foreign Trade and the National Economy* (New Haven: Yale University Press, 1963); and Sidney Ratner, *The Tariff in American History* (New York: Van Nostrand, 1972). On domestic markets in an age of mass consumption, penetrating studies include Harold Barger, *Distribution's Place in the American Economy Since 1869* (Princeton: Princeton University Press, 1955); Paul David and Peter Solar, "History of the Cost of Living in America," *Research in Economic History,* 2 (1977);

Jean Gottmann, *Megalopolis* (New York: Twentieth Century Fund, 1971); and Herman P. Miller, *Rich Man, Poor Man* (New York: Crowell, 1971).

Information on demobilization and reconversion of the U.S. and other wartime economies to peacetime goals can be found in Herman Van der Wee, *Prosperity and Upheaval: The World Economy, 1945–1980* (Berkeley: University of California Press, 1984). For important insights on postwar economic changes and rigidities, see David C. Mowery and Nathan Rosenberg, *Technology and the Pursuit of Economic Growth* (New York: Cambridge University Press, 1989); Mancur Olson, *The Rise and Decline of Nations* (New Haven: Yale University Press, 1982); and Harold G. Vatter, *The U.S. Economy in the 1950s* (New York: W. W. Norton, 1963). Another important article is Michael Edelstein, "What Price Cold War? Military Spending and Private Investment in the U.S., 1946–1979," *Cambridge Journal of Economics*, 14 (1990).

Part V

The Postindustrial Economy and the New World Order

1945–1990s

WORLD WAR II, BY CRIPPLING AMERICA'S AL-LIES AND devastating its enemies, had thrust the United States by 1945 into a position of economic and political leadership for much of the world. Meeting the challenges of leadership called for maintaining a strong and growing economy at home while building a liberal, freer trading and financial order internationally. Each of these tasks was complicated by the Cold War—the ideological, economic, and political conflict between the market economies of the capitalist world and the centrally planned economies of the Communist world.

The nature of the postwar challenges almost inevitably led to a greatly enlarged role for government in the processes of decision making. Memories of the Great Depression were still fresh in 1945. The federal government, buoyed by newly developed economic theories that explained how depressions could occur and how they might be avoided by governmental economic policies, committed itself to fostering economic growth, full employment, and price stability. The remarkable U.S. economic expansion during the war, though an unusual experience under atypical circumstances, seemed to many observers to demonstrate the validity of the new Keynesian theories that rationalized government intervention to stabilize the economy.

The new world economic order envisioned by American leaders also called for more government involvement in economic life, as did the Cold War. If world trade was to grow, trading barriers erected by national governments had to be brought down, and new international institutions, organizations, and agreements had to be created to support the flows of goods, services, productive resources, and finance among nations. If communism was to be contained, the United States and its Allies had to sustain a high level of diplomatic and military preparedness. Accepting these international responsibilities also meant accepting a relatively greater role for government in economic affairs.

Thus, the central focus of this most recent era in U.S. economic history is on government in the economy. Government, of course, is an ever-present factor in economic history. In the U.S. case, government had significant roles in every previous era—in the colonial movement toward economic and political independence; in the transportation and industrial revolutions of 1790 to 1860; in the rise of big business and especially in the reactions to it during the years from 1860 to 1914; and in the era of prosperity, depression, and two world wars lasting from 1914 to 1945. But it was only after 1945 that Americans would allow that their government had continuing responsibilities for macroeconomic stabilization at home and for maintaining—and defending—a liberal, market-oriented economic order internationally. How government decision makers met these challenges is the major theme of the half-century of U.S. economic history from the mid-1940s to the early 1990s.

During the first two postwar decades, as we will see in Chapter 21, the decisions made by U.S. policymakers enjoyed considerable success, with prosperity and stable economic growth at home and economic recovery, growth, and the containment of communism abroad. Around the mid-1960s, however, the reach of U.S. decision makers began to exceed their grasp. One result was the Great Inflation period of 1965 to 1982, the focus of Chapter 22. In reaction to that experience, the 1980s brought major economic policy shifts that in many ways replaced the problems of the inflationary era with new ones, while not returning the United States to the prosperous and stable economic conditions of 1946 to 1965 (topics addressed in Chapter 23).

However, the Cold War, which profoundly affected the American and world economies during the half-century after World War II, finally came to an end in the early 1990s. The ongoing adjustment to this development will likely call for reduced allocations of U.S. economic resources to national defense, even though the post–Cold War world, with its revival of nationalism and other political-economic complications in many areas, soon demonstrated that it could hardly be described as "an outbreak of peace." Americans will also have to adjust to continuing structural changes in the domestic and world economies. These are some of the challenges that decision makers in all parts of the U.S. economy will face in the 1990s and beyond.

Chapter 21

The Good Years
1945–1965

WHEN WORLD WAR II ENDED, THE UNITED States was in a uniquely strong position to affect the course of economic history, at home and abroad. Domestically, American decision makers used that position to build a mixed economy, with reliance on private markets to guide most economic decisions but using government policies to promote economic growth, achieve economic stability, and raise economic well-being across all the diverse groups comprising American society. In the international sphere, the strength and prosperity of the U.S. economy became the basis for decisions by American leaders to ensure the recovery of other countries from the war, to build a liberal trading and financial order, and, in response to the outbreak of the Cold War, to contain the threat of Communist expansionism.

In retrospect, the most successful of these policy decisions was that of containing communism. As the 1980s gave way to the 1990s, the Cold War, a dominating influence on American and world economic life after 1945, finally came to an end with the collapse of communism and its threat to a liberal world order. This marked the end of an era, in economic and other areas of history. The end of an era is a time for looking back. Therefore, before turning to the main themes and some of the details of U.S. economic history after 1945, let us consider a broad perspective on America's position in the world at that date, how it got there, and how that position changed from the 1940s to the 1990s.

A Perspective on the U.S. Economy in the Twentieth Century

In the years immediately following World War II, the U.S. economy produced a larger proportion of the world's goods and services than any one nation had ever done before (or likely will do ever again). Americans, who represented only 6 percent of the world's population, accounted for about half of the total world economic output. The unique American position was a result of two factors: U.S. economic growth sustained at high rates since the early nineteenth century and the different impacts of World War II on the U.S. economy and that of other leading economic powers. Long-term U.S. growth, extensively studied in this text, made the American economy the world's largest by the late nineteenth century, and that growth and leading position were maintained into the twentieth century. The catastrophes of the second and fourth decades—World War I and the Great Depression—slowed the growth of the world economy but did not detract from the United States's leading position in it because most of the developed industrial countries were affected in similar ways by slower world economic growth.

The era of World War II was a different matter. On the eve of the war, the United States, though only partly recovered from the Depression, remained the largest and in many areas the most technologically advanced economy. During and immediately after the war, the U.S. economy—President Franklin Roosevelt's arsenal of democracy—grew much faster than the economies of other leading nations. Just how much faster is evident in the index numbers of real output growth shown in Table 21–1. By 1948, U.S. output was 65 percent larger than it was a decade earlier, in contrast to the output of Western Europe, which, dragged down by the economic collapse of defeated Germany, was 13 percent below 1938 levels. The Japanese economy suffered a collapse second only to Germany's. The Soviet Union, a member of the alliance against fascism during the war years, followed a pattern similar to that of the victorious Western European allies: little real growth from 1938 to 1948 followed by more rapid growth from 1948 to 1950. The U.S. economy also grew between 1948 and 1950, but not as fast as those of many of its allies in the war and not nearly as fast as those of defeated Germany and Japan.

Table 21–1 *Changes in Real GNP in the United States, Western Europe, Japan, and the Soviet Union, 1938–1950 (Index: 1938 = 100)*

Country	1938	1948	1950
United States	100	165	179
United Kingdom	100	106	114
France	100	100	121
West Germany	100	45	64
Italy	100	92	104
Belgium	100	115	124
Netherlands	100	114	127
Switzerland	100	125	131
Norway	100	122	131
Sweden	100	133	148
Total	100	106	114
Japan	100	63	72
Soviet Union	100	105	128

SOURCE: Adapted from data in Herman Van der Wee, *Prosperity and Upheaval: The World Economy, 1945–1980* (Berkeley: University of California Press, 1986), p. 30.

The pattern of relative growth among nations that was evident shortly after the war continued in the decades after 1950. The United States continued to grow, but its European wartime Allies grew faster and its former enemies, Germany and Japan, as well as much of the rest of the world, grew faster still. As these developments unfolded in the post-1945 decades, many Americans began to fret over their slower-growing economy, to bemoan a loss of international competitiveness in many areas, and to worry about becoming a nation in economic decline. To be sure, major economic problems did confront American economic decision makers between the 1940s and the 1990s, as we shall see in this and the following two chapters, and many of them could perhaps have been avoided by better decisions. But a longer perspective on the last half-century should draw attention to three important points that serve to temper concerns about America's decline.

First, an American economy in which 6 percent of the world's people produced half the world's economic output just after World War II was most unusual. The United States could have continued with such a share under circumstances that would be not only difficult to imagine but also ones that likely would have been inconsistent with world peace, political stability, and economic prosperity.

Second, U.S. decision makers had no interest in a continuance of the unique position of their economy in the world right after the war. Instead, working with other nations bilaterally and through international organizations, these decision makers worked to rebuild a liberal world economic order like the one that had served the interests of most nations and the growth of the world economy before 1914. In this they were successful, despite the complications of a Cold War that divided the world into two power blocs and a largely less-developed Third World for nearly half a century.

Third, in the early 1990s, the U.S. economy, after a half-century of continued growth, remained the world's largest and most productive in terms of output per labor hour and overall living standards. The economies of many other nations had grown faster, and a few had nearly caught up with the American economy in productivity and living standards. But in the world of the 1990s, Americans numbering less than 5 percent of the world's population still produced about a quarter of the world's goods and services, which is on the order of what they did in 1914. In this sense, as in others, the United States and the rest of the world in the 1990s have returned to a more typical relationship with one another than was the case in 1945, or indeed at any time since the early years of the twentieth century.

Building a Freer World-Trading Order

The world economy grew and prospered along with that of the United States in the decades before 1914. Then it broke down in the two world wars and the Great Depression of the 1914 to 1945 period. High-level U.S. decision makers during and after World War II were determined not to allow a repeat of the disastrous nationalistic political and military policies of the previous era. As noted earlier in the chapter, they were in a unique position to achieve this goal. Most of the cards were in their hands. U.S. economic and military powers were by far the strongest in the world. The economies of the nation's wartime Allies were weak in comparison, whereas those of its enemies were devastated.

Politically, the keystone of the new world order was the United Nations, formed in 1945. Economically, the key developments were new institutions, organizations, and policies designed in the short run to bring about recovery from the effects of the war and in the long run to foster freer world trade, orderly international financial transactions, and worldwide economic growth.

The Bretton Woods Agreements

The economic arrangements began to be put into place at an international monetary conference in the summer of 1944, before the war ended. Meeting in July of that year at the Mount Washington Hotel in the tiny resort town of Bretton Woods in northern New Hampshire, U.S. and British delegations—the latter included the eminent economist John Maynard Keynes—hammered out agreements to create a new international economic and financial order. The U.S. dollar, for obvious reasons based on the size and strength of the American economy, became the key international currency. Other countries agreed to fix the exchange rate of their national currencies in relation to the dollar and therefore in relation to each other. The United States, which then held the greater part of the world's stock of monetary gold, agreed to maintain an international gold price of $35 per ounce and to

exchange its gold for dollars when dollars were presented through official channels by other nations. This was a gold-bullion exchange standard based on the dollar. It differed from the pre-1914 gold standard in that gold reserves were nationalized. Gold coins were no longer used as money by ordinary citizens, including those of the United States, where gold coins had already been nationalized—called in by the federal government—in 1933. The gold price of $35 per ounce had been established in 1934, when the United States, to aid recovery from the Depression, devalued the dollar to 59 percent of its former gold value.

To make the new world economic and financial order work, the Bretton Woods agreements created an International Monetary Fund (IMF) and an International Bank for Reconstruction and Development (which came to be known as the World Bank). The IMF was—and is—essentially a credit union in which member countries pool funds that then can be lent as foreign-exchange reserves to individual member countries experiencing short-term adverse payments balances in their international transactions. With such IMF aid, a country could avoid either devaluing its currency, thereby disrupting international trade and finance, or the alternative of contracting its own economy, with consequent increases in unemployment and domestic political unrest. The IMF bought a country time while it put its economic house in order, often with advice on how to do so from the IMF. Its objectives were stable international currency values and an ending of restrictions on foreign-exchange transactions.

The World Bank was and remains an investment bank. It was intended to make or guarantee long-term loans that would finance projects to promote economic development in the receiving nation. As the dominant economic power when these institutions were created, the United States made the largest subscriptions of funds to the IMF and the World Bank, and both of the new international institutions set up their headquarters in Washington, D.C.

The General Agreement on Tariffs and Trade

By themselves, the Bretton Woods institutions could aid freer world trade and finance only so far. If nations continued to maintain high tariffs on imports from other nations, their effects would be muted. Here again U.S. decision makers took the lead. They had begun to move for lower trading barriers in the Trade Agreements Act of 1934, which was renewed in 1945 for three years. Armed with this renewed authority, the U.S. government in 1946 called for an international meeting, held in Geneva, Switzerland, under UN auspices, to reduce import duties. The result of that meeting in 1947 was the General Agreement on Tariffs and Trade. GATT facilitated negotiations between and among nations to reduce tariff barriers and to apply tariffs in a nondiscriminatory way. The "most favored nation" clause, for example, held that any GATT signatory could ask for and receive the same lower duty on imports that one nation had granted to another in bilateral bargaining. Within the GATT framework, eight "rounds" of international bargaining to reduce tariffs were organized between 1947 and 1992. The most recent, the so-called Uruguay Round, continues at this writing. Five of the rounds, beginning in Geneva, were held from 1947 to 1962, followed by the Kennedy Round during 1963 to 1967, the Tokyo Round during 1973 to 1980, and the Uruguay Round that began in 1986. Together these rounds reduced tariffs on the items they covered from an average of 40 percent after World War II to 4 percent in the 1990s. The tariff reductions were a boon to the expansion of world trade.

The European Community

One exception under the 1947 GATT protocols allowed suspension of the most-favored-nation clause if a group of countries wished to form a customs union or free-trade area. This exception led in later years to formation of a number of trading blocs that liberalized trade among their constituent countries while protecting the bloc from external competition. The most significant of these blocs to emerge after World War II was the European Common Market—later called simply the European Community or EC—created by the 1957 Treaty of Rome. Originally made up of France, West Germany, Italy, and the three smaller Benelux nations, the European Community later expanded to include twelve nations, with further additions likely in the 1990s and later.

The plan of the European Community was first to achieve a customs union, then full economic integration, and finally political integration of the member states. By the late 1960s, the customs union was in place. Its main features affecting the United States and the rest of the world were a common external tariff and a common agricultural policy. These were protectionist measures contrary to the American goal of freer world trade. But the United States went along with—even supported—the creation of the European Community because a stronger and more united Europe moving toward freer internal trade would be a bulwark against Communist expansionism. Thus, the Cold War had ramifications for the international economic policies of the United States. The nations of the European Community shared many of the political goals of U.S. decision makers, especially Communist containment. They also viewed the protectionist features of EC policies as ways of narrowing the productivity and income gaps between their countries and the United States.

U.S. Trade and Balance of Payments

As the largest trading nation, even though international trade was a relatively small component of its economy compared to most other nations, the United States was one, but far from the only, beneficiary of the freer trading order it had done so much to construct. During the two postwar decades covered in this chapter, 1946 to 1965, U.S. merchandise exports increased from $11.8 billion to $26.5 billion, on the whole a rather moderate expansion that indicated an emerging problem of international competitiveness for U.S. producers in international markets. Imports of goods to the United States grew considerably faster than U.S. exports, from $5.1 billion to $21.5 billion. Annual merchandise trade balances were always positive—or in mercantilist terms, "favorable"—in these years; that is, exports exceeded imports. More remarkably, the net income from U.S. investments abroad (over and above payments to foreigners on assets they owned in the United States) rose ninefold, from $0.6 billion to $5.4 billion between 1946 and 1965. These trade and investment income surpluses allowed U.S. businesses to invest billions of dollars in productive facilities in other countries. At the same time, they made it possible for the U.S. government to provide billions of dollars of economic and military aid to many nations. U.S. trade and current account surpluses allowed an outflow of dollars that lubricated the machinery of world trade without threatening the integrity of the international financial system.

The government-sponsored transfers of dollars and other forms of aid to foreign countries, which included the celebrated Marshall Plan aid to war-torn Europe during the period 1948 to 1951, were related to a second theme of the U.S. role in the world after 1945. As it led the world toward a freer trading and financial order, the United States also led an alliance of democratic nations in the Cold War against the Communist bloc led by the Union of Soviet Socialist Republics (USSR), the successor state to the Russian empire under the czars, which had been taken over by the Communists in 1917.

The Cold War and the Containment of Communism

After World War II, the Soviet Union, which from 1941 on had been an ally in the struggle against fascism, adopted a hostile position toward its former allies, chiefly the United States. The so-called Iron Curtain divided Europe north to south, from the Baltic to the Adriatic seas. The USSR installed pro-USSR Communist regimes with centrally planned and controlled economies in countries east of the Iron Curtain and aided Communist insurgencies attempting to take political, economic, and military control of other countries. Communist expansionism threatened the interests, values, and freedoms of the United States and its allies. As the hostile and expansionist motives of Stalin, the Soviet dictator, became clearer, the U.S. response, formulated by 1947, became one of containing communism. The Western- and Eastern-world allies of the United States during the war, as well as the defeated nations, joined in the policy of containment under American leadership.

Together, the United States and its allies in the Cold War in the end were more successful than they had ever expected to be. At the end of the 1980s and into the early 1990s, the Communist empire created by Stalin fell apart, and its old component states in Eastern Europe and the former Soviet Union worked to replace their centrally planned economies with market-based arrangements. From 1945 to 1990, however, the economic and other costs of the Cold War to the West and to the Eastern bloc were great. A large share of the costs of defending the West and its eastern allies fell on the United States as the leader of the Western alliance to contain communism.

An early step in U.S. Cold War decision making, one consistent with the policy of restoring free trade and finance, was the Marshall Plan. A precursor to this was a 1946 State Department program for turning over $8 billion of U.S. surplus property in devastated areas of Europe and Asia to governments there to aid them in relief, rehabilitation, and reconstruction. Nevertheless, by 1947, Western Europe's postwar economic recovery had stalled. This raised fears that the Communists, through insurrections or possibly through democratic political processes, might come to power in those countries.

At Harvard's commencement exercises in June 1947, George C. Marshall, the U.S. Secretary of State and a World War II hero, announced the U.S. plan to aid Europe's recovery. Congress approved the Marshall Plan, which during the 1948 to 1951 period contributed more than $13 billion of U.S. economic aid to the nations of Western Europe, including Italy and the Western-occupied zones of Germany. Marshall Plan aid helped to stimulate a remarkable economic recovery of those countries. The United States used its economic leverage to push Europe's postwar decision makers toward greater reliance on market mechanisms as opposed to government economic controls, an outcome that helped to sustain their growth in subsequent years and decades. Some analysts argue that this nudge toward market-based economic decision making was more important than the resource aid itself. Many postwar European leaders remembered the chaotic economic conditions between the world wars and probably would have been tempted to turn toward extensive governmental economic planning and less reliance on markets in the absence of the U.S. influence.

In 1949, at the time of the Marshall Plan, the United States spearheaded the move for the North Atlantic Treaty Organization (NATO), a mutual defense alliance of a number of Western European countries as well as Iceland, Canada, and the United States. Directed at countering Communist expansionism NATO set the pattern for other regional defense alliances created and led in later years by the United States, which largely financed and equipped them. American military personnel and equipment were stationed throughout the world, and military aid was given to numerous nations. After China, the world's most populous nation, fell to the Communists in 1949, major hot wars were waged against Communist expansionism

in Korea (1950 to 1953) and Vietnam (1964 to 1973), as well as a number of lesser actions. In these and other ways, the Cold War devoured huge quantities of American economic resources for nearly half a century.

Costs of the Cold War

How much did the Cold War cost? Figure 21–1 represents a first pass at answering this question. It shows the fraction of U.S. GNP devoted to national defense between 1947 and 1991. From 1947 to 1950, after the postwar demobilization was virtually complete and before the Cold War heated up, defense spending averaged about 5 percent of GNP. It was somewhat more than one-third of all federal spending in these years. From 1951 to 1960, expenditures on national defense soared to more than 10 percent of GNP, reaching a Cold War peak of nearly 14 percent in 1953, the last year of the war in Korea. In the 1950s, defense absorbed roughly 60 percent of the federal budget. From 1961 to the early 1970s, which included the years of war in Vietnam, just under 10 percent of GNP and just under half of federal spending were devoted to defense. After the Vietnam War, defense spending fell back to about 5 percent of GNP by the late 1970s. It rose to between 6 percent and 7 percent of GNP during President Ronald Reagan's defense buildup in the 1980s, but by the early 1990s the defense-spending-to-GNP ratio had fallen once again to levels prevalent in the late 1940s. From 1960 to 1990, defense spending declined as a proportion of the federal budget from about half to less than one quarter, not because defense spending fell—in fact, it rose a great deal—but because other categories of federal spending increased even more rapidly. Most of the drop in defense spending as a share of all federal spending occurred by the mid-1970s, roughly a decade after the Great Society and other welfare-state programs born in the 1960s had swelled federal nondefense spending.

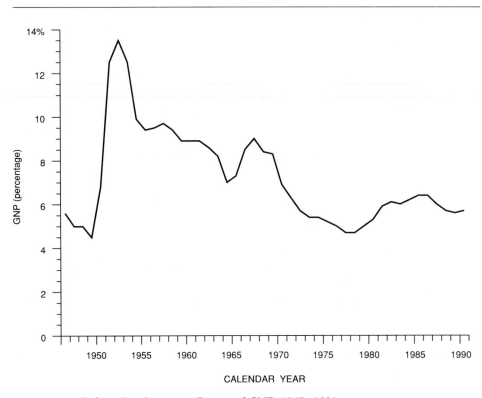

Figure 21–1 *Defense Purchases as a Percent of GNP, 1947–1991*
SOURCE: Adapted from *Historical Statistics of the United States, Bicentennial Edition*, 1975; *Economic Report of the President*, 1991, 1992 (Washington, D.C.: GPO).

Not all of the defense spending of the decades after 1945 can be attributed to the Cold War. But most of it can. In the first decade of the twentieth century, before World War I launched three-quarters of a century of world turmoil, the United States was already a military as well as an economic power. It spent about 40 percent to 50 percent of its federal budget on defense then, just as it did in the 1960s. But that spending amounted to only about 1 percent of GNP in the years from 1901 to 1910, as compared with 5 percent or more after 1945. Using that simpler and more peaceful world early in the century as a benchmark, one may conclude that four-fifths or more of

the vast amount the United States spent on defense between World War II and the 1990s was the result of the Cold War.

There were other Cold War costs as well, ones less easily measurable in dollars or as shares of the U.S. economic product. Defense spending on the Cold War scale created powerful groups with vested interests in it. Dwight D. Eisenhower, himself a military hero of World War II, in his 1961 farewell address as president warned Americans that in their midst was being created a "military-industrial complex" with interests of its own that might not match those of the nation. Military and civilian careers, jobs at military bases and in

The Cold War. These citizens are protesting against military spending and the mentality created by the Cold War outside of San Francisco's City Hall in 1960. Inside, Congress's House Un-American Activities Committee (HUAC) was holding hearings. HUAC promoted fears of Communist subversion within the United States; after being renamed the House Internal Security Committee in 1969, it was abolished in 1975. (UPI/The Bettmann Archive)

defense plants and laboratories, financial returns to those who invested in the defense industries, and even university research budgets depended in greater or lesser degrees on Cold War spending. The interest groups represented in this listing—there were others as well—tended to support higher and higher levels of defense and defense-related spending because they benefited directly or indirectly from it.

Although the military-industrial complex absorbed a significant portion of U.S. resources without creating goods and services that satisfied basic human needs, not all of the effects of the Cold War detracted from that nonmilitary goal. Military research and development created know-how applicable in a number of civilian industries; for example, in aerospace and electronics, including computers. And defense considerations in the 1950s contributed to such worthwhile developments as the interstate highway system (so called "interstate and defense highways") and increased federal spending on education (e.g., the National Defense Education Act of 1958). Political satirists of the time—an era in which even worthwhile causes did not lead automatically to demands for federal spending programs—noted that the federal government would not deliver better highways and education on their own merits but that each could easily be gotten in the name of defense. Such was the Cold War mentality. Studies have shown that the Cold War was paid for mainly by reduced consumption rather than by reductions in investment and capital formation.[1] If so, American living standards in the Cold War era every year were several percentage points lower than they might have been. There can be little doubt, moreover, that while it lasted, the Cold War, for good or ill, contributed greatly to the expanded role of governmental decision making in American economic life.

Government Accepts Responsibility for Economic Stabilization

Between 1945 and 1965, U.S. decision makers gradually came to accept the idea that the federal government could stabilize and even fine-tune the performance of the U.S. economy. Doubts would arise about this idea after 1965, and notions of fine-tuning were abandoned by the 1980s, but government's acceptance of responsibility for economic stabilization remained into the 1990s as one of the more significant changes that occurred in the United States during the twentieth century.

Fiscal Policies Before the 1960s

The effects of World War II's massive military spending on the U.S. economy, as explained in Chapter 20, were dramatic, especially in the reduction of unemployment. As of 1940, the last prewar year for the United States, unemployment had not been below a rate of 14 percent since 1930. In 1942, it fell to less than 5 percent and, in 1944, to less than 2 percent. The government's wartime spending program was directed by considerations other than economic recovery. But viewed as an experiment in large-scale fiscal stimulation of the economy, the program contained clear lessons for economists, policymakers, and the citizenry.

Employment Act of 1946.   The fiscal lessons of the Depression and the war were not wasted. Soon after the war, the Employment Act of 1946 committed the federal government to the promotion of economic stability. The act stated that "it is the continuing policy and responsibility of the Federal Government to use all practical means . . . to promote maximum employment, production, and purchasing power." Although the goals specified were subject to different interpretations, they were widely considered to mean full employment, healthy economic growth, and stability of the general price level. To aid federal decision makers in formulating policies to achieve these goals, the act established the President's Council of Economic Advisers and a congressional Joint Economic Committee composed of members of both houses to monitor the economy and economic policies.

A view held by many Americans at the end of World War II was that the depressed economic conditions of the 1930s would return once the greatly expanded levels of wartime spending were phased out. Government spending on goods and services did in fact contract sharply, from an annual rate of almost $100 billion in early 1945 to only $35 billion a year later. But only a brief and mild slowdown resulted. In 1946, as wartime price controls began to be dismantled, the economy recovered rapidly. The driving force of the expansion was pent-up demand on the part of consumers who had accumulated large amounts of liquid assets—money, near monies, and government securities—during the war, while at the same time stinting on their consumption as resources were channeled into the war effort. With the war over, consumers went on a buying spree. Prices rose rapidly from 1945 to 1948, and unemployment remained below 4 percent.

Early Postwar Recessions.   The business cycle, however, was not a thing of the past. In

1948 to 1949, and again in 1953 to 1954, 1957 to 1958, and 1960 to 1961, the economy slipped into recessions characterized by rising rates of unemployment and underutilized productive capacity. But the important point for a historical perspective on these times is that the early post–World War II recessions were much milder in terms of price and unemployment changes than were the prewar downturns of 1920 to 1921, 1929 to 1933, and 1937 to 1938.

A good part of the credit for the greater economic stability of the two decades after World War II can perhaps be given to the expanded economic role of government, including its explicit commitment to promote stability. But one must be careful not to exaggerate the effects of that commitment. In the two decades in question, the commitment may have had more effect on the confidence of consumers, investors, and business in general than on discretionary government policy decisions to promote stability when it appeared to be threatened. The sheer size of the government in the economy and how it interacted with the rest of it, even in the absence of discretionary policy changes, go far toward explaining the improvement in economic stability.

Automatic Fiscal Stabilizers. To understand why this was the case in the early postwar decades, we must distinguish between *automatic* and *discretionary stabilization policies.* In the fiscal area, much of the credit for greater postwar stability must be given to the automatic fiscal stabilizers rather than to discretionary policy actions. Expenditure stabilizers included such payments as unemployment compensation, which went up when unemployment rose and went down when the economy improved without any discretionary policy actions. Tax stabilizers moved automatically in the opposite direction: Individual and corporate income tax receipts as well as payroll and excise tax collections fell off with declining incomes during economic downturns and then rose as the economy recovered and moved toward full employment. The result was that fluctuations in the balance of the government's budget automatically stabilized private incomes relative to fluctuations in aggregate national product. Because levels of government spending on all items, including unemployment compensation and Social Security transfers, as well as levels of taxation had risen greatly relative to the size of the economy since the 1930s, the automatic fiscal stabilizers played a large role in stabilizing the postwar economy.

Discretionary Fiscal Policy. Discretionary fiscal policy actions—conscious decisions to vary government spending or taxes for purposes of promoting economic stability—were generally less important than automatic budgetary changes before the 1960s. When discretionary changes occurred, they were often motivated by considerations other than economic stability. Thus, the 1948 income tax cut, which helped to stabilize the economy during the first postwar recession of 1948 to 1949, was based more on a general public desire—ever present in peacetime in the United States—for lower taxes rather than on a policy decision to fight the impending recession. This tax cut was passed over the veto of President Harry S Truman, who worried about the possible inflationary consequences of a tax cut as well as the need to finance Cold War defense expenditures. And tax cuts during the 1953 to 1954 recession had been previously scheduled and likely would have occurred without the recession, which itself was caused by rapid reductions in federal spending at the end of the Korean War. In the 1957 to 1958 and 1960 to 1961 recessions, President Eisenhower's concerns over inflation, similar to Truman's in 1948, led to rather tight fiscal and monetary policies.

Although the theory of discretionary fiscal policy for economic stabilization was increasingly understood by economists and policymakers in the postwar years, practical political and economic constraints severely limited its application before the 1960s. Concern for balanced budgets was one of these constraints. Even when budget deficits were small and the result of economic weakness, many people considered them to represent profligacy on the part of government and called for reduced expenditures or higher taxes. Such policy measures, of course, were the direct opposites of what the theory of a stabilizing fiscal policy called for. Another constraint involved the inevitable lags in policy action and implementation: The need for action had first to be recognized, then appropriate action had to be decided on and implemented, and finally, with a further lag, would come the economic effects of the action. By the time a policy actually affected the economy, conditions might well have changed and the intended stabilizing policy could turn out to be destabilizing. Hence, except in war or a prolonged depression, the ability of discretionary fiscal actions to reduce the duration and severity of postwar recessions was limited in both theory and practice. But the automatic stabilizers worked fairly well.

Monetary Policy (1945–1960)

An independent monetary policy in the postwar era was not possible until 1951, when the Federal Reserve System was released from its obligation, entered into during World War II, to peg interest rates on government securities at low levels. After much bickering between the Fed, which saw the need to let interest rates rise from extremely low wartime levels in order to stave off inflation, and the Treasury, which wanted low rates in order to minimize the interest cost of a federal debt greatly enlarged by the war, the two parties reached an agreement—the Treasury-Fed Accord of 1951. It freed the Fed to pursue the stabilizing monetary policies it deemed appropriate.

After 1951 and into the early 1960s, the Fed's monetary policies attempted to promote stability by "leaning against the wind." In practice, this meant that the Fed attempted to restrain an expanding economy from overheating with inflationary consequences and to counteract recessions with low-interest, easy-money policies. The main concern of the Fed during the 1950s was inflation, and in retrospect it did a creditable job on this front. Toward the end of the 1950s, however, the Fed's image became somewhat tarnished when it contributed to the 1957 to 1958 recession by failing to ease monetary and credit conditions after the downturn had occurred. It then contributed to the 1960 to 1961 recession by returning to a restrictive policy in 1959, before recovery from the previous recession was complete. These mishaps led many economists and politicians at the time to conclude that the Fed was slowing down U.S. economic growth through excessive restraint on monetary and credit expansion.

The Triumph of Discretionary Stabilization Policies (1961–1965)

The recessions of 1957 to 1958 and 1960 to 1961, coming so close together, furnished important political issues during the presidential campaign of 1960. When John F. Kennedy won a narrow victory after a campaign in which he promised "to get this country moving again," he brought with him to Washington economic advisers who believed more strongly than their predecessors in active fiscal and monetary policies to promote stability and growth. Increases in defense spending aided the recovery from recession in 1961, and in 1962 a tax credit and liberalized depreciation rules were implemented to encourage business investment. In 1963, with unemployment remaining over 5.5 percent, the Kennedy administration proposed a major cut in individual and corporate income taxes. Coming at a time of a deficit in the federal budget, this was a startling proposal to many observers. But the case for the tax cut was carefully explained by administration economists, and the measure became law in early 1964, shortly after Kennedy's tragic assassination.

Effects of the 1964 Tax Cut. The tax cut of 1964 worked. Between 1963 and 1966, the economy grew at rates of 5 percent to 6 percent per year, prices were relatively stable, and unemployment declined from 5.7 percent to 3.8 percent. Monetary policy cooperated with fiscal policy during the long expansion that began in 1961 and picked up steam after the tax cut. Rather than "leaning against the wind" as it had done in the 1950s, the Fed allowed the money supply to expand at higher rates in these years. Monetarist economists argued that this monetary expansion, as much or more than the tax cut, was the true basis of the higher rate of growth. Perhaps so, but a further monetarist argument contending that the inflation that began in the mid-1960s was also caused by higher monetary growth starting in 1961 is on weaker ground. Prices were relatively stable from 1961 to 1965, and other events were more likely causes of the higher rate of inflation after 1965 (see Chapter 22).

Fiscal Dividends? By the mid-1960s, the economists who advised the Kennedy and Johnson administrations were proud of their economic management. They could point out to those who remained unpersuaded that despite the 1964 tax cut (in the economists' view, because of the tax cut!) the federal fiscal deficits of 1965 and 1966 were substantially reduced from earlier levels. Rising incomes more than offset the decline in income tax rates as far as federal revenue was concerned. The economists held out the promise of an even better future. Because tax revenues would continue to rise with economic growth, they argued that it would be possible and even necessary for the government again and again to

cut tax rates or, alternatively, to increase government spending without increasing taxes. These so-called fiscal dividends would have to be paid out to prevent the federal budget from becoming a drag on economic growth. Unfortunately, as we will see in Chapter 22, things did not turn out to be quite so rosy after 1965.

Major Developments in the Labor Markets After 1945

Since 1945, a number of key changes have occurred in American labor markets. The baby boom that began just after the war was one change of long-term importance because it would swell the ranks of entrants to the labor markets in the 1960s and 1970s. Equally important for the long-term, women began to enter the labor force in ever greater numbers after the war. (Other important developments affecting labor markets, including the improvements that occurred in the status of black and other minority workers as well as the rise in the relative shares of employment and output of the service sector of the economy compared to the goods-producing components, are discussed in Chapter 22.)

The Post–World War II Baby Boom

For nearly two decades after 1945, the birthrate in the United States moved up to the higher levels—about 25 per thousand members of the population—that had been typical early in the century but not seen after the early 1920s. By way of contrast, the birthrate was only 18 per thousand during the Depression decade of the 1930s. The death rate declined steadily in these decades, from about 18 per thousand at the turn of the century to 11 per thousand in the 1930s and to less than 10 per thousand after 1945.

The result of these various demographic changes in the 1950s was a surge in U.S.

population growth to a rate—more than 1.7 percent per year—not seen since the period prior to World War I early in the century. In American history before 1914, surges in population growth from period to period usually depended on surges in immigration. The post–World War II phenomenon was different. In that era, immigration to the United States from other countries was trivial as a result of restrictive immigration legislation dating back to the 1920s. Instead, the population surge was the result of what came to be known as the baby boom, which lasted into the early 1960s. For perspective, we note that by the end of the 1960s, the birthrate had fallen back to the levels of the 1930s, and from the early 1970s to the early 1990s, it moved even lower, to about 15 or 16 per thousand.

The baby boom was a surprise to demographers. The long-term trends in the modern economic history of economically developed nations have been for both the birthrate and the death rate to fall and for populations to grow at a lower rate because the former fell more than the latter. In explanations of the trends, a falling death rate is typically related to rising living standards and to advances in health and medicine. A falling birthrate, similarly, is related to such factors as the rising relative costs of children in increasingly urbanized societies and, in particular, to greater opportunities and better wages for women—potential mothers—which give them incentives to pursue jobs and careers in the labor markets and to postpone childbearing.

Explaining the Baby Boom. So what explains the baby boom? It occurred as American society was becoming more urban and less rural and as more opportunities in the labor market were opening up for women. The most intriguing answer is proposed by Richard Easterlin, an economic historian and demographer, who stresses the relative prosperity of the U.S. economy after World War II as compared with

the depressed years of the 1930s.[2] Young adults after World War II were living in an era of expanding job opportunities, upward social mobility, and rising living standards that contrasted markedly with the depressed economic conditions and social crises that they and their parents had experienced from the late 1920s through the war. Moreover, because of the low birthrate that had prevailed in the era of their own births, this generation of young adults was not large in relation to the postwar economic opportunities that confronted it. Therefore, the greater well-being of these young adults after 1945 compared to their childhood years led them to enjoy more of everything—cars, homes, television sets, and—yes—babies.

The children of the young adults of the postwar era, the baby boomers born from 1946 to the early 1960s, lived well as children but would be much more numerous than their parents' generation when they began to enter the labor market in the 1960s. It was unlikely, Easterlin argued at that time, that the baby boomers' economic expectations and their opportunities would match those of their parents. More likely, they would be the opposite: high expectations and lower opportunities, merely because there were so many of the baby boomers. Easterlin therefore predicted a drop in the birthrate as the boomers coped with a more crowded labor market and lower relative incomes, and he turned out to be right.

Long-Term Effects of the Baby Boom. The baby boom had, and in the 1990s indeed still is having, a large impact on the U.S. economy. While it was occurring in the postwar era, the baby boom increased demands for all sorts of goods and services associated with children and large families: more and larger homes, second autos—preferably station wagons—to haul the kids around, more schools and colleges, more pediatricians, fast food at the proliferating drive-ins, and many more consumer

The Baby Boom and Suburbanization. This 1949 photo shows Levittown, Long Island, a community near New York City that did not exist three years earlier. Techniques of mass producing defense workers' housing during the war were applied to the problem of a postwar housing shortage. Express highways provided routes to and from work. Farm land near cities was converted to higher-valued uses. (UPI/The Bettmann Archive)

goods. In later decades, as we shall see in Chapter 22, it led to large increases in young and inexperienced workers, to a slower growth of real earnings, to concerns about job creation and the quality of jobs, and even to concerns about low savings rates and the long-term financing of the Social Security system (which in the next century will have to pay retirement and health benefits to rapidly growing numbers of retirees). Unusual demographic events such as the baby boom have many implications for economic life when they occur and for decades afterward.

The Rise of Women's Labor Force Participation

Another important change in the labor market in the half-century after World War II was the ever-growing proportion of American women who chose to work for pay. As Table 21–2 in-

dicates, between 1890 and 1940, women's labor force participation—the fraction of working-age women who were in the labor force—gradually rose from 19 percent to 26 percent. Then it jumped to 35 percent over the two decades ending in 1960. This was merely the start. By 1990, nearly 58 percent of working-age women were in the labor force.

Breakdown of Marriage Bars. What accounts for the rapid rise of female participation after 1940? An important clue is exhibited in Table 21–2. Single women's participation rates, though well above the rates of married women, changed only slightly between 1940 and 1960. But the participation rate of married women more than doubled, from 14 percent to 31 percent in these years. Claudia Goldin, the compiler and analyst of these data, concludes that social norms discouraging married women from working began to break down in

Table 21–2 *Female Labor Force Participation Rates, 1890–1990*

Year	All Women	Single Women	Married Women
1890	19%	11%	5%
1900	21	44	6
1920	24	46	9
1930	25	51	12
1940	26	46	14
1950	30	51	22
1960	35	48	31
1970	42	51	40
1980	51	62	50
1990	58	57[a]	58

[a]1990 data: single women category includes widowed, divorced, and separated.
SOURCES: Data for 1890 to 1980 are adapted from Claudia Goldin, *Understanding the Gender Gap: An Economic History of American Women* (New York: Oxford University Press, 1990), p. 17; data for 1990 are adapted from *Economic Report of the President 1992* (Washington, D.C.: GPO, 1992), p. 337; and U.S. Bureau of the Census, *Statistical Abstract of the United States 1991*, 111th ed. (Washington, D.C.: GPO, 1991), p. 390.

these decades.[3] Female school teachers, airline flight attendants, and women in a number of other occupations were no longer required by "marriage bars" to leave the labor force when they married. Contributing to the breakdown of the old norms were the tight labor markets of the 1940s and 1950s. These resulted in large measure from the same demographic factors that were connected with the baby boom. The low birthrate of the prewar era coupled with the war and postwar prosperity brought about expanded job opportunities for all potential workers, women included, after 1940. From 1940 to 1960, according to Goldin's findings, the largest increases in women's labor force participation were in the older age groups, thirty-five years and up. Participation rates of younger women, fifteen to thirty-four years in age, grew much less. These younger married women concentrated instead on being mothers of the baby boomers.

Anti-discrimination Legislation. After 1960, more and more of the baby boom mothers—and eventually their daughters—entered the labor force. By 1979, over half of all working-age American women were in it. Some were unemployed, however, and so it was not until 1985 that, for the first time in U.S. history, more than half of all working-age women were actually employed for pay. The steady rise of female participation resulted in part from continued changes in social norms about women's roles in the home, the family, and the workplace. These included reductions in barriers to a woman's ability to choose work, including some prompted by legislation. In 1961, John F. Kennedy appointed a Presidential Commission on the Status of Women, and some of its recommendations, based on findings of discrimination against women in both private- and public-sector jobs, led to the Equal Pay Act of 1963. Shortly thereafter, Title VII of the 1964 Civil Rights Act prohibited discrimination in hiring, promotion, and other conditions of employment on the basis of race, color, religion, sex, or national origin. The act led to the establishment of the Equal Employment Opportunity Commission (EEOC) to receive and investigate complaints of job-market discrimination. Such complaints rose rapidly in the early 1970s, when about a third of them were related to sex discrimination.

Other factors associated with increased women's labor force participation were the decisions of many married couples to have few or no children as well as the rising divorce rate in the 1960s and 1970s. The cause-effect relationships between decisions to work and decisions about desired numbers of children and about divorce are difficult to disentangle, but the results of those decisions were clearly evident in the labor statistics. From the 1960s to the 1990s, the rising numbers of women in the la-

Female Workers in the 1960s.   After World War II, increasing numbers of American women entered and stayed in the labor force. The workers pictured here illustrate another theme of the postwar economy as well: They are assembling portable tactical radar systems for a defense contractor on Long Island, New York. (UPI/Bettmann Newsphotos)

bor market both reflected and reinforced the baby boom in bringing about a rapid growth of the labor force and a rise in its proportion of young and inexperienced workers. Job opportunities for women expanded across a wider range of employers and economic sectors than had been the case earlier, but as young and first-time entrants to the labor market, women were often on the lowest rungs of job ladders.

The Gender Gap.   An important consequence of these characteristics of female entrants and of remaining elements of job-market discrimination was the "gender gap," the difference between men's and women's earnings. Table 21–3 presents the post–World War II trends in earnings. The gender gap barely changed from the 1950s to the 1980s. What changes there were indicate an increase in the gender gap from 1955 to 1973, followed by a decrease in the gap later in the 1970s. The first real evidence of a narrowing of the gender gap

Table 21–3 *Ratio of Female to Male Full-Time Earnings, All Occupations, 1955–1989*

Year	Median Yearround Earnings	Median Weekly Wage and Salary Income
1955	0.64	—
1961	0.60	—
1967	0.58	—
1973	0.57	0.62
1979	0.60	0.63
1984	0.64	0.68
1989	0.68	0.70

SOURCES: Adapted from Claudia Goldin, *Understanding the Gender Gap: An Economic History of American Women* (New York: Oxford University Press, 1990), pp. 60–61; and U.S. Bureau of the Census, *Statistical Abstract of the United States 1991*, 111th ed. (Washington, D.C.: GPO, 1991), pp. 415, 417.

came in the 1980s. The data are consistent with rising female labor force participation resulting from entry of many women workers who at first were young or inexperienced. By the

1980s, as more and more working women accumulated job experience, the gap began to narrow. Despite the gains, women's earnings in 1990 averaged only 70 percent of men's, indicating that a substantial gender gap remained a feature of American labor markets in the 1990s.

Two Decades of Stable Growth

In 1965, Americans looked back on two postwar decades of stable economic growth at home as well as a world economy recovered from World War II and making strides in economic development in most areas. On the domestic front, the U.S. economy in real terms doubled in size between 1946 and 1965. GNP (in 1958 dollars) rose from $313 billion to $618 billion, an annual rate of growth of 3.7 percent. Real product per person rose 44 percent, or about 2 percent per year, even as the baby boom generation increased the denominator without directly adding much to the numerator. Productivity (real output per labor hour in the private domestic economy) rose even faster, about 3 percent per year. Inflation was low: After a sharp rise when wartime price controls were removed, the Consumer Price Index advanced less than 2 percent per year on average between 1948 and 1965. There were,

as noted earlier in the chapter, four brief recessions with troughs in 1949, 1954, 1958, and 1961. But real product per person fell barely at all during the first three and actually rose a little on a year-to-year basis in the 1960 to 1961 recession. The worst year for unemployment came in 1958, when the rate reached 6.6 percent. Unemployment rates of 4 percent to 5 percent were more typical of the period. If not quite full employment, they were at least close to it.

Internationally, the economic institutions and policies put in place under American leadership at the end of World War II also enjoyed considerable success. The freer world trading and financial order led to remarkable economic recoveries in Japan and Western Europe even before the advent of the European Economic Community. And Cold War policies contained the spread of communism in Europe and, at considerable costs, in Korea, though Communist threats were still evident in other parts of Asia as well as in Africa and Latin America. The ideological and political tensions of the Cold War, as well as the end of colonialism and the resurgence of nationalism in the less developed countries of the Third World, created many problems for international economic and political relations in these decades. But they were not so great as to stifle economic growth and development in most of the world.

Summary

The economic momentum and international leadership that were legacies of World War II for the United States carried over into the postwar years. Fears that a depressed economy like that of the 1930s would return after the war were quickly dissolved by a postwar economic expansion that for two decades featured high rates of growth, some of the best advances in productivity in U.S. economic history, and

minimal rates of inflation. Americans who lived at that time knew that the economy was in much better shape than it had been for many years. In 1958, John Kenneth Galbraith termed the United States "the affluent society" in a book so titled, though his point was that it was much more affluent privately than publicly.[4] And Walt Rostow, in his 1960 book, *The Stages of Economic Growth: A Non-Communist*

Manifesto, whose subtitle indicated how far the Cold War had penetrated all areas of consciousness, said that the United States was the first economy in history to reach the stage of "high mass consumption."[5]

American self-confidence, wealth, know-how, and Cold War concerns all came together in President John F. Kennedy's 1961 challenge—which was met successfully—to put an astronaut on the moon before the end of the 1960s. The years from 1945 to 1965 for the United States were ones of great optimism and solid economic accomplishments, though tempered by Cold War politics and fears. From the perspective of the 1990s, what conclusion might we draw about this earlier era, when some of the leading worries about the economy (in addition to Galbraith's private-public imbalance) were annual growth rates of 3 percent when they could have been 4 percent, and inflation rates that seemed to creep up toward 2 percent or 2.5 percent? Not bad perhaps. We might even say without risking overstatement that these indeed were good years for most Americans; however, African-Americans, other minorities, and women still had to work for equal opportunity.

Endnotes

1. See, for example, Michael Edelstein, "What Price Cold War? Military Spending and Private Investment in the U.S., 1946–1979," *Cambridge Journal of Economics,* 14 (1990), 421–37.

2. Richard Easterlin, *Birth and Fortune: The Impact of Numbers on Personal Welfare* (New York: Basic Books, 1980).

3. Claudia Goldin, *Understanding the Gender Gap: An Economic History of American Women* (New York: Oxford University Press, 1990).

4. John Kenneth Galbraith, *The Affluent Society* (Boston: Houghton Mifflin, 1958).

5. Walt Rostow, *The Stages of Economic Growth: A Non-Communist Manifesto* (Cambridge: Cambridge University Press, 1960).

Suggested Readings

The Employment Act of 1946 established the President's Council of Economic Advisers; the reports of the Council, a major part of each year's *Economic Report of the President* (Washington, D.C.: GPO, annually beginning in 1947), provide a running commentary on the state of the U.S. economy as well as analysis and interpretation of longer-term domestic and international economic problems confronting the United States and the world. Another valuable feature of the *Report* is a comprehensive collection of "Statistical Tables Relating to Income, Employment, and Production" covering, typically, several decades. Other basic sources of economic data with more detail and even longer periods of coverage are U.S. Department of Commerce publications: *Survey of Current Business* (Washington, DC: Bureau of Economic Analysis, monthly); U.S. Bureau of the Census, *Statistical Abstract of the United States* (Washington, D.C.: GPO, annually); and U.S. Bureau of the Census, *Historical Statistics of the United States—Colonial Times to 1970,* Bicentennial Edition, (Washington, D.C.: GPO, 1975).

For a long-run perspective on the world economy and the place of the United States in it, see Angus Maddison, *Phases of Capitalist Development* (Oxford: Oxford University Press, 1982). Herman Van der Wee, *Prosperity and Upheaval: The World Economy, 1945–1980* (Berkeley: University of California Press, 1986), treats the post–World War II decades from an international perspective. Robert Gilpin, *The Political Economy of International Relations* (Princeton: Princeton University Press, 1987), provides a detailed account of international trade and financial policies after 1944. On the Marshall Plan, see Michael J. Hogan, *The Marshall Plan: America, Britain, and the Reconstruction of Western Europe, 1947–1952* (New York: Cambridge University Press, 1987).

Economic and other effects of the Cold War are viewed in a sweeping historical context by historian Paul Kennedy, *The Rise and Fall of the Great Powers: Economic Change and Military Conflict from 1500 to 2000* (New York: Random House, 1987). Michael Edelstein, "What Price Cold War? Military Spending and Private Investment in the U.S., 1946–1979," *Cambridge Journal of Economics,* 14 (1990), discusses the ways in which the Cold War was paid for. See also Robert A. Pollard, *Economic Security and the Origins of the Cold War, 1945–1980* (New York: Columbia University Press, 1985).

The evolution of the federal government's acceptance of responsibility for economic stabilization is the subject of Herbert Stein's *The Fiscal Revolution in America,* rev. ed. (Lanham, Md.: AEI Press, 1990; first published in 1969). See also Nicholas Spulber, *Managing the American Economy: From Roosevelt to Reagan* (Bloomington: Indiana University Press, 1989) and Hugh S. Norton, *The Quest for Economic Stability: Roosevelt to Reagan* (Columbia: University of South Carolina Press, 1985). Details on the 1950s are given by Iwan W. Morgan, *Eisenhower versus "The Spenders": The Eisenhower Administration, the Democrats, and the Budget, 1953–60* (New York: St. Martin's Press, 1990).

On the changed approach to economic policy in the 1960s, see Walter W. Heller, *New Dimensions in Political Economy* (Cambridge: Harvard University Press, 1966); James Tobin, *National Economic Policy* (New Haven: Yale University Press, 1966), and Arthur M. Okun, *The Political Economy of Prosperity* (New York: W. W. Norton, 1969).

The post–World War II baby boom is analyzed by Richard Easterlin in *Birth and Fortune: The Impact of Numbers on Personal Welfare* (New York: Basic Books, 1980), and in *The American Baby Boom in Historical Perspective* (New York: National Bureau of Economic Research, 1962), and by Louise B. Russell, *The Baby Boom Generation and the Economy* (Washington, D.C.: Brookings Institution, 1982).

Economic analysis of the position of women in the American economy throughout the nation's history is provided by Claudia Goldin, *Understanding the Gender Gap: An Economic History of American Women* (New York: Oxford University Press, 1990). Alice Kessler Harris, *Out to Work: A History of Wage-Earning Women in the United States* (New York: Oxford University Press, 1982) is also valuable. The post–World War II labor market in general is treated by Richard B. Freeman, "The Evolution of the American Labor Market, 1948–80," in Martin Feldstein, ed., *The American Economy in Transition* (Chicago: University of Chicago Press, 1980), a volume that has other valuable essays on the postwar economy as well.

Economist Alice Rivlin's recent book, *Reviving the American Dream: The Economy, the States, and the Federal Government* (Washington, D.C.: Brookings Institution, 1992), is more about the economic problems Americans face in the 1990s, but she also provides a penetrating perspective on the early postwar decades, which she terms "The Good News Years," as well as "The Disappointing Years" of the 1970s and 1980s, which we discuss in Chapters 22 and 23.

Chapter 22

The Great Inflation, 1965–1982

THE SUCCESSFUL POLITICAL ECONOMY FASHIONED by U.S. decision makers during the two decades after the Second World War began to unravel in the mid-1960s. On the domestic front, stable economic growth with advancing levels of productivity and living standards and minimal price inflation gave way to a regime of sharper expansions and contractions, a marked slowing in the advance of productivity and living standards, and a price inflation unprecedented in U.S. history. The inflation reached double-digit levels—annual price-level increases of 10 percent or more—during the mid- and late 1970s. In this *Great Inflation*, our focus in this chapter, one finds the source of many problems for the American economy from 1965 to 1982 and beyond.

International economic and political developments both affected and were affected by the disturbing changes in the U.S. domestic economy. The American inflation was exported to the rest of the world, leading to the breakdown and then the collapse in 1973 of the Bretton Woods system of fixed exchange rates among the national currencies of the leading trading nations. On top of that, political instability in the Middle East and the formation of a strong cartel by the Organization of Petroleum Exporting Countries (OPEC) resulted in two oil price shocks—sharp increases in the prices of crude petroleum, a vital commodity in world trade, in 1973 and 1979. Higher oil prices after 1973 added to the inflationary pressures that were already building, and they compounded the problems of decision makers who had to cope with them.

The collapse of Bretton Woods and the oil price shocks created new strains for the liberal trading and financial order constructed under American leadership after World War II. That order had already been strained by an unfortunate turn in U.S. Cold War policy. Containing the spread of communism suffered a setback in what many considered the misdirected effort and ultimate failure of U.S. policy in the long and costly Vietnam War of 1964 to 1973. (The negative impact of a continuing Cold War on the Soviet economy was not to evident to Western observers at the time, though it did become evident later on.)

By the end of the 1970s, the American economy was in a mess. At home it faced stagflation—excessive unemployment and inflation. Internationally, the U.S. position weakened in trade and finance. The economic optimism of the early 1960s, tempered as it was by Cold War realities, gave way to a malaise (a word used by President Jimmy Carter to describe the country's condition during his administration from 1977 to 1981) concerning America's economic situation and prospects, as well as its ability to continue in a role of economic and political leadership in the world.

Dimensions of the Great Inflation

The Great Inflation that began around 1965 lasted for seventeen years, until 1982, when the Federal Reserve's attempts to break its momentum, which began in 1979, achieved success. Monetary policy then shifted course in the direction of stimulating a U.S. economy mired in its most severe recession since the 1930s. By 1982, however, the price level, as measured by all three of the commonly used price indexes—consumer prices, producer prices (finished goods), and the gross domestic product (GDP) deflator—was about three times its level in 1965. In other words, a U.S. dollar had one-third the purchasing power it possessed in 1965. Put still another way, the rate of inflation over the seventeen-year period was about 6.5 percent per year, continuously compounded. At no other point in U.S. history was a rate of price advance of this magnitude sustained for such a long period of time.

Inflation continued after 1982, but at much reduced rates. From 1982 to 1991, the consumer price index and the GDP deflator each rose about 40 percent, or at a rate of about 3.7 percent per year. Producer prices rose considerably less rapidly, at a rate of about 2.2 percent per year. These were high rates compared to those before 1965, but after the Great Inflation most Americans welcomed them.

How the Great Inflation Began

Policy Decisions: Guns and Butter

What went wrong? Several decisions made by federal policymakers in the mid-1960s set in motion a troubling sequence of events that plagued the American economy for decades thereafter. One was the widely supported decision to make a quantum leap toward the welfare state in the form of a host of Great Society programs proposed by President Lyndon Johnson and enacted by Congress between 1964 and 1968. The Great Society represented a revival of the New Deal's reformist spirit that had been dormant politically after the 1940s. Second, there was the 1964 decision, prompted by Cold War considerations, to escalate dramatically the military involvement of the United States in the long-running conflict in Vietnam. However, neither of these decisions by itself was directly responsible for the initiation of the Great Inflation. The real culprit of the story was the decision, more implicit than explicit, to finance both the Great Society and the Vietnam War mainly through inflation, rather than by means of tax increases or reduced government spending in other areas.

Thus, in the mid-1960s, U.S. federal decision makers attempted to provide Americans with both more butter and more guns through massive increases in government spending financed by money creation. Such a policy would have been consistent with price stability only if there had been underutilized economic resources at the time, as had been the case when World War II began. But by the mid-1960s, the U.S. economy was close to fully utilizing its available resources. Under these circumstances, then, massive increases in government spending without adequate provision for financing through higher taxes resulted in increased inflation.

The mechanism of inflation was relatively simple. As the federal government raised its demands from the American economy, interest rates rose. The Federal Reserve System, operating on a Keynesian economic analysis predicting that higher interest rates would choke off economic growth, responded to rising interest rates by expanding the money supply. The Fed had previously moved toward higher rates of monetary growth in the early 1960s under prodding from the Kennedy administration, which wanted to reduce unemployment and raise the rate of economic growth. However, unlike the period after 1965, there was slack in the economy's use of resources, and more money financed real growth without increasing the rate of inflation. After 1965, higher monetary growth served to raise the price level. As the inflation got going, private economic decision makers came to have expectations of continued and possibly increased inflation, and they acted accordingly. Lenders, for example, demanded higher interest rates for lending money to protect against the expected inflation. The Fed responded by further increases in money growth, and in doing so it sustained the inflationary momentum through the 1970s.

Increased Government Spending

The root of the inflation problem, then, was the federal government's attempt after 1965 to provide both more guns and more butter in an economy that was fully utilizing its resources.

How much and when did government spending grow? And for what purposes? The impetus from the escalation of U.S. involvement in Vietnam was concentrated in the years 1965 to 1968, when defense spending leapt from $50 billion to $82 billion. Defense spending then remained around the 1968 level until U.S. forces withdrew from Vietnam starting in 1973, and the conflict ended with Communist victory in 1975. Increases in nondefense spending resulting mainly from the Great Society and other welfare state programs were larger in magnitude and persisted longer. Federal nondefense expenditures were about $75 billion in 1965. By 1968, when the Vietnam buildup was largely completed, nondefense expenditures were $100 billion. In 1970, they were some $127 billion. During the 1970s, federal nondefense spending doubled roughly every five years, reaching $277 billion in 1975 and $540 billion in 1981.

Effect on Taxpayers

By 1980s' standards (as we will see in Chapter 23), these massive increases in government spending were achieved with relatively small increases in fiscal deficits and the national debt, though Americans at the time thought the increases were large in comparison to previous experience. The largest Great Society programs were financed in part by new and increased taxes, especially taxes on payrolls. The main reason deficits did not soar, however, was the method of inflationary finance. As individual incomes and business profits rose with inflation, taxpaying units subject to progressive taxation were pushed into higher tax-rate brackets (referred to as the "bracket creep"); as a result, they paid relatively more of their incomes to the government, even though in real or price-level-adjusted terms they were hardly richer.

Eventually, the technique of nondebated, nonlegislated tax increases resulted in a taxpayers' revolt, not the first in American history but unique in the twentieth century. The revolt broke out first at the state and local levels in 1978. State and local expenditures increased nearly as fast as federal expenditures between 1965 and 1980—from $72 billion to $337 billion—in part because the Great Society measures increased demands on these lower levels of government as well as those at the federal level. State and local transfer payments to individuals, for example, grew at well over 13 percent per year from 1965 to 1980, whereas traditional purchases of goods and services (for education, roads, and the like) grew at "only" 10 percent per year. And, just as at the federal level, inflation increased state and local revenues from income, sales, and property taxes. Although these taxes were not as progressive as federal taxes, they nonetheless had the effect of increasing the taxes that income earners, consumers, and property owners paid when they did not seem to be better off in real terms and therefore had little empathy for persons on welfare. Hence, ethnic and other social cleavages in American society reinforced inflation in helping to fuel the taxpayers' revolt. By 1980, the revolt spread to the national level with the election of a conservative, anti-tax president—Ronald Reagan. The Reagan administration brought about a decided shift in methods of federal finance during the 1980s (see Chapter 23).

The Great Society Programs

The Great Society programs were indirect causes of the Great Inflation. The military escalation in Vietnam and the means by which it and the Great Society programs were financed were the main causes. Wars accompanied by inflation, as documented in earlier chapters, were not new in U.S. history. But the Great Society measures were new. Like the New

Deal programs of the 1930s, these programs represented a quantum jump in government's functions and its disposition of economic resources. But unlike the New Deal programs of the Great Depression, the Great Society programs came at a time of great economic prosperity. This occurred in part because many Americans at the time thought that the New Deal's economic and social reforms had not been completed when World War II forced them to be placed on the backburners. If anything, reformers thought, the affluence of postwar America made further reforms no less necessary and even more affordable. The Great Society was foreshadowed as early as 1961, when an expanded program of Aid to Families with Dependent Children (AFDC) was enacted. It initially involved direct public assistance to poor families with children. In later years, it became the largest program of direct transfers of funds to poor families and a pillar of the American welfare state.

Two influential books published in 1962 drew attention to some of the arguments for an expanded government role in economic life. Michael Harrington's *The Other America: Poverty in the United States* drew attention to the widespread poverty present in the midst of an affluent society.[1] Rachel Carson's *The Silent Spring* drew attention to the ways in which modern agricultural and industrial processes and products were poisoning the earth's land, water, and air; in the process, she launched the environmental movement of the latter half of the twentieth century.[2] And, of course, it was obvious to many Americans—from Supreme Court justices to poor farmers and laborers— that continuing racial discrimination denied all manner of opportunity, including economic opportunity, to African-American citizens.

However, an important contributing factor to the changes brought about by the Great Society was the 1963 assassination of President John F. Kennedy. His successor, Lyndon Johnson, a dedicated New Dealer and a master

politician, persuaded Congress to pass legislation that carried through Kennedy's program in civil rights, tax reduction, and education. Then Johnson, after winning the 1964 presidential election by a tremendous popular majority, induced Congress in 1965 to enact his own Great Society program.

Medicare and Medicaid

Two of the leading and later most expensive of all the Great Society programs came in the area of health. Medicare, approved by Congress in 1965, provided national health insurance for elderly and disabled persons regardless of their incomes. Under Medicare—an expansion of the social insurance reforms of the New Deal—the elderly and disabled continue to receive medical care from private-sector practitioners and hospitals, but the federal government paid their bills.

Medicaid, a companion measure, provided publicly funded health insurance for poor persons of all ages. Medicaid was administered by the states with a combination of federal and state financing, whereas the federal government ran Medicare and financed it through increases in Social Security payroll taxes. Both initiatives, like Social Security, were entitlement programs—that is, the government obligated itself to pay what medical bills came in regardless of whether it had the money. If not, it had to find the money.

Both the Medicare and Medicaid programs expanded the demand for medical care without doing anything to increase the supply. The consequences for medical costs and government expenditures were predictable: Spending soared beyond expectations. Medicare and Medicaid became two of the costliest programs in the government budget.

The War on Poverty

Another set of Great Society programs fell under the rubric of the *War on Poverty*. Harrington

Poverty in an Affluent Society.   These slums in Washington, D.C., are not far from the nation's Capitol.
(UPI/Bettmann Newsphoto)

was only one of many commentators to bring the nation's attention to the poverty that persisted in an otherwise affluent society. Congress, following President Johnson's recommendations, passed the Economic Opportunity Act of 1964, which created an Office of Economic Opportunity (OEO) to supervise a variety of antipoverty programs. These included Head Start, a preschool program; a Job Corps to train youth; Upward Bound, a program to aid poor high schoolers to get into college; Vista, a domestic counterpart of the Peace Corps that Kennedy had launched to send Americans to aid less-developed nations; a Model Cities program for urban redevelopment; a legal services program for the poor; and a Food Stamp program to subsidize food purchases. Unlike the AFDC, the War on Poverty programs did not in general directly transfer money to poor citizens. Rather, they provided services organized and financed by government to the poor in the

hope that they would escape poverty by bettering themselves. Many of these poverty initiatives were dropped as opposition formed to their community-based action programs and as the Vietnam buildup strained the federal budget. Although reductions in poverty rates occurred at the time of the War on Poverty, some argued that they were more the result of economic growth during the 1960s. Whatever the case, when growth slowed in the 1970s and 1980s, poverty rates rose.

Aid to Education, Transportation, Civil Rights, and Other Areas

Under the Great Society label, the Johnson administration provided increased federal aid to education at all levels, from poor elementary school districts to needy college students. New cabinet-level Departments of Transportation (DOT) and of Housing and Urban Develop-

ment (HUD) were added to the executive branch. Programs were enacted to protect the environment; in 1970 under the Nixon administration, these were brought together in the new Environmental Protection Agency (EPA). The Great Society even encompassed the arts, letters, and the broadcast media by establishing the National Endowments for the Arts and the Humanities and the Corporation for Public Broadcasting. And in its civil rights legislation, the Great Society took major steps to expand economic, political, and social opportunities for minority citizens (as we will see later in the chapter). Compared to programs such as Medicare, Medicaid, and Social Security, these other Great Society initiatives were not costly items in the federal budget, but they did represent a marked expansion of governmental functions. And with a few exceptions, such as the War on Poverty, they remained in the federal budget as ongoing programs.

Regulation: Old and New

The era of the Great Society witnessed not only the installation of new and expensive social welfare programs; from the mid-1960s to the early 1970s, the federal government also introduced new regulatory agencies and added them to the panoply of existing agencies that had been formed from the 1880s through the 1930s. These new agencies differed from the old ones. They dealt with economic, social, and environmental regulation in ways that cut across business and industry lines. In contrast, the older agencies were directed for the most part toward specific industries, and their regulatory focus was mainly economic—rates (prices) to be charged, entry and exit of firms, and levels and quality of service.

The old federal regulation included such agencies as the Interstate Commerce Commission (ICC, created in 1887), which regulated railroads and, later, trucking and water carriers; the Federal Trade Commission (FTC, established in 1914), which dealt with antitrust issues, advertising and branding, and allegations of unfair competition; and the Federal Power Commission (FPC, set up in 1920), which dealt initially with waterpower issues but whose jurisdiction was expanded to include the production and interstate transmission of electric power and natural gas. In the 1970s—a time of great national concern over energy supplies and costs—the FPC was renamed the Federal Energy Regulatory Commission (FERC). To these old regulatory agencies the New Deal of the 1930s added the Federal Communications Commission (FCC) in 1934, the Securities and Exchange Commission (SEC) in 1934, and the Civil Aeronautics Board (CAB) in 1938 to regulate broadcasting and other telecommunications, the securities industry, and air transportation, respectively. It was these older regulatory agencies that became the main targets of the deregulation movement that arose in the late 1970s and the 1980s (see Chapter 23).

The new regulation of the Great Society era included the creation of the Equal Employment Opportunity Commission (EEOC) in 1964, the Environmental Protection Agency (EPA) in 1970, the Occupational Safety and Health Administration (OSHA) of the Department of Labor in 1970, and the Consumer Product Safety Commission (CPSC) in 1972. These new agencies brought regulation to bear on broad concerns of an affluent society: equal opportunity, a clean environment, and health and safety in workplaces, homes, and just about every other place. Translating these social concerns into effective regulation proved to be controversial and problematical in the years and decades after the agencies were formed. The agencies' supporters praised their efforts to bring about a fairer, cleaner, safer, and healthier America. But opponents saw the new regulations as raising the costs of doing business and the prices of goods and services; other charges were that the regulations caused losses of jobs and a general weakening of U.S. competitiveness in the world economy.

Domestic Policy Reactions to the Great Inflation

The Great Inflation of 1965 to 1982 proved to be a humbling experience for the makers of U.S. economic policy. In the mid-1960s, they exuded optimism about the ability of fiscal and monetary policies to fine-tune the economy to achieve full employment, growth, and price stability. They held out the possibility of fiscal dividends: Economic growth and progressive taxation would generate growing federal revenues unless tax rates were cut. But the Vietnam War and the Great Society initiatives intervened and quickly demonstrated that there were other, more pressing uses for fiscal dividends.

As the inflation rate crept upward, inflation itself became a key problem for policymakers. From the late 1960s to the early 1980s, a series of policy shifts and experiments were put into place in repeated attempts to slow the inflation, but with few exceptions they proved ineffective. The policy zigzags did, however, add to economic instability. The recessions of 1973 to 1975 and 1980 to 1982, for example, were much more severe in terms of declining output and rising unemployment than had been the case in the earlier post–World War II recessions.

Decline of Fiscal Policy

Most of all, one sees in these policies a gradual abandonment or lessening of the faith in the fiscal policy that had been so great in the mid-1960s. In retrospect, the decline of fiscal policy is not surprising. It always faced problems of lags in recognizing a need for a change of di-

rection, in making the change, and in having the change take hold. The Great Society created further drawbacks to fiscal policy, for when the government introduced expensive new entitlement programs and expanded old ones, it lost a good measure of discretionary control over its spending. And when, as a consequence of this loss of control over spending, fiscal deficits soared, arguments for using discretionary tax cuts to stabilize the economy lost much of their force. How could taxes be cut, or spending increased, to fight a downturn in the economy if the government budget was already taking in far less money through taxation than it needed to pay its growing bills? When the economy was expanding and possibly experiencing inflation, a policy of reducing budget deficits by explicit increases in income taxes was not usually considered. The decline of even this kind of limited fiscal policy meant that much of the battle against inflation fell on drastic measures such as peacetime wage and price controls, which contradict the basic operating principles of a market economy, and on the monetary policy of the Federal Reserve System. During the 1970s, neither proved equal to the task of stopping the inflation.

Stagflation

The problem of these years was called *stagflation*—the simultaneous presence of persistent inflation and high unemployment. In the macroeconomic theories that guided economic policy at the time, stagflation was not supposed to be a problem. An economy, if it had a macroeconomic problem, was supposed to have either unemployment or inflation, but not both at the same time. Economists reconciled the two elements of stagflation with theories emphasizing inflationary expectations. For example, if lenders expected an existing inflation to continue or increase in its rate, they would attempt to protect the real value of the purchasing power they lent by demanding higher interest rates on loans. Rising interest rates, as a response to inflation and inflationary expectations, would then slow the economy and raise unemployment. Thus stagflation was explained. But how was it to be fought?

Wage-Price Controls and Price Shocks. By 1971, when neither traditional fiscal nor monetary policies appeared capable of eliminating stagflation, the Nixon administration decided to attack inflationary expectations by means of the extreme policy of a temporary wage-and-price freeze, followed by several phases of more or less flexible wage and price controls that lasted until 1974. But when unemployment failed to respond as expected, from 1972 to early 1974 the Federal Reserve pursued rapid monetary expansion. This action by itself would likely have accelerated inflation within the loose framework of price controls. But the inflation rates of 1973 to 1974, the highest in over a quarter-century, were also fueled, so to speak, by two price shocks coming from abroad. One was a large jump in crude petroleum prices engineered by the OPEC cartel in response to Middle Eastern conflict between Israel and the Arab states. The other was a sharp increase in the prices of agricultural commodities resulting from crop failures in other countries, especially the Soviet Union, historically a large grain producer.

Rising Federal Budget Deficits. Attempts to fight the soaring inflation of 1973 to 1974 by traditional means, namely tighter monetary and fiscal policies, produced the then worst recession since the 1930s. The years 1974 and 1975 saw negative real growth, with unemployment among civilian workers rising to an average rate of 8.5 percent in 1975. Policies were therefore reversed once again, with a tax cut in 1975 and the resumption of high rates of monetary expansion. The economy recovered from 1975 through 1979, but this recovery was marked by renewed inflation at still higher rates and by only modest declines in unemployment rates. It was also marked by federal budget deficits that rose to the $40 billion to $80 billion range in a period of economic expansion and another oil price shock in 1979. The latter event was a temporary disturbance. The former one, however, pointed to a longer-term change in the way government interacted with the economy. Before the Vietnam military escalation and the Great Society's expansion of entitlement and other programs raised government spending, federal budgets generally had declined during periods of economic recovery and expansion.

The Federal Reserve Changes Course, 1979

The increasing momentum of inflation from 1965 to 1981 was not broken until the severe recession of 1981 to 1982, when unemployment rates rose to more than 10 percent of the labor force. The main player in this drama was the Federal Reserve. Throughout the years of the Great Inflation up to 1979, the Fed had over and over again reacted to rising unemployment by reducing interest rates in an attempt to stimulate the economy. But this policy entailed monetary expansion, and so it served mainly to raise the rate of inflation and push interest rates higher still. It was based on the Fed's misinterpretation of the causes and effects of rising interest rates.

In late 1979, the Fed changed its policies under the direction of its newly appointed chairman, Paul Volcker, a respected economist with extensive practical experience in private and governmental finance. Volcker turned the Fed toward a policy of targeted reductions in monetary growth while allowing interest rates to find their own levels in financial markets. In response, market interest rates from 1980 to 1982 went through the roof, reaching their highest levels in U.S. history. In 1981, commercial banks charged their best customers a

Gasoline Rationing in the 1970s.   When Middle Eastern political instability and a cartel of oil producing countries restricted the flow of crude oil to the United States, American authorities tried for a time to control prices of petroleum products below market clearing levels and to allocate supplies administratively rather than through market mechanisms. The resulting "shortages" manifested themselves in long lines of motorists at filling stations such as this one in Los Angeles. (UPI/The Bettmann Archive)

prime rate that average 18.9 percent, while the federal government itself at one point covered its growing deficit by borrowing money for 20 years at 15.8 percent. This was the harsh medicine, dispensed by the Fed, that produced a deep recession and finally broke the back of the inflationary momentum of the preceding fifteen years.

Inflation and Domestic Finance

Rise of Interest Rates

A broad outline of the course of U.S. interest rates between 1945 and 1991 is shown in Fig-

ure 22–1 by the yields of prime corporate and U.S. government bonds. Several points can be made from the evidence in the figure. One is that U.S. financial markets are well integrated; here that can be seen in the parallel movements of the two yield series—one for private debt and the other for public debt. Another point is that interest rates rose from the depressed and pegged levels in effect during and after World War II, but they then leveled off in the early 1960s when the economy expanded at good rates and prices were stable. Then, after 1965, interest rates commenced a steep ascent (interrupted only briefly by two recessions) that carried them by 1981 to levels that were about three times higher than the levels

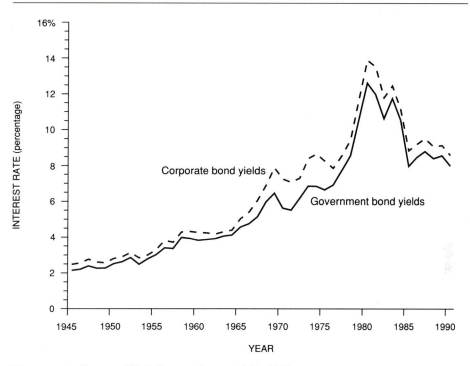

Figure 22–1 *Course of U.S. Interest Rates, 1945–1991*
SOURCE: Data for 1946 to 1989: Sidney Homer and Richard Sylla, *A History of Interest Rates,*
3rd ed. (New Brunswick, NJ: Rutgers University Press, 1991), pp. 370–71, 375–76; data for
1990 to 1991: *Federal Reserve Bulletin* (March 1992), p. A24.

of the early 1960s. After 1981, nominal interest rates fell but only to levels in the early 1990s that had been reached around 1970 when the Great Inflation was well underway.

Credit Crunches, Disintermediation, and Financial Innovation.   Levels and trends of interest rates since 1945 corresponded fairly well with the levels and trends of inflation. Interest rate movements were dramatic and they had dramatic effects on both financial markets and the U.S. and world economies. One financial effect of inflation and rising interest rates was a weakening of a variety of U.S. financial institutions, especially those that held the U.S.

public's deposits and made various types of loans. These were the commercial banks and the various thrift institutions—saving and loan associations (S&Ls), mutual savings banks, and credit unions. After the New Deal financial reforms of the 1930s, these institutions were regulated in the interest rates they could pay depositors. When market rates rose during the Great Inflation, depositors discovered that they could profit by withdrawing funds from the depository institutions and placing them into financial instruments with unregulated rates (e.g., Treasury bills) or into new, unregulated institutions that arose to do it for them. The former activity, called *disintermediation,* was intimately related to the occasional "credit crunches" of the late 1960s and the 1970s, when some would-be borrowers were unable to get credit from banks and thrifts. The new institutions that arose on top of disintermediation to compete with banks and thrifts were the money market mutual funds. They accepted people's deposits withdrawn from depository institutions as shares in the funds, invested the proceeds in short-term money market instruments paying the shareholders a market yield well above the regulated rates paid by banks and thrifts, and even allowed the shareholders to write checks on their fund balances. A lot of this was made possible by the new computer technologies applied to financial institutions.

Money market mutual funds did not exist before 1973. By 1981, they held more than $200 billion and by 1991 more than $500 billion of assets. Much of this money came out of banks and thrifts or would have gone into them in the absence of inflation and regulation. They continued to gain funds even after the government in 1980 and 1982, in response to the squeeze on banks and thrifts, relaxed some of the regulations that had caused the depository institutions to lose market share. Among the reasons were continuing problems for financial institutions that had their roots in the era of the Great Inflation (see Chapter 23).

Depressed Stock Market

Nonfinancial corporations also faced difficulties as a result of rising interest rates in that era. Rising interest rates made bonds and other fixed-income investments relatively more attractive than stocks as investments. One consequence—surprising to many because stocks had long been reputed as a hedge against inflation—was that stock prices made only limited gains between 1965 and the early 1980s. The Standard & Poor's composite index of common stock prices increased only 2 per-

cent annually from 1965 to 1980, a period when inflation averaged more than 6 percent per year. Another index, the popular Dow-Jones Industrial Average of thirty blue-chip stock prices, was lower in 1982 than it had been in 1965.

Depressed stock prices made it difficult for corporations to raise external capital by selling stock. Instead, they turned to issuing bonds and, increasingly over the inflationary years, to short-term loans in order to finance their needs. Although interest rates were high, the interest expenses paid out, unlike dividends, were tax deductible, and so the government shared in the costs of borrowing. But the huge volume of borrowing that resulted raised the weight of debt in corporate capital structures and increased the vulnerability to bankruptcy, which became a problem in the less inflationary 1980s. Depressed stock prices also led to a wave of corporate mergers and takeovers during the 1980s, as financiers and other corporate investors bought up companies at bargain prices in financial markets, usually by issuing still more debt (see Chapter 23).

International Reactions to the U.S. Inflation

The Great Inflation quickly undermined the Bretton Woods system of fixed exchange rates, a cornerstone of the post–World War II trade and finance. During the two decades from 1945 to 1965, the world's postwar dollar shortage gradually was transformed into a dollar surplus. U.S. military and economic aid transferred dollars to friendly and neutral countries in these years as a part of the Cold War strategy of containing the spread of communism. Some of these dollars were spent on U.S. exports, but growing amounts were held on reserve by foreign nations. More dollars flowed out as American multinational corporations invested in foreign countries; these flows were only partly offset by returns on the investments and by foreign investment in the United States. Until the mid-1960s, however, the world's dollar surplus was manageable. A Eurodollar market even emerged in Europe, where dollars could be lent and borrowed beyond the reach of U.S. financial regulations.

An Overvalued Dollar

In the late 1960s, rising U.S. inflation meant that dollars, including the dollars held by foreigners, bought less than before. With the system of fixed exchange rates, the dollar became overvalued. In turn, overvalued dollars made imports look cheap to Americans, but they also made U.S. exports appear more expensive to foreigners. The results were a sharp deterioration in the U.S. balance of trade with the rest of the world, international currency speculation against the dollar (betting that it would be devalued or other currencies revalued upward), and a rise of protectionist sentiments within the United States. By 1971, the United States imported more goods than it exported for the first time in decades.

Collapse of Bretton Woods System

President Richard Nixon made a bold and blunt response to these developments on 15 August 1991, as a part of his new economic policy that included the domestic wage and price controls referred to earlier in the chapter. Nixon suspended international convertibility of the dollar into gold and imposed a temporary 10 percent surcharge on imports into the United States. The suspension of dollar–gold convertibility effectively ended the Bretton Woods system, though it limped on until 1973 by means of adjustments that turned out to be ineffective. After 1973, the dollar had its value in terms of other currencies determined daily in world currency markets, in much the same way that corporate shares were priced daily in

the stock markets. Flexible exchange rates introduced a new element of uncertainty into international trade and finance. And the surcharge on imports was, of course, a retreat from the goals of freer trade and lower tariffs that U.S. policymakers had espoused since the 1930s. The Great Inflation thus weakened the U.S. commitment to freer trade and played into the hands of protectionists at home and abroad.

Flexible Exchange Rates and Oil Imports

It was hoped in the early 1970s that the new regime of flexible exchange rates determined by market forces would stabilize relative currency values and promote orderly adjustments of trade and payments imbalances. That hope was dashed by continued U.S. inflation in the 1970s, and in particular by the great outflow of dollars from the United States after the leaps in oil prices engineered by the OPEC cartel in 1973 and 1979. Because the United States imported vast quantities of oil, the world was again flooded with dollars. The trade-weighted value of the dollar by 1980 was only a little over 70 percent of its value in 1971. Against strong currencies, the fall of the dollar was steeper: A dollar bought 3.9 German marks in 1969 but only 1.8 in 1979; over the same period, the dollar fell in relation to the Japanese yen from 358 to 220. Ordinarily, a cheaper dollar might have been expected to increase U.S. exports and reduce imports, thus cutting U.S. international trade and payments deficits. But because the bill for vastly more expensive oil imports was so large, these deficits at the end of the 1970s were greater than they had been a decade earlier.

The Slowing of Productivity Growth

Accompanying the Great Inflation was a marked slowing in the long-term growth of

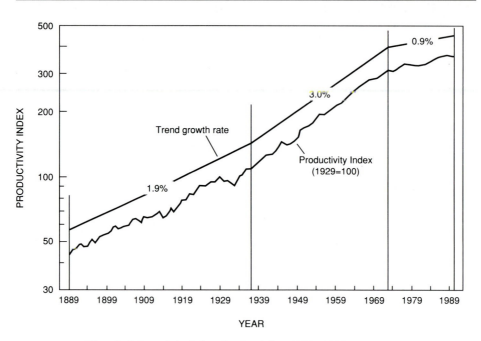

Figure 22–2 *Historical Growth in Labor Productivity, 1889–1989*
Labor productivity has increased steadily over the past century, but productivity growth has slowed in recent years.
NOTE: Labor productivity is private business sector GDP per hour. Percentages are average annual rates of change for periods indicated.
SOURCES: Council of Economic Advisers, *Economic Report of the President, 1992* (Washington, D.C.: GPO, 1992), p. 91.

American labor productivity—that is, the economic output generated per hour worked. Because growing productivity historically has been the major source of increases in living standards, the productivity slowdown became one of the more vexing economic problems of the American economy during the late twentieth century. The historical dimensions of the productivity slowdown are evident in Figure 22–2. Productivity in the U.S. economy grew at nearly 2 percent per year from 1889 to 1937, at 3 percent per year from 1937 to 1973, and at less than 1 percent per year from 1973 to the start of the 1990s. The year 1973 is often selected as the point of transition to lower pro-

ductivity growth because that growth slowed in nearly all large industrial countries after the oil and agricultural shocks of that year. But a detailed examination of the underlying U.S. data indicates that the slowdown actually began in the United States in the mid-1960s. This is demonstrated by the data in Table 22–1, which compares productivity growth over five-, seven-, and ten-year intervals from 1960 to 1990.

Many factors were cited by observers as possible contributors to the slowing of productivity growth. One was the increasing relative importance of the service sector compared to the goods-producing sector, a development dis-

Table 22–1 *The Productivity Slowdown, 1960–1990: Percent Changes in Business Sector, Output per Person over Ten-, Seven-, and Five-Year Intervals*

Period	Ten-Year Intervals	Seven-Year Intervals	Five-Year Intervals
		Percent Change	
1960–1970	33%		
1970–1980	13		
1980–1990	11		
1962–1969		22%	
1969–1976		14	
1976–1983		4	
1983–1990		7	
1960–1965			20%
1965–1970			11
1970–1975			10
1975–1980			3
1980–1985			8
1985–1990			3

SOURCE: Calculated from data in *Economic Report of the President, 1992* (Washington, D.C.: GPO, 1992), pp. 348–49.

cussed later in the chapter. Since productivity growth historically has been greater in goods production than in services, an increased consumer preference for services relative to goods could itself slow productivity growth. Another set of factors emphasized labor force changes after the mid-1960s, in particular the large numbers of baby boomers, women, and minorities who entered the work force around that time. To the extent that these workers lacked experience or had lower average skill levels than the rest of the labor force, they reduced the average quality of American labor and thus may have slowed the rate of productivity advance.

Still another set of factors involved a slowing in the rate of capital accumulation resulting from low U.S. savings and investment rates, and from government budget deficits that absorbed savings without adding to the capital stock. The Council of Economic Advisers, for example, noted in its 1992 *Report* that capital per worker in the U.S. private business sector grew by 2.4 percent a year from 1959 to 1973, and productivity by 2.8 percent. From 1973 to the 1990s, the corresponding figures were 0.8 percent and 0.9 percent. The Council also pointed out that six other leading economies—those of Canada, France, Germany, Italy, Japan, and the United Kingdom—had higher rates of growth of capital per worker than the United States as well as higher rates of productivity growth.[3] These countries' levels of productivity, while lower absolutely than American levels, were gaining and in some cases drawing close to parity with the U.S. levels.

Additional factors cited by some analysts in attempting to account for the productivity slowdown included a slowing in the rate of technological progress (though that is something difficult both to define and to measure) and an alleged increase in natural resource scarcity. The latter was a popular explanation during the food and energy crises of the 1970s, but most present-day economists dismiss it as incorrect. Natural resources, compared to other economic resources, became cheaper, not more expensive, over the course of the twentieth century.

Because productivity growth slowed in most large industrial economies during the 1970s and 1980s, one must be careful not to overemphasize U.S. economic conditions and policies in explaining the slowdown. Those conditions and policies could, of course, be pertinent to an explanation of the relatively low growth of U.S. productivity compared to other countries. And, given the large size and role of the United States in the world economy, it is possible that the greater international economic and financial instability that the United States unleashed from the mid-1960s on could have slowed productivity everywhere.

The Rise of Services and the Decline of Manufacturing

In 1950, about half of the workers in the United States produced goods and the other half delivered services. By 1990, about a quarter of U.S. workers produced goods and three-quarters delivered services (see Table 22–2). Although this fundamental shift in employment has been termed the "rise of the service economy," it is clear from the data that the service sector was already large in the U.S. economy by the end of World War II. In fact, by examining shares of production (GDP) instead of shares of employment (see Table 22–3), we find that in 1950 more than half (55 percent) of production represented services and only 45 percent was goods. By the end of the 1980s, service output approached three-quarters of total GDP, whereas goods output by 1988 had fallen to only 28 percent of it.

The Lesson of Agriculture

The data in Tables 22–2 and 22–3 merit further study, for they reveal much about a major long-term trend in modern economic history. During the second half of the twentieth century, the agricultural sector (including forestry and fisheries) continued in the relative decline it had exhibited throughout U.S. history. By 1990, less than 3 percent of workers labored in agriculture, and they produced about 2 percent of U.S. output. The data indicate why workers left agriculture: Since the output share of agriculture is less than the employment share, workers in general are more productive and earn more in nonagricultural pursuits. The labor market thus continues to guide labor away from farming, as it has for at least two centuries. There is, to be sure, another way to look at these data. The American farmer is in fact extremely efficient and productive. On average, the farmer feeds forty or so other Americans and on top of that produces surpluses for export to other countries. By this standard, the American farmer is the most productive farmer in the world. Still, the farmer's labor tends to be even more productive of economic value in nonagricultural pursuits, which is why the agricultural sector has become so small a part of the total economy.

What has been true of agriculture in recent decades has also been true, though not in quite so extreme a way, of the goods-producing sector in general. Only construction has about held its own as a share of employment and output after 1950. Manufacturing and mining, two sectors almost synonymous with an industrial economy, exhibit declines in their output and employment shares that parallel those in agriculture. This suggests that the United States has indeed become, as some analysts argue, a postindustrial society—one in which providing services rather than making goods is the dominant economic activity.

Table 22–2 *Changing Shares of Employment in the Goods and Services Sectors, 1950–1990 (percent of total employment)*

	Goods Sectors					Services Sectors					
Year	Agriculture, Forestry, and Fisheries	Manufacturing	Construction	Mining	Total	Transportation, Communication, and Public Utilities	Wholesale and Retail Trade	Finance, Insurance, and Real Estate	Other Services	Government	Total
1950	13.7%	29.1%	4.5%	1.7%	49.0%	7.7%	17.9%	3.6%	10.2%	11.5%	51.0%
1960	9.2	28.2	4.9	1.2	43.5	6.7	19.1	4.4	12.4	14.0	56.5
1970	4.7	26.1	4.8	0.9	36.5	6.1	20.2	4.9	15.5	16.9	63.5
1980	3.6	21.6	4.6	1.1	30.8	5.6	21.7	5.5	19.1	17.3	69.2
1990	2.8	16.9	4.5	0.6	24.8	5.1	22.9	6.0	25.0	16.2	75.2

SOURCE: Calculated from data in *Economic Report of the President, 1992* (Washington, D.C.: GPO, 1992), pp. 332, 344–45.

Table 22–3 *Changing Shares of Output (GDP) in the Goods and Services Sectors, 1950–1988 (percent of total output)*

	Goods Sectors					Services Sectors					
Year	Agriculture, Forestry, and Fisheries	Manufacturing	Construction	Mining	Total	Transportation, Communication, and Public Utilities	Wholesale and Retail Trade	Finance, Insurance, and Real Estate	Other Services	Government	Total
1950	7.4%	29.7%	4.5%	3.3%	44.9%	9.1%	18.2%	10.9%	8.6%	8.4%	55.2%
1960	4.3	28.7	4.5	2.5	40.0	9.1	16.8	13.4	9.9	10.7	59.9
1970	3.2	25.6	4.8	1.7	35.5	8.6	17.0	14.1	11.6	13.2	64.5
1980	2.9	21.7	5.1	4.0	33.7	9.0	16.4	15.0	14.0	12.0	66.4
1988	2.1	19.5	4.8	1.7	28.0	9.1	16.1	17.1	18.0	11.7	72.0

SOURCES: 1950 to 1970 figures are calculated from data in U.S. Bureau of the Census, *Historical Statistics of the United States, Bicentennial Edition* (Washington, D.C.: GPO, 1975), p. 233; 1980 to 1988 figures are calculated from data in U.S. Bureau of the Census, *Statistical Abstract of the United States, 1991* (Washington, D.C.: GPO, 1992), p. 432.

Manufacturing's Decline. The gate at the United States Steel Corporation's Youngstown, Ohio, works is padlocked in this 1980 photo. Steelworkers attempted unsuccessfully to buy the plant and keep it going; the company shut it down and made plans to dismantle it. (UPI/The Bettmann Archive)

Manufacturing Follows the Pattern of Agriculture

The relative decline of U.S. manufacturing is also indicated by the data in Tables 22–2 and 22–3. Because many people still consider manufacturing to be the backbone of the American economy, this decline is much lamented. Similarly, in earlier eras of history, the relative decline of agriculture was lamented, especially by rural people and those—the French physiocrats and Thomas Jefferson come to mind—who thought that agriculture was the backbone of their economies two centuries ago and disdained the rise of commerce and manufacturing.

Proponents and defenders of U.S. manufacturing have attributed its decline to foreign competition, to a lack of manufacturing investment, or to a reduction in the quality of American labor. These have been among the problems of recent U.S. economic history, and much could have been done that wasn't done to revitalize U.S. manufacturing and labor. Nonetheless, a longer historical perspective suggests that these problems can be exaggerated. The relative decline of manufacturing in the total economy was evident in the 1950s and 1960s, when most economists considered the U.S. economy to be performing well. A fundamental fact of the postindustrial society appears to be that its members express a preference for relatively fewer goods, including manufactures, and relatively more services in the total economic pie. To deny that fact is to swim against the tides of history.

Misleading Constant-Dollar Output Indexes. Some do deny the fact, however. Indexes of manufacturing's share of economic output in constant dollars—for example, in 1958, 1972, or 1982 prices—indicate a relative constancy. The problem with this way of arguing that manufacturing did not really decline is that the "constant" share in fact declined over time as the base was updated. Over recent decades, manufacturing's constant share in 1958 dollars was about 30 percent. In 1972 dollars it was about 24 percent. In 1982 dollars it was about 21 percent. In other words, the "constant" share declined over time. Constant-dollar indexes of economic output have their uses, but one of them should not be to deny that U.S. manufacturing is in a state of decline relative to the rest of the economy.

The explanation of the paradox of a constant share that declines over time is that higher productivity levels in manufacturing than in services reduce the prices of manufactured goods relative to the prices of services. The prices of computers, television sets, automobiles, and airplanes have fallen relative to the prices of medical, legal, and domestic services as well as the cost of college tuition. Earlier in history the same was true, but relative output of manufactures increased even faster than relative prices fell and the manufacturing sector increased in size, in both current and constant dollars.

But that does not seem to happen in a postindustrial society, in which people demand more services even at higher relative prices. Therefore, the current-dollar shares of output shown in Table 22–3 are better indicators than constant-dollar shares of how the structure of the U.S. economy has changed over recent decades. They confirm the relative decline of manufacturing after World War II that is equally evident in the employment shares shown in Table 22–2.

Paradoxes of Industrial Policies. Another paradox is that policies suggested and sometimes implemented during the 1970s, 1980s, and 1990s, intended to stem the relative decline of manufacturing in the U.S. economy, had the opposite effect. More capital investment and more investment in workers' education, training, and skills increased manufacturing productivity and hastened the sector's relative decline. This happened historically in agriculture as well. Increases in agricultural productivity freed resources that had been in agriculture to move to other sectors, and agriculture became an increasingly smaller part of the whole economy. In postwar America, the same has been happening to manufacturing.

Other industrial policies faced different but equally formidable obstacles. Policies that tried to increase exports ran afoul of the fact that many other nations were now competing in the world's export markets for manufactures. Those that restricted imports of manufactures gave temporary boosts to the protected industries, firms, and workers, but only at a high cost to consumers of their products. When the automobile industry reeled under competition from imports in the late 1970s, for example, voluntary restraints on imports from Japan (which resulted in higher U.S. car prices to consumers but preserved jobs), cost U.S. consumers an estimated amount per job saved

that was several times the earnings of an automobile worker in that job.

Productivity in Services

The service industries that have risen—the other side of the coin of the relative decline of goods production—defy simple categorization. Many service-sector jobs—for example, in trade and personal services, the jobs of clerks, waiters, bellhops, and the like—could be characterized as requiring low skills, having low productivity, and paying low wages. Other service-sector jobs, however, require great training, skills, and talents—those of physicians, lawyers, investment bankers, entertainers, and professors—and pay relatively high wages and salaries. Because services in general had lower productivity growth than goods production, the increasing relative share of services in total output itself damped the growth of labor productivity after the mid-1960s. But that cannot be a big part of the explanation of the productivity slowdown because services were a large and growing component of the economy before 1965, when productivity growth was considerably greater. In those years, such innovations as supermarkets, regional shopping malls, and standardized, reusable shipping containers raised productivity in trade and transportation services. Modern information and communications services seem equally capable of permitting increases in service productivity. Recent history suggests that higher rates of growth in economy-wide productivity, if they come at all, will likely come from improvements in service productivity simply because services are the largest and fastest-growing part of the economy. Nonetheless, the problems of balancing job losses against productivity gains and of finding new employment opportunities for lower-skilled workers displaced by productivity-increasing technologies have long been and will remain difficult ones to solve.

African-Americans in the Labor Market

America's black population had its economic and other opportunities limited for more than two centuries by the institution of slavery. Opportunities thereafter continued to be limited for more than another century by policies and practices, official and unofficial, of racial discrimination. As a result, a black-white earnings gap existed throughout American history, similar in nature to the gender gap in wages discussed in Chapter 21. Half a century ago, the racial gap in earnings was large. In 1940, as Table 22–4 indicates, the earnings of black male workers were only 43 percent of those of white males. After 1940, however, there were impressive improvements in the economic status of black workers relative to whites. The relative gains of blacks were especially strong in the 1940s and the period from 1960 to 1980, with little change coming in the 1950s and the 1980s. By 1980, black males earned 73 percent of white male earnings. The racial gap in earnings was still substantial, but it was also substantially smaller than it had been forty years earlier. Black female workers also gained: In 1989, their median weekly earnings were 90

Table 22–4 *Black Male Wages as a Percentage of White Male Wages, 1940–1990*

Year	Percent Black/White
1940	43%
1950	55
1960	58
1970	64
1980	73
1990	72

SOURCES: Data for 1940 to 1980 are adapted from James P. Smith and Finis R. Welch, "Black Economic Progress After Myrdal," *Journal of Economic Literature*, 27 (June 1989): 522; data for 1990 are from *Economic Report of the President 1992—Annual Report of the Council of Economic Advisers* (Washington, D.C.: GPO, 1992), pp. 102–103.

percent of those of white females. However, as noted in Chapter 21, female workers in general earned only 70 percent as much as males in 1989.

Black Migrations

What accounted for the decline of the racial gap in earnings? In part, it was African-American migration, both from low-wage agriculture to higher-wage nonagricultural jobs and from the low-wage South of 1940 to other regions of the country having higher wage levels. Migration was a key factor in the narrowing of the racial earnings gap during the 1940s. When that decade began, three-fourths of African-Americans lived in the South; when it ended, the proportion was less than two-thirds. Many blacks left agriculture and the South during and after World War II for better paying jobs in industry and urban areas outside the South.

Schooling

Another factor that narrowed the racial earnings gap was the gain in average years of schooling for blacks relative to whites. In 1940, black males in the working ages of sixteen to sixty-four, for example, on average had only half the years of schooling of whites. After 1940, average years of schooling rose for whites and blacks, but they rose much faster for blacks. By 1960, the black males in the sixteen-to-sixty-four age group had three-fourths the average years of schooling of whites; by 1980, they had 87 percent. Since education tends to make workers more productive and is therefore correlated with earnings, the relative educational gains of African-Americans over the past half-century made a major contribution to the narrowing of the racial earnings gap.

Antidiscrimination Laws

The gains in the earnings of African-American workers between 1960 and 1980 were also buoyed by the advances in civil rights, some of the greatest achievements of the Great Society. Title VII of the 1964 Civil Rights Act, as noted in Chapter 21's discussion of the gender gap in earnings, forbade discrimination in employment and led to the creation of an Equal Employment Opportunity Commission. That era also saw the establishment of the Office of Federal Contract Compliance to monitor the antidiscrimination and affirmative-action responsibilities of government contractors. Black political power was raised by the Voting Rights Act of 1965. These and other federal actions effectively opened up greater economic opportunities for African-Americans, especially in the South where racial discrimination had often had the force of state and local law behind it. Between 1965 and 1975, as the walls of segregation came tumbling down, there were substantial gains in the earnings of southern blacks relative to those of southern whites.

Much of the national convergence in these years was the result of black workers' gains in the South, where half of all blacks, despite the earlier migrations, continued to live after 1970.

The lack of progress in narrowing the racial earnings gap after the mid- to late 1970s, which contrasts with the gains made during the 1980s in narrowing the gender gap in earnings, resulted from slower economic growth, and especially from reduced employment opportunities in decaying central cities and other areas where African-Americans increasingly lived and worked. The relative decline of manufacturing and the rise of the services sector also contributed. Black workers, despite their educational advances, were still disproportionately employed in unskilled and low-skilled jobs compared to whites, and the services sector differentially rewarded highly skilled workers compared to the manufacturing sector.

Summary

The goals of high-level U.S. decision makers from the mid-1960s through the 1970s were worthy ones. Internationally, they sought to continue to promote freer trade and contain Communist expansionism without plunging the world into another world war. At home they hoped to continue the policies of their predecessors that had promoted growth, reasonably full employment, and price stability. And they wanted to eliminate poverty, expand opportunities for minorities, provide health care for the elderly and the poor, make workplaces and consumer products safer, and protect the environment.

Some of these goals were reached. Others were not. It was an ambitious agenda, one that would perhaps have been difficult to achieve in full under the best of circumstances. What was achieved was done so at a greater cost

than was necessary when federal decision makers failed to heed one of the first lessons of elementary economics—that an economy utilizing all of its resources in the production of butter and guns does not have the option to have more of both. By failing to decrease some areas of spending or to increase taxation, federal decision makers unleashed a period of inflation in the United States and the world that made more difficult the achievement of every one of their goals. It was a tribute to the resiliency of the American economy that it came through an era of errant though well-intended economic, social, and military policies (along with others that advanced income security and welfare) as well as it did. Nonetheless, by 1980, many Americans were tired of the not-so-hidden taxes imposed by inflation and with methods of government that did not seem to be able to cope with the inflationary forces they had unleashed. The 1980s, as a result,

brought major shifts in the directions of governmental economic policies.

Endnotes

1. Michael Harrington, *The Other America: Poverty in the United States* (New York: Macmillan, 1962).
2. Rachel Carson, *The Silent Spring* (Boston: Houghton Mifflin, 1962).

3. "Annual Report of the Council of Economic Advisers," in *Economic Report of the President, 1992* (Washington, D.C.: GPO, 1992), pp. 91–95.

Suggested Readings

A number of the Suggested Readings at the end of Chapter 21 are pertinent as well to the topics covered in this chapter and the next. For an account of economic policy during the Johnson administration (1963–1969), see James E. Anderson and Jared E. Hazelton, *Managing Macroeconomic Policy: The Johnson Presidency* (Austin: University of Texas Press, 1986). An interesting study of what has come to be known as "the political business cycle" is Edward R. Tufte, *Political Control of the Economy* (Princeton: Princeton University Press, 1978). For an early evaluation of the Great Society, see Eli Ginzberg and Robert M. Solow, eds., *The Great Society: Lessons for the Future* (New York: Basic Books, 1974); a later one is Henry J. Aaron, *Politics and the Professors: The Great Society in Perspective* (Washington, D.C.: Brookings Institution, 1978). A more negative evaluation of several initiatives of the Great Society is provided by Charles Murray, *Losing Ground: American Social Policy, 1950–1980* (New York: Basic Books, 1984). For a pessimistic perspective on the growth of government in this and earlier eras of U.S. history, see Robert Higgs, *Crisis and Leviathan: Critical Episodes in the Growth of American Government* (New York: Oxford University Press, 1987).

U.S. monetary policy and inflation from the 1890s to the 1980s are discussed by Robert A. Degen, *The American Monetary System: A Concise Survey of Its Evolution since 1896* (Lexington, Mass.: Lexington Books, 1987). For a detailed account of the dramatic effects of inflation on U.S. and world interest rates, see Sidney Homer and Richard Sylla, *A History of Interest Rates*, 3rd ed. (New Brunswick, NJ: Rutgers University Press, 1991). A study of economic policy in the 1960s and 1970s is Alan Blinder, *Economic Policy and the Great Stagflation* (New York: Academic Press, 1979). Some inside views of policymakers in the Nixon and Ford administrations, 1969–1977, are offered by George P. Schultz and Kenneth W. Dam, *Economic Policy Beyond the Headlines* (New York: W. W. Norton, 1977). Benjamin M. Friedman discusses financial market developments through the late 1970s in "Postwar Changes in the American Financial Markets," Martin Feldstein, ed., *The American Economy in Transition* (Chicago: University of Chicago Press, 1980). The oil price shocks of the 1970s are among the subjects treated by Richard H. K. Vietor, *Energy Policy in America since 1945: A Study in Business-Government Relations* (New York: Cambridge University Press, 1984).

Wage and price controls as methods of coping with inflation in this and earlier periods are the subjects of Karl Brunner and Alan Meltzer, eds., *The Economics of Price and Wage Controls* (Amsterdam: North Holland, 1976), and Hugh Rockoff, *Drastic Measures: A History of Wage and Price Controls in the United States* (New York: Cambridge University Press, 1984). Two accounts specific to the 1970s experience are Arnold R. Weber and Daniel J. B. Mitchell, *The Pay Board's Progress: Wages and Controls in Phase II* (Washington, D.C.: Brookings Institution, 1978), and John T. Dunlop et al., eds., *The Lessons of Wage and Price Controls* (Cambridge: Harvard University Press, 1978).

The old and new regulations are surveyed by Thomas K. McCraw, "Regulatory Agencies," in Glenn Porter, ed., *Encyclopedia of American Economic History: Studies of the Principal Movements and Ideas*, vol. 2 (New York: Scribner's, 1980), a reference work that is also valuable for most of the topics covered in this book. More detail on the principal architects of modern American regulatory policies is given in McCraw's *Prophets of Regulation* (Cambridge: Harvard University Press, 1984). A long-term perspective on governmental intervention in the market economy is given by Jonathan R. T. Hughes, *The Governmental Habit Redux: Economic Controls from Colonial Times to the Present* (Princeton: Princeton University Press, 1991). Specific aspects of the new regulation are covered in Peter Asch, *Consumer Safety Legislation: Putting a Price on Life and Limb* (New York: Oxford University Press, 1988); Charles Noble, *Liberalism at Work: The Rise and Fall of OSHA* (Philadelphia: Temple University Press, 1986); and Bruce Yandle, *Political Limits of Environmental Regulation* (New York: Quorum Books, 1989).

For a long-term perspective on the productivity slowdown of recent decades, see William J. Baumol, Sue Anne Batey Blackman, and Edward N. Wolff, *Productivity and American Leadership: The Long View* (Cambridge: The MIT Press, 1989). An early attempt to analyze the slowdown is Edward F. Denison, *Accounting for Slower Economic Growth: The United States in the 1970s* (Washington, D.C.: Brookings Institution, 1979). Angus Maddison, "Growth and Slowdown in Advanced Capitalist Economies: Techniques of Quantitative Assessment," *Journal of Economic Literature*, 25 (1987) demonstrates that the United States was not the only economy to suffer from declining productivity growth in the period.

A study of the rise of the services sectors in the overall economy, though now somewhat dated, is Victor R. Fuchs, *The Service Economy* (New York: National Bureau of Economic Research, 1968). A more recent discussion stressing the importance of productivity growth in services and the long-term relative decline of manufacturing is Hudson Institute, *Workforce 2000: Work and Workers for the 21st Century* (Indianapolis: Hudson Institute, 1987).

Recent economic analyses of the changing position of African-Americans in the labor force include James P. Smith and Finis R. Welch, "Black Economic Progress after Myrdal," *Journal of Economic Literature*, 27 (June 1989); a Symposium on the Economic Status of African-Americans in *The Journal of Economic Perspectives*, 4 (1990); and John J. Donahue III and James Heckman, "Continuous versus Episodic Change: The Impact of Civil Rights Policy on the Economic Status of Blacks," *Journal of Economic Literature*, 29 (1991). Earlier studies include Jay Mandle, *The Roots of Black Poverty* (Durham, N.C.: Duke University Press, 1978) and Stanley M. Masters, *Black-White Income Differentials* (New York: Academic Press, 1973). For discussions of continuing economic problems of African-Americans, see Richard B. Freeman and Harry J. Holzer, eds., *The Black Youth Employment Crisis* (Chicago: University of Chicago Press, 1986) and William J. Wilson, *The Truly Disadvantaged: The Inner City, The Underclass and Public Policy* (Chicago: University of Chicago Press, 1987).

Chapter 23

Deficits, Debts, and Defaults, 1980–1992

G REAT SHIFTS IN THE DIRECTIONS OF FEDERAL ECO-
nomic and other policies did much to
determine the course of the American
economy during the 1980s and early 1990s.
Some of these shifts were reactions to problems caused by the great inflation of 1965 to
1982 (see Chapter 22). In that category were
tighter monetary policies, changes in the financial regulatory system, and some aspects of
the major reforms of the federal tax system. A
more basic objective of tax reform, however,
was to increase the incentives for Americans to
earn, save, and invest more and thereby increase the rate of economic growth—so-called
supply-side economics. Other policy changes
likewise were directed toward increasing
growth. They represented reversals of the
trends that had been in place for decades and
included the movement to deregulate regulated industries, to roll back some of the
welfare-state institutions of the New Deal and
the Great Society, and in general to reduce the
role of government in economic life. However,
defense expenditures in constant 1987 dollars
rose 50 percent between 1980 and 1987, after
barely changing at all during the previous
seven years. These huge increases in defense
were based on the view that the Cold War
needed more vigorous prosecution, justifying
greatly expanded government spending on the
military.

It is obvious, then, that the policy shifts of
the 1980s were based on deliberate decisions to
change the course of U.S. economic history in
a major way. But what were the results of
those shifts for the economy? If one examines
broad indicators of economic performance,
such as the growth of real output, the labor
force and employment, the rate of inflation,
and the unemployment rate, there were some
differences as well as similarities between the
1980s and earlier decades (see Table 23–1).
Real output grew slightly less than it did in the
1970s, and at substantially lower rates than in
the 1950s and 1960s. The labor force and em-

ployment grew at roughly the same rates as
they had during the 1960s. The first members
of the baby boom generation (born during the
1945 to 1965 period) began to enter the labor
force in the mid-1960s, and the last of them
entered it during the early 1980s, which likely
accounts for the similarities of the two decades. It was during the 1970s that the full
force of the baby boomers' arrival in the labor
market was felt.

The unemployment rate in 1990 differed little from its level in 1960 and 1970. The inflation
rate of the 1980s was well below that of the
1970s, but more than twice the inflation rates
of the 1950s and 1960s. Thus, some, but not all,
of the broad indicators of economic performance suggest that the 1980s were not very
different from earlier decades. The differences
that are evident in the data appear to be something like an average of the experience of earlier decades.

What tentative conclusion might be drawn
about the economic impact of the 1980s policy
shifts? Perhaps the modern American economy is like a great ship at sea. The gusting
winds of changed economic policies may alter
its course a little, and storms may rock it.
When these pass, the ship adjusts itself to get
back to its long-term course. Its passengers
and crew, however, do not forget the winds
and storms when the calm returns. For the
United States, the calm after the winds and
storms of the 1980s was unusual in two respects. First, the Cold War came to an end,
removing the political and military factors that
had been a tremendous burden for the United
States and the world for half a century. Second, the U.S. economy stood dead in the water from 1989 through 1991, with a real GDP
that barely changed over those three years.
The recession that hit in mid-1990 seemed to
end in early 1991, but more than a year later
(mid-1992) there were few visible signs of
recovery—an unusual experience in the history of U.S. recessions. This was a legacy that

Table 23–1 *Decadal Changes in Major Economic Indicators, 1950–1990 (percent change in decade, except for unemployment rates)*

Period	Percent Change					
	Real GDP	Population	Labor Force	Employment	Consumer Price Index	Unemployment Rate (end of decade)
1950–60	38%	19%	12%	10%	23%	5.5%
1960–70	46	14	19	20	24	4.9
1970–80	31	11	29	26	112	7.1
1980–90	29	10	17	19	59	5.5

Source: Calculated from data in *Economic Report of the President, February 1992* (Washington, D.C.: GPO 1992), pp. 299, 331, 332, 361. For 1950 to 1960, the growth rate of real GNP is substituted for that of real GDP, which is unavailable in the source.

the policies of the 1980s transmitted to the 1990s. But let us turn from the peculiar calm of the early 1990s to the course alterations, winds, and storms that preceded it.

Monetary Policy: Tight Money

The Federal Reserve System, as noted in Chapter 22, changed its operating procedures in late 1979 in an attempt to fight the Great Inflation during its worst, double-digit phase. The procedural change involved the decisions to aim at reducing the growth of monetary aggregates and to allow interest rates to find their own levels in private financial markets. During the preceding inflationary years, the Fed had often aimed at bringing down interest rates to fight a weak economy and rising unemployment, only to find that the money it created in the process increased inflation and drove up interest rates.

In one sense, the 1979 change in monetary policy appeared to be ineffective. None of the several measures of the money stock grew at very different rates over the four or five years after 1979 than they had in the four or five years before that year. According to the theories of

the monetarist school of economists, which had gained considerable credence in earlier years by correctly predicting the inflationary results of high rates of monetary growth, the period after 1979 should not have been very different from the period that preceded it. But it was, and the simpler monetarist theories therefore lost some of their credibility.

Decline of Inflation Rates

What seems to have happened after 1979 is this: Expectations of worsening inflation interacted with the Fed's policy (endorsed by the Reagan administration in 1981) of controlling monetary growth to drive interest rates up to unprecedented levels from 1979 to 1982. Soaring interest rates created distress for many users of credit and plunged the American economy into its worst post-1945 recession in 1981 to 1982, when monthly unemployment rates rose to double-digit levels. This deep recession finally reduced inflationary expectations and brought down the rate of inflation. As measured by the GDP deflator, the broadest of all price indexes, the rate of inflation fell from 10 percent in 1981 to 6.2 percent in 1982, its lowest level in a decade. In 1983, a year of recovery, the GDP inflation rate fell to 4.1 percent; it remained approximately in a 3 percent to 4 percent range for the next decade. In short, from the decade before 1982 to the decade after it, the rate of U.S. inflation was cut in half. The drop in inflation rates was both greater and more rapid than most economists had thought possible after the Great Inflation of 1965 to 1982.

Stagnation of 1989–1992

Although lower inflation rates, and the lower interest rates that followed reductions in inflationary expectations, were welcomed as the 1980s progressed, both remained high by historical standards. The Fed sought to reduce the inflation rate still further by a policy of slower monetary growth, particularly during and after 1987, when economist Alan Greenspan succeeded Paul Volcker as Federal Reserve Board chairman. During the next five years, the economy responded by ceasing to grow, but little progress was made in reducing inflation below the 3 percent to 4 percent range. The 1990 to 1991 recession, and slow real growth after it ended, were widely attributed to the Fed's none-too-successful efforts to wring remaining inflation out of the economy.

From 1979 to 1992, monetary policy was essentially the only domestic stabilization policy of a discretionary nature employed by the United States. The inflationary era led to a loss of faith in the ability of fiscal policies to promote economic stability. During the 1980s, fiscal policies were directed toward goals other than short-run stability. Tax policy changes were aimed at raising long-term growth. Expenditure policies were intended primarily to build up national defense and to fund continuing welfare-state programs. The most striking fiscal change of the 1980s was that tax policy and expenditure policy came to have virtually no relationship to each other. Income tax rates were cut and the tax system reformed for one set of reasons; expenditures increased for an-

other set of reasons. The notable results of these policies were large fiscal deficits and a soaring national debt.

Fiscal Policy: Deficits and Debt

Ronald Reagan was elected president in 1980 in good measure because he promised to change the by then largely discredited policies associated with the previous era of inflation. And change them he and his administration did. The Reagan program, announced in 1981, called for (1) supply-side tax cuts intended to increase Americans' incentives to work and produce by allowing both workers and businesses to keep more of what they earned, (2) expenditure cuts and a reallocation of government spending toward defense and away from nondefense categories, (3) deregulation of many regulated activities (though this policy change antedated Reagan's administration as explained later in the chapter), and (4) support for the Federal Reserve's anti-inflation policies that had been put into effect before Reagan came to office.

Economic Recovery Tax Act

The cornerstone of the Reagan program was the Economic Recovery Tax Act (ERTA) of 1981. This supply-side tax-cut measure, phased in over three years (1981 to 1983), sharply reduced marginal income tax rates across all income brackets. For example, the top marginal tax rate, 70 percent in 1981, was cut to 50 percent in 1982. The legislation also attacked the problem of "bracket creep" inherited from the previous era of inflation (see Chapter 22) by indexing tax exemptions, deductions, and bracket income thresholds to changes in the Consumer Price Index. And, to stimulate savings and investment, the 1981 law among other changes introduced a greatly accelerated depreciation of capital assets and a more favorable tax treatment of capital gains.

All in all, ERTA was a major tax cut. The federal Office of Management and Budget later estimated that the 1981 changes reduced Treasury revenues by $750 billion between 1981 and 1986. From the 1981 to 1984 fiscal years (October 1–September 30), there was little change in individual income tax revenues and a decline in corporate income tax collections—despite continued inflation (albeit at lower rates) and a recovery from the recession of 1981 to 1982.

Expenditure Growth and the Defense Buildup

At the same time, Reagan's program began a decade-long defense-spending increase. Defense expenditures rose from $158 billion in 1981 to $253 billion in 1985 and to about $300 billion in both 1989 and 1990. The Reagan administration had hoped to pay for its defense buildup (1) by reducing other areas of government spending and (2) through the increased revenues that were expected to follow from the supply-side economic growth unleashed by the 1981 tax cuts. But these hopes were not realized. Although the economy did enjoy a long expansion from 1982 to 1990, it was not a robust expansion. Real GDP growth for the whole decade of 1980 to 1990 was actually lower than that for 1970 to 1980 (refer again to Table 23–1). In the lower tax environment of the 1980s—even after the 1981 tax cuts were partly offset by revenue-increasing adjustments in 1982 and by higher payroll taxes enacted in 1983—an ordinary rate of economic growth gave rise to a substantially lower growth of federal revenues than would have been the case if taxes not been cut so much in 1981. In fiscal year 1990, federal revenues were about $100 billion lower than they would have been under the pre-1981 tax code. The 1981 cuts by themselves would have made the 1990 shortfall about $300 billion, but they were offset by post-1981 income and payroll tax in-

creases that brought in about $200 billion more in 1990.

Nondefense Expenditures. What about the Reagan goal of reallocating government spending away from nondefense areas and toward defense? Like the hoped-for increase in economic growth rates to higher levels, it did not materialize. Defense spending rose 90 percent from 1981 to 1990. But in these same years, overall federal nondefense spending grew nearly as fast—83 percent—and represented by far the largest component of federal spending in both years (77 percent in 1981 and 76 percent in 1990). The Reagan administration was successful in getting Congress to pass its politically popular tax cuts, but it was unsuccessful in persuading Congress to enact nondefense expenditure cuts as an offset to increased defense spending. Some small cuts that were enacted in discretionary programs led quickly to visible social problems: rising poverty rates and the appearance of homeless persons in many cities and towns. Other, larger components of spending were placed in off-limits categories for political reasons by the administration and Congress. These categories included the welfare-state entitlement programs, such as Medicare (where spending increased 50 percent from 1981 to 1990) and Social Security (where spending increased 78 percent). Because the welfare programs paid benefits to elderly Americans of all classes and incomes, it was deemed impolitic to cut them.

Interest Expenditures. The fastest-growing major category of federal spending during the 1980s, however, was not a politically popular entitlement program but rather federal interest expenditures, which rose 168 percent between 1981 to 1990, from $68.8 billion to $184.2 billion. Because federal spending—defense and nondefense—rose much faster than federal tax revenues throughout the 1980s and early 1990s, the resulting deficiency had to be borrowed. And the borrowing increased the national debt, on which interest had to be paid, at unprecedented rates (at least in peacetime) and by unprecedented absolute amounts. Figure 23–1 charts a half-century of federal fiscal deficits (and surpluses, of which there were few, the last occurring in 1969). The figure shows, for example, the large deficits of World War II, the mix of small deficits and surpluses of the first two decades of the postwar era, and the tendency of deficits to rise during the 1970s. The most striking feature of the figure, however, is the sharp rise in the deficit during the early 1980s and its continuance at unusually high and increasing levels into the 1990s. The United States had its first deficit of

more than $100 billion in 1982, the first full year of the Reagan tax cuts, and that was the lowest deficit to occur in the next decade. The 1991 deficit was a new record—$269 billion—and the government's estimates of the deficits for 1992 and 1993 were new records as well—in the $300 billion to $400 billion range.

The National Debt

The continuing flow of yearly deficits gave rise to an increasing national debt—the stock of Treasury bills, notes, and bonds outstanding and drawing interest. Figure 23–2 charts the gross federal debt for the same half-century as

Figure 23–1 *Federal Budget Deficits and Surpluses, 1940–1993*

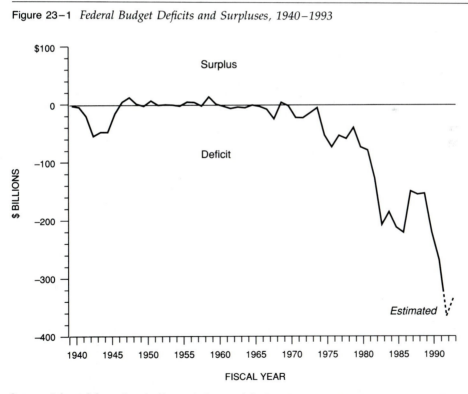

SOURCE: Adapted from data in *Economic Report of the President, 1992* (Washington, D.C.: GPO, 1992), p. 385.

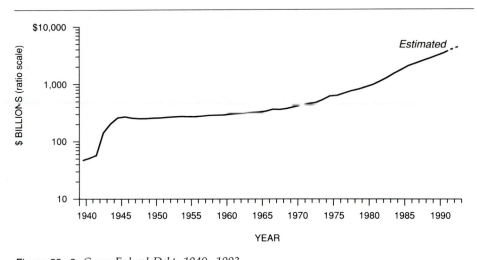

Figure 23–2 *Gross Federal Debt, 1940–1993*
SOURCE: Adapted from data in *Economic Report of the President, 1992* (Washington, D.C.: GPO, 1992), p. 385.

Figure 23–1's deficits. The debt rose from $48 billion to $271 billion between 1939 and 1946, mostly the result of World War II borrowing. Two decades later, it had increased by some $70 billion, to $340 billion in 1966. During the next fifteen years, 1966 to 1981, the gross federal debt roughly tripled, to $994 billion. Then it more than quadrupled between 1981 and 1992, to more than $4000 billion.

Although the deficit and debt data lend some perspective to federal fiscal policies during the past half-century, in many respects they are misleading. For example, the gross debt data do not reveal that the government debt is in part owned by government agencies, such as the Federal Reserve System and the Social Security Trust Fund. Thus, around 1990, the debt held by the public was only about three-quarters of the total gross debt. (Publicly held debt, however, also quadrupled between 1981 and 1992.) Another drawback of the deficit and debt data is that they are not adjusted for the falling value of the dollar, whose purchasing power was greatly reduced by inflation during the half-century after 1940. Finally,

the data say little about the capacity to service the debt; that is, to pay the interest on it and perhaps even to pay it down in the future should budget surpluses materialize (as they did, it will be recalled from Chapter 15, every year for a quarter-century after the Civil War).

Ratio of National Debt to GDP.   Some of the problems in interpreting long-term trends in deficits and debts can be overcome by relating the debt to the size of the U.S. economy, since the economy ultimately is the base on which the government can draw to service the debt. The ratio of the gross federal debt to GDP over the past half-century is charted in Figure 23–3. In 1991, the gross debt was about 64 percent of GDP. The debt/GDP ratio was much higher at the end of World War II, at which time the debt was 123 percent of GDP. The ratio declined for a quarter-century after the war, before leveling off in the 1970s at about 35 percent of GDP. Then the debt/GDP ratio rose steadily throughout the 1980s toward 70 percent in the early 1990s. Thus, the fiscal policies of the United States during the Reagan (1981 to 1989) and

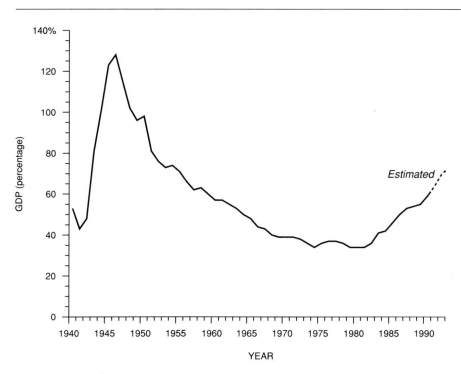

Figure 23–3 *Ratio of Federal Gross Debt to Gross Domestic Product, 1940–1993 (in percentages)*
SOURCE: Adapted from data in *Economic Report of the President, 1992* (Washington, D.C.: GPO, 1992), p. 385.

Bush (1989 to 1993) administrations approximately doubled the ratio of national debt to GDP in twelve years. Except for the World War II era, the ratio in the early 1990s was the highest in U.S. history. The shift in fiscal policy that began with the Reagan tax cuts in 1981 was one of the most dramatic changes to occur in two centuries of American economic policy.

Effects of the U.S. Economic Policy Shifts

High Real Interest Rates

The dramatic shifts in federal economic policies during the early 1980s had equally dra-

matic effects on the U.S. and world economies for the remainder of that decade and into the 1990s. Federal Reserve monetary policies shifted toward an anti-inflation, tight-money stance late in 1979, and with only a few temporary reversals maintained that stance into the 1990s. In 1981, fiscal policies shifted in the opposite direction as taxes were cut, expenditures were increased, and the resulting budgetary shortfalls were covered by increased borrowing in financial markets. The effects of these policies—tight money coupled with large budget deficits covered by borrowing—combined to raise interest rates to some of the highest levels in U.S. history. Nominal interest rates peaked during the years 1980 to 1982, when the Federal Reserve used tight money to break the inflationary momentum built up during the previous fifteen years. After 1982, when inflation rates fell to much lower levels, nominal interest rates also fell but more slowly than did inflation rates. As a result, real interest rates remained quite high by historical standards during the 1980s and early 1990s. The economic effects of this long period of high real interest rates were both international and domestic in nature.

International Effects

The Balance of Payments and Foreign Investment. High real interest rates during the early 1980s greatly increased the attractiveness to foreigners of investing in U.S. assets. As foreign investors bought dollars to invest in those assets, the international value of the dollar, which had been battered down during the high-inflation, low-real-interest-rate environment of the 1970s, made a dramatic recovery. For example, a dollar on average was worth about 1.8 German marks in 1980 but 3 marks in 1985, or about 4.2 French francs in 1980 but nearly 9 francs in 1985.

The rise of the foreign-exchange value of the dollar in these years led to a historic shift in international trade and investment patterns. For decades the United States had earned current account credits by exporting more goods and services than it imported and from the earnings of its investments abroad. That began to change during the era of the Great Inflation (1965 to 1982), but as late as 1980 and 1981 there were still positive, if small, current account credits. From 1981 to early 1986, however, the soaring value of the dollar, itself the result of high U.S. interest rates, made imported products cheaper to Americans and U.S. products more expensive to foreigners. The current account balance went from a $1 billion surplus in 1980 to a peak deficit of $160 billion by 1987. Thereafter, a fall in the value of the dollar in foreign-exchange markets alleviated the problem somewhat, but in 1989 the trade and current account deficits remained above $100 billion.

The federal government's policies of high real interests during the 1980s generated two unintended results in the international economic relations of the United States. First, a strong dollar reduced exports, increased imports, and reduced the competitiveness of American producers and products in both domestic and foreign markets. Second, as foreigners responded to high U.S. interest rates by investing in U.S. assets (such as U.S. Treasury bonds, stocks, buildings, factories, and land), the United States in just a few years went from being the largest creditor nation in the world to the largest international debtor. At the beginning of the 1980s, U.S. investments abroad (at current or replacement cost) were nearly $400 billion greater than foreigners' investments in the United States. By the mid-1980s, the two stocks of assets were about equal. Then, by the late 1980s, foreigners owned about $400 billion more of U.S. assets than Americans owned abroad. This was one of the more dramatic turnarounds of a country's foreign investment position in the history of international finance.

What had happened in the 1980s was that Americans—in both the governmental and private sectors—were borrowing and creating debt to a much greater extent than could be financed by U.S. savings. The Reagan administration had hoped that its tax program would increase Americans' incentives to save and that faster economic growth would enlarge the pie out of which greater savings would come. Unfortunately for the plan, the long expansion of the economy from 1982 to 1990 was at a typical rather than an usually high rate, and so the Reagan tax program provided far greater incentives to invest, often with borrowed money, than to save. Continued inflation

Imports and Jobs. Unionized workers from Pennsylvania are protesting against imports of goods they produce. Federal economic policies during the early 1980s led to a rise in the dollar's international value and to soaring imports and weak exports. But the rising U.S. trade deficits gave foreigners dollars that they lent back, which, in part, assisted the federal government in financing its budget deficit. (UPI/The Bettmann Archive)

along with economic expansion after 1982 created incentives for investing with borrowed money to purchase real assets—houses, land, commercial buildings, and so on. Inflation reduced the real value of the debt incurred, while economic expansion made it easier to rent or sell the real assets to others at higher prices. These were among the reasons the 1980s were marked by an explosion of private as well as public debt.

The private savings rates of Americans, as conventionally measured, actually declined during the 1980s (though some analysts fault the conventional measurements for not adequately taking capital gains, governmental pension savings, and other factors into account). And, of course, the large federal deficits provided by fiscal policy represented increased negative savings. Since Americans could not finance all of the debt that was being created by their private and public sectors, foreign purchasers made up the difference, which amounted to a sum that approached $1 trillion.

The LDC Debt Crisis. The oil price shocks of the 1970s led to large financial windfalls for the members of OPEC and other oil producers, far more than could be invested or consumed in the oil-producing countries without disrupting their economies. The windfalls, or "petrodollars," as they were called, thus had to be "recycled." Petrodollars (oil was priced in dollars in world markets) were deposited in leading U.S. and foreign banks, which then lent them to their loan customers. Among the largest of these customers in the decade after 1973 were the governments of the less-developed countries (LDCs) of Latin America, Asia, and Africa. The petrodollar sums to be recycled were huge. The government debt of developing nations appeared for political, economic, and financial reasons to be a good place to put them. The LDCs had long been recipients of foreign aid from the developed industrial nations, and the world inflation of the late 1960s and 1970s seemed to guarantee that the commodities the LDCs produced and exported would continue to rise in price so that these countries would have no difficulty repaying their loans.

From 1979 to 1982, however, the Federal Reserve fought the U.S. inflation by pushing the United States, still the world's largest economy by a good measure, into a deep recession with tight money and soaring interest rates. While that was happening, the Reagan tax cuts kept real interest rates high by raising demands for funds to finance U.S. private investment and the federal fiscal deficit. The U.S. recession reduced imports from the LDCs, and as the disinflation spread from the United States to the rest of the world, commodity prices in world trade leveled off and in some cases fell. These results of U.S. policy curtailed the ability of LDCs to repay their loans while at the same time raising their debt service requirements because interest rates charged on the loans made to LDCs were often tied to the level of U.S. interest rates. (Variable-rate financing was one of the innovations that the financial world created in the 1970s in its efforts to cope with inflation.)

The LDC debt crisis broke out in 1982, when Mexico announced that it was unable to service its foreign debt. By then oil prices— Mexico was a major oil exporter—were falling

for several reasons, including the U.S. recession, the energy deregulation programs in the United States, and the slow but eventually effective moves toward energy conservation that resulted from the sharply higher oil prices of the 1970s. Soon other large LDC borrowers— Venezuela, Brazil, Argentina, and Chile among them—followed Mexico into default by being unable to service their debts. International banks and institutions such as the IMF then turned to working out arrangements with the governments of the developed countries and the LDCs to reschedule and write down the LDC debts. The process would take many years. The more immediate effects were a curtailment of lending to LDCs by the international banks and a weakening of the banks' balance sheets and competitiveness. Large U.S. money center banks were among the major losers from the LDC debt crisis.

Parallel Domestic Financial Crises

The LDC debt crisis had a counterpart within the United States, which remained a large energy producer even though it imported more and more of its requirements. The jump in energy prices engineered by OPEC in the 1970s led to an investment boom in the energy-producing industries of the U.S. "oil patch" states of the South, Southwest, and West. Local banks in these states funded much of the investment, though they often resold their loans to larger banks in American financial centers. When oil and other energy prices fell, many of these loans went into default or became "nonperforming." Bank failures broke out in the oil patch and spread to money centers. In 1984, the Continental Illinois Bank of Chicago, then the nation's seventh largest bank, essentially failed because of bad loans to energy producers. It was taken over by the government, though its depositors were bailed out because the bank was considered to be "too big to fail."

Another domestic counterpart of the LDC debt crisis arose in U.S. agriculture. American farmers, like agricultural producers in the LDCs, benefited from rising agricultural commodity prices during the inflation and foreign crop failures of the 1970s. Many of them incurred higher debts to purchase more land and equipment, because they expected that the prices of the products they produced would continue to increase or at least remain high. Like the primary product producers in the LDCs, their hopes were dashed by the high-interest and disinflation policies introduced in the early 1980s. Farm foreclosures increased, and many banks and other financial institutions that had lent heavily to farmers experienced financial difficulties and in some cases failure.

Domestic Effects

The Savings and Loan Crisis. The U.S. savings and loan (S&L) crisis of the 1980s, which continued to be worked out in the 1990s, furnished what is likely the most telling example of how the policy shifts of the 1980s, made to counter problems created by the earlier inflationary era, resulted in making problems worse instead of alleviating or solving them. America's savings and loan associations, so-called thrift institutions or S&Ls, for decades took the deposits of savers and employed them primarily in making mortgage loans to homebuyers. Most S&Ls were local in their orientation, a typical manifestation of the long U.S. tradition of having many small and locally oriented financial institutions (in contrast to having only a few large institutions with extensive branch systems, as is common in many other countries).

The distinctive feature of the S&Ls as financial institutions was that their deposits could be withdrawn on short notice but their mortgage loans were made for long periods of time, typically twenty to thirty years. When the Great Inflation after 1965 led to much higher interest rates, many S&Ls were pushed toward insolvency. Higher interest rates reduced the value of their holdings of mortgage loans that had been made at lower rates in the past. At the same time, the federal government regulated the rates that S&Ls could pay depositors at levels that became lower and lower relative to unregulated market rates, which were increasing in response to inflation. The unregulated market—including the money market mutual funds that arose during the 1970s to offer savers higher, unregulated rates—drained deposits from S&Ls. Hence, the S&Ls became trapped in a dilemma caused by inflation and rising interest rates. If their deposit rates were deregulated and they paid market rates to savers, their interest costs would exceed the interest they earned on their long-term mortgages made at lower average rates. If, instead, their deposit rates continued to be regulated at levels below market rates, they would lose deposits and would have to sell off their mortgages at prices below their nominal value in order to pay depositors. Either way, their costs would exceed their revenues, their profits would disappear, and they would fail. By 1980, many S&Ls were in deep trouble.

America's decision makers, public and private, refused to recognize the nature of the dilemma faced by the S&Ls and their imminent if not actual bankruptcy by 1980. If they had, the S&Ls might have been closed down, liquidated, or reorganized at that time. Instead, deregulation was seen as the way out. In the last year of the Carter administration, 1980, Congress enacted the Depository Institutions Deregulation and Monetary Control Act (DIDMCA). This was followed in 1982, under the Reagan administration, by the Garn-St. Germain Depository Institutions Act. Together these two acts phased out regulation of the interest rates that S&Ls (and other regulated financial institutions) could pay depositors,

The Savings and Loan Debacle.   This Maryland state-insured savings and loan association failed in 1985. Depositors, fearing depletion of the insurance fund, line up to withdraw their funds. Soon thereafter, savings and loans were failing throughout the United States, depleting federal deposit insurance funds. The federal government enacted a plan to bail out the depositors at a cost of more than $200 billion to taxpayers. (UPI/The Bettmann Archive)

made S&Ls more like banks and money market mutual funds by allowing them to offer checking accounts, and—to increase the appeal of S&L deposits over money market investments—raised federal insurance of deposits from $40,000 to $100,000 per account. These changes made it easier for S&Ls to attract and keep deposits. In addition, the two deregulatory acts expanded the asset powers of the thrift institutions. To the traditional fixed-rate mortgage loans were added the authority to make adjustable-rate mortgage (ARM) loans, as well as consumer loans, commercial real estate loans, ordinary commercial loans such as banks offered, and even to take equity positions in business ventures.

In short, at a time when their net worths were being destroyed by rising interest rates, the S&Ls were granted new powers to compete for federally insured deposits and to enter previously off-limits areas of lending and in-

vestment, which in many respects were far riskier than the traditional fixed-rate residential mortgage. No effort was made, however, to have deposit insurance premiums reflect the risks that might be taken by the newly liberated S&Ls. And, because in the political economy of the time regulation was deemed the problem and deregulation the solution, no effort was made to increase net-worth standards (i.e., capital requirements) or regulatory supervision of thrift institutions. The S&Ls were permitted to try to recoup their previous losses and restore their profitability by taking more risks in their investing of government-insured deposits. It was a gamble, a coin flip for which "heads" meant that the S&Ls won and "tails" meant that the government and the citizenry it represented lost. By the mid- to late 1980s, it became clear in many instances that the government had lost. The S&Ls made loans that could not be serviced or repaid, deposit insurance funds were depleted, and a bailout of S&L depositors became necessary (it would cost taxpayers a discounted value, in 1990 dollars, estimated in 1992 at more than $200 billion). The policy shifts of the 1980s did not create the S&L problem; that happened during the previous era of high inflation. But the policy decisions of the early 1980s did make the problem much worse than it might have been. The S&L crisis was an unprecedented financial debacle.

Wall Street, Mergers and Acquisitions, and Junk Bonds.

Corporate America, like other sectors of the economy, was buffeted by the storms of the inflationary era from the mid-1960s to the early 1980s. An overvalued dollar combined with rising costs and prices and the productivity slowdown to make the products of many American corporations less competitive in domestic and foreign markets than they would have been without the complications caused by U.S. inflation. Corporate critics and other analysts often argued that U.S. corporations needed to invest more and modernize their factories to compete with European and Japa-

nese firms having later vintages of capital. But the inflationary era brought rising interest rates and depressed stock prices, raising the cost of capital to American firms. For example, as noted in Chapter 22, indexes of stock prices were little higher, and in some cases actually lower, in 1982 than they had been in 1965. In these circumstances, some corporations concluded that the best way to increase the value of their shares was to buy them back in the stock market. More importantly for the 1980s, if corporations wanted to expand, it often appeared cheaper for them to buy existing companies than to invest in newly constructed facilities.

This was the background of the great wave of mergers, acquisitions, and corporate buyouts that took place in the 1980s. It was the fourth such wave in U.S. history, after those of the late 1890s, 1920s, and 1960s. The dimensions of the 1980s wave are given in Table 23–2. The peak years were from 1984 to 1988, though there was a drop in merger activity in 1987, when stock prices raced up before crashing in October, followed by a peak in dollar volume and large deals in 1988. Thereafter,

Table 23–2 *Corporate Mergers and Acquisitions, 1980–1988*

Year	Number of Mergers and Acquisitions	Value (in $ billions)	Number Valued in Excess of $1 Billion
1980	1,565	$ 33.0	3
1981	2,326	67.3	8
1982	2,296	60.4	9
1983	2,387	52.8	7
1984	3,158	126.0	19
1985	3,428	145.4	26
1986	4,323	204.4	34
1987	3,701	167.5	30
1988	3,487	226.6	42
Total	26,671	$1,083.4	178

Source: Adapted from data in Walter Adams and James Brock, *Dangerous Pursuits: Mergers and Acquisitions in the Age of Wall Street* (New York: Pantheon, 1989), p. 12.

some of the scandals and criminal activity (insider trading and the like) that came to light reduced the financing available and put a damper on the merger wave.

The 1980s merger wave was supported in part by the stance of the Reagan administration toward less government interference in the economy. The government's merger guidelines were relaxed, the Antitrust Division of the Justice Department had its staff cut in size, and few of the merger deals where challenged on antitrust grounds. Concerns about reductions of competition in the United States were lessened for some by the realizations that the American economy was one of the most open in the world and international competition for American firms was therefore much greater than it had been earlier in history. Others, however, saw the mergers as disrupting firms, eliminating jobs, and reducing competition.

Wall Street investment bankers played prominent roles in many of the merger deals—as advisers to corporations on mergers and acquisitions, as financers, and as organizers of leveraged buyouts (LBOs) and hostile takeovers. In a leveraged buyout, a corporation's assets became collateral for loans incurred to buy out its stockholders. Hostile takeovers separated underperforming managements— and some good ones—from the corporate assets they controlled. Those who took over hoped to profit—the bankers from arranging and financing the deals, and the new managers and stockholders from more efficient deployments of the firms' assets. But a high reliance on debt as against equity in merger financing increased the debt burdens of corporations, and some analysts argued that alleged efficiency gains came less from operational improvements than from wage cuts and layoffs of workers.

The so-called *junk bond,* a low-grade, high-yield, high-risk form of debt, was an important source of merger and LBO finance. Junk bonds were hardly new, but they went from minor to major financial status during the 1980s. An innovative financier, Michael Milken of the Drexel, Burnham, Lambert investment-banking house, persuaded many institutional and individual investors that the returns on junk bonds would amply compensate for their risk. Milken created a market in which issuers and buyers of junk bonds could trade. However, when the economy slowed at the end of the 1980s and some issuers of junk bonds defaulted, the market for junk bonds collapsed. Milken's firm failed, and he was convicted of violations of securities laws and went to prison.

The 1980s merger wave was widely criticized for its excesses and the legal and ethical transgressions of some who participated in it. And many of the gains that were supposed to have resulted from it were not so apparent in the stagnating economy of the early 1990s. But the merger wave may have had some positive effects. Inefficient corporate managements were disciplined by takeovers and threats of takeovers. For decades a fragmented U.S. financial system and a financial regulatory system had made it difficult for investors to discipline managers except by selling their holdings of corporate stock. Many managerial groups retained corporate earnings and invested them in low-return projects, which increased the size of their firms and their own prestige, instead of paying them out to the owner-stockholders. These managers sometimes paid themselves high salaries and fringe benefits even when their firms' profits and stock prices were not performing well. The merger wave may have reinstituted elements of investor control of firms after a long era of managerial dominance.

Mergers, however, did not eliminate all managerial abuses of power. In some cases, they may have even increased such abuses. And the merger wave's explosion of private debt, coming on top of the explosion of federal deficits and debt, weakened corporate capital structures and left a debt and debt-service overhang that helped to keep real interest rates at high levels and contributed to the slowing of U.S. economic growth in the late 1980s and early 1990s.

The Deregulation Movement

The movement for the deregulation of regulated businesses began to be embodied in legislation in the late 1970s, yet it continued into the 1980s when most of its effects became apparent. Some of these effects were discouraging, as the earlier discussion of the S&L crisis indicates. In other areas, however, deregulation did work to promote competition, to expand consumer choice, and to encourage innovation.

The Transportation Industries

The Airline Deregulation Act of 1978 gave airline companies the power to set fares competitively. It also allowed free entry by new airline companies and by existing companies into new markets. Before that time, the Civil Aeronautics Board (CAB) set fares, allocated routes, and regulated entry. The interstate airline business had been a largely noncompetitive cartel enforced and regulated by the government. Economists had earlier noted this, but Congress did not begin to question the results of CAB regulation until the mid-1970s. It then began to ask why non-CAB-regulated fares between cities within large states (especially California and Texas) were substantially lower than CAB-regulated fares on routes of similar distances between cities in different states. The answers pointed to the cartel enforced by the CAB in the interests of existing airline companies as against the interests of consumers and potential entrants. This led to the 1978 act, which was opposed by many airline companies that had found federal regulation congenial.

After deregulation, average airline fares changed frequently, falling in most major markets but rising in smaller ones. Airlines entered into and exited from particular routes and new firms entered—and left—the industry. Some airline companies eventually failed. Others were merged into stronger carriers. Most studies of the effects of airline deregulation conclude that consumers benefited from lower fares and increased service, even though overcrowded airports and frequent fare and schedule changes complicated the air traveler's life.

The Motor Carrier Act of 1980 had much the same effects on the trucking industry. Under ICC trucking regulation before 1980, many interstate shippers found that it was cheaper to own and use their own trucks than to use ICC-regulated carriers, even though the private carriers' trucks had to return empty from their destinations. This was a clear sign that trucking regulation inflated costs to shippers using ICC-regulated common carriers. The growth of private trucking meant that only about a third of truck traffic actually fell under ICC-regulation. After the ICC's regulatory authority was limited in 1980, licensed interstate carriers expanded. By 1990, there were more than forty thousand licensed carriers compared with only seventeen thousand in 1980. Since a major part of the U.S. transportation bill was for trucking services, increased competition had major benefits for shippers and consumers.

The Staggers Act of 1980 curtailed the power of the ICC to set freight rates for railroads. For decades the ICC had stifled competition and innovation in the modes of transportation it regulated, with American railroads being especially devastated by government mandates and controls. With reduced regulation after 1980, U.S. railroads once again became innovative and competitive in transportation markets, particularly in the western parts of the country. The rejuvenation of America's railroads remains one of the less noticed effects of the deregulatory movement, but one that may be more noticed in the years ahead.

Other Industries

Deregulation and greater competition came as well to the energy and telecommunications industries during the 1980s. In most cases, consumer choices were expanded, prices became more competitive, and innovations—for example, fax machines, portable and cellular telephones, answering machines, and expanded cable television services—were introduced. The S&L crisis slowed the deregulation movement, especially in finance, by the end of the 1980s. And the newer forms of environmental and social regulation described in Chapter 22 were relatively untouched by deregulation. Nonetheless, for several industries, deregulation reversed a century-long assertion of greater federal control over private business.

The Decline of Organized Labor

Organized labor suffered a blow in 1981, when President Reagan decided to fire more than eleven thousand striking air-traffic controllers and give their jobs to newly hired replacements. But in truth, the union movement by then was already in a state of decline. Union members were not only a declining fraction of the U.S. labor force; their absolute numbers were also shrinking. After legislative gains during the New Deal of the 1930s and employment gains during and after World War II, organized labor accounted for about one-quarter of the total U.S. labor force in the years from 1950 to 1970. During those two decades union membership in absolute terms increased from about fifteen million to twenty-one million workers. Between 1970 and 1989, however, union membership declined to about seventeen million workers. In the same period, the

total U.S. labor force, swelled by baby boomers and increasing numbers of women workers, grew by more than forty million. Thus, the unionized share of the labor force was cut nearly in half, to about 14 percent, by the end of the 1980s. (About two million workers were represented by unions even though they were not union members.)

There were several reasons for organized labor's decline. The most important was the rise of the services sector, analyzed in Chapter 22. The services sector was never as intensively unionized as was goods production, especially manufacturing. Within services, the only category in which organized labor enjoyed much success in recent decades was government. In 1989, some 6.4 million governmental employees were members of unions, and they accounted for about 38 percent of all U.S. union membership. In the private economy, union membership declined in all the major categories of goods and services employment.

Another factor, the shift of manufacturing in recent decades from the so-called "rust belt" of the Northeast to the so-called "sunbelt" of the South and West, hastened the decline of organized labor. Many of the sunbelt states had antiunion traditions and right-to-work laws, which made it illegal to require union membership as a condition of employment even when unions won recognition in employee elections.

Some scandals in union management and evidences of corruption in union leadership also undermined political and worker support for unions. So did the growing problem of U.S. competitiveness in domestic and foreign markets; unions in industries subject to international competition began to fear that their gains in collective bargaining contracts would lead to an export of jobs to other countries. And, finally, as government took on greater responsibilities for monitoring safety in the workplace and retirement arrangements, there seemed to be less need for unions to do so. All of these late twentieth-century trends in labor

Christmas in New York City, 1987. A homeless person sleeps in the doorway of a store for rent. Policy changes of the 1980s increased homelessness and led to a glut of commercial property. (UPI/The Bettmann Archive)

worked to undermine the status and extent of the organized union movement.

Trends in Economic Welfare

Slower economic growth, especially as manifested in the productivity slowdown after the mid-1960s, reduced the gains in the welfare of Americans from what they had experienced in the prosperous and noninflationary decades after World War II. Median family incomes (in real, inflation-adjusted terms) grew only 24 percent between 1967 and 1990, or at a rate of less than 1 percent per year on a compounded basis. In the two previous decades, the gain was close to 3 percent per year. Median household income grew even slower, only some 16 percent over the same period. The years of high inflation ending in deep recession from 1973 to 1982 were particularly devastating to living standards; in those years, real median family income actually fell. The recovery from 1982 to 1990 reversed the decline, but in 1990 real median family income (around $36,000) was only 6 percent higher than it was in 1973.

Few families, of course, are on the median. Trends in the distribution of income reveal a more complex story. From the 1940s to the 1970s, for example, there was a slight tendency toward greater equality in income distribution; after the early 1970s, though, that trend reversed. During the 1980s, a move toward greater inequality gained momentum. From 1973 through 1989, average real family income increased 16 percent, but the gain for the top fifth of the distribution was 26 percent and that of the top 5 percent of the distribution was 34 percent. Since the top components of the distribution had above-average gains, the lower ones had to have below-average gains. The lowest 20 percent, for instance, was particularly hard hit, experiencing a slight decline in average real income between 1973 and 1990. The federal government's calculations of poverty rates bear out this result. The official poverty rate fell from 22 percent to 11 percent between 1959 and 1973, then it rose to 15 percent in 1983 and was close to 14 percent in 1990 (even after seven years of economic growth).

Among the reasons for increased inequality in the distribution of income were increasing numbers of two-income professional couples and an increased differential in the earnings of skilled, highly educated, professional workers compared to those of less-skilled, less-educated, blue-collar workers. The distribution of wages and salaries across all occupations became less equal. Here, the weakening of organized labor may have been a factor, but whether this was a cause or a symptom of increased inequality remains an unanswered question. The Reagan tax cuts and other policies of the 1980s accelerated the trend toward greater inequality in income distribution.

Upper-income groups received the lion's share of the benefits of lower taxes, while administration policies cut back on payments to welfare recipients and other "social safety net" programs, the value of which had already been falling in real terms since the early 1970s. Soaring interest rates of the inflationary 1970s and the relatively high rates of the 1980s also contributed to increased income inequality, for those with higher incomes and holdings of wealth received the largest shares of interest income.

Summary

The 1980s witnessed a reversal of many of the trends in U.S. economic policy of the previous half-century. In general, the new policies were a reaction to the Great Inflation of 1965 to 1982 and to the welfare policies of the New Deal and the Great Society. Tight money directly attacked inflation. Tax cuts alleviated some of the negative effects of inflation on nominal and real after-tax incomes. The deficits, debts, and defaults that resulted from this policy mix helped to keep real interest rates at high levels throughout the decade and into the 1990s. Inflation was greatly reduced from the levels of the 1970s but was still high by earlier U.S. standards. Fiscal stimulus from tax cuts and increased spending led to a recovery and a long economic expansion after the 1981 to 1982 recession. But that stimulus tapered off toward the end of the 1980s, while high real interest rates continued. As a result, the U.S. economy experienced a recession in 1990 to 1991 and little real growth from 1989 to 1992.

In the early 1990s, the U.S. economy was still coping with the deficits, debts, and defaults created by the legacies of the 1980s. Since the Cold War had come to an end, the main challenges facing America's economic decision makers in the early 1990s were how to revive a stagnant, debt-ridden economy while adjusting to new domestic and international realities.

Suggested Readings

While it is perhaps too soon to expect balanced historical accounts of the 1980s, there is no shortage of written materials on that decade. An interesting dialogue between political scientists and economists treating the decade's monetary policies, budget deficits, welfare policies, tax reforms, the savings and loan crisis, and international trade problems is featured in Alberto Alesina and Geoffrey Carliner, eds., *Politics and Economics in the Eighties* (Chicago: University of Chicago Press, 1991). William Greider, *Secrets of the Temple: How the Federal Reserve Runs the Country* (New York: Simon and Schuster, 1987), offers a fascinating account of how the Fed, under Paul Volcker, broke the momentum of inflation at the start of the decade but contributed in the process to subsequent financial problems. Volcker presents his own reflections on these topics in Paul Volcker and Toyoo Gyohten, *Changing Fortunes: The World's Money and the Threat to American Leadership* (New York: Times Books, 1992).

Insiders' accounts of how the Reagan revolution in economic policy was supposed to work and failed to do so are provided, respectively, by Reagan appointees Paul Craig Roberts, *The Supply Side Revolution: An Insider's Account of Policymaking in Washington* (Cambridge: Harvard University Press, 1984), and David Stockman, *The Triumph of Politics: How the Reagan Revolution Failed* (New York: Harper & Row, 1986). Agreeing essentially with Stockman are economists Alan Blinder in two books, *Hard Heads, Soft Hearts: Tough-Minded Economics for a Just Society* (Reading, Mass: Addison Wesley, 1987) and *Growing Together: An Alternative Economic Strategy for the 1990s* (n.p., Whittle Direct Books, 1991), and Benjamin M. Friedman, *Day of Reckoning: The Consequences of American Economic Policymaking Under Reagan* (New York: Random House, 1988). Another economist provides cogent analyses of most U.S. economic problems of recent decades and doses of pessimism about the prospects for solving them: Paul Krugman, *The Age of Diminished Expectations: U.S. Economic Policy in the 1990s* (Cambridge: The MIT Press, 1991). But the editor of *The Wall Street Journal* sees the 1980s as a decade of positive change and accomplishment: Robert L. Bartley, *The Seven Fat Years* (New York: The Free Press, 1992).

For a concise and well-reasoned account of budget deficits and the soaring national debt, see Robert Heilbroner and Peter Bernstein, *The Debt and the Deficit* (New York: W. W. Norton, 1989). Lester Thurow, *Head to Head: The Coming Economic Battle Among Japan, Europe, and America* (New York: Morrow, 1992) studies the economic problems the United States faces in global competition with Japan and the nations of the European Community.

The background of the LDC debt crises of the 1980s is featured in Barry Eichengreen and Peter Lindert, eds., *The International Debt Crisis in Historical Perspective* (Cambridge: The MIT Press, 1989). The savings and loan crisis receives a clear and informed treatment by an economist who served as a member of the Federal Home Loan Bank Board in its midst: Lawrence J. White, *The S & L Debacle: Public*

Policy Lessons for Bank and Thrift Regulation (New York: Oxford University Press, 1991).

The frenetic activity in the money and capital markets of Wall Street during the 1980s is the subject of many books. Among those that bring a sense of economic and historical perspective to their topics are Walter Adams and James Brock, *Dangerous Pursuits: Mergers and Acquisitions in the Age of Wall Street* (New York: Pantheon Books, 1989); Henry Kaufman, *Interest Rates, the Markets, and the New Financial World* (New York: Times Books, 1986); James Grant, *Money of the Mind: Borrowing and Lending in America from the Civil War to Michael Milken* (New York: Farrar Straus & Giroux, 1992); and Alan J. Auerbach, ed., *Corporate Takeovers: Causes and Consequences* (Chicago: University of Chicago Press, 1988).

On regulation and the movement to deregulate, see the lengthy chapter on economist Alfred Kahn and the Civil Aeronautics Board in Thomas K. McCraw, *Prophets of Regulation* (Cambridge: Harvard University Press, 1984); Richard H. K. Vietor, "Contrived Competition: Airline Regulation and Deregulation, 1925–1988," *Business History Review,* 64 (1990); Elizabeth E. Bailey, David R. Graham, and Daniel P. Kaplan, *Deregulating the Airlines* (Cambridge: The MIT Press, 1985); Severin Borenstein, "The Evolution of U.S. Airline Competition," *Journal of Economic Perspectives,* 6 (1992); John Richard Felton and Dale G. Anderson, eds., *Regulation and Deregulation of the Motor Carrier Industry* (Ames: Iowa State University Press, 1989), and Albro Martin, *Railroads Triumphant,* (New York: Oxford University Press, 1992).

Organized labor and its decline are the subjects of Richard B. Freeman and James L. Medoff, *What Do Unions Do?* (New York: Basic Books, 1984); Gordon L. Clark, *Unions and Communities Under Seige: American Communities and the Crisis of Organized Labor* (New York: Cambridge University Press, 1989); Michael Goldfield, *The Decline of Organized Labor in the*

United States (Chicago: University of Chicago Press, 1987); Gilbert J. Gall, *The Politics of Right to Work: The Labor Federations as Special Interests, 1943–1979* (Westport, Conn.: Greenwood Press, 1988); and Robert H. Zieger, *American Workers, American Unions, 1920–1985* (Baltimore: Johns Hopkins University Press, 1986).

Informed discussions of changes in income distribution and living standards include Frank Levy, *Dollars and Dreams: The Changing American Income Distribution* (New York: W. W. Norton, 1988); Robert E. Litan, Robert Z. Lawrence, and Charles L. Schultze, *American Living Standards: Threats and Challenges* (Washington, D.C.: Brookings Institution, 1989); and the analysis of the Council of Economic Advisers in *Economic Report of the President, 1992* (Washington, D.C.: GPO, 1992). A cogent analysis of the debate over income distribution is given by Paul R. Krugman, "Behind the Numbers," *The American Prospect* (Fall 1992). In the same issue are stimulating articles on the logic of public investment in the 1990s.

Index